11/12

no map 3/13

Fodor's 2013

WASHIN
D.C.

D0674990

Fodor's Travel Publications   New York, Toronto, London, Sydney, Auckland
www.fodors.com

FODOR'S WASHINGTON, D.C. 2013

Editorial Contributors: Beth Kanter, Mike Lillis, Allison Lombardo, Kathryn McKay, Elana Schor, Cathy Sharpe, Renee Sklarew

Editors: Stephen Brewer, Robert I.C. Fisher, Penny Phenix

Production Editor: Jennifer DePrima
Maps & Illustrations: David Lindroth, Mark Stroud, *cartographers;* Rebecca Baer, *map editor;* William Wu, *information graphics*
Design: Fabrizio La Rocca, *creative director*; Tina Malaney, Chie Ushio, Jessica Ramirez, *designers*; Melanie Marin, *associate director of photography;* Jennifer Romains, *photo research*
Cover Photo: (U.S. Capitol Rotunda): Richard T. Nowitz/age fotostock
Production Manager: Angela L. McLean

ISBN 978-0-307-92937-2

ISSN 0743-9741

SPECIAL SALES
This book is available at special discounts for bulk purchases for sales promotions or premiums. Special editions, including personalized covers, excerpts of existing books, and corporate imprints, can be created in large quantities for special needs. For more information, write to Special Markets/Premium Sales, 1745 Broadway, MD 3-1, New York, NY 10019, or e-mail specialmarkets@randomhouse.com.

AN IMPORTANT TIP & AN INVITATION
Although all prices, opening times, and other details in this book are based on information supplied to us at press time, changes occur all the time in the travel world, and Fodor's cannot accept responsibility for facts that become outdated or for inadvertent errors or omissions. So **always confirm information when it matters,** especially if you're making a detour to visit a specific place. Your experiences—positive and negative—matter to us. If we have missed or misstated something, **please write to us.** Share your opinion instantly through our online feedback center at fodors.com/contact-us.

CONTENTS

MAPS

ABOUT THIS GUIDE

Fodor's Ratings

Everything in this guide is worth doing—we don't cover what isn't—but exceptional sights, hotels, and restaurants are recognized with additional accolades. Fodor's Choice★ indicates our top recommendations; ★ highlights places we deem highly recommended; and **Best Bets** call attention to notable hotels and restaurants in various categories. Care to nominate a new place? Visit Fodors.com/contact-us.

Trip Costs

We list prices wherever possible to help you budget well. Hotel and restaurant price categories from $ to $$$$ are noted alongside each recommendation. For hotels, we include the lowest cost of a standard double room in high season. For restaurants, we cite the average price of a main course at dinner or, if dinner isn't served, at lunch. For attractions, we always list adult admission fees; discounts are usually available for children, students, and senior citizens.

Hotels

Our local writers vet every hotel to recommend the best overnights in each price category, from budget to expensive. Unless otherwise specified, you can expect private bath, phone, and TV in your room. **For expanded hotel reviews, facilities, and deals visit Fodors.com.**

TripAdvisor ⊚⊚

Our expert hotel picks are reinforced by high ratings on TripAdvisor. Look for representative quotes in this guide, and the latest TripAdvisor ratings and feedback at Fodors.com.

Ratings		Hotels & Restaurants	
★	Fodor's Choice	🏨	Hotel
★	Highly recommended	↳	Number of rooms
ℭ	Family-friendly	⦿⦿	Meal plans
Listings		✕	Restaurant
✉	Address	⌑	Reservations
✉	Branch address	⌂	Dress code
☎	Telephone	▭	No credit cards
🖷	Fax	$	Price
⊕	Website		
✎	E-mail	**Other**	
⊡	Admission fee	⇨	See also
☉	Open/closed times	☞	Take note
Ⓜ	Subway	⅄	Golf facilities
⊹	Directions or Map coordinates		

Restaurants

Unless we state otherwise, restaurants are open for lunch and dinner daily. We mention dress code only when there's a specific requirement and reservations only when they're essential or not accepted. **To make restaurant reservations, visit Fodors.com.**

Credit Cards

The hotels and restaurants in this guide typically accept credit cards. If not, we'll say so.

Experience
Washington, D.C.

WASHINGTON, D.C. TODAY

Classically majestic and stunningly beautiful, the Capitol, the White House, and the Supreme Court stand at the heart of Washington, D.C. They are powerful, steadfast symbols of the stability and strength of the nation. But the city that revolves around this axis is in a constant state of change, lived on a more human scale.

Today's D.C....

...is obsessed with politics. The historic 2008 election of President Barack Obama captivated the overwhelmingly Democratic D.C. in ways not seen in years. Yet the pendulum swung back in 2010 when Republicans trounced the Democrats at the polls, splitting control of Congress between the parties, magnifying the city's historic power struggles and creating a legislative standoff that's practically defined Capitol Hill for two years running. With the partisan soap opera at their doorstep—and with D.C.'s economy revolving around the federal government—many Washingtonians are happily enchanted by their unique political milieu. Yet, ironically, locals are also somewhat distanced from the nation's affairs due to their lack of a vote in Congress. Recent efforts to grant such a vote were thwarted by Republicans, making

the city's unofficial motto, "Taxation without Representation," seem destined to remain apt for some time.

Perhaps for that reason, many D.C. residents focus more intently on local politics. And Washington's mayors—from Marion Barry and his illicit drug habits to Adrian Fenty and his controversial schoolteacher firings—have provided plenty of spice over the years. Not to be outdone, current Mayor Vincent Gray ignited scandal immediately when reports of cronyism and campaign finance abuse surfaced just weeks after he took office. As of this writing, the federal investigation into "Graygate" continues—as does D.C.'s string of colorful mayors.

...is in demographic flux. Two recent population trends highlight the changing face of Washington: First, the 2010 Census found that the number of residents increased, relative to 10 years earlier, for the first time in five decades. And second, in 2011 the District's black population fell below 50 percent for the first time since 1960, when Washington became the first majority-black city in the country. Hardly unrelated, the trends reveal that, after years fleeing D.C. due to high crime rates and underperforming

D.C.: JUST THE FACTS

THE PEOPLE
Population, city: 617,996

Population, metro area: 5,582,170

Median age: 35.1

Ethnic makeup: African-American 49.9%; non-Hispanic white

34.8%; Hispanic 9.1%; Asian 3.5%; multiracial 2.7%

Infant mortality rate: 12.8 per 1,000 births

Literacy: 81% (est.)

Crime rate: 61.1 offenses per 1,000 residents

Type of government: Limited representational democracy with no voting members of Congress; elected mayor and nine-member council

Workforce: 331,098 (67.1%)

Per capita income: $42,078

schools, more and more suburban families are opting to live in the city where they work. These younger professionals—mostly white, mostly drawn by the government and related industries—have helped bolster Washington's economy, but not without a price. Indeed, the gentrification—heightened by enormous stadium projects like Nationals Park—has reached deep into the traditionally black areas of Northeast and Southeast, stirring resentments, driving up costs, and pricing many longtime residents out of their childhood homes. The changes have flown largely under the radar, but are starting to get more attention as local officials seek ways to strengthen local commercial interests without sacrificing decades of community and culture.

. . . is fitness crazy. Long agitated by D.C.'s unflattering designation as "Hollywood for ugly people," Washingtonians have fought back in recent years with a surging interest in fitness and health. Quite aside from the numerous gyms popping up all over the city—and ignoring, for a moment, the countless joggers constantly circling the Mall—local residents have adopted a slew of activities to get outside and stay in shape. Like to play kickball?

There are teams scattered all over the city. Enjoy Ultimate Frisbee? There's a league for that, too. Rugby? Got it. Even bocce—the age-old Italian sport of lawn bowling—has inspired a passionate following and launched formal competitions around town. The District's many parks and green spaces cater perfectly to that game of pickup football (or *futbol*), and the city's wild embrace of bike sharing has been complemented by the creation of bike-only lanes on some of its most traveled thoroughfares. Add a long list of burgeoning indoor crazes to the mix—everything from yoga to Pilates to Zumba—and you've got a city intent on shedding its wonks-only reputation.

. . . is stuck in traffic. It's official: The roads around D.C. are among the most poorly planned in the country, snarling traffic at all hours and creating the nation's longest commute outside of Los Angeles. Spend an hour in gridlock on the Beltway—or 30 minutes in a cab just to get across town—and you'll understand why more locals are flocking to the Metro and even bike sharing to get around the city. Visitors to D.C., it is often suggested, can preserve both time and sanity by doing the same.

Unemployment: 9.9% (Jan. 2012)

Major industries: Government, law, tourism, high-tech, higher education

Official motto: *Justitia Omnibus* (Justice for All)

Official food: The half-smoke, a large, smoked link sausage most famously found at Ben's Chili Bowl on U Street

THE LAND

Land area: 61 square miles

Nicknames: The District, D.C., Inside the Beltway

Latitude: 38 N

Longitude: 77 W

Elevation: From sea level to 420 feet

Natural hazards: Lobbyists, motorcades, lack of congressional representation

WASHINGTON, D.C. PLANNER

Safety Tips	Getting Your Bearings

Safety Tips

D.C. is a relatively safe city, but crimes do occur, even in typically "safe" neighborhoods. The best way to protect yourself is to stick to well-lighted and populated areas and avoid walking alone after dark.

Many of the city's business and government districts become deserted at night, but the public transportation system is exceptionally safe, with only a few incidents of crime reported each year.

When to Go

D.C. has two delightful seasons: spring and autumn. In spring the city's ornamental fruit trees are blossoming, and its many gardens are in bloom. Summers can be uncomfortably hot and humid. By autumn most of the summer crowds have left and you can enjoy the sights in peace.

Winter weather is mild by East Coast standards, but a handful of modest snowstorms each year bring this southern city to a standstill.

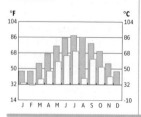

Getting Your Bearings

Four Quadrants: The address system in D.C. takes some getting used to. The city is divided into the four quadrants of a compass (NW, NE, SE, SW), with the U.S. Capitol at the center. Because the Capitol doesn't sit in the exact center of the city (the Washington Monument does), Northwest is the largest quadrant. Northwest also has most of the important landmarks, although Northeast and Southwest have their fair share.

Numbered Streets and Lettered Streets: Within each quadrant, numbered streets run north to south, and lettered streets run east to west (the letter *J* was omitted to avoid confusion with the letter *I*).

The streets form a fairly simple grid—for instance, 900 G Street NW is the intersection of 9th and G streets in the northwest quadrant of the city. Likewise, if you count the letters of the alphabet, skipping J, you can get a good sense of the location of an address on a numbered street. For instance, 1600 16th Street NW is close to Q Street, Q being the 16th letter of the alphabet if you skip J.

In short, this means it's vital to know which quadrant you're headed to, because 14th Street NW is a long way from 14th Street NE—about 28 blocks, in fact.

Avenues on the Diagonal: As if all this weren't confusing enough, Major Pierre L'Enfant, the Frenchman who originally designed the city, threw in diagonal avenues recalling those of Paris.

Most of D.C.'s avenues are named after U.S. states. You can find addresses on avenues the same way you find those on numbered streets, so 1200 Connecticut Avenue NW is close to M Street, because M is the 12th letter of the alphabet when you skip J. Furthering the chaos, L'Enfant devised a number of traffic circles as well—aesthetically pleasing additions that can nonetheless frustrate even the best out-of-town drivers.

Getting Around

Car Travel: Driving in D.C. can be a headache. Traffic is usually congested, and the road layout is designed for frustration, with one-way streets popping up at just the wrong moment. Once you've reached your destination, the real challenge begins: D.C. must be among the most difficult cities in America in which to find parking. All of this means that you'd be wise to use public transit whenever possible.

Metro and Bus Travel: The Washington Metropolitan Area Transit Authority operates a network of subway lines (known locally as the Metro) and bus routes throughout D.C. Most popular tourist attractions are near Metro stops, though certain areas are only accessible by bus, most notably Georgetown and Adams Morgan in Northwest, and the Atlas District in Northeast.

Metro fares depend on the distance traveled and range from $1.95 to $5 during "peak" hours—which include the morning and evening commutes and the after-midnight hours of weekends—and from $1.60 to $2.75 at all other times. Some good news: holders of popular SmarTrip cards get a 25¢ discount on all rides. Some bad news: a 20¢ surcharge is added to rides taken during "peak of the peak" hours, meaning the height of the workday rush. Bus fares are $1.70 (exact change only) for regular routes, and $3.85 for express routes, though SmarTrip users get a 20¢ discount on each. A special bus, the 5A, runs from D.C. to Dulles airport for $6. SmarTrip cards also grant free transfers between buses and 50¢ discounts on transfers between buses and the Metro. One-day passes on the Metro are available for $9, while weekly passes range up to $47, depending on hourly restrictions. All can be purchased online. Weekly bus tickets run $15, available only through SmarTrip.

Washington Metropolitan Area Transit Authority
☎ 202/637–7000 ⊕ www.wmata.com.

Taxi Travel: In 2012, the city tweaked taxi rates to accommodate driver complaints. Under that proposal (which was not finalized as of this writing), there is a $3 minimum base charge, with rates increasing 27¢ for every eighth of a mile ($2.16 per mile)—up from the previous rate of 25¢ per sixth of a mile. To help ease the pain on riders, the city proposed to scrap a number of unpopular surcharges, including the $1.50 for cabs hailed by phone, the $1.50 for each additional passenger, the $1 fuel surcharge and the $1 to carry small pets.

Taxi Information District of Columbia Taxicab Commission
☎ 202/645–6018 ⊕ www.dctaxi.dc.gov.

Getting Here

D.C. is served by three airports: **Ronald Reagan Washington National Airport (DCA)** in Virginia, 4 miles south of Downtown Washington; **Dulles International Airport (IAD)**, 26 miles west of Washington, D.C.; and **Baltimore/Washington International–Thurgood Marshall Airport (BWI)** in Maryland, about 30 miles to the northeast.

Amtrak trains arrive and depart from Union Station, in Northeast D.C.

Visitor Information

Washington, DC Convention and Tourism Corporation ✉ *4th fl., 901 7th St., NW, Downtown* ☎ *202/789–7000, 800/422–8644* ⊕ *www.washington.org.*

The Smoking Ban

Smoking has been banned in restaurants, bars, nightclubs, and taverns since 2007. It is allowed outside—with a caveat. Introduced in 2010, property owners—both commercial and residential—may post signs barring smoking within 25 feet of their property. The law, however, is widely considered unenforceable, and many bars and restaurants still invite patrons to light up outside, leading to the increased popularity of establishments with rooftop bars or back decks.

WHAT'S WHERE

1 **The Mall.** This expanse of green is at the heart of D.C., stretching from the Capitol to the Washington Monument, and is lined by some of America's finest museums. D.C.'s most famous monuments are concentrated west of the Mall and along the Tidal Basin.

2 **The White House Area and Foggy Bottom.** There's great art at the Corcoran and Renwick galleries, as well as performances at the Kennedy Center, and a whiff of scandal at the Watergate.

3 **Capitol Hill and Northeast D.C.** The Capitol itself, along with the Supreme Court and Library of Congress, dominates this area. Follow Hill staffers to find restaurants, bars, and a thriving outdoor market. Also explore the ever-growing H Street Corridor, aka the Atlas District.

4 **Downtown.** The Federal Triangle and Penn Quarter attract visitors to museums and galleries by day. By night, crowds head to the Verizon Center and Chinatown's bars, restaurants, and movie theaters.

5 **Georgetown.** The capital's wealthiest neighborhood is great for strolling, shopping, and partying, with the scene centering on Wisconsin and M streets. The C&O Canal starts here, providing recreation in and out of the water.

6 **Dupont Circle and Logan Circle.** This hub of fashionable restaurants and shops is also home to the most visible segment of the gay community. The Kalorama neighborhood is an enclave of embassies, luxurious homes, and small museums. Moving east, beautiful Logan Circle is largely residential, though a few hip new bars and eateries are just a short block away.

7 **Adams Morgan.** One of D.C.'s most ethnically diverse neighborhoods has offbeat restaurants and shops and a happening nightlife. Grand 19th-century apartment buildings and row houses have lured young professionals here.

8 **U Street Corridor.** Revitalization has brought trendy boutiques and hip eateries to the area around 14th and U, which was a hotbed of African-American culture in the early 20th century.

9 **Upper Northwest.** This mostly residential swath of D.C. holds two must-see attractions: the National Cathedral and the National Zoo.

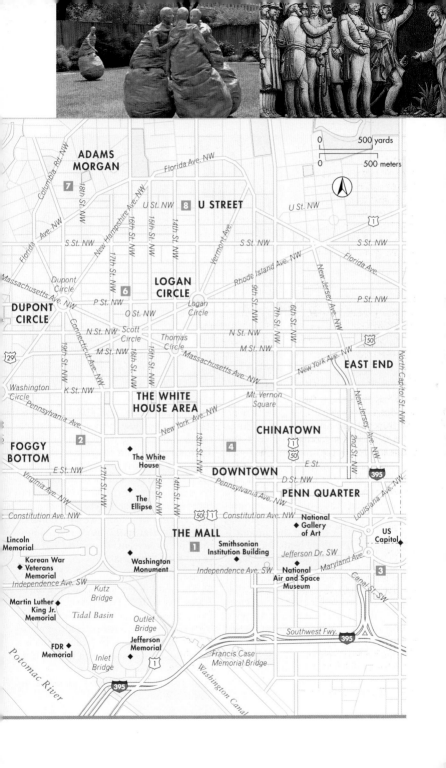

WASHINGTON, D.C. TOP ATTRACTIONS

Capitol

(A) Home of the Senate and the House of Representatives, the marble Capitol is an architectural marvel filled with frescoes and statues. Tours begin at the new Capitol Visitor Center. The Capitol grounds are equally stunning—Frederick Law Olmsted, the landscape architect famous for New York City's Central Park, designed them. A tour of the interior is impressive, but nothing beats attending a live debate on the House or Senate floor.

Washington Monument

(B) This 555-foot, 5-inch obelisk is visible from nearly everywhere in the city. From the top, it also offers unparalleled views. Unfortunately, damage suffered during a rare East Coast earthquake closed the monument to the public in August 2011, with the reopening set for late 2013.

Lincoln, Jefferson, and FDR Memorials

(C) The key to these memorials is to stop, stand, and read the writing on the walls. There's nothing quite like reading the Gettysburg Address while the massive marble statue of Lincoln broods behind you. Ponder the first lines of the Declaration of Independence at the Jefferson Memorial, and remember the line "We have nothing to fear but fear itself" as you encounter the stark monuments to poverty and war at the FDR Memorial.

White House

(D) The best-known address in the United States may be 1600 Pennsylvania Avenue. Every president but George Washington has lived here, and many heads of state have passed through its hallowed halls. The self-guided tour lets you follow their footsteps through the historic rooms. Note that it takes advance planning to visit the White House.

National Cathedral

(E) Like its medieval European counterparts, this 20th-century cathedral has a nave, transepts, and vaults that were built stone by stone. Unlike those historic buildings, the National Cathedral has a gargoyle in the shape of Darth Vader.

Dumbarton Oaks

(F) If you enjoy formal gardens, visit the 10-acre grounds of Dumbarton Oaks, one of the loveliest spots for a stroll.

Arlington National Cemetery

(G) The hills across the Potomac from the Tidal Basin are the final resting place for some 340,000 members of the armed services. A visit here can be both sobering and moving.

Smithsonian Museums

(H) Mostly flanking the National Mall, these illustrious galleries hold everything from Kermit the Frog to the *Spirit of St. Louis* and the Hope Diamond to Rodin's *Burghers of Calais*.

Martin Luther King Jr. Memorial

The newest addition to the Mall, this 30-foot sculpture of solid granite pays tribute to King, the giant of the civil rights movement killed by an assassin's bullet in 1968. President Barack Obama dedicated the memorial in October of 2011.

Vietnam Veterans, Korean War Veterans, and World War II Memorials

Touch a name of a Vietnam vet, see your reflection alongside the statues of Korean War soldiers, search for the stories of those who lost their lives in World War II. These memorials are interactive and unforgettable.

National Zoo

The pandas may be the zoo's most famous attraction, but they're not the only highlight. Monkeys, elephants, lions, and other exotic residents never fail to delight.

GREAT ITINERARIES

ONE DAY IN D.C.

If you have a day or less (and even a dollar or less!) in D.C., your sightseeing strategy is simple: take the Metro to the Smithsonian stop and explore the area around the Mall. You'll be at the undisputed heart of the city—a beautiful setting in which you'll find America's greatest collection of museums, with the city's spectacular monuments and the halls of government a stone's throw away.

Facing the Capitol, to your left are the **Museum of Natural History**, the **National Gallery of Art**, and the **National Archives**. To your right are the **Museum of African Art**, the **Hirshhorn Museum**, the **National Air and Space Museum**, and more. Head in the other direction, toward the **Washington Monument**, and you're also on your way to the **World War II Memorial**, the **Lincoln Memorial**, the **Vietnam Veterans Memorial**, and more monuments to America's presidents and its past. A lover of American history and culture could spend a thoroughly happy month, much less a day, wandering the Mall and its surroundings.

If you're here first thing in the morning: You can hit monuments and memorials early. They're open 24 hours a day and staffed beginning at 8 am. The outdoor sculpture garden at the Hirshhorn opens at 7:30, and the Smithsonian Institution Building ("the Castle") opens at 8:30. In the Castle you can grab a cup of coffee, watch an 18-minute film about D.C., and see examples of objects from many of the 18 Smithsonian museums.

If you only have a few hours in the evening: Experience the beauty of the monuments at dusk and after dark. Many people think they're even more striking when the sun goes down. National Park Service rangers staff most monuments until midnight.

FIVE DAYS IN D.C.

Day 1

With more time at your disposal, you have a chance both to see the sights and to get to know the city. A guided bus tour is a good way to get yourself oriented; if you take one of the hop-on, hop-off tours we recommend, you'll get genuine insights without a lot of tourist hokum. ⇨ *See Day Tours and Guides in Travel Smart Washington, D.C.*

Because you can get on and off wherever you like, it's a good idea to explore **Georgetown** and the **Washington National Cathedral** while on a bus tour; neither of which is easily accessible by Metro.

Day 2

Devote your next day to the Mall, where you can check out the museums and monuments that were probably a prime motivation for your coming to D.C. in the first place. There's no way you can do it all in one day, so just play favorites and save the rest for next time. Try visiting the monuments in the evening: they remain open long after the museums are closed and are dramatically lighted after dark.

Keep in mind that the **National Museum of Natural History** is the most visited museum in the country, while the **National Air and Space Museum**, the **National Gallery of Art**, and the **Museum of American History** aren't too far behind; plan for crowds almost anytime you visit. If you visit the **U.S. Holocaust Memorial Museum**, plan on spending two to three hours. If you're with kids on the Mall, take a break by riding the carousel.

Cafés and cafeterias within the museums are your best option for lunch. Two excellent picks are the Cascade Café at the **National Gallery of Art** and the Mitsitam Café at the **National Museum of the American Indian**, where they serve creative dishes inspired by native cultures. Just north of the Mall, the newly opened **Newseum** features a food court with a menu designed by celebrity chef Wolfgang Puck. If you've got more time (and more money to spend), drop by the Source, a ritzy Puck-owned restaurant behind the museum.

If the weather permits—and you're not already weary with museum fatigue—consider the healthy walk from the **Washington Monument** to the **Lincoln Memorial** and around the **Tidal Basin**, where you can see the **Jefferson Memorial**, the **FDR Memorial**, and the new **Martin Luther King Jr. Memorial**. Nearby, nestled north of the Mall's reflecting pool, is **"The Wall,"** a sobering black granite monolith commemorating the 58,272 Americans who never returned from the Vietnam War.

Day 3

Make this your day on **Capitol Hill**, where you'll have the option of visiting the **Capitol**, the **U.S. Botanic Gardens**, the **Library of Congress**, the **Supreme Court**, and the **Folger Shakespeare Library**.

Call your senators or congressional representative (or your country's embassy, if you are a visitor from outside the U.S.) for passes to see Congress in session. There's also the option of venturing into one of the congressional office buildings adjacent to the Capitol, where congressional hearings are almost always open to the public. (Visit ⊕ *www.house.gov* and ⊕ *www.senate.gov* for schedules). Likewise, check the Supreme Court's website (⊕ *www.supremecourtus.gov*) for dates of oral arguments. If you show up at court early enough, you might gain admission for either a short (three-minute) visit or the full morning session.

Day 4

Head to the **National Zoo** and say good morning to the pandas. If the weather is bad, you can still enjoy the numerous indoor animal houses. Then hop on the Metro to **Dupont Circle** for lunch. Walk west on tree-lined P Street NW to **Georgetown**, where you can shop, admire the architecture, and people-watch.

If you got a good dose of Georgetown on your first day, consider instead hopping on the Metro to the **International Spy Museum**, a Chinatown attraction that tends to be less crowded after 2 pm. From there you can easily walk to the **Smithsonian American Art Museum** and **National Portrait Gallery**, which stay open until 7.

Day 5

Spend the morning at **Arlington National Cemetery**. While you're there, don't miss the changing of the guard at the Tomb of the Unknowns, every hour or half hour, depending on the time of year. A short detour north of the cemetery brings you to the **Marine Corps War Memorial**, a giant bronze rendering of American soldiers planting the flag on Iwo Jima during World War II—one of the most famous images in U.S. military history.

After your quiet, contemplative morning, head back across the Potomac to spend the afternoon in **Adams Morgan** and **Dupont Circle**. Lunch at one of Adams Morgan's Ethiopian, El Salvadoran, or Mexican restaurants, and take in the Dupont Circle art scene—there's an assortment of offbeat galleries tucked into the side streets, as well as the renowned **Phillips Collection**.

D.C. WITH KIDS

D.C. is filled with kid-friendly attractions. These sights are sure winners:

American Museum of Natural History

Say hello to Henry. One of the largest elephants ever found in the wild, this stuffed beast has greeted generations of kids in the rotunda of this huge museum dedicated to natural wonders. Take your kid to the O. Orkin Insect Zoo, home to live ants, bees, centipedes, tarantulas, roaches (some as large as mice), and other critters you wouldn't want in your house.

Bureau of Engraving and Printing

Any youngster who gets an allowance will enjoy watching as bills roll off the presses. Despite the lack of free samples, the self-guided, 35-minute bureau tour is one of the city's most popular attractions.

DC Ducks

What do you get when you cross a tour bus with a boat? A duck, of course—DC Ducks, that is. Tour the city by both land and water without leaving your seats aboard these unusual amphibious vehicles: standard 2.5-ton GM trucks in watertight shells with propellers.

Discovery Theater

Within the Smithsonian's Ripley Center on the Mall, this lively theater began as a low-key puppet show before expanding to feature more than 300 programs a year exploring art, science and global heritage—everything from robots to the Wright Brothers to African drums.

International Spy Museum

This museum takes the art of espionage to new levels for junior James Bonds and Nancy Drews. Even the most cynical pre-teens and teenagers are usually enthralled with all the cool gadgetry. Note that this museum is best for older tweens and teens—if you bring along a younger sibling, you could be in for a workout: there aren't many places to sit down, and strollers aren't allowed in the museum.

Mount Vernon

Farm animals, a hands-on discovery center, an interactive museum, and movies about the nation's first action hero make George Washington's idyllic home a place where families can explore all day.

National Air and Space Museum

There's a good reason why this place is one of the most popular museums in the world: kids love it. The 23 galleries here tell the story of aviation and space from the earliest human attempts at flight. All three gift shops sell freeze-dried astronaut food—not as tasty as what we eat on Earth, but it doesn't melt or drip. If you've never crunched into ice cream, it's worth the experience.

National Museum of American History

Oh say you can see . . . the flag that inspired "The Star Spangled Banner," Oscar the Grouch, the ruby-red slippers from *The Wizard of Oz,* an impressive collection of trains, and more pieces of Americana than anyone can digest in a day.

National Zoo

Known more for its political animals than its real animals, D.C. nevertheless has one of the world's foremost zoos. If your child is crazy about animals, this is an absolute must—it's huge!

Paddleboat the Tidal Basin

What better way to see the Jefferson Memorial and the world-famous cherry trees—gifts from Japan—than from the waters of the tidal basin? The paddleboats get the kids and you off your feet and into the sun!

D.C. LIKE A LOCAL

If you want to "go native" and get a sense for D.C. as the locals know it, try these experiences.

Catch a Flick

Summers in D.C. add a refreshing twist to the typical dinner-and-a-movie date night. In July and August locals head to several outdoor venues to see classic films alfresco. The Mall's Screen on the Green is the most popular, but NoMa's Summer Screen, just north of Union Station, pulls an ever-growing audience as well. Several movie halls around the city play host to Filmfest DC (⊕ *www.filmfestdc.org*), an increasingly popular April festival boasting an always-eclectic assortment of works from amateur and professional filmmakers worldwide.

Dine on Ethiopian Food

The District's many Ethiopian expats have introduced the community to their unique African cooking. The best restaurants, such as Etete, have long been clustered in the U Street neighborhood, but Ethiopic, a relative newcomer in the Atlas District, is rewriting those rules. Meat and vegetarian dishes are ladled onto a large round of spongy *injera* bread, and diners eat with their hands, ripping off pieces of bread to scoop up the delectable stews. Using your hands instead of utensils adds to the sensual appeal of this cuisine.

Go for a Bike Ride

Your typical Mall-and-monuments tourist may not know that D.C. is home to several great bike trails—and the city's bike share program (⊕ *www.capitalbikeshare.com*), introduced in 2010, makes it easier than ever for visitors to take advantage. The Capitol Crescent Trail and Rock Creek Trail are popular routes between D.C. and Maryland. For more ambitious cyclists, the Custis Trail in Arlington links D.C. to the 45-mile Washington & Old Dominion (W&OD) trail in Virginia, while the Chesapeake & Ohio (C&O) towpath runs for nearly 185 miles between D.C. and western Maryland. From there, the most hardcore peddlers can catch the Great Allegheny Passage trail, which extends another 150 traffic-free miles to Pittsburgh. On a warm, sunny day, expect to find the local paths bustling with cyclists, rollerbladers, and strollers.

Hang Out on U Street

You won't find many tourists in the U Street neighborhood, and many locals have only recently discovered the area. During the day, browse through the unique boutiques that line 14th and U streets NW, or read the *Washington City-Paper* at one of the many cafés. In the evening, select from trendy or ethnic restaurants, post up at a local bar like Dodge City, a newish hipster hangout, catch a popular indie band at the 9:30 Club, or some jazz at Bohemian Caverns.

Shop at an Outdoor Market

Instead of sleeping in on a Saturday morning, grab your trusty canvas bag and a wad of cash and head to one of D.C.'s outdoor markets. The best-known venue, Eastern Market on Capitol Hill, underwent a modernization and restoration project after a devastating fire in 2007, and the building is gorgeous. It is *the* place to buy a quick meal or picnic ingredients and mingle with residents. On weekends there are craft, flea, and produce markets. The Dupont Circle farmers' market and Georgetown flea market—both year-round venues—are also popular with residents. And the Maine Avenue Fish Market in Southwest is a must-visit for seafood lovers. Get there early to see the fishermen unload their catch.

FREE IN D.C.

For thrifty visitors, D.C. can be a dream come true. All the Smithsonian museums and national memorials are free, as are many other museums—too many, in fact, to list here. Many top attractions are also gratis, like Ford's Theatre and Dumbarton Oaks. Summertime is heaven for budget travelers, with free outdoor concerts and festivals every week.

Free Attractions
Anderson House
Dumbarton Oaks (free from November 1 to March 14)
Folger Shakespeare Library
Ford's Theatre
Kenilworth Aquatic Gardens
Kennedy Center tours
Library of Congress
National Arboretum
National Zoo
Old Post Office Pavilion
Old Stone House
Rock Creek Park
Supreme Court of the United States
U.S. Botanic Garden
U.S. Capitol/Capitol Visitors Center
Washington National Cathedral
White House

Free Performances
The **Kennedy Center** hosts performances every day at 6 pm on the Millennium Stage. Also, every September the Prelude Festival kicks off the Kennedy Center's fall schedule with many free events. Choral and church groups perform at the **National Cathedral**, often at no charge.

In summer, folk, pop, and rock bands perform on Monday and Thursday nights atop **Fort Reno Park**. You can also hear jazz in the **National Gallery of Art's sculpture garden** on Friday evenings in summer—a diversion enormously popular among locals, so get there early if you want to secure some lawn space. The Carter Barron Amphitheatre in **Rock Creek Park** hosts a series of free shows and concerts throughout spring and summer, with tickets distributed at the facility's box office the day of the events. To catch free performances of the **Shakespeare Theatre Company,** sign up online for the group's Free-for-All lottery, which awards same-day tickets for the company's performances at the Sidney Harman Hall in Chinatown. Performances of military music take place around the city. From June through August the U.S. Navy Band, U.S. Air Force Band, U.S. Marine Band, and U.S. Army Band take turns playing concerts on the grounds of the **U.S. Capitol** weekdays at 8 pm. You can also see the U.S. Marine Band every Friday night from May through August during the Evening Parade at the Marine Barracks.

Almost every day of the year, the **Politics and Prose** independent bookstore on Connecticut Avenue invites fiction and nonfiction authors to the store for book readings, talks, and Q&A sessions. Another indie bookstore, **Busboys and Poets**, offers a wide variety of readings, films, and political discussions almost every night as well.

Free Festivals
D.C. is a city of festivals, many of which are free to the public (food and souvenirs cost extra). For a complete list of annual events, visit the Washington, D.C. Convention and Tourism Corporation at ⊕ *www.washington.org.*

Half-Price Tickets
TICKETPlace (⊕ *www.ticketplace.org,* or call in, Wednesday–Sunday, at ✉ *407 7th Street NW, between D and E Streets*) sells half-price tickets to D.C.'s theater and music events.

SIGHTSEEING TOURS

If ever there was a "do it yourself" city, it's D.C. The Metro system is safe and easy to navigate and most of the major sights and museums are concentrated in a single area. Armed with a Metro map, a guide to the Mall, and a comfortable pair of shoes, you can do it all, all by yourself.

Nevertheless, sometimes a guided tour just makes more sense, especially when it comes to experience, insider knowledge, and a parking pass. So consider one if your trip matches one of the situations here. ⇨ *See Travel Smart Washington, D.C. for more information.*

If this is your first trip...

The Metro might be the most convenient way to get around, but it is notably lacking in city views. If you'd like to get the lay of the land with ease, **Old Town Trolley Tours** and the **Tourmobile** buses operated by the National Park Service offer hop-on, hop-off convenience and are perfect for your first day in the city.

A bike tour, with a company such as **Bike the Sights**, offers a gentle ride with show-stopping scenery. Visitors might also consider D.C.'s bike-share program, which offers short-term memberships of 24 hours (for $7), three days ($15) or 30 days ($25). Additional costs will be tacked on, however, depending on how long you actually use the bike. If you want a more automated journey, Capital Segway, City Segway Tours, and Segs in the City all offer guided rides around the major tourist sights. They average between $70 and $80 for a two-to-three-hour tour, but prices, services, and durations differ between companies.

If you want an insider's look...

Arranging constituent visits to the **White House** and to the sessions of **Congress** is one of the duties of your representative and senators. Contact their offices (⊕ *www.house.gov* and ⊕ *www.senate.gov*) in advance to arrange your visit. If you are a visitor from another country, your embassy in D.C. can make the arrangement for you, given enough notice.

Several other government buildings, like the **State Department,** require advance reservations for a tour.

If you just can't get enough...

Mad about political gossip? Hear the juicy bits from Washington's rumor mill with **Gross National Product's Scandal Tours,** featuring stops at the Tidal Basin, where a powerful congressman and his stripper girlfriend ran afoul of the law, and the Watergate, where the country's most infamous burglary led to the fall of a president. Or, for a more extensive history lesson, take a multiday tour with **Smithsonian Associates,** for a walk through the battles and strategies that shaped Civil War history. Stops include such historic sites as Manassas National Battlefield Park in Virginia, Antietam National Battle Field in Maryland, and Harpers Ferry, West Virginia, site of John Brown's last stand.

If you want a new perspective...

You know what the Potomac looks like from the city, but have you ever seen the monuments from the river? **Thompson Boat Center** offers hourly and daily rentals on canoes and kayaks. Pack a lunch and paddle over to Roosevelt Island for a picnic.

HAPPY HOUR IN D.C.

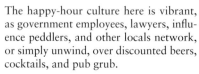

The happy-hour culture here is vibrant, as government employees, lawyers, influence peddlers, and other locals network, or simply unwind, over discounted beers, cocktails, and pub grub.

The trend is especially pronounced on Capitol Hill, where staffers and their powerful bosses can hop from a desk to a barstool in a matter of minutes. But every neighborhood in D.C. has its popular after-work haunts.

For Politicos

A few blocks behind the Capitol, the **Pour House** (✉ *319 Pennsylvania Ave. SE* ☎ *202/546–0779*), **18th Amendment** (✉ *613 Pennsylvania Ave., SE* ☎ *202/543–3622*), and **Tune Inn** (✉ *331 Pennsylvania Ave. SE* ☎ *202/543–2725*) all offer lively happy hours frequented by the hoards of congressional staffers streaming home from work. Nearby, the **Capitol Lounge** (✉ *231 Pennsylvania Ave. SE* ☎ *202/547–2098*) barely even pretends to cater to those outside the Hill. A popular draw is "Politics and Pints Trivia" night. Just a stone's throw from Union Station, the **Union Pub** (✉ *201 Massachussetts Ave. NE* ☎ *202/546–7200*) boasts a large front patio where similar crowds gather to sip suds and watch passersby. Two neighboring Irish pubs—the **Dubliner** and **Kelly's Irish Times** (✉ *14 F St. NW* ☎ *202/543–5433*)— come furnished with all the Gaelic trimmings, including fish-and-chips and Guinness on tap.

For Sophisticates

Penn Quarter's **Proof**, a pioneer of D.C.'s wine-bar scene, is a posh and popular spot to impress a date. Casual newcomer **Cork** (✉ *1720 14th St. NW* ☎ *202/265–2675*), which offers 50 wines by the glass near U Street, was an instant hit—and has the crowds to prove it. And the long, sleek bar at Cleveland Park's **Bardeo** (✉ *3311 Connecticut Ave. NW* ☎ *202/244–6550*) is the perfect perch from which to sample their extensive selection of wine "flights."

For the beer lover, **Granville Moore's Brickyard** is a crowd favorite in the emerging Atlas District. The bustling bar features an evolving roster of Belgian brews—the perfect accompaniment to their delicious mussels. At **Brasserie Beck**, Downtown, the sommelier will happily walk you through the extensive list of Belgian beer options, as are the friendly bartenders at Dupont Circle's spacious **Bistrot du Coin.**

For Insomniacs

Missed happy hour? No worries. There are a number of bars in town offering specials for night owls. **Clyde's** (✉ *707 7th St. NW* ☎ *202/349–3700*) in Chinatown and the **Old Ebbitt Grill** near the White House are two. Both feature half-price raw-bar specials after 11 pm on most weekdays. **Agora** (✉ *1527 17th St. NW* ☎ *202/332–6767*) goes a step further, featuring $3 beers and $4 cocktails to accompany their post-11 pm food specials. Also, don't miss **Hank's Oyster Bar** near Dupont Circle, which offers $1 late-night oysters.

A Bit of the Outdoors

A number of bars in town lure patrons to happy hour with a more universally appealing feature: the roof deck. Around U Street, **Local 16, Marvin,** and **Nellie's** all jump during happy hour, as young locals returning from work stop off to take the edge off. The **Reef** (✉ *2446 18th St. NW* ☎ *202/518–3800*) in Adams Morgan also offers a bustling open-air rooftop bar, while the roof deck at the **Cleveland Park Bar and Grill** (✉ *3421 Connecticut Ave. NW* ☎ *202/806–8940*) in Upper Northwest features TVs for the sports fan.

INSIDE THE SAUSAGE FACTORY: HOW LAWS ARE MADE

1

Amid the grand marble halls of the Capitol building, members of Congress and their aides are busy crafting the country's policies. It's not a pretty process; as congressional commentators have quipped, laws are like sausages—it's best not to know how either is made. But for iron stomachs, here's a brief tour through Washington's sausage factory.

The Lightbulb Stage

Most laws begin as mere proposals that any of Congress's 535 members may offer in the form of bills. Many are trivial, such as renaming post-office branches. Others are vital, like funding the federal government. Once introduced, all proposals move to congressional committee.

Congressional Committees and Committee Hearings

Thousands of proposals are introduced each year, but almost all die in committee. Congress has nowhere near enough time to entertain each bill, so committee leaders must prioritize. Many bills are dismissed for ideological reasons; for example, conservative proposals to privatize Social Security have little chance moving through committees headed by liberal Democrats. Many other bills simply lack urgency. Efforts to rein in fuel costs, for instance, are popular when gas prices are high, but lose steam when costs fall. Lobbying and special-interest money is another factor dictating the success or failure of individual bills.

More fortunate bills continue to the committee hearing stage, where experts discuss the merits and drawbacks. These hearings—staged in the congressional office buildings adjacent to the Capitol—are usually open to the public; check ⊕ *www. house.gov* and ⊕ *www.senate.gov* under the "committee" headings for schedules.

Committee members then vote on whether to move bills to the chamber floor.

Passing the House, Senate, and White House

A bill approved by committee still faces three formidable tests before becoming a law: it must pass the full House, the full Senate, and usually the White House.

Complicating matters, each legislative chamber has different rules for approving bills. In the House, proposals need only a simple majority, whereas in the Senate a minority can block a bill simply by debating it indefinitely (watch *Mr. Smith Goes to Washington* for a dramatic example). Senate leaders can end filibusters, but to do it requires support from 60 out of the 100 senators—a heavy lift if the majority party doesn't have 60 members of its own. President Barack Obama's controversial economic stimulus bill, for example, passed only after Democrats (who then held 58 seats) convinced three Republicans to support the proposal.

A bill passed by both the House and the Senate then proceeds to the White House. The president can either sign it—in which case it becomes law—or veto it, in which case it returns to Congress. Lawmakers can override the veto, but two-thirds of each chamber must support the override to transform a vetoed bill into law. When President George W. Bush twice vetoed a popular children's health care proposal, for example, House supporters couldn't rally the two-thirds majority to override it. The bill became law only when Obama, a supporter, took over the White House.

If all this sounds complicated, it is. Then again, no one poking around a sausage ever said it's easy to decipher the parts.

D.C. IN THE MOVIES

1 *In the Line of Fire.* A Secret Service agent (Clint Eastwood) tries to protect the president from an assassin (John Malkovich). Eastwood memorably says to Lincoln "Wish I could have been there for you, pal" at the **Lincoln Memorial.**

2 *The Day the Earth Stood Still.* The movie begins with a flying saucer landing outside the **White House.**

3 *Nixon.* Oliver Stone's biopic depicts the life of Richard Nixon (Anthony Hopkins) from childhood to presidency to scandal, with many **White House** scenes.

4 *All the President's Men.* The story of the **Watergate** scandal; the notorious hotel's entrance and parking lot were shot on location.

5 *Mr Smith Goes to Washington.* James Stewart battles with senators on **Capitol Hill.** Patriotism and faith in the people ultimately triumph over murky politics.

6 *Strangers on a Train.* Alfred Hitchcock's film features **Union Station,** where two strangers plot the perfect crime.

7 *The Exorcist.* The 75 steps at **Prospect and 36th streets** that lead down to M Street in **Georgetown** are second in fame only to Rocky's in Philadelphia.

8 *Wedding Crashers.* Owen Wilson's character crashes the wedding of the treasury secretary's daughter. See the mansion at ⊠ **3122 P Street NW in Georgetown.**

9 *Enemy of the State.* Will Smith, playing a lawyer, finds himself accidentally in possession of evidence of a politically motivated murder. Jason Lee is chased through **Adams Morgan** and the **Dupont Circle underpass.**

10 *Dr Strangelove.* A U.S. general goes insane and launches nuclear war on the U.S.S.R. In this Cold War satire set in the **Pentagon,** Peter Sellers plays the three would-be heroes: the U.S. president, a British officer, and Dr. Strangelove.

11 *Transformers: Dark of the Moon.* The third installment of the action series made headlines when a yellow Camero (aka Bumblebee) collided with a D.C. police SUV during filming near the **Capitol.**

12 *State of Play.* This thriller depicts a reporter (Russell Crowe) chasing a story of congressional corruption, dirty defense contracts, and murder. The film includes scenes in **Mt. Pleasant,** the **Maine Avenue Fish Market,** and Ben's Chili Bowl.

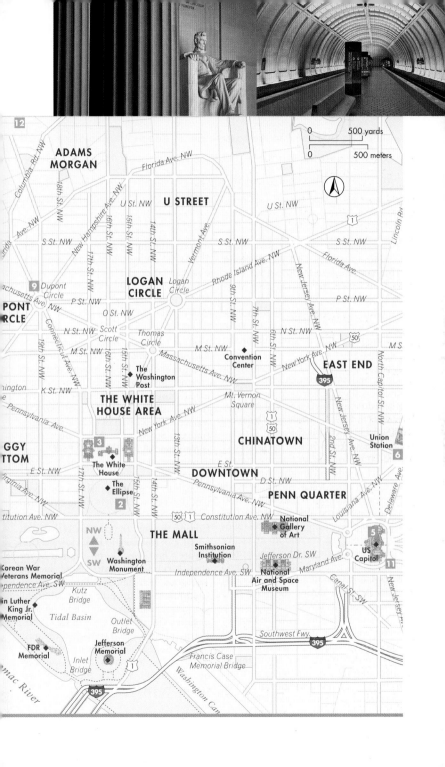

WASHINGTON, D.C. BLACK HISTORY WALK

A walk along U Street and the eastern rim of Adams Morgan gives a taste of D.C. that most tourists never get. This tour through "Black Broadway" bounces from lively commercial streets brimming with hip bars, cafés, and boutiques to quiet, tree-lined residential blocks and highlights African-American culture and history.

"Black Broadway"—U Street Corridor

The **African-American Civil War Memorial** at 10th and U streets is the perfect place to start; it has its own Metro stop. More than 200,000 names of black soldiers who fought for their freedom surround the small memorial. A block west sits **Bohemian Caverns**, a landmark restaurant and lounge that once hosted such jazz greats as Louis Armstrong, Ella Fitzgerald, Billie Holiday, and native son Duke Ellington. You can still catch live jazz here; check the schedule and return in the evening. Across 11th Street is **Washington Industrial Bank**, which thrived by offering African-Americans a service that others in the city wouldn't: the option to borrow money. One block south and another west you'll find the **12th Street YMCA**, the oldest black Y in the country (1853). Head back to U Street to explore the **African-American Civil War Museum**, featuring wonderful photographs from the era and an extensive on-site database for searching individual soldiers. Next, grab a half-smoke at **Ben's Chili Bowl**. A D.C. landmark, Ben's refused to close its doors during the fierce riots that followed the 1968 assassination of Dr. Martin Luther King Jr. While most of U Street was being destroyed, Ben's fed the policemen and black activists trying to keep order. Next door is the **Lincoln Theater**, another exceptional jazz venue and, from 1922 until desegregation, one of the largest and most elegant "colored-only" theaters. Given the area's history, it's probably little wonder that 15th and U marked the epicenter of the spontaneous celebration that erupted in the streets following the 2008 election of Barack Obama, the country's first African-American president.

North of U Street

Venture north one block to marvel at **St. Augustine's Catholic Church**—a gorgeous, two-tower cathedral now home to a black congregation that seceded from its segregated church (St. Matthews) in 1858. Feel free to walk inside to glimpse the striking stained-glass portrait of a black St. Augustine and St. Monica. A few steps north is **Meridian Hill (or Malcolm X) Park**, where a number of civil rights marches have originated over the years. If you're lucky enough to be strolling through on a Sunday, don't miss the lively drum circle that forms spontaneously in the afternoon. Cutting through the park to 16th Street, you'll spot **Meridian Hill Hall**, Howard University's first coed dorm. Alumni of the elite African-American school include Thurgood Marshall and Toni Morrison. Continuing north, past some beautiful working embassies, you'll find **All Souls Unitarian Church**. Its pastor in the 1940s, Reverend A. Powell Davies, led the push to desegregate D.C. schools. President William Taft and Adlai Stevenson were once members, and the church bell was cast by the son of Paul Revere.

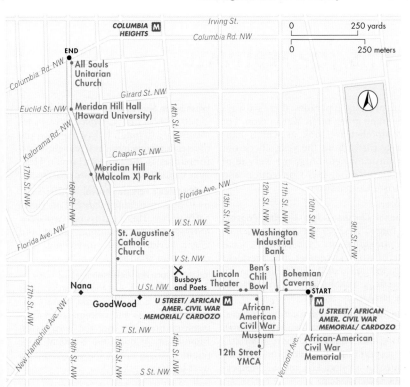

Highlights:	U Street was the center of black culture before Harlem was Harlem. See where Duke Ellington played, indulge in a half-smoke at Ben's Chili Bowl, and learn a bit about African-American history along the way.
Where to Start:	African-American Civil War Memorial on the Metro's Green or Yellow line.
Length:	About 1.5 miles; 1–2 hours, with window-shopping.
Where to Stop:	All Souls Unitarian Church. The S1, S2, or S4 bus lines on 16th Street will whisk you back Downtown.
Best Time to Go:	While the sun is up, though the nightlife on U Street is an attraction in itself.
Worst Time to Go:	Avoid walking through Meridian Hill Park after dark.
Shopping Detour:	Check out Nana (✉ 1528 U St. NW between 15th and 16th Sts., upstairs) for new and vintage women's clothing, and browse Goodwood (✉ 1428 U St. NW between 14th and 15th Sts.) for antique wood furniture and estate jewelry.

D.C.'S TOP FESTIVALS

From protests to parades, there's always something going on in Washington. For a comprehensive look at what's happening throughout the year, check out ⊕ *www.washington.org*, the website of the Washington, DC Convention and Tourism Corporation.

Winter

National Christmas Tree Lighting/Pageant of Peace (☎ *202/208–1631* ⊕ *www. thenationaltree.org* ☉ *December*). Each year in early December, the president lights the tree at dusk on the Ellipse, with concerts, a Yule log, and Nativity scene held later in the month.

Restaurant Week (⊕ *www.washington.org/ restaurantwk* ☉ *January and August*). During this promotion, more than 200 top restaurants offer lunch and dinner menus for around $20 and $35 respectively—often a steal.

Spring

National Cherry Blossom Festival (☎ *877/44– BLOOM* ⊕ *www.nationalcherryblossom festival.org* ☉ *Late March–early April*). Washington's most eye-catching annual festival opens with a Japanese lantern-lighting ceremony at the Tidal Basin. Some years, the cherry trees actually cooperate with the festival's planners and bloom on schedule.

Filmfest DC (☎ *202/234–3456* ⊕ *www. filmfestdc.org* ☉ *Early–mid-April*). 2013 will mark the 27th anniversary of this international festival, which seems to grow more popular each year.

Summer

Capital Pride Festival (☎ *202/719–5304* ⊕ *www.capitalpride.org* ☉ *Early June*). This weeklong festival, the nation's fourth-largest celebrating gay, lesbian, bisexual, and transgendered citizens, features a parade with eye-catching floats.

Washington Shakespeare Theatre Free for All (☎ *202/547–1122* ⊕ *www.shakespeare theatre.org* ☉ *June*). For two weeks, the theater company mounts free nightly performances at the Sidney Harman Hall, near Chinatown. Tickets are required.

Smithsonian's Folklife Festival (☎ *202/633– 6440* ⊕ *www.folklife.si.edu* ☉ *Late June– early July*). This engrossing two-week festival includes traditional dance and music performances, storytelling, and ethnic food of all sorts.

Independence Day Celebration (☎ *202/619– 7222* ☉ *July*). July 4 at the nation's capital begins with a grand parade along Constitution Avenue and culminates in awe-inspiring fireworks over the Washington Monument. At dusk, the National Symphony Orchestra plays from the Capitol's west lawn.

Fall

National Book Festival (☎ *202/707–1940* ☉ *Late September*). Sponsored by the Library of Congress, this two-day event attracts some of the world's top authors, poets, and illustrators to the National Mall, where visitors can get books signed, snap photos with their favorite scribes, or just swim the seas of literature. It's a great place for kids.

Veterans Day (☎ *703/607–8000 Cemetery Visitor Center, 202/619–7222 National Park Service* ☉ *November 11*). Services take place at Arlington National Cemetery, the Vietnam Veterans Memorial, and the U.S. Navy Memorial. A wreath-laying ceremony is held at 11 am at the Tomb of the Unknowns.

Neighborhoods

WORD OF MOUTH

"D.C. is wonderful . . . Just try not to overdo. You won't see everything. You can't see every exhibit in every museum. Pace yourself,
see what you are interested in, and take long lunches and breaks."
　　　　　　　　　　　　　　　　　　　　　　　—con_brio

Updated by
Renee Sklarew

Washington is a city of vistas—a marriage of geometry and art. Unlike other large cities, it isn't dominated by skyscrapers. The result: the world's first planned capital is also one of its most beautiful.

HOW D.C. CAME TO BE

The city that invented American politicking, back scratching, and delicate diplomatic maneuvering is itself the result of a compromise. Tired of its nomadic existence after having set up shop in eight locations, Congress voted in 1785 to establish a permanent federal city. Northern lawmakers wanted the capital on the Delaware River, in the North; Southerners wanted it on the Potomac, in the South. A deal was struck when Virginia's Thomas Jefferson agreed to support the proposal that the federal government assume the war debts of the colonies if New York's Alexander Hamilton and other northern legislators would agree to locate the capital on the banks of the Potomac.

George Washington himself selected the site of the capital, a diamond-shape, 100-square-mile plot that encompassed the confluence of the Potomac and Anacostia rivers, not far from his estate at Mount Vernon. To give the young city a head start, Washington included the already thriving tobacco ports of Alexandria, Virginia, and Georgetown, Maryland, in the District of Columbia. In 1791 Pierre-Charles L'Enfant, a French engineer who had fought in the Revolution, created the classic plan for the city.

It took the Civil War—and every war thereafter—to energize the city, by attracting thousands of new residents and spurring building booms that extended the capital in all directions. Streets were paved in the 1870s, and the first streetcars ran in the 1880s. Memorials to famous Americans such as Lincoln and Jefferson were built in the first decades of the 20th century, along with the massive Federal Triangle, a monument to thousands of less-famous government workers.

THE MALL
AMERICA'S TOWN GREEN

It could be said that the Mall—the heart of almost every visitor's trip to Washington—has influenced life in the U.S. more than any other expanse of lawn. The Mall is a picnicking park, a jogging path, and an outdoor stage for festivals and fireworks. People come here from around the globe to tour the illustrious Smithsonian Institution museums, celebrate special events, or rally to make the world a better place.

The AIDS Memorial Quilt on the Mall in 1996.

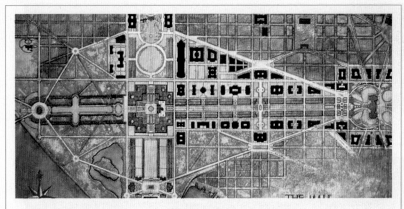

FROM TRASH HEAP TO TOURIST ATTRACTION: A BRIEF HISTORY OF THE MALL

Even before becoming the birthplace of American political protest, the Mall was a hotly contested piece of real estate. More than a century of setbacks and debate resulted not in Pierre L'Enfant's vision of a house-lined boulevard, but rather the premier green space you see today.

In 1791, Pierre Charles L'Enfant designed Washington, D.C., with a mile-long Grand Avenue running west from the Congress building. According to his plan, the boulevard would be lined with homes for statesmen and open green spaces, including a central garden bordered by a dense grove of trees.

L'Enfant's grandiose plan took more than 100 years to become a reality. By 1850, the area we now know as the Mall had not become a park, but was used instead as a storage area for lumber, firewood, and trash. With President Fillmore's permission, a group of businessmen hired landscape designer Andrew Jackson Downing to plan a national park featuring natural-style gardening. Sadly, Downing was killed in 1852, and his plan was never fully implemented.

Despite this setback, progress continued. The first Smithsonian museum on the Mall, the National Museum (now the Arts and Industries Building), opened to the public in 1881, and after 35 years of construction, the Washington Monument was completed in 1884.

A victory for the Mall occurred in 1901, when the Senate Park Commission, or McMillan Commission, was created to redesign the Mall as the city's ceremonial center. The McMillan plan embraced L'Enfant's vision of formal, public spaces and civic art, but replaced his Grand Avenue with a 300-foot expanse of grass bordered by American elms. It also called for cultural and educational institutions to line the Mall. Finally, a modified version of L'Enfant's great open space in the heart of Washington would become a reality.

The National Park Service assumed management of the Mall in 1933. In the latter half of the twentieth century, new museums and monuments opened on the Mall to create the public gathering place, tourist attraction, and tribute to our nation's heroes that we know today.

Above, McMillan Plan for the Mall, Washington, D.C., 1902.

HISTORIC RALLIES ON THE MALL

1894: Coxey's Army, a group of unemployed workers from Ohio, stage the first-ever protest march on Washington.

1939: Contralto Marian Anderson gives an Easter Sunday concert on the grounds of the Lincoln Memorial after the Daughters of the American Revolution bar her from performing at their headquarters because she's black.

1963: The Lincoln Memorial is the site of Martin Luther King Jr.'s inspirational I Have a Dream speech during the March on Washington.

1971: The Vietnam Veterans Against the War camp out on the Mall to persuade Congress to end military actions in Southeast Asia.

1972: The first Earth Day is celebrated on April 22 on the National Mall.

1987: The AIDS Memorial Quilt is displayed for the first time in its entirety. It returns to the Mall in 1988, 1989, 1992, and 1996.

1995: Nearly 400,000 African-American men fill the Mall, from the Capitol to the Washington Monument, during the Million Man March.

Top, Matin Luther King Jr. delivers his I Have a Dream speech.

Center, Vietnam War Veterans protest.

Bottom, Million Man March.

WHAT ABOUT THE MONUMENTS?

Visitors often confuse the Mall with the similarly named National Mall. The Mall is the expanse of lawn between 3rd and 14th Streets, while the National Mall is the national park that spans from the Capitol to the Potomac, including the Mall, the monuments, and the Tidal Basin. To reach the monuments, head west from the Mall or south from the White House and be prepared for a long walk. To visit all the monuments in one day requires marathon-level stamina and good walking shoes; to visit the monuments and the Mall in the same day would be the Ironman of tourism. ⇨ For more about D.C.'s monuments and memorials, see Chapter 4.

TOP 15 THINGS
TO DO ON THE MALL

1. Ride the old-fashioned carousel in front of the Smithsonian Castle.

2. Watch the fireworks on the Fourth of July.

3. See the original *Spirit of St. Louis,* and then learn how things fly at the National Air and Space Museum.

4. Gross out your friends at the Natural History Museum's Insect Zoo.

5. Gawk at Dorothy's ruby slippers, Kermit the Frog, Abraham Lincoln's top hat, and Lewis and Clark's compass at the American History Museum.

6. Twirl around the ice skating rink in the National Gallery of Art's sculpture garden.

7. View astonishing wooden masks at the Museum of African Art.

8. Taste North, South, and Central American dishes at the National Museum of the American Indian's Mitsitam Café.

9. Exercise your First Amendment rights by joining a rally or protest.

10. Peek at the many-armed and elephant-headed statues of Hindu gods at the Sackler Gallery.

11. Pose with sculptures by Auguste Rodin and Henry Moore at the Hirshhorn Sculpture Garden.

12. Learn how you make money—literally—at the Bureau of Engraving and Printing.

13. Follow the lives of the people who lived and died in Nazi Germany at the Holocaust Memorial Museum.

14. Eat, drink, watch, listen, and learn at an outdoor cultural festival.

15. Picnic and people-watch on the lawn after a hard day of sightseeing.

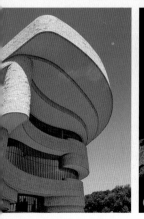

VISITING THE MUSEUMS ON THE MALL

MAKE THE MOST OF YOUR TIME

With 12 museums spread out along 11 city blocks, you can't expect to see everything in one day. Few people have the stamina for more than half a day of museum- or gallery-hopping at a time; children definitely don't. To avoid mental and physical exhaustion, try to devote at least two days to the Mall and use these itineraries (and our listings in Chapter 3) to make the best use of your time.

Historical Appeal: For a day devoted to history and culture, start with the **Holocaust Museum**, grabbing lunch at its excellent cafeteria. After refueling, the next stop is the **American History Museum**, which reopened in late 2008 after extensive renovations. Or, cross the length of the Mall to visit the **Museum of the American Indian** instead.

Art Start: To fill a day with paintings and sculptures, begin at the twin buildings of the **National Gallery of Art**. Enjoy the museum's sculpture while you dine in the garden's outdoor café. You'll find a second sculpture garden directly across the Mall at the **Hirshhorn**. If you like the avant-garde, visit the Hirshhorn's indoor galleries; for a cosmopolitan collection of Asian and African art and artifacts, head instead to the **Sackler Gallery** and **Museum of African Art**.

Taking the Kids: The most kid-friendly museum of them all, the **National Air and Space Museum** is a must-see for the young and young-at-heart. There's only fast food in the museum, but the **Museum of the American Indian** next door has healthier options. If your young bunch can handle two museums in a day, cross the lawn to the **Natural History Museum**. This itinerary works well for science buffs, too.

THE BEST IN A DAY

Got one day and want to see the best of the Smithsonian? Start at the **Air and Space Museum**, then skip to the side-by-side **Natural History** and **American History Museums**. Picnic on the Mall or hit the museum cafeterias.

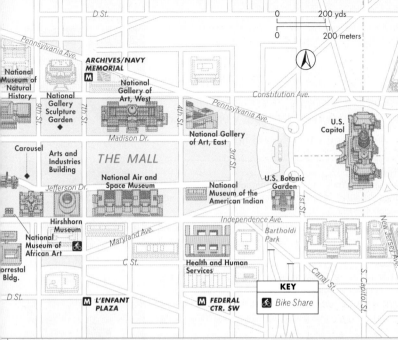

NOT ANOTHER HOT DOG! A Survival Guide to Eating Well on the Mall

Even locals wonder where to grab a decent bite to eat when touring the Smithsonian Museums. Hot dogs, soft pretzels, and ice cream from a cart don't make for a nutritious lunch. On a weekday, the streets north of Constitution Avenue offer easy-to-find lunch spots, but virtually all are closed on weekends.

Here are some places for better dining by the Mall, though several require a few blocks' walk.

On the Fly food carts offer eco-friendly, often organic snacks. Find one by the Sackler Gallery.

Museum of the American Indian: The Mitsitam Café—the name means "let's eat" in the language of the Delaware and Piscataway people—is one of the best museum cafeterias on the Mall. Food stations serve native-inspired sandwiches, entrees, soups, and desserts from five regions of the western hemisphere.

Pavilion Café: Located in the National Gallery's Sculpture Garden, this eatery offers indoor and outdoor seating with views of the artwork and fountain/ice rink outside. The menu includes salads, sandwiches, and pizzas. You'll also find more food options inside the National Gallery.

Pennsylvania Avenue SE: If lunchtime finds you on the east end of the Mall, head past the Capitol to Pennsylvania Avenue SE. Between Second and Fourth Streets, you'll find plenty of pubs, cafés, and sandwich shops. It's a bit of a hike, but well worth the shoe leather.

Old Post Office Pavilion: The food court here is open seven days a week. The selection is predictable—sushi, pizza, deli, bagels, Chinese food—but they provide cheap fare for a variety of tastes.

Ronald Reagan Building and International Trade Center: The food court here is another option, but is closed on Sundays during the winter.

ANNUAL EVENTS

The Mall's spacious lawn is ideal for all kinds of outdoor festivals. These annual events are local favorites and definitely worth a stop if you're in town while they're happening.

St. Patrick's Day Parade

WINTER

Ice Skating: Whirl and twirl at the outdoor ice rink in the National Gallery of Art's Sculpture Garden. *Mid-November through mid-March*

St. Patrick's Day Parade: Dancers, bands, and bagpipes celebrate all things Irish along Constitution Avenue. *Mid-March*

SPRING

National Cherry Blossom Festival: When the cherry trees burst into bloom, you know that spring has arrived. Fly a kite, watch a parade, and learn about Japanese culture in a setting sprinkled with pink and white flowers. *Late March through early April*

Cherry Blossom Festival

SUMMER

Smithsonian Folklife Festival: Performers, cooks, farmers, and craftsmen demonstrate cultural traditions from around the world. *Around July 4*

Independence Day: What better place to celebrate the birth of our nation than in the capital city? Enjoy concerts and parades on the Mall, then watch the fireworks explode over the Washington Monument. *July 4*

Smithsonian Folklife Festival

Screen on the Green: Film favorites are shown on a gigantic movie screen on Monday nights. Bring a blanket and picnic dinner to better enjoy the warm summer evenings. *Mid-July through mid-August*

FALL

Black Family Reunion: D.C. celebrates African-American family values. Pavilions showcase businesses owned by African-Americans and events and performances feature black entertainers, celebrities, and experts. *September*

Independence Day Reenactment

National Book Festival: Meet your favorite author in person at the Library of Congress' annual literary festival. Over 70 writers and illustrators participate in readings, live interviews, and events for kids. *September*

Marine Corps Marathon: The "Marathon of the Monuments" starts in Virginia but winds its way around the entire National Mall. It's as fun to cheer as it is to run. *Late October*

Marine Corps Marathon

PLANNING YOUR VISIT

National Cherry Blossom Festival Parade

KEEP IN MIND

■ All of the museums on the Mall are free to the public.

■ Since September 11, 2001 security has increased, and visitors will need to go through screenings and bag checks, which create long lines during peak tourist season.

■ Two museums require timed-entry passes: the Holocaust Museum from March through August, and the Bureau of Printing and Engraving. If you've got a jam-packed day planned, it's best to get your tickets early in the morning or in advance.

GETTING HERE AND GETTING AROUND

Metro Travel: You can access the Mall from several Metro stations. On the Blue and Orange lines, the Federal Triangle stop is convenient to the Natural History and American History museums, and the Smithsonian stop is close to the Holocaust Memorial Museum and Sackler Gallery. On the Yellow and Green lines, Archives/Navy Memorial takes you to the National Gallery of Art. The L'Enfant Plaza stop, accessible from the Blue, Orange, Yellow, and Green lines, is the best exit for the Hirshhorn and Air and Space Museum.

Bus Travel: Walking from the Holocaust Memorial Museum to the National Gallery of Art is quite a trek. Many visitors take advantage of the Mall Express hop-on, hop-off bus run by ANC Tours/Martz Gray Line (⊕ www.anctours.com/MallExpress.php), which run 9–6:30 Mar.–Sept. and 9–4:30 Oct.–Feb.

Car Travel: Parking is hard to find along the Mall. You can find private parking garages north of the Mall in the Downtown area, where you'll have to pay to leave your car. If you're willing to walk, limited free parking is available on Ohio Drive SW near the Jefferson Memorial and East Potomac Park.

HELP, THERE'S A PROTEST ON THE MALL!

Since the 1890s, protesters have gathered on the Mall to make their opinions known. If you're not in a rallying mood, you don't have to let First Amendment activities prevent you from visiting the Smithsonian museums or enjoying a visit to the Mall.

■ **Use the back door:** All of the Smithsonian museums have entrances on Constitution or Independence Avenues, which do not border the Mall's lawn. Use these doors to gain admission without crossing the Mall itself.

■ **Know you're protected:** The Mall is a national park, just like Yosemite or Yellowstone. The National Park Service has a responsibility to visitors to make sure they can safely view park attractions. To this end, demonstrators are often required to keep main streets open.

■ **Avoid the crowds:** Even the biggest rallies don't cover the entire National Mall. If the crowd is by the Capitol, head west to visit the Lincoln Memorial. If protestors are gathered around the Washington Monument, visit the Jefferson Memorial on the opposite side of the Tidal Basin. There's plenty to see.

THE WHITE HOUSE AREA
AND FOGGY BOTTOM

Sightseeing
★★★★★
Dining
★★★☆☆
Lodging
★★☆☆☆
Shopping
★☆☆☆☆
Nightlife
★★☆☆☆

Foggy Bottom includes some of D.C.'s most iconic attractions, the top being the White House. The home of every U.S. president but George Washington, the 132-room mansion is as impressive in real life as it is on television. It may be tough to decide what to see first of the monuments and parkland of the National Mall and Tidal Basin, as well as some of Washington's smaller museums. Adding to the variety, you'll find the Kennedy Center, the infamous Watergate complex, and George Washington University's campus. Peppered among the government buildings, museums, monuments, and university buildings are also some of D.C.'s oldest houses, revealing the area's surprisingly residential character.

WHITE HOUSE AREA WALK

Seeing everything this neighborhood has to offer could easily occupy the greater part of a day, or more, so prioritize and be prepared for lots of walking. This walk takes you past the core area around the White House and then offers two ways to continue exploring the neighborhood—either checking out the monuments on the National Mall and Tidal Basin or the government buildings west of the White House. In good weather the monuments are particularly enticing, but there are interesting tours of some of the government buildings as well. Many sites require advance reservations and few are kid-friendly, but history and art buffs shouldn't miss these hidden gems.

A statue of Andrew Jackson during the Battle of New Orleans presides over Lafayette Square.

Whether you choose to focus your time on monuments or government buildings, it's easy to wind up at the **John F. Kennedy Center for the Performing Arts** for an evening performance. Along the Potomac River, the Kennedy Center is both a memorial to the late president and a bustling cultural center with six theaters for the performance of music, dance, opera, and dramatic arts. Time your visit well, and you could catch one of the free concerts at 6 pm daily.

CORE WHITE HOUSE AREA

Arriving at either the Farragut West or McPherson Square Metro stop, you quickly reach the trees and flower beds of **Lafayette Square**, an intimate oasis amid Downtown Washington. The park was named for the Marquis de Lafayette, the young French nobleman who came to America to fight in the Revolution. His **statue** is in the southeast corner of the park. In the center, the large **statue of Andrew Jackson** is the second equestrian statue made in America.

St. John's Episcopal Church has sat across from the park since 1816. Every president since Madison has visited the church, and many have worshipped here regularly. The **Decatur House** just west of the square was the first private residence on Lafayette Square, and now houses the National Center for White House History, plus a museum that shows the living quarters as they were in the Federal period and in the Victorian era.

Looking south, the **White House,** at 1600 Pennsylvania Avenue, is straight ahead across the park. Tops on every first-timer's D.C. to-do list should be a visit to this most famous home. Plan ahead: you must make arrangements for admission months in advance with your member of Congress or embassy. For more information, stop at the **White House**

GETTING ORIENTED

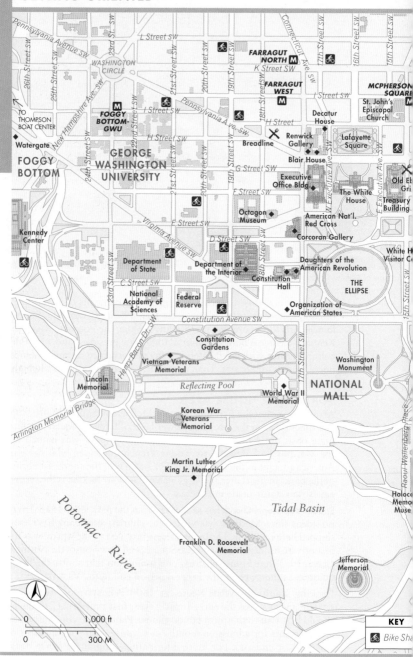

Pennsylvania Avenue SW
26th Street SW
25th Street SW
23rd St. SW
L Street SW
WASHINGTON CIRCLE
Pennsylvania Ave. SW
New Hampshire Ave. SW
21st Street SW
20th Street SW
19th St. SW
18th Street SW
L Street SW
K Street SW
FARRAGUT NORTH M
Connecticut Ave. SW
17th Street SW
16th Street SW
15th Street SW
FARRAGUT WEST M
I Street SW
MCPHERSON SQUARE M
TO THOMPSON BOAT CENTER
M **FOGGY BOTTOM-GWU**
I Street SW
H Street
Decatur House
St. John's Episcopal Church
Watergate
H Street SW
Breadline
Renwick Gallery
Lafayette Square
FOGGY BOTTOM
GEORGE WASHINGTON UNIVERSITY
G Street SW
Blair House
Old El Gri
Virginia Avenue SW
E Street SW
F Street SW
Executive Office Bldg.
The White House
W Executive Ave. SW
E Executive Ave. SW
Treasury Building
Kennedy Center
Octagon Museum
American Nat'l. Red Cross
White H Visitor C
D Street SW
Corcoran Gallery
Department of State
Department of the Interior
8th Street SW
Daughters of the American Revolution
15th Street SW
C Street SW
National Academy of Sciences
Federal Reserve
Constitution Hall
THE ELLIPSE
Constitution Avenue SW
Organization of American States
Henry Bacon Dr. SW
Constitution Gardens
Vietnam Veterans Memorial
Washington Monument
Lincoln Memorial
Reflecting Pool
World War II Memorial
NATIONAL MALL
7th Street SW
Arlington Memorial Bridge
Korean War Veterans Memorial
Martin Luther King Jr. Memorial
Raoul Wallenberg Place
Potomac River
Tidal Basin
Holoca Memo Muse
Franklin D. Roosevelt Memorial
Jefferson Memorial

0 —— 1,000 ft
0 —— 300 M

KEY
Bike Sha

GREAT EXPERIENCES IN THE WHITE HOUSE AREA

Corcoran Gallery of Art: The great 19th-century American painters were inspired by the sublime majesty of the American West. See the most-definitive works—Albert Bierstadt's *Mount Corcoran* and Frederick Church's *Niagara*.

John F. Kennedy Center for the Performing Arts: See a free performance by anyone from the Joffrey Ballet to the National Symphony Orchestra here on the Millennium Stage, daily, 6 pm.

The Renwick Gallery: If the White House tour doesn't satisfy your inner decorating diva, perhaps the Tiffany objets d'art, intricately carved antique tables, and opulent Victorian Grand Salon here will do the trick.

Thompson's Boat Center: Take in Washington's marble monuments, lush Roosevelt Island, and the Virginia coastline with a canoe ride down the Potomac.

The White House: You have to plan weeks, if not months, in advance, and you're only allowed into 9 of the 132 rooms, but there's no denying the kick of touring 1600 Pennsylvania Avenue—especially around Christmas.

GETTING HERE

The White House can be reached by the Red Line's Farragut North stop or the Blue and Orange lines' McPherson Square and Farragut West stops. Foggy Bottom has its own Metro stop, also on the Blue and Orange lines. A free shuttle runs from the station to the Kennedy Center. Many of the other attractions are a considerable distance from the nearest subway stop. If you don't relish long walks or time is limited, check the map to see if you need to make alternate travel arrangements to visit specific sights.

PLANNING YOUR TIME

Touring the area around the White House could easily take a day or even two, depending on how long you visit each of the museums along the way.

If you enjoy history, you may be most interested in the **Decatur House, DAR Museum,** and **State Department**. If it's art you crave, devote the hours to the **Corcoran** and **Renwick** galleries instead. Save the **Kennedy Center** for the evening.

QUICK BITES

The Corcoran Gallery's Todd Gray's Muse. Chef Todd Gray serves a lunch of salads, sandwiches, and small plates. ⊠ *500 17th St. NW, White House area* ☎ *202/639–1786* ⊕ *www.todd graysmuse.com* ⊗ *Closed Mon. and Tues. No dinner.*

Breadline. The menu changes daily, but you'll always find sweet breakfast treats and savory lunchtime salads and sandwiches. ⊠ *1751 Pennsylvania Ave. NW, White House area* ☎ *202/822–8900* ⊕ *www. breadline.com* ⊗ *Closed weekends* Ⓜ *Farragut West.*

Old Ebbitt Grill. The haunt of former presidents is still a popular watering hole for politicos, journalists, and off-duty Secret Service agents. ⊠ *675 15th St. NW, White House area* ☎ *202/347–4800* ⊕ *www.ebbitt.com.*

2

Visitor Center, in the Department of Commerce building on Pennsylvania Avenue between 14th and 15th streets NW.

The White House is flanked by two imposing buildings that you can view but not enter. To the east, the **Treasury Building** is the largest Greek Revival edifice in Washington. Robert Mills, the architect responsible for the Washington Monument and the Patent Office (now the Smithsonian American Art Museum), designed the grand colonnade that stretches down 15th Street. The building's southern facade has a **statue of Alexander Hamilton,** the department's first secretary. To the west, the granite edifice that looks like a wedding cake is the Eisenhower **Executive Office Building,** styled after the Louvre. Built as a headquarters of the State, War, and Navy departments, it now houses offices for the vice president and other members of the executive branch. The building was the site of both the first presidential press conference in 1950 and the first televised press conference five years later.

> **CITY VIEW**
>
> For a different view of the city without waiting in line, don't miss the view from the roof of the Kennedy Center. There's also a café and restaurant there.

As you go past the Executive Office Building, note the green canopy marking the entrance to **Blair House** opposite, the residence used by heads of state visiting Washington. Farther along, the **Renwick Gallery** of the Smithsonian American Art Museum exhibits American crafts and decorative arts.

Seventeenth Street leads you to the **Corcoran Gallery of Art.** The Beaux-Arts building houses an impressive collection of American, European, and contemporary art, photography, and decorative arts. One block west, at 18th Street, the **Octagon Museum**—actually a six-, not eight-sided building—is where President James and Dolley Madison lived temporarily, after the British burned the White House in 1814. Today, it portrays life in the city at the birth of the nation's new capital.

You could detour here to the left, cut across the Ellipse and see the White House and its perfect south lawn and vegetable garden from the other side. On the southern end stand a weather-beaten **gatehouse** that once stood on Capitol Hill and the **Boy Scouts Memorial.** By the southeast corner of the White House lawn, the **Tecumseh Sherman Monument** depicts the Civil War general mounted on his steed, surrounded by four sentries.

Otherwise, farther down 17th Street, a tour of the **Daughters of the American Revolution (DAR)** headquarters lets you peek into a few of the 31 period rooms—each decorated in a style unique to one state and one time period—and the Beaux-Arts auditorium now used as a genealogy library. The museum on the first floor hosts changing exhibitions.

Continuing south on 17th Street, the headquarters of the **Organization of American States,** which is made up of nations from North, South, and Central America, contains a patio adorned with a pre-Columbian–style fountain and lush tropical plants. This tiny rain forest is a good place to rest when Washington's summer heat is at its most oppressive.

Punctuating the skyline like an exclamation point, the Washington Monument can be seen from 30 miles away.

A MONUMENTAL STROLL

At this point you probably want to make the choice between monuments and government buildings. If you choose the former, carefully cross the speeding highway that is Constitution Avenue and reach the peace and tranquillity of the **National Mall**, home of D.C.'s monuments and memorials. Heading east, you can't miss the **Washington Monument.** The elegant obelisk built in memory of George Washington dominates the skyline. The monument's pyramidion top and supporting structure is under repair due to a 5.8-magnitude earthquake in 2011; there is no access to the top and a fence surrounds the structure to protect visitors from falling debris. The monument is scheduled to reopen in late 2013.

To the west, see the **World War II Memorial** and continue along the **Reflecting Pool**, with the imposing **Lincoln Memorial** dominating the view ahead of you. On either side are the **Korean War** and **Vietnam Veterans Memorials** and **Constitution Gardens.** If you can, make time to visit the **Tidal Basin**, home to the **Roosevelt** and **Jefferson** memorials, and the city's newest memorial, honoring **Martin Luther King Jr.** Each spring the cherry trees around the Tidal Basin burst into pink-and-white blooms, and the city celebrates the beauty of this gift from Japan with a two-week **Cherry Blossom Festival.**

GOVERNMENT BUILDINGS

If you forgo the monuments, take Constitution Avenue to the west instead. The headquarters of many government departments and national organizations reside along the blocks between E Street and Constitution Avenue west of the Ellipse. Several offer tours or exhibits for the public, but always check whether advance reservations are required, and bring photo ID.

Virginia Avenue takes you up past the **Department of the Interior,** which contains a museum with exhibits based on the work of its branches, such as the Bureau of Land Management, National Park Service, and U.S. Geological Survey. Turn left on C Street to the **Federal Reserve Building,** which displays special art exhibitions that are only worth visiting if you're fascinated with the subject or want to see the inside of the Fed; reserve in advance. Set back from the Fed, you'll find the **National Academy of Sciences.** It offers two galleries of science-related art. Robert Berks's sculpture of Albert Einstein outside the building has broader appeal and a shady resting spot; the creator of the theory of relativity looks—dare we say?—cuddly.

You must reserve a tour at the **State Department** three months in advance, but it's worth the effort. A docent takes you to the top floor's **Department of State's Diplomatic Reception Rooms**—usually reserved for heads of state and special honorees, and the great halls and gathering spaces are furnished with American antiques and art.

Away from the White House and federal buildings, northern Foggy Bottom is the home of **George Washington University.** The university has no separate campus, but occupies many of the modern buildings and 19th-century houses between 19th and 24th streets south of Pennsylvania Avenue.

Near the Kennedy Center along the water, the **Watergate** made history on the night of June 17, 1972, but the apartment-office complex doesn't look so scandalous in person. Famous—and infamous—residents have included Attorney General John Mitchell and presidential secretary Rose Mary Woods of Nixon White House fame, as well as such D.C. insiders as Jacob Javits, Ruth Bader Ginsberg, Bob and Elizabeth Dole, Monica Lewinsky, and Condoleezza Rice. You'll also find shops and restaurants here.

If looking at the Potomac makes you yearn to get closer, the **Thompson's Boat Center,** at the end of Virginia Avenue, rents canoes, sailboats, and kayaks in the warmer months. Bike rentals are also available.

WHITE HOUSE AREA WITH KIDS

Touring the **White House** is as much of a thrill for kids as it is for adults. If you didn't plan your visit in advance, you can still get a look at White House life at the **White House Visitor Center,** where videos and photos capture first families. Unlike the actual White House, kids can roam around here and sit on the furniture.

At the **Daughters of the American Revolution Museum** kids five to seven can discover what life was like as a colonial child when they take part in the twice-monthly Colonial Adventure program.

In summer, give kids a break from touring the monuments with an afternoon boat ride on the **Tidal Basin.** If you're feeling a bit more intrepid, you can rent canoes from **Thompson's Boat Center** and paddle along the Potomac.

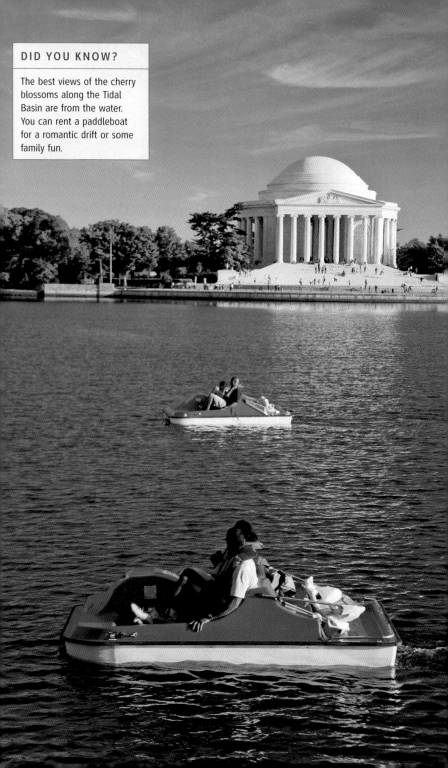

CAPITOL HILL AND NORTHEAST D.C.

Sightseeing
★★★★☆

Dining
★★★☆☆

Lodging
★★★☆☆

Shopping
★★★☆☆

Nightlife
★★★★☆

The people who live and work on "the Hill" do so in the shadow of the edifice that lends the neighborhood its name: the gleaming white Capitol. This is where political deals and decisions are made. Lining the streets behind these venerable buildings are some of the bars and pubs where off-duty senators, members of Congress, and lobbyists do some of their business.

Beyond these grand buildings lies a vibrant and diverse group of neighborhoods with charming residential blocks lined with Victorian row houses and a fine assortment of restaurants, bars, and shops, not to mention D.C.'s favorite market and newest sporting attraction. A little farther afield, the rapidly gentrifying H Street Corridor to the north and east offers hip, happening, and edgy shopping, dining, and nightlife.

CAPITOL HILL WALK

Capitol Hill's exact boundaries are disputed. Although most say it's bordered to the west, north, and south by the Capitol, H Street NE, and I Street SE, respectively, extending east only to 14th Street, some real-estate speculators argue that the trendy neighborhood extends east to the Anacostia River. What's clear is that Capitol Hill's historic-preservation movement is hard at work, restoring more and more 19th-century houses and fighting the urban blight that creeps in around the edges of this historic part of Washington.

There's a lot to see here, but you can easily explore the streets in a couple of hours. A good place to start is **Union Station**, easily accessible on the Metro Red Line. The Beaux-Arts station, modeled after a Roman bath, dominates the northwest corner of Capitol Hill. Thanks to a restoration project completed in 1988, the city's main train station has turned into a minimall, with shops, restaurants, and bike rentals. In the station's front plaza sits a steely-eyed Christopher Columbus at the base of a column on the **Columbus Memorial Fountain,** designed by Lorado Taft.

Next door, the **National Postal Museum** will delight philatelists. The Smithsonian takes a playful approach to stamp collecting and the history of the U.S. Postal Service with its interactive exhibits. On the other side of Union Station, the **Thurgood Marshall Federal Judiciary Building** is worth a quick peek. The atrium, designed by architect Edward Larabee Barnes, encloses a garden of bamboo five stories tall.

Following Delaware Avenue south, you come right up to the Capitol, the point from which the city is divided into quadrants: northwest, southwest, northeast, and southeast. North Capitol Street, which runs north from the Capitol, separates northeast from northwest; East Capitol Street separates northeast and southeast; South Capitol Street separates southwest and southeast; and the Mall (Independence Avenue on the south and Constitution Avenue on the north) separates northwest from southwest.

The massive **U.S. Capitol** sits majestically at the east end of the Mall, and is the foremost reason to visit Capitol Hill. Although the free tour (⊕ *tours.visitthecapitol.gov*) takes you through the impressive rotunda, Statuary Hall, and Old Senate Chamber, to see your legislators at work you need to arrange in advance for (free) gallery passes—contact your senator or representative's office. If you're a visitor from outside the United States, contact your embassy. Stop in at the **Capitol Visitor Center,** located underneath the Capitol, for guided tours, information, and to view the 13-minute orientation film. Enter on the east side of the building. The imposing buildings to the north and south of the Capitol house the offices of senators and representatives.

In front of the Capitol, three monuments flank a reflecting pool. In the center the **Ulysses S. Grant Memorial** is one of the largest sculpture groups in the city. To the south stands the **James A. Garfield Monument,** and to the north a **Peace Monument** commemorating sailors who died in the Civil War. Across Constitution Avenue a monolithic carillon forms the **Robert A. Taft Memorial,** dedicated to the longtime Republican senator and son of the 27th president.

Across from the Garfield Memorial, the **United States Botanic Garden** is the oldest botanic garden in North America. After touring the conservatory, be sure to wander through the rose, butterfly, water, and regional gardens of the **National Garden.** Another lovely spot, the **Bartholdi Fountain,** was created by Frederic-Auguste Bartholdi, sculptor of the Statue of Liberty. The aquatic monsters, sea nymphs, tritons, and lighted globes all represent the elements of water and light.

Continue east on Independence Avenue, then north on 1st Street, where the Jefferson Building of the Library of Congress and the U.S. Supreme Court sit side by side. The **Library of Congress** has so many books, recordings, maps, manuscripts, and photographs that it actually takes three buildings to get the job done. The **Jefferson Building** is only part open to the public. Here you can view the **Great Hall,** peek into the **Main Reading Room,** and wander through changing exhibitions related to the library's holdings. You can line up to hear oral arguments inside

GETTING ORIENTED

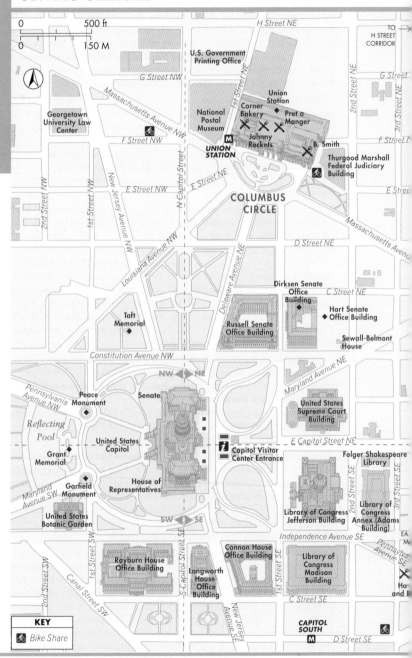

0 ——— 500 ft
0 ——— 150 M

H Street NE

TO
H STREET
CORRIDOR

U.S. Government
Printing Office

G Street NW

G Street

Georgetown
University Law
Center

Massachusetts Avenue NW

National
Postal
Museum

Corner
Bakery

Union
Station

Pret a
Manger

2nd Street NE

3rd Street NE

G Street NE

F Street NW

F Street I

UNION
STATION

Johnny
Rockets

B. Smith

Thurgood Marshall
Federal Judiciary
Building

E Street NW

E Street NE

COLUMBUS
CIRCLE

E Stree

2nd Street NW

1st Street NW

New Jersey Avenue NW

N Capitol Street

D Street NE

Massachusetts Avenu

Louisiana Avenue NW

Delaware Avenue NE

Dirksen Senate
Office
Building

C Street NE

Taft
Memorial

Russell Senate
Office Building

Hart Senate
Office Building

Sewall-Belmont
House

Constitution Avenue NW

NW   NE

Maryland Avenue NE

Pennsylvania
Avenue NW

Peace
Monument

Senate

United States
Supreme Court
Building

Reflecting
Pool

United States
Capitol

E Capitol Street NE

Grant
Memorial

Capitol Visitor
Center Entrance

Folger Shakespeare
Library

Maryland
Avenue SW

Garfield
Monument

House of
Representatives

Library of Congress
Jefferson Building

2nd Street SE

3rd Street SE

Library of
Congress
Annex (Adams
Building)

United States
Botanic Garden

SW   SE

Independence Avenue SE

EA
M

Pennsylvania
Avenue SE

1st Street SW

Canal Street SW

Rayburn House
Office Building

S Capitol Street SE

Longworth
House
Office
Building

Cannon House
Office Building

1st Street SE

Library of
Congress
Madison
Building

Hav
and I

2nd Street SW

New Jersey Avenue SE

C Street SE

CAPITOL
SOUTH

D Street SE

KEY

🚲 Bike Share

GREAT EXPERIENCES ON CAPITOL HILL AND NORTHEAST D.C.

The Capitol: See democracy in action. Watch congressmen and -women debate, insult, and wrangle their way through the job of making laws in the House and Senate chambers.

Eastern Market: One of D.C.'s most beloved weekend destinations is the place to pick up fresh produce, flowers, and locally made crafts.

The Hawk 'n' Dove: Order a pint and listen in as congressional staffers gripe about their famous bosses and locals debate the Redskins' Super Bowl chances at this quintessential D.C. bar and Capitol Hill institution. Closed for renovations at this writing, it's scheduled to reopen later in 2012.

The Library of Congress: Take a break from debate to contemplate the Gutenberg Bible, the lavishly sculpted Great Hall, and the splendor of the gilded Main Reading Room.

The Supreme Court: Round out your firsthand look at the three branches of government by watching the justices hear precedent-setting arguments.

United States Botanic Garden: Wrinkle your nose at the corpse flower, explore the jungle, gawk at the orchids, or stroll the paths of the new National Garden.

GETTING HERE

From the Red Line's Union Station, you can easily walk to most destinations on Capitol Hill. From the Blue and Orange lines, the Capitol South stop is close to the Capitol and Library of Congress, and the Eastern Market stop leads to the market and the Marine Corps Barracks. Bus numbers 30, 32, 34, 35, 36, and Circulator buses run from Friendship Heights through Georgetown and Downtown to Independence Avenue, the Capitol, and Eastern Market. A streetcar, which is slated to come into service in July 2013, will link Union Station with H Street's nightlife. Street parking is available.

PLANNING YOUR TIME

Touring Capitol Hill should take you about three hours, allowing for about an hour each at the **Capitol**, the **Botanic Garden**, and the **Library of Congress**.

If you want to see **Congress** in action, contact your legislator (or your country's embassy, if you are visiting from abroad) in advance, and bear in mind that the House and Senate are usually not in session in August.

Supreme Court cases are usually heard October through April, Monday through Wednesday, two weeks out of each month.

QUICK BITES

Library of Congress's Madison Building Cafeteria. Breakfast and lunch are served on the sixth floor, with a stunning view. ✉ *Madison Building, Library of Congress, Independence Ave., SE, between 1st and 2nd Sts., Capitol Hill* ☎ *202/707–8300* ⊕ *www.loc.gov* ☉ *Sat. and Sun.* Ⓜ *Capitol South.*

Tortilla Cafe. Inexpensive Salvadoran/Mexican specialties include an all-day breakfast. ✉ *210 7th St. SE, Capitol Hill* ☎ *202/547–5700* ⊕ *www.tortillacafe.com.*

The food court at Union Station offers everything from pizza to sushi.

2

Bustling Union Station is a great place to grab a bite and people-watch.

the **Supreme Court Building** when court is in session, but portions of the majestic building's first two floors are worth visiting year-round, with exhibits, lectures, a visitor's film, gift shop, and small cafeteria.

Behind the Library of Congress, the **Folger Shakespeare Library** holds an enormous collection of works by and about Shakespeare and his times, as well as a reproduced 16th-century theater and gallery that are open to visitors (the books are not). North of the Folger on 2nd Street, the **Sewall-Belmont House** was the headquarters of the historic National Woman's Party and contains exhibits and artifacts from the suffrage and women's rights movements.

SOUTH AND EAST OF THE CAPITOL

Away from the Capitol, you'll find some enticing attractions, including one of D.C.'s oldest communities and a thriving market. This area is well served by the Metro, though you can get around on foot.

East of 2nd Street, the neighborhood changes dramatically from large-scale government buildings to 19th-century town houses. Among them is the first Washington home of the abolitionist and writer **Frederick Douglass,** at 320 A Street NE, which you can visit by appointment.

Follow Pennsylvania Avenue south between 2nd and 4th streets to the main commercial thoroughfare. Restaurants, bars, and coffee shops frequented by those who live and work on the Hill line these blocks. Reaching Seward Square, take C Street one block to **Eastern Market** on the corner of 7th Street; it has been a feature of D.C. life since 1873. The main building, gutted by fire in 2007, has reopened after a $22-million restoration and modernization project. Here you can find an array of farmers, flower vendors, and other merchants who sell their fresh

A 24-foot-high catwalk at the U.S. Botanic Garden offers views of the lush jungle canopy.

produce and crafts to locals and tourists alike. The market is open all week, but really buzzes on weekends. Seventh Street takes you back to Pennsylvania Avenue, the Eastern Market Metro station, and to the historic **Barracks Row** neighborhood. Along 8th Street, Barracks Row was the first commercial center in Washington, D.C. The Barracks were built after 1798 and rebuilt in 1901, but this neighborhood housed a diverse population of newly arrived immigrants even before the Civil War. On the north side of the street you'll find the barracks and, opposite, a variety of shops and restaurants. The **Marine Corps Barracks and Commandant's House,** the nation's oldest continuously active marine installation, is the home of the U.S. Marine Band. On Friday evenings from May through August you can attend the hour-long ceremony performed on the parade deck by the **Marine Band** (the "President's Own") and the **Drum and Bugle Corps** (the "Commandant's Own"). You can reserve a seat (at ⊕ *www.marines.mil*), but it's not really necessary—there's usually plenty of room.

Right at the end of 8th Street, on the bank of the Anacostia River, you will find the 115-acre **Washington Navy Yard,** the Navy's oldest outpost onshore. On its premises are the **Navy Museum and Art Gallery,** which chronicles the history of the U.S. Navy and exhibits Navy-related paintings, sketches, and drawings. From the Navy Yard, walk to the new Southeast Waterfront Riverwalk, where the decommissioned U.S. Navy destroyer *Barry* is open for touring. The Navy Yard visitor's entrance is at 11th and O streets SE. It's a little farther west along M Street SE to the new **Nationals Park,** home of the Washington Nationals. Opened in spring 2008, the ballpark cost more than $600 million. It offers interactive tours on nongame days and throughout the off-season. From here it's just a short walk to the Navy Yard Metro station.

NORTHEAST D.C.

On the outskirts of Capitol Hill you'll find gritty neighborhoods improving at varying rates. Although there are sights worth exploring here, some of them are a long walk from the Capitol—drive or take public transportation instead. The new streetcar link from Union Station eastward along H Street, under construction at this writing, should be operational in the summer of 2013.

The **H Street Corridor**, also known as the **Atlas District**, after the Atlas Performing Arts Center, is a diverse, edgy, and evolving stretch of nightlife between 12th and 14th streets NE. This is a rapidly gentrifying neighborhood with restaurants, shops, and bars opening, and a younger crowd moving in. Here you'll find a mix of the original, the hip, and the unexpected. In September it's the venue for the annual H Street Music Festival, celebrating the developing arts, entertainment, and fashion scene.

Following E Street east to 17th Street, you will find the **Congressional Cemetery**, established in 1807 "for all denomination of people," which was the first national cemetery created by the government. You can take a self-guided walking tour of the premises. Farther upriver, and due east from the Capitol on East Capitol Street, **RFK Stadium** is the home of the D.C. United soccer team.

Farther to the north, the National Shrine of the Immaculate Conception and Franciscan Monastery are open for tours of the buildings and tranquil gardens. Get there by car, H6 bus, or take the Metro to Brookland station. Although there is no food service at the shrine, restaurants and a market can be found nearby on 12th Street NE.

CAPITOL HILL WITH KIDS

Capitol Hill offers plenty for kids to do. After they've had their fill of history, they can commune with nature, hit a home run, and sample sweet treats.

There are lots of locally made toys and games to see and touch at **Eastern Market**. Street performers entertain while kids indulge in blueberry pancakes with ice cream at the **Market Lunch** counter.

At the **United States Botanic Garden**, kids can become Junior Botanists; they receive a free adventure pack with cool tools to use during their visit and afterwards at home, as well as access to a secret website. There's also a family guide available.

Catch a game at **Nationals Park** or take a tour on a nongame day. You'll see the Nationals dugout, the clubhouse, and press box, plus you can throw a pitch in the bullpen and test out the batting cages.

Or take a tour with **DC Ducks**: during the 1½-hour ride in an amphibious vehicle over land and water, a wise-quacking captain mixes historical anecdotes with trivia.

DOWNTOWN

Sightseeing
★★★★☆
Dining
★★★★☆
Lodging
★★★★☆
Shopping
★★★☆☆
Nightlife
★★★★☆

Downtown D.C. is where government, commerce, and entertainment meet. The streets are wide, the buildings are as tall as they get in Washington, and it is here that D.C. feels most like a big city. It's an extensive area, encompassing some distinct districts, and packed with historic and cultural attractions, with still more development in the pipeline. Downtown is compact; you can see the main sights in an hour and a half, not counting time spent inside museums. Travel light—you'll have to have your bag screened before entering almost everywhere.

DOWNTOWN WALK

The Downtown area can be divided into several sections, each with its own personality. **Federal Triangle** is the wedge-shape area south of Pennsylvania Avenue, north of Constitution Avenue, and east of 15th Street. It's the neighborhood's serious side, with imposing gray buildings and all-business mentality. **Penn Quarter** makes up the area directly to the north of Pennsylvania Avenue. This is Downtown's party side, where restaurants and bars mix with popular museums and the burgeoning theater district. **Chinatown** gives the neighborhood an international flair, and **Judiciary Square,** immediately to the east, is like a stern older uncle frowning about the goings-on.

FEDERAL TRIANGLE AND JUDICIARY SQUARE

Begin at **Metro Center,** the core of D.C.'s Metro system and its busiest station; from here most of Downtown is a short walk away. Take 12th Street south to **Federal Triangle.** The mass of government buildings was constructed between 1929 and 1938 in order to consolidate government workers in one place, and construction continued right into the

GETTING ORIENTED

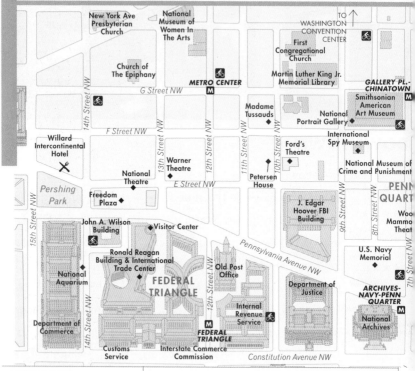

New York Ave Presbyterian Church

National Museum of Women In The Arts

TO
WASHINGTON CONVENTION CENTER

First Congregational Church

Church of The Epiphany

METRO CENTER

Martin Luther King Jr. Memorial Library

G Street NW

GALLERY PL.- CHINATOWN

Smithsonian American Art Museum

14th Street NW

F Street NW

Madame Tussauds

National Portrait Gallery

Willard Intercontinental Hotel

13th Street NW

12th Street NW

11th Street NW

International Spy Museum

Ford's Theatre

National Museum of Crime and Punishment

Warner Theatre

10th Street NW

PENN QUARTER

National Theatre

E Street NW

Petersen House

Wool Mammo Theat

Pershing Park

Freedom Plaza

J. Edgar Hoover FBI Building

15th Street NW

John A. Wilson Building

Visitor Center

9th Street NW

8th Street NW

7th Street NW

U.S. Navy Memorial

Pennsylvania Avenue NW

Ronald Reagan Building & International Trade Center

Old Post Office

ARCHIVES- NAVY-PENN QUARTER

National Aquarium

FEDERAL TRIANGLE

Department of Justice

Department of Commerce

14th Street NW

12th Street NW

Internal Revenue Service

National Archives

FEDERAL TRIANGLE

Customs Service

Interstate Commerce Commission

Constitution Avenue NW

GETTING HERE

Take the Metro to Federal Triangle or Archives-Navy Memorial to visit the government buildings along Pennsylvania Avenue. The Gallery Place–Chinatown stop gives direct access to the Verizon Center, Chinatown, and the American Art and Spy museums. Judiciary Square has its own stop, and Metro Center is the best choice for the National Theatre and Penn Quarter. Bus routes crisscross the area as well. Street parking is available; it's easier to find on nights and weekends away from the main Chinatown and Verizon Center area.

GREAT EXPERIENCES DOWNTOWN

International Spy Museum: Indulge your inner James Bond with a look at 007's Aston Martin from *Goldfinger*—along with more serious toys used by the CIA, FBI, and KGB.

The National Archives: After seeing the Declaration of Independence, Constitution, and Bill of Rights, lose yourself in the Public Vault, where you can find everything from the Emancipation Proclamation to *Mad* magazine.

National Portrait Gallery and Smithsonian American Art Museum: These sister museums have something for everyone, from presidential portraits to old-timey "crazy quilts."

Newseum: Find out how the headlines are made, and read the front pages from all over the country, displayed in front of the building.

Theater District: Catch performances, ranging from Shakespeare to the avant-garde, in Penn Quarter's answer to Broadway.

2

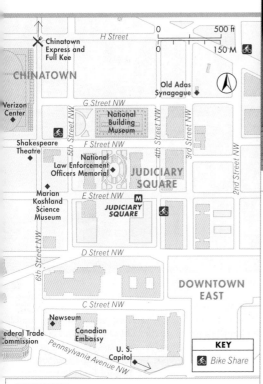

PLANNING YOUR TIME

Downtown is densely packed with major attractions—far too many to see in one day. You'll need at least an hour inside each attraction, so pick the two that appeal most and stroll past the rest. Art lovers might focus on the **National Portrait Gallery** and **Smithsonian American Art Museum**; history buffs might limit themselves to touring the **National Archives** and the **National Building Museum**; families with kids may prefer the **International Spy Museum**; and media junkies will want to visit the **Newseum** and the **Marian Koshland Science Museum**, which looks at the science behind media headlines.

SAFETY

Downtown's blocks of government and office buildings become something of a ghost town when the working day is done. You may prefer not to walk alone in this area after dark. The recently revitalized Penn Quarter still carries some vestiges of its grittier past, so stick to the main commercial areas at night.

QUICK BITES

Cheap eats abound in Chinatown.

Chinatown Express. Watch the chef stretching noodles by the window before you head into Chinatown Express to try some. ⊠ *746 6th St. NW, Chinatown* ☎ *202/638–0424.*

Food courts. There are food courts in Penn Quarter, eat at National Place *(1331 Pennsylvania Ave., NW 202/662–1250)* and Federal Triangle at the **Ronald Reagan Building** *(⊠ 1300 Pennsylvania Ave. NW,Downtown* ☎ *202/312–1300).*

Ming's Restaurant. Favorite for late-night dining with authentic, exotic Cantonese cuisine, along with Japanese and Sushi. ⊠ *617 H St. NW, Chinatown* ☎ *202/289–1001.*

Willard Intercontinental Hotel. The historic Willard Intercontinental Hotel serves breakfast and lunch at **Café du Parc,** tea in **Peacock Alley,** and drinks in the **Round Robin & Scotch Bar.** ⊠ *1401 Pennsylvania Ave. NW, Downtown* ☎ *202/628–9100.*

Savvy visitors skip the lines at the Washington Monument for the view from the Old Post Office Pavilion.

1990s. The neighborhood was formerly known as Murder Bay for its notorious collection of rooming houses, taverns, tattoo parlors, and brothels. When city planners moved in, they chose a uniform classical architectural style for the new buildings. As you pass by, give a nod to the **John A. Wilson Building, Internal Revenue Service Building, Department of Justice**, and Apex Building, which houses the **Federal Trade Commission**. These buildings aren't open to the public.

Ahead of you, the **Ronald Reagan Building and International Trade Center** houses the most secure tourist office and food court you'll ever see. You need to show a photo ID and go through a security checkpoint in order to collect brochures and subway schedules. It's also home to the Capitol Steps, who perform political comedy sketches on Friday and Saturday nights. The Old Post Office Pavilion, saved from demolition in 1973, has a food court and shops. The building is set to be developed into a luxury hotel by Donald Trump in 2014, but the observation deck in the clock tower—one of Washington's best-kept secrets—will remain open to the public. Although it's not as tall as the Washington Monument, the view from the Old Post Office's clock tower is nearly as impressive, and it's usually not crowded. The windows are bigger, and—unlike those at the monument—they're open, allowing cool breezes to waft through.

Nearby, the **Department of Commerce** houses the **National Aquarium** in its basement, a location as underwhelming as the aquarium itself. Slightly hidden across the street is a tiny and delightful shady oasis, **Pershing Park**, a pleasant area with picnic tables and a pond. Diagonally across the street the **Freedom Plaza**, named in honor of Martin Luther King Jr., is often the favored site for protests and concerts, and is inlaid with a map from L'Enfant's original 1791 plan for the Federal City. To compare L'Enfant's vision with today's reality, stand in the middle of the map's Pennsylvania Avenue and look west. L'Enfant had planned an unbroken vista from the Capitol to the White House, but the Treasury Building, begun in 1836, ruined the view. Turning to the east, you can see the U.S. Capitol sitting on the former Jenkins Hill.

Follow Pennsylvania Avenue, the nation's symbolic Main Street, known for inaugural and other parades and civic demonstrations, toward the Capitol. On your left, the **J. Edgar Hoover Federal Bureau of Investigation Building** has been a favorite attraction for visitors interested in espionage and the persecution of bad guys. Sadly, tours have been suspended indefinitely for security reasons, so consider the Museum of Crime and Punishment a worthy alternative. The **National Archives** on the right display the original Declaration of Independence, Constitution, and Bill of Rights. One of Washington's newest and most dynamic museums, the **Newseum,** opened its doors in 2008. The seven-level building with 14 main galleries showcases 500 years of journalism history with multimedia displays. The spectacular stone-and-glass edifice next door is the Canadian Embassy.

Fourth Street takes you across Judiciary Square, where you will find city and federal courthouses, as well as the **National Law Enforcement Officers Memorial.** To the east, the small **Marian Koshland Science Museum** explores and explains the science behind current news headlines. Across the street the **National Building Museum** is known as much for its impressive interior hall as for its exhibits on architecture and the building arts. The **Old Adas Israel Synagogue** on 3rd Street is the oldest synagogue in D.C.

A couple of blocks to the west, new galleries, restaurants, and other cultural hot spots have taken over much of the real estate. Look out for the **Shakespeare Theatre Company's** performing arts center, the **Sydney Harman Hall.** The area surrounding the **Verizon Center** sports arena has cinemas, restaurants, and shops. Expect crowds on weekend evenings. From here, you're only a block away from the Gallery Place/Chinatown Metro stop; continue north on 7th Street to Chinatown.

CHINATOWN AND PENN QUARTER

Chinatown begins just north of the Verizon Center. This compact neighborhood is marked by the ornate, 75-foot Friendship Arch at 7th and H streets and Chinese characters on storefronts such as Ann Taylor Loft and Starbucks. Nearly every Cantonese, Szechuan, Hunan, and Mongolian restaurant has a roast duck hanging in the window, and the shops here sell Chinese food, arts and crafts, and newspapers. Nearby, **Martin Luther King Jr. Memorial Library** is the only D.C. building designed by the illustrious modernist architect Ludwig Mies van der Rohe. From here detour west on G Street and north on 13th Street to see the **National Museum of Women in the Arts,** which showcases works by female artists from the Renaissance to the present (it has the only Frida Kahlo in the city), and don't miss its new and changing outdoor sculpture installation by women artists alongside the building on New York Avenue.

South of Chinatown, below G Street, **Penn Quarter** begins. This neighborhood has blossomed into one of the hottest addresses in town for nightlife and culture. The **National Portrait Gallery** and the **Smithsonian American Art Museum** are the main cultural draws. The fun and interactive **International Spy Museum** across the street displays the largest collection of spy artifacts in the world.

A block west along E Street brings you out to Washington's theater district, home to the venerable **Ford's Theatre,** the **Warner Theatre,** which has its own walk of fame on the sidewalk out front, and the **National Theatre.** The progressive **Woolly Mammoth Theatre Company** is nearby on 7th and D streets.

Tours of **Ford's Theatre, the Center for Education and Leadership,** and the **Petersen House** take you back to the night of Lincoln's assassination and explore the lasting legacy of his presidency. John Wilkes Booth and his coconspirators plotted out the dirty deed at **Suratt Boarding House** a few blocks away in Chinatown.

DOWNTOWN WITH KIDS

If you happen to time your visit with a monthly KidSpy workshop at the **International Spy Museum,** your junior James Bonds and young Nancy Drews can assume a new identity complete with disguise, go on a spy mission, meet real spies, and more. This is a great museum for tweens, but younger kids may not get it.

Teens will relish the creepy interactive exhibits at the Crime and Punishment Museum.

The **National Building Museum** takes building blocks to new heights as kids can strap on a tool belt and design their own cities.

At the **National Archives** kids can gawk at the Declaration of Independence, Constitution, and Bill of Rights; suddenly school history isn't so abstract.

The **Newseum** lets kids experience the stories behind the headlines, and they can even "broadcast" the news in front of the camera. Older kids can pick out big story headlines from world events they lived through.

Both the **National Portrait Gallery** and **Smithsonian American Art Museum** have something for everyone, from presidential portraits to art made from aluminum foil, bottle caps, and even television sets.

GEORGETOWN

Sightseeing
★★★☆☆

Dining
★★★★★

Lodging
★★★★☆

Shopping
★★★★★

Nightlife
★★★★★

At first glance, Washington's oldest and wealthiest neighborhood may look genteel and staid, but don't be fooled: this is a lively part of town. By day, Georgetown is D.C.'s top shopping destination, with everything from eclectic antiques and housewares to shoes and upscale jeans. By night, revelers along M Street and Wisconsin Avenue eat, drink, and make merry. This neighborhood was made for strolling with its historic tree-lined streets and views of the Potomac from waterfront parks. Although the coveted brick homes north of M Street are the province of Washington's high society, the rest of the neighborhood offers ample entertainment for everyone.

GEORGETOWN WALK

Georgetown can be thought of in four sections: the shopping and nightlife area along **M Street,** the **university,** the **historic residential** neighborhoods, and the **waterfront.** The most popular and crowded area is the first, located mainly on M Street and Wisconsin Avenue. The C&O Canal is a sylvan spot for a bike ride, morning jog, or pleasant paddle, while the riverfront restaurants and parks at Washington Harbour let you enjoy the water views exertion-free. The neighborhood can be comfortably explored in an afternoon, though you may want to linger here.

M Street is a fitting introduction to the area that is known for its high-end clothing boutiques, antiques stores, and fancy furniture shops, now squeezing cheek-to-jowl with chain stores such as J. Crew and Banana

GETTING ORIENTED

GREAT EXPERIENCES IN GEORGETOWN

C&O Canal: Walk or bike along the path here, which offers bucolic scenery from the heart of Georgetown all the way to Maryland.

Dumbarton Oaks: Stroll through the 10 acres of formal gardens—Washington's loveliest oasis.

M Street: Indulge in some serious designer retail therapy (or just window-shopping). Reward your willpower or great find with a great meal afterward—all on the same street.

Tudor Place: Step into Georgetown's past with a visit to the grand home of the Custis-Peter family. On view are antiques from George and Martha Washington's home at Mount Vernon and a 1919 Pierce Arrow roadster.

Washington Harbour and Waterfront Park: Come on a warm evening to enjoy sunset drinks while overlooking the Watergate, Kennedy Center, and Potomac River.

GETTING HERE

There's no Metro stop in Georgetown, so you have to take a bus or taxi or walk to this part of Washington. It's about a 15-minute walk from Dupont Circle or the Foggy Bottom Metro station. Perhaps the best transportation deal in Georgetown is the Circulator. For a buck you can ride from Union Station along Massachusetts Avenue and K Street to the heart of Georgetown. Or try the Georgetown Circulator route, which connects M Street to the Dupont Circle and Rosslyn Metro stops. The Circulator runs daily at varying hours (⊕ www.dccirculator.com).

Other options include the G2 Georgetown University Bus, which goes west from Dupont Circle along P Street, and the 34 and 36 Friendship Heights buses, which go south down Wisconsin Avenue and west down Pennsylvania Avenue toward Georgetown.

PLANNING YOUR TIME

You can easily spend a pleasant day in Georgetown, partly because some sights (**Tudor Place, Dumbarton Oaks, Oak Hill Cemetery,** and **Dumbarton House**) are somewhat removed from the others and partly because the street scene, with its shops and people-watching, invites you to linger.

Georgetown is almost always crowded. It's not car-friendly either, especially at night; driving and parking are always difficult. The wise take the Metro to Foggy Bottom or Dupont Circle and then walk 15 minutes from there, or take a bus or taxi.

QUICK BITES

Ching Ching Cha. If the crowds of Georgetown become overwhelming, step into Ching Ching Cha, a Chinese teahouse where tranquillity reigns supreme. In addition to tea, lunch and dinner may be ordered from a simple menu with light, healthful meals. ✉ *1063 Wisconsin Ave. NW, Georgetown* ☎ *202/333–8288* ⊕ *www.chingchingcha.com.*

Wisey's. Wisey's is the more central outpost of university favorite **Wisemiller's Delicatessen.** There are a few tables in the small storefront. Healthy choices include panini, wraps, and salads, and smoothies and specialty teas are also available. ✉ *1440 Wisconsin Ave. NW, Georgetown* ☎ *202/333–4122* ⊕ *www.wiseystogo.com.*

Republic or cheap and chic H&M and Zara. Slightly out of place amid the modern shops and cafés, the 18th-century **Old Stone House** and garden on M Street are thought to be the oldest in the city.

RESIDENTIAL GEORGETOWN AND GU

Leaving the throngs behind for now, 31st Street takes you north into the heart of residential Georgetown where impossibly small cottages stand side by side with rambling mansions. At Q Street, **Tudor Place** was once the home of Thomas Peter, son of Georgetown's

WE HAVE A SITUATION

West of Wisconsin Avenue on M Street, a somewhat uninspiring shopping mall—the Shops at Georgetown Park—occupies the site selected in the 1960s by the White House as the Situation Room with the first hotline to Moscow. Today's Situation Room is in the basement of the White House's West Wing; the staff of senior officers monitors and deals with world and U.S. crises.

first mayor, and his wife, Martha Custis, Martha Washington's granddaughter. A house tour lets you see many of Martha Washington's Mount Vernon possessions, as well as a 1919 Pierce Arrow roadster.

Farther up 31st Street, **Dumbarton Oaks** (no relation to Dumbarton House) can rightfully claim to be one of the loveliest spots in Washington, D.C. The 10 acres of formal gardens and English parkland may inspire a romantic proposal or a game of hide-and-seek, and the well-placed benches offer quiet nooks to rest weary feet or have a tête-à-tête. The attached museum is also well worth a visit.

To the east, **Montrose Park** entertains kids, dogs, and picnickers with wide lawns, tennis courts, and a playground. The funerary obelisks, crosses, and gravestones of **Oak Hill Cemetery** mark the final resting place for actor, playwright, and diplomat John H. Payne and William Corcoran, founder of the Corcoran Gallery of Art. A short detour east on Q Street, **Dumbarton House** is a distinctive example of Federal-era architecture and furnishings. One block farther along Q Street, **Mount Zion Cemetery** was featured in David Baldacci's novel *The Collectors*.

Circling back, Wisconsin Avenue leads you downhill past a variety of small boutiques and cafés toward the intersection with M Street. Instead of following it the whole way, make a right on O Street, where you will find **St. John's Church,** one of the oldest churches in the city. Thirty-third Street brings you down to N Street to see some of the finest Federal-era architecture in D.C. **Cox's Row** is a group of five Federal houses, between 3339 and 3327 N Street, named after Colonel John Cox, a former mayor of Georgetown who built them in 1817.

N street gives way to **Georgetown University.** Founded in 1798, it is the oldest Jesuit school in the country. The imposing, Victorian Healy Hall at its entrance was named for Patrick Healy, the president of Georgetown University in 1873, who was the biracial son of a slave and white Irish slave-owner. About 12,000 students attend the university, known now as much for its perennially successful basketball team as for its fine programs in law, medicine, foreign service, and the liberal arts.

Known for its great window-shopping, Georgetown is a notoriously difficult place to park.

Turn left at 36th Street to return to M Street, perhaps via the undeniably spooky 75 steps that featured prominently in the horror movie *The Exorcist*. Find them past the old brick streetcar barn at No. 3600. Down on the western end of M Street, you'll find the small **Francis Scott Key Memorial Park**, honoring the Washington attorney who penned the national anthem during the War of 1812.

M STREET AND THE WATERFRONT

Walk back along M Street toward Washington Harbour, taking in the shops and restaurants along the way. The small **Museum of Contemporary Art** in **Canal Square**, a converted 1850s warehouse, is located here. You might be tempted to stop at **Leopold's Kafe & Konditorei** at the end of Cady's Alley, and linger on its shady terrace. A short detour down Wisconsin Avenue will take you to **Grace Episcopal Church** where many 19th-century residents prayed.

Georgetown's **C&O Canal** links the Potomac with the Ohio River. A sandy red path along the bank makes for a scenic walk or bike ride—look out for great blue herons and turtles lounging in the sun. Every summer the National Park Service offers rides on mule-drawn canal boats. Two miles west of the Key Bridge along the canal towpath, **Fletcher's Boat House** rents kayaks, canoes, and bikes. You can also follow the canal through the heart of Georgetown, running parallel with M Street. As you connect with Thomas Jefferson Street, note the Georgetown **Masonic Museum** on Thomas Jefferson Street, which harks back to the area's past as a working-class city populated by tradespeople, laborers, and merchants. You might want to stop for tea and cake at the fun and funky **Baked and Wired** on the same street. Head south on 31st

A History of Georgetown

The area that would come to be known as George (after George II), then George Towne, and finally Georgetown was part of Maryland when it was settled in the early 1700s by Scottish immigrants, many of whom were attracted by the region's tolerant religious climate.

Georgetown's position—at the farthest point up the Potomac that's accessible by ship—made it an ideal transit and inspection point for farmers who grew tobacco in Maryland's interior. In 1789 the state granted the town a charter, but two years later Georgetown—along with Alexandria, its counterpart in Virginia—was included by George Washington in the Territory of Columbia, site of the new capital.

While Washington struggled, Georgetown thrived. Wealthy traders built their mansions on the hills overlooking the river; merchants and the working class lived in modest homes closer to the water's edge.

In 1810 a third of Georgetown's population was African-American—both free people and slaves. The Mt. Zion United Methodist Church on 29th Street is the oldest organized black congregation in the city, and when the church stood at 27th and P streets it was a stop on the Underground Railroad (the original building burned down in the mid-1800s).

Georgetown's rich history and success instilled in all its residents a feeling of pride that persists today. When Georgetowners thought the dismal capital was dragging them down, they asked to be given back to Maryland, the way Alexandria was given back to Virginia in 1845.

Tobacco's star eventually fell, and Georgetown became a milling center, using waterpower from the Potomac. When the Chesapeake & Ohio (C&O) Canal was completed in 1850, the city intensified its milling operations and became the eastern end of a waterway that stretched 184 miles to the west.

The canal took up some of the slack when Georgetown's harbor began to fill with silt and the port lost business to Alexandria and Baltimore, but the canal never became the success that George Washington had envisioned.

In the years that followed, Georgetown was a malodorous industrial district, a far cry from the fashionable spot it is today. Clustered near the water were a foundry, a fish market, paper and cotton mills, and a power station for the city's streetcar system.

It still had its Georgian, Federal, and Victorian homes, though, and when the New Deal and World War II brought a flood of newcomers to Washington, Georgetown's tree-shaded streets and handsome brick houses were rediscovered. Pushed out in the process were many of Georgetown's renters, including many of its black residents.

Today, some of Washington's most famous residents call Georgetown home, including former *Washington Post* executive editor Ben Bradlee, political pundit George Stephanopoulos, Senator (and 2004 presidential nominee) John Kerry, and *New York Times* op-ed doyenne Maureen Dowd, who lives in a townhouse where President Kennedy lived as a senator.

In the 19th century mules pulled boats loaded with 100 tons of coal along the C&O Canal towpath.

Street toward the Potomac to take a rest on a bench under the trees in the **Georgetown Waterfront Park.**

Following the Potomac east to K Street between 30th and 31st streets you will find **Washington Harbour,** a riverfront development specializing in restaurants and bars with scenic views of the river, the Watergate complex, and the Kennedy Center. Boat trips to Mount Vernon, the National Harbor, and Alexandria leave from here, offering a waterfront perspective of the city's monuments.

If you have dallied and evening approaches, you'll be in good company. By night the hungry, the thirsty, and the ready-to-party pound the pavement on this side of D.C. You'll find Vietnamese, Thai, Middle Eastern, and Ethiopian restaurants here, as well as burgers and fries at a variety of grubby pubs. After hours, college students and recent graduates overrun the bars, but a few lounges do cater to a more mature, upscale crowd.

GEORGETOWN WITH KIDS

Georgetown may not seem like the most kid-friendly part of D.C., but with nice weather the **Waterfront Park** and **C&O Canal** offer pleasant walks and picnic opportunities. If your toddlers and young children need a playground fix, north of M Street at 27th, you'll find the **Rose Park** "Tot Lot," complete with climbing frames and sandpit. **Montrose Park** to the north also has a playground.

DUPONT CIRCLE AND LOGAN CIRCLE

Sightseeing
★★★★☆
Dining
★★★★★
Lodging
★★★★☆
Shopping
★★★★☆
Nightlife
★★★★☆

Dupont Circle is the grand hub of D.C., literally. This traffic circle is essentially the intersection of the main thoroughfares of Connecticut, New Hampshire, and Massachusetts avenues. More important though, the area around the circle is a vibrant center for urban and cultural life in the District.

Along with wealthy tenants and basement-dwelling twentysomethings, museums, art galleries, and embassies call this upscale neighborhood home. Offbeat shops, specialty bookstores, coffeehouses, and restaurants of all ethnicities and price ranges lend the area a funkier, more urban feel.

The Logan Circle neighborhood runs to the east along P Street and stretches north along the 14th Street Corridor. You'll find more sidewalk cafés, nightlife, shopping, as well as a handful of sights and two theaters, Source DC and Studio Theatre.

Add to the mix stores and clubs catering to the neighborhood's large gay community and this area becomes a big draw for nearly everyone. Perhaps that's why the fountain at the center of the Dupont traffic island is such a great spot for people-watching.

DUPONT CIRCLE WALK

Two hours should be enough to walk the main sights here; longer if you want to linger in some of the neighborhood's fascinating small museums and enticing cafés.

Take the Metro to the dramatic Dupont Circle Q Street exit and you'll find yourself in the heart of it all. If you arrive on a Sunday morning you'll emerge into Dupont Circle's year-round **farmers' market** at the corner of Q and 20th streets. The large island in the middle of the traffic circle a few paces down Connecticut Avenue is a lively urban park, vibrant with rollerbladers, chess players, street performers, and a marble fountain created by Daniel Chester French. On sunny days the surrounding benches are pleasant spots for people-watching, newspaper reading, or relaxing with a cup of coffee or a snack. Also nearby is the one-of-a-kind bookstore **Kramerbooks & Afterwords**, which has a broad and eclectic selection of reading material, as well as a popular café, open daily and throughout the night on Friday and Saturday.

NORTHWEST OF DUPONT CIRCLE

Head up the main north–south artery of Connecticut Avenue, lined with shops, restaurants, and cafés that are busy day and night. Turning left onto R Street you'll pass number 2131, an understated white-painted town house, home to FDR and Eleanor Roosevelt between 1916 and 1920. Detour a block south on 21st Street to find the **Phillips Collection**, founded as the first permanent museum of modern art in the country, with a collection including works by Renoir, Degas, Van Gogh, Picasso, Klee, and Matisse.

Along R Street lie a variety of art galleries. Nestled among them the nonprofit **Fondo Del Sol Visual Arts Center** is devoted to the cultural heritage of Latin America and the Caribbean. Detour east on R Street for the **National Museum of American Jewish Military History,** which displays weapons, uniforms, medals, recruitment posters, and other military memorabilia related to American Jews serving in the U.S. military.

At the west end of R Street, **Sheridan Circle** and Massachusetts Avenue are home to a cluster of embassies in striking villas. North on Massachusetts Avenue, you'll see some very unrestrained architecture, including the **Cameroon Embassy,** housed in a fanciful castle with a conical tower, bronze weather vane, and intricate detailing around the windows and balconies (this building is under renovation, and Cameroon has temporarily relocated but may ultimately be evicted by the owners, Harvard).

S Street edges into the Kalorama district. The **Woodrow Wilson House** shows the former president's home pretty much as he left it. On display are many gifts from foreign dignitaries. Next door, the **Textile Museum** hosts special exhibitions as well as its permanent collection of fabric arts, and a shop stuffed with beautiful things; the museum is moving to Foggy Bottom in 2014.

Just south of Sheridan Circle the **Bison Bridge** is guarded by four bronze statues of the shaggy mammals. Nearby, the **Anderson House** was bequeathed by Larz and Isabel Anderson to the Society of the Cincinnati, an exclusive club of the descendents of Revolutionary War officers. Next door, the **Walsh-McLean House** was once home to Evalyn Walsh-McLean, the last private owner of the Hope Diamond (now in the National Museum of Natural History). Head back to Connecticut Avenue for tempting opportunities for tea, lunch, or a snack before continuing on.

SOUTHEAST OF DUPONT CIRCLE

Past Dupont Circle, heading down Massachusetts Avenue toward Scott Circle, you'll pass the **Brookings Institution** and the Johns Hopkins University D.C. campus buildings. The **Christian Heurich House Museum,** once known as the Brewmaster's Castle, was the home of a German-born beer magnate and is nearby on New Hampshire Avenue. **Scott Circle** is decorated with statues of General Winfield Scott, Daniel Webster, and S. C. F. Hahnemann. If you walk to the south side of the circle and

GETTING ORIENTED

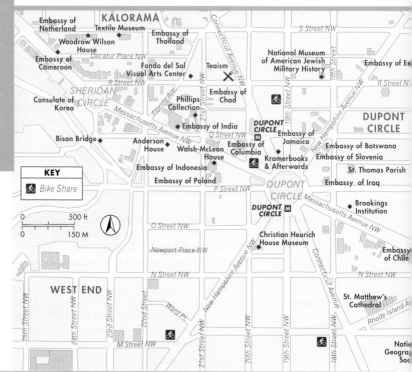

QUICK BITES

Kramerbooks & Afterwords. At this independent bookstore and café you can relax over dinner or a drink after browsing. ✉ *1517 Connecticut Ave. NW, Dupont Circle* ☎ *202/387–1400* ⊕ *www.kramers.com.*

Teaism. In addition to several dozen varieties of tea, there's a selection of seafood and vegetarian entrées, many available in bento boxes and seasoned with tea. ✉ *2009 R St. NW, Dupont Circle* ☎ *202/667–3827* ⊕ *www.teaism.com.*

GREAT EXPERIENCES AROUND DUPONT CIRCLE AND LOGAN CIRCLE

Anderson House: Glimpse into the life of a fabulously wealthy U.S. diplomat and his glamorous, art-loving wife at their magnificent mansion in the early 1900s.

Dupont Circle: Grab a cup of coffee and a *CityPaper* and take in the always-buzzing scene around the fountain.

Logan Circle: Take in a contemporary play at the Studio Theatre, then stay out late in the restaurants and bars on 14th and P Streets.

National Geographic Society: See *National Geographic* magazine come to life in rotating exhibits at the society's Explorers Hall.

Phillips Collection: Admire masterpieces such as Renoir's *Luncheon of the Boating Party* and Degas's *Dancers at the Barre* at the country's first museum of modern art.

2

CARDOZO/SHAW

S Street NW

R Street NW

Corcoran Street NW

Q Street NW

16th Street NW

13th Street NW

Vermont Avenue NW

Church Street NW

Studio
◆Theatre

P Street NW

LOGAN
CIRCLE

LOGAN
CIRCLE

15th Street NW

Rhode Island Avenue NW

Q Street NW

O Street

Mary McLeod Bethune
Council House ◆

13th Street NW

12th Street NW

16th Street NW

Embassy
Australia

Embassy
of Tunisia

N Street NW

14th Street NW

Vermont Avenue NW

SCOTT
CIRCLE

Massachusetts Avenue NW

THOMAS
CIRCLE

M Street NW

Metropolitan African
Methodist Episcopal
Church

Washington
Post Building

A GOOD WALK: KALORAMA

To see the embassies and luxurious homes that make up the Kalorama neighborhood, begin your walk at the corner of S and 23rd streets.

Head north up 23rd, keeping an eye out for the emergency call boxes now turned into public art.

At the corner of Kalorama Road, head west, but don't miss the Tudor-style mansion at 2221 Kalorama Road, now home to the French ambassador.

Turn right on Kalorama Circle, where you can look down over Rock Creek Park and into Adams Morgan. Kalorama means "beautiful view" in Greek, and this is the sight that inspired the name.

From here you can retrace your steps, or take Kalorama Circle back to Kalorama Road, turn right, and make a left on Wyoming to bring you back to 23rd.

GETTING HERE

Dupont Circle has its own stop on the Metro's Red Line. Exit on Q Street for the Phillips Collection, Anderson House, and Kalorama attractions. Take the Connecticut Avenue exit for the National Geographic Society, Christian Heurich House museum, or shopping between Dupont Circle and Farragut North. Follow P Street to the east for Logan Circle. On-street parking is available on the residential streets away from the circle but gets harder to find on weekend evenings.

PLANNING YOUR TIME

Visiting the Dupont Circle area takes at least half a day, although you can find things to keep you busy all day and into the evening. You'll likely spend the most time at the **Phillips Collection, Anderson House,** and **Woodrow Wilson House.** The hours will also fly if you linger over lunch or indulge in serious browsing in area shops.

look down 16th Street, you'll get a familiar view of the columns of the White House, six blocks away. Nearby, down 17th Street, the **National Geographic Society** brings its magazines to life with interactive exhibits, photo galleries, and live shows.

A few sights lie clustered on or near M Street south of Scott Circle, including two noteworthy religious institutions. The **Metropolitan African Methodist Episcopal Church** is one of the most influential African-American churches in the city. The Renaissance-style **St. Matthew's Cathedral** is the seat of Washington's Roman Catholic diocese, and the historic site of President Kennedy's funeral Mass.

SEE AND BE SCENE

Dupont's gay scene is concentrated mainly on 17th Street. A variety of gay-friendly, lively, and offbeat bars and restaurants stretch between P and R streets, many with outdoor seating perfect for people-watching. JR's Bar and Grill and Cobalt are favorites. D.I.K. Bar is the place to be on the Tuesday before Halloween for the annual High Heel Drag Race down 17th Street. At the informal block party, elaborately costumed drag queens strut their stuff along the route from Church to Queen streets and then race to the finish line.

LOGAN CIRCLE

Sometimes called MidCity, the epicenter of this neighborhood is at the intersection of P and 14th Streets. This is where the bars and restaurants buzz by day and spill out onto the sidewalks at night. In the 2000s, gentrification took hold and brought to life a once derelict neighborhood. Revitalized it certainly is, but take a moment to notice the layers of history.

Logan Circle itself can be found to the east along P Street, a circle of brooding redbrick Victorian mansions, and surrounding streets where many prominent African-Americans once lived. One block south of the circle on Vermont Avenue, the **Mary McLeod Bethune Council House** features exhibits on the achievements of African-American women.

Around the corner on 14th, you'll come across the highly regarded **Studio Theater,** a number of contemporary art galleries, more boutiques, and music venues, all part of 14th Street's thriving arts scene, continuing right up to U Street.

DUPONT CIRCLE WITH KIDS

Dupont Circle isn't overflowing with activities for kids. But if you're there on a Sunday morning for the **farmers' market** on the corner of Q and 20th streets, you may be able to get them excited about fruits and vegetables. If not, the homemade ice cream and cookies will certainly do the trick.

Stead Park is at 16th, and P Street has a lighted basketball court and newly renovated playground.

ADAMS MORGAN

Sightseeing
★☆☆☆☆

Dining
★★★★☆

Lodging
★☆☆☆☆

Shopping
★★★☆☆

Nightlife
★★★★★

To the urban and hip, Adams Morgan is a beacon of light in an otherwise stuffy landscape. D.C. may have a reputation for being staid and traditional, but drab suits, classical tastes, and bland food make no appearance here. Adams Morgan takes its name from two elementary schools that came together in 1958 after desegregation. It remains an ethnically diverse neighborhood with a United Nations of cuisines, offbeat shops, and funky bars and clubs.

It's also the city's Latin Quarter. The area wakes up as the sun goes down, and young Washingtonians in their weekend best congregate along the sidewalks, crowding the doors of this week's hot bar or nightclub. Typical tourist attractions are sparse, but the scene on a Saturday night has its own appeal. If you're here on the second Saturday in September, sample the vibrant neighborhood culture at the Adams Morgan Day Festival.

ADAMS MORGAN WALK

This walk centers around the heart of Adams Morgan on 18th Street and its intersection with Columbia Road, where the dining and nightlife scene stretches for several blocks. The streets are narrow and appear to be under periodic reconstruction. You can easily see Adams Morgan in an hour or two, so you may want to combine it with a trip to Dupont Circle or U Street, perhaps winding up here in the evening when this neighborhood gets hopping. Outside this central area, Adams Morgan starts to feel gritty at night, and most visitors never venture farther.

If you arrive from Dupont Circle, you'll walk north up 18th Street. As soon as you reach the stretch of restaurants, cafés, shops, and bars, you've reached Adams Morgan proper. The neighborhood's restaurant corridor lies on 18th Street south of Columbia Road and the parts of Columbia Road and Calvert Street directly adjacent. The city's most

GETTING ORIENTED

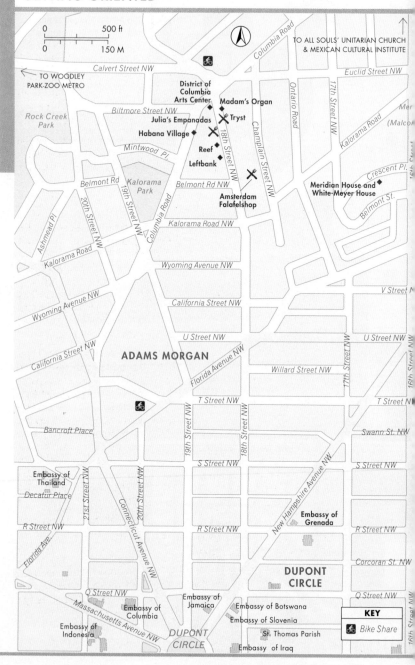

Columbia Road

TO ALL SOULS' UNITARIAN CHURCH
& MEXICAN CULTURAL INSTITUTE

Calvert Street NW

Euclid Street NW

TO WOODLEY
PARK-ZOO METRO

District of
Columbia
Arts Center

Madam's Organ

Biltmore Street NW

Julia's Empanadas

Tryst

Rock Creek
Park

Habana Village

Mintwood Pl.

Reef

Leftbank

18th Street NW

Champlain Street NW

Ontario Road

17th Street NW

Kalorama Road

Crescent Pl.

Belmont Rd

Belmont Rd NW

Kalorama
Park

19th Street NW

20th Street NW

Amsterdam
Falafelshop

Meridian House and
White-Meyer House

Belmont St.

Ashmead Pl.

Belmont Rd

Columbia Road

Kalorama Road NW

Kalorama Road

Wyoming Avenue NW

Wyoming Avenue NW

California Street NW

V Street N

California Street NW

U Street NW

U Street NW

ADAMS MORGAN

Florida Avenue NW

Willard Street NW

17th Street NW

T Street NW

T Street N

Bancroft Place

19th Street NW

18th Street NW

Swann St. NW

Bancroft Place

S Street NW

S Street NW

16th Street NW

Embassy of
Thailand

21st Street NW

20th Street NW

Embassy of
Grenada

Decatur Place

R Street NW

Connecticut Avenue NW

New Hampshire Avenue NW

R Street NW

R Street NW

Florida Ave.

Corcoran St. NW

**DUPONT
CIRCLE**

Q Street NW

Q Street NW

Massachusetts Avenue NW

Embassy of
Columbia

Embassy of
Jamaica

Embassy of Botswana

Embassy of Slovenia

Embassy of
Indonesia

**DUPONT
CIRCLE**

St. Thomas Parish

Embassy of Iraq

KEY	
🚲	Bike Share

0   500 ft
0   150 M

GREAT EXPERIENCES IN ADAMS MORGAN

Eat ethnic food: Adams Morgan rivals U Street with its plentiful and delicious Ethiopian restaurants. If you'd rather dine using utensils, you can choose among Japanese, Brazilian, Mexican, Indian, and other ethnic cuisines.

Hang out like a local: The residents of Adams Morgan make an art of relaxing. Follow their lead and settle into one of Tryst's overstuffed armchairs with a laptop or a copy of the *New Republic* and a coffee, or kill hours browsing the "rare and medium-rare" selections at Idle Time Books.

Move to the beat: Every evening from 3 to 9 pm and on Sunday afternoon, drummers from all walks of life form the Drum Circle in Meridian Hill Park, bashing out the beats while some dance and others simply sit back and watch.

Stay out all night: If you want to party on until the break of dawn, this is the place to do it. Don't miss the live music at Madam's Organ, the salsa dancing at Habana Village, and the cool kids making the scene at the Black Squirrel or Bourbon.

GETTING HERE

Like Georgetown, Adams Morgan has no Metro stop. It's a pleasant 15-minute walk from the Woodley Park/Zoo Metro station: walk south on Connecticut, then turn left on Calvert Street, and cross over Rock Creek Park on the Duke Ellington Bridge. Or you can get off at the Dupont Circle Metro stop and walk east to (and turn left onto) 18th Street.

The heart of Adams Morgan is at the intersection of Adams Mill Road, Columbia Road, and 18th Street. Don't even dream about finding parking here on weekend evenings.

If you take the Metro, remember that stations close at midnight, or 3 am on Friday and Saturday nights. If you're not ready to turn in by then, you'll need to hail a cab.

PLANNING YOUR TIME

A window-shopping wander around Adams Morgan can occupy the better part of an afternoon. And if you take advantage of the restaurants and nightlife here, there's no telling when your head will hit the pillow.

The few tourist attractions in this area aren't time-intensive, but they can be a long walk from restaurants.

QUICK BITES

Amsterdam Falafelshop. The bargain-priced menu consists entirely of top-it-yourself falafels in pita, Dutch-style french fries, and brownies. It's open until 4 am on weekends. ⊠ *2425 18th St. NW, Adams Morgan* ☎ *202/234–1969* ⊕ *www.falafelshop.com.*

Julia's Empanadas. One handmade empanada may fill you up, but you'll be tempted to try a few, including the sweet, fruit-filled varieties. They're served in a paper bag to-go, so you can comfortably eat standing up, or walk to a nearby park to people-watch. ⊠ *2452 18th St. NW, Adams Morgan* ☎ *202/328–6232* ⊕ *www.juliasempanadas.com.*

Tryst Coffeehouse-Bar-Lounge. Everybody feels at home relaxing on the old couches and comfy chairs. There's live jazz Monday to Wednesday 8–11 pm. ⊠ *2459 18th St. NW, Adams Morgan* ☎ *202/232–5500* ⊕ *www.trystdc.com.*

diverse eats are served along these few blocks—a succession of Salvadoran *pupusas* (stuffed tortillas), Ethiopian *injera* (pancakelike sourdough bread), French ratatouille (savory vegetable stew), and West African *moi moi* (black-eyed pea cakes) unrivaled in the city.

Adams Morgan's bar and club scene caters mostly to a young crowd in their twenties. The popular clubs often have lines out the door, and walking down 18th Street around midnight is a little like trying to drive on the Beltway at rush hour. If you're game for a drink, try **Bourbon** for a huge selection of wine, microbrews, 150 kinds of whiskey, and an outdoor patio, or the **Reef** with its unpretentious atmosphere, colorful fish tanks, and rooftop bar. The multistory **Madam's Organ** is a neighborhood institution, with live music every night, and **Habana Village** is one of the best places in the city for Cuban cuisine, salsa dancing, and Latin music.

> **LOOK UP**
>
> As you walk around Adams Morgan, note the many colorful and striking murals. Champorama Mural is one of the best; it is located in a tiny park just off 18th Street on the corner of Kalorama Road and Champlain Street. Among others, Toulouse Lautrec is on 18th near Belmont Street. Find more on Columbia Road, including the oldest remaining mural in the neighborhood at 17th Street.

The shops on 18th Street feed an appetite for the offbeat. Here you can find collectibles such as Mission furniture, Russel Wright crockery and Fiesta ware, aerodynamic art deco armchairs, Bakelite telephones, kidney-shape coffee tables, and oddball salt and pepper shakers. On the west side of 18th Street are antiques shops as well as secondhand shops set up in alleys or warehouses. Nearby is the **District of Columbia Arts Center,** a combination art gallery and performance space.

Columbia Road to the east between 16th and 18th is the area's Latin Quarter, as bilingual as it gets in Washington. At tables stretched along the street, vendors hawk watches, leather goods, knockoff perfumes, CDs, sneakers, clothes, and handmade jewelry. On Saturday morning a market springs up on the plaza at the southwest corner of 18th and Columbia, with stands selling fruits, vegetables, flowers, and fresh bread, not to mention exotic delicacies from the food stands.

At the corner of 16th and Columbia, **All Souls' Unitarian Church** was a cornerstone of the civil rights movement and community activism during the 20th century. Heading south on 16th, the **Mexican Cultural Institute** promotes Mexican art, culture, and science. Farther down the street the public can explore two mansions owned by the Meridian International Center, a nonprofit promoting international understanding. The **Meridian and White-Meyer Houses** hold periodic art exhibits with an international flavor. On the opposite side of 16th Street, **Meridian Hill Park,** also known as **Malcolm X Park,** was once considered a possible location for the White House. Stop off here for shade and city views among the fountains and statues of Joan of Arc and Dante.

2

U STREET CORRIDOR

Sightseeing
★★☆☆☆
Dining
★★★★☆
Lodging
★☆☆☆☆
Shopping
★★★★☆
Nightlife
★★★★★

Home-style Ethiopian food, offbeat boutiques, and live music are fueling the revival of the U Street area. Just a few years back, this neighborhood was running on fumes, surviving on memories of its heyday of black culture and jazz music in the first half of the 20th century.

The neighborhood was especially vibrant from the 1920s to the 1950s, when it was home to jazz genius Duke Ellington, social activist Mary McLeod Bethune, and poets Langston Hughes and Georgia Douglas Johnson. The area's nightclubs hosted Louis Armstrong, Cab Calloway, and Sarah Vaughn. In the 1950s Supreme Court Justice Thurgood Marshall, then still a lawyer, organized the landmark *Brown v. Board of Education* case at the 12th Street YMCA. Now the crowds are back, and this diverse neighborhood faces the threat of yuppification.

U STREET CORRIDOR WALK

You'll need a couple of hours to explore U Street fully, especially if you want to stop in the African-American Civil War Museum. You're likely to spend most of your time along U Street itself, detouring here and there to see the sights just a couple of blocks away. Don't stray too far off the main drag, especially at night.

Beginning at the 10th Street exit of the U Street/Cardozo Metro station, you emerge right at the **African-American Civil War Memorial,** honoring the black soldiers who fought in the Union Army. For more on that story, walk two blocks west to the **African-American Civil War Museum,** which tells the tale of Africans in America from the slave trade through the civil rights movement with numerous photos and documents. Don't miss the **Duke Ellington Mural** on the western side of the building.

Once the hub of black cultural life, with first-run movies and live performances, the **Lincoln Theater** now functions as a theater and event venue. The 12th Street YMCA has been made over to the **Thurgood Marshall Center,** which houses a museum on the history of African-Americans

GETTING ORIENTED

KEY

🚲 Bike Share

W Street NW

V Street NW

✕ Busboys and Poets

Ben's Chili Bowl

Lincoln Theater ◆ ✕

Bohemian Caverns ◆

9:3 Clu

New Hampshire Avenue NW

Vermont Avenue NW

U Street NW

U Street/ Cardozo Ⓜ African-American Civil War Museum

Ⓜ **U Street/ Cardozo**

African-American Civil War Memorial

Etefe

DC

15th Street NW

14th Street NW

16th Street NW

12th Street

11th Street NW

T Street NW

◆ Source Theater

Thurgood Marshall Center

Swann Street NW

CARDOZO

Westminster St.

10th Street NW

S Street NW

◆ Black Cat

13th Street NW

TO HOWARD → UNIVERSITY

R Street NW

Corcoran Street NW

Vermont Avenue NW

11th Street NW

Q Street NW

Church Street NW

Rhode Island Avenue NW

P Street NW

16th Street NW

LOGAN CIRCLE

LOGAN CIRCLE/SHA

O Street NW

P Street NW

O Street NW

Rhode Island Avenue NW

14th Street NW

13th Street NW

SCOTT CIRCLE

N Street NW

Embassy of Tunisia

Massachusetts Avenue NW

Vermont Avenue NW

12th Street NW

11th Street NW

10th Street NW

16th Street NW

15th Street NW

M Street NW

THOMAS CIRCLE

Massachusetts Ave.

0   500 f

0   150 M

GREAT EXPERIENCES ON U STREET CORRIDOR

African-American Civil War Memorial and Museum: Learn about the lives of slaves and freedmen, and discover whether your ancestors fought in black regiments during the Civil War.

Ben's Chili Bowl: If you can top it with chili, it's on the menu. This D.C. institution has perfected its recipe over the last 50 years and satisfies meat eaters and vegetarians alike.

Boutiques: Whether you're after funky footwear or flashy housewares, hit the shops on U and 14th streets for trendy finds.

Ethiopian food: Nothing brings you closer to your meal than eating with your hands. Use the spongy *injera* bread to scoop up delectable dishes from East Africa.

Jazz and live music: Music greats like Duke Ellington made this neighborhood famous back in the 1920s. Relive the glory years at a jazz performance at Bohemian Caverns or HR 57, or rock out to today's music at the 9:30 Club or Black Cat.

GETTING HERE

The Green Line Metro stops at 13th and U, in the middle of the main business district. To get to the African-American Civil War Memorial, get out at the 10th Street exit. Parking can be found on the residential streets north and south of U Street, but as the area gets more popular, spots are getting harder to find on weekend nights.

The area is within walking distance from Dupont Circle and Adams Morgan, but at night you're better off on the bus or in a cab, especially if you're alone. The 90, 92, and 93 buses travel from Woodley Park through Adams Morgan to 14th and U, while the 52 and 54 buses travel north from several Downtown Metro stops up 14th Street (check ⊕ www.wmata. com for information).

PLANNING YOUR TIME

You'll need half a day at most to see U Street's attractions and visit its boutiques. You can also fill an evening with dinner on U Street, a show at the **9:30 Club** or **Bohemian Caverns,** and drinks afterward. If you're not driving, allow plenty of time for public transportation.

QUICK BITES

Ben's Chili Bowl. The quintessential meal here is the chili half-smoke, a spicy grilled hot dog covered with mustard, onions, and, of course, chili. ⊠ *1213 U St. NW, U St. Corridor* ☎ *202/667–0909* ⊕ *www.benschilibowl.com* Ⓜ *U Street (Green Line).*

Busboys and Poets. This bookstore–cum–restaurant–cum–coffee lounge serves up a menu of sandwiches, pizzas, and burgers. Events that liven up your meal include literary readings, openmike nights, and musical performances. ⊠ *2021 14th Street, NW, U St. Corridor* ☎ *202/387–7638* ⊕ *www.busboysandpoets. com* Ⓜ *U Street Cardozo (Green Line).*

SAFETY

The commercial district here borders a much less gentrified area. The blocks between 10th and 16th streets are well lighted and busy, but the neighborhood gets grittier to the north and east. Use your street sense, especially at night. It's wise to splurge on a cab late at night.

in the U Street/Shaw neighborhood. Duke Ellington fans can find his former homes at 1805 and 1813 13th Street.

Although the neighborhood was nearly destroyed in the rioting that followed the 1968 assassination of Martin Luther King Jr., U Street has recently reclaimed some of its former pulse. **Bohemian Caverns** combines an elegant restaurant with an underground music venue and upstairs club. It's been hosting jazz greats since 1926. On V Street, the **9:30 Club** attracts big-name rock bands and lesser-known indie artists alike to one of the East Coast's coolest concert halls. South on 14th Street, the **Black Cat** rocks out with independent and alternative bands from the city and around the world. **DC9** hosts an eclectic mix of local and national bands and DJs. Find it on the corner of 9th and U.

A longtime center for African-American life in the District, U Street is now home to many of the city's East African immigrants, who've brought their culinary traditions to the neighborhood restaurants. Clubs have expanded beyond jazz to include all kinds of rock music, and new shops have popped up to bring in even more business. Standout restaurants in D.C.'s unofficial Little Ethiopia such as **Etete** tempt diners with spongy *injera* bread and hearty meat and vegetarian dishes. Multiculti dining is in abundance here, but the city's humble roots are not yet forgotten; the granddaddy of Washington diners, **Ben's Chili Bowl**, has been serving chili, chili dogs, chili burgers, and half-smokes (spicy sausages served in a hot-dog bun) since 1958. A sign inside used to let you know that only Bill Cosby eats at Ben's for free, until November 2008, when the Obama family was added to the list. Ben's even has its own neighborhood visitor center and a second bar and restaurant in the next building.

U Street's shopping scene has garnered attention in recent years as well. Most of the boutiques are clustered on U Street between 14th and 16th streets. Pop in and out of the little shops to find cutting-edge footwear, Asian furnishings, playful housewares, and eclectic or vintage clothing. Fourteenth Street has some rich pickings as well and you could happily detour all the way south to **Logan Circle**, past the **Source Theater** and **Black Cat** music venue. East of the commercial district, the historically black Howard University has been educating African-American men and women since 1867. Notable graduates include authors Zora Neale Hurston and Toni Morrison, opera singer Jessye Norman, and Nobel Peace Prize–winner Ralph Bunche.

U STREET CORRIDOR WITH KIDS

U Street really comes into its own at night, but tweens and teens can have a good time here during the day. Kids of any age can have a great lunch at Ben's Chili Bowl, and they're warmly welcomed in Etete as well. Teens might like browsing the eclectic shops on U Street and down 14th Street. For a sweet treat, check out the **ACKC Cocoa Gallery**, a bright and welcoming chocolate café on 14th Street.

UPPER NORTHWEST

Sightseeing
★★★★☆

Dining
★★☆☆☆

Lodging
★★☆☆☆

Shopping
★★★★☆

Nightlife
★☆☆☆☆

The upper northwest corner of D.C. is predominantly residential and in many places practically suburban. However, there are several good reasons to visit the leafy streets, including the National Zoo and National Cathedral. If the weather is fine, spend an afternoon strolling through Hillwood Gardens or tromping through Rock Creek Park's many acres. You'll have to travel some distance to see multiple attractions in one day, but many sights are accessible on foot from local Metro stops.

UPPER NORTHWEST WALK

Upper Northwest isn't a neighborhood; it is a geographic grouping of several neighborhoods, including Cleveland Park, Woodley Park, Tenleytown, and Foxhall. The majority of attractions lie on or near Connecticut Avenue north of Woodley Park or on Massachusetts Avenue north of Georgetown. The **Kreeger Museum** is the exception, with its location in Foxhall, northwest of Georgetown. This area divides into three walks. Either focus on the zoo and surrounding area, or head up to the cluster of museums and landmarks around Cleveland Park and Massachusetts Avenue. Alternatively, Rock Creek Park offers shady walks and activities for kids, or hit the shops at the edge of D.C. Using the bus or Metro or driving will allow you to see more of the area in a day.

ZOO AND SURROUNDINGS

The **National Zoo** is a reason in itself to head uptown; take the Metro to the Cleveland Park station. Although recent attention has focused on giant pandas Tian Tian and Mei Xiang, the Smithsonian's free zoological park is full of red pandas, clouded leopards, and Japanese giant

Hillwood Estate's Japanese garden provides a tranquil spot for quiet contemplation.

salamanders, as well as the traditional lions, tigers, and bears. The zoo makes for a picturesque stroll on warm days, but be prepared for some hills to climb and crowds on sunny weekends.

South of the zoo lies **Woodley Park**, a residential neighborhood filled with stately apartment buildings. The stretch of Connecticut Avenue between Calvert and Woodley Road is notable for its popular array of restaurants and the **Wardman Tower**, a cross-shape tower built in 1928 as a luxury apartment building. Once known for its famous residents, it's now part of the Marriott Wardman Park Hotel. **Woodley**, a Georgian mansion that served as the summer home of four presidents, lies on Cathedral Avenue between 29th and 31st streets. At Woodley Park/Zoo Metro, the Red Line takes you back Downtown.

CLEVELAND PARK AND MASSACHUSETTS AVENUE

These attractions are more scattered, so allow a bit more time, and plan to drive or take the bus or Metro.

A 20-minute walk uphill from the Van Ness Red Line stop or an easy drive or cab ride away, the **Hillwood Estate, Museum and Gardens** displays cereal heiress Marjorie Merriweather Post's collection of 18th- and 19th-century French and Russian decorative art. The grounds and gardens equal the art collection in beauty and size. Also in this area, **Howard University Law School** is famed for its African-American graduates, such as Oliver Hill, Thurgood Marshall, and Charles Hamilton Houston.

Farther south you could combine several attractions on Massachusetts Avenue. The **Islamic Mosque and Cultural Center**, with its 162-foot-high minaret, is the oldest Islamic house of worship in D.C. The **Khalil Gibran Memorial Garden** combines Western and Arab symbols in

GETTING ORIENTED

TO FRIENDSHIP
HEIGHTS
Garrison St. NW

Wisconsin Ave. NW
Belt Rd. NW
42nd St. NW
43rd St. NW
39th St.
38th St.
Fessenden St. NW

River Rd. NW
Fort Reno
Park
Everett
St. NW
Ellicott St. NW
Linnean Ave. NW

Reno
Reservoir
Davenport St. NW
Davenport St. NW

Nebraska Ave. NW
Chesapeake St. NW
Connecticut Ave. NW
36th St.
Brandywine St. NW

Murdock Mill Rd. NW
45th St. NW
4th St. NW
Albemarle St. NW
Appleton St. NW
Albemarle St. NW

TENLEYTOWN–AU
Alton Pl. NW
Audubon Ter. NW
Soapstone Valley
Park

Alton Pl. NW
43rd St.
Tenley
Circle
39th St. NW
Yuma St. NW
Reno Rd. NW
**University
of the
District of Columbia**
Howard
University Law
School

Yuma St. NW
Windom Pl. NW
38th St. NW
37th St. NW
36th St. NW
Van Ness St. NW
Hillwood E
Muse
Ga

Warren St. NW

Van Ness St. NW
VANESS–UDC
Upton St. NW

Tindall St.
Tilden St. NW

Nebraska Ave. NW
Melvin Hazen
Park
Rodman St. NW

Ward
Circle
Wisconsin Ave. NW
**CLEVELAND
PARK**
Porter St.

American
University
Porter St. NW
**CLEVELAND
PARK**

Glover-
Archbold
Park
Ordway St. NW

Newark St. NW
Newark St. NW

Macomb St. NW
Massachusetts Ave. NW
Idaho Ave. NW
Macomb St. NW
34th St.
33rd St.
**WOODLEY
PARK**

Lowell St. NW
Lowell St. NW
Connecticut

Klingle St. NW
Woodley Rd.

Cathedral Ave. NW
**Washington National
Cathedral**
TO WOODLEY
PARK–ZOO METRO

WESLEY HEIGHTS
Hawthorne St. NW
32nd St.
Cathedral Ave. NW

39th St. NW
**St. Sophia
Cathedral**
Garfield St. NW
Woodley

Glover-
Archbold
Park
Foxhall Rd.
Fulton St. NW
35th St.
34th Pl. NW
34th St. NW
Circle
Cleveland Ave. NW
Woodland Dr.

Davis Pl.

Kreeger
Museum
Calvert St. NW
40th St. NW
39th Pl. NW
39th St. NW
Observatory
**U.S. Naval
Observatory**
Kahil Gibran
Memorial Garden

FOXHALL
37th St. NW
Wisconsin Ave. NW
Massachusetts Ave. NW
Rock

0   400 yards
0   400 meters
KEY
Bike Share
Dumbarton
Oaks Park
Islamic Mosq
and Cultural Cent

Rock Cre
Park

GREAT EXPERIENCES IN UPPER NORTHWEST

House museums: The Hillwood Estate, Museum, and Gardens showcases cereal heiress Marjorie Merriweather Post's collection of Imperial Russian art and Fabergé eggs, and 25 gorgeous acres of formal French and Japanese gardens. Chagalls, Picassos, and Monets inside contrast with the architecture at the modernist Kreeger Museum.

National Zoo: Visit the giant pandas, elephants, lions, and other members of the animal kingdom while you enjoy a stroll outdoors.

Shopping in Friendship Heights: The city's most glamorous shopping lines Wisconsin Avenue at the Maryland border. Want to actually buy something? Plenty of stores cater to shoppers on a budget, too.

U.S. Naval Observatory: View the heavens through one of the world's most powerful telescopes (on Monday evenings with a reservation).

Washington National Cathedral: Look for the Darth Vader gargoyle on the soaring towers of this cathedral, then relax among the rosebushes in the Bishop's Garden. Concerts are held here, too.

GETTING HERE

Connecticut Avenue attractions, such as the zoo, are accessible from the Red Line Metro stops between Woodley Park/Zoo and Van Ness. The Friendship Heights Bus travels north from Georgetown along Wisconsin Avenue and takes you to the National Cathedral.

Parking can be tricky along Massachusetts Avenue; to see these sights, it's often more practical for good walkers to hoof it up the street or take the N2, N3, N4, or N6 bus between Dupont Circle and Friendship Heights. For more-outlying sights, driving or cabbing it may be the best way to visit.

PLANNING YOUR TIME

The amount of time you spend at the zoo is up to you; animal enthusiasts could easily spend a full day here. You may want to plan your trip around daily programs, such as the elephant-training session or the small-mammal feeding.

For other itineraries, be sure to leave room in your schedule for travel between sights and, if you have a car, for parking. To maximize your time, call ahead to inquire whether on-site parking is available and when the next tour will begin.

QUICK BITES

The blocks immediately surrounding the Woodley Park and Cleveland Park Metro stations are chockablock with restaurants and ice-cream stores.

If you've got the time, skip lunch at the zoo's eateries and head north or south on Connecticut to find a wealth of dining options, then head back.

FINDING A RESTROOM AT THE ZOO

At the National Zoo, unlike most everywhere else in D.C., public restrooms can be found in four convenient locations: in the Panda Plaza, next to the Zoo Police Station, inside the visitor center, and inside Amazonia.

remembrance of the Lebanese-born poet. Opposite the garden, the **U.S. Naval Observatory** makes a stand for science. Continuing north, the Greek Orthodox **St. Sophia Cathedral** is noted for the handsome mosaic work on the interior of its dome. Dominating the skyline, the **Washington National Cathedral** is the sixth-largest cathedral in the world. Its Gothic decor features fanciful gargoyles, including one shaped like Darth Vader. In 2011 the Cathedral sustained damage caused by

GETTING TO THE ZOO

If you're just going to the zoo, leave the Metro at Cleveland Park instead of Woodley Park/Zoo for a shorter downhill walk. At the end of your visit, return downhill to the Metro via Woodley Park/Zoo. If the zoo doesn't wipe you out, tag on a trip to Adams Morgan, easily accessible on foot from the Woodley Park/Zoo Metro stop.

an earthquake but still hosts services and offers tours, including a tour and tea in the **Pilgrim Observation Gallery.**

ROCK CREEK PARK, FOXHALL, AND OUTER D.C.

Although the 1,800 acres of **Rock Creek Park** span much of Washington and into Maryland, two of the main driving entrances are in Upper Northwest. Take Tilden Road to get to the Peirce Mill and Military Road to reach the nature center and planetarium. The park is accessible to pedestrians throughout the city.

When the weather is clear, two parks in this area are worth a visit. The 183-acre **Glover-Archbold Park** features a 3.5-mile nature trail. The highest point in the District, **Fort Reno Park** hosts free outdoor concerts in summer.

Tucked away in the Foxhall neighborhood, the **Kreeger Museum** showcases the small but impressive collections of paintings, sculpture, and African art collected by wealthy businessman David Kreeger. Tour the hall where he entertained famous musicians and the dining room decorated entirely with Monets. Reserve in advance except on Friday and Saturday.

At the Maryland border, the intersection of Wisconsin and Western avenues forms **Friendship Heights.** This shopping-mall district is the place to pick up the latest finds at Tiffany, Jimmy Choo, Louis Vuitton, and Neiman Marcus. TJ Maxx and Loehmann's provide designer deals.

UPPER NORTHWEST WITH KIDS

At the **National Zoo** the Kids Farm and Pizza Garden keep kids busy learning how to take care of animals and where food comes from.

Rock Creek Nature Center and Planetarium (✉ *5300 Glover Rd. NW* ◷ Closed Mon. and Tues.) offers a variety of hands-on experiences for kids in the **Discovery Room.** They can look inside beehives, create rainstorms, and crawl inside a volcano. Fish and amphibian feeding time is 4 pm. The **planetarium** has weekend shows for kids.

At the **National Cathedral,** kids can see gargoyles pulling just about every face imaginable. The **Children's Chapel** is designed to the scale of a six-year-old child, and the Space Window contains a piece of rock from the moon.

Museums

WORD OF MOUTH

"Most visitors go to the museums along the Mall, and they are wonderful, but during high-tourist-traffic times they are also very crowded. There are many equally wonderful museums in other parts of town."

—fkranzberg

Updated by
Renee Sklarew

The internationally renowned collections of the Smithsonian—137 million objects, specimens, and artworks displayed in the world's largest museum complex—make Washington one of the great museum cities. The holdings of the 19 Smithsonian museums range from a 65-million-year-old *Tyrannosaurus rex* skeleton to masterpieces by Da Vinci and Picasso, the Hope Diamond, the original "Star-Spangled Banner," and the space shuttle *Discovery*—and all are on view for free.

Add in the legendary art treasures of the National Gallery, the Phillips Collection, the Corcoran, and Dumbarton Oaks, and Washington D.C. becomes a true feast for the eyes.

PLANNING

HITTING THE HIGHLIGHTS
Nowhere else can you see the Declaration of Independence and the Constitution, both displayed at the National Archives. Touch a moon rock beneath the *Spirit of St. Louis* at the National Air and Space Museum. The masterpieces of Monet and Matisse at the National Gallery of Art are must-sees, as are Thomas Jefferson's desk and Dorothy's ruby slippers at the National Museum of American History.

For modern art, it's tough to beat the constantly changing Hirshhorn Museum, where an Alexander Calder mobile might hover over a multimedia installation by today's hottest talent. For intimately grouped masterpieces, head to the Phillips Collection. Lovers of architecture and design shouldn't miss a pilgrimage to the National Building Museum.

VISITING THE SMITHSONIAN

Most of the 19 Smithsonian museums are open between 10 and 5:30 more than 360 days a year, and all are free (there may be charges for some special exhibits). To get oriented, start with a visit to the Smithsonian building—aka the "Castle," for its towers-and-turrets architecture—which has information on all the museums.

SPECIAL EVENTS

The Smithsonian museums regularly host an incredible spectrum of special events, from evenings of jazz to dance nights to food and wine tastings, films, lectures, and events for families and kids. A full schedule is available at ⊕ *www.si.edu/events*. Popular events include live jazz on Friday evenings in summer from 5 to 8:30 at the National Gallery of Art sculpture garden and Take Five performances every third Thursday from 5 to 7 at the Smithsonian American Art Museum. Every four months the Hirshhorn Museum throws a wildly popular after-hours party with DJs, sound-and-light art installations, a cash bar, and a dance floor.

MUSEUMS WITH KIDS

At the Museum of Natural History they'll meet a giant *T. rex*, see live tarantulas, explore butterfly gardens, take in an IMAX movie, or even brave a sleepover. They'll conduct lively experiments at Spark!Lab or watch live demonstrations of important events in American history at the Museum of American History, and they can see famous spaceships, fighter planes, and the Space Shuttle *Discovery* at the National Air and Space Museum. At the Corcoran Gallery of Art, interactive exhibitions and **Free Summer Saturdays** are for younger visitors, while "Conversation Starters" are self-guided tour brochures for parents. The Freer Gallery of Art and Hirshhorn Museum offer free art workshops for kids and teens. The National Building Museum showcases such interactive exhibits as the Building Zone, and at the D.A.R. Museum kids can play games and try on costumes from the time of the American Revolution. Groove to Tot-Rock and other family-friendly performances at Discovery Theater in the Ripley Center next to the Smithsonian Castle.

MUSEUMS WITH LATE HOURS

Corcoran Gallery of Art, Thursday until 9 pm.

International Spy Museum, April–October, daily until 7 pm.

Museum of Crime and Punishment, Friday and Saturday daily until 8 pm, Sunday through Thursday until 7 pm.

Phillips Collection, Thursday until 8:30 pm.

BEST GIFT SHOPS

National Air and Space Museum. This is the largest of all the Smithsonian museum stores.

National Building Museum. With shelves filled with Alessi kitchenware, handmade jewelry, and slickly photographed tomes on architecture, design lovers and modernists will be in heaven.

National Gallery of Art. Here you can find one of the country's largest selections of books on art and art history, along with posters, prints, stationery, and gifts.

3

CORCORAN GALLERY OF ART

✉ *500 17th St. NW, White House area* ☎ *202/639-1700* ⊕ *www.corcoran.org* ✉ *$10; extra admission for special exhibitions* ⊙ *Wed., Fri., and weekends 10–5; Thurs. 10–9* Ⓜ *Farragut West or Farragut North.*

TIPS

■ There are free docent-led tours Wednesday through Saturday at noon, Thursday evenings at 7, and weekends at 3.

■ Purchase advance tickets for special exhibitions, which tend to be popular.

■ Todd Gray's Muse at the Corcoran restaurant is set in the marble-columned atrium and is a great place for a sophisticated meal; enjoy Market Brunch on the first and third Sunday of every month, featuring live entertainment.

■ The shop offers exhibition catalogs, art and design books, apparel, toys, prints and more, as well as original art by students and alumni of the Corcoran School of Art and Design.

The Corcoran looks like a museum and acts like a gallery, blending classic elegance and experimental edge. Washington's first art museum is housed in a marble Beaux-Arts mansion, and is home to an important collection of 18th-, 19th-, and 20th-century European and American art.

As the parent of the Corcoran School of Art and Design, the museum is also devoted to showcasing cutting-edge contemporary art, from established superstars to undiscovered talents.

HIGHLIGHTS

A prize collection of masterworks by the great early American artists, including John Copley, Gilbert Stuart, Rembrandt Peale, Mary Cassatt, and John Singer Sargent, is in constant rotation, but you're always guaranteed to see a selection of the most-important pieces, displayed in gilded frames in high-ceilinged rooms.

Experience the breadth of postwar art with works by Cy Twombly, Lee Bontecou, Andy Warhol, and Ellsworth Kelly.

Photography is one of the museum's great strengths: recent exhibits of works by Richard Avedon and William Eggleston drew sellout crowds.

The exhibition space Gallery 31 shows work by students, faculty, and alumni of the highly reputed Corcoran School of Art and Design.

THE FREER AND SACKLER GALLERIES

✉ *Freer: 12th St. and Jefferson Dr. SW, The Mall* ☎ *202/633–4880* ✉ *Sackler: 1050 Independence Ave. SW, The Mall* ☎ *202/312–1012* ⊕ *www.asia.si.edu* 🎫 *Free* ⊙ *Daily 10–5:30* Ⓜ *Smithsonian.*

3

TIPS

■ The Freer and Sackler galleries are home to the largest Asian art research library in the United States, open to the public five days a week without appointment.

■ Free highlight tours meet at the information desks at 11, noon, and 1 daily, except Wednesday and federal holidays. There are often a variety of other free tours as well; ask at the information desks.

■ The museums regularly host films, concerts, readings, and other events; check the website to see what's on.

■ Take advantage of the Freer's wide menu of excellent brochures on everything from Islamic art and Japanese painting to South Asian sculpture and Near Eastern ceramics.

■ At the ImaginAsia workshops, held most weekends at the Arthur M. Sackler Gallery, children ages six to 14 work on projects such as origami and printing blocks.

Home to one of the world's finest collections of Asian art, the Smithsonian's Freer Gallery of Art was made possible by an endowment from Detroit industrialist Charles Lang Freer. Opened in 1923, the collection includes more than 27,000 works of art from the Far and Near East. When Freer endowed the gallery, he insisted the collection could not be lent out, nor could objects from outside the collections be displayed. Because of the restrictions, a second museum was built to house the Asian art collection of Arthur M. Sackler, with works from the Middle East and Southeast Asia. A lower-level gallery connects the two museums.

HIGHLIGHTS

Pick a jade carving or a painted silk scroll from the collections of Imperial Chinese decorative arts.

Study ancient Biblical manuscripts, including Egyptian gospel parchments from the 4th century, and the colorful Adoration of the Magi parchment from 13th-century Armenia.

Behold the bodhisattva: a 12th-century Japanese sculpture of a Buddhist approaching Nirvana.

Ogle the curves of the 10th-century Indian bronze sculptures of the dancing god Shiva and his wife, the goddess Parvati.

The museum houses the world's largest collection of paintings by James McNeill Whistler. Be sure to see the Peacock Room, a jewel box of a space that Whistler designed, with gold murals on peacock blue walls, and a peacock-feather-pattern gold-leaf ceiling.

Manuscripts of 15th-century Persian love poetry, in exquisite calligraphy accompanied with intricate gold and silver paintings, are a must-see in the Sackler Gallery.

HIRSHHORN MUSEUM AND SCULPTURE GARDEN

✉ *Independence Ave. and 7th St. SW, The Mall* ☎ *202/633–2829* ⊕ *www.hirshhorn.si.edu* 💳 *Free* ⏱ *Museum daily 10–5:30, sculpture garden daily 7:30–dusk* Ⓜ *Smithsonian or L'Enfant Plaza (Maryland Ave. exit).*

TIPS

■ The sculpture garden makes an inspiring spot for a picnic.

■ Docents lead impromptu 30-minute tours between noon and 4. Every Friday at 12:30 there is a free gallery talk and tour focusing on a current exhibition.

■ Have a question? Seek out the museum's Interpretive Guides, who wear question-mark badges.

■ Teens should check out the ArtLab, a design studio where they can experiment with new technology and learn digital-media techniques.

■ About three times a year, to coincide with a major installation, the museum hosts Hirshhorn After Hours events: parties that last until midnight and feature performance art, live music, dancing, and gallery talks.

■ The museum regularly screens independent and experimental films.

Conceived as the nation's museum of modern and contemporary art, the Hirshhorn is home to nearly 12,000 works by masters who include Pablo Picasso, Piet Mondrian, and Willem de Kooning, as well as contemporary superstars Damien Hirst and Olafur Eliasson. The art is displayed in a round 1974 poured-concrete building designed by Gordon Bunshaft, dubbed the "Doughnut on the Mall" when it was built. Most of the collection was bequeathed by the museum's founder, Joseph H. Hirshhorn, a Latvian immigrant who made his fortune in uranium mines.

HIGHLIGHTS

The internationally renowned sculpture collection has masterpieces by Henry Moore, Alberto Giacometti, and Constantin Brancusi. Outside, sculptures dot a grass-and-granite garden. Among them is a 32-foot-tall yellow cartoon brush-stroke sculpture by pop-art iconographer Roy Lichtenstein that has become a beloved local landmark. Among other works are Jeff Koons's *Kiepenkerl* and Auguste Rodin's *Burghers of Calais*.

Inside, the third level is the place to see masterworks from the museum's permanent collection, such as Alexander Calder's intriguing mobiles, Joan Miró's whimsical dreamscapes, and Sol LeWitt's wall drawings.

The second level houses exhibits that rotate about three times a year, curated by museum staff and devoted to particular artists or themes.

The lower level houses thematic installations featuring recent and experimental works from the permanent collection, as well as the Black Box, a space for moving image installations by international artists.

INTERNATIONAL SPY MUSEUM

✉ *800 F St. NW, East End*
☎ *202/393–7798* ⊕ *www.
spymuseum.org* ✉ *Permanent
exhibition only, adults $19.95;
seniors $14.95; children 7–17
$13.95; ages 6 and under free;
Operation Spy only, $14.95*
⊙ *Apr.–Sept., daily 9–8; Oct.–
Mar., daily 10–6; hours subject
to change; check website
before visiting* Ⓜ *Gallery Pl./
Chinatown.*

3

TIPS

■ Advance tickets (purchased
at the museum or on its
website) are highly recommended. All tickets are date
and time specific. Tickets are
most likely available (and your
visit less crowded) on Tuesday,
Wednesday, and Thursday or
daily after 2 pm. Allow about
two hours for a visit.

■ This is a great museum for
kids age 10 and up; younger
ones might not get it. At the
popular monthly KidSpy workshop for kids ages 10–14, participants can assume a cover
identity and disguise, make a
portable lie detector, crack a
cipher, check out surveillance
electronics, and more.

■ The museum regularly
hosts films, events, and lectures by espionage experts. A
GPS-guided walking tour, Spy
in the City, takes "agents" 12
years and older on a mission
outside the museum walls.

It's believed that there are more spies in Washington
than in any other city in the world, making it a fitting
home for this museum, which displays the world's largest collection of spy artifacts. Museum advisers include
top cryptologists; masters of disguise; and former CIA,
FBI, and KGB operatives. Exhibits range from the coded
letters of Revolutionary War überspy Benedict Arnold
to the KGB's lipstick pistol, to high-tech 21st-century
espionage toys, showcased with theatrical panache in a
five-building complex (one, the Warder-Atlas Building,
housed Washington's Communist party in the 1940s).

HIGHLIGHTS

The Secret History of History exhibit takes you through
the espionage behind the headlines, from Moses's use of
spies in Canaan to Abraham Lincoln's employment of
the Pinkerton National Detective Agency as a full-scale
secret service in the Civil War, to the birth of Lenin's
state-run espionage ring—later known as the KGB.

There's a heavy mix of flash and fun, with toys used by
actual operatives as well as James Bond's Aston Martin
and tales of celebrity spies like singer Josephine Baker,
chef Julia Child, and actress Marlene Dietrich.

The story of Cold War espionage is displayed in a maze
of mirrors, a flashy but apt visual metaphor for the
deadly game of spying and counterspying that gripped
the United States and Soviet Union. Weapons of Mass
Disruption is right up to date on cyber attacks and the
modern spy game of theft and destruction of intelligence.

Operation Spy, a one-hour "immersive experience,"
works like a live-action game, dropping you into the
middle of a high-stakes foreign intelligence mission.
Each step of the operation—which includes decrypting
secret audio files, a car chase, and interrogating a suspect agent—is taken from actual intelligence operations.

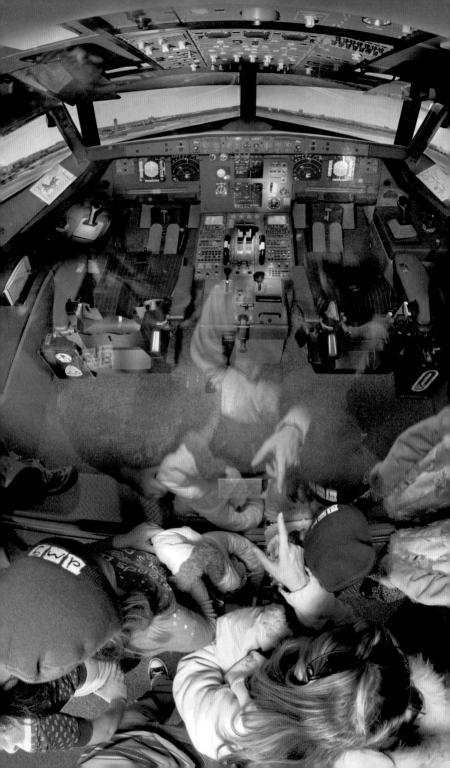

NATIONAL AIR AND SPACE MUSEUM

(above) Neil Armstrong and Buzz Aldrin's spacesuits.
(left) You can see into the cockpit of the Airbus A320.

The country's second most-visited museum, attracting 9 million people annually to its vast and diverse collection of historic aircraft and spacecraft, is the perfect place to amaze the kids with giant rocket ships, relive the glory days of fighter jets, and even learn to fly. Its 22 galleries tell the story of humanity's quest for flight—from the Wright brothers' experiments with gliders to space exploration.

PLANNING YOUR TIME

If you only have an hour take the free ninety-minute docent-led tour of the museum's highlights, which leaves daily at 10:30 and 1 from the Welcome Center.

To get the most from the museum, plan your must-sees in advance and allow plenty of time—at least two hours—to take everything in. The museum has three basic types of exhibits: aircraft and spacecraft; galleries of history and information; and experiences, such as IMAX films and hands-on workshops. An ideal visit would include a mix of these.

Before your visit, buy timed tickets online up to two weeks in advance for the popular IMAX films and planetarium shows to bypass the long lines and sold-out screenings.

When you arrive at the museum, consult the guides at the welcome desk; they can help you fine-tune your plan. If you didn't buy tickets for IMAX online, buy them now.

If you're traveling with kids, arrive early to avoid lines and pick up a kids' guide with games and activities at the welcome desk. Hit the wow-factor exhibits like the **Milestones of Flight** and **Space Race** first but leave time for the hands-on **How Things Fly** gallery, and IMAX and planetarium shows. Strollers are allowed through the security checkpoint; there is a family bathroom on the first floor near the food court and a baby changing station near the **Early Flight** gallery.

If you just can't get enough, the **Steven F. Udvar-Hazy Center,** a companion museum near Dulles International Airport, features a massive hangar filled with hundreds more aircraft, spacecraft, and aviation artifacts.

✉ Independence Ave. and 6th St. SW, The Mall ☎ 202/633–1000, 202/633-4629 movie information, 202/633-5285 TDD ⊕ www.nasm.si.edu 🎟 Free, IMAX or Planetarium $9, IMAX feature film $15 flight simulators $7-$8 ⊙ Daily 10–5:30, Mar 28–Sept 5 open most days to 7:30

MUSEUM HIGHLIGHTS

AIRCRAFT AND SPACECRAFT

First stop: the **Milestones of Flight** gallery at the entrance contains museum superstars like the **Spirit of St. Louis**, in which Charles Lindbergh made the first solo transatlantic flight; **Sputnik**, the first satellite in space; and the giant **U.S. Pershing II** and **Soviet SS-20** nuclear missiles.

Albatros D.va

Next, make like Buzz Lightyear and head to infinity and beyond with a walk through the **Skylab Orbital Workshop**, the largest component of America's first space station in the **Space Race** gallery. Also on display are an arsenal of rockets and missiles, from the giant **V-2 rocket** to the devastatingly accurate **Tomahawk Cruise missile**. The Apollo Lunar Module is also a must-see in **Exploring the Moon**.

Sputnik replica

HISTORY AND SCIENCE

Even those who don't like history flock to the fascinating **Wright Brothers** gallery to see the first machine to achieve piloted flight, the **Wright 1903 Flyer** and the new **Pioneers of Flight** gallery.

For history buffs, the **Great War in the Air**, **World War II**, and **Sea-Air Operations** galleries are essential, with legendary fighter planes such as the **Supermarine Spitfire**.

In the history of space exploration, **Apollo to the Moon** is packed with artifacts from moon missions.

Is there life on Mars? Find out in the science-oriented **Explore the Universe**, **Looking at Earth**, and **Moving Beyond Earth** galleries.

IMAX AND PLANETARIUM SHOWS

Lift off with an **IMAX** film. You'll feel like you've left the ground with the swooping aerial scenes in **To Fly!** and **Fighter Pilot**. Or take a trip into deep space with **3D Sun**. In the **Albert Einstein Planetarium**, you can watch the classic tour of the nighttime sky as well as shows like **Cosmic Collisions** and **Black Holes**.

HANDS-ON

Learn to fly in the interactive **How Things Fly** exhibit geared towards kids and families. Test your top gun skills at one of the popular **Flight Simulators** where you'll get full-on fighter plane experience—barrel rolls and all.

TOURING TIPS

Avoid the Crowds: Between April and September (and on holiday weekends) the museum is slammed with visitors; it is least crowded September to March. It's always a good idea to come before noon to beat the rush.

Where to Eat: A huge food court offers McDonald's, pizza, and sandwiches, and is the most simple and practical eating option around.

Souvenirs: The three-story museum store is the largest in all the Smithsonian museums, and one of the best. Along with souvenirs, books, and collectors' items, it also displays a model of the USS Enterprise, used in the filming of the first Star Trek television series. If you have kids, don't start your tour here or you may never leave!

Flight Simulators: Tickets can be purchased at the IMAX box office or in the **Flight Simulators** gallery.

Soviet SS-20 nuclear missile.

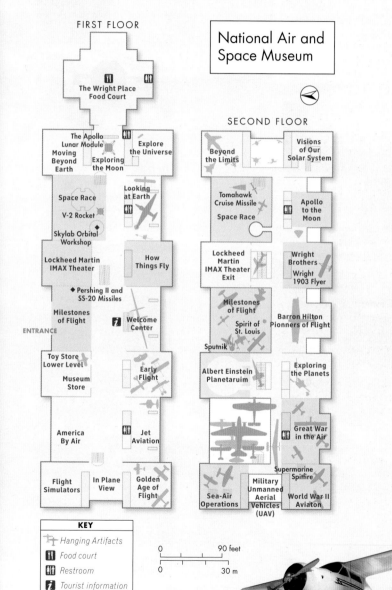

Apollo capsule   Breitling Orbiter   Apollo 11 module   Lockheed Vega

National Air and Space Museum

FIRST FLOOR

The Wright Place Food Court

The Apollo Lunar Module

Moving Beyond Earth

Exploring the Moon

Explore the Universe

Space Race
V-2 Rocket

Skylab Orbital Workshop

Looking at Earth

Lockheed Martin IMAX Theater

How Things Fly

◆ Pershing II and SS-20 Missiles

Milestones of Flight

Welcome Center

ENTRANCE

Toy Store
Lower Level

Museum Store

Early Flight

America By Air

Jet Aviation

Flight Simulators

In Plane View

Golden Age of Flight

SECOND FLOOR

Beyond the Limits

Visions of Our Solar System

Tomahawk Cruise Missile

Space Race

Apollo to the Moon

Lockheed Martin IMAX Theater Exit

Wright Brothers

Wright 1903 Flyer

Milestones of Flight

Spirit of St. Louis

Barron Hilton Pionners of Flight

Sputnik

Albert Einstein Planetaruim

Exploring the Planets

Great War in the Air

Supermarine Spitfire

Albert Einstein Planetaruim

Military Unmanned Aerial Vehicles (UAV)

Sea-Air Operations

World War II Aviaton

KEY

- Hanging Artifacts
- Food court
- Restroom
- Tourist information

0   90 feet

0   30 m

Staggerwing

NASM TALKS TO FODOR'S

The original 1903 Wright Flyer.

Boeing F4B-4

Gen. John R. Daily (USMC, Ret.), director of the National Air and Space Museum, talks to Coral Davenport about what interests him at the Air and Space Museum.

BE AMAZED

"I would like visitors to take away a better understanding of the importance of air, aviation, and space in the leadership role of this country and technology. Also, an education in the four forces of flight—gravity, lift, thrust, and drag. **How Things Fly** is a physics lab designed to be understandable for kids, but I've watched so many adults be amazed as they learn the basics of the physics of flight in that gallery."

FLY THROUGH THE AGES

"The history is extremely important—but of them all, the **Wright Brothers** gallery is probably the most important. Also, the **Golden Age of Flight** gallery, about the period when aviation was young, and people were doing crazy things—wing walking, barnstorming. The **World War II** galleries are also a big draw. I think a lot of parents and grandparents most closely relate to those galleries. They bring their families and tell stories about what it was like flying air raids over Germany."

MAKING CONNECTIONS

"This is a personal museum. There are attachments between individuals and artifacts. Sometimes families come in because Dad wants to look at his old airplane. But the designers have put together rich cross-cultural exhibits—showing the historic, but also the cultural and social impacts of aviation. They show what people were wearing, how developments in aviation led to fads and movements. It's hard to tie it all together sometimes but this museum helps people make those connections."

FAVORITE PLANE

"The **Boeing F4B-4** in Sea-Air Operations is my favorite plane—my father flew that exact plane the year I was born. It's a pre-World War II airplane. When you compare that to the **X-15** or the **Bell X-1**, you see the tremendous leap that aviation took in the middle of the century, as a result of World War II."

1960s flight attendant uniform

NATIONAL AIR AND SPACE MUSEUM STEVEN F. UDVAR-HAZY CENTER

For more giant jets and spaceships, you won't want to miss the museum's **Udvar-Hazy Center** at Washington Dulles International Airport in northern Virginia. The center showcases the museum's growing collection of historic air- and spacecraft, which is much too large to fit into the building on the Mall.

Unlike the museum on the Mall, the Udvar-Hazy Center focuses on one thing: planes and rockets, hung as though in flight throughout two vast multi-level hangars. This focus makes the center more appealing for families with kids too young to take in detailed historic narratives. It is also much less crowded than the Mall museum.

One giant three-level hangar is devoted to historic aircraft, such as the **Lockheed SR-71 Blackbird,** the fastest jet in the world; the sassy-looking **DeHavilland Chipmunk,** a prototype aerobatic airplane; the sleek, supersonic **Concorde,** and the **Enola Gay,** which in 1945 dropped the first atomic bomb to be used in war on Hiroshima, Japan.

A second space hangar is largely taken up by the space shuttle **Enterprise,** as well as satellites, space stations, and space missile launchers. There is also an 8-story **IMAX** theater.

✉ 14390 Air and Space Museum Parkway, Chantilly, VA ☎ 202/633–1000, 866/868–7774 movie information, 202/633–5285 TDD ⊕ www.nasm.si.edu ✆ Free, IMAX feature film $15, Planetarium or IMAX show $9, flight simulators $7–$8 ⊘ Daily 10–5:30

TOURING TIPS

Getting Here: You'll need a car as there is no nearby Metro or bus stop. The drive takes about 30–40 minutes from D.C. Take I-66 West to Route 28 North (Exit 53B); drive 5 mi and exit at the Air and Space Museum Parkway, follow signs to the museum. Parking is $12.

Airport Shuttle: You can combine a morning visit with an afternoon departure flight from nearby Dulles Airport. There are 15-minute shuttles every hour between the airport and museum for 50¢. A taxi ride costs about $10.

When you arrive: Head to the welcome desk for a customized "Flight Plan" to guide you around the museum. Allow at least an hour to tour and another 45 minutes to see an **IMAX** film.

With Kids: Pick up museum guides with games and activities for kids ages 9 and up at the welcome desk.

Where to Eat: There is a McDonald's and McCafe with slightly healthier fare on the second floor.

(top) Space Shuttle Enterprise; (bottom) DeHavilland Chipmunk.

3

IN FOCUS NATIONAL AIR AND SPACE MUSEUM

NATIONAL ARCHIVES

✉ *Constitution Ave. between 7th and 9th sts., The Mall* ☎ *866/272–6272, 877/444–6777 tours and reservations* ⊕ *www.nara.gov* 🎟 *Free* ⊘ *Mar. 15–Labor Day, daily 10–7; Labor Day–Mar. 14, daily 10–5:30; tours weekdays at 9:45* Ⓜ *Archives/Navy Memorial.*

TIPS

■ Reservations to visit the Archives are highly recommended: without one, you could wait up to an hour to get in. Reservations for guided tours, or for a self-guided visit, must be made at least six weeks in advance. March, April, May, and the weekends around Thanksgiving and Christmas are the busiest. Expect to spend 90 minutes here, viewing the charter documents and touring the permanent exhibit. Before your tour, check out the informative introductory film at the McGowan Theater.

■ The Archives are open to anyone. Family genealogists can find birth, death, military, and census records, immigrant ships' passenger lists, letters, and maps since the beginning of the nation's history. Archivists can help you track down ancestors' records or anything else you're looking for.

The National Archives are at once monument, museum, and the nation's memory. Headquartered in a grand marble edifice on Constitution Avenue, the National Archives and Records Administration is charged with preserving and archiving the most historically important U.S. government records. At 33 facilities nationwide, including 13 presidential libraries, the Archives preserves 10 billion paper records dating back to 1775 and billions of recent electronic records.

HIGHLIGHTS

The star attractions, which draw a million viewers every year, are the Declaration of Independence, Constitution, and Bill of Rights. These are housed in the Archives' rotunda, each on a marble platform, encased in bulletproof glass, and floating in argon, an inert gas, which protects the irreplaceable documents. To the right of the rotunda, displayed with great majesty, is the 1297 Magna Carta, the document of English common law whose language inspired the Constitution: this is one of four remaining originals.

The permanent exhibit showcases the breadth of the Archives' holdings. You can find anything from the Emancipation Proclamation to the first issue of *Mad* magazine (used as evidence in congressional hearings on juvenile delinquency). The Public Vaults have more than a thousand originals or facsimiles on display. The Archives' 500,000 film and audio recordings include films of flying saucers, used as evidence in congressional UFO hearings, and tapes of the Nuremberg trials and Congress debating Prohibition.

Many exhibits are interactive and kid-friendly. One room of letters from children to U.S. presidents includes a letter from seventh-grader Andy Smith, asking Ronald Regan for federal funds to clean up a disaster area—his room.

NATIONAL BUILDING MUSEUM

✉ *401 F St. NW, between 4th and 5th Sts., Downtown* ☎ *202/272–2448* ⊕ *www.nbm.org* 💳 *Free; temporary exhibits $8; Building Zone $8* ⊙ *Mon.–Sat. 10–5, Sun. 11–5, Building Zone until 4* Ⓜ *Judiciary Sq. or Gallery Pl./ Chinatown.*

TIPS

■ Free historic building tours are offered daily at 11:30, 12:30, and 1:30.

■ Interactive Discovery Cart programs for children ages five and up are offered at 10:30 and 2:30 on Saturday and 11:30 and 2:30 on Sunday.

■ Before entering the building, walk down its F Street side. The terra-cotta frieze by Caspar Buberl between the first and second floors depicts soldiers marching and sailing in an endless procession around the building. The architect, U.S. Army Corps of Engineers' General Montgomery C. Meigs, lost his eldest son in the Civil War, and, though the frieze depicts Union troops, he intended it as a memorial to all who were killed in the bloody war.

■ Find the café in the museum's Great Hall, and don't miss the highly regarded shop.

National Building Museum is the nation's premier organization devoted to the built environment. The open interior of the mammoth redbrick edifice is one of the city's great spaces, and has been the site of many presidential inaugural balls. The eight central Corinthian columns are among the largest in the world, rising to a height of 75 feet. Although they resemble Siena marble, each is made of 70,000 bricks that have been covered with plaster and painted. For years, the annual *Christmas in Washington* TV special has been filmed here.

HIGHLIGHTS

The permanent exhibit *Washington: Symbol and City* tells the story of the birth and evolution of the backwater that eventually became the nation's capital (beginning by debunking the myth that Washington was built on a swamp!). You can touch the intricately detailed models of the White House, the Capitol, the Washington Monument, and the Lincoln and Jefferson memorials, and look at original drawings, building plans, maps, videos, and photographs that trace the city's architectural history.

Among the most popular permanent exhibits is the Building Zone, where kids ages two to six can get a hands-on introduction to building by constructing a tower, exploring a playhouse, or playing with bulldozers and construction trucks.

House and Home takes visitors on a tour of houses both familiar and surprising, through past and present, exploring American domestic life and residential architecture.

There are also temporary exhibits: recent ones have covered environmentally sustainable architecture and Lego architecture; the upcoming *Designing for Disaster* demonstrates plans for disaster-resilient communities.

NATIONAL GALLERY OF ART, WEST BUILDING

✉ *4th St. and Constitution Ave. NW, The Mall* ☎ *202/737–4215* ⊕ *www.nga.gov* ⊡ *Free* ☉ *Mon.–Sat. 10–5, Sun. 11–6* Ⓜ *Archives/Navy Memorial.*

The two buildings of the National Gallery hold one of the world's foremost collections of art from the 13th to the 21st centuries. If you want to view the museum's holdings in (more or less) chronological order, it's best to start in the West Building. Opened in 1941, the domed museum was a gift to the nation from industrialist and treasury secretary Andrew Mellon. The rotunda, with 24 marble columns surrounding a fountain topped with a statue of Mercury, sets the stage for the masterpieces on display in more than 100 galleries.

HIGHLIGHTS

The only painting by Leonardo da Vinci on display in the Americas, *Ginevra de' Benci* is the centerpiece of the collection's survey of Italian Renaissance paintings and sculpture; it also includes Raphael's *Alba Madonna* and Sandro Botticelli's *Adoration of the Magi*.

The masters of painting light, Rembrandt van Rijn and Johannes Vermeer, anchor the magnificent collection of Dutch and Flemish works.

The 19-century French Galleries house masterworks by such superstars as Vincent Van Gogh, Paul Cézanne, Claude Monet, Auguste Renoir, and Edgar Degas. The gallery is organized into groupings that showcase the bold innovations that occured during the era of Impressionism and Post-impressionism.

THE SCULPTURE GARDEN

Walk beneath flowering trees in the sculpture garden, on the Mall between 7th and 9th streets. Granite walkways take you through a shaded landscape and sculptures from the museum's permanent collection, including Roy Lichtenstein's playful *House I* and Miró's *Personnage Gothique, Oiseau-Eclair*. The huge central fountain, pure magic on hot summer days, is converted to an outdoor skating rink in winter.

NATIONAL GALLERY OF ART, EAST BUILDING

✉ *Constitution Ave. between 3rd and 4th Sts. NW, The Mall* ☎ *202/737–4215* ⊕ *www. nga.gov* 🎟 *Free* ⊘ *Mon.–Sat. 10–5, Sun. 11–6* Ⓜ *Archives/ Navy Memorial.*

3

TIPS

■ To reach the East Building, you can take the underground concourse, lined with gift shops and a cafeteria, but to best appreciate the building's architecture, enter from outside: exit the West Building through its eastern doors and cross 4th Street.

■ To preserve the Matisse cutouts, the works are on view only between 10 and 3 Monday through Saturday and 11 to 3 on Sunday in the East Building Concourse.

■ Don't miss Multiverse by Leo Villareal, a complex light sculpture visitors experience as they pass through the walkway between the East and West buildings. The work features approximately 41,000 LED nodes that run through channels along the 200-foot-long space.

■ Free docent-led tours leave from the information desk weekdays at 11:30 and 1:30, and weekends at 11:30 and 3:30.

■ The cheat-sheet "What to See in An Hour" pinpoints 15 highlights of the East Building.

The East Building opened in 1978 in response to the changing needs of the National Gallery, especially to house a growing collection of modern art. The trapezoidal shape of the site prompted architect I. M. Pei's dramatic approach: two interlocking spaces shaped like triangles provide room for galleries, auditoriums, and administrative offices. Despite its severe angularity, Pei's building is inviting. The ax-blade-like southwest corner has been darkened and polished smooth by thousands of hands irresistibly drawn to it. Inside, the sunlit atrium is dominated by a colorful 76-foot-long Alexander Calder mobile, the perfect introduction to galleries filled with masterworks of modern and contemporary art.

HIGHLIGHTS

Masterpieces from every famous name in 20th-century art—Pablo Picasso, Jackson Pollock, Piet Mondrian, Roy Lichtenstein, Joan Miró, Georgia O'Keeffe, and dozens of others—fill the galleries.

The bold shapes and brilliant teals and fuschias of Henri Matisse's giant paper cutouts make them among the most innovative, important, and purely enjoyable works of modern art. The National Gallery's collection of these is considered the world's greatest.

Huge, color-drenched Mark Rothko works are a perennial favorite—the gallery owns more than 300 paintings and 600 works on paper by the iconic American modernist.

World-class temporary exhibitions are a big draw. Recent years have seen the collected works of Andy Warhol, Paul Gaugin, Canaletto, Robert Frank, Martin Puryear, Jan Lievens, and Hendrick Avercamp.

NATIONAL MUSEUM OF AMERICAN HISTORY

✉ *Constitution Ave. and 14th St. NW, The Mall* ☎ *202/633–1000* ⊕ *www.americanhistory.si.edu* 🎫 *Free* ☉ *Daily 10–5:30 with occasional extended hrs to 7:30 pm, check website* Ⓜ *Smithsonian or Federal Triangle.*

TIPS

■ Head to the welcome center on the second floor or to the information desk on the first floor to pick up a map, learn about tours and demonstrations, and find out if a free performance is scheduled.

■ During the high season and on holidays, expect waits of up to 20 minutes for the Star-Spangled Banner and the First Ladies' Dresses. To see pop-culture memorabilia without the wait, check out displays in the lower-level entrance, including costumes worn by Humphrey Bogart, Lauren Bacall, and Clint Eastwood, along with Harry Potter's robe.

■ The Stars and Stripes Café serves sandwiches, salads, pizza, and burgers, and the Constitution Café serves coffee, ice cream, sandwiches, and snacks.

■ The main museum store is on the first floor; another is on the third floor with military-inspired books, apparel, and gifts; and you can also find mementoes in the Popular Culture store near the Mall entrance on the second floor.

The 3 million artifacts in the country's largest American history museum explore America's cultural, political, and scientific past, with holdings as diverse and iconic as Abraham Lincoln's top hat, Thomas Edison's lightbulbs, Julia Child's entire kitchen, and Judy Garland's ruby slippers from *The Wizard of Oz.*

HIGHLIGHTS

The centerpiece of the Star-Spangled Banner gallery is the banner that in 1814 was hoisted to show that Fort McHenry had survived 25 hours of British rocket attacks, inspiring Francis Scott Key to write the lyrics that became the national anthem.

For political and military history, visit the American Presidency, Gunboat Philadelphia, and Price of Freedom: Americans at War galleries.

"American Stories" showcases historic and cultural touchstones of American history through more than 100 objects from the museum's vast holdings: a walking stick used by Benjamin Franklin, a sunstone capital from a Mormon temple, Lincoln's gold pocket watch, Archie Bunker's chair, Muhammad Ali's boxing gloves, a fragment of Plymouth Rock, and Kermit the Frog.

This is the only museum in the world with an active program of using its historical musical instruments for live performances; the Smithsonian Chamber Music Society holds regular concerts.

NATIONAL MUSEUM OF THE AMERICAN INDIAN

✉ *4th St. and Independence Ave. SW, The Mall* ☎ *202/633–1000* ⊕ *www.americanindian. si.edu* ⊒ *Free* ⊙ *Daily 10–5:30* Ⓜ *L'Enfant Plaza.*

3

TIPS

■ Visit between 10 and 2 on a sunny day to see the central atrium awash in rainbows created by the light refracted through prisms in the ceiling aligned with Earth's cardinal points.

■ From roasted venison and Peruvian seviche to pork pibil tacos and quinoa salad, the museum's Mitsitam Native Foods Cafe offers a modern perspective on foods that have been grown, raised, and harvested in North and South America for thousands of years.

■ Free tours are offered daily, and the museum's 6,000-square-foot imagiNA-TIONS Activity Center includes hands-on activities throughout the year, including an interactive quiz show modeled after Jeopardy! and an igloo-building exercise.

The Smithsonian's newest museum, opened in 2004, stands apart visually and conceptually from the other cultural institutions on the Mall. The undulating exterior, clad in pinkish-gold limestone from Minnesota, evokes natural rock formations shaped by wind and water.

Inside, four floors of galleries cover 10,000 years of history of the thousands of native tribes of the Western Hemisphere. However, only 5% of the museum's holdings are on display at any one time, and they are arranged to showcase specific tribes and themes, rather than a chronological history. Some visitors find this approach confusing, but touring with one of the Native American guides can help bring the history and legends to life.

HIGHLIGHTS

Live music, dance, theater, and storytelling are central to experiencing this museum. Tribal groups stage performances in the two theaters and sunlit ceremonial atrium.

The *Our Universe* exhibit tells the unique creation legends of eight different tribes, with carvings, costumes, and videos of tribal storytellers. The stories rotate to give exposure to the different tribes of the Americas.

Central to the native story is the transformation that convulsed the tribes of America in 1492, the year of first contact with Europeans. The exhibits focusing on the native world before and after "first contact" are among the most compelling.

NATIONAL MUSEUM OF NATURAL HISTORY

✉ *Constitution Ave. and 10th St. NW, The Mall* ☎ *202/633–1000* ⊕ *www. mnh.si.edu* 🎟 *Free; IMAX $9; Butterfly Pavilion $6 adults, $5 kids, free Tues.* ⊙ *Museum daily 10–5:30, Mar.–Sept. until 7.30; Discovery Room Tues.– Fri. noon–2:30, weekends 10:30–3:30* Ⓜ *Smithsonian or Federal Triangle.*

TIPS

■ The IMAX theater shows two- and three-dimensional natural history films throughout the day. Buy advance tickets at the box office when you arrive, then tour the museum.

■ The Butterfly Pavilion makes a great photo op. Timed tickets sell out fast—buy them in advance online or when you arrive. The pavilion is free on Tuesday, but still requires a timed ticket.

■ Both the Discovery Room and Forensic Anthropology Lab have hands-on research activities and workshops for kids.

■ Watch paleontologists at work in the glassed-in fossil labs between Dinosaur Hall and the Life in the Ancient Seas gallery.

This is one of the world's great natural history museums. In 2010, the museum celebrated its centenary, and now boasts 23 exhibition halls, one of the largest IMAX screens in the world, giant dinosaur fossils, glittering gems, creepy-crawly insects, and other natural delights—more than 126 million specimens in all—and attracts more than 7 million visitors annually.

HIGHLIGHTS

Get between *Tyrannosaurus rex* and his dinner, a feisty *Triceratops*. The two giant fossils are poised for action, as are the other occupants of the popular Dinosaur Hall, which range from a 72-foot-long *Diplodocus longus* to a tiny *Thescelosaurus neglectus* (a small dinosaur so named because its disconnected bones sat for years in a college drawer before being reassembled).

Watch out for the cheetah above you on the tree branch in Mammal Hall, which explains mammals' evolution, diversity, and role in the food chain with 274 taxidermy mounts.

See a perfectly preserved giant squid and the vivid ecosystem of a living coral reef in Ocean Hall, the museum's largest exhibit. Tours are offered weekends at 11 and 2. The Ocean Explorer theater simulates a dive into the depths of the sea.

Drool over the jewels of the National Gem Collection in the Janet Annenberg Hooker Hall of Geology, Gems and Minerals: Marie Antoinette's earrings; the Rosser Reeves ruby; and the Hope Diamond, a rare 45.52-carat blue gem donated by Harry Winston in 1958.

Walk among hundreds of brilliantly colored butterflies in the Butterfly Pavilion, which requires a separate admission. For a different kind of entomological experience, check out giant millipedes and furry tarantulas in the O. Orkin Insect Zoo, named for the pest-control magnate who donated money to modernize the exhibits.

NATIONAL PORTRAIT GALLERY

✉ *8th and F Sts. NW, Downtown* ☎ *202/633–8300* ⊕ *www.npg.si.edu* ✉ *Free* ☾ *Daily 11:30–7* Ⓜ *Gallery Pl./Chinatown.*

3

TIPS

■ The Portrait Gallery and American Art Museum are two different entities within the same building—the art complements the portraits, setting up a rich dialogue between the two.

■ The elegant covered courtyard has a café and is frequently the site of performances and special events. At the "Portrait Connection" computer kiosks, you can search a database of the gallery's collections. Look up the portrait's subject, and the database can tell you where in the gallery it is and show you an image, even if it's not currently on exhibit.

■ There are free docent-led tours most weekdays at 11:45, 1, and 2:15, and most Saturdays and Sundays at 11:45, 1:30, and 3:15. Check the website to confirm times. At the Lunder Conservation Center on the third and fourth floors, you can watch conservators preserving and restoring works.

Devoted to the intersection of art, biography, and history, this museum has on view hundreds of images of men and women who have shaped U.S. history. There are prints, paintings, photos, and multimedia sculptures of subjects from George Washington to Madonna. This museum shares the landmark Old Patent Office Building with the Smithsonian American Art Museum.

HIGHLIGHTS

Built between 1836 and 1863, and praised by Walt Whitman as the "noblest of Washington buildings," this gracious marble edifice is considered one of the country's finest examples of Greek Revival architecture.

The museum has the only complete collection of presidential portraits outside the White House, starting with Gilbert Stuart's iconic "Lansdowne" portrait of George Washington. Interesting perspectives include the plaster cast of Abraham Lincoln's head and hands; political cartoonist Pat Oliphant's sculpture of George H. W. Bush bowling; and Shepard Fairey's red, white, and blue *Obama Hope* portrait of President Barack Obama.

The American Origins exhibit chronicles the first contact between Europeans and Native Americans, the Founding Fathers, and historic figures through the Industrial Age. Subjects include Benjamin Franklin (the painting, by Joseph Duplessis, is the basis for Franklin's likeness on the $100 bill); Native American diplomat Pocahontas; and Thomas Edison in his workshop.

From a sculpture of 20th-century icon Gertrude Stein to Andy Warhol's Marilyn Monroe prints, to Madonna's 1985 *Time* magazine cover, the third-floor gallery of **Twentieth-Century Americans** offers a vibrant tour of the people who shaped the country and culture of today.

NEWSEUM

✉ *555 Pennsylvania Ave. NW, Downtown* ☎ *888/639–7386* ⊕ *www.newseum.org* 🎫 *$21.95 adults* ◷ *Daily 9–5* Ⓜ *Archives/Navy Memorial.*

TIPS

■ ABC's This Week is filmed here every Sunday morning; museum visitors are welcome to watch it live on the giant screen in the atrium.

■ Celebrity chef Wolfgang Puck designed the menu for the food court, as well as for the well-reviewed restaurant The Source, adjoining the museum.

■ The best way to tour the museum is by viewing the orientation films on the ground floor, then taking the elevator up to the top floor and working your way down.

■ Tickets for the Newseum are valid for two consecutive days (but walk-in visitors are welcome); purchasing them in advance on the website gains you 10 percent off the ticket price.

■ The top-floor terrace offers one of the best views of the Capitol and looks directly down onto Pennsylvania Avenue.

The Newseum opened to great fanfare in 2008, in a landmark $450 million glass-and-silver structure on Pennsylvania Avenue, set smack between the White House and the Capitol: a fitting location for a museum devoted to the First Amendment and the role of a free press in democracy. Visitors enter into a 90-foot-high media-saturated atrium, overlooked by a giant breaking-news screen and a news helicopter suspended overhead.

From there, 15 galleries display 500 years of the history of news, including exhibits on the First Amendment; global news; the rise of multimedia; and the way radio, television, and the Internet transformed how we find out about the world. The space and the exhibits are high-tech, multimedia, and sometimes shamelessly fun, though among them are powerful evocations of 9/11 and the Journalists Memorial, honoring journalists killed while reporting the news.

HIGHLIGHTS

The largest piece of the Berlin Wall outside Germany, including a guard tower, is permanently installed in an exhibit explaining how a free press was a key contributor to the fall of the wall.

Fifteen state-of-the art theaters, including an eye-popping "4-D" theater and another with a 90-foot-long screen, show features, news, sports, and documentaries throughout the day.

In the Interactive Newsroom you can create your own newscast or be a photographer in an action news event.

The greatest and most powerful press photos are on display at the Pulitzer Prize Photographs gallery.

PHILLIPS COLLECTION

✉ *1600 21st St. NW, Dupont Circle* ☎ *202/387–2151*
🌐 *www.phillipscollection.org*
🎫 *Free for permanent collection weekdays; admission varies weekends and for special exhibitions.* 🕐 *Tues., Wed., Fri., and Sat. 10–5; Thurs. 10–8:30; Sun. 11–6* Ⓜ *Dupont Circle.*

3

TIPS

■ The Phillips is open on Thursday until 8:30 pm. On the first Thursday of the month, the museum hosts Phillips after 5, combining live music, gallery talks, entertainment, and a cash bar. Reservations are advised.

■ The museum holds Sunday-afternoon concerts, a tradition since 1941, in its oak-paneled music room from October through May. Advance reservations are recommended.

■ Take a break in the café, overlooking the museum courtyard.

■ There are tours of the museum, all at noon: Spotlight Talks, 15 minutes focusing on one artwork, Tuesday to Fridays; introduction to the permanent collection on Saturdays; tours of special exhibitions on Sundays. Tours are included in admission.

■ Download the Phillips's free app (using the museum's public Wi-Fi) to learn more about the works in the galleries during your visit.

The first museum of modern art in the country, the masterpiece-filled Phillips Collection is unique in origin and content. It opened in 1921 in the Georgian Revival mansion of collector Duncan Phillips, who wanted to showcase his art in a museum that would stand as a memorial to his father and brother. Having no interest in a painting's market value or its faddishness, Phillips searched for pieces that impressed him as outstanding products of a particular artist's unique vision. At the heart of the collection are impressionist and modern masterpieces by Pierre-Auguste Renoir, Vincent van Gogh, Paul Cézanne, Edgar Degas, Pablo Picasso, Paul Klee, Pierre Bonnard, and Henri Matisse. By combining works of different nationalities and periods in displays that change frequently, the Phillips makes for a museum-going experience that is as intimate as it is inspiring. The domestic scale and personal atmosphere encourage visual conversations among the works.

HIGHLIGHTS

The collection's most famous piece is Renoir's magnificent work of Impressionism, *Luncheon of the Boating Party*. Other celebrity works include Degas's *Dancers at the Barre*, van Gogh's *Entrance to the Public Garden at Arles*, and Cézanne's intense, piercing self-portrait.

The glowing, chapel-like Rothko Room emerged from a bond between Phillips and modern master Mark Rothko. Rothko said he preferred to exhibit his paintings in smaller, more intimately scaled rooms, and Phillips designed the gallery specifically to the artist's preferences.

Jacob Lawrence's epic *Migration Series* portrays the mass movement of African Americans from the rural South to the industrial North beginning in World War I.

SMITHSONIAN AMERICAN ART MUSEUM

✉ *8th and G Sts. NW,*
Downtown ☎ *202/633–7970*
⊕ *www.americanart.si.edu*
🎟 *Free* ⊙ *Daily 11:30–7:30*
Ⓜ *Gallery Pl./Chinatown.*

TIPS

■ Much of the museum's holdings are in storage, but you can view more than 3,000 works in its Luce Foundation Center. At computer kiosks set among the glass cases, you can look up any work in the center to find out more about the artist and the work.

■ At the Lunder Conservation Center, visitors can watch the museum's conservators at work and learn more about preservation.

■ Look out for 21st Century Consort, a series of ticketed concerts inspired by artworks on view with preconcert discussions.

■ The Courtyard Café offers dining, drinks, and snacks.

■ There are free docent-led tours every day at 12:30 and 2.

■ The museum regularly holds lectures, films, and evenings of live jazz in its auditorium and courtyard. Check the website for a schedule.

The world's most comprehensive collection of American art spans three centuries, from the colonial period to today. Among the artists represented are John Singleton Copley, Winslow Homer, Mary Cassatt, Georgia O'Keeffe, Edward Hopper, David Hockney, Christo and Jeanne-Claude, Jenny Holzer, Kerry James Marshall, Cory Arcangel, and Robert Rauschenberg. This museum occupies a National Historic Landmark building it shares with the National Portrait Gallery.

HIGHLIGHTS

The American folk-art galleries are filled with fabulous pieces, from the ceramic Elvis Presley–shape jug and the enormous intricately crafted tinfoil altarpiece, to the Coke-bottle quilt sewn by a grandmother from Yakoo County, Mississippi.

The collection galleries on the second floor link artworks to major moments in America's past, from the American Colonies and the founding of the new republic, to western expansion and discovery, to the Civil War and late 19th-century America, to early modernism.

American art came into its own by the late 19th and early 20th centuries. The museum has the largest collection of New Deal art and the finest collection of American Impressionist paintings, including the light-filled canvases of Mary Cassatt and Childe Hassam, Gilded Age portraits by John Singer Sargent, and masterpieces by Winslow Homer and James McNeill Whistler.

The museum's Lincoln Gallery on the third floor features modern and contemporary paintings and sculpture, including *For SAAM* by Jenny Holzer, Robert Indiana's seminal *The Figure Five*, David Hockney's *Snails Space with Vari-Lites, "Painting as Performance,"* and Nam June Paik's *Electronic Superhighway: Continental US, Alaska, Hawaii,* a billboard-size video wall.

UNITED STATES HOLOCAUST MEMORIAL MUSEUM

✉ *100 Raoul Wallenberg Pl. SW, enter from Raoul Wallenberg Pl. or 14th St. SW* ☎ *202/488–0400, 800/400–9373 for tickets* ⊕ *www. ushmm.org* ✉ *Free* ☉ *Daily 10–5:30* Ⓜ *Smithsonian.*

3

TIPS

■ Like the history it covers, the museum can be profoundly disturbing; it's not recommended for children under 11, although Daniel's Story, in a ground-floor exhibit not requiring tickets, is designed for children ages eight and up.

■ Plan to spend two to three hours here, and get here well before last entry to the permanent collection at 4:30.

■ On Wednesdays at 1 pm, March—August, experience the "First Person" eyewitness testimonies given by volunteer survivors.

■ Timed-entry passes (distributed on a first-come, first-served basis at the 14th Street entrance starting at 10 or available in advance through the museum's website) are necessary for the permanent exhibition March–August. Allow extra time to enter the building in spring and summer, when long lines can form.

Museums usually celebrate the best that humanity can achieve, but this museum instead documents the worst. A permanent exhibition tells the stories of the millions of Jews, Gypsies, Jehovah's Witnesses, homosexuals, political prisoners, the mentally ill, and others killed by the Nazis between 1933 and 1945. The exhibitions are detailed and graphic; the experiences memorable and powerful.

HIGHLIGHTS

The presentation is as extraordinary as the subject matter: upon arrival, you are issued an "identity card" containing biographical information on a real person from the Holocaust. As you move through the museum, you read sequential updates on your card.

Hitler's rise to power and the spread of European anti-Semitism are thoroughly documented in the museum's early exhibits, with films of Nazi rallies, posters, newspaper articles, and recordings of Hitler's speeches immersing you in the world that led to the Holocaust.

You are confronted with the gruesome, appalling truths of the Holocaust in the deeply disturbing exhibit **The Final Solution,** which details the Nazis' execution of 6 million Jews. Exhibits include film footage of scientific experiments done on Jews, artifacts such as a freight car like those used to transport Jews from Warsaw to the Treblinka death camp, and crematoria implements. There are films and audio recordings of Holocaust survivors telling their harrowing stories.

After this powerful experience, the adjacent Hall of Remembrance, filled with candles and hand-painted tiles dedicated to children who died in the Holocaust, provides a much-needed space for quiet reflection.

OTHER MUSEUMS

Anderson House. A palatial home that's a mystery even to many longtime Washingtonians, Anderson House isn't an embassy, though it does have a link to that world. Larz Anderson was a diplomat from 1891 to 1913 and his career included postings to Japan and Belgium. Anderson and his heiress wife, Isabel, toured the world, picking up objects that struck their fancy. They filled their residence, which was constructed for them in 1905, with the booty of their travels. Visitors to Anderson House will receive a guided tour of the first and second floors, gorgeously furnished with the Andersons' eclectic collection of furniture, tapestries, paintings, sculpture, historic artifacts, and Asian art, and will learn about entertaining in Gilded Age Washington. Among the highlights of the house are several floor-to-ceiling murals that reveal the splendor of the era as well as the Andersons' patriotism and pastimes. The house also regularly displays temporary exhibitions. ⊠ *2118 Massachusetts Ave. NW, Dupont Circle* ☎ *202/785–2040* ⊕ *www.societyofthecincinnati. org* ⊠ *Free* ☾ *Tues.–Sat. 1–4* Ⓜ *Dupont Circle.*

Art Museum of the Americas. Changing exhibits highlight modern and contemporary Latin American and Caribbean artists in this small gallery, part of the Organization of American States. A public garden connects the art museum and the OAS building. ⊠ *201 18th St. NW, White House area* ☎ *202/458–6016* ⊕ *www.museum.oas.org* ⊠ *Free* ☾ *Tues.–Sun. 10–5* Ⓜ *Farragut West.*

Christian Heurich House Museum. This opulent Romanesque Revival mansion, also known as the Brewmaster's Castle, was the home of Christian Heurich, a German immigrant who made his fortune in the beer business. Heurich's brewery was in Foggy Bottom, where the Kennedy Center stands today. The building is considered one of the most intact Victorian houses in the country, and all the furnishings were owned and used by the Heurichs. The interior is an eclectic gathering of plaster detailing, carved wooden doors, and painted ceilings. The downstairs Breakfast Room, which also served as Heurich's *bierstube* (or beer hall), is decorated like a Ratskeller and adorned with German sayings such as "A good drink makes old people young."

Heurich must have taken proverbs seriously. He drank beer daily, had three wives, and lived to be 102. The house, which is now run as the nonprofit Heurich House Museum, offers weekly guided tours and is available for special event rentals. ⊠ *1307 New Hampshire Ave. NW, Dupont Circle* ☎ *202/429–1894* ⊕ *www.heurichhouse.org* ⊠ *$5* ☾ *Tours Thurs. and Fri. at 11:30 and 1, Sat. at 11:30, 1, and 2:30* Ⓜ *Dupont Circle.*

☾ **Daughters of the American Revolution Museum (DAR).** The headquarters of the Daughters of the American Revolution, the Beaux-Arts-style Memorial Continental Hall was the site of the DAR's annual congress until the larger Constitution Hall was built. An entrance on D Street leads to the museum, where the 30,000-item collection includes fine examples of colonial and Federal furniture, textiles, quilts, silver, china, porcelain, stoneware, earthenware, and glass. Thirty-one period rooms are decorated in styles representative of various U.S. states, ranging from an 1850 California adobe parlor to a New Hampshire attic filled with 18th- and 19th-century toys. Two galleries—one featuring changing exhibitions—hold decorative arts. Docent tours are available weekdays 10–2:30 and Saturday 9–5. In the **Touch of Independence** education center for children, families can explore early American life through period games and costumes. During the Colonial Adventure tours, held the first and third Sunday of the month at 1:30 and 3 from September through May, costumed docents use the objects on display to teach children ages five to seven about day-to-day life in colonial America. Reservations are required two weeks in advance. Experience hands-on crafts, games, and a tour on **Fun Family Saturdays** every third Saturday, September to June. ⊠ *1776 D St. NW, White House area* ☎ *202/628-1776* ⊕ *www.dar.org* ☜ *Free* ⊙ *Weekdays 9:30–4, Sat. 9–5* Ⓜ *Farragut West.*

Decatur House on Lafayette Square. Decatur House, home to the National Center for White House History, is located across from the White House and was the first and last private residence on Lafayette Square. The distinguished neoclassical house is the work of Benjamin Henry Latrobe, the country's first professional architect and engineer who is most famous for his construction of the Capitol and design of many of its beautiful interior spaces. Decatur House is one of the oldest surviving homes in Washington, and one of only three remaining residential buildings designed by Latrobe.

Built for naval hero Stephen Decatur and his wife, Susan, in 1819, the house bore witness to many historic events in the century and a half that followed. Planning to start a political career, Decatur built this home near the White House, but died tragically 14 months later after a famous duel with Commodore James Barron. Later occupants of the house included diplomats and statesmen, Baron de Tuyll, Henry Clay, Martin Van Buren, and the Beales, a prominent western family whose modifications of the building include a parquet floor with the state seal of California. Wealthy hotel and tavern owner John Gadsby purchased the Decatur House as a retirement home in 1836, adding a large two-story dependency in the rear of the property, used as quarters for numerous enslaved individuals in his household—the only extant slave quarters in Washington. ⊠ *748 Jackson Pl. NW, White House area* ☎ *202/842-0920* ⊕ *www.decaturhouse.org* ☜ *$5* ⊙ *Check website or call for up-to-date tour information during renovation* Ⓜ *Farragut W.*

Drug Enforcement Administration Museum. Just across the street from the Fashion Centre at Pentagon City—a destination in itself for shoppers—is the DEA Museum, within the U.S. Drug Enforcement Administration's headquarters. The exhibit provides a 150-year tour of the effect of drugs on American society, starting with quaint 19th-century ads for opium-laced patent medicines and "cocaine tooth drops" (opiates, cannabis, and cocaine were unregulated then). But documentation of these addictive substances' medical dangers, as well as the corrosive political effect of the opium trade, which China detested, is hard-hitting. A similar contrast is found between the period feel of artifacts from a 1970s head shop and displays on the realities of present-day drug trafficking. Besides teaching the history of drug abuse in America, the museum chronicles the work of the DEA and its predecessors. ⊠ *700 Army Navy Dr., at Hayes St., Pentagon City, Arlington, Virginia* ☏ *202/307–3463* ⊕ *www.deamuseum.org* ◱ *Free* ⊙ *Tues.–Fri. 10–4* ⊙ *Federal holidays* Ⓜ *Pentagon City.*

Dumbarton Oaks. Career diplomat Robert Woods Bliss and his wife, Mildred, bought this property and home in 1920, employing famous landscape architect Beatrix Farrand to tame the sprawling grounds into acres of splendid gardens. With the help of various architects, the Blisses also removed additions to the 1801 mansion to create a colonial revival home. In 1940, the Blisses gave their estate to Harvard University, built a wing for their collections, and established a research institution and library. Their world-renowned collections of Byzantine and pre-Columbian art are small but choice, reflecting the enormous skill and creativity developed at roughly the same time in two very different parts of the world. The Byzantine collection includes beautiful examples of both religious and secular items executed in mosaic, metal enamel, and ivory. Pre-Columbian works include artifacts and textiles from Mexico and Central and South America by peoples such as the Aztec, Inka, Maya, and Olmec, arranged in an enclosed glass pavilion designed by Philip Johnson. Also on public view are the lavishly decorated Music Room, with Bliss objects, and the Rare Book Room.

In 1944, one of the most important events of the 20th century took place here when representatives of the United States, Britain, China, and the Soviet Union met in the Music Room to lay the groundwork for the United Nations. For more information on the gardens of Dumbarton Oaks, ⇨ *see Sports and the Outdoors.* ⊠ *1703 32nd St. NW, Georgetown* ☏ *202/339–6401, 202/339–6409 Tours* ⊕ *www. doaks.org* ◱ *Museum, free; gardens, free Nov. 1–Mar. 14, $8 Mar. 15–Oct. 31* ⊙ *Tues.–Sun. 2–5; garden tours, Tues., Wed., and Thurs. at 2:15; museum tours ($8) by advance reservation, Tues., Wed., and Thurs.*

Folger Shakespeare Library. The Folger Library's collection of works by and about Shakespeare and his times is second to none. The reading rooms are open only to academic researchers, but the white-marble art deco building, decorated with sculpted scenes from the Bard's plays, is well worth a look. Inside is a reproduction of a 16th-century inn-yard theater—the site for performances of chamber music, baroque opera, and Shakespearean plays—and a gallery, designed in the manner of an Elizabethan Great Hall, that holds rotating exhibits from the library's collection. One of the Folger's Shakespeare First Folios is always on view and may be thumbed through digitally in the Great Hall. A manicured Elizabethan garden on the grounds is open to the public, and the gift shop features many collectibles featuring the Bard and English theater. The building was designed by architect Paul Philippe

Cret and dedicated in 1932. Henry Clay Folger, the library's founder, was Standard Oil's president and chairman of the board. ✉ *201 E. Capitol St. SE, Capitol Hill* ☎ *202/544–4600* ⊕ *www.folger. edu* 🎟 *Free* 🕙 *Mon.–Sat. 10–5, Sun. 12–5* Ⓜ *Capitol South.*

Fodor's Choice
★ **Ford's Theatre National Historic Site.** The events that took place here on the night of April 14, 1865, shocked the nation. During a performance of *Our American Cousin,* John Wilkes Booth entered the state box at **Ford's Theatre** and shot Abraham Lincoln in the back of the head. The stricken president was carried across the street to the house of tailor William Petersen. Charles Augustus Leale, a 23-year-old surgeon, was the first man to attend the president. To let Lincoln know that someone was nearby, Leale held his hand throughout the night. Lincoln died the next morning. The theater and Petersen's house are now the anchors of an ambitious block-long, Lincoln-centered cultural campus commemorating the president. The theater, which stages performances throughout the year, is restored to look as it did when Lincoln attended, including the presidential box draped with flags as it was on the night he was shot. The portrait of George Washington on the box is the same one over which Lincoln sat; its frame has a nick made by Wilkes's spur as he leapt from the box to the stage. In the restored **Petersen House** you can see the room where Lincoln died and the parlor where his wife, Mary Todd, waited in anguish through the night.

The centerpiece of the **Center for Education and Leadership** is a jaw-dropping, three-story tower of 6,800 books written about Lincoln. In the center, visitors take an immersive step back in time, to April 15, 1865, entering a 19th-century street scene where they find a reproduction of Lincoln's funeral train car and see its route to Springfield, Illinois. Visitors also learn about the manhunt for John Wilkes Booth and his coconspirators' trial, and they interact with an "escape map" to the tobacco barn where Booth was captured. Exhibits also explore the fate of Lincoln's family after his death, explain the milestones of Reconstruction, and describe Lincoln's legacy and his enduring impact on U.S. and world leaders. A visit ends with a multiscreened video wall that shows how Lincoln's ideas resonate today.

Visits to Ford's Theatre National Historic Site require a free, timed-entry ticket. Same-day tickets are available at the theater box office beginning at 8:30 am on a first-come, first-served basis. You can also reserve tickets in advance through Ticketmaster (⊕ *www.ticketmaster.com*) with a $2.50 fee per ticket. ✉ *511 10th St. NW, Downtown* ☎ *202/426–6924* ⊕ *www.fords.org* 🎟 *Free* 🕙 *Daily 9–5; theater closed to visitors during rehearsals and matinees, generally Thurs. and weekends* Ⓜ *Metro Center or Gallery Pl./Chinatown.*

Frederick Douglass National Historic Site. **Cedar Hill,** the Anacostia home of abolitionist Frederick Douglass, was the first Black National Historic Site that Congress designated. Douglass, a former slave who delivered rousing abolitionist speeches at home and abroad, resided here from 1878 until his death in 1895. The house has a wonderful view of Washington across the Anacostia River and contains many of Douglass's personal belongings. The home has been meticulously restored to its original grandeur; you can view Douglass's hundreds of books displayed on his custom-built bookshelves, and Limoges china on the Douglass family dining table. A short film on Douglass's life is shown at a nearby visitor center. Entry to the home requires participation in a 30-minute ranger-led tour, for which you must arrive 20 minutes in advance; reserve by phone or online. ⊠ *1411 W St. SE, Anacostia* ☎ *202/426-5961 Cedar Hill tours, 202/547-4273 museum tours* ⊕ *www.nps.gov/ frdo* ⊒ *$1.50* ☉ *Mid-Oct.–mid-Apr., daily 9–4:30; mid-Apr.–mid-Oct., daily 9–5; check website for tour times* Ⓜ *Anacostia.*

★ **Hillwood Estate, Museum and Gardens.** Long before the age of Paris Hilton, cereal heiress Marjorie Merriweather Post was the most celebrated socialite of the 20th century, famous for her fabulous wealth and beauty, as well as her passion for collecting art and creating some of the world's most lavish homes. Of these, the 25-acre Hillwood Estate, which Merriweather Post bought in 1955, is the only one now open to the public. The 36-room Georgian mansion, where she regularly hosted presidents, diplomats, and royalty, is sumptuously appointed, with a formal Louis XVI drawing room, private movie theater and ballroom, and magnificent libraries filled with portraits of the glamorous hostess, her family, and acquaintances, as well as works from her rich art collection. She was especially fascinated with Russian art, and her collection of Russian icons, tapestries, gold and silver work, and Fabergé eggs is considered to be the largest and most significant outside of Russia. She devoted equal attention to her gardens: you can wander through 13 acres of them. ⇨ *For more information about the gardens, see the Gardens section in Sports and the Outdoors.* You should allow two to three hours to take in the estate, gardens, and museum shop. Reservations are recommended on spring weekends for tours and lunch or tea in the café. The estate is best reached by taxi or car (free parking is available on the grounds). It's a 20- to 30-minute walk from the Metro. ⊠ *4155 Linnean Ave. NW, Upper Northwest* ☎ *202/686–5807, 202/686–8500* ⊕ *www.hillwoodmuseum.org* ⊒ *House and grounds, $15* ☉ *Feb.–Dec., Tues.–Sat. 10–5* Ⓜ *Van Ness/UDC.*

Kreeger Museum. The cool white domes and elegant lines of this postmodern landmark stand in stark contrast to the traditional feel of the rest of the Foxhall Road neighborhood. Designed in 1963 by iconic architect Philip Johnson, the building was once the home of GEICO insurance executive David Lloyd Kreeger and his wife Carmen. Music is a central theme of the art and the space: the Kreegers wanted a showpiece residence that would also function as a gallery and recital hall. The art collection includes works by Renoir, Degas, Cézanne, and Munch, African artifacts, and outstanding examples of Asian art. The domed rooms also have wonderful acoustics, and serve as an excellent performance venue for the classical concerts that are regularly performed here. Information about upcoming performances is available on the museum's website. The museum is not reachable by Metro; you need to take a car or taxi to get here. ⊠ *2401 Foxhall Rd. NW, Upper Northwest* ☏ *202/338–3552* ⊕ *www.kreegermuseum.org* ⊠ *$10* ⊙ *Sat. 10–4, optional tours at 10:30, noon, and 2; Tues.–Thurs., tours at 10:30 and 1:30 by reservation only. Closed Aug. to Labor Day.*

Madame Tussauds. A branch of the famous London-based waxworks franchise focuses on U.S. presidential history. You can see and pose for pictures with uncanny likenesses of the Founding Fathers or any of the presidents, including Barack Obama and his wife, or sit inside the Oval Office, painstakingly re-created in wax. The Glamour Room is populated with waxen re-creations of Julia Roberts, JLo, and Brad Pitt, among others. Purchase tickets online for the best daily discount. ⊠ *1025 F St. NW, Downtown* ☏ *202/942–7300* ⊕ *www. madametussaudsdc.com* ⊠ *$21* ⊙ *Mon.–Thurs. 12–6, Fri.–Sun. 10–6* Ⓜ *Metro Center or Gallery Pl./Chinatown.*

Marian Koshland Science Museum. Sponsored by the National Academy of Sciences, this small but engaging museum invites teens and adults to interact with current scientific issues in a thought-provoking setting. Visitors have the opportunity to use science and math to solve problems and engage in conversation. In *Earth Lab: Degrees of Change* you'll examine the energy sector and employ strategies to lower carbon dioxide emissions to a level that will significantly reduce the impact of climate change. Take on the role of policy maker in a simulation game and decide what actions you want to take and compare your plans with other players. *The Life Lab* encourages visitors to think about decisions throughout their life and explore how the brain develops. There's a driving simulator and a 3-D look inside the brain, plus exhibits on infectious disease and DNA sequencing.

Although the interactive exhibits are fun and educational, they are aimed at ages 13 and up. ⊠ *525 E St. NW, Downtown* ☏ *202/334–1201* ⊕ *www.koshland-dc.org* ⊠ *$7* ⊙ *Wed.–Mon. 10–5* Ⓜ *Gallery Pl./Chinatown or Judiciary Sq.*

National Aquarium. Established in 1873, the National Aquarium is the nation's first public aquarium, welcoming visitors since 1932 to its location inside the lower level of the Department of Commerce Building. The Aquarium is home to *America's Aquatic Treasures*, and houses more than 250 species, including sharks, eels, amphibians, and loggerhead turtles. Special exhibits highlight the animals and habitats of the National Marine Sanctuaries Program and freshwater ecosystems of the United States and its territories.

This intimate 45-minute aquatic experience is a fun outing for children, but seekers of a transcendent aquarium experience will probably be happier visiting the Baltimore National aquarium, which is routinely ranked among the nation's best. ⊠ *14th St. and Constitution Ave. NW, Downtown* ☏ *202/482–2825* ⊕ *www.nationalaquarium.com* ⊠ *$9.95* ⊙ *Daily 9–5; sharks fed Mon., Wed., and Sat. at 2; piranhas fed Tues., Thurs., and Sun. at 2; alligators fed Fri. at 2* Ⓜ *Federal Triangle.*

◔ **National Geographic Museum.** Founded in 1888, the National Geographic Society is best known for its magazine, and a welcoming 13,000-square-foot exhibition space gives visitors the feeling of stepping into its pages. The National Geographic Museum has child-friendly interactives and is home to a rotating display of objects from the society's permanent collections—cultural, historical, and scientific—as well as traveling exhibitions. ✉ *17th and M Sts. NW, Dupont Circle* ☎ *202/857–7588, 202/857–7689 group tours* ⊕ *www.nationalgeographic.com* ✈ *Free, special exhibitions $8* ☉ *Mon.–Sat, 10-6, Sun. 10–5* Ⓜ *Farragut North.*

◔ **National Museum of African Art.** This unique underground building houses stunning galleries, a library, photographic archives, and educational facilities. Rotating exhibits present African visual arts, including sculpture, textiles, photography, archaeology, and modern art. Long-term installations explore the sculpture of sub-Saharan Africa, the art of Benin, the pottery of Central Africa, the archaeology of the ancient Nubian city of Kerma, and the artistry of everyday objects. The museum's educational programs for both children and adults include films with contemporary perspectives on African life, storytelling programs, festivals, and hands-on workshops, such as traditional basket-weaving, that bring Africa's oral traditions, literature, and art to life. Workshops and demonstrations by African and African-American artists offer a chance to meet and talk to practicing artists. The well-stocked museum shop sells collectibles, pottery, art, jewelry, books and maps. ✉ *950 Independence Ave. SW, The Mall* ☎ *202/633–1000* ⊕ *africa.si.edu* ✈ *Free* ☉ *Daily 10–5:30* Ⓜ *Smithsonian.*

National Museum of Crime and Punishment. America's history of crime and the judicial system are explored in exhibits that demonstrate tactics used by law enforcement, forensic scientists, crime-scene investigators, and the consequences for committing a crime. Exhibits range from a medieval torture chamber to the getaway car used by bank robbers Bonnie and Clyde. With more than 100 interactives, you can put your hands in pillory stocks, take a lie-detector test, enter a jail cell, and experience a simulated crime-scene investigation. From pirates, witches, and Wild West outlaws, to white-collar criminals, serial killers, and computer hackers, many displays involve reading, are at times grim, and better for older children. Created in partnership with *America's Most Wanted* host John Walsh, the lower level of the museum includes a behind-the-scenes look at the program.

The museum recommends purchasing advance tickets on the website: tickets are spaced hourly with a specific date and time. ✉ *575 7th St. NW, Downtown* ☎ *202/621–5550* ⊕ *www.crimemuseum.org* ✈ *$17.95 online, $19.95 box office walk up* ☉ *Sept. 5–May 20, Sun.–Thurs. 10–7, Fri. and Sat. 10–8; May 21–Sept. 4, Mon.–Thurs. 9–7, Fri. and Sat. 9–8, Sun. 10–7* Ⓜ *Gallery Pl./Chinatown.*

National Museum of Women in the Arts. Works by female artists from the Renaissance to the present are showcased at this museum. The beautifully restored 1907 Renaissance Revival building was designed by Waddy B. Wood; it was once a Masonic temple, for men only. In addition to displaying traveling shows, the museum has a collection that includes paintings, drawings, sculpture, prints, and photographs by Frida Kahlo, Camille Claudel, Mary Cassat, Alma Thomas, Judy Chicago, Magdalena Abakanowicz, Nan Goldin, Louise Dahl-Wolfe, Helen Frankenthaler, and Élisabeth Vigée-Lebrun. The museum also oversees the New York Avenue Sculpture Project, the first outdoor sculpture corridor in D.C., featuring changing installations by women artists. The Museum Shop sells products celebrating women artists, and also fair-trade art, jewelry, and home accents created by the International Women Artisans Initiative. The Mezzanine Cafe offers lunch fare and desserts, as well as brunch the first Sunday of the month, and the museum hosts a variety of programs for kids and teens, as well as adults. ⊠ *1250 New York Ave. NW, Downtown* ☎ *202/783–5000* ⊕ *www.nmwa.org* ⊠ *$10* ☉ *Mon.– Sat. 10–5, Sun. noon–5* Ⓜ *Metro Center.*

> **WORD OF MOUTH**
>
> "I was completely taken aback by how much I enjoyed the New-seum. I spent two hours there Sunday and almost three hours on Monday ($20 ticket is good for two consecutive days). I liken this to a children's discovery museum, only for adult news junkies."
>
> —amyb

Old Stone House. What was early American life like? Here's the capital's oldest window into the past. This fieldstone house, thought to be Washington's oldest surviving building, was built in 1765 by a cabinetmaker named Christopher Layman. According to some still-unsubstantiated claims, this may have been George Washington's Engineering Headquarters or Suters Tavern; it is known that this oasis in busy Georgetown was used as both a residence and place of business by a succession of occupants. Five of the house's rooms are furnished with the simple, sturdy artifacts—plain tables, spinning wheels, and so forth—of 18th-century middle-class life. The National Park Service maintains the house and its lovely gardens, where you can picnic among fruit trees and perennials. ⊠ *3051 M St. NW, Georgetown* ☎ *202/426–6851* ⊕ *www. nps.gov/olst* ⊠ *Free* ☉ *Wed.–Sun. 12–5.*

Pope John Paul II Cultural Center. A shrine to former Pope John Paul II, who served for 27 years, the center pays homage to John Paul's life, his tireless work (he held 738 audiences with heads of state), and outreach to people of all ages and nations. Polish and the first non-Italian pope in four centuries, John Paul presided over the fall of communism. Currently under renovation, the center will remain open during renovation with temporary exhibits. A visit to the center, a mile from the Metro, can easily be combined with a visit to the National Shrine of the Immaculate Conception. ⊠ *3900 Harewood Rd. NE, Northeast D.C.* ☎ *202/635–5400* ⊕ *www.jp2shrine.org* ⊠ *Free* ☉ *Tues. and Thurs. 10–5, Mon., Wed., Fri. by appointment only* Ⓜ *Brookland/ Catholic University.*

President Lincoln's Cottage. In June 1862 President Lincoln moved from the White House to this Gothic Revival cottage on the grounds of the Soldiers' Home to escape the oppressive heat of Washington and to grieve for the loss of his son Willie. Lincoln and his wife lived in the cottage from June to November of 1862, 1863, and 1864—a quarter of his presidency. Considered the most significant historic site of President Lincoln's presidency outside the White House, it was here that the president developed the Emancipation Proclamation. Tours attempt to re-create a visit to the cottage similar to what Lincoln's many visitors in the 1860s experienced, and to take visitors inside Lincoln's mind as he anguished over the Civil War and emancipation.

The 150th anniversary of the Emancipation Proclamation is commemorated through exhibits, including an illustration of how present-day abolitionists work to stop modern slavery, with first-hand accounts by survivors of human trafficking.

Tours are given every hour from 11 to 3, Monday through Saturday, and every hour noon to 4 on Sunday. Only 20 spots are available per tour; make advance reservations through the website.

Although the museum is reachable by Metro and bus, it's much easier to drive or take a cab. Visitors may also picnic on the cottage grounds, which have been landscaped to look as they did when Lincoln lived here. ⊠ *Armed Forces Retirement Home, Rock Creek Church Rd. and Upshur St. NW, Upper Northwest* ☏ *202/829–0436* ⊕ *www. lincolncottage.org* 🎫 *$15* 🕙 *Mon.–Sat. 9:30–4:30, Sun. 10:30–4:30* Ⓜ *Georgia Ave./Petworth.*

Renwick Gallery. The Renwick Gallery is a luscious French Second Empire–style building across the street from the White House and the Eisenhower Executive Office Building. But even with such lofty neighbors, this fanciful gingerbread house, which has the words "dedicated to art" engraved above the entrance, is still the most appealing architecture on the block. Designed by James Renwick in 1859 to hold the art collection of Washington merchant and banker William Wilson Corcoran, the National Historic Landmark building today is a branch of the Smithsonian American Art Museum, housing the museum's collection of decorative art and crafts. The building's interior matches the architecture—much red velvet and gold trim—but the exquisitely crafted works on display have a modern and witty edge. Larry Fuente's 1988 sculpture *Game Fish* is a marlin fashioned entirely out of vintage toys—Superman and Gumby are represented, as well as dice, yo-yos, and dominoes. Best of all is Kim Schahmann's 1993–1999 *Bureau of Bureaucracy*: a beautifully crafted wooden cabinet full of cupboards to nowhere, bottomless drawers, drawers within drawers, hidden compartments, and more, a wonderful metaphor for the labyrinthine workings of government. The Grand Salon houses a display of landscapes, portraits, and allegorical works. ⊠ *Pennsylvania Ave. at 17th St. NW, White House area* ☏ *202/633–2850* ⊕ *www.americanart.si.edu* 🎫 *Free* 🕙 *Daily 10–5:30* Ⓜ *Farragut West.*

Sewall-Belmont House. The Sewall House has stood strong on Capitol Hill for more than 200 years. Early occupants of the house participated in the formation of Congress and witnessed the construction of the U.S. Capitol and Supreme Court. In 1929, the National Women's Party (NWP) purchased the house and it soon evolved into a center for feminist education and social change. For more than sixty years, the trailblazing NWP utilized the strategic location of the house to lobby for women's political, social, and economic equality. Today, an expansive collection of artifacts from the women's suffrage and equal rights campaigns brings the story of the Women's Rights movement to life. The innovative tactics and strategies these women devised became the blueprint for women's progress throughout the twentieth century. ⊠ *144 Constitution Ave. NE, Capitol Hill* ☎ *202/546–1210* ⊕ *www. sewallbelmont.org* ⊴ *$5* ⊗ *Wed.–Sun. noon–4* Ⓜ *Union Station.*

☾ **Smithsonian Anacostia Community Museum.** The Smithsonian's only neighborhood museum is located in Anacostia, a historically black neighborhood in Southeast Washington, far off the tourist track. The museum is devoted to the rich experience of contemporary African American culture in the nation and the capital, which has long had a majority black population. It has evolved into an interactive museum documenting, preserving, and interpreting African American history from local and community history perspectives using video, fine art, crafts, and photography. The museum's facade features traditional African design elements: brickwork patterns evoke West African kente cloth, and the concrete cylinders reference the stone towers of Zimbabwe and are ornamented with diamond patterns like those found on the adobe houses of Mali. A free weekend shuttle operates in summer from the National Mall. The museum is close to the Frederick Douglas National Historic Site and Kenilworth Aquatic Gardens. ⊠ *1901 Fort Pl. SE, Anacostia* ☎ *202/633–4820* ⊕ *anacostia.si.edu* ⊴ *Free* ⊗ *Daily 10–5* Ⓜ *Anacostia, then W2/W3 bus.*

Smithsonian Institution Building. The original home of the Smithsonian Institution is this red sandstone, Medieval Revival style building, better known as the Castle. It was designed by James Renwick Jr., the architect of St. Patrick's Cathedral in New York City. Although British scientist and founder James Smithson never visited America, his will stipulated that should his nephew, Henry James Hungerford, die without an heir, Smithson's entire fortune would go to the United States, "to found at Washington, under the name of the Smithsonian Institution, an establishment for the increase and diffusion of knowledge." The museums on the Mall are the Smithsonian's most visible example of this ideal, but the organization also sponsors traveling exhibitions and maintains research posts in outside-the-Beltway locales, such as the Chesapeake Bay and the tropics of Panama.

■**TIP**➔ Today the Castle houses the Smithsonian Information Center, which can help you get your bearings and decide which attractions to visit. A 10-minute video gives an overview of the Smithsonian museums and the National Zoo, and the exhibition *The Smithsonian Institution: America's Treasure Chest* features objects representing all the museums that reveal the breadth and depth of the Smithsonian's collections. The center opens at 8:30 am, 1 1/2 hours before the other museums, so you can plan your day without wasting sightseeing time. It also offers smaller temporary exhibitions, a good café, and a store. ⊠ *1000 Jefferson Dr. SW, The Mall* ☎ *202/633–1000* ⊕ *www.si.edu* ⊴ *Free* ⊗ *Daily 8:30–5:30* Ⓜ *Smithsonian.*

☾ **Smithsonian National Postal Museum.** The National Museum of Natural History has the Hope Diamond, but the National Postal Museum has the envelope wrapping used to mail the gem to the Smithsonian. Exhibits, underscoring the important part the mail has played in America's development, include horse-drawn mail coaches, railway mail cars, airmail planes, and a collection of philatelic rarities, along with more than 5 million stamps. Learn about stamp collecting and tour *Systems at Work,* an exhibit that demonstrates how mail has gone from the mailbox to its destination for the past 200 years and features a high-def film highlighting amazing technologies. The exhibit *Mail Call* shows the history of the military postal system from the Revolutionary War to today, including a video called "Missing You—Letters from Wartime." The museum takes up only a portion of what is the old Washington City Post Office, designed by Daniel Burnham and completed in 1914. Nostalgic odes to the noble mail carrier are inscribed on the exterior of the marble building; one of them, "The Letter," eulogizes the "Messenger of sympathy and love / Servant of parted friends / Consoler of the lonely / Bond of the scattered family / Enlarger of the common life." Tours are offered most days at 11 and 1 from the information desk. ⊠ *2 Massachusetts Ave. NE, Capitol Hill* ☎ *202/633–5555* ⊕ *www. postalmuseum.si.edu* ⊠ *Free* ☾ *Daily 10–5:30* Ⓜ *Union Station.*

Textile Museum. The museum showcases weavings, carpets, and tapestries that date from 3,000 BC to the present. Rotating exhibits are taken from a permanent collection of 19,000 historic and ethnographic items that include Coptic and pre-Columbian textiles, Kashmir embroidery, and Turkman tribal rugs. The museum also hosts traveling exhibitions, accompanied by demonstrations and other educational events, and at least one yearly show of modern textiles, such as quilts or fiber art. The museum has a tiny store packed with handmade textiles from around the world, books, and gifts. ⊠ *2320 S St. NW, Dupont Circle* ☎ *202/667–0441* ⊕ *www.textilemuseum.org* ⊠ *Suggested donation $8* ☾ *Tues.–Sat. 10–5, Sun. 1–5* Ⓜ *Dupont Circle.*

Tudor Place. Stop at Q Street between 31st and 32nd streets; look through the trees to the north, to the top of a sloping lawn, and you can see the neoclassical Tudor Place, designed by Capitol architect Dr. William Thornton and completed in 1816. On the house tour you can see the largest collection of George and Martha Washington items outside Mt. Vernon, Francis Scott Key's desk, and spurs belonging to soldiers who were killed in the Civil War. You can only visit the house by guided tour (given hourly), but afterward you can wander freely, with map or audiotour through the formal garden, full of roses and boxwoods, many planted in the early 19th century. ⊠ *1644 31st St. NW, Georgetown* ☎ *202/965–0400* ⊕ *www.tudorplace.org* ⊠ *$8, includes admission to garden; garden only, $3* ☾ *House Feb.–Dec., Tues.–Sat. 10–4, Sun., noon–4; Garden Feb.–Dec., Mon.–Sat. 10–4, Sun. noon–4.*

☾ **Washington Navy Yard.** A 115-acre historic district with its own street system, the Washington Navy Yard is the Navy's oldest outpost on shore. Established in 1799 as a shipbuilding facility, the district was burned by the Americans during the War of 1812 to keep the British from capturing the base and the four Navy ships docked there. Rebuilt and converted to weapons production by the mid-19th century, the Navy Yard became integral to the defense of Washington during the Civil War, and the Lincoln assassination conspirators were held there. Charles Lindbergh landed at the Navy Yard after his famous transatlantic flight.

The Navy Yard gradually fell into disuse until the 1960s, when it was revived as a thriving administrative and cultural center. It currently houses the Navy Museum. Outside the base, on 8th Street, you can see the historic, impressive Home of the Commandants, home of the commandant of the Marines Corps, and the historic Marine Barracks.

The public entrance to the Navy Yard is on 11th and O streets; visitors 16 and older must show valid government-issued identification (a drivers license or passport). Take Metro (Orange/Blue line to Eastern Market station) or the DC Circulator Union Station to Navy Yard route (every day except Sunday, stop is closer to entrance on M and 8th streets). Personal vehicles are permitted into the Navy Yard on weekends, but there's also metered public parking under the Southeast Freeway on 8th Street, and an abundance of restaurants and eclectic shops steps away in Barracks Row. Every Friday night after 8 in summer, the U.S. Marine Band hosts a parade of music and marching. ⊠ *O and 11th Sts. SE, Northeast D.C.* ⬛ *Free* ☉ *Weekdays 9–5, weekends 10–5* Ⓜ *Eastern Market or Navy Yard.*

Navy Museum. These displays in Building 76 of the Navy Yard chronicle the history of the U.S. Navy from the Revolution to the present. Exhibits range from the fully rigged foremast of the USS *Constitution* (better known as *Old Ironsides*) to a U.S. Navy Corsair fighter plane dangling from the ceiling. All around are models of fighting ships, a real Vietnam-era Swift boat, working periscopes, displays on battles, and portraits of the sailors who fought them. In front of the museum is a collection of guns, cannons, and missiles, and the decommissioned U.S. Navy destroyer *Barry* floats a short distance away on RiverWalk by the Anacostia River. The **Navy Art Collection,** including many works by Navy artists, is also housed in the museum.

To tour the Navy Museum you must enter through the visitor's gate at 11th and O streets SE and show a valid photo ID; you'll receive a pass and map of the surroundings. Check the museum website for any changes in entry information. ⊠ *805 Kidder Breese St. SE, entrance on 11th and O Sts. SE, Southeast* ☎ *202/433–4882 Navy Museum, 202/433–4882 USS Barry* ⊕ *www.history.navy.mil* ⬛ *Free* ☉ *Weekdays 9–5, weekends 10–5* Ⓜ *Eastern Market.*

Navy Art Collection inside the Navy Museum. This collection exhibits Navy-related paintings, sketches, and drawings, many created during combat by Navy artists. ☎ *202/433–3815* ⊕ *www.history.navy.mil.*

Woodrow Wilson House. President Wilson and his second wife, Edith Bolling Wilson, retired in 1921 to this Georgian Revival house designed by Washington architect Waddy B. Wood. (Wood also designed the Department of the Interior and the National Museum of Women in the Arts.)

President Wilson suffered a stroke toward the end of his second term, in 1919, and upon leaving office, lived out the last few years of his life on this quiet street. Edith made sure he was comfortable; she had a bed constructed that had the same dimensions as the large Lincoln bed Wilson had slept in while in the White House. She also had the house's trunk lift (a sort of dumbwaiter for trunks) converted to an Otis elevator so the partially paralyzed president could move from floor to floor. When the streetcars stopped running in 1962, the elevator stopped working; it had received its electricity directly from the streetcar line. It has since been restored and is back in service today for visitors with accessibility needs.

Wilson died in 1924—Edith survived him by 37 years—and bequeathed the house and its contents to the National Trust for Historic Preservation. On view inside are such items as a Gobelins tapestry, a baseball signed by King George V, and the shell casing from the first shot fired by U.S. forces in World War I. The house also contains memorabilia related to the history of the short-lived but influential League of Nations, including the colorful flag Wilson hoped would be adopted by that organization. ⊠ *2340 S St. NW, Dupont Circle* ☎ *202/387–4062* ⊕ *www.woodrowwilsonhouse.org* ✉ *$10 adults* ☉ *Tues.–Sun. 10-4* Ⓜ *Dupont Circle.*

4

Monuments and Memorials

WORD OF MOUTH

"We started our walk from the Washington Monument to the World War II Memorial, where a group of veterans were gathered, to the Vietnam Veterans Memorial, Korean War Veterans Memorial, and the Lincoln Memorial at the end. It was a plus for the kids to get a chance to speak with the veterans."

—Amy

Updated
by Kathryn
McKay

Washington is a monumental city. In the middle of traffic circles, on tiny slivers of park, and at street corners and intersections, you find statues, plaques, and simple blocks of marble honoring the generals, artists, and statesmen who helped shape the nation. Of these tributes, the greatest and grandest are clustered west of the Mall on ground reclaimed from the marshy flats of the Potomac—which also happens to be the location of Washington's most striking display of cherry trees.

These memorials now look like part of the landscape, but their beginnings were often controversial. From the Lincoln Memorial to the Martin Luther King Jr. Memorial, they sparked sometimes-fierce debate over how and why America should enshrine its history. Over time, though, the memorials become icons of unquestionable significance.

Visit the memorials on the Mall and Tidal Basin at night for fewer crowds and cooler air. Although you won't get the views, the lighting is particularly beautiful on the Lincoln and Jefferson memorials. Inside the Lincoln, lights and shadows play across his face, making him look even more thoughtful.

Across the Potomac, Arlington National Cemetery memorial has a power all its own. Though it pays tribute to great Americans, including Robert and John F. Kennedy, what's most striking about the cemetery is its "sea of stones"—the thousands upon thousands of graves holding men and women who served in the U.S. military.

PLANNING

PLANNING YOUR TIME

It takes about four or five hours to tour the monuments west of the Mall, with time to relax on a park bench and grab a snack from a vendor or one of the snack bars east of the Washington Monument, near the Lincoln Memorial.

If you're visiting during the first two weeks in April, take extra time around the Tidal Basin and the Washington Monument to marvel at the cherry blossoms. From mid-April through November, you might want to spend an hour on a paddleboat in the Tidal Basin. In summer, consider taking a Martz Gray Line bus and travel between the monuments in air-conditioned comfort.

Across the Potomac, Arlington National Cemetery merits a couple of hours on its own.

ASK A RANGER

You may think of park rangers as denizens of the woods, but they're a conspicuous presence at Washington's memorials—look for the olive-green and gray uniforms. Rangers lead talks about each memorial run by the Park Service (every hour on the hour, from 10 am to 11 pm) unless they are short-staffed, which does happen. They are an invaluable source of information; don't hesitate to ask questions of them. Kids can get Junior Park Ranger activity booklets from the ranger booths at the Lincoln, Roosevelt, Vietnam, World War II, and King memorials.

TOURS

Washington Walks (⊕ *www.washingtonwalks.com*) has tours with witty commentary that cover most of the major monuments and memorials. They operate from April through October, and each two-hour tour costs $15. **DC by Foot** (⊕ *www.dcbyfoot.com*) offers free (work for tips) walking tours of the memorials. Tours meet at the northeast corner of 15th Street and Constitution Avenue NW (next to the Department of Commerce) at 10 am most days, but check the website for details. **Bike and Roll Washington, DC** (⊕ *www.bikethesites.com*) conducts tours on wheels from late March through November. The cost is $40–$45 for adults, $25–$35 for children 12 and under; price includes bike rental, helmet, bottled water, and snack.

MONUMENTAL SOUVENIRS

At **Arlington National Cemetery** there are gift shops at the visitor center, the Women in Military Service for America Memorial, and the Arlington House. The National Park Service contracts with a private company that operates gift shops and bookstores at or near the **FDR Memorial** (the largest), **Jefferson Memorial, Lincoln Memorial,** Martin Luther King Jr. Memorial, and **Washington Monument.** The books are different at each shop, but the souvenirs tend to be the same.

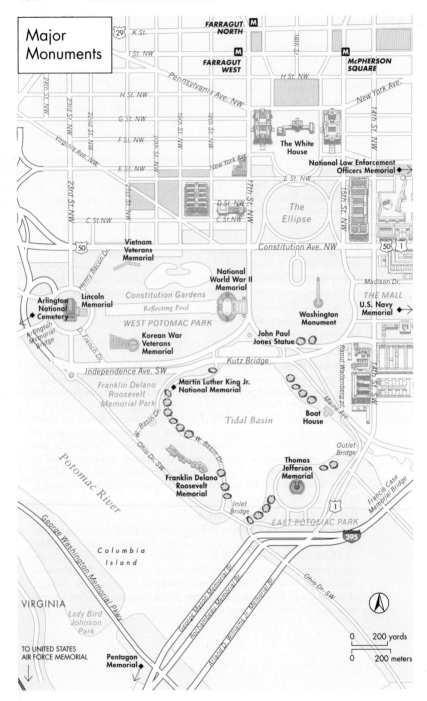

Major Monuments

ARLINGTON, THE NATION'S CEMETERY

The most famous, most visited cemetery in the country is the final resting place for more than 330,000 Americans, from unknown soldiers to John F. Kennedy. With its tombs, monuments, and "sea of stones," Arlington is a place of ritual and remembrance, where even the most cynical observer of Washington politics may find a lump in his throat or a tear in his eye.

EXPERIENCING THE SEA OF STONES

In 1864, a 200-acre plot directly across the Potomac from Washington, part of the former plantation home of Robert E. Lee, was designated America's national cemetery. Today, the cemetery covers 624 acres.

Today, Arlington's major monuments and memorials are impressive, but the most striking experience is simply looking out over the thousands upon thousands of headstones aligned across the cemetery's hills.

Most of those buried here served in the military—from reinterred Revolutionary War soldiers to troops killed in Iraq and Afghanistan. As you walk through the cemetery, you're likely to hear a trumpet playing taps or the report of a

gun salute. An average of 27 funerals a day are held here, Monday through Friday. There currently are some 300,000 graves in Arlington; it's projected that the cemetery will be filled by 2060.

FINDING A GRAVE

At the Visitors Center, staff members and computers can help you find the location of a specific grave. You need to provide the deceased's full name and, if possible, the branch of service and year of death.

4

WHO GETS BURIED WHERE

With few exceptions, interment at Arlington is limited to active-duty members of the armed forces, veterans, and their spouses and minor children. In Arlington's early years as a cemetery, burial location was determined by rank (as well as, initially, by race), with separate sections for enlisted soldiers and officers. Beginning in 1947, this distinction was abandoned. Grave sites are assigned on the day before burial; when possible, requests are honored to be buried near the graves of family members.

ABOUT THE HEADSTONES

Following the Civil War, Arlington's first graves were marked by simple whitewashed boards. When these decayed, they were replaced by cast-iron markers covered with zinc to prevent rusting. Only one iron marker remains, for the grave of Captain Daniel Keys (Section 13, Lot 13615, Grid G-29/30).

In 1873, Congress voted in the use of marble headstones, which continues to be the practice today. The government provides the standard-issue stones free of charge. Next of kin may supply their own headstones, though these can only be used if space is available in one of the sections where individualized stones already exist.

THE SAME, BUT DIFFERENT

Regulation headstones can be engraved with one of 45 symbols indicating religious affiliation. In section 60, the headstones of soldiers killed in Afghanistan and Iraq reflect the multicultural makeup of 21st-century America. Along with a variety of crosses and the Star of David, you see the nine-pointed star of the Baha'i; a tepee and three feathers representing the Native American faiths; the Muslim crescent and star; and other signs of faith. (Or lack of it. Atheism is represented by a stylized atom.)

Opposite: Sea of Stones; Upper left: Burial ceremony; Bottom left: A soldier placing flags for Memorial Day. Right: Coast Guard headstone.

PLANNING YOUR VISIT TO ARLINGTON

ARLINGTON BASICS

Getting Here: You can reach Arlington on the Metro, by foot over Arlington Memorial Bridge (southwest of the Lincoln Memorial), or by car—there's a large parking lot by the Visitors Center on Memorial Drive. Also, the Martz Gray Line bus (☎ 800/862–1400 ⊕ www.graylinedc.com) and Old Town Trolley (☎ 202/832–9800 ⊕ www.old towntrolley.com) both have Arlington National Cemetery stops in their loops.

☉ Apr.–Sept., daily 8–7; Oct.–Mar., daily 8–5.

🎫 Cemetery free, parking $1.75 per hr for the first three hours, $2.50 per hr thereafter. Tourmobile Arlington Tour $7.50, Old Town Trolley $35.

☎ 877/907–8585 for general information and to locate a grave.

⊕ www.arlingtoncemetery.mil

✗ No food or drink is allowed at the cemetery. There are water fountains in the Visitor Center, and from fall through spring a water fountain operates near the amphitheater at the Tomb of the Unknowns. You can also purchase bottled water at the Women's Memorial.

TOURING OPTIONS

Your first stop at the cemetery should be the Visitor Center, where you can pick up a free brochure with a detailed map. Once there you have a choice: tour by bus or walk.

Arlington by Bus. Martz Gray Line tour buses leave every 15 to 25 minutes from just outside the Visitor Center April through September, daily 8:30–6:30, and October through March, daily 8:30–4:30. The 40-minute tour includes stops at the Kennedy grave sites, the Tomb of the Unknowns, and Arlington House. Your bus driver will provide basic facts about the cemetery.

Arlington on Foot. Walking the cemetery requires some stamina, but it allows you to take in the thousands of graves at your own pace. On the facing page is a walking tour that includes the major points of interest. Audio tours are available in the Visitor Center.

Above: 3rd Infantry Honor Guard

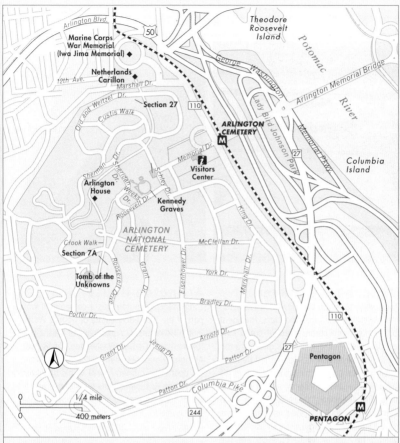

A WALKING TOUR

■ Head west from the Visitors Center on Roosevelt Drive and turn right on Weeks Drive to reach the **Kennedy graves;** just to the west is **Arlington House.** (¼ mile)

■ Take Crook Walk south, following the signs, to the **Tomb of the Unknowns;** a few steps from the tomb is **Section 7A,** where many distinguished veterans are buried. (³⁄₁₀ mile)

■ To visit the graves of soldiers killed in Afghanistan and Iraq, take Roosevelt Drive past Section 7 and turn right on McClellan Drive, turn right when you get to Eisenhower Drive, then go left onto York Drive. The graves will be on your right. (⁶⁄₁₀ mile)

■ Walk north along Eisenhower Drive, which becomes Schley Drive; turn right onto Custis Walk, which brings you to **Section 27,** where 3,800 former slaves are buried. (¾ mile)

■ Leave the cemetery through the Ord and Weitzel Gate, cross Marshall Drive carefully, and walk to the 50-bell **Netherlands Carillon,** where there's a good vista of Washington. To the north is the **United States Marine Corps War Memorial,** better known as the **Iwo Jima Memorial.** (¼ mile)

ARLINGTON'S MAIN ATTRACTIONS

The Kennedy Graves

Once while taking in the view of Washington from Arlington National Cemetery, President John F. Kennedy commented, "I could stay here forever." Seeing Kennedy's grave is a top priority for most visitors. He's buried beneath an eternal flame, next to graves of two of his children who died in infancy, and of his wife, Jacqueline Kennedy Onassis. Across from them is a low wall engraved with quotations from Kennedy's inaugural address. Nearby, marked by simple white crosses, are the graves of Robert F. Kennedy and Ted Kennedy.

The gas-fueled flame at the head of John F. Kennedy's grave was lit by Jacqueline Kennedy during his funeral. A continuously flashing electric spark reignites the gas if the flame is extinguished by rain, wind, or any other cause.

Many visitors ask where Kennedy's son John F. Kennedy Jr. is buried. His ashes were scattered in the Atlantic Ocean, near the location where his plane went down in 1999.

Arlington House

Long before Arlington was a cemetery, it was part of the 1,100-acre estate of George Washington Parke Custis, a grandchild of Martha and (by marriage) George Washington. Custis built Arlington House between 1802 and 1818. After his death, the property went to his daughter, Mary Anna Randolph Custis, who wed Robert E. Lee in 1831. The couple made Arlington House their home for the next 30 years.

In 1861 Lee turned down the position of commander of the Union forces and left Arlington House, never to return. Union troops turned the house into an Army headquarters, and 200 acres were set aside as a national cemetery. By the end of the Civil War headstones dotted the estate's hills. Ultimately, there would be more than 16,000.

At this writing, most furnishings have been removed temporarily as the house undergoes renovation, but walk through and speak to the ranger on duty. The views from Arlington House remain spectacular. ☎ 703/235–1530 ⊕ www.nps.gov/arho ▭ Free ⊗ Daily 9:30–4:30.

Robert E. Lee

Tomb of the Unknowns

The first burial at the Tomb of the Unknowns, one of the cemetery's most imposing monuments, took place on November 11, 1921. In what was part of a world-wide trend to honor the dead after the unparalleled devastation of World War I, an unidentified soldier was interred under the large white-marble sarcophagus. Unknown servicemen killed in World War II and Korea joined him in 1958.

The Memorial Amphitheater west of the tomb is used for ceremonies on Veterans Day, Memorial Day, and Easter. Decorations awarded to the unknowns are displayed in an indoor trophy room.

One of the most striking activities at Arlington is the precision and pageantry of the changing of the guard at the Tomb of the Unknowns. From April through September, soldiers from the Army's U.S. Third Infantry (known as the Old Guard) change guard every half hour during the day. For the rest of the year, and at night all year long, the guard changes every hour.

The Iwo Jima Memorial

Ask the tour bus driver at Arlington where the Iwo Jima is, and you might get back the quip "very far away." The memorial commonly called the Iwo Jima is officially named the United States Marine Corps War Memorial, and it's actually located just north of the cemetery. Its bronze sculpture is based on one of the most famous photos in American military history, Joe Rosenthal's February 23, 1945, shot of five marines and a navy corpsman raising a flag atop Mt. Suribachi on the Japanese island of Iwo Jima. By executive order, a real flag flies 24 hours a day from the 78-foot-high memorial. ☎ *703/289-2500*

On Tuesday evening at 7 PM from early June to mid-August there's a Marine Corps sunset parade on the grounds of the Iwo Jima Memorial. On parade nights a free shuttle bus runs from the Arlington Cemetery visitors' parking lot.

The Old Guard are not making a fashion statement in their sun-glasses—they're protecting their eyes from the sun's glare off the white marble of the tomb.

FRANKLIN DELANO ROOSEVELT MEMORIAL

⊠ *900 Ohio Dr. SW, West
side of Tidal Basin, The Mall*
☎ *202/426–6841* ⊕ *www.nps.
gov* ☒ *Free* ☉ *24 hrs; staffed
daily 9:30 am–11:30 pm*
Ⓜ *Smithsonian.*

TIPS

■ If you come with a toddler, head straight to the third room. Though youngsters can't sit on Roosevelt's lap, they can pet Fala, Roosevelt's Scottish terrier. The tips of Fala's ears and his nose shine from all the attention.

■ Allow about 30 minutes at this memorial. Take your time walking through the most expansive presidential memorial in Washington and read the lines from FDR's speeches.

■ This was the first memorial designed to be wheelchair accessible. Several pillars with Braille lettering and tactile images help the visually impaired.

■ This memorial presents great opportunities for family photographs. You can strike a pose while petting Fala, joining the men in the breadline, or listening to Roosevelt's fireside chat.

■ At night the lighting over the waterfalls creates interesting shadows, and there's not as much noise from airplanes overhead.

Unveiled in 1997, this 7.5-acre memorial to the 32nd president includes waterfalls and reflecting pools, four outdoor gallery rooms—one for each of Roosevelt's presidential terms (1933 to 1945)—and 10 bronze sculptures. The granite megaliths connecting the galleries are engraved with some of Roosevelt's famous statements, including, "The only thing we have to fear is fear itself."

HIGHLIGHTS

Congress established the Franklin Delano Roosevelt Memorial Commission in 1955, and invited prospective designers to look to "the character and work of Roosevelt to give us the theme of a memorial." Several decades passed before Lawrence Halprin's design for a "walking environmental experience" was selected. It incorporates work by artists Leonard Baskin, Neil Estern, Robert Graham, Thomas Hardy, and George Segal, and master stone carver John Benson.

The statue of a wheelchair-bound Roosevelt near the entrance of the memorial was added in 2001. Originally, the memorial showed little evidence of Roosevelt's polio, which he contracted at age 39. He used a wheelchair for the last 24 years of his life, but kept his disability largely hidden from public view. The statue was added after years of debate about whether to portray Roosevelt realistically or to honor his desire not to display his disability.

You're encouraged to touch the handprints and Braille along the columns in the second room, which represent the working hands of the American people.

A bronze statue of First Lady Eleanor Roosevelt stands in front of the United Nations symbol in the fourth room. She was a vocal spokesperson for human rights and one of the most influential women of her time.

KOREAN WAR VETERANS MEMORIAL

✉ *Daniel French Dr. SW and Independence Ave. SW, West end of Mall, The Mall* ☎ *202/426–6841* ⊕ *www.nps. gov/kwvm* ✉ *Free* ☉ *24 hrs; staffed daily 9:30 am–11:30 pm* Ⓜ *Foggy Bottom.*

TIPS

■ Allow about 10 or 15 minutes at this memorial.

■ A sign at the entrance to the memorial indicates the time of the next park ranger-led interpretive talk.

■ You can get service information on the soldiers who died in the Korean War from the touch-screen computer at the memorial information booth. Further information about veterans and casualties is available at www.korean-war.org.

■ It may be tempting for kids to trek through the field with the statues, but it's not allowed. They can strike a pose next to the wall and see their reflection added to those of the 19 soldiers.

■ Visit the shop in the nearby Lincoln Memorial for books and souvenirs relating to the Korean War.

This memorial to the 1.5 million United States men and women who served in the Korean War (1950–53) highlights the high cost of freedom. Nearly 37,000 Americans were killed on the Korean peninsula, 8,000 were missing in action, and more than 103,000 were wounded. The privately funded memorial was dedicated on July 27, 1995, on the 42nd anniversary of the Korean War Armistice. Compare this memorial to the more intimate Vietnam Veterans Memorial and the grandiose World War II Memorial.

HIGHLIGHTS

In the *Field of Service*, 19 oversize stainless-steel soldiers toil through a rugged triangular terrain toward an American flag; look beneath the helmets to see their weary faces. The reflection in the polished black granite wall to their right doubles their number to 38, symbolic of the 38th parallel, the latitude established as the border between North and South Korea in 1953, as well as the 38 months of the war.

Unlike many memorials, this one contains few words, but what's here is poignant. The 164-foot-long granite wall etched with the faces of 2,400 unnamed servicemen and servicewomen says simply, "Freedom is not free." The plaque at the base of the flagpole reads, "Our nation honors her sons and daughters who answered the call to defend a country they never knew and a people they never met." The only other words are the names of 22 countries that volunteered forces or medical support, including Great Britain, France, Greece, and Turkey.

The adjacent circular Pool of Remembrance honors all who were killed, captured, wounded, or missing in action; it's a quiet spot for contemplation.

4

LINCOLN MEMORIAL

✉ 23rd St. SW and Independence Ave. SW, West end of Mall, The Mall ☎ 202/426–6841 ⊕ www.nps.gov/linc 🖥 Free ◷ 24 hrs; staffed daily 9:30 am–11:30 pm Ⓜ Foggy Bottom.

TIPS

■ The power of pennies? On the lower level of the memorial is a small museum financed with pennies collected by schoolchildren.

■ Lincoln's face and hands look especially lifelike because they're based on castings done in his lifetime. Those who know sign language might recognize that the left hand is shaped like an A and the right like an L. It's unlikely this was intentional, but the sculptor, Daniel Chester French, did have a deaf son.

■ Marchers flock to the Lincoln every year, drawing attention to various causes.

■ Lincoln's famous Emancipation Proclamation, which set the stage for ending slavery, is on display several times per year at the National Archives (Constitution Ave., between 7th and 9th streets) See where Lincoln was shot (on April 14, 1865) at Ford's Theatre (511 10th St. NW).

Many consider the Lincoln Memorial the most inspiring monument in Washington, but that hasn't always been the case: early detractors thought it inappropriate that a president known for his humility should be honored with what some felt amounts to a grandiose Greek temple. The memorial was intended to be a symbol of national unity, but over time it has come to represent social justice and civil rights.

HIGHLIGHTS

Daniel Chester French's statue of the seated president gazes out over the Reflecting Pool. The 19-foot-high sculpture is made of 28 pieces of Georgia marble.

The surrounding white Colorado-marble memorial was designed by Henry Bacon and completed in 1922. The 36 Doric columns represent the 36 states in the Union at the time of Lincoln's death; their names appear on the frieze above the columns. Over the frieze are the names of the 48 states in existence when the memorial was dedicated. Alaska and Hawaii are represented with an inscription on the terrace leading up to the memorial. At night the memorial is illuminated, creating a striking play of light and shadow across Lincoln's face.

Two of Lincoln's great speeches—the second inaugural address and the Gettysburg Address—are carved on the north and south walls. Above each is a Jules Guerin mural: the south wall has an angel of truth freeing a slave; the unity of North and South is opposite.

The memorial's powerful symbolism makes it a popular gathering place: In its shadow Americans marched for integrated schools in 1958, rallied for an end to the Vietnam War in 1967, and laid wreaths in a ceremony honoring the Iranian hostages in 1979. It may be best known, though, as the site of Martin Luther King Jr.'s "I Have a Dream" speech.

MARTIN LUTHER KING JR. MEMORIAL

✉ *1964 Independence Ave. SW, The Mall* ☏ *202/426–6841,* ⊕ *www.nps.gov/mlkm* 🎟 *Free* ⊙ *24 hrs; staffed daily 9:30 am–11:30* Ⓜ *Smithsonian.*

TIPS

■ Allow about 20 to 30 minutes at this memorial, which was designed as a place for reflection.

■ Cross West Basin Drive to visit the park ranger station and gift shop, which sells books on MLK for all ages and a variety of keepsakes.

■ Walk over to the Lincoln Memorial, where you can stand on the same step where King delivered his "I Have a Dream" speech. A plaque marks the exact spot.

■ Contrary to popular belief, King wasn't the first African American with a memorial in D.C. That honor goes to Mary McLeod Bethune, founder of the National Council of Negro Women and an informal adviser to FDR. Bethune is depicted in a 17-foot-tall bronze statue (Lincoln Park, East Capitol and 12th Sts. NE).

A "King" now stands tall among the presidents on the National Mall. At the dedication on October 16, 2011, President Barak Obama said, "This is a day that would not be denied." The memorial opened 15 years after Congress approved it in 1996 and 82 years after the famed civil rights leader was born in 1929.

HIGHLIGHTS

Located strategically between the Lincoln and Jefferson memorials and adjacent to the FDR Memorial, the crescent-shape King Memorial sits on a 4-acre site on the curved bank of the Tidal Basin.

There are two main ways to enter the memorial. From West Basin Drive, walk through a center walkway cut out of a huge boulder, the Mountain of Despair. From the Tidal Basin entrance, a 28-foot tall granite boulder shows King looking out toward Jefferson. The symbolism of the mountain and stone are explained by King's words: "With this faith, we will be able to hew out of the mountain of despair a stone of hope." The centerpiece stone was carved by Chinese sculptor Lei Yixin; his design was chosen from more than 900 entries in an international competition. Fittingly, Yixin first read about King's "I Have a Dream" speech at age 10 while visiting the Lincoln Memorial.

The themes of democracy, justice, hope, and love are reflected through quotes on the south and north walls and on the Stone of Hope. The quotes reflect speeches, sermons, and writings penned by King from 1955 through 1968. Waterfalls in the memorial reflect King's use of the biblical quote: "Let justice roll down like waters and righteousness like a mighty stream."

4

NATIONAL WORLD WAR II MEMORIAL

✉ *17th St. SW and Home Front Dr. SW, between Independence Ave. SW and Constitution Ave. NW, The Mall* ☎ *202/426–6841* ⊕ *www.wwiimemorial. com* ✉ *Free* ⊙ *24 hrs* Ⓜ *Smithsonian.*

TIPS

■ Look for veterans. Perhaps the best part of visiting this memorial might be the last opportunities to see men and women who fought in World War II and are part of what former NBC news anchor Tom Brokaw called "The Greatest Generation."

■ Computers at the National Park Service kiosk behind the Pacific side of the memorial contain information about soldiers who lost their lives in the war.

■ Kids might be bored here. You can engage their attention by asking them to look carefully at the bas-reliefs for a dog and a radio as large as today's big-screen televisions. Then try to find Kilroy, the cartoonlike character who appears to be looking over a ledge (hint: He's in two places). The image and the phrase "Kilroy was here" were popular graffiti left by U.S. soldiers during the war.

Dedicated just before Memorial Day in 2004, this symmetrically designed monument honors the 16 million Americans who served in the armed forces, the more than 400,000 who died, and all who supported the war effort at home.

HIGHLIGHTS

An imposing circle of 56 granite pillars, each bearing a bronze wreath, represents the U.S. states and territories of 1941–45. Four bronze eagles, a bronze garland, and two 43-foot-tall arches inscribed with "Atlantic" and "Pacific" surround the large circular plaza. The roar of the water comes from the Rainbow Pool, here since the 1920s but newly renovated as the centerpiece of the memorial. There are also two fountains and two waterfalls.

The Field of Stars, a wall of 4,000 gold stars, commemorates the more than 400,000 Americans who lost their lives in the war.

Although the parklike setting and the place of honor between the Washington Monument and the Lincoln Memorial may seem appropriate, some people were critical when the site for the memorial was announced, because they felt it would interrupt the landscape between the two landmarks and because it uses some of the open space that had been the site of demonstrations and protests.

Bas-relief panels tell the story of how World War II affected Americans by depicting women in the military, V-J Day, medics, the bond drive, and more activities of the time. The 24 panels are divided evenly between the Atlantic front and the Pacific front.

THOMAS JEFFERSON MEMORIAL

✉ *Tidal Basin, south bank, off Ohio Dr. SW, The Mall* ☎ *202/426–6841* ⊕ *www.nps. gov/thje* ▭ *Free* ⊙ *Daily 8 am–midnight* Ⓜ *Smithsonian.*

4

TIPS

■ Check out the view of the White House from the memorial's steps—it's one of the best.

■ Jefferson was the second president to live in the White House, but the first full-term occupant.

■ Park ranger programs are offered throughout the day, and you can ask questions of the ranger on duty.

■ Learn more about Jefferson by visiting the exhibit called Light and Liberty on the memorial's lower level. It chronicles highlights of Jefferson's life and has a timeline of world history during his lifetime.

■ Allow 15 minutes to walk here from the Metro. The memorial is the southernmost of Washington's major monuments and memorials, and it's a full four blocks and a trip around the Tidal Basin from the nearest Metro stop, Smithsonian.

■ Limited free parking is available under the 14th Street Bridge, off Ohio Drive near where it intersects with East Basin Drive.

In the 1930s Congress decided that Thomas Jefferson deserved a monument positioned as prominently as those honoring Washington and Lincoln. Workers scooped and moved tons of the river bottom to create dry land for the spot directly south of the White House where the monument was built. Jefferson had always admired the Pantheon in Rome, so the memorial's architect, John Russell Pope, drew on it for inspiration. His finished work was dedicated on the bicentennial of Jefferson's birth, April 13, 1943.

HIGHLIGHTS

Early critics weren't kind to the memorial—rumor has it that it was nicknamed "Jefferson's muffin" for its domed shape. The design was called outdated and too similar to that of the Lincoln Memorial. Indeed, both statues of Jefferson and Lincoln are 19 feet, just 6 inches shorter than the statue of Freedom atop the Capitol.

The bronze statue of Jefferson, standing on a 6-foot granite pedestal, looms larger than life. It wasn't always made of bronze. The first version was made of plaster, because bronze was too expensive and was needed for the war. The statue you see today was erected in 1947.

You can get a taste of Jefferson's keen intellect from his writings about freedom and government inscribed on the marble walls surrounding his statue.

Many people may be surprised to learn that Jefferson didn't list being president as one of his greatest accomplishments. When he appraised his own life, Jefferson wanted to be remembered as the "Author of the Declaration of American Independence, of the Statute of Virginia for religious freedom, and Father of the University of Virginia."

VIETNAM VETERANS MEMORIAL

✉ *Constitution Gardens, 23rd St. NW and Constitution Ave. NW, The Mall* ☎ *202/426-6841* ⊕ *www.nps.gov/vive* 🎫 *Free* ☉ *24 hrs; staffed daily 9:30 am–11:30 pm* Ⓜ *Foggy Bottom.*

TIPS

■ Names on the wall are ordered by date of death. To find a name, consult the alphabetical lists found at either end of the wall. You can get assistance locating a name at the white kiosk with the brown roof near the entrance.

■ At the wall, rangers and volunteers wearing yellow caps can look up the names and supply you with paper and pencils for making rubbings. Every name on the memorial is preceded (on the west wall) or followed (on the east wall) by a symbol designating status. A diamond indicates "killed, body recovered." A plus sign (found by a small percentage of names) indicates "killed, body not recovered."

■ If you're visiting with older children or teens, be prepared for questions about war and death. Sometimes children think all 58,272 soldiers are buried at the monument. They aren't, of course, but the wall is as evocative as any cemetery.

"The Wall," as it's commonly called, is one of the most visited sites in Washington. The names of more than 58,000 Americans who died in the Vietnam War are etched in its black granite panels, creating a somber, dignified, and powerful memorial. It was conceived by Jan Scruggs, a former infantry corporal who served in Vietnam, and designed by Maya Lin, then a 21-year-old architecture student at Yale.

HIGHLIGHTS

Thousands of offerings are left at the wall each year: many people leave flowers, others leave personal objects such as the clothing of soldiers or letters of thanks from schoolchildren. The National Park Service collects and stores the items. In 2007 Congress approved the establishment of a memorial center to display many of the items left near the wall, but as of this writing, architectural plans still haven't been approved.

The statues near the wall came about in response to controversies surrounding the memorial. In 1984 Frederick Hart's statue of three soldiers and a flagpole was erected to the south of the wall, with the goal of winning over veterans who considered the memorial a "black gash of shame." A memorial plaque was added in 2004 at the statue of three servicemen to honor veterans who died after the war as a direct result of injuries suffered in Vietnam, but who fall outside Department of Defense guidelines for remembrance at the wall.

The Vietnam Women's Memorial was dedicated on Veterans Day 1993. Glenna Goodacre's bronze sculpture depicts two women caring for a wounded soldier while a third woman kneels nearby; eight trees around the plaza commemorate the eight women in the military who died in Vietnam.

WASHINGTON MONUMENT

✉ *15th St. NW, between Constitution Ave. NW and Independence Ave. SW, The Mall* ☎ *202/426–6841, 877/444–6777 for advance tickets* ⊕ *www.nps.gov/ wamo; www.recreation.gov for advance tickets* 🎟 *Free; $1.50 service fee per advance ticket* ⊙ *Closed until late 2013 or 2014. On reopening, hours will be daily 9–5* Ⓜ *Smithsonian.*

TIPS

■ You can still look down on D.C. at the Old Post Office Pavilion (100 Pennsylvania Ave. NW at 12th St.) or the Washington National Cathedral's Pilgrim Observation Gallery (Massachusetts and Wisconsin Aves. NW).

■ When the monument reopens, it will use a free timed-ticket system for the elevator ride. A limited number of tickets will be available each day at the marble lodge on 15th Street. In spring and summer, lines are likely to start hours before the monument opens.

■ Maps below viewing-station windows point out some of Washington's major buildings, but you might want to bring a more detailed map (available at the monument's bookstore).

This beloved landmark closed on Tuesday August 23, 2011, after a rare but powerful 5.8 magnitude earthquake hit 320 miles away in Bristol, Virginia. The quake sent tremors that rattled the mighty monument, leaving visible cracks and structural damage. Repair work is expected to last at least until the end of 2013.

The 555-foot, 5-inch Washington Monument punctuates the capital like a huge exclamation point and was part of Pierre L'Enfant's plan for Washington (his intended location proved to be marshy, so it was moved 100 yards southeast to firmer ground; a stone marker indicates L'Enfant's original site). Construction began in 1848 and continued, with interruptions, until 1884. The design called for an obelisk rising from a circular colonnaded building, but the idea was eventually abandoned. Upon its completion, the monument was the world's tallest structure.

HIGHLIGHTS

Six years into construction, members of the anti-Catholic Know-Nothing Party stole and smashed a block of marble donated by Pope Pius IX. This action, combined with funding shortages and the onset of the Civil War, brought construction to a halt. After the war, building finally resumed, and though the new marble came from the same Maryland quarry as the old, it was taken from a different stratum with a slightly different shade.

When the monument reopens, an elevator will once again whiz to the top of the monument in 70 seconds—a trip that in 1888 took 12 minutes via steam-powered elevator. From the viewing stations at the top you can take in most of the District of Columbia, as well as parts of Maryland and Virginia.

4

DID YOU KNOW?

Each year on July 4, the National Symphony Orchestra goes out with a bang, ending its performance with Tchaikovsky's "1812 Overture" and using real cannons (with blanks)!

OTHER MEMORIALS

District of Columbia War Memorial. Despite its location and age, visitors have often overlooked this memorial on the National Mall that was dedicated by President Herbert Hoover in 1931. Unlike the neighboring memorials on the National Mall, this relatively small structure isn't a national memorial. The 47-foot-high memorial is dedicated to the 499 men and women (military and civilian) from Washington,

D.C., who died in the Great War. Unofficially referred to as the World War I memorial, the open-air marble dome was in disrepair and hidden by trees for decades. Through the American Recovery and Reinvestment Act of 2009, the memorial was restored to its original grandeur and is now maintained by the National Park Service. On November 10, 2011, the memorial, which had the John Phillip Sousa band playing at its original dedication, was rededicated as local musicians from the Duke Ellington School of the Arts performed. ⊠ *Independence Ave. SW, North side, between World War II Memorial and Lincoln Memorial, The Mall* ☎ *202/426–6841* ⊕ *www.nps.gov* ⊘ *24 hrs; staffed daily 9:30 am–11:30 pm* Ⓜ *Foggy Bottom.*

National Law Enforcement Officers Memorial. These 3-foot-high walls bear the names of approximately 20,000 American police officers killed in the line of duty since 1791. On the third line of panel 13W are the names of six officers killed by William Bonney, better known as Billy the Kid. J. D. Tippit, the Dallas policeman killed by Lee Harvey Oswald, is honored on the ninth line of panel 63E. Other names include the 72 officers who died due to 9/11. Directories there allow you to look up officers by name, date of death, state, and department. Call to arrange for a free tour. A National Law Enforcement Museum is in the works, scheduled for completion by early 2014; until then, a small visitor center (⊠ *400 7th St. NW*) has a computer for looking up names, a display on the history of law enforcement, and a small gift shop. For a self-guided cell phone tour, call ☎ *202/747–3461.* ⊠ *400 block of E St. NW, Penn Quarter* ☎ *202/737–3400* ⊕ *www.lawmemorial.org* ☎ *Free* ⊘ *Weekdays 9–5, Sat. 10–5, Sun. noon–5* Ⓜ *Judiciary Square.*

Pentagon Memorial. Washington's own "9/11 memorial" commemorates the 184 people who perished when the hijacked American Airlines Flight 77 crashed into the northwest side of the Pentagon. Benches engraved with the victims' names are arranged in order by date of birth and where they were when they died. The names of the victims who were inside the Pentagon are arranged so that visitors reading their names face the Pentagon, and names of the victims on the plane are arranged so that visitors reading their names face skyward. Designed by Julie Beckman and Keith Kaseman, the memorial opened to the public on September 11, 2008, the seventh anniversary of the attacks. Volunteer docents periodically stand near the entrance and answer questions. Parking for the memorial is extremely limited and not well marked; take the Metro instead. ✉ *1 Rotary Rd., Pentagon, Arlington, Virginia* ☎ *301/740–3388* ⊕ *www.whs.mil/memorial* ✉ *Free* ⊗ *24 hrs; restroom facilities 7 am–10 pm* Ⓜ *Pentagon.*

United States Air Force Memorial. Three stainless-steel, asymmetrical spires slice through the skyline up to 270 feet, representing flight, the precision of the "bomb burst" maneuver performed by the Air Force Thunderbirds, and the three core values of the Air Force: integrity, service, and excellence. The spires are adjacent to the southern portion of Arlington National Cemetery and visible from the Tidal Basin and I–395 near Washington. At the base of the spires is an 8-foot statue of the honor guard, a glass wall engraved with the missing man formation, and granite walls inscribed with Air Force values and accomplishments. ✉ *1 Air Force Memorial Dr., off Columbia Pike, Arlington, Virginia* ☎ *703/979–0674* ⊕ *www.airforcememorial.org* ✉ *Free* ⊗ *Apr.–Sept., daily 8 am–11 pm; Oct.–Mar., daily 8 am–9 pm* Ⓜ *Pentagon.*

United States Navy Memorial. Although Pierre L'Enfant included a Navy Memorial in his plans for Washington, D.C., it wasn't until 1987 that one was built. The main attraction here is an 860-ton, 100-foot-in-diameter granite map of the world, known as the Granite Sea. It's surrounded by fountains, benches, and six ship masts. The *Lone Sailor*, a 7-foot-tall statue, stands on the map in the Pacific Ocean between the United States and Japan. The Naval Heritage Center, next to the memorial in the Market Square East Building, displays videos and exhibits of uniforms, medals, and other aspects of Navy life. If you've served in the Navy, you can enter your record of service into the Navy Log here. The theater shows a rotating series of Navy-related movies throughout the day. Bronze relief panels on the Pennsylvania Avenue side of the memorial depict 26 scenes commemorating events in the nation's naval history and honoring naval communities. ■ TIP➔ The panels are at a perfect height for children to look at and touch; challenge your child to find these items: a helicopter, a seagull, a U.S. flag, a sailor with binoculars, a dog, penguins, and seals. If you look carefully at the flagpole nearest the entrance to the Heritage Center, you'll see a time capsule, scheduled to be opened in 2093. ✉ *701 Pennsylvania Ave. NW, Downtown* ☎ *202/737–2300* ⊕ *www.navymemorial.org* ✉ *Free* ⊗ *24 hrs; Naval Heritage Center Daily 9:30–5* Ⓜ *Archives/Navy Memorial.*

Official Washington

WORD OF MOUTH

"I think the National Cathedral is absolutely beautiful, and attending one of the Sunday services in the nave of the cathedral is inspiring."
—furledleader

"The Library of Congress is a fabulous building with magnificent architecture. Our guide made the tour very interesting with great stories for young and old."

—europeannovice

Updated by
Cathy Sharpe

Given the heightened security concerns of present-day Washington, it might come as a surprise to learn that most government institutions continue to welcome the general public. The Founding Fathers' mandate of a free and open government lives on—just with metal detectors and bag searches. Though security checks are no one's idea of fun, most people find them a small price to pay for the opportunity to get a firsthand look at the government in action. Being in the famous halls of the Capitol, the White House, or the Supreme Court is a heady experience. It's one part celebrity sighting and one part the world's best civics lesson.

Although the Capitol, White House, and Supreme Court get the lion's share of the attention, other government institutions hold their own, sometimes-quirky appeal. Art enthusiasts can gaze in wonder at the works on display at the Red Cross headquarters and the Interior Department, while military buffs can retrace the footsteps of four- and five-star generals in the seemingly endless hallways of the Pentagon.

If you're fascinated by finance, you'll want to plan ahead for visits to the Bureau of Engraving and Printing, the Federal Reserve, and the Department of Treasury. You need to sign up three months in advance for a tour of the Department of State, but your advance work will be rewarded with a visit to the plush Diplomatic Reception Rooms, where few sightseers tread.

PLANNING

WHEN TO PLAN AHEAD

You can visit many of Washington's government offices, but you have to do some advance planning in many cases—not just for the White House and Congress, but for places that are less high-profile as well. *Here's a rundown of how far in advance you need to make arrangements.*

SITE	TIME IN ADVANCE
Capitol Tour	Morning of visit–3 months
Congressional session	2 weeks–2 months
White House (spring, summer, December)	6 months
White House (other times)	1–2 months
Supreme Court	Morning of visit
American Red Cross	1 week
Department of Interior	2–4 weeks
Department of State	3 months
Federal Reserve	5 days
Pentagon	8 days–3 months
Treasury Building	1–2 months

NO ADVANCE PLANNING REQUIRED

Two of the most impressive places in Washington don't require advance reservations. The **Library of Congress** and the **Washington National Cathedral** are architectural and artistic treasures.

The cathedral was dubbed at its creation a "House of Prayer for All People," and does indeed draw people from all over the world seeking comfort and reflection. Statues of George Washington and Abraham Lincoln make it clear that this is a place where church and state are welcome to coexist. With its murals, paintings, sculptures and statues, and, of course, millions of books and manuscripts, the Library of Congress is truly impressive. Even if you're not a bookworm, the free docent-led tour is one of the best things going in the city.

CAPITOL VISITOR CENTER

One of the most visited attractions, the **Capitol Visitor Center** is the starting point for tours of the Capitol and where you'll discover a plethora of historical treasures, including a table used by Abraham Lincoln during his 1865 inaugural address. Crowds in the spring and summer can number in the thousands, so plan for at least three hours here. The five-football-fields-size underground complex is a destination in itself, with the model of the statue of *Freedom*, a 530-seat dining room that serves the famous Senate bean soup, and exhibits on the Capitol. Tours of the Capitol run Monday through Saturday from 8:50 to 3:20. Allow extra time to go through security.

To visit the Capitol, you'll need to either reserve tickets online at ⊕ *www.visitthecapitol.gov* or contact your representative or senator.

OFFICIAL WASHINGTON WITH KIDS

Before visiting the Capitol, have a discussion with your kids about Congress's role in the government and the Capitol's place in history. Then during the tour, encourage them to move up front to see and hear better.

Kids can email the president at *president@whitehouse.gov* or send a letter to the White House. The president and first lady even have their own zip code: 20500.

Kids get a kick out of seeing currency printed at the **Bureau of Engraving and Printing.** At the gift shop they can buy bags of shredded bills and get a postcard-size rendering of a dollar with their face in the place of George Washington's.

WHITE HOUSE EVENTS

DECEMBER AT THE WHITE HOUSE

The White House is decorated for Christmas during December every year. Even before you enter the State Dining Room, you can smell the gingerbread. The White House gingerbread-house tradition began during the Nixon administration, and has been continued ever since.

Since 1961 the Christmas tree in the Blue Room (another stands in the East Room) has reflected themes. In 1974 the Fords' Christmas tree ornaments emphasized thrift and recycling. In 1991 the Bushes' tree featured needlepoint figurines. Holiday cards created by military children, as well as ornaments with patches, medals and badges representing all branches of the military adorned the Obamas' 2011 Christmas tree.

■ TIP→ December is far and away the most difficult time of year to secure a tour. The White House is able to accommodate fewer than 10% of the tour requests it receives.

EASTER EGG ROLL

Kids have been rolling Easter eggs at the White House since at least 1878. Over the years the Egg Rolls have evolved into elaborate affairs with bands and bunnies. The event is held the Monday after Easter, from 8 am to 7 pm on the South Lawn of the White House. Tickets are distributed via an online lottery system. Each group has to include at least one child 13 years old or under and no more than two adults.

For the most up-to-date information on the Easter Egg Roll, call the White House 24-hour information line at ☎ *202/456–7041.*

PLANNING A VISIT

To visit the White House, you have to make arrangements through your representative or senator. You can find their contact information on the Web at ⊕ *www.house.gov* and ⊕ *www.senate.gov.* (You can probably also find them in your local phone book.)

Don't be reluctant to contact your congresspeople—it's part of their job, and they have lots of experience handling such requests. Some will even invite you to meet with them and talk about your interests and concerns.

Continued on page 163

ON THE HILL, UNDER THE DOME: EXPERIENCING THE CAPITOL

In Washington, the Capitol literally stands above it all: by law, no other building in the city can reach the height of the dome's peak.

Beneath its magnificent dome, the day-to-day business of American democracy takes place: senators and representatives debate, coax, and cajole, and ultimately determine the law of the land.

For many visitors, the Capitol is the most exhilarating experience Washington has to offer. It wins them over with a three-pronged appeal:

■ It's the city's most impressive work of architecture.

■ It has on display documents, art, and artifacts from 400 years of American history.

■ Its legislative chambers are open to the public. You can actually see your lawmakers at work, shaping the history of tomorrow.

THE CAPITOL THROUGH THE CENTURIES

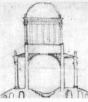

(Clockwise from top left) Moving into the new Capitol circa 1800; 19th–century print by R. Brandard; Thornton sketch circa 1797; the Capitol before the dome.

1792 - 1807
A Man with a Plan

William Thornton, a physician and amateur architect from the West Indies, wins the competition to design the Capitol. His plan, with its central rotunda and dome, draws inspiration from Rome's Pantheon. On September 18, 1793, George Washington lays the Capitol's cornerstone. In November 1800, Congress moves from Philadelphia to take up residence in the first completed section, the boxlike area between the central rotunda and today's north wing. In 1807, the House wing is completed, just to the south of the rotunda; a covered wooden walkway joins the two wings.

1814 - 1826
Washington Burns

In 1814, British troops march on Washington and set fire to the Capitol, the White House, and other government buildings. The wooden walkway is destroyed and the two wings gutted, but the walls remain standing after a violent rainstorm douses the flames. Fearful that Congress might leave Washington, residents fund a temporary "Brick Capitol" on the spot where the Supreme Court is today. By 1826, reconstruction is completed under the guidance of architects Benjamin Henry Latrobe and Charles Bulfinch; a low dome is made of wood sheathed in copper.

1850s - 1880s
Domed if You Do

North and south wings are added through the 1850s and '60s to accommodate the growing government of a growing country. To maintain scale with the enlarged building, work begins in 1885 on a taller, cast-iron dome. President Lincoln would be criticized for continuing the expensive project during the Civil War, but he calls the construction "a sign we intend the Union shall go on."

(Clockwise from top left) The east front circa 1861; today the Capitol is a tourist mecca with its own visitor center; *Freedom* statue.

Expanding the Capitol

1960s - Today

The east front is extended 33½ feet, creating 100 additional offices. In 1983 preservationists fight to keep the west front, the last remaining section of the Capitol's original facade, from being extended; in a compromise the facade's crumbling sandstone blocks are replaced with stronger limestone. In 2000 the ground is broken on the subterranean Capitol Visitor Center, to be located beneath the grounds to the building's east side. The extensive facility, three-fourths the size of the Capitol itself, was finally completed on December 2, 2008 to the tune of $621 million.

Freedom atop the Capitol Dome

The twin-shelled Capitol dome, a marvel of 19th-century engineering, rises 285 feet above the ground and weighs 4,500 tons. It can expand and contract as much as 4 inches in a day, depending on the outside temperature.

The allegorical figure on top of the dome is *Freedom*. Sculpted in 1857 by Thomas Crawford, *Freedom* was cast with help from Philip Reid, a slave. Crawford had first planned for the 19½-foot-tall bronze statue to wear the cloth liberty cap of a freed Roman slave, but Southern lawmakers, led by Jefferson Davis, objected. An "American" headdress composed of a star-encircled helmet surmounted with an eagle's head and feathers was substituted. A light just below the statue burns whenever Congress is in session.

Before the visitor center opened, the best way to see the details on the *Freedom* statue atop the Capitol dome was with a good set of binoculars. Now, you can see the original plaster model of this classical female figure up close. Her right hand rests on a sheathed sword, while her left carries a victory wreath and a shield of the United States with 13 stripes. She also wears a brooch with "U.S." on her chest.

THE CAPITOL VISITOR CENTER

The enormous and sunlit Capitol Visitor Center (CVC) is the start for all Capitol tours, and brings a new depth to the Capitol experience with orientation theaters, an interactive museum, and live video feeds from the House and Senate. It also provides weary travelers with welcome creature comforts, including a 530-seat restaurant.

DESIGN

At 580,000 square feet, the visitor center is approximately three-quarters the size of the 775,000-square-foot Capitol. The center's belowground location preserves the historic landscape and views designed by Frederick Law Olmsted in 1874. Inside, skylights provide natural light and views of the majestic Capitol dome. The center opened in December 2008, three years late and $356 million over budget.

EMANCIPATION HALL

The center's largest space is a gorgeous sunlit atrium called Emancipation Hall in honor of the slaves who helped to build the Capitol in the 1800s. The plaster model of the *Freedom* statue, which tops the Capitol's dome, anchors the hall. Part of the Capitol's National Statuary Hall collection is also on display here.

MUSEUM

Other attractions include exhibits about the Capitol, historical artifacts, and documents. A marble wall displays historic speeches and decisions by Congress, like President John F. Kennedy's famous 1961 "Man on the Moon" speech and a letter Thomas Jefferson wrote to Congress in 1803 urging the funding of the Lewis and Clark Expedition.

KIDS AT THE CVC

The Capitol Visitor Center is a great place for families with children who may be too young or too wiggly for a tour of the Capitol. In the Exhibition Hall, the 11-foot tall touchable model of the Capitol, touch screen computers, and architectural replicas welcome hands-on exploration.

Challenge younger kids to find statues of a person carrying a spear, a helmet, a book, and a baby.

Tweens can look for statues of the person who invented television, a king, a physician, and a representative who said, "I cannot vote for war."

PLANNING YOUR CAPITOL DAY

BEAN SOUP AND MORE

A favorite with legislators, the Senate bean soup has been served every day for more than 100 years in the exclusive Senate Dining Room. It's available to the general public in the restaurant of the CVC (⊙ Open 7:30 AM–4 PM) on a rotating basis. You can also try making your own with the recipe on the Senate's Web site (⊕ www.senate.gov).

LOGISTICS

To tour the Capitol, you can book free, advance passes at ⊕ www.visitthecapitol.gov or through your representative's or senator's offices. In addition, a limited number of same-day passes are available at the CVC's Information Desk or at tour kiosks on the east and west fronts of the Capitol. Tours run every 15 minutes; the first tour begins at 8:50 and the last at 3:20, Monday through Saturday. The center is closed on Sunday.

Plan on two to four hours to tour the Capitol and see the visitor center. You should arrive at least 30 minutes before your scheduled tour to allow time to pass through security. Tours, which include a viewing of the orientation film *Out of Many, One*, last about one hour.

If you can't get a pass to tour the Capitol, the Capitol Visitor Center is still worth a visit.

To get passes to the chambers of the House and Senate, contact your representative's or senator's office. Many will also arrange for a staff member to give you a tour of the Capitol or set you up with a time for a Capitol Guide Service tour. When they're in session, some members even have time set aside to meet with constituents. You can link to the e-mail of your representative at ⊕ www.house.gov and of your senators at ⊕ www.senate.gov.

SECURITY

Expect at least a 30-minute wait going through security when you enter the Capitol Visitor Center. Bags can be no larger than 14 inches wide, 13 inches high, and 4 inches deep, and other possessions you can bring into the building are strictly limited. Take a look at the full list of prohibited items on ⊕ www.visitthe-capitol.gov. There are no facilities for storing prohibited belongings before you pass through security, but there is a coat check inside the center. For more information, call ☎ 202/226–8000, 202/224–4049 TTY.

GETTING HERE— WITHOUT GETTING VOTED IN

The Union Station, Capitol South and Federal Center, SW Metro stops are all within walking distance of the Capitol. Follow the people wearing business suits— chances are they're headed your way. Street parking is extremely limited, but Union Station to the north of the Capitol has a public garage and there is some metered street parking along the Mall to the west of the Capitol.

TOURING THE CAPITOL

National Statuary Hall

To see the Capitol you're required to go on a 30- to 40-minute tour conducted by the Capitol Guide Service. The first stop is the Rotunda, followed by the National Statuary Hall, the Hall of Columns, the old Supreme Court Chamber, the crypt (where there are exhibits on the history of the Capitol), and the gift shop. Note that you *don't* see the Senate or House chambers on the tour. (Turn the page to learn about visiting the chambers.) The highlights of the tour are the first two stops. . . .

THE ROTUNDA

You start off here, under the Capitol's dome. Look up and you'll see *Apotheosis of Washington,* a fresco painted in 1865 by Constantino Brumidi. The figures in the inner circle represent the 13 original states; those in the outer ring symbolize arts, sciences, and industry. Further down, around the Rotunda's rim, a frieze depicts 400 years of American history. The work was started by Brumidi in 1877 and continued by another Italian, Filippo Costaggini. American Allyn Cox added the final touches in 1953.

NATIONAL STATUARY HALL

South of the Rotunda is Statuary Hall, which was once the chamber of the House of Representatives. When the House moved out, Congress invited each state to send statues of two great deceased residents for placement in the hall. Because the weight of the statues threatened to make the floor cave in, and to keep the room from being cluttered, more than half of the sculptures have ended up in other spots in the Capitol. Ask your guide for help finding your state's statues.

ARTIST OF THE CAPITOL

Constantino Brumidi (1805-80) devoted his last 25 years to frescoing the Capitol; his work dominates the Rotunda and the Western Corridor. While painting the section depicting William Penn's treaty with the Indians for the Rotunda's frieze *(pictured above),* a 74-year-old Brumidi slipped from the 58-foot scaffold, hanging on until help arrived. He would continue work for another four months, before succumbing to kidney failure.

TRY THIS

Because of Statuary Hall's perfectly elliptical ceiling, a whisper uttered along the wall can be heard at the point directly opposite on the other side of the room. Try it when you're there—if it's not noisy, the trick should work.

ONE BIG HAWAIIAN

With a solid granite base weighing six tons, Hawaii's Kamehameha I in Statuary Hall is among the heaviest objects in the collection. On Kamehameha Day (June 11, a state holiday in Hawai'i), the statue is draped with leis.

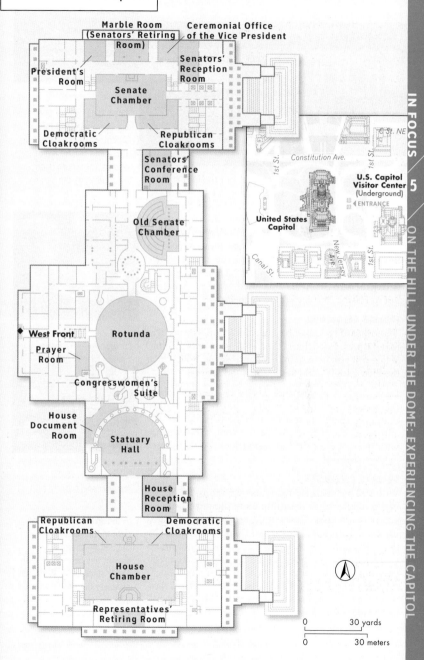

United States Capitol

Marble Room
(Senators' Retiring Room)

Ceremonial Office
of the Vice President

President's Room

Senators' Reception Room

Senate Chamber

Democratic Cloakrooms

Republican Cloakrooms

Senators' Conference Room

Old Senate Chamber

West Front

Rotunda

Prayer Room

Congresswomen's Suite

House Document Room

Statuary Hall

House Reception Room

Republican Cloakrooms

Democratic Cloakrooms

House Chamber

Representatives' Retiring Room

C St. NE

1st St.

Constitution Ave.

1st St.

U.S. Capitol Visitor Center (Underground)

ENTRANCE

United States Capitol

New Jersey Ave.

Canal St.

1st St.

0   30 yards

0   30 meters

GOING TO THE FLOOR

A tour of the Capitol is impressive, but the best part of a visit for many people is witnessing the legislators in action. Free gallery passes into the House and Senate chambers have to be obtained from your representative's or senator's office. They aren't hard to come by, but getting them takes some planning ahead. Once you have a pass, it's good for any time the chambers are open to public, for as long as the current Congress is sitting. Senate chambers are closed when the Senate is not in session, but the House is open.

HOUSE CHAMBER
The larger of two chambers may look familiar: it's here that the president delivers the annual State of the Union. When you visit, you sit in the same balcony from which the First Family and guests watch the address.

Look carefully at the panels above the platform where the Speaker of the House sits. They're blue (rather than green like the rest of the panels in the room), and when the House conducts a vote, they light up with the names of the representatives and their votes in green and red.

SENATE CHAMBER
With 100 members elected to six-year terms, the Senate is the smaller and ostensibly more dignified of Congress's two houses. Desks of the senators are arranged in an arc, with Republicans and Democrats divided by the center aisle. The vice president of the United States is officially the "president of the Senate," charged with presiding over the Senate's procedures. Usually, though, the senior member of the majority party oversees day-to-day operations, and is addressed as "Mr. President" or "Madam President."

Judiciary Committee

House session

SWEET SPOT IN THE SENATE

In the sixth desk from the right in the back row of the Senate chamber, a drawer has been filled with candy since 1968. Whoever occupies the desk maintains the stash.

THE SUPREME COURT

✉ *One 1st St. NE, Capitol Hill*
☎ *202/479–3030* ⊕ *www.supremecourt.gov* 📧 *Free*
🕐 *Weekdays 9–4:30; court in session Oct.–June* Ⓜ *Union Station or Capitol South.*

TIPS

■ The Washington Post carries a daily listing of what cases the court will hear. The court displays its calendar of cases a month in advance on its website; click on "Oral Arguments."

■ You can't bring your overcoat or electronics such as cameras and cell phones into the courtroom, but you can store them in a coin-operated locker.

■ When court isn't in session, you can hear lectures about the court, typically given every hour on the half hour from 9:30 to 3:30.

■ On the ground floor you can also find revolving exhibits, a video about the court, a gift shop, an information desk, and a larger-than-life statue of John Marshall, the longest-serving chief justice in Supreme Court history. Rumor has it that some lawyers visit the statue of John Marshall to rub the toe of his shoe for good luck on their way to arguing before the court.

It wasn't until 1935 that the Supreme Court got its own building: a white-marble temple with twin rows of Corinthian columns designed by Cass Gilbert. Before then, the justices had been moved around to various rooms in the Capitol; for a while they even met in a tavern. William Howard Taft, the only man to serve as both president and chief justice, was instrumental in getting the court a home of its own, though he died before the building was completed. Today you can sit in the gallery and see the court in action. Even when court isn't in session, there are still things to see.

HIGHLIGHTS

The court convenes on the first Monday in October and hears cases until April. There are usually two arguments a day at 10 and 11 in the morning, Monday through Wednesday, in two-week intervals.

On mornings when court is in session, two lines form for people wanting to attend. The "three-to-five-minute" line shuttles you through, giving you a quick impression of the court at work. The full-session line gets you in for the whole show. If you want to see a full session, it's best to be in line by at least 8:30. For the most-contentious cases, viewers have been known to queue up the night before. In May and June the court takes to the bench Monday morning at 10 to release orders and opinions. Sessions usually last 15 to 30 minutes and are open to the public.

How does a hardworking Supreme Court justice unwind? Maybe on the building's basketball court, known as "the highest court in the land." It's not open to the public, but try to imagine Antonin Scalia and Ruth Bader Ginsburg trading elbows in the lane.

5

THE WHITE HOUSE

✉ *1600 Pennsylvania Ave. NW, White House area* ☎ *202/208–1631, 202/456–7041 24-hr info line* ⊕ *www.whitehouse.gov* 🖅 *Free; reservations required* ⊙ *Tours Tues.–Thurs. 7:30–11, Fri. 7:30–12, Sat. 7:30–1* Ⓜ *Federal Triangle, Metro Center, or McPherson Sq.*

TIPS

■ To see the White House you need to contact your representative or senator. Tours are scheduled on a first-come, first-served basis. Requests should be made up to six months in advance (especially during spring and summer) and no less than 21 days in advance. You'll be asked for the names, birth dates, and Social Security numbers of everyone in your group, and you'll be told where to meet and what you can bring.

■ On the morning of your tour, call the White House Visitors Office information line for any updates; tours are subject to last-minute cancellation. Arrive 15 minutes early. Your group will be asked to line up in alphabetical order. Everyone 18 years or older must present government-issued photo ID. Going through security will probably take as long as the tour itself: 20 to 25 minutes.

America's most famous house was designed in 1792 by Irishman James Hoban. It was known officially as the Executive Mansion until 1902, when President Theodore Roosevelt rechristened it the White House, long its informal name. The house has undergone many structural changes: Andrew Jackson installed running water, James Garfield put in the first elevator, and Harry Truman had the entire structure gutted and restored, adding a second-story porch to the south portico.

HIGHLIGHTS

The self-guided tour includes rooms on the ground floor, but the State Floor has the highlights. The East Room is the largest room in the White House, the site of ceremonies and press conferences; this is also where Theodore Roosevelt's children roller-skated and one of Abraham Lincoln's sons harnessed a pet goat to a chair and went for a ride. The portrait of George Washington that Dolley Madison saved from torch-carrying British soldiers in 1814 hangs in the room, and the White House Christmas tree stands here every winter. The only president to get married in the White House, Grover Cleveland, was wed in the Blue Room. The second daughter of President Cleveland and First Lady Frances, Esther, holds the distinction of being the only child born in the White House. The Red Room, decorated in early-19th-century American Empire style, has been a favorite of first ladies. Mary Todd Lincoln had her coffee and read the morning paper here. In 1961, First Lady Jacqueline Kennedy undertook an extensive restoration of the White House to preserve and showcase the historical and architectural significance of the home and its contents. The East Garden, which now bears her name, honors her contributions.

The White House

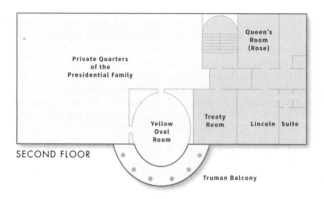

SECOND FLOOR

Queen's Room (Rose)

Private Quarters of the Presidential Family

Yellow Oval Room

Treaty Room

Lincoln | Suite

Truman Balcony

5

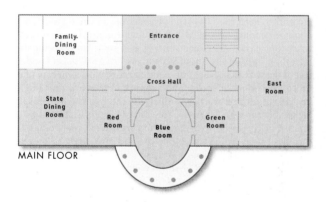

MAIN FLOOR

Family Dining Room

Entrance

Cross Hall

East Room

State Dining Room

Red Room

Blue Room

Green Room

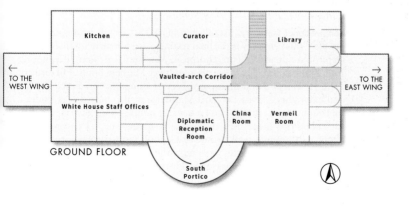

GROUND FLOOR

Kitchen

Curator

Library

← TO THE WEST WING

Vaulted-arch Corridor

→ TO THE EAST WING

White House Staff Offices

Diplomatic Reception Room

China Room

Vermeil Room

South Portico

OTHER GOVERNMENT OFFICES AND INSTITUTIONS

American Red Cross. The national headquarters for the American Red Cross is composed of four buildings. Guided tours show off the oldest, a neoclassical structure of blinding-white marble built in 1917 to commemorate women who cared for the wounded on both sides during the Civil War. Three stained-glass windows designed by Louis Comfort Tiffany illustrate the values of the Red Cross: faith, hope, love, and charity. Other holdings included on the 60-minute tour include an original Norman Rockwell painting, sculptures, and two signature quilts. Weather permitting, the tour includes a visit to the courtyard. ⊠ *430 17th St. NW, White House area* ☎ *202/303–4233* ⊕ *www.redcross.org/museum/history/visitorinfo.asp* ☜ *Free* ◷ *Tours only, Wed. and Fri. 10 and 2* Ⓜ *Farragut West.*

↻ **Bureau of Engraving and Printing.** Paper money has been printed here since 1914, when the bureau relocated from the redbrick-towered Auditors Building at the corner of 14th Street and Independence Avenue. In addition to paper currency, military certificates and presidential invitations are printed here, too. You can only enter the bureau on tours, which last about 40 minutes. From March through August, free same-day timed-entry tour passes are issued starting at 8 am (plan on being in line no later than 7 am) at the Raoul Wallenberg Place SW ticket booth. For the rest of the year, tickets are not required and visitors simply wait in line—up to two hours in spring and summer, longer if a tour bus unloads just as you arrive; waits will likely be short in the off-peak months, September through February. You also can arrange a tour through your senator or representative; these tours are offered year-round, Monday through Friday at 8:15 and 8:45 am and also every 15 minutes from 4 to 4:45 pm, April through August. ⊠ *14th and C Sts. SW, The Mall* ☎ *202/874–2330, 866/874–2330 tour information* ⊕ *moneyfactory.gov/tours/washingtondctours.html* ☜ *Free* ◷ *Sept.–Feb., tours weekdays every 15 minutes 9–10:45 and 12:30–2, visitor center weekdays 8:30–3:30; Mar.–Aug., tours weekdays every 15 minutes 9–7, visitor center weekdays 8:30–7:30.* Ⓜ *Smithsonian.*

Congressional Cemetery. Established in 1807 "for all denomination of people," this cemetery is the final resting place for such notables as U.S. Capitol architect William Thornton, Marine Corps march composer John Philip Sousa, Civil War photographer Mathew Brady, FBI director J. Edgar Hoover, and many members of Congress. Air Force veteran and gay rights activist Leonard Matlovich is also buried here under a tombstone that reads "When I was in the military, they gave me a medal for killing two men and a discharge for loving one." The cemetery is about a 20-minute walk from the Capitol. On Saturdays from April through October, you can join one of the free docent-led tours at 11 or the Civil War–themed tours led by Historian Steve Hammond at 1. You also can take a self-guided tour highlighting everything from the War of 1812 to women of arts and letters; copies of the tours are available at the cemetery gatehouse. Narrated cell-phone tours are available by dialing ☎ *202/747–3474.* ⊠ *1801 E St. SE, Capitol Hill* ☎ *202/543–0539*

⊕ *www.congressionalcemetery.org* ☽ *Daily dawn–dusk; office weekdays 10–2, Sat. 10–1* Ⓜ *Stadium Armory or Potomac Ave.*

Department of Agriculture. Although there's not a lot to see inside, this gargantuan complex does have a one-room visitor center with displays and audio stations that highlight the nation's agricultural policies. ✉ *Independence Ave. between 12th and 14th Sts. SW, The Mall* ☎ *202/720–2791* ⊕ *www.dm.usda.gov/oo/visitorcenter* 💳 *Free* ☽ *Weekdays 9–3* Ⓜ *Smithsonian.*

Department of the Interior. The outside of the building is plain, but inside a wealth of art reflects the department's work. Heroic oil paintings of dam construction, gold panning, and cattle drives line the hallways. Exhibits in the **Department of the Interior Museum** outline the work of the Bureau of Land Management, the U.S. Geological Survey, the Bureau of Indian Affairs, the National Park Service, and other department branches. The museum is currently closed for renovations, and public programs are offered in other parts of the main building once or twice a month. On Tuesdays and Thursdays at 2, you can view more than 75 of the museum's dramatic murals created in the 1940s by photographer Ansel Adams and other artists such as Maynard Dixon and John Steuart Curry. Reservations are required for the Murals Tour; call at least two weeks in advance. The Indian Craft Shop across the hall from the museum sells Native American pottery, dolls, carvings, jewelry, baskets, and books. ✉ *1849 C St. NW, White House area* ☎ *202/208–4743* ⊕ *www.doi.gov/interiormuseum* 💳 *Free* ☽ *Weekdays 8:30–4:30; craft shop also open 3rd Sat. 10–4* Ⓜ *Farragut West.*

Department of State. U.S. foreign policy is administered by battalions of brainy analysts in the huge Department of State building (often referred to as the State Department). All is presided over by the secretary of state, who is fourth in line for the presidency (after the vice president, speaker of the House, and president pro tempore of the Senate). On the top floor are the opulent Diplomatic Reception Rooms, decorated like the great halls of Europe and the rooms of wealthy colonial American plantations. Furnishings include a Philadelphia highboy, a Paul Revere bowl, and the desk on which the Treaty of Paris, which ended the Revolutionary War, was signed in 1783. ■ **TIP→ To visit the reception rooms, register online for a tour three months in advance.** The tours are recommended for visitors 13 and over. ✉ *2201 C St. NW, Foggy Bottom* ☎ *202/647–3241* ⊕ *https://receptiontours.state.gov* 💳 *Free* ☽ *Tours weekdays at 9:30, 10:30, and 2:45* Ⓜ *Foggy Bottom.*

Federal Reserve Building. This imposing marble edifice, its bronze entryway topped by a massive eagle, was designed by Folger Library architect Paul Cret. Its appearance seems to say, "Your money's safe with us." Even so, there's no money here, as the Fed's mission is to set interest rates and keep the economy on track. The stately facade belies a friendlier interior, with a varied collection of art and three special art exhibitions every year. ✉ *20th St. and Constitution Ave. NW, Foggy Bottom* ☎ *202/452–3778 for art exhibition reservations at least 5 days in advance, 202/452–3324 to arrange building tours for groups of 10 or more at least 2 wks in advance* ⊕ *www.federalreserve.gov/finearts* ✉ *Free* ☉ *Weekdays 10–3:30 during art exhibitions* Ⓜ *Foggy Bottom.*

★ **Library of Congress.** The largest library in the world has more than 151 million items on approximately 650 miles of bookshelves. Only 23 million of its holdings are books—the library also has 3 million recordings, 13 million photographs, 5.4 million maps, and 66 million manuscripts. Also here is the Congressional Research Service, which, as the name implies, works on special projects for senators and representatives.

Built in 1897, the copper-domed **Thomas Jefferson Building** is the oldest of the three buildings that make up the library. Like many other structures in Washington, the library was criticized by some as being too florid, but others praised it as the "book palace of the American people," noting that it "out-Europed Europe" in its architectural splendor. The dome, topped with the gilt "Flame of Knowledge," is certainly decorative, with busts of Dante, Goethe, Nathaniel Hawthorne, and other great writers perched above its entryway. The *Court of Neptune*, Roland Hinton Perry's fountain at the base of the front steps, rivals some of Rome's best fountains.

The Jefferson Building opens into the Great Hall, richly adorned with mosaics, paintings, and curving marble stairways. The grand, octagonal Main Reading Room, its central desk surrounded by mahogany readers' tables under a 160-foot-high domed ceiling, inspires researchers and readers alike. Computer terminals have replaced card catalogs, but books are still retrieved and dispersed the same way: readers (16 years or older) hand request slips to librarians and wait patiently for their materials to be delivered. Researchers aren't allowed in the stacks, and only members of Congress and other special borrowers can check books out. Items from the library's collection—which includes one of only three perfect Gutenberg Bibles in the world—are on display in the Jefferson Building's second-floor Southwest Gallery and Pavilion. Information about current and upcoming exhibitions, which can include oral-history projects, presidential papers, photographs, and the like, is available by phone or Web. ■ TIP➔ To even begin to come to grips with the scope and grandeur of the library, one of the free hourly tours is highly recommended. Well-informed docents provide fascinating information about the library's history and holdings; they can decode the dozens of quirky allegorical sculptures and paintings throughout the building.

✉ *Jefferson Bldg., 1st St. and Independence Ave. SE, Capitol Hill* ☎ *202/707–9779* ⊕ *www.loc.gov* 🎟 *Free* ☉ *Mon.–Sat. 8:30–4:30; reading room hrs may extend later. Free tours Mon.–Sat. at 10:30, 11:30, 1:30, and 2:30, and weekdays at 3:30* Ⓜ *Capitol South.*

Pentagon. The headquarters of the United States Department of Defense is the largest low-rise office building in the world. Approximately 24,000 military and civilian workers arrive daily. Astonishingly, the mammoth structure, completed in 1943, took less than two years to construct.

Following the September 2001 crash of hijacked American Airlines Flight 77 into the northwest side of the building, the damaged area was removed in just over a month and repaired in a year. In 2008, the two-acre Pentagon Memorial, with its 184 benches commemorating those lost in the attack, was dedicated. The memorial is open 24 hours a day, Monday through Sunday. Tours of the Pentagon are free and offered Monday though Friday, 9 to 3. Book reservations online through the Pentagon Tour Office or through your congressperson's office at least two weeks, but no more than three months, in advance. ✉ *I–395 at Columbia Pike, and Rte. 27, Suburban Virginia* ☎ *703/697–1776* ⊕ *pentagon.afis.osd.mil* Ⓜ *Pentagon.*

Ronald Reagan Building and International Trade Center. This $818 million, 3.1-million-square-foot colossus is the largest federal building to be constructed in Washington since the Pentagon, and the first to be designed for use by both the government and the private sector. A blend of classical and modern architecture, the Indiana-limestone structure replaced what for 50 years had been an enormous parking lot. The Reagan Building houses the Environmental Protection Agency, the U.S. Customs Service, and the U.S. Agency for International Development. Free guided tours are offered Mondays, Wednesdays, and Fridays at 11. The building has a food court on the lower level, and a theatrical group, the Capitol Steps, performs works of political satire in the Amphitheater on Friday and Saturday nights at 7:30. During the summer months, check out Live!, a free concert series, on Woodrow Wilson Plaza, performed daily from noon to 1:30. A farmers' market, with demonstrations by local chefs, takes over the plaza on Fridays. ✉ *1300 Pennsylvania Ave. NW, Downtown* ☎ *202/312-1300* ⊕ *www.itcdc.com* 🎟 *Free* ☉ *Tours: Mon., Wed., and Fri. at 11* Ⓜ *Federal Triangle.*

Treasury Building. Once used to store currency, this is the largest Greek Revival edifice in Washington. Robert Mills, the architect responsible for the Washington Monument and the Patent Office (now the Smithsonian American Art Museum), designed the grand colonnade that

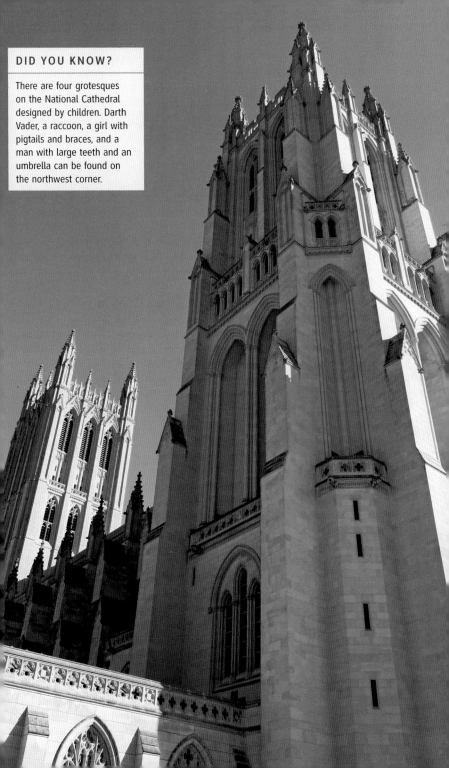

There are four grotesques on the National Cathedral designed by children. Darth Vader, a raccoon, a girl with pigtails and braces, and a man with large teeth and an umbrella can be found on the northwest corner.

stretches down 15th Street. After the death of President Lincoln, the Andrew Johnson Suite was used as the executive office by the new president while Mrs. Lincoln moved out of the White House. Other vestiges of the building's earlier days are the two-story marble Cash Room and the gilded west dome. One-hour

tours arranged through your congressperson are available most Saturdays at 9, 9:45, 10:30, and 11:15; participants must be U.S. citizens or legal residents. ✉ *15th St. and Pennsylvania Ave. NW, White House area* ☎ *202/622–2000* ⊕ *www.treasury.gov/resource-center/faqs* Ⓜ *McPherson Sq. or Metro Center.*

Fodor's Choice ★ **Washington National Cathedral.** Construction of the sixth-largest cathedral in the world began in 1907, and what is officially known as the Cathedral Church of St. Peter and St. Paul was finished and consecrated in 1990. Like its 14th-century Gothic counterparts, the stunning National Cathedral has a nave, flying buttresses, transepts, and vaults that were built stone by stone. The cathedral is Episcopalian, but it's the site of frequent ecumenical and interfaith services. State funerals for Presidents Eisenhower, Reagan, and Ford were held here, and the tomb of Woodrow Wilson, the only president buried in Washington, is on the nave's south side. ■TIP➜ The expansive view of the city from the Pilgrim Observation Gallery is exceptional. You can even enjoy a traditional afternoon English tea in the gallery most Tuesdays and Wednesdays following a one-hour cathedral tour.

The compact, English-style **Bishop's Garden** provides a counterpoint to the cathedral towers with boxwoods, ivy, tea roses, yew trees, and an assortment of arches, bas-reliefs, and stonework from European ruins.

The cathedral's **Flower Mart** is held annually on the first Friday and Saturday in May and is one of Washington's premier festivals. Each year, one Washington embassy is honored and festival goers are treated to the culture, traditions, food, and art of the selected country, though lobster rolls are traditionally on offer on the Friday evening of the festival. This is one of only two times during the year that you can climb the 333 steps to the cathedral's tower.

In 2011, the cathedral sustained earthquake damage. Over the next five years, stone carvers will repair or replace damaged carvings with limestone from the same quarry that supplied material for the building of the cathedral. ✉ *Wisconsin and Massachusetts Aves. NW, Upper Northwest* ☎ *202/537–6200, 202/537–6207 tour information* ⊕ *www.nationalcathedral.org* ◳ *Suggested tour donation $10* ⊙ *Weekdays 10–5:30, Sat. 10–4:30, Sun. 8–4 (8–1 for worship only). Tours: weekdays 10–11:30 and 1–3:30, Sat. 10–11:30 and 12:45–3, Sun. 1–2:30 (tours are every 30 mins). Gardens open daily dawn–dusk* Ⓜ *Cleveland Park or Tenleytown-AU. Take any 30 series bus.*

SEX! POWER! MONEY!

★ ★ ★

SCANDALOUS WASHINGTON

Newt Gingrich's 2012 presidential bid ended with disclosures that he had had an affair with his now-third wife, Callista (pictured with him above), while still married to his second, plus the "Tiffanygate" shadow cast by his $500,000 loan from the jeweler.

Every "gotcha!" headline since President Nixon's burglars at the Watergate has been affixed with a "-gate," but Washington's memory of kickbacks, sleaze, and dirty deeds goes back centuries further. Before there was Monica, there was Marilyn; before Marilyn, there was Carrie and Peggy and Nan. Most people are familiar with Whitewater, but what of the Star Route and Teapot Dome? The history of the United States is thick with plots, scams, and bad behavior. Herewith, selections from Washington's long and democratic history of scandal.

SEX!

Petticoat Tales

Margaret "Peggy" Eaton

Fanne Fox

Ooh la la, whispered Washington's society matrons, when President Andrew Jackson's war secretary John Henry Eaton fell for Margaret "Peggy" Timberlake, a young widow he had known for years. Pretty, charming Peggy had a fast reputation for 1829, and soon rumors flew about the circumstances of her husband's death, the paternity of her two children, and Eaton. It was all idle gossip—until Eaton married her, after which the other Cabinet wives shunned her, and the social stir of insult and offense all but shut down business at the White House for *two years.* In 1831, the Cabinet resigned en masse and Jackson was finally able to get some work done. As for Peggy? After Eaton's death, she sparked another scandal, by marrying her granddaughter's 19-year-old dance instructor. *(Location: Peggy Eaton is buried in Oak Hill Cemetery, 3001 R St. NW)*

Naked Ambition

In 1974, Wilbur Mills spent his days chairing the House Ways and Means Committee—and his nights with a stripper known as "Fanne Fox, the Argentine Firecracker." A typical Capitol romance, until his car was stopped one night by police, and his lady friend leapt from the car and into the Tidal Basin, leaving a drunken Mills to his fate. Surprisingly, Mills' political career survived—until he appeared later that year, drunk, onstage with Fox at a Boston burlesque. *(Location: Tidal Basin)*

Hail to the Cheat

Warren Harding

President Bill Clinton was hardly the first and likely not the worst of the White House philanderers. That dubious honor may go to President Warren Harding, a legendary Lothario who is purported to have carried on with paramours Carrie Phillips and Nan Britton (among others) in some unlikely places, including a White House closet. (When his wife Florence came by, a Secret Service agent warned him with a discreet knock on the door.) Relative propriety in the 1920's press meant that any blue dresses remained unreported, but Harding may have left behind a more incriminating piece of evidence—an illegitimate daughter, Elizabeth Ann. *(Location: White House)*

POWER!

Former CIA officer Valerie Plame

Reporters Bob Woodward, left, and Carl Bernstein, whose reporting of the Watergate scandal won them a Pulitzer Prize, sit in the newsroom of the *Washington Post* on May 7, 1973.

He Really Bugs Me

The Big Kahuna of Washington scandals had humble beginnings, in the discovery of a taped-open door at the Watergate Hotel one night in June of 1972. The door led to burglars, on a mission to bug the Democratic National Committee, and the burglars led through the Republican party machine straight to the White House and President Richard "Tricky Dick" Nixon. Two young reporters, Bob Woodward and Carl Bernstein, uncovered the most impossible-seeming story of the century, and their secret meetings with anonymous leaker "Deep Throat" (W. Mark Felt) are the stuff of legend. One of many fond memories of the moment when Washington lost America's trust: Nixon's immortal, and untruthful, declaration, "I am not a crook." *(Location: Watergate Hotel, Virginia Ave., near 27th St. NW)*

I Spy . . .

When Valerie Plame had her CIA cover blown in 2003 by a syndicated columnist, Washington's shady nexus of journalists, politicians, and sneaky leaks was, too. Vice President Dick Cheney's chief aide, Lewis "Scooter" Libby, was convicted, but only of lying to investigators. We may never know why Plame was targeted—perhaps because of her husband's criticism of the Bush Administration over the Iraq war. Plame chronicled her story in a 2007 book, which was dramatized in a 2010 movie called *Fair Game.*

From Ronald with Love

OLIVER L NORTH
DOB 10 7 43

Oliver North

Two wrongs *can* make a right: a right-wing guerilla organization, that is. President Ronald Reagan likened Nicaragua's Contras to the Founding Fathers. Too bad funding the insurgent group was illegal. So was a secret deal the White House made to sell arms to Iran. When it was discovered in 1986 that the cash from Iran had been funneled to the Contras, the Gipper had some explaining to do. Luckily for him, National Security Council aide Oliver North had a shredder, and he wasn't afraid to use it. North's secretary, Fawn Hall, took care of the rest by smuggling out remaining suspect documents in her boots and skirt. *(Location: Old Executive Office Building, 17th & F Streets NW)*

MONEY!

Teapot Dome scandal cartoon by Clifford Kennedy Berryman

William Adams Richardson

A Cozy Deal

It may seem old hat today—access to public resources awarded in a no-bid contract to cronies of someone in the president's inner circle—but in 1922 it was front-page news. Interior Secretary Albert Fall had authority over the Teapot Dome strategic oil reserve transferred from the Department of the Navy to Interior, and once he was in charge, he leased the land to Mammoth Oil. The deal was technically legal—what *wasn't* was the $404,000 kickback he got for arranging it. Fall nearly succeeded in keeping his stake quiet, until he raised suspicions by having the office of the lead Senate investigator ransacked. *(Location: Department of Interior, 1849 C St. NW)*

Secretary of Shame

In 1872, the House of Representatives was so determined to remove War Secretary William Belknap that it voted to impeach him, even after he had already resigned. The high-living general was caught having awarded a lucrative military trading post appointment in exchange for kickbacks; the quarterly bribes he took came to ten times his official salary. The House's venom waxed poetic: legislators voted unanimously that the Secretary was "basely prostituting his high office to his lust for private gain." Belknap resigned in disgrace—and tears—and committed suicide in 1890. *(Location: House of Representatives)*

Taxman to Axman

When Treasury Secretary William Richardson hired contractor-cum-bounty hunter John Sanborn in 1872 to help the IRS collect taxes, the idea was simple. Sanborn chased down tax cheats, and was allowed to keep half of the take for his trouble. But when he ran out of tax evaders and went after honest companies, Richardson turned a blind eye—in exchange for his own cut.

The Sheik of Bribery

If Middle Eastern "businessmen" looking suspiciously like FBI agents offered *you* cash for favors, you might smell a rat—particularly if their business cards read "Abdul Enterprises." But in 1978, seven legislators gave just such men the benefit of the doubt, and had their trusting natures (and brazen avarice) rewarded with bribery convictions. Hint: Next time, guys, check the shiny shoes.

Where to Eat

WORD OF MOUTH

"We went to Hank's Oyster Bar and Grill for fried oyster dinner . . . Oh boy, this was delicious! I am not usually a fan of fried food, but the oysters were so plump and perfectly cooked, they were divine."

—LBloom

Updated by
Elana Schor

As host to visitors and transplants from around the world, Washington benefits from the constant infusion of different cultures. Despite D.C.'s lack of true ethnic neighborhoods and the kinds of restaurant districts found in many other cities, you *can* find almost any cuisine here, from Burmese to Ethiopian. Just follow your nose.

Although most neighborhoods lack a unified culinary flavor, make no mistake: D.C. is a city of distinctive areas, each with its own style. Adams Morgan, for example, is known for its small family-run eateries. You'll find Ethiopian restaurants next to Italian trattorias and French bistros. These small ethnic spots open and close frequently; it's worth taking a stroll down the street to see what's new. The Chinatown area is often disparaged by D.C. natives for lacking the authenticity of New York's or San Francisco's, but although its Asian kitchens are outdone by those in the less accessible Virginia suburbs, its Latin American and Middle Eastern food more than bridges the gap.

Downtown, you'll find many of the city's blue-chip law firms and deluxe, expense-account restaurants, as well as stylish lounges, microbrew pubs, and upscale eateries that have sprung up to serve the crowds that attend games at the Verizon Center.

Wherever you venture forth in the city, there are a few trends worth noting: Spanish tapas eateries and other restaurants serving small tasting portions are bigger than ever. You'll find this style of eating pervasive, whether you're at a Greek, Asian, or American restaurant. High-end restaurants in town also have begun to add bar menus with smaller plates that are much less expensive than their entrées, but created with the same finesse.

Though Italian, French, and fusion spots continue to open at a ferocious pace, Washingtonians are always hungry to try something new, whether it's Chinese smoked lobster, fiery Indian curry, or crunchily addictive Vietnamese spring rolls.

PLANNING

EATING OUT STRATEGY

Where should we eat? With hundreds of D.C. eateries competing for your attention, it may seem like a daunting question. But fret not—our expert writers and editors have done most of the legwork. The 100-plus selections here represent the best this city has to offer—from hot dogs to haute cuisine. Search "Best Bets" for top recommendations by price, cuisine, and experience. Sample local flavor in the neighborhood features. Or find a review quickly in the alphabetical-by-neighborhood listings. Delve in, and enjoy!

RESERVATIONS

Plan ahead if you're determined to snag a sought-after reservation. Some renowned restaurants are booked weeks in advance. But you can get lucky at the last minute if you're flexible—and friendly. Most restaurants keep a few tables open for walk-ins and VIPs. Show up for dinner early (5:30 pm) or late (after 10 pm) and politely inquire about any last-minute vacancies or cancellations. If you're calling a few days ahead of time, ask if you can be put on a waiting list. Occasionally, an eatery may ask you to call the day before your scheduled meal to reconfirm: don't forget, or you could lose out.

HOURS

Washington has less of an around-the-clock mentality than other big cities, with many big-name restaurants shutting down between lunch and dinner and closing their kitchens by 11 pm. Weekend evenings spent Downtown can also be a hassle for those seeking quick bites, because many popular chain eateries cater to office workers and shut down on Friday at 6 pm. For a midnight supper, the best bets are Dupont Circle and the U Street Corridor, while families looking for late lunches should head north from the Mall to find kitchens that stay open between mealtimes.

WHAT TO WEAR

As unfair as it seems, the way you look can influence how you're treated—and where you're seated. Generally speaking, jeans and a button-down shirt will suffice at most table-service restaurants in the $–$$ range. Moving up from there, some pricier restaurants require jackets, and some insist on ties. In reviews, we mention dress only where men are required to wear a jacket or a jacket and tie. But even when there's no formal dress code, we recommend wearing jackets and ties in $$$ and $$$$ restaurants. If you have doubts, call the restaurant and ask.

PRICES

If you're watching your budget, be sure to ask the price of daily specials recited by the waiter or captain. The charge for specials at some restaurants is noticeably out of line with the other prices on the menu. Beware of the $10 bottle of water; ask for tap water instead. And always review your bill.

If you eat early or late you may be able to take advantage of a prix-fixe deal not offered at peak hours. Most upscale restaurants offer great lunch deals with special menus at cut-rate prices designed to give customers a true taste of the place.

UPPER NORTHWEST
casual neighborhood joints

ADAMS MORGAN AND U STREET CORRIDOR
ethnic eats and quirky bars

GEORGETOWN
mix of white-tablecloth and no-tablecloth eateries

DUPONT CIRCLE
upscale, stylish restaurants with lively bar scene

CHINATOWN
tapas-style restaurants with eclectic cuisine

FOGGY BOTTOM
cheap cafés popular with students

DOWNTOWN
revitalized arts district with upscale eateries

CAPITOL HILL
pub grub and cafés aplenty for harried staffers

Sheridan Circle

Columbia Rd.

Florida Ave.

16th St.

New Hampshire Ave.

Yermont Ave.

Florida Ave.

Massachusetts Ave.

Dupont Circle

Rhode Island Ave.

Logan Circle

Scott Circle

Thomas Circle

Rock Creek

M St.

Connecticut Ave.

M St.

Whitehurst Fwy.

Washington Circle

K St.

15th St.

14th St.

New York Ave.

Pennsylvania Ave.

23rd St.

Theodore Roosevelt Island

Virginia Ave.

Constitution Ave.

THE MALL

Reflecting Pool

Independence Ave.

THE MONUMENTS

Arlington Memorial Br.

Columbia Island

Tidal Basin

CAPITOL HILL

Potomac River

Francis Case Memorial Br.

Washington Canal

VIRGINIA

| 0 | 500 yards |
| 0 | 500 meters |

Credit cards are widely accepted, but many restaurants (particularly smaller ones Downtown) accept only cash. If you plan to use a credit card, it's a good idea to double-check its acceptability when making reservations or before sitting down to eat.

Prices in the reviews are the average cost of a main course at dinner or, if dinner is not served, at lunch.

TIPPING AND TAXES

In most restaurants, tip the waiter 16%–20%. (To figure the amount quickly, just double the sales tax noted on the check—it's 10% of your bill.) Tip at least $1 per drink at the bar and $1 for each coat checked. Never tip the maître d' unless you're out to impress your guests or expect to pay another visit soon.

If you're dining with a group, make sure not to overtip: review your check to see if a gratuity has been added, as many restaurants automatically tack on an 18% tip for groups of six or more.

DINING WITH KIDS

Though it's unusual to see children in the dining rooms of D.C.'s most elite restaurants, eating with youngsters in the nation's capital does not have to mean culinary exile. Many of the restaurants reviewed here are excellent choices for families and are marked with a ☾ symbol.

SMOKING

Smoking is banned in all restaurants and bars, with the exception of a few spaces that have enclosed and ventilated rooms—usually for cigar aficionados.

USING THE MAPS

Throughout the chapter, you'll see mapping symbols and coordinates (⊕ 3:F2) after property names or reviews. To locate the property on a map, turn to the Washington, D.C. Dining and Lodging Atlas at the end of this chapter. The first number after the ⊕ symbol indicates the map number. Following that is the property's coordinate on the map grid.

6

BEST BETS FOR WASHINGTON, D.C., DINING

With thousands of restaurants to choose from, how will you decide where to eat? Fodor's writers and editors have selected their favorite restaurants by price, cuisine, and experience in the lists here. You can also search by neighborhood for excellent eating experiences—just peruse the following pages. Or find specific details about a restaurant in the full reviews, which are listed alphabetically by neighborhood later in the chapter.

Fodor's Choice ★

2941 Restaurant, $$$, p. 221
Blue Duck Tavern, $$, p. 196
Central Michel Richard, $$, p. 203
Citronelle, $$$$, p. 212
Hank's Oyster Bar, $$, p. 213
Inn at Little Washington, $$$$, p. 221
Komi, $$$$, p. 214
Nora, $$$$, p. 214
Palena, $$$$, p. 220
Rasika, $$, p. 210
Ray's Hell Burger, $, p. 222
Sweetgreen, $, p. 215
Zaytinya, $$, p. 210

Best By Price

$

Ben's Chili Bowl, p. 217
Etete, p. 218

Good Stuff Eatery, p. 199
Ray's Hell Burger, p. 222
Rocklands, p. 213
Sweetgreen, p. 215
Teaism, p. 206
Bistrot du Coin, p. 213
Granville Moore's Brickyard, p. 199
Kushi, p. 209

$$

Blue Duck Tavern, p. 196
Central Michel Richard, p. 203
Estadio, p. 216
Hank's Oyster Bar, p. 213
Jaleo, p. 209
Matchbox, p. 209
Zaytinya, p. 210

$$$

2941 Restaurant, p. 221

Art and Soul, p. 197

$$$$

1789 Restaurant, p. 211
Charlie Palmer Steak, p. 198
Citronelle, p. 212
CityZen, p. 204
Inn at Little Washington, p. 221
Komi, p. 214
Nora, p. 214
Obelisk, p. 215
Palena, p. 220

Best By Cuisine

AFRICAN

Etete, $, p. 218
Ethiopic, $, p. 198

AMERICAN

2941 Restaurant, $$$, p. 221
Blue Duck Tavern, $$, p. 196

Cashion's Eat Place, $$$, p. 217
Inn at Little Washington, $$$$, p. 221
Ted's Bulletin, $, p. 201

ASIAN (VARIOUS)

Full Kee, $, p. 208
Kushi, $, p. 209
Teaism, $, p. 206

BELGIAN

Belga Café, $$, p. 197
Brasserie Beck, $$$, p. 201
Granville Moore's Brickyard, $, p. 199
Marcel's, $$$$, p. 197

ECLECTIC

Ardeo, $$, p. 219
Komi, $$$$, p. 214
Palena, $$$$, p. 220

FRENCH

Bistro Bis, $$$, p. 198
Bistro Français, $$, p. 211
Central Michel Richard, $$, p. 203

GREEK/TURKISH

Cava, $$, p. 198
Zaytinya, $$, p. 210

INDIAN

Heritage India, $, p. 220
Rasika, $$, p. 210

ITALIAN

Bibiana Osteria and Enoteca, $$, p. 201

Cafe Milano, $$$$, p. 212

Obelisk, $$$$, p. 215

Posto, $$$, p. 217

JAPANESE

Kaz Sushi Bistro, $$$, p. 205

Kushi, $, p. 209

Sushi-Ko, $$, p. 213

LATIN AMERICAN

Ceiba, $$, p. 203

Cuba Libre, $$$, p. 208

PIZZA

2 Amys, $, p. 219

Matchbox, $$, p. 209

Pizzeria Paradiso, $, p. 215

Seventh Hill, $, p. 200

SEAFOOD

Black Salt, $$$, p. 220

Hank's Oyster Bar, $$, p. 213

Johnny's Half Shell, $$$, p. 199

Kinkead's, $$$, p. 196

Pearl Dive Oyster Palace, $$, p. 219

SOUTHERN

Georgia Brown's, $$, p. 204

Hill Country, $$, p. 208

Oohhs & Aahhs, $, p. 218

Zola, $$$, p. 211

SPANISH

Estadio, $$, p. 216

Jaleo, $$, p. 209

Taberna del Alabardero, $$$, p. 206

STEAK

Cafe Milano, $$$$, p. 212

The Capital Grille, $$$$, p. 203

Charlie Palmer Steak, $$$$, p. 198

The Palm, $$$$, p. 215

Best By Experience

BEST BRUNCH

Belga Café, $$, p. 197

Birch & Barley, $$, p. 216

Black Salt, $$$, p. 220

Georgia Brown's, $$, p. 204

BEST FOR BUSINESS

The Capital Grille, $$$$, p. 203

Charlie Palmer Steak, $$$$, p. 198

The Palm, $$$$, p. 215

BEST HOTEL DINING

Blue Duck Tavern, $$, p. 196

Citronelle, $$$$, p. 212

CityZen, $$$$, p. 204

Poste, $$$, p. 209

BEST POLITICO-WATCHING

Cafe Milano, $$$$, p. 212

Charlie Palmer Steak, $$$$, p. 198

Posto, $$$, p. 217

BEST WITH KIDS

Ben's Chili Bowl, $, p. 217

Five Guys, $, p. 212

Good Stuff Eatery, $, p. 199

Kramerbooks & Afterwords, $$, p. 214

The Market Lunch, $, p. 200

Rocklands, $, p. 213

CAPITAL CLASSICS

1789 Restaurant, $$$$, p. 211

Ben's Chili Bowl, $, p. 217

Occidental Grill, $$$$, p. 205

GOOD FOR GROUPS

Heritage India, $, p. 220

Hill Country, $$, p. 208

Zaytinya, $$, p. 210

GREAT VIEWS

2941 Restaurant, $$$, p. 221

Charlie Palmer Steak, $$$$, p. 198

MOST ROMANTIC

1905, $$, p. 217

Birch & Barley, $$, p. 216

Ethiopic, $, p. 198

Komi, $$$$, p. 214

PRETHEATER

Jaleo, $$, p. 209

Rasika, $$, p. 210

QUIET MEAL

Equinox, $$$, p. 204

Obelisk, $$$$, p. 215

Palena, $$$$, p. 220

Taberna del Alabardero, $$$, p. 206

SPECIAL OCCASION

2941 Restaurant, $$$, p. 221

Citronelle, $$$$, p. 212

CityZen, $$$$, p. 204

TRENDY

Marvin, $$, p. 218

Rasika, $$, p. 210

Westend Bistro by Eric Ripert, $$$, p. 197

Zaytinya, $$, p. 210

WINE BARS

Bistrot Lepic, $$, p. 219

Sonoma, $$, p. 200

Vidalia, $$$, p. 216

6

CAPITOL HILL AND NORTHEAST D.C.

"The Hill," as locals know it, was once an enclave of congressional boardinghouses in the shadow of the Capitol building, but is now D.C.'s largest historic district, with an eclectic mix of restaurants.

The neighborhood's central location has kept it an integral and thriving part of D.C. from the beginning. With the House, Senate, Supreme Court, Library of Congress, and other offices nearby, government is a constant presence.

Around the Capitol South Metro station, government offices end and neighborhood dining begins. Here, along tree-lined streets, you'll find neighborhood bars and restaurants that cater to lunch and happy-hour crowds during the week and local residents on weekends.

Neighborhood establishments and all-American pubs line historic Barracks Row (⊠ *8th St. SE*), with Eastern Market anchoring the homey House side of the Hill; the Senate end is given a more hustle-and-bustle vibe with the chain dining of Union Station.

WORLD FLAVOR

Travel to one of Barracks Row's restaurants with international flair: **Belga Café** (⊠ *514 8th St. SE ✛ 2:H6*), with 84 Belgian beer varieties is "the godfather of beer," says executive chef Bart Vandaele. Pair yours with smoked foie gras or shrimp-stuffed tomatoes. Upstairs, **Banana Café** (⊠ *3500 8th St. SE ✛ 2:H6*) is a rousing piano bar; downstairs it's a Cuban restaurant. The **Starfish Café** (⊠ *539 8th St. SE ✛ 2:H6*) combines Creole and Caribbean cuisines, with selections like seviche and crab cakes, while **Tortilla Café** (⊠ *210 7th St. SE ✛ 2:H6*) specializes in Salvadorean tamales known as *pupusas*.

CAPITOL HILL HOTSPOTS

NONPARTISAN PUBS

Escape politics as usual at these bars and eateries favored by lobbyists, senators, and congressional representatives.

Tune Inn (⊠ *331 Pennsylvania Ave. SE ✛ 2:H5*) is Capitol Hill's last remaining dive bar. Here "you can plop down on a bar stool and be next to absolutely anybody," according to owner Lysa Nardelli. That "anybody" could be a senator or a congressional intern. The bar has a taxidermy theme, with stuffed deer heads decorating the walls. Stuffed deer backsides mark the location of restrooms.

The nearby **Pour House** (⊠ *319 Pennsylvania Ave. SE ✛ 2:H5*) is a local favorite of young congressional aides who crowd its wood-paneled walls to watch sports and unwind after a long day of political combat. The menu is predictable—think cheesy spinach dip and spicy buffalo wings—but the vibe is universally comforting and the "Top of the Hill" rooftop lounge offers plenty of room to shoot pool.

The Monocle (⊠ *107 D St. NE ✛ 2:G3*) has been serving up "tablecloth" dining to senators and staff since 1960. The restaurant's location, a quick dash from the Senate office at the Capitol, gives it an insider-y feel. Head to the bar for jumbo salads, roasted oysters, and fried calamari.

H IS FOR HIPSTER

Follow H Street away from the Capitol and you'll find the new Atlas District, where eclectic bars bring out politicos in heels and kids in sneakers. Live music complements the Creole bordello vibe at the **Red Palace** (⊠ *1212 H St. NE ✛ 2:H2*), where you can wash down a gut-busting "burporken" sandwich of beef, pork, and chicken with local brews, while the **Pug** (⊠ *1234 H St. NE ✛ 2:H2*) offers $3 beers all day long and hipster-cool games like Rock-'em Sock-'em Robots. Elsewhere, **Taylor Gourmet** (⊠ *1116 H St. NE ✛ 2:H2*) keeps the neighborhood satisfied with its belly-busting sub sandwiches, stuffed with house-roasted meats and sharp provolone.

HAUTE CONGRESS

Since America's founding, the Capitol has been ruled by tradition: everyone sits in assigned seats, speaks according to seniority, and expects indigestion from the congressional cafeterias. But that last custom became a thing of the past in 2007, when the dining spots in the House of Representatives received a classy makeover courtesy of the Manhattan catering firm Restaurant Associates. The day-old pizza was replaced with fresh grilled fish and build-your-own tacos; the limp iceberg lettuce replaced with arugula, snap peas, and hand-tossed *panzanella* (bread and tomato) salad. Any visitor to the Capitol can feast at the renovated cafeterias alongside legislators and their aides, though operating hours can vary depending on the day. The posh remodeling at the Senate's three cafés added a fresh gelato station and popcorn stand—but history buffs can rest assured the bean soup that has been a menu staple since 1901 is still available.

6

DOWNTOWN, CHINATOWN, AND WHITE HOUSE AREA

Don't let the staid steak houses and saloons fool you—the capital power brokers who dine Downtown also have a taste for the quirky and fun. The area is experiencing a boom of high-concept openings.

At the popular Latin restaurant Ceiba, *above*, fans rave about the seviche and caipirinhas.

Until recently, tourists who trekked north from the Mall hungry for something more than Smithsonian cafeteria food were stranded Downtown with little but high-end options. Now young Washingtonians are taking advantage of residential development and moving off Capitol Hill to Downtown, pulling trendy and affordable dining choices up north.

Chinatown and nearby Penn Quarter are the nerve center of the area, thanks to the Verizon Center and a row of popular clothing stores, but the crowds mean an inevitable wait for tables.

If you're in the mood to splurge without feeling like a stuffed shirt, perennials like **Oceanaire Seafood Room** (⊠ *1201 F St. NW* ✛ *2:C3*) and **Ceiba** (⊠ *701 14th St. NW* ✛ *2:B3*) have a more relaxed vibe on weekends.

MARKET SHARE

The nation's capital may be an urban jungle, but its farmers' markets are rightly revered for offering an oasis of fresh food from northern Virginia. Penn Quarter's outdoor bazaar takes over 8th Street NW between D and E streets every Thursday from 3 pm to 7 pm between April and November, transporting shoppers into the country-side with grape tomatoes from Endless Summer Harvest, and goat cheese from Blue Ridge Dairy.

D.C. FOODIES ARE BUZZING ABOUT . . .

FRESH FOOD FINDS

The **Passenger** (✉ *1021 7th Street NW* ✛ *2:D1*) is home to our favorite mixologists on the Eastern seaboard, who can turn even the most bizarre cocktail requests ("a drink like springtime" and "something set on fire" were recently overheard) into magic in a glass. Their kimchi hot dog makes a perfect accompaniment.

Visitors to the Senate side of the capital who are seeking a quick bite should not miss **Toscana Cafe** (✉ *601 2nd St. NE* ✛ *2: H3*), where the sunny outdoor patio complements the sumptuous sandwiches.

STARS OF THE KITCHEN

Meet three of Downtown Washington's best, and enjoy their most special dishes.

Jose Andres. Since he began serving up tapas from **Jaleo** (✉ *480 7th St. NW* ✛ *2:D3*) kitchen in 1993, Andres has become a capital legend. The biggest of his many talents: enticing skeptical Americans to embrace the octopus, a favorite of his native Spain. It never misses.

Alain Ducasse. The youngest chef in history to win three Michelin stars, this debonair Frenchman has chosen a worthy partner in the St. Regis hotel company. Ducasse's unifying theme at the new **Adour** (✉ *923 16th St. NW* ✛ *1:G6*) is "cuisine designed with wine in mind"—but with a $370 Osetra caviar on the menu, drama is also the order of the day.

Laurent Tourondel. This wizard of the grill charged south from Manhattan for his latest outpost of the lavish **BLT Steak** (✉ *1625 I St. NW* ✛ *2:A2*), where the free baskets of warm Gruyère-cheese popovers are so wildly in demand that you can now take a copy of the recipe home.

FOOD CHAIN

Most visitors to D.C. pack their days with as many events as possible, often leaving little time for an exciting new food experience. But even quick bites can become adventurous for those who know when to pass up McDonald's in favor of a quirky local chain. The capital's three best homegrown franchises have convenient Downtown locations. **Firehook Bakery** (✉ *912 17th St. NW* ✛ *2:A2* ✉ *555 13th St. NW* ✛ *2:B3*) is known for its cold salads, such as lemon orzo and curried chicken, and decadent cookies—try the Presidential Sweet, made with dried cherries. **Marvelous Market** (✉ *1800 K St. NW* ✛ *1:F6*) serves everything from pesto lasagna to a ham, Brie, and cornichon sandwich that would be right at home in Paris. **Wasabi** (✉ *908 17th St. NW* ✛ *1:G6*) is a sushi shop with kicky mod interior that wraps its tuna rolls in takeout-friendly cellophane. Raw-fish skeptics can choose chicken soup with udon noodles or teriyaki salmon.

6

GEORGETOWN

Georgetown's picturesque Victorian streetscapes make it D.C.'s most famous neighborhood, with five-star restaurants in historic row houses and casual cafés sandwiched between large national chain stores.

At its beginnings in the mid-1700s, Georgetown was a Maryland tobacco port. Today the neighborhood is D.C.'s premier shopping district, as well as a tourist and architectural attraction. The neighborhood's restaurants range from upscale Italian to down-home barbecue. Residents' resistance to opening a Metro station in the area was once a touchy subject, but more frequent bus service on the DC Circulator from Dupont Circle has eased any sense of cultural xenophobia among the well-heeled locals.

Georgetown's main thoroughfares, M Street NW and Wisconsin Avenue NW, are always bustling with university students, professionals, and tourists. On a given day you may encounter political activists on the sidewalks, wedding parties posing for photos, and gossiping teens laden with shopping bags.

SWEET SPOT

Chocoholics go ga-ga for **Leonidas Fresh Belgian Chocolates** (✉ *1531 Wisconsin Ave. NW* ✛ *1:A4*), which imports 80 varieties of chocolates from Belgium, including its popular champagne truffle. For a cool treat, stop at **Thomas Sweet Ice Cream** (✉ *3214 P St. NW* ✛ *1:B4*). Before committing to a flavor, sample our favorites: tiramisu and coconut. Replacing **CakeLove** as the city's best sugar rush is **Georgetown Cupcake** (✉ *3301 M St. NW* ✛ *1:A5*), where two stylish sisters dish out palm-size euphoria made with Madagascar vanilla and Valhrona chocolate.

NEIGHBORHOOD FAVES

ELEGANT, COUNTRY INN:
The **1789 Restaurant** (✉ *1226 36th St. NW* ✛ *1:A5*), jacket required, is housed in a Federal building off M Street, serving American classics. Each of the restaurant's five dining rooms offers a different historical experience, from the John Carroll Room, displaying early maps of the city, to the Civil War–inspired Manassas Room.

ASIAN TEAHOUSE:
Ching Ching Cha (✉ *1063 Wisconsin Ave. NW* ✛ *1:B5*) offers 70 types of Chinese and Japanese teas, using traditional tea ware and serving techniques. Recline on thick pillows with a pot of orchid-scented Snow Dragon tea, nibbling on steamed dumplings and traditional Chinese desserts.

BUSTLING TRATTORIA:
Papa Razzi (✉ *1066 Wisconsin Ave. NW* ✛ *1:B5*), a perennial crowd-pleaser, is in the oldest standing firehouse in D.C. Fans rave about the thin-crust, wood-fired pizzas and the award-winning "Cesare" salad.

RIVERFRONT DINING

Dining along the Potomac River offers fresh seafood and a stunning view of D.C. From any restaurant along the riverfront boardwalk, you can see the Kennedy Center, Roosevelt Island, and the Key Bridge. **Nick's Riverside Grille** (✉ *3050 K St. NW* ✛ *1:B6*) makes a mean oyster po'boy sandwich for lunch, and specializes in grilled seafood at dinner. Farther down the boardwalk at **Tony and Joe's Seafood Place** (✉ *3000 K St. NW, Suite 10* ✛ *1:B6*), don't miss the Sunday Champagne Brunch with a live jazz band. Watch the sunset while enjoying a glass of wine at **Sequoia** (✉ *3000 K St. NW, Suite 100* ✛ *1:B6*), an upscale restaurant favored by high-ranking politicians. The Asian-accented American menu features standouts like duck-and-pine-nut dumplings.

FRUGAL FOODIE

Frugal foodies enviously eyeing Washington's finest kitchens may be surprised to find affordable alternatives in Georgetown. If you've been priced out of the $28 seafood at **Black Salt**, try the casual and beachy **Tackle Box** (✉ *3245 M St. NW* ✛ *1:B5*), where delicate bluefish with pesto and grilled corn on the cob cost less than half the price.

If you're hankering for the delectable Middle Eastern fare of **Zaytinya**, go for **Quick Pita** (✉ *1210 Potomac St. NW* ✛ *1:A5*), where the unstylish name belies a top-flight tabbouli salad and succulent grilled meats for less than $10 per meal.

The golden charms of **Brasserie Beck's** high-class beer menu are mirrored at **Birreria Paradiso** (✉ *3282 M St. NW* ✛ *1:A5*), a den of Belgian brews casually hidden beneath a neighborhood pizzeria.

6

DUPONT CIRCLE AND FOGGY BOTTOM

A mixture of funky and formal, Dupont Circle and Foggy Bottom represent the progressive and the historic sides of Washington. But in the true sense of bipartisanship, dining options are as diverse as this town's political leanings.

Stop into Teaism, a café and retail shrine to tea, located in a converted town house, for more than 50 varieties of loose-leaf teas. Tea-friendly sweets and snacks are also available.

Dupont Circle defies the staid, conservative reputation of Washington, turning D.C. Technicolor in the evening hours. The high-rent, liberal-minded neighborhood has hip art galleries, bookstores, and yoga studios that draw a mix of yuppies and activists. There's no shortage of flamboyant characters and political rallies in this always-bustling enclave. If possible, make reservations for sit-down meals, and expect crowds, especially on weekends.

The history-steeped Foggy Bottom area boasts architectural landmarks like the Watergate Hotel. Around George Washington University there's cheaper, college-friendly fare like burrito joints and coffee shops. Nearby, the Kennedy Center draws a more mature crowd with tastes that have evolved past ramen noodles and nachos.

TASTY TIDBITS

The capital's reigning carbohydrate kings hold court on weekdays at **Bread Line** (✉ 1751 Pennsylvania Ave. NW ⊹ 1:F6), where the fresh sourdough baguettes are irresistibly fluffy and the baked goods fit for Marie Antoinette. The indoor eating area is large but no-frills, so most locals order takeout and make a picnic with their couscous, spicy lamb flatbreads, and chocolate-mascarpone Oreos.

LUNCH LIKE A LOCAL

Take a break from the memorials and take in another kind of sightseeing: people-watching. See Washingtonians cavorting in their natural habitats at these popular spots.

Near the Phillips Collection, **Firefly** (✉ *1310 New Hampshire Ave. NW ⊹ 1:E4*) puts forth a hip, cozy atmosphere, and a menu of comforting fare like Waldorf salad with poached shrimp, seared-tuna club sandwich with avocado, and for dessert, caramelized banana split. The check, presented in a glass jar with holes poked into the lid, makes getting the bill almost endearing.

The Mediterranean-accented **Rosemary's Thyme Bistro** (✉ *1801 18th St. NW ⊹ 1:F3*) has a fiercely loyal following that comes for sidewalk dining and stellar happy-hour specials. Grab a spot on the patio and sample fresh favorites like the spinach ravioli or the feta-meta salad.

Eschew the ubiquitous chains and get your midday fuel at **Burger, Tap, and Shake** (✉ *2200 Pennsylvania Ave. NW ⊹ 1:D6*), where college kids scarf down traditional cheeseburgers and their parents up the ante with gourmet riffs like the "Apache Sweat Lodge," a patty with New Mexican green chile, and the "Evil Empire" milkshake that comes spiked with vanilla vodka. ∎TIP→ "BTS," as fans call it, starts serving bright and early at 7:30 am.

PRETHEATER DINNER DEALS

The intimate **Notti Bianche** (✉ *824 New Hampshire Ave. NW ⊹ 1:D6*) in the G.W. University Inn serves indulgent Italian cuisine. The $32 three-course prix-fixe theater menu is available from 5 pm to 7 pm every day.

The French restaurant **Marcel's** (✉ *2401 Pennsylvania Ave. NW ⊹ 1:D5*) serves a $58 three-course pretheater dinner menu that includes round-trip executive car service to and from the Kennedy Center.

FRO-YO 2.0

The Hollywood-inspired craze for low-sugar, all-natural frozen desserts has made traditional ice cream a thing of the past in the District. Whether you're familiar with the dessert sensation—lower-calorie than richer cones such as Häagen-Dazs—Dupont Circle is home to two places that will satisfy your craving for the good stuff. **Dolcezza** (✉ *1704 Connecticut Ave. NW ⊹ 1:E3*) serves more than a dozen flavors of gelato and sorbet replete with local, organic ingredients so fresh you'll feel downright virtuous while indulging. The Thai coconut milk and salted caramel are particular favorites. Its wacky competitor, **Mr. Yogato** (✉ *1515 17th St. NW ⊹ 1:G4*), serves a wider range of flavors, such as pomegranate and strawberry, and features a rotating cast of free toppings. It is run by a former rocket scientist who gives discounts to those who stump him on *Seinfeld* trivia and features a Ghirardelli hot-chocolate bar in the winter months.

6

ADAMS MORGAN, U STREET CORRIDOR

The busy and bustling 18th Street in Adams Morgan is a popular nighttime destination for dinner and drinks.

Libations trump legislation in the nightlife-centric U Street/Adams Morgan area. This irreverent side of the District is characterized by bumping bars and an up-all-night attitude.

U Street links Shaw, centered near Howard University's campus, to Adams Morgan, and is known for indie rock clubs, edgy bars, and trendy restaurants. Although the urban hipster vibe is being threatened by skyrocketing rents and the intrusion of chain stores, you'll still find more tattoos and sneakers than pinstripes and pearls here.

In Adams Morgan legions of college kids descend on 18th Street for abundant drink specials and dance clubs. Quaint ethnic cafés (Ethiopian, French, Italian) are bustling during evening hours. But as the night wears on the crowds gravitate to greasy spoons and "jumbo slice" pizza joints. The next culinary frontier lies just east along Columbia Road, where the Salvadoran immigrant community dines on its native cuisine while young families flock to hearty local pubs for their ample portions.

ERNEST CUISINE

Named for a Hemingway character with an irresistible zest for life, the chic bistro **Bar Pilar** (✉ *1833 14th St. NW* ✛ *1:H2*) pays homage to its favorite author with simple but stunning small plates that harken back to Hemingway's Key West heyday. Think cold sugar baby watermelons and red wine–braised chicken with leeks.

A NIGHT ON THE TOWN

In this town you can get drinks, eat dinner, go dancing, and listen to live music all in one venue. Paint the town red (or blue) at one of our favorite U Street or Adams Morgan spots.

Start out the night at **Café Saint-Ex** (✉ *1847 14th St. NW* ✚ *1:H3*) by dining on farm-friendly American dishes, then head downstairs to dance off dinner with the help of a rotating cast of DJs in the often crowded but always rollicking downstairs bar.

Local 16 (✉ *1602 U St. NW* ✚ *1:G2*) may have experimented with its menu (currently American with international influences), but its status as a neighborhood hot spot has never wavered. After dinner, the intimate restaurant becomes a jumping nightclub as DJs start spinning and the crowd spills out onto a balcony patio crowned by palm trees.

The multitasking **Busboys and Poets** (✉ *2021 14th St. NW* ✚ *1:H2*)—a coffee shop, restaurant, bar, performance space, and progressive bookstore—wears many hats without scrimping on taste. Try the simple yet divine peanut-butter-and-honey-on-challah sandwich for a low-key lunch, or stay for the homemade meat loaf (most entrées are in the $10 to $15 range) and a live jazz show.

The walls rattle with the echo of bumping bodies at the **Wonderland Ballroom** (✉ *1101 Kenyon St. NW* ✚ *1:H1*) during its überpopular weekend DJ sessions, while the beat slows down on Sunday with live music. The all-American menu features burgers and fries as good as Coney Island's and savory brunch salads.

The spirit of storytelling lives on, along with stellar crab cakes and mint juleps, at the Southern-themed **Eatonville** (✉ *2121 14th St. NW* ✚ *1:H2*). Here, the monthly Food and Folklore series pairs a special prix-fixe menu with a lecture on the cultural traditions of the African-American community.

BRUNCH BONANZA

Brunch is a cherished ritual on the Adams Morgan/U Street strip, where bars mop up last night's spilled beer and fire up the French toast. Some of the most unforgettable brunches can be found in otherwise second-string kitchens, such as **Smoke & Barrel** (✉ *2471 18th St. NW* ✚ *1:F1*), a barbecue joint by night that turns out stellar huevos rancheros by day, and **Perry's** (✉ *1811 Columbia Rd. NW* ✚ *1:F1*), which pairs its pancakes with a rip-roaring drag queen revue. The array of up-and-coming shops in both neighborhoods makes for perfect afternoon strolling. After downing spicy sausage-and-egg sandwiches at **Bourbon** (✉ *2321 18th St. NW* ✚ *1:F1*), you can cruise nearby vintage fashion outpost **Meeps** (✉ *2104 18th St. NW* ✚ *1:F2*). Nothing helps work off the waffles of **Tabaq Bistro** (✉ *1336 U St. NW* ✚ *1:H2*) like a jaunt through **Lettie Gooch** (✉ *1517 U St. NW*), a bohemian boutique beloved by D.C. fashionistas.

6

UPPER NORTHWEST

Lions, tigers, and lobbyists...oh my! After the requisite cooing over the pandas and other cuddly creatures at the National Zoo, consider wandering around this popular neighborhood to observe locals eat, drink, and play.

Many Hill staffers, journalists, and other inside-the-Beltway types live along this hilly stretch of Connecticut Avenue. Eateries and shops line the few blocks near each of the Red Line Metro stops. Restaurants in Cleveland Park range from tiny takeout spots like **Vace Italian Delicatessen,** one of the few places in town to get a great slice of pizza, to nearby **Ardeo** (✉ *3311 Connecticut Ave. NW* ✛ *1:D1*), an upscale Modern American restaurant where you stand a good chance of spying your favorite Sunday-morning talk-show guests at a nearby table.

Ethnic dining is also abundant here, especially in Cleveland Park. Lined up along the stately stretch of modern row houses are diverse dining options ranging from Afghan to Thai.

BOOKS AND BITES

Hungry bibliophiles will want to make a lunchtime pilgrimage to **Politics & Prose** (✉ *5015 Connecticut Ave. NW* ✛ *1:D1*), one of the country's best independent bookstores. P&P boasts a full calendar of author readings, a refreshingly well-read staff, and a cozy basement café with free Internet access, dozens of tea selections, and tasty sandwiches. The café, **Modern Times**, also serves pastries and vegetarian sushi made on-site. Our favorite sandwiches are the English Roast, made with marinated roast beef, cheddar cheese, arugula, mango chutney, and plum tomatoes, and the salami and Gorgonzola panini.

DINNER AND A MOVIE

In a town teeming with monuments and memorials, Cleveland Park's **AMC Loews Uptown 1** (✉ *3426 Connecticut Ave. NW*)—known to locals simply as "The Uptown"—is a shrine to the glamour of days gone by. From the red-velvet curtain to the massive balcony to the 70-foot-long and 40-foot-high screen, this art deco movie palace is a throwback to a time when the experience of seeing a movie could be as romantic as the picture you came to see.

■TIP→ Shows sell out quickly, and coveted balcony seats fill up fast. Avoid the dreaded sold-out sign by heading to the box office early. Then, with tickets in hand, enjoy dinner at one of the many nearby restaurants.

Just a block away, **Indique** (✉ *3512–14 Connecticut Ave. NW* ✣ *1:D1*) offers a $20 three-course pretheater menu from 5:30 to 7 pm. Choices at the attractive, upscale Indian spot might include tandoori chicken tikka, Tamilnad fish curry, and mango ice cream. A sister restaurant, **Indique Heights**, recently arrived a few miles north in suburban Maryland.

Across the street, the rustic Italian enoteca **Dino** (✉ *3435 Connecticut Ave. NW* ✣ *1:D1*), is known both for its ambience and its award-winning wine list. The daily changing menu always includes a wide selection of cured meats, cheeses, and *fritti*, or fried items.

Spices Asian Restaurant & Sushi Bar (✉ *3333-A Connecticut Ave. NW* ✣ *1:D1*) is a popular neighborhood pan-Asian spot offering everything from Peking duck to pad thai noodles in a bustling, bistro-esque space.

For a one-dish meal that's quick and refreshing, stop into **Nam-Viet** (✉ *3419 Connecticut Ave. NW* ✣ *1:D1*). The atmosphere is minimal, but you probably won't care after tucking into juicy, salty-sweet caramelized pork chops or spicy rice-noodle soup filled with seared fish or beef.

GOLDEN GLOVER

Located just north of Georgetown and west of Cleveland Park, the Glover Park neighborhood is fast becoming Washington's home for sleeper culinary hits. You'll need a car, but any visitor eager to avoid crowds during high season should hightail it to **Surfside** (✉ *2444 Wisconsin Ave. NW* ✣ *1:A2*), where the steak burritos and mango salsa will evoke California dreaming. At **Breadsoda** (✉ *2233 Wisconsin Ave. NW* ✣ *1:A2*) the pool tables, Ping-Pong, and Nintendo Wii help patrons work off the hefty spicy turkey sandwiches. "A taste of the South for your mouth" is the kitschy motto of **Kitchen** (✉ *2404 Wisconsin Ave. NW* ✣ *1:A2*), where sweet potato and scallion hush puppies are served in a thick, piquant Mississippi-style barbecue sauce.

RESTAURANT REVIEWS

Listed alphabetically within neighborhood. Use the coordinate at the end of the review (✛ 2:B2) to locate a property on the Where to Eat and Stay map.

THE WHITE HOUSE AREA AND FOGGY BOTTOM

$$

MODERN
AMERICAN

Fodor'sChoice

★

✕ **Blue Duck Tavern.** Many chefs are fond of artisanal and local ingredients. Chef Sebastien Archambault is so committed to the cause that fixings are often strewn across marble counters in the restaurant's show kitchen. By now diners have gotten used to watching pastry chefs churn ice cream to be served minutes later in glass ice buckets, but sweets—and watching for the town's biggest political names to claim their favorite tables—aren't the only pleasures. The kitchen, located in the Park Hyatt Hotel, wows with Modern American riffs like a double-cut pork chop with huckleberry jam, an oven-roasted marrowbone with creamy insides, and rightly titled "champion" collard greens. The dining room is stylish, done up with Shaker furniture and quilts. ⑤ *Average main: $25* ✉ *1201 24th St. NW, Foggy Bottom* ☎ *202/419–6755* ⊕ *www.blueducktavern.com* ⌂ *Reservations essential* Ⓜ *Foggy Bottom/GWU* ✛ *1:D5.*

$

MODERN
AMERICAN

✕ **Founding Farmers.** Inside this ultramodern take on the old-school farmhouse, sustainability is the culinary mantra. Local farms provide much of the fresh vegetables in the jam-packed salads (try the muscular Late Harvest, crowned by balsamic-roasted onions and blue cheese) and environmentally responsible practices are used to catch every type of fish on the menu. The sheer number of offerings can make for a disorienting experience, with 16 options for pastas and flatbreads alone, but its combination of affordability and reliability is unmatched in the neighborhood. ■TIP➔ Visitors with early museum call times are also well-served by the 7 am start of its top-notch breakfast. Vegans will be particularly pleased with the array of meat- and egg-free options, and cocktail lovers are advised to try any of the smashing "recession-proof cocktails," all top-shelf and well priced. ⑤ *Average main: $16* ✉ *1924 Pennsylvania Ave. NW, Foggy Bottom* ☎ *202/822-8783* ⊕ *www.wearefoundingfarmers.com* ⌂ *Reservations essential* Ⓜ *Foggy Bottom/GWU* ✛ *1:E6.*

$$$

SEAFOOD

✕ **Kinkead's.** This multichambered seafood restaurant has a raw bar downstairs, with a more casual array of dishes to bridge from lunch into dinner, and more formal dining rooms upstairs, but the mood of quiet elegance remains. The open kitchen upstairs allows you to watch chef Bob Kinkead and company turn out an eclectic menu inspired by Kinkead's New England roots and by the cuisines of Asia and Latin America. Don't miss the signature dish—salmon encrusted with pumpkin seeds and served with a ragout of crab, shrimp, and corn. Save room for dessert, because the lemon sampler, which includes a meringue tart and pudding cake, is a knockout. ⑤ *Average main: $28* ✉ *2000 Pennsylvania Ave. NW, Foggy Bottom* ☎ *202/296–7700* ⊕ *www.kinkead.com* ⌂ *Reservations essential* ☾ *No lunch weekends* Ⓜ *Foggy Bottom/GWU* ✛ *1:E6.*

$$$$ ✕ **Marcel's.** Chef Robert Wiedmaier trained in the Netherlands and Bel-
BELGIAN gium, and in this, his first solo venture, his French-inspired Belgian
cooking focuses on robust seafood and poultry preparations served in
three or more courses. Don't miss the mussels, if they're available, and
take advantage of the perfectly seared diver scallops served with delicate
Japanese citrus sauce. The duck breast is a marvel, its succulent dark
meat coated in flavorful *jus* that melts into the accompanying risotto
cake. In season, be sure to order the fig tart with citrus crème anglaise
and honey-cinnamon ice cream. $ *Average main: $115* ✉ *2401 Pennsyl-*
vania Ave. NW, Foggy Bottom ☎ *202/296–1166* ⊕ *www.marcelsdc.com*
⌕ *Reservations essential* ☾ *No lunch* Ⓜ *Foggy Bottom/GWU* ✛ *1:D5.*

$$$ ✕ **Westend Bistro by Eric Ripert.** Where else but the Ritz-Carlton Hotel
MODERN would you find the chef of New York City's award-winning restau-
AMERICAN rant Le Bernardin? Eric Ripert, directing his former Manhattan star
Joe Palma in the kitchen, is wowing the swells of Foggy Bottom with
comfort food such as fish burgers with saffron aioli and a salad of local
greens gussied up with truffle vinaigrette. Two caveats: side dishes must
be ordered à la carte, and the handmade cocktails are a skyscraping
$13 per glass. The bourbon-based Scarlet Oak, spiked with homemade
sorghum soda, and a tangerine tequila named after the chef are par-
ticularly irresistible. $ *Average main: $29* ✉ *1190 22nd St. NW, Foggy*
Bottom ☎ *202/974–4900* ⊕ *www.westendbistrodc.com* ⌕ *Reservations*
essential ☾ *No lunch weekends* Ⓜ *Foggy Bottom/GWU* ✛ *1:E5.*

6

CAPITOL HILL AND NORTHEAST D.C.

$$$ ✕ **Art and Soul.** Best known as Oprah's longtime personal chef, Art
MODERN Smith is now serving the Washingtonian crowd at this funky Southern-
AMERICAN fried spot, located in the Liaison Capitol Hill. The signature dish here
is the hoecake, a once modest slab of fried cornmeal scarfed down
by overworked and cash-strapped field workers during the 19th century. Smith and executive chef Wes Morton gussy up their hoecakes
with a rotating cast of toppings: lately poached quince with walnut
and a creamy, dreamy goat cheese-and-figs have been spotted pairing
nicely with the bar's artisanal cocktails. Low Country classics such as
shrimp with grits and fried chicken cloaked in decadent pepper gravy
are also on hand. $ *Average main: $28* ✉ *415 New Jersey Ave. NW,*
Capitol Hill ☎ *202/393–7777* ⊕ *www.artandsouldc.com* Ⓜ *Union Sta-*
tion ✛ *2:F3.*

$$ ✕ **Belga Café.** You can go traditional with mussels and the crispiest of
BELGIAN french fries or dabble in what the chef calls Euro-fusion at this sleek
café done up with dark wood, exposed brick, and creamy chairs and
linens. Classic dishes such as *waterzooi* (Flemish beef stew) and leg
of rabbit cooked with beer are expertly turned out, along with newer
takes such as seared scallops with young carrots, red beets, and orange
sauce. Belgium's love of well-made beer is reflected in the three-page list.
Crowds at lunch and dinner—and especially for the überpopular waffle-
centric brunch—sometimes mean a short wait, even with a reservation.
$ *Average main: $23* ✉ *514 8th St. SE, Capitol Hill* ☎ *202/544–0100*
⊕ *www.belgacafe.com* Ⓜ *Eastern Market* ✛ *2:H6.*

$$$ ✕**Bistro Bis.** A zinc bar, spacious brown-leather booths, and a glass-
FRENCH front display kitchen create great expectations at Bistro Bis, the second
restaurant from Jeffrey Buben, owner of the much-acclaimed Vidalia.
The seasonal menu seamlessly merges Modern American standards with
French bistro classics. For a first course, be sure to try the steak tartare.
Main-course hits on the menu, which changes frequently to reflect mar-
ket and seasonal choices, include classic steak frites, trout with caramel-
ized shallots, and lamb shank with black olives and polenta. But don't
be fooled by its daylong hours and convenient location—the mood
is more meet-the-parents than family-friendly. $ *Average main: $29*
✉ *Hotel George, 15 E St. NW, Capitol Hill* ☎ *202/661–2700* ⊕ *www.
bistrobis.com* ⌢ *Reservations essential* Ⓜ *Union Station* ✛ *2:F3.*

$$ ✕**Cava.** This modern mecca for mezes (small plates for sharing) deliv-
MEDITERRANEAN ers delicious and chic Mediterranean without the whiz-bang conceits of
Zaytinya, its competitor for the title of tops in D.C. The entire Greek
catalogue is here for the taking, from fluffy *taramosalata* (salmon roe
dip) with a touch of citrus to rich, melt-in-your-mouth spinach pie to
pita-clad lamb souvlaki topped by a puff of thick Greek yogurt. There
are few surprises on the menu, save for the gloriously salty halloumi
cheese topped with mint, but the leather-lined room and gallant service make the traditional dishes feel new again. There are two other
locations: in Rockville, Maryland, and the Clarendon neighborhood
of Arlington, Virginia; the latter is accessible by public transportation.
$ *Average main: $22* ✉ *527 8th St. SE, Capitol Hill* ☎ *202/543–9090*
⊕ *dc.cavamezze.com* ⌢ *Reservations not accepted* ⊗ *No lunch Mon.*
Ⓜ *Eastern Market* ✛ *2:H6.*

$$$$ ✕**Charlie Palmer Steak.** It's hard not to feel like a master of the universe
STEAKHOUSE when ensconced in this coolly elegant dining room in the imposing
shadow of the Capitol. Oversize floral arrangements, tones of blue-
gray, a dramatic glass-enclosed wine cellar, and quasi-Danish modern
furniture form a backdrop to the contemporary cuisine. Dry-aged rib
eye, marinated hanger steak, and porterhouse steak with chanterelle
mushrooms are the meaty choices. But goat cheese-stuffed agnolotti
pasta and butter-steeped lobster make a good showing, too, as do sides
such as mashed Yukon Golds and Brussels sprouts dusted in sharp
pecorino. The crème brûlée trio finishes things off nicely. $ *Average
main: $38* ✉ *101 Constitution Ave. NW, Capitol Hill* ☎ *202/547–8100*
⊕ *www.charliepalmer.com* ⊗ *Closed Sun. No lunch Sat.* Ⓜ *Union Station* ✛ *2:F4.*

$ ✕**Ethiopic.** The spongy rolls of sourdough *injera* bread (a ubiquitous
AFRICAN carbohydrate on Ethiopian plates) used in place of utensils can make
traditional Ethiopian feel decidedly undelicate, but the bright surroundings and friendly service here make for a downright romantic experience. Venture off the well-beaten path of spicy lamb and lentils to try
the spicy chickpea dumplings or fragrant simmered split peas, laden
with garlic and served in a clay pot. For devoted meat lovers, the rosemary notes in the *beef tibs* (a type of hearty steak cut) and the chicken
legs' rich red pepper sauce will crown a memorable, affordable meal.
The full bar also serves potent Ethiopian beers. Be warned: the still-
gentrifying neighborhood of H Street NE is not an ideal place to walk

alone at night. $ *Average main: $14* ⌧ *401 H St. NE, Capitol Hill* ☎ *202/675–2066* ⊕ *www.ethiopicrestaurant.com* ⊘ *Closed Mon. No lunch Tues.–Thurs.* Ⓜ *Union Station* ✛ *2:H2.*

$ ✕ **Good Stuff Eatery.** Fans of Bravo's *Top Chef* will first visit this brightly
AMERICAN   colored burgers-and-shakes shack hoping to spy charismatic TV chef
☺   Spike Mendelsohn, but they will return for the comfort-food favorites. The lines can be long, as it has quickly become a favorite lunch
spot of congressional aides, but Spike's inventive beef dishes—including
the "Blazin' Barn" Asian burger topped with Thai basil and pickled
radish—are worth the wait. After placing your order cafeteria-style,
remember to grab several of the fresh dipping sauces for the tasty
thyme-and-rosemary-seasoned hand-cut skinny fries or Vidalia onion
rings. Just as important, leave room for a toasted marshmallow or
chocolate malted shake that's as thick as the ones you remember from
childhood. $ *Average main: $6* ⌧ *303 Pennsylvania Ave. SE, Capitol Hill* ☎ *202/543–8222* ⊕ *www.goodstuffeatery.com* ⊘ *Closed Sun.*
Ⓜ *Eastern Market* ✛ *2:H5.*

$ ✕ **Granville Moore's Brickyard.** This Belgian beer hall with a gourmet soul
BELGIAN   is worth a visit despite its location in D.C.'s Atlas District, an area that
can be seedy after dark. Snag a seat at the bar or at one of the first-
come, first-served tables, and linger over unfiltered artisanal brews that
range from Chimay to the obscure, lip-smacking Brasserie des Rocs.
The food is terrific, specifically the pots of steamed mussels served with
crunchy, twice-fried frîtes paired with homemade dipping sauces. The
bison burger, warm apple-stuffed hush puppies, and wild boar pat-
ties are indulgent without crossing the line into predictable pub grub.
$ *Average main: $14* ⌧ *1238 H St. NE, Capitol Hill* ☎ *202/399–2546*
⊕ *www.granvillemoores.com* ⌲ *Reservations not accepted* ⊘ *No lunch*
Ⓜ *Union Station* ✛ *2:H2.*

$ ✕ **Jimmy T's Place.** This D.C. institution is tucked in the first floor of an
AMERICAN   old row house only five blocks from the Capitol. Sassy waiters, talk-
☺   ative regulars, and this small diner's two boisterous owners, who run
the grill, pack the place daily. Soak in the local culture or read the paper
as you enjoy favorites such as grits, bacon, omelets, or the homey eggs
Benedict, made with a toasted English muffin, a huge piece of ham,
and lots of hollandaise sauce. The anything-goes atmosphere makes
it a great place for kids. Breakfast is served all day, with recession-
friendly prices that rarely rise into the double digits. $ *Average main:
$6* ⌧ *501 E. Capitol St. SE, Capitol Hill* ☎ *202/546–3646* ⊟ *No credit
cards* ⊘ *Closed Mon. and Sat. No dinner* Ⓜ *Eastern Market* ✛ *2:H5.*

$$$ ✕ **Johnny's Half Shell.** A 2010 move from Dupont Circle to more spa-
SEAFOOD   cious quarters on Capitol Hill may have diminished the neighborhood
charm of this seafood bar, but it at least made it easier to get a table. The
Southern-tinged mid-Atlantic fare—pristine Kumamoto oysters, flavor-
ful seafood stews, fried oyster po'boys, and a stellar pickled-onion-and-
blue-cheese-topped "Baltimore" hot dog, only available at lunch—is as
wonderful as ever. And the pastry chef turns out a worthy coconut cake.
Not surprisingly, the crowd is heavy on politicos drawn as much by
the buzz and big-band tunes. Members of Congress can also be found
downing a quick Gruyère-cheese omelet during breakfast on weekdays,

often in the company of top campaign contributors. $ *Average main: $29* ✉ *400 N. Capitol St. NW, Capitol Hill* ☎ *202/737–0400* ⊕ *www. johnnyshalfshell.net* ⊗ *Closed Sun.* Ⓜ *Union Station* ✣ *2:F3.*

$

AMERICAN

☾

✕ **The Market Lunch.** For a perfect Saturday morning or afternoon on the Hill, take a walk around the Capitol, a stroll through Eastern Market, and then dig in to a hefty pile of blueberry buckwheat pancakes from Market Lunch. The casual counter service and informal seating make it ideal for kids. Favorites include ham, eggs, grits, or pancakes in the morning and crab cakes, fried shrimp, or fish for lunch. Expect long lines and plan to be in line by noon on Saturday in order to ensure availability of every dish. Eastern Market's post-fire renovation in 2009 gave Market Lunch a spruced-up new home. ■TIP→ Follow convention and order quickly, eat, and give up your seat for the next customer. $ *Average main: $14* ✉ *Eastern Market, 225 7th St. SE, Capitol Hill* ☎ *202/547– 8444* ⌲ *Reservations not accepted* ▭ *No credit cards* ⊗ *Closed Mon. No dinner, brunch Sat. only* Ⓜ *Eastern Market* ✣ *2:H6.*

$

ITALIAN

✕ **Seventh Hill.** When this hand-tossed-pizza spot first opened, it seemed like a risky bet given the high bar set by capital favorites such as Matchbox and 2 Amys. But the breezy charm of this casual bistro, epitomized by its gregarious *pizzaiolo* (trained pizza chef) Anthony Pilla, quickly vaulted its pies to the top of the heap. Each is named for a nearby neighborhood—the zesty mating of basil and anchovies on the "SW Waterfront" pie is matched only by the creamy goat cheese of the "Eastern Market"—but the signature dish may well be Pilla's special "love bread." ■TIP→ Patrons who match Pilla's charm quip for quip are often rewarded with a free round of "love" grub. It comes out of his wood-fired oven with a different herb ratio each time, but the warm spools of salty goodness are true to their name. You're sure to fall in love with this welcoming spot. $ *Average main: $16* ✉ *327 7th St. SE, Capitol Hill* ☎ *202/544–1911* ⊕ *www.montmartredc.com/seventhhill* ⌲ *Reservations not accepted* ⊗ *Closed Mon.* Ⓜ *Eastern Market* ✣ *2:H6.*

$$

WINE BAR

✕ **Sonoma.** This chic multilevel wine bar has pours aplenty (in both tasting portions and full glasses) along with well-thought-out charcuterie boards piled with prosciutto and fluffy, grill-charred *focaccia* bread. There's more-conventional fare, too, like a juicy roasted chicken with humble but hearty lentils. By day the crowd skews to Senate staffers, by night the place becomes a hipster scene in the bar on the second level—think low tables and sofas—while a youngish crowd shares cheese plates and sips $3 Italian beers in the crowded street-level dining room. $ *Average main: $20* ✉ *223 Pennsylvania Ave. SE, Capitol Hill* ☎ *202/544–8088* ⊕ *www.sonomadc.com* ⌲ *Reservations essential* ⊗ *No lunch weekends* Ⓜ *Capitol S* ✣ *2:H5.*

$

ASIAN

✕ **Sticky Rice.** The capital's hip young things usually begin their nights out with cocktails, not high-concept food, but this kitschy den of sushi and karaoke is a popular exception. Between the trippy wall-mounted light sculptures and the gigantic gong that rings with every order of a mind-altering "sake bomb," a night out here is always exciting. New customers are thrilled to trade in those predictable California rolls for a Dirty South, made with tempura-battered sweet potatoes, or a Billy Goat's Gruff, where fresh yellowtail is slathered in goat cheese and dosed with piquant ponzu sauce. Those expecting thrilling service, however, may leave frustrated. $ *Average main: $15* ✉ *1224 H St. NE, Capitol Hill* ☎ *202/397–7655* ⊕ *www.stickyricedc.com* ⌖ *Reservations essential* Ⓜ *Union Station* ✛ *2:H2.*

$ ✕ **Ted's Bulletin.** Extra, extra! This cheeky homage to mid-20th-century
AMERICAN diners is styled after a newspaper office, with menus printed in broad-
Ⓒ sheet format and specials mounted on the wall in mismatched plastic lettering. But one bite of the grilled cheese with tomato soup or the "Burgh" burger, served on Texas toast with coleslaw and a fried egg, will convince you that the kitchen's skills are no joke. Kids will love the 16 clever milk shake flavors, and their parents will love the nine extra shakes that come with a kick of liquor added. (The Nutty Professor, made with Frangelico, is worth writing home about.) Thecommander –in chief is a fan, stopping by for a cheeseburger in 2011. $ *Average main: $13* ✉ *505 8th St. SE, Capitol Hill* ☎ *202/544–8337* ⊕ *www. tedsbulletin.com* ◷ *No lunch Mon.–Fri.* Ⓜ *Eastern Market* ✛ *2:H6.*

DOWNTOWN

$$ ✕ **Bibiana Osteria and Enoteca.** The fingerprints of Ashok Bajaj, creator
ITALIAN of Chinatown's überpopular Rasika, are all over this modern kitchen specializing in hearty Florence-inspired cuisine. The 120-seat dining room is decked out in Bajaj's favored spare tones and metallic accents, while servers remain uncommonly attentive and knowledgeable. And in a city where Italian spots too often hit obvious notes such as brick-oven pizzas, Bibiana's customers can try presentations such as buttery burrata mozzarella with pureed zucchini and blue crab served atop linguine colored jet-black by squid ink. The surroundings may be rich, but the ample portions and sensible prices make for a recession-friendly splurge. $ *Average main: $18* ✉ *1100 New York Ave. NW, entrance at 12th and H Sts., Downtown* ☎ *202/216–9550* ⊕ *www.bibianadc.com* ◷ *No lunch Sat. Closed Sun.* Ⓜ *Metro Center* ✛ *2:C2.*

$$ ✕ **Bombay Club.** One block from the White House, the beautiful Bombay
INDIAN Club tries to re-create the refined aura of British private clubs in colonial India. Potted palms and a bright blue ceiling above white plaster moldings adorn the dining room. On the menu are unusual seafood specialties and a large number of vegetarian dishes, but the real standouts are the aromatic curries. The bar, furnished with rattan chairs and dark-wood paneling, serves hot hors d'oeuvres at cocktail hour. The attire tends toward upscale business-casual. $ *Average main: $20* ✉ *815 Connecticut Ave NW,Downtown* ☎ *202/659–3727* ⊕ *www.bombayclubdc. com* ⌖ *Reservations essential* ◷ *No lunch Sat.* Ⓜ *Farragut W* ✛ *1:G6.*

$$$ ✕ **Brasserie Beck.** Give in to sensory overload at this homage to the
BELGIAN railway dining rooms that catered to the prewar European elite. Every detail of Beck's interior exudes luxury, from the vintage-accented clocks that stand above mahogany booths to the exposed stainless-steel kitchen (now rechristened the "epicurean solarium"). The food is just as rich as you'd expect: entrée-size salads with bacon and egg, *fruits de mer* platters laden with enough shellfish for a small army, and a dizzying lineup of artisanal beers. The production is impressive, and you'll remember the food fondly after returning home—but you might consider a

6

JOSÉ ANDRÉS'S KID-FRIENDLY D.C.

José Andrés is a busy man. He is the award-winning chef and owner of ThinkFoodGroup, a collection of restaurants including D.C.-based **Zaytinya, Oyamel, Jaleo,** and **minibar by José Andrés.** When he's not opening restaurants, writing books, or guest lecturing at the prestigious Harvard University, you can find the affable chef spending time with his wife and three daughters at his home just outside D.C.

Fodor's: What are some of your favorite local restaurants to take your kids?
José Andrés: 2 Amy's Pizza has great Margheritas with mozzarella and tomatoes imported from Italy. My daughters love the burgers at **Palena.** It's a very fancy restaurant but they have this informal café, with four or six tables in the front. They also love sushi. We don't go to just one place, but they like **Kaz Sushi** and **Sushi-Ko.**

Fodor's: There are so many great attractions in D.C. and many of them are free, how do you decide which ones to visit with your kids?
Andrés: They like to go to the museums. There's so many of them but we may go to the **National Air and Space Museum,** which is very cool. I think Washington as a cultural city is very undervalued; you get so much for how little it costs you. The new **Newseum** is awesome because there you can be a news anchor for a day. It's not like we go to the same one every month but those are some of the ones. In Bethesda there's a very cool **Imagination Stage** (⊕ www.imaginationstage.org). It's in Bethesda, and anyone visiting D.C. should know it's only a subway ride away from Downtown. They always

have amazing plays. It's a full theater exclusively for kids; they don't have that in many places.

Fodor's: When you're visiting National Mall museums, where do you go for lunch?
Andrés: On the Mall there's plenty of restaurants to go to on the right and left. And lately we have some food trucks coming to D.C. like the **Red Hook Lobster Truck.** My daughters like those lobster rolls. You have to go on the Web and check where they are and they're never in the same place, but they're very good.

Fodor's: What are the best family-friendly stops on Capitol Hill?
Andrés: It's always good to know what they're doing at the **Library of Congress.** It's not kid-friendly all the time but there are things for kids sometimes, so it's good to check the Web. But if you're going to Capitol Hill, you can get a good burger by Spike Mendolsohn at **Good Stuff Eatery.** It's great. His mother is there—it's a family affair. He's bringing new life to that part of town.

Fodor's: How about good spots for kids on Dupont Circle?
Andrés: I would recommend the farmers' market in Dupont. To me that's very important because every meal of my first two children; every single puree that they ate when they were one or two years old, came from that market. It's the place to be, and it's good to go and hang around, and you can try some crab cakes, or buy some flowers, or some tomatoes, or some apples or ice cream on a Sunday morning between 9 and 1.

fast the next day. $\boxed{\$}$ *Average main: $26* ✉ *1101 K St. NW, Downtown* ☎ *202/408–1717* ⊕ *www.beckdc.com* Ⓜ *McPherson Sq.* ✛ *2:C1.*

$ ✗ **Burma.** Myanmar, the country formerly known as Burma, is bordered
ASIAN   by India, Thailand, and China, which gives a good indication of the
cuisine at this Chinatown restaurant. Curry and tamarind share pride
of place with lemon, cilantro, and soy seasonings. Batter-fried eggplant
and squash are paired with complex, peppery sauces. Green-tea-leaf
and other salads leave the tongue with a pleasant tingle. Such entrées as
mango pork and tamarind fish are equally satisfying. The style and feel
of the place aren't much, but this quiet gem has a worthwhile escape
from the hustle and bustle of the neighborhood. $\boxed{\$}$ *Average main: $12*
✉ *740 6th St. NW, 2nd fl., Downtown* ☎ *202/638–1280* ☉ *No lunch
weekends* Ⓜ *Gallery Pl./Chinatown* ✛ *2:D2.*

$$$$ ✗ **The Capital Grille.** A few blocks from the U.S. Capitol, this New Eng-
STEAKHOUSE   land–tinged steak house is a favorite among Republican congressmen.
Politics aside, the cuisine, wine list, and surroundings are all top-shelf.
Don't let the meat hanging in the window distract you from the fact that
this restaurant has a lot more to offer than fine dry-aged porterhouse
cuts and delicious cream-based potatoes. For instance, don't miss the
panfried calamari with hot cherry peppers. A second location in Tysons
Corner has the same menu but a slightly different wine list. $\boxed{\$}$ *Average
main: $50* ✉ *601 Pennsylvania Ave. NW, Downtown* ☎ *202/737–6200*
⊕ *www.thecapitalgrille.com* ⌀ *Reservations essential* ☉ *No lunch Sun.*
Ⓜ *Archives/Navy Memorial* ✛ *2:D4.*

$$ ✗ **Ceiba.** At this popular Latin restaurant you'll probably want to start
LATIN AMERICAN   with a mojito or a pisco sour cocktail, then taste the tuna tartar taqui-
tos or crab-and-salt cod croquettes. This is a menu meant for grazing,
but the main courses, like rib eye with chimichurri sauce and *feijoada*
(stew of beans and meat) made from pork shanks, still satisfy. Also stel-
lar are desserts such as buttermilk key lime tart with pineapple sorbet
and cinnamon-dusted churros to dip in Mexican hot chocolate. Island-
theme murals, angular cream banquettes, an open kitchen, and vaulted
ceilings set the scene. ■**TIP**→ For a more casual experience, try the early-
and late-evening happy hours, where first-come, first-serve seats in the
lounge are easier to come by. $\boxed{\$}$ *Average main: $24* ✉ *701 14th St. NW,
Downtown* ☎ *202/393–3983* ⊕ *www.ceibarestaurant.com* ☉ *Closed
Sun. No lunch Sat.* Ⓜ *Metro Center* ✛ *2:B3.*

$$ ✗ **Central Michel Richard.** French powerhouse chef Michel Richard has
FRENCH   set up camp Downtown with this semicasual bistro offering up Franco-
Fodor's Choice   American spin-offs like fried chicken, tomato-and-goat cheese torte, and
★   a ginger-flecked Ahi tuna burger. Rows of hams hang in a glass case.
Light fixtures are subtly stamped with the word "Central." A jazzy
portrait of Richard (think Andy Warhol) stares down from one wall.
The mood is playful and low-key; cocktails and champagne flow. And
there are even a few carryovers from Richard's more formal Citronelle
in Georgetown like "Michel's Chocolate Bar," the chef's sinful house-
made riff on a Kit Kat wafer. $\boxed{\$}$ *Average main: $25* ✉ *1001 Pennsylvania
Ave. NW, Downtown* ☎ *202/626–0015* ⊕ *www.centralmichelrichard.
com* ⌀ *Reservations essential* ☉ *No lunch weekends* Ⓜ *Archives/Navy
Memorial* ✛ *2:C3.*

6

$$$$
AMERICAN

✕ **CityZen.** The Mandarin Hotel's rarefied dining room has fast become a destination for those serious about food. In a glowing space with soaring ceilings, chef Eric Ziebold, formerly of Napa Valley's famed French Laundry, creates luxe fixed-price, four-course meals from the finest ingredients. Unexpected little treasures abound, such as scrambled eggs with white truffles shaved at the table and buttery miniature Parker House rolls. Main courses could include bacon-wrapped quail over poached cherries or sweet butter-poached Maine lobster salad with turnips, and desserts such as Meyer lemon soufflé seem spun out of air. To take full advantage of the dining experience, opt for a six-course tasting menu. ⑤ *Average main: $95 ⊠ Mandarin Oriental, 1330 Maryland Ave. SW, Downtown* ☎ *202/787–6148* ⊕ *www.mandarinoriental.com/ washington/dining/cityzen ⌂ Reservations essential* ☉ *Closed Sun. and Mon. No lunch* Ⓜ *Smithsonian* ✛ *2:B6.*

$$$
AMERICAN

✕ **Equinox.** Virginia-born chef-owner Todd Gray looks to area purveyors for hard-to-find heirloom and local foodstuffs at his low-key American eatery. The furnishings and the food are simple and elegant, rebounding nicely following a 2009 fire that destroyed part of the kitchen. The fresh ingredients speak for themselves: grilled lamb rib eye with a puree of local Blue Ridge chestnuts, roasted black bass with baby carrots and clams, and simply sautéed oysters from the nearby Rappahannock River. Wine pairings are available for an extra fee, and an à la carte menu ($$) is available at lunch, led by a fresh vegetable platter that is can't-miss for meat avoiders. ⑤ *Average main: $34 ⊠ 818 Connecticut Ave. NW, Downtown* ☎ *202/331–8118* ⊕ *www.equinoxrestaurant.com ⌂ Reservations essential* ☉ *No lunch weekends* Ⓜ *Farragut W* ✛ *2:A2.*

$
ECLECTIC

✕ **G Street Food.** Like Washington, D.C.'s layout and architecture, this upscale cafeteria takes a cue from Europe. The cosmopolitan menu echoes the best of the Continent's eclectic café scene; breakfasts range from Italian potato-and-egg panini to Norwegian lox, and lunch ups the ante with a daily sausage selection and a French-inspired "tartine of the day." Asian cuisine gets its due as well, and an Indian curry cauliflower salad packs a flavorful punch greater than its low price tag. Lines here can look oppressive at midday, as government workers come flocking for falafel and fresh-cut fries, but stick around and you'll be rewarded with a midday meal that's smarter, and often more affordable, than the chain spots. ⑤ *Average main: $9 ⊠ 1706 G St. NW, Downtown* ☎ *202/408–7474* ⊕ *www.gstreetfood.com ⌂ Reservations not accepted* ☉ *No dinner. Closed weekends* Ⓜ *Farragut W* ✛ *1:F6.*

$$
SOUTHERN

✕ **Georgia Brown's.** An elegant New South eatery and a favorite hangout of local politicians—First Lady Michelle Obama famously broke bread here with the mayor's wife and Second Lady Jill Biden—Georgia Brown's serves shrimp Carolina-style (head intact, with steaming grits on the side); thick, rich crab soup; and specials such as grilled salmon and slow-cooked green beans with bacon. Fried green tomatoes are filled with herb cream cheese, and a pecan pie is made with bourbon and imported Belgian dark chocolate. ■ TIP➔ The Sunday "jazz brunch" adds live music and a decadent chocolate fondue fountain to the mix. The airy, curving dining room has white honeycomb windows and unusual ceiling ornaments of bronze ribbons. ⑤ *Average main: $25 ⊠ 950 15th*

St. NW, Downtown ☎ *202/393–4499* ⊕ *www.gbrowns.com* ✍ *Reservations essential* ✹ *No lunch Sat.* Ⓜ *McPherson Sq.* ✛ *2:A2.*

$$ ✗ **The Hamilton.** Words don't do justice to the remodeling of a former
ECLECTIC warehouse-like Borders bookstore into this delightfully classy cavalcade of culinary hits bolstered by a belowground live music hall where New Orleans trumpeteers and gospel singers perform into the night. Hungry for a sandwich? The olive-laden muffuletta will take you back to Louisiana. Prefer a salad? The salmon version takes a trip to the Mediterranean, with bulgur wheat and feta. And if dessert's your game, the mud pie profiterole is simply sublime. If you're still hungry after a show, get this: Food is served 24 hours a day, seven days a week. ⑤ *Average main: $20* ✉ *600 14th St. NW, Downtown* ☎ *202/787–1000* ⊕ *www. thehamiltondc.com* ✍ *Reservations essential* ✛ *2:B3.*

$$$ ✗ **Kaz Sushi Bistro.** Traditional Japanese cooking is combined with often
JAPANESE inspired improvisations ("freestyle Japanese cuisine," in the words of chef-owner Kaz Okochi) at this serene location. For a first-rate experience, sit at the sushi bar and ask for whatever is freshest and best. The chef's years of experience preparing fugu—the potentially poisonous blowfish, available only in winter—means you're in good hands, though the experience is pricey. A less risky splurge is the series of four escalating tasting menus, which also puts you in the master's hands, at a price that depends on the market price for each small cut of fish. It's not all sushi here; innovations include coriander-crusted calamari and Asian short ribs. ⑤ *Average main: $26* ✉ *1915 I St. NW, Downtown* ☎ *202/530–5500* ⊕ *www.kazsushibistro.com* ✹ *Closed Sun. No lunch Sat.* Ⓜ *Farragut W* ✛ *1:F6.*

$$$$ ✗ **Occidental Grill.** One of the most venerable restaurants in the city is
AMERICAN located inside the hotel that once helped coin the phrase "lobbyist" for its lively ground-floor social scene. The kitchen's walls are covered with photos of politicians and other notables who have come here for the food and the attentive service. The standbys are best—Caesar salad, grilled swordfish or scallops, duck breast, roasted chicken. More than half of the menu is seafood. ⑤ *Average main: $35* ✉ *Willard InterContinental, 1475 Pennsylvania Ave. NW, Downtown* ☎ *202/783–1475* ⊕ *www. occidentaldc.com* ✍ *Reservations essential* Ⓜ *Metro Center* ✛ *2:B3.*

$$ ✗ **Old Ebbitt Grill.** People flock here to drink at the several bars, which
AMERICAN seem to go on for miles, and to enjoy well-prepared buffalo wings, hamburgers, and Reuben sandwiches. The Old Ebbitt also has Washington's most popular raw bar, which serves farm-raised oysters. Pasta is homemade, and daily fresh fish or steak specials are served until 1 am. Despite the crowds, the restaurant never feels cramped, thanks to its well-spaced, comfortable booths. Service can be slow at lunch; if you're in a hurry, try the café-style Ebbitt Express next door. ⑤ *Average main: $25* ✉ *675 15th St. NW, Downtown* ☎ *202/347–4800* ⊕ *www.ebbitt. com* Ⓜ *Metro Center* ✛ *2:B3.*

$ ✗ **Paul.** This chic, quick café is the Parisian equivalent of Starbucks, but
FRENCH that doesn't mean Americans of all walks of life won't be blown away by the fluff of its cheese *gougeres* puffs, the heft of its salty-sweet *croque monsieur* sandwich, and the delicate crunch of its almond-flour *macaron* cookies. A recently opened spin-off in Georgetown has not sapped

6

the appeal of Paul's perfect pastry, so lengthy waits are to be expected during the lunch rush. But when you compare its price and quality to other Downtown lunch options after a morning of museum trekking, nothing comes close. $ *Average main: $10* ⊠ *801 Pennsylvania Ave. NW, Downtown* ☎ *202/524–4500* ⊕ *www.paul-usa.com* ⚕ *Reservations not accepted* ✛ *2:D4.*

$ ✕ **Pho 14.** As the city's population of upwardly mobile strivers migrates

VIETNAMESE north, so do affordable, crowd-pleasing gems like this outpost for huge bowls of soothing (or spicy, depending on your preference) Vietnamese noodle soup. Standing-room-only crowds for the watermelon-size servings of beef, vegetable, shrimp, or chicken recently eased after the owners, riding high on local word of mouth, took over the grocery store next door and doubled in size. Hearty *banh mi* sandwiches and stir-fries are worthy choices if *pho* soup doesn't appeal. Suggest this to the Washingtonians you're visiting and watch them be impressed by your local prowess. $ *Average main: $12* ⊠ *1436 Park Rd. NW, Downtown* ☎ *202/986–2326* ⊕ *www.dcpho14.com* ⚕ *Reservations not accepted* ✛ *2:B1.*

$$$ ✕ **Taberna del Alabardero.** A lovely formal dining room, skillful service,

SPANISH and sophisticated cooking make this restaurant one of Washington's best. Start with tapas, made even tastier by a half-off happy hour that goes until 6:30 pm on weekdays: rice studded with escargot and wild mushrooms, or smoky grilled chorizo. Proceed to a hefty bowl of chestnut soup or egg-soaked brioche and venture on to authentic paella and fine Spanish country dishes. French-toast-like *torrijas* are a light ending to this rich fare. The plush interior and handsome bar make things romantic and help attract a well-heeled clientele. $ *Average main: $30* ⊠ *1776 I St. NW, at 18th St., Downtown* ☎ *202/429–2200* ⊕ *www.alabardero. com* ☾ *Closed Sun. No lunch weekends* Ⓜ *Farragut W* ✛ *1:F6.*

$ ✕ **Teaism.** This informal teahouse stocks more than 50 teas (black, white,

ASIAN and green) imported from India, Japan, and Africa, but it also serves

☾ healthful and delicious Japanese, Indian, and Thai food as well as tea-friendly sweets like ginger scones, plum muffins, and salty oat cookies. You can mix small dishes—tandoori kebabs, tea-cured salmon, Indian flat breads—to create meals or snacks. There's also a hefty burger or *ochazuke,* green tea poured over seasoned rice. The smaller Connecticut Avenue branch (enter around the corner, on H Street; closed on weekends), tucked neatly on a corner adjacent to Lafayette Park and the White House, is a perfect spot to grab lunch after touring the nation's power center. Breakfast is served daily. $ *Average main: $11* ⊠ *400 8th St. NW, Downtown* ☎ *202/638–6010* ⊕ *www.teaism.com* Ⓜ *Archives/ Navy Memorial* ✛ *2:D3.*

$$$$ ✕ **Wolfgang Puck's The Source.** Wolfgang Puck's first foray into Washing-

MODERN ton, D.C., provides diners with two dining experiences. The downstairs

AMERICAN area is home to an intimate lounge where guests can order specialty cocktails, hand-rolled pizza crowned by homemade sausage, and a juicy quartet of miniature burgers with featherlight fries or tempura onion straws. Brunch is served here on Saturday (11:30 am–3 pm). Upstairs the focus is on Asian haute cuisine: think wok-fried sea bass with Thai chilis and suckling pig tender enough to fall off your fork. The service

D.C. FOOD TRUCKS

The nation's capital loves celebrity chefs and pricey bistros, but its latest romance is both affordable and accessible: food trucks. The mobile food rush reached its peak in 2010, when local brick-and-mortar restaurateurs attempted to fight the trucks' appeal by passing an ordinance to keep them from staying too long in one place. That battle continues, but visitors keen to try the best D.C. trucks can always take advantage of Twitter. Even nonmembers of the networking site are free to visit the trucks' pages to track their locations—and in many cases, check out menus to see whether chicken vindaloo or red velvet cupcakes are on the docket at these favorite spots.

Red Hook Lobster Pound (⊕ *twitter.com/lobstertruckdc*) is the Washington outpost of a popular Brooklyn, New York, spot that purveys rolls filled with überfresh shellfish from Maine (tossed with light mayo) and Connecticut (kissed by creamy butter) variations. Add a decadent chocolate whoopie pie for dessert, and try the equally good shrimp roll for $7 less.

Fojol Brothers (⊕ *twitter.com/fojolbros*) calls itself a "traveling culinary carnival," and with good reason—the quartet of cooks behind its African-Indian fusion eats are fond of fake mustaches that complete their masquerade as chefs from mythical Benethopia and Merlindia. But there's nothing faux about the fragrant flavors of their buttered chicken, berbere lentils, and pumpkin stews.

Sauca (⊕ *twitter.com/wheresauca*) is a global celebration of the sandwich, with each day bringing a new and delightful filling for its tangy flatbread. The Vietnamese pork *banh mi*, accented by pickled vegetables and peanut sauce, and the beef shawarma spiked by garlicky *chimmichurri* sauce, are standouts on a memorable menu.

6

is so dedicated it borders on slavish. Don't miss the lacquered duck with huckleberries and the mango soufflé dessert. ⑤ *Average main: $45* ✉ *575 Pennsylvania Ave. NW, Downtown* ☏ *202/637–6100* ⊕ *www.wolfgangpuck.com* ⚑ *Reservations essential* ☾ *Closed Sun. No lunch Sat.* Ⓜ *Archives/Navy Memorial* ✛ *2:D4.*

CHINATOWN

$$$ ✕ **America Eats Tavern.** Hard economic times have sparked a boomlet in
AMERICAN New Deal nostalgia around the capital, and nothing epitomizes financial-crisis chic like this embrace of Americana created by celebrity chef José Andrés to showcase "the lost dishes that sustained those who came before us," as the menu puts it. In practice, that means crowd-pleasing executions of more mundane classics—think Cobb and Waldorf salads—and riskier return engagements, such as the piquant Hangtown fry of oysters, eggs, and bacon. At **Minibar** ($$$$), a six-stool bar on the second floor, you can explore a less wallet-conscious tasting menu of about 30 creative morsels, such as a foie-gras "lollipop" coated with cotton candy, conjured up before your eyes. ■**TIP**➔ Minibar is arguably the most adventurous dining experience in the city, which means you have to reserve at least a month in advance. ⑤ *Average main: $30* ✉ *405 8th*

St. NW, Chinatown ☎ *202/393–0812* ⊕ *www.americaeatstavern.com* ☖ *Reservations essential* ✛ *2:D3.*

$$$ ✕ **Cuba Libre.** The mascot of Philadelphia import Guillermo Pernot's
LATIN AMERICAN rollicking new supper club is a winking Rita Hayworth lookalike in a
ruffled gypsy dress, a perfect symbol of the Technicolor bravado that
marks his bold "Nuevo Cubano" cuisine. The fish is served with cheeky
accompaniments such as candied peanut salsa on seviche and Haitian
eggplant salad on truffled asparagus, while even old-school standards
such as empanadas and guacamole are tweaked for the postmodern
era. But playing with tradition pays off—the creamy five-seafood paella
is pure magic, and the grilled pineapple mojito puts the old-fashioned
style to shame. One important tip: The vivacious bar scene, even on
weeknights, makes this a less-advisable trip for families or those seeking
a quieter night; only those 21 and older are admitted on weekends after
9 pm. Ⓢ *Average main: $26* ⊠ *801 9th St. NW, Chinatown* ☎ *202/408–
1600* ⊕ *cubalibrerestaurant.com* ☖ *Reservations essential* ☾ *No lunch
Sat. and Sun. Brunch weekends only* Ⓜ *Gallery Pl./Chinatown* ✛ *2:D2.*

$ ✕ **Full Kee.** Many locals swear by this standout from the slew of
CHINESE mediocre Chinese joints in the area. The style-free interior can be
off-putting to some—reminiscent of the fluorescent-lit dives of Man-
hattan's Chinatown—but the cuisine is top-notch. Addictively salty
shrimp or scallops in garlic sauce cry out for a carryout to enjoy again
later, as do the wide assortment of Cantonese-style roasted meats.
■ TIP➔ Order from the house specialties, not the tourist menu; the meal-
size soups garnished with roast meats are the best in Chinatown. Tried-
and-true dishes include the steamed dumplings, crispy duck, eggplant
with garlic sauce, and sautéed leek flower. Ⓢ *Average main: $14* ⊠ *509
H St. NW, Chinatown* ☎ *202/371–2233* ⊕ *www.fullkeedc.com* ▬ *No
credit cards* Ⓜ *Gallery Pl./Chinatown* ✛ *2:D2.*

$$ ✕ **Graffiato.** Mike Isabella brought a rock-star cool to his stint on *Top
MODERN ITALIAN Chef,* and his venture down I–95 gave the same instant pizzazz to Wash-
ington's often-staid culinary scene. Everyone does wood-fired pizzas,
but Graffiato (the Italian word for "scratched," an excellent summary
of its artful-grunge ambience) does a Jersey Shore pie inspired by Isabella's home state that piles pink cherry-pepper aioli onto fried calamari.
Everyone does cheese plates, but Graffiato kicks theirs up with house-
made dulce de leche–garlic jam that's so good you'll beg to take a jar
home. The good news is that you can; the better news is that this TV
name lives up to the hype. Just don't expect to hear much over the Bon
Jovi that keeps the party going during prime dinner hours. Ⓢ *Average
main: $25* ⊠ *707 6th St. NW, Chinatown* ☎ *202/289–3600* ⊕ *graffia-
todc.com* ☖ *Reservations essential* ✛ *2:D2.*

$$ ✕ **Hill Country.** Barbecue partisans, put down your forks! Few who stop
BARBECUE by this bustling hive of smoky brisket and gooey ribs can deny that
it does Texas meat right—right down to the pay-by-the-pound ethos
that lets you sample one slice of lean beef and one scoop of gooey
shoepeg corn pudding alongside a small, succulent game hen cooked
over a can of beer, so tender it drips juice down your chin. But this
family-friendly retreat cleans up into a social destination come nightfall,
when live music takes the stage and Wednesday becomes a rollicking

country-western karaoke night. $ *Average main: $18* ✉ *410 7th St. NW, Chinatown* ☎ *202/556–2050* ⊕ *www.hillcountry.com* ⊹ *2:D3.*

$$ ✕ **Jaleo.** You are encouraged to make a meal of the long list of tapas at
SPANISH this lively Spanish bistro, although the six types of handcrafted paella are the stars of an ample entrée menu. Tapas highlights include the *gambas al ajillo* (sautéed garlic shrimp), fried potatoes with spicy tomato sauce, and the grilled chorizo. Adventurers are encouraged to sample the octopus with paprika; sangria lovers should slide up to the bar for a refreshing $4 glass during the popular 4:30–7 pm happy hour. Two spin-off locations, in Bethesda, Maryland, and Arlington, Virginia, are equally memorable. $ *Average main: $20* ✉ *480 7th St. NW, Chinatown* ☎ *202/628–7949* ⊕ *www.jaleo.com* Ⓜ *Gallery Pl./Chinatown* ⊹ *2:D3.*

$ ✕ **Kushi.** The boisterous chatter in this warehouse of a dining room may
JAPANESE make for a less-than-calm dinner, but crowds are buzzing with good reason over their fresh sashimi and succulent grilled meats. For pleasing prices of $3 or so, the *izakaya* side of the restaurant turns out smoky wood-fired skewers of pork belly, sticky yam, squid, and crispy duck. Velvety tuna and thick yellowtail rule the raw-fish menu, and rare Eastern liquors such as Choya Kokutu dark rum make for clever cocktails. Teens will get a kick out of this breath of chic air in the often staid D.C. dining scene, and the twenties crowd will appreciate the late-night hours. $ *Average main: $16* ✉ *465 K St. NW, Chinatown* ☎ *202/682–3123* ⊕ *www.eatkushi.tumblr.com* Ⓜ *Gallery Pl./Chinatown* ⊹ *2:E1.*

$$ ✕ **Matchbox.** The miniburgers, served on toasted brioche buns with a
AMERICAN huge mound of fried onion strings, get the most press, but the main
🐾 clue to what to order at this convivial triple-decker bar-restaurant is the glowing wood-burning pizza oven. The personal pizzas are "New York–style," with a thin, crisp crust. You probably won't mistake them for the very best of New York, but the spicy "Fire and Smoke" pie does the Big Apple one better. Homey plates such as braised short ribs with wasabi mashed potatoes and New England seafood stew add substance to the menu. There's a great lineup of draft beers and oddball martinis arranged by "girly" and "manly," plus a kitchen that stays open late on weekends. $ *Average main: $22* ✉ *713 H St. NW, Chinatown* ☎ *202/289–4441* ⊕ *www.matchboxdc.com* Ⓜ *Gallery Pl./Chinatown* ⊹ *2:D2.*

$$ ✕ **Oyamel.** The specialty at this Mexican stunner is *antojitos*, literally
MEXICAN translated as "little dishes from the street." But the high ceilings, gracious service, and gorgeous Frida Kahlo–inspired interior are anything but street, and even the smallest of dishes is bigger than life when doused with chocolatey *mole poblano* sauce or piquant lime-cilantro dressing. Standouts include house-made margaritas topped with a clever salt foam, the Veracruz red snapper in a hearty olive-tomato confit, and grasshopper tacos—yes, those are bugs basted in tequila and pepper sauce . . . and they're delightful. $ *Average main: $21* ✉ *401 7th St. NW, Chinatown* ☎ *202/628–1005* ⊕ *www.oyamel.com* Ⓜ *Archives/Navy Memorial* ⊹ *2:D3.*

$$$ ✕ **Poste.** Inside the trendy Hotel Monaco, Poste woos diners with a
MODERN towering skylighted space that until 1901 was the General Post Office.
AMERICAN Homing in on Modern American brasserie fare, chef Robert Weland conjures up such satisfying dishes as foie-gras terrine and pan-roasted

6

sirloin with truffled frites, but his crowning glory is the recently launched "20 Bites" tasting menu. In season, panfried softshell crabs are not to be missed. For dessert there's a dream of an apple tart topped with caramel ice cream. In warmer months the neoclassical courtyard is a serene spot for fruit-infused cocktails and brunch, with a well-known build-your-own Bloody Mary bar. Year-round, the lively bar inside attracts scenesters with booths on raised platforms. ⓢ *Average main: $30 ⊠ Hotel Monaco, 555 8th St. NW, Chinatown* ☎ *202/783–6060* ⊕ *www.postebrasserie.com* Ⓜ *Gallery Pl./Chinatown* ✛ *2:D3.*

$$$
MODERN
AMERICAN

✕ **PS 7's.** This restaurant manages to be at once swanky yet youthful, and its bar scene is hip but low-key, with inventive cocktails and nibbles like miniature Vietnamese *banh mi* sandwiches, spinach salad with tender chunks of bacon and fried onions, and an irresistible "nutty goat" flatbread. In the elegant sunken dining room the menu reads like a tasting menu, but the portions are hardly tiny. The diner calls the shots. Kobe beef is shaped into whimsical ravioli-esque shapes thanks to hand-stretched chestnut pasta. And the place is not without a touch of whimsy courtesy of portholelike fish tanks filled with gold-fish in the restrooms. ⓢ *Average main: $30 ⊠ 777 I St. NW, Chinatown* ☎ *202/742–8550* ⊕ *www.ps7restaurant.com* ☾ *Closed Sun. No lunch Sat.* Ⓜ *Gallery Pl./Chinatown* ✛ *2:D2.*

$$
INDIAN
Fodor's Choice
★

✕ **Rasika.** This trendy Indian restaurant pairs an adventurous wine list with spicy fare in a supersleek setting. The chef, London export Vikram Sunderam (from Bombay Brasserie), comes from a town where curries never get short shrift. He has prepared a menu of traditional delights, like a fiery green masala chicken, alongside newer, more inspired ones, like green chili mussels, black cod with star anise, and fried spinach leaves with sweet yogurt sauce. Libations at the bar are concocted with as much creativity as the food. Muted shades of cream, apple green, and cinnabar and dangling crystals evoke the subcontinent in a stylish, modern way. ⓢ *Average main: $22 ⊠ 633 D St. NW, Chinatown* ☎ *202/637–1222* ⊕ *www.rasikarestaurant.com* ☾ *Closed Sun. No lunch Sat.* Ⓜ *Archives/Navy Memorial* ✛ *2:D3.*

$
CAFÉ

✕ **Taylor Gourmet.** When is a sandwich more than just meat and cheese on bread? When it's crafted with the attention to detail and fine ingredients that have become the hallmark of this Philadelphia-inspired instant classic. Taylor's substitution-friendly staff piles fresh roasted turkey, ham, chicken cutlets, and cold cuts beneath emerald arugula, juicy roasted red peppers, and waves of provolone so finely aged it snaps on the palate. If the Vine Street Expressway (chicken, prosciutto, pesto) or the Callow-hill (spicy house-made meatballs in marinara sauce) don't grab you, the delicate pasta salads or eye-popping egg sandwiches—available during breakfast and late-night hours—will make you a believer. Other locations can be found on H Street NE and K Street NW, in the bottom of the massive CityVista complex. ⓢ *Average main: $11 ⊠ 1908 14th St. NW, U Street Corridor* ☎ *202/588–7117* ⊕ *www.taylorgourmet.com* ✛ *2:B1.*

$$
MIDDLE EASTERN
Fodor's Choice
★

✕ **Zaytinya.** This sophisticated urban dining room with soaring ceilings is a local favorite for meeting friends or dining with a group. Zaytinya, which means "olive oil" in Turkish, devotes practically its entire menu to Turkish, Greek, and Lebanese small plates, known as meze.

To get the full experience, make a meal of three or four of these, such as the popular braised lamb shank with eggplant puree, or the crispy potatoes drizzled in finger-licking yogurt. ■**TIP→** So many options make this a great choice for vegetarians and meat lovers alike. Reservations for times after 6:30 are not accepted; come prepared to wait on Friday and Saturday nights, and practice your pouncing technique for when a roomy bar table comes open. ⑤ *Average main: $21* ✉ *701 9th St. NW, Chinatown* ☎ *202/638–0800* ⊕ *www.zaytinya.com* Ⓜ *Gallery Pl./ Chinatown* ✛ *2:D2.*

$$$
SOUTHERN

✕ **Zola.** Swanky and chic, Zola channels a 1940s vibe with its snug banquettes, oval bar carts, and dramatic red flourishes. Food is fun without being over-the-top, and the best dishes hew to the Southern bent that first characterized its kitchen. Try the brown butter trout with charred arugula or the hay-smoked venison, a touch of farm-to-table flair that shines through the upscale setting. Dessert is also a standout, with an Irish stout sundae and cooling lychee soup tops on the list. A new happy-hour menu also offers affordable small bites after 9:30pm—perfect for hungry theatergoers leaving a show. ⑤ *Average main: $27* ✉ *800 F St. NW, Chinatown* ☎ *202/654–0999* ⊕ *www.zoladc.com* ◔ *No lunch weekends* Ⓜ *Gallery Pl./Chinatown* ✛ *2:D3.*

6

GEORGETOWN

$$$$
AMERICAN

✕ **1789 Restaurant.** This dining room with Early American paintings and a fireplace could easily be a room in the White House. But all the gentility of this 19th-century town-house restaurant is offset by the down-to-earth food on the menu, which changes daily. The soups, including the pumpkin stew with local maple syrup, are flavorful. Rack of lamb and fillet of beef are specialties, and the seafood dishes are excellent. Service is fluid and attentive. Try the bread pudding and apple strudel for a sweet finish. ⑤ *Average main: $39* ✉ *1226 36th St. NW, Georgetown* ☎ *202/965–1789* ⊕ *www.1789restaurant.com* ⌲ *Reservations essential* ⌂ *Jacket required* ◔ *No lunch* ✛ *1:A5.*

$$
CAJUN

✕ **Bayou.** New Orleans and Washington, D.C., might seem to have little in common, but both cities share a common love of carousing after hours and belt-stretching cuisine. The urban marriage is consummated beautifully at this two-level po'boy palace, where live bands frequently turn the top floor into a mini–Bourbon Street. Down below, though, the food rules—such as a pork chop done right by its Andouille sausage—Brussels sprouts hash and a fried green tomato appetizer hearty enough to join the entrée menu. Daily specials, such as Wednesday gator night, round out the down-home picture. ⑤ *Average main: $21* ✉ *2519 Pennsylvania Ave. NW, Georgetown* ☎ *202/223–6941* ⊕ *www.bayouonpenn.com* ◔ *Closed Mon.* ✛ *1:D5.*

$$
FRENCH

✕ **Bistro Français.** Washington's chefs head to Bistro Français for minute steak, sirloin with black-pepper or red-wine sauce, and rotisserie chicken. Daily specials may include *suprême* of salmon with broccoli mousse and beurre blanc. In the less formal café, sandwiches and omelets are available in addition to entrées. The bistro also has fixed-price lunches ($$) and early and late-night dinner specials ($$) that include a glass of wine and appetizer, as well as a champagne brunch on weekends. ■**TIP**➜ It stays open until 3 am on weekdays and 4 am on weekends. $ *Average main: $25* ✉ *3128 M St. NW, Georgetown* ☎ *202/338–3830* ⊕ *www.bistrofrancaisdc.com* ☾ *Brunch weekends only* ✛ *1:B5.*

$$$$
ITALIAN

✕ **Cafe Milano.** By night you're likely to rub shoulders with local social-ites, professional sports stars, visiting celebrities, and the Euro-trendy crowd at Cafe Milano's cheek-by-jowl bar. Expect authentic, sophisti-cated Italian cooking and a pricey wine list. Specialties are fried stuffed olives and smelts, thin-crust pizzas, sumptuous pasta dishes such as lobster with linguine and braised veal ravioli, air-dried ricotta, and the type of beautifully composed and dressed salads favored by ladies who lunch. $ *Average main: $40* ✉ *3251 Prospect St. NW, Georgetown* ☎ *202/333–6183* ⊕ *www.cafemilano.net* ✛ *1:A5.*

$$$$
FRENCH
Fodor'sChoice
★

✕ **Citronelle.** See all the action in the glass-front kitchen at chef Michel Richard's flagship California-French restaurant. Appetizers might include foie gras with lentils prepared three ways, and main courses run to lobster medallions with lemongrass, saddle of lamb crusted with herbs, and 72-hour braised Texas short ribs. Desserts are luscious: a crunchy napoleon with filament-like pastry and the special "chocolate bar," Richard's dense, rich take on a Snickers candy bar. A chef's table in the kitchen gives you a ringside seat (reserve at least a month ahead). The three-course menu costs $110 per person, with an even more adven-turous *Promenade Gourmande* option available for $190, or $280 with wine pairings. The bar menu ($$–$$$) has morsels such as mushroom "cigars" and Serrano ham. $ *Average main: $190* ✉ *Latham Hotel, 3000 M St. NW, Georgetown* ☎ *202/625–2150* ⊕ *www.citronelledc. com* ⌦ *Reservations essential* 🎩 *Jacket required* ☾ *No lunch* ✛ *1:B5.*

$
AMERICAN
☺

✕ **Five Guys.** One of the quirky traditions of this homegrown fast-food burger house is to note on the menu board where the potatoes for that day's fries come from, be it Maine, Idaho, or elsewhere. The place gets just about everything right: from the grilled hot dogs and hand-patted burger patties—most folks get a double—to the fresh hand-cut fries with the skin on and the high-quality toppings such as sautéed onions and mushrooms. Add an eclectic jukebox to all of the above and you've got a great burger experience. There are a number of locations around D.C. including Dupont Circle, Downtown, Columbia Heights, and Chi-natown. $ *Average main: $6* ✉ *1335 Wisconsin Ave. NW, Georgetown* ☎ *202/337–0400* ⊕ *www.fiveguys.com* ✛ *1:B4.*

$$
AUSTRIAN

✕ **Kafe Leopold.** Forget all the clichés about heavy Austrian fare served by waiters in lederhosen. Leopold is about as Euro trendy as it gets, with an all-day coffee and drinks bar, an architecturally hip dining space, and a chic little patio complete with a minifountain. Food is pared-down Mitteleuropean: wine soup, crisp Wiener schnitzel paired with peppery greens, an endive salad with mustard dressing. In the middle of design-obsessed Cady's Alley, the café draws an artsy city crowd that's content to sit and watch the scene evolve, just as it's done in Europe. Brunch is a particularly popular setting for such people-watching manna. $ *Av-erage main: $18* ✉ *3315 M St. NW, Georgetown* ☎ *202/965–6005* ⊕ *www.kafeleopolds.com* ⌦ *Reservations not accepted* ✛ *1:A5.*

$ VIETNAMESE **Miss Saigon.** Shades of mauve and green, black art deco accents, and potted palms decorate this Vietnamese restaurant, where attention is lavished on the food and its presentation. Begin with crisp spring rolls or chilled garden rolls, and then proceed to exquisite salads of shredded green papaya topped with shrimp or chicken. Daily specials include imaginative preparations of the freshest seafood. In addition, "caramel"-cooked and grilled meats are standouts. Prices are moderate, especially for lunch, but you may have to order several dishes to have your fill. *Average main: $17 3057 M St. NW, Georgetown 202/333–5545 www.ms-saigonus.com Foggy Bottom/GWU 1:B5.*

$ BARBECUE **Rocklands.** This tiny branch of the popular local barbecue chain does mostly takeout business, but even when eaten with plastic silverware, the baby back ribs and smoked half chicken are still as tender as advertised. Disposable coolers are also sold here, perfect for filling up with corn bread and potato rolls and picnicking by the waterfront. Those who think that barbecue can never deliver a new taste will be humbled by the Pearl, a portable stack of macaroni-and-cheese, barbecued pork, and baked beans that sounds excessive but hits the spot. Locations in Northern Virginia's Arlington and Alexandria neighborhoods are equally reliable. *Average main: $13 2418 Wisconsin Ave. NW, Georgetown 202/333–2558 www.rocklands.com 1:A2.*

6

$$ JAPANESE **Sushi-Ko.** At the city's self-touted first raw-fish restaurant, daily specials are always innovative: sesame oil–seasoned trout layered with crisp wonton crackers, and a sushi special might be salmon topped with a touch of mango sauce and a sprig of dill. You won't find the restaurant's delicious ginger, mango, or green-tea ice cream at the local Baskin-Robbins, but you will find another location of this stylish retreat in wealthy Chevy Chase, just north of the Maryland-D.C. border. *Average main: $24 2309 Wisconsin Ave. NW, Georgetown 202/333–4187 www.sushikorestaurants.com Reservations essential No lunch Sat.–Mon. 1:A2.*

DUPONT CIRCLE AND LOGAN CIRCLE

DUPONT CIRCLE

$ FRENCH **Bistrot du Coin.** An instant hit in its Dupont Circle neighborhood, this moderately priced French bistro with a monumental zinc bar is noisy, crowded, and fun. The comforting, traditional bistro fare includes starter and entree portions of mussels in several different preparations. Steaks, garnished with a pile of crisp fries, are the main attraction, but you might also try the herb raviolis or *magret de canard* (a maple-infused duck breast with pepper-cream sauce). Wash it down with house Beaujolais, Côtes du Rhône, or an Alsatian white. *Average main: $17 1738 Connecticut Ave. NW, Dupont Circle 202/234–6969 www.bistrotducoin.com Brunch weekends only Dupont Circle 1:E3.*

$$ SEAFOOD Fodor's Choice ★ **Hank's Oyster Bar.** The watchword is simplicity at this popular and chic take on the shellfish shacks of New England. A half-dozen oyster varieties are available daily on the half shell, both from the West Coast and local Virginia waters, alongside another half-dozen daily fish specials, from bouillabaisse to tuna tartare. An amuse-bouche

of cheddar Goldfish crackers adds a touch of whimsy. Don't be shy about asking for seconds on the complimentary baking chocolate presented along with your check—the kitchen doesn't serve sweets, but it doesn't need to. $ *Average main: $21* ✉ *1624 Q St. NW, Dupont Circle* ☎ *202/462–4265* ⊕ *www.banksdc.com* ☉ *No brunch weekdays* Ⓜ *Dupont Circle* ✛ *1:G4.*

$$$$ ✕ **Komi.** Johnny Monis, the young, energetic chef-owner of this small, personal restaurant, offers one of the most adventurous dining experiences in the city. The multicourse prix fixe, which can run up to two-dozen small dishes at the chef's discretion, showcases contemporary fare with a distinct Mediterranean influence. ■**TIP**➜ Reservations open 30 days in advance—and the longer you wait, the smaller your chance at a coveted table. Star plates include fresh sardines with pickled lemons, suckling pig over apples and bacon with polenta, and mascarpone-filled dates with sea salt. It doesn't come cheap, and don't expect a menu available online, or even after you arrive, but do expect the four-hour ride of your foodie life in Monis's renowned hands. $ *Average main: $135* ✉ *1509 17th St. NW, Dupont Circle* ☎ *202/332–9200* ⊕ *www. komirestaurant.com* ⌕ *Reservations essential* ☉ *Closed Sun. and Mon. No lunch* Ⓜ *Dupont Circle* ✛ *1:G4.*

MODERN
AMERICAN
Fodor's Choice
★

$$ ✕ **Kramerbooks & Afterwords.** This popular bookstore-cum-café is a favorite neighborhood breakfast spot. ■**TIP**➜ It's also a late-night haunt on Friday and Saturday, when it's open around the clock. There's a simple menu with soups, salads, and sandwiches, but many people drop in just for cappuccino and dessert. The "dysfunctional family sundae"—a massive brownie soaked in amaretto with a plethora of divine toppings—is especially popular. Catch a live music performance—everything from rock to the blues—here Wednesday through Saturday from 8 pm to midnight. $ *Average main: $19* ✉ *1517 Connecticut Ave. NW, Dupont Circle* ☎ *202/387–3825* ⊕ *www.kramers.com* Ⓜ *Dupont Circle* ✛ *1:F4.*

CAFÉ
☾

$ ✕ **Nooshi.** Always packed, with long lines waiting for tables and takeout, this attractive Pan-Asian noodle house has remarkably good Chinese, Japanese, Thai, Indonesian, Malaysian, and Vietnamese dishes. Try the Thai drunkin noodles, which are soused in sake; Nasi Goreng, a spicy fried rice with chicken satay; or the Vietnamese rice noodles with grilled chicken. After the restaurant added its extensive sushi menu, it changed its name to Nooshi (noodles plus sushi). $ *Average main: $16* ✉ *1120 19th St. NW, Dupont Circle* ☎ *202/293–3138* ⊕ *www.nooshidc.com* ☉ *No lunch Sun.* Ⓜ *Farragut N* ✛ *1:F5.*

ASIAN

$$$$ ✕ **Nora.** Chef and founder Nora Pouillon helped pioneer the sustainable-food revolution with the first certified organic restaurant in the country, and her seasonal, sustainable ingredients are out of this world. Settle into the sophisticated and attractive quilt-decorated dining room and start with the artichoke and cherry tomato tart or a locally grown salad. Entrées such as pepper-crusted steak and roasted salmon with parsnips emphasize the well-balanced, earthy ingredients. A four-course tasting menu is available, with a reduced price for vegetarians. $ *Average main: $38* ✉ *2132 Florida Ave. NW, Dupont Circle* ☎ *202/462–5143* ⊕ *www.noras.com* ⌕ *Reservations essential* ☉ *Closed Sun. No lunch* Ⓜ *Dupont Circle* ✛ *1:E3.*

AMERICAN
Fodor's Choice
★

$$$$
ITALIAN

✕ **Obelisk.** Come here for eclectic Italian cuisine in a setting so quietly stunning you'll remember it for years. The three-course prix fixe ($$$$), your only option, changes every day, combining traditional dishes with chef Peter Pastan's innovations. Representative main courses are lamb with garlic and sage, and braised grouper with artichoke and thyme. The dining room is tiny and the warm and attentive service makes this feel like a hidden gem. $ *Average main: $75* ⊠ *2029 P St. NW, Dupont Circle* ☎ *202/872–1180* ⌒ *Reservations essential* ⊗ *Closed Sun. and Mon. No lunch* Ⓜ *Dupont Circle* ✛ *1:E4.*

$$$$
ITALIAN

✕ **The Palm.** A favorite lunchtime hangout of power brokers, from politics to media, the Palm has walls papered with caricatures of the famous patrons who have dined there. Main attractions include gargantuan steaks and Nova Scotia lobsters, several kinds of potatoes, and New York cheesecake. One of the Palm's best-kept secrets is that it's also a terrific old-fashioned Italian restaurant. Try the veal Marsala for lunch or, on Thursday, the tasty shrimp in marinara sauce. $ *Average main: $48* ⊠ *1225 19th St. NW, Dupont Circle* ☎ *202/293–9091* ⊕ *www. thepalm.com* ⌒ *Reservations essential* ⊗ *No lunch weekends* Ⓜ *Dupont Circle* ✛ *1:F5.*

$
ITALIAN
☾

✕ **Pizzeria Paradiso.** A trompe-l'oeil ceiling adds space and light to a simple interior at the ever-popular Pizzeria Paradiso, which has spin-off locations in Georgetown and suburban Alexandria, Virginia. The restaurant sticks to crowd-pleasing basics: pizzas, panini, salads, and desserts. Although the standard pizza is satisfying, you can enliven it with fresh buffalo mozzarella or unusual toppings such as potatoes, capers, and mussels. Gluten allergies are accommodated with special dough, available on request. Wines are well chosen and well priced. The intensely flavored gelato is a house specialty. $ *Average main: $17* ⊠ *2003 P St. NW, Dupont Circle* ☎ *202/223–1245* ⊕ *www. eatyourpizza.com* Ⓜ *Dupont Circle* ✛ *1:E4.*

$
ECLECTIC
Fodor's Choice
★

✕ **Sweetgreen.** When three Georgetown University graduates carved out a closet-sized niche to sell freshly made salads and tart frozen yogurt, no one in the city batted an eyelash. Since that time, their empire has opened locations in Maryland and Virginia while expanding into healthful, tasty "market sides" that use all local ingredients, such as spicy kale and balsamic roasted sweet potatoes. The guacamole salad, which brilliantly deposits every flavor of the Mexican dip onto mixed greens, remains a classic. But everything else about this franchise is breaking new ground. $ *Average main: $9* ⊠ *1512 Connecticut Ave. NW, Dupont Circle* ☎ *202/387–9338* ⊕ *www.sweetgreen.com* Ⓜ *Dupont Circle* ✛ *1:E4.*

$$$
MODERN
AMERICAN

✕ **Tabard Inn.** Fading portraits and overstuffed furniture make the lobby lounge look like an antiques store, but this hotel restaurant's culinary sensibilities are thoroughly modern. The menu, which changes daily, consistently offers interesting seafood and vegetarian options. A popular entrée is the house-made squid-ink pasta with scallops, rock shrimp, and parsley. A vegetarian option might be sweet potato and Parmesan ravioli thickened with fragrant sage butter. ■**TIP→** In good weather you can eat in the quaint, tranquil courtyard during first-come, first-serve breakfast hours. $ *Average main: $28* ⊠ *Hotel Tabard Inn, 1739 N St.*

6

NW, Dupont Circle ☎ *202/331–8528* ⊕ *www.tabardinn.com/restaurant* Ⓜ *Dupont Circle* ✛ *1:F4.*

$$$ ✕ **Vidalia.** There's a lot more to Chef Jeffrey Buben's distinguished res-
SOUTHERN   taurant than the sweet Vidalia onion, which is a specialty in season. Inspired by the cooking and the ingredients of the South and the Chesapeake Bay region, Buben's version of New American cuisine revolves around the best seasonal fruits, vegetables, and seafood he can find. Try the seared foie gras with pickled cherries, the shrimp on yellow grits, or the sensational lemon chess pie. The sleek modern surroundings, including a wine bar, are equal to the food. Ⓢ *Average main: $33* ✉ *1990 M St. NW, Dupont Circle* ☎ *202/659–1990* ⊕ *www.vidaliadc.com* ☉ *Closed Sun. July and Aug. No lunch weekends* Ⓜ *Dupont Circle* ✛ *1:F5.*

LOGAN CIRCLE

$$ ✕ **Birch & Barley.** In a city where culinary classicism is too often code
AMERICAN   for predictable steaks and pastas, this earth-toned kitchen is a welcome throwback to the age before zany fusion ingredients turned dinner into science class. The six entrées, as well as rotating flatbread and pasta duos, are odes to autumnal flavors that pair perfectly with the 555 (yes, that's not a typo) varieties of artisan beers on offer. Try the ricotta cavatelli topped by melt-in-your-mouth short ribs or the succulent Brat burger with creamy Emmentaler and kick back for a leisurely, romantic repast. Just save room for the delightful desserts, particularly the house-made versions of childhood classics such as the Snickers bar and pudding pop. Ⓢ *Average main: $23* ✉ *1337 14th St. NW, Logan Circle* ☎ *202/567–2576* ⊕ *www.birchandbarley.com* 🥢 *Reservations essential* ☉ *Closed Mon. Brunch Sun. only* Ⓜ *Shaw/Howard U.* ✛ *1:H4.*

$$ ✕ **Estadio.** The name of this polished palace means "stadium," and its
SPANISH   gorgeously baroque interior, which surrounds a high-wire open kitchen, makes a perfect stage for energetic and flavorful new uses of top-notch ingredients. The menu, developed by chef Haidar Karoum and owner Mark Kuller during research jaunts through Spain, is a master class in tapas, with a sherry-glazed halibut punched up by garlicky romesco sauce and tortilla Espanola smoother than any served in Barcelona. The bar menu is equally inventive, though watch out for smaller-than-normal wine pours. Try the quirky alcoholic "slushitos" to get a delightful adult twist on the beloved Slurpee. For dessert, don't miss the sweet-and-salty sherry ice cream float with pumpkinseed brittle. Ⓢ *Average main: $25* ✉ *1520 14th St. NW, Logan Circle* ☎ *202/319–1404* ⊕ *www. estadio-dc.com* Ⓜ *U St./Cardozo* ✛ *1:H3.*

$$ ✕ **Masa 14.** This modern lounge blends Asian and Latin American fla-
ASIAN FUSION   vors, with a menu of memorable small plates. The masa-panko-crusted calamari comes with a kick of Madras curry, and savory pork belly tacos are served on an Asian bun. The cocktail list, headlined by more than 100 varieties of tequila, is the star of the city's longest bar (65 feet). The only thing missing from this collaboration between raw-fish guru Kaz Okochi and fusion impresario Richard Sandoval is a full-time sushi chef—but with house music thumping and bartenders shaking fresh libations, few patrons realize their spicy tuna wasn't hand-rolled. ■ TIP➔ The prix-fixe all-you-can-eat-and-drink brunch is a rare find in any city, and a challenge worth taking. Ⓢ *Average main: $20* ✉ *1825 14th St.*

NW, Logan Circle ☎ *202/328–1414* ⊕ *www.masa14.com* ⊘ *No lunch. No brunch weekdays* Ⓜ *U Street/Cardozo* ✛ *1:H3.*

$$$ ✕ **Posto.** Now that the Obama administration has anointed this breezy,
ITALIAN   classic Italian kitchen its new power-dining palace, keep one eye on the
door in case the attorney general or White House political adviser comes
popping in for a piece of wood-fired picante pizza. If spicy salami isn't
your thing, the array of salads are convincing evidence that Italian food
need not be carbohydrate-centric. The bustling aisles are often less than
romantic, and service can be scattershot when a VIP is in the room, but
if you're looking for a great meal with a side order of Capitol culture,
there's no better place to be. $ *Average main: $26* ⊠ *1515 14th St. NW,
Logan Circle* ☎ *202/332–8613* ⊕ *www.postodc.com* ⬥ *Reservations
essential* ⊘ *No lunch* Ⓜ *U Street/Cardozo* ✛ *1:H4.*

ADAMS MORGAN

$$$ ✕ **Cashion's Eat Place.** Walls are hung with family photos, and tables
AMERICAN   are jammed with regulars feasting on up-to-date homestyle cooking.
Founder and capital cuisine superstar Ann Cashion recently sold the
spot to her longtime sous chef, but the Eat Place has remained a neighborhood favorite. The menu changes daily, but roast chicken, steak,
and seafood are frequent choices. Side dishes, such as garlicky mashed
potatoes, sometimes upstage the main course. If it's available, order the
chocolate terrine layered with walnuts, caramel, mousse, and ganache.
■ TIP➜ If you're dining with a local, make sure to ask for the 10% "neighborhood discount." $ *Average main: $30* ⊠ *1819 Columbia Rd. NW, Adams
Morgan* ☎ *202/797–1819* ⊕ *www.cashionseatplace.com* ⬥ *Reservations essential* ⊘ *Closed Mon. No lunch* Ⓜ *Woodley Park/Zoo* ✛ *1:F1.*

6

U STREET CORRIDOR

$$ ✕ **1905.** This spot's logo features an antiqued key, which is the per-
ECLECTIC   fect symbol for a dining experience so intimate you'll want to keep it
a closely guarded secret. Young chef Matthew Richardson unites the
flavors of France, Greece, and Italy with all-American touches for his
intelligent comfort food. Spinach pie is served with a piquant heirloom
bean cake, while the ubiquitous bistro burger gets an exotic makeover
thanks to mushrooms cooked into the patty and a coat of brie. The
dining room's refurbished Victorian-era fixtures and wallpaper create
a romantic buzz that recalls the Moulin Rouge—in fact, canoodling
couples like to sip absinthe in the more private window booths. $ *Aver-
age main: $21* ⊠ *1905 9th St. NW, U Street Corridor* ☎ *202/332–1905*
⊕ *1905dc.com* ⬥ *Reservations essential* ⊘ *No lunch. Closed Sun. and
Mon.* Ⓜ *U St./Cardozo* ✛ *1:H2.*

$ ✕ **Ben's Chili Bowl.** Long before U Street became hip, Ben's was serving
AMERICAN   chili. Chili on hot dogs, chili on Polish-style sausages, chili on burgers,
ⓒ   and just plain chili. Add cheese fries if you dare. The faux-marble bar
and shiny red-vinyl stools give the impression that little has changed
since the 1950s, but don't be fooled—this favorite of President Obama
and his aides has rocketed into the 21st century with an iPhone app
and kiosks at Nationals baseball games. Turkey and vegetarian burgers

and meatless chili are the menu's more upscale nods to modern times. Ben's closes at 2 am Monday through Thursday, at 4 am on Friday and Saturday. It serves no breakfast on Sunday but stays open until 11 pm. Southern-style breakfast is served from 6 am weekdays and from 7 am on Saturday. $ *Average main: $6* ⊠ *1213 U St. NW, U Street Corridor* ☎ *202/667–0909* ⊕ *www.benschilibowl.com* ⊟ *No credit cards* Ⓜ *U St./Cardozo* ✛ *1:H2.*

$$ ✕ **Cork.** This rustic, dimly lighted slip of a wine bar brings chic cuisine
MODERN   to the still-gentrifying streets of the city's hippest neighborhood. The
AMERICAN   wine list features rare varietals—most under $10 per glass. Even tee-totalers will find much to love among the menu's classic dishes. The duck confit in beet vinaigrette and avocado bruschetta with pistachio oil are particular standouts, and the goat cheesecake has made its inventor locally famous. The one thing missing: intimacy. Expect long waits on weekends, and to stand uncomfortably close to fellow tipplers at the bar. It's best to call 30 minutes before you arrive. $ *Average main: $20* ⊠ *1720 14th St. NW, U Street Corridor* ☎ *202/265–2675* ⊕ *www.corkdc.com* ☾ *No lunch. Closed Mon.* Ⓜ *U Street/Cardozo* ✛ *1:H3.*

$ ✕ **Etete.** The best of the city's Ethiopian restaurants, Etete doesn't hold
AFRICAN   back on the spices. Savory pastries known as *sambusas* are filled with
☖   fiery lentils, and ginger brightens a stew of vegetables. The sharing of dishes and the mode of eating—rather than using utensils diners tear off pieces of *injera*, a spongy pancakelike bread to scoop up stews and sautées—make for exotic and adventurous dining at this style-conscious eatery. $ *Average main: $14* ⊠ *1942 9th St. NW, U Street Corridor* ☎ *202/232–7600* ⊕ *www.eteterestaurant.com* Ⓜ *U St./Cardozo* ✛ *1:H2.*

$$ ✕ **Marvin.** The owner of this quirky club and restaurant named after soul
BELGIAN   singer Marvin Gaye is Eric Hilton, a D.C. local who became a national celebrity as half of the DJ supergroup Thievery Corporation. Inspired by Gaye's sojourn to Belgium in the 1980s, the menu combines soul food with traditional French classics—think chicken and waffles and fall-apart poached monkfish. The food is so good it'll bust your belt. After dinner, sample a Belgian beer and shake your booty on the upstairs dance floor. At Sunday brunch, try the stellar shrimp and grits or the lighter watercress salad. $ *Average main: $22* ⊠ *2007 14th St. NW, U Street Corridor* ☎ *202/797–7171* ⊕ *www.marvindc.com* ⬤ *Reservations essential* ☾ *No lunch. Brunch Sun. only* Ⓜ *U St./Cardozo* ✛ *1:H2.*

$ ✕ **Oohhs & Aahhs.** No-frills soul food is what you can find at this
SOUTHERN   friendly eat-in/take-out place where the price is right and the food is delicious. Ultrarich macaroni and cheese, perfectly fried chicken, and smoky-sweet beef ribs just beg to be devoured. Sides like collard greens have a healthy bent, cooked with vinegar and sugar rather than the traditional salt pork. Smack in the middle of the U Street area, the place is both a neighborhood hangout and destination for those missing the perennial dishes that Mama always made best. $ *Average main: $17* ⊠ *1005 U St. NW, U Street Corridor* ☎ *202/667–7142* ⊕ *www.oohhsnaahhs.com* ⊟ *No credit cards* ☾ *Closed Sun. and Mon.* Ⓜ *U St./Cardozo* ✛ *1:H2.*

$$ ✕**Pearl Dive Oyster Palace.** Chef Jeff Black does serve a po'boy at his
CREOLE dazzlingly decorated follow-up to the popular Black Salt, but that's
about as working-class as it gets at this polished homage to the bivalve.
Oysters come raw, with a pair of perfect dipping sauces—for about
$1 each, during happy hour—or warm in five irresistible guises, from
bacon-wrapped to crusted in cornmeal and sprinkled with sweet
potato. If you eschew shellfish, Black has you covered with a grass-
fed steak lovingly bedecked in blue cheese. Expect to get the best and
pay for it here, where craft cocktails are $12 and each warm apple
pie serving comes baked into its own mini-skillet. Upstairs, the well-
heeled crowd endures lengthy table waits with Peroni on tap at the
breezy Black Jack bar. ⑤ *Average main: $25* ✉ *1612 14th St. NW, U
Street Corridor* ☎ */319–1612* ⊕ *www.pearldivedc.com* ⚓ *Reservations
essential* ✛ *2:B1.*

UPPER NORTHWEST

$ ✕**2 Amys.** Judging from the long lines here, the best pizza in D.C. is
PIZZA uptown. Simple recipes allow the ingredients to shine through at this
☾ Neapolitan pizzeria. You may be tempted to go for the D.O.C. pizza
(it has *Denominazione di Origine Controllata* approval for Neapolitan
authenticity), but don't hesitate to try the daily specials. Roasted pep-
pers with anchovies and deviled eggs with parsley-caper sauce have by
now become classics. At busy times the wait for a table can exceed an
hour, and the noisy din of a packed house may discourage some din-
ers. ⑤ *Average main: $13* ✉ *3715 Macomb St. NW, Upper Northwest*
☎ *202/885–5700* ⊕ *www.2amyspizza.com* ⚓ *Reservations not accepted*
☾ *No lunch Mon.* ✛ *1:A2.*

$$ ✕**Ardeo.** The trendy American Ardeo and its loungelike counterpart,
MODERN the wine bar Bardeo, sit side by side in the ever-popular culinary
AMERICAN strip of Cleveland Park. Ardeo is known for its clean design, professional and knowledgeable staff, and creative menu. Everything is
skillfully prepared, from gnocchi with sugar pumpkin to crab salad
and a roasted organic chicken. Bardeo has similar options in smaller
portions, and great wine offerings, including more than 20 wines by
the glass. ⑤ *Average main: $22* ✉ *3311 Connecticut Ave. NW, Upper
Northwest* ☎ *202/244–6750* ⊕ *www.ardeobardeo.com* Ⓜ *Cleveland
Park* ✛ *1:D1.*

$$ ✕**Bistrot Lepic.** Relaxed and upbeat, with bright yellow walls and col-
FRENCH orful paintings, this small, crowded neighborhood bistro is French in
every regard—starting with the flirty servers. Traditional bistro fare has
been replaced with potato-crusted salmon served with French grapes
and ouzo-grape sauce. Some standards, like veal cheeks, remain. The
wine is all French, with many wines available by the glass. The wine bar
on the second floor has a menu of small plates such as terrine of foie
gras, smoked-trout salad, and onion-bacon tart. On this level, seating
is first-come, first-served, with a smaller menu than the one available to
downstairs customers with reservations. ⑤ *Average main: $24* ✉ *1736
Wisconsin Ave. NW, Glover Park* ☎ *202/333–0111* ⊕ *www.bistrotlepic.
com* ⚓ *Reservations essential* ✛ *1:A3.*

6

$$$ ✕ **Black Salt.** Just beyond Georgetown in the residential neighborhood
SEAFOOD of Palisades, Black Salt is part fish market, part gossipy neighborhood
hangout, part swanky restaurant. Fish offerings dominate, and vary
from classics like oyster stew and fried Ipswich clams to more-offbeat
fixings like Pacific butterfish with piquillo pepper, lobster with Kaffir
lime, and a butterscotch *pot de crème* for dessert. The place can get
crowded and loud, and reservations are a must for weekends. Regu-
lars consider a meal at the bar a good fallback—especially when the
house-made ginger-mascarpone French toast is on hand during the out-
of-this-world brunch. ⑤ *Average main: $31* ✉ *4883 MacArthur Blvd.,
Upper Northwest* ☎ *202/342–9101* ⊕ *www.blacksaltrestaurant.com*
🍽 *Reservations essential* ⊗ *No lunch Sun. Brunch Sun. only* ✛ *1:A2.*

$ ✕ **Heritage India.** You feel like a guest in a foreign land dining at this
INDIAN restaurant: there's incredible attention to detail in everything from the
tapestried chairs to the paintings of India and the traditional tandoori
and curry dishes. Try the *khazana,* an assortment of curries served with
rice pilaf. Bottles of wine are half price on weeknights, and you may
still be able to claim a clever "stimulus package" that gives returning
customers a discount. A spin-off Thai bistro is also located in the Glover
Park outpost, while a sister location in Dupont Circle is similarly popu-
lar with bargain diners. ⑤ *Average main: $16* ✉ *2400 Wisconsin Ave.
NW, Upper Northwest* ☎ *202/333–3120* ⊕ *www.heritageindiausa.com*
🍽 *Reservations essential* ✛ *1:A2.*

$$ ✕ **New Heights.** This inviting restaurant has 11 large windows that over-
MODERN look nearby Rock Creek Park. The sophisticated contemporary cooking
AMERICAN has changed hands among multiple chefs in recent years, but all blend
bold world flavors into the traditional American dishes. Grilled strip
steak goes exotic with ginger and shiitake mushrooms, while roasted
chicken breast flirts with candied cashews on the side. Fans of experimental desserts will appreciate the cinnamony Mexican *churros* served
with raspberry "dust." ⑤ *Average main: $25* ✉ *2317 Calvert St. NW,
Upper Northwest* ☎ *202/234–4110* ⊕ *www.newheightsrestaurant.com*
Ⓜ *Woodley Park/Zoo* ✛ *1:D1.*

$$$$ ✕ **Palena.** Chef Frank Ruta and pastry chef Ann Amernick met while
MODERN working in the White House kitchens. At their contemporary American
AMERICAN restaurant the French- and Italian-influenced menu changes seasonally.
Fodor's Choice Among the can't-miss presentations are chestnut ravioli with shiitake
★ mushrooms, raw diver scallops with creme fraiche, and roasted venison with quince. Comforting desserts such as a tangy German apple
cake or a chocolate torte are a perfect match for the earthy cooking.
■ TIP➜ Four- or six-course tasting menus are available. Reservations are
not accepted for the equally fabulous café, where the inexpensive menu
includes a cheeseburger with truffles, foie-gras terrine, and an extravagant platter of fries, onion rings, and paper-thin fried Meyer lemon
slices. ⑤ *Average main: $75* ✉ *3529 Connecticut Ave. NW, Cleveland
Park* ☎ *202/537–9250* ⊕ *www.palenarestaurant.com* 🍽 *Reservations
essential* ⊗ *Restaurant closed Sun. and Mon. No lunch (except in café,
weekends only)* Ⓜ *Cleveland Park* ✛ *1:D1.*

SUBURBAN VIRGINIA

$$$
MODERN
AMERICAN
Fodor's Choice
★

✕ **2941 Restaurant.** Soaring ceilings, a woodsy lakeside location, and a koi pond make this one of the most striking dining rooms in the area. The playful cooking continually surprises, with plates like short rib–spiked fondue and scallops with lentils, free-range chicken, a pumpkin baked Alaska crowned by candied cranberries, and little gifts from the kitchen like rainbow-hue house-made cotton candy. It's a family affair, too. The chef's father makes the artisanal breads that run from rosemary olive to cherry almond. You can order à la carte or splurge on one of the tasting menus. Those seeking a thriftier experience can head to the bar, where an abridged menu is offered. $ *Average main: $27* ✉ *2941 Fairview Park Dr., Falls Church, Virginia* ☎ *703/270–1500* ⊕ *www.2941.com* ⌣ *Reservations essential* ☾ *No lunch weekends* ✛ *1:A6.*

$$$
AMERICAN

✕ **Ashby Inn.** If there's a recipe for a perfect country inn, Chef Tarver King and co-owner/sommelier Neil Wavra have it. Head an hour west from D.C., and your reward is extraordinary comfort food. Dishes are made with eclectic pairings of fresh local ingredients and presented in an intimate setting. Steelhead trout, for example, comes with granola, ham, and green apples, while fennel shortbread tops a citrus dessert intensely christened "cocoa and blood." Sunday brunch is from noon to 2:30. $ *Average main: $34* ✉ *692 Federal St., Paris, Virginia* ☎ *540/592–3900* ⊕ *www.ashbyinn.com* ☾ *Closed Mon.–Tues. No lunch Sun. Brunch Sun. only* ✛ *1:A6.*

$$$
MODERN
AMERICAN

✕ **Fyve Restaurant Lounge.** This formerly staid dining room in the Ritz-Carlton got a modern makeover that matches the inventive cuisine stylings of new chef Frederic Chartier, who cut his teeth running the kitchen at culinary legend Eric Ripert's Blue restaurant on Grand Cayman Island. Warm tones of red and orange accentuate the sensuality of the Italian-inspired menu. Standout dishes include the tangy cheese and artichoke terrine with balsamic vinaigrette and an organic chicken in fragrant bacon sauce. At breakfast, the cranberry brioche French toast is another favorite. $ *Average main: $28* ✉ *Ritz-Carlton, 1250 S. Hayes St., Pentagon City, Arlington, Virginia* ☎ *703/415–5000* ⊕ *www. fyverestaurant.com* ✛ *2:B6.*

$$$$
AMERICAN
Fodor's Choice
★

✕ **Inn at Little Washington.** A 90-minute drive from the District takes you past hills and farms to this English-style country manor, where the service matches the setting. A seven-course dinner might begin with tiny canapés such as a mini-BLT on house-made bread, and soup follows—perhaps chilled fruit or creamy leek. Braised duck and seared foie gras over watercress might come next, then squab over garlic polenta. Desserts, including the "palette" of pastel-hue sorbets, are fanciful, and the cheese plate is delivered on a life-size, mooing faux cow. A "gastronaut" menu, including wine pairings, takes the foodie fun to more acrobatic heights, with such offerings as bitter chocolate-dusted lamb loin on salsify purée with ratatouille. $ *Average main: $180* ✉ *Middle and Main Sts., Washington, Virginia* ☎ *540/675–3800* ⊕ *www.theinnatlittlewashington.com* ⌣ *Reservations essential* ☾ *No Lunch. Closed Tues. Jan.–Apr., and June–Sept.* ✛ *2:A6.*

6

$

AMERICAN

Fodor's Choice

★

✗ **Ray's Hell Burger.** The ambience is nothing to write home about, but the succulent beef—freshly ground in-house every day—at this unassuming suburban spot is nothing short of sublime. Owner Michael Landrum, who pioneered the no-frills foodie-mecca concept at Ray's the Steaks just down the street, is nothing short of fanatical about quality and variety, and here he backs up the hype with toppings that range from marinated mushrooms to fluffy, tangy blue cheese. Burgers can be ordered blackened, Cajun, or grilled, and all come with watermelon. Fries and beer are now available here too, which didn't dissuade President Obama and Vice President Biden, whose "working lunch" at Ray's caused such crowds that Landrum had to move to a bigger location. $ *Average main: $10* ⊠ *1725 Wilson Blvd., Arlington, Virginia* ☎ *703/841–0001* ⊕ *rayshellburger.com* ⌲ *Reservations not accepted* ⊗ *No lunch Mon.* Ⓜ *Court House or Rosslyn* ✛ *2:B6.*

Dining and Lodging Atlas

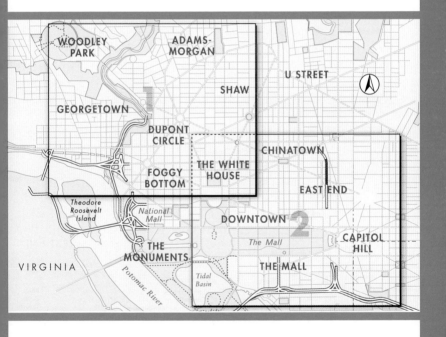

WOODLEY PARK

ADAMS-MORGAN

U STREET

SHAW

GEORGETOWN

DUPONT CIRCLE

CHINATOWN

THE WHITE HOUSE

FOGGY BOTTOM

EAST END

Theodore Roosevelt Island

National Mall

DOWNTOWN

CAPITOL HILL

THE MONUMENTS

VIRGINIA

Potomac River

Tidal Basin

The Mall

THE MALL

KEY	
☐	Hotels
■	Restaurants
■	Restaurant in Hotel
M	Metro Station

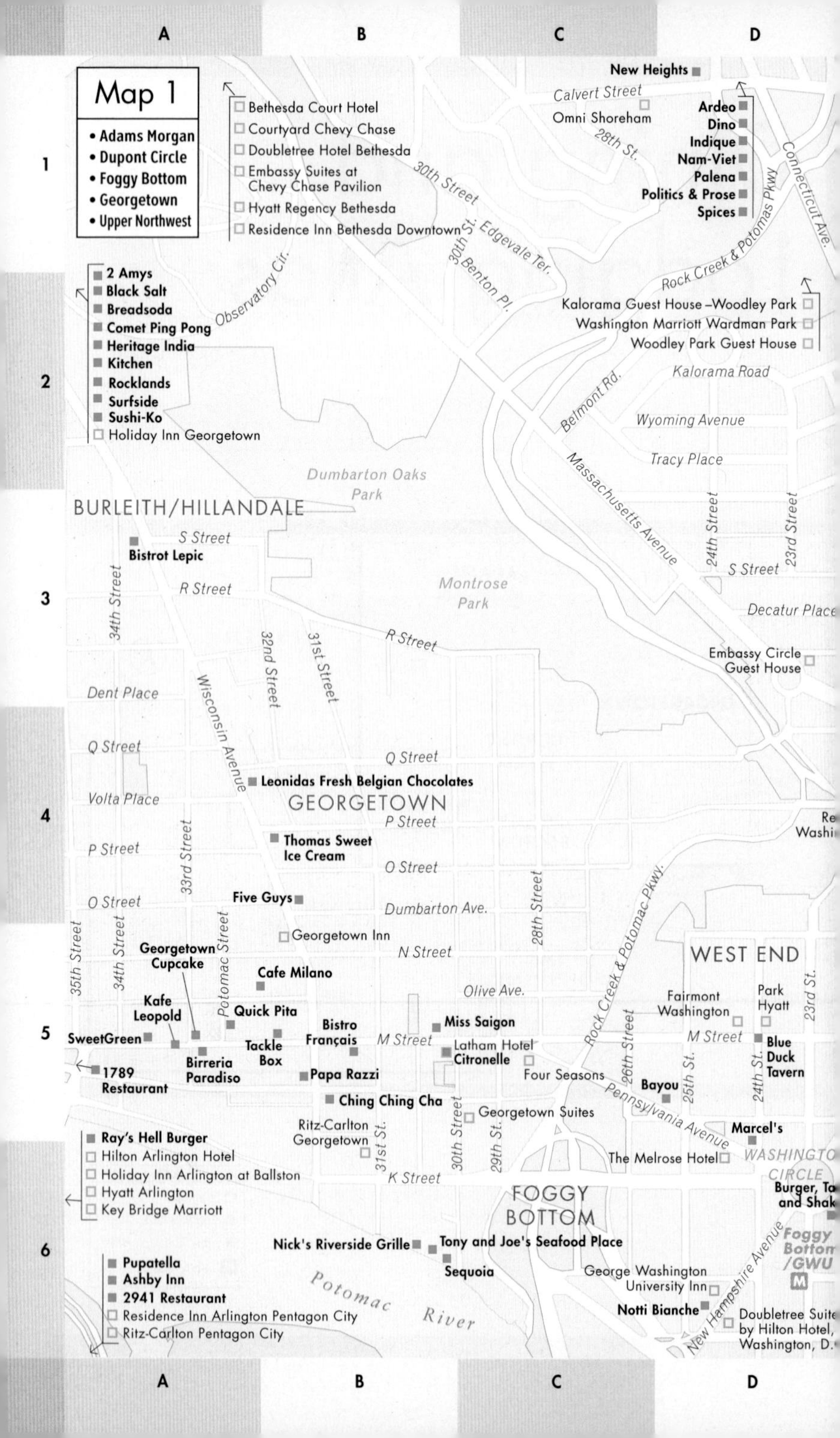

Map 1

- Adams Morgan
- Dupont Circle
- Foggy Bottom
- Georgetown
- Upper Northwest

New Heights

Calvert Street

Omni Shoreham

28th St.

Ardeo
Dino
Indique
Nam-Viet
Palena
Politics & Prose
Spices

Rock Creek & Potomas Pkwy.

Connecticut Ave.

- 2 Amys
- Black Salt
- Breadsoda
- Comet Ping Pong
- Heritage India
- Kitchen
- Rocklands
- Surfside
- Sushi-Ko
- ☐ Holiday Inn Georgetown

Bethesda Court Hotel
Courtyard Chevy Chase
Doubletree Hotel Bethesda
Embassy Suites at
  Chevy Chase Pavilion
Hyatt Regency Bethesda
Residence Inn Bethesda Downtown

30th Street

30th St. Edgevale Ter.

30th St. Benton Pl.

Kalorama Guest House –Woodley Park ☐
Washington Marriott Wardman Park ☐
Woodley Park Guest House ☐

Kalorama Road

Wyoming Avenue

Belmont Rd.

Tracy Place

Massachusetts Avenue

24th Street

23rd Street

Dumbarton Oaks
Park

BURLEITH/HILLANDALE

S Street

■ Bistrot Lepic

34th Street

R Street

32nd Street

31st Street

R Street

Montrose
Park

S Street

Decatur Place

Dent Place

Wisconsin Avenue

R Street

Embassy Circle
Guest House

Q Street

Q Street

Volta Place

33rd Street

■ Leonidas Fresh Belgian Chocolates

GEORGETOWN

P Street

P Street

28th Street

Re___
Washi___

P Street

■ Thomas Sweet
  Ice Cream

O Street

O Street

35th Street

34th Street

Five Guys

Dumbarton Ave.

N Street

WEST END

Georgetown
Cupcake

Potomac Street

☐ Georgetown Inn

Olive Ave.

Fairmont
Washington

Park
Hyatt

23rd St.

Kafe
Leopold

Cafe Milano

Quick Pita

Miss Saigon

M Street

26th Street

24th St.

Blue
Duck
Tavern

SweetGreen

Tackle
Box

Bistro
Français

Latham Hotel
Citronelle

M Street

Birreria
Paradiso

Papa Razzi

Four Seasons

25th St.

Bayou

■1789
Restaurant

Ching Ching Cha

Georgetown Suites

Marcel's

Ritz-Carlton
Georgetown

31st St.

30th Street

29th St.

Pennsylvania Avenue

WASHINGTON
CIRCLE

■ Ray's Hell Burger
☐ Hilton Arlington Hotel
☐ Holiday Inn Arlington at Ballston
☐ Hyatt Arlington
☐ Key Bridge Marriott

K Street

The Melrose Hotel ☐

Burger, Ta__
and Shak__

FOGGY
BOTTOM

Foggy
Botto__
/GWU
Ⓜ

Nick's Riverside Grille ■

Tony and Joe's Seafood Place

George Washington
University Inn

New Hampshire Avenue

■ Pupatella
■ Ashby Inn
■ 2941 Restaurant
☐ Residence Inn Arlington Pentagon City
☐ Ritz-Carlton Pentagon City

Sequoia

Potomac

River

Notti Bianche

Doubletree Suite__
by Hilton Hotel,
Washington, D.__

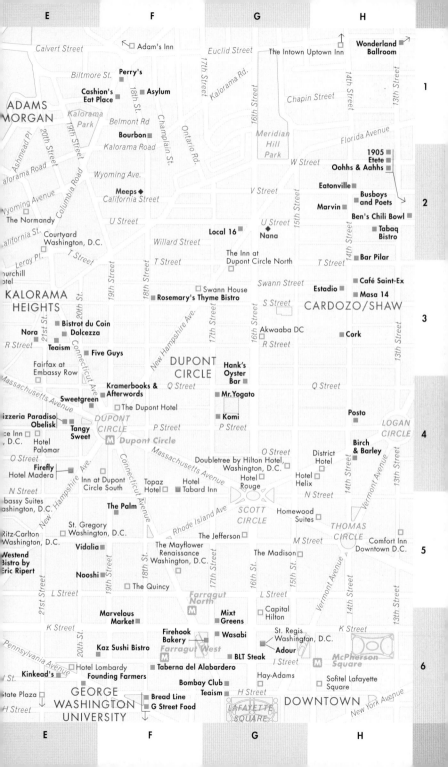

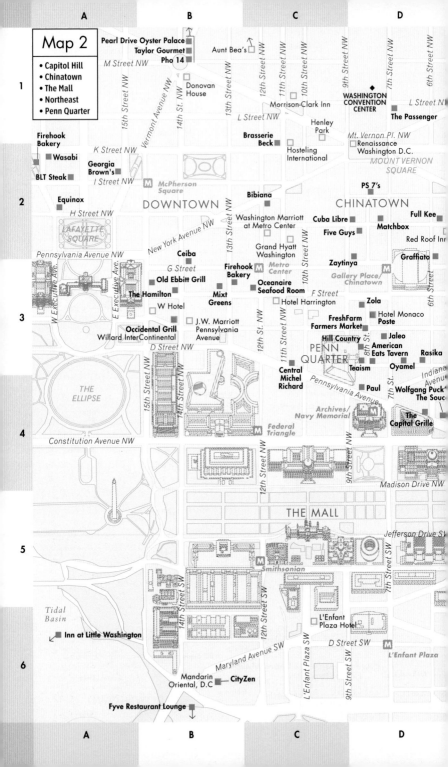

Map 2

- Capitol Hill
- Chinatown
- The Mall
- Northeast
- Penn Quarter

Column A:

Firehook Bakery
Wasabi
BLT Steak
Equinox
LAFAYETTE SQUARE
Pennsylvania Avenue NW
THE ELLIPSE
Tidal Basin
Inn at Little Washington

Column B:

Pearl Drive Oyster Palace
Taylor Gourmet
Pho 14
M Street NW
Donovan House
13th Street NW
L Street NW
K Street NW
Georgia Brown's
I Street NW
McPherson Square
DOWNTOWN
New York Avenue NW
Ceiba
G Street
Old Ebbitt Grill
The Hamilton
W Hotel
Occidental Grill
Willard InterContinental
J.W. Marriott Pennsylvania Avenue
D Street NW
14th Street NW
15th Street NW
12th Street NW
12th St. NW
11th Street NW
13th Street NW
Firehook Bakery
Mixt Greens
Oceanaire Seafood Room
Metro Center
Federal Triangle
THE MALL
Smithsonian
14th Street SW
12th Street SW
Maryland Avenue SW
Mandarin Oriental, D.C
CityZen
Fyve Restaurant Lounge

Column C:

Aunt Bea's
12th Street NW
11th Street NW
10th Street NW
Morrison-Clark Inn
L Street NW
Henley Park
Brasserie Beck
Hosteling International
Bibiana
Washington Marriott at Metro Center
Grand Hyatt Washington
Hotel Harrington
FreshFarm Farmers Market
Hill Country
PENN QUARTER
Central Michel Richard
Cuba Libre
Five Guys
Zaytinya
10th Street NW
F Street NW
Teaism
American Eats Tavern
Pennsylvania Avenue
Paul
Archives/ Navy Memorial
L'Enfant Plaza Hotel
L'Enfant Plaza SW
9th Street SW
D Street SW
L'Enfant Plaza

Column D:

9th Street NW
7th Street NW
6th Street NW
WASHINGTON CONVENTION CENTER
L Street N
The Passenger
Mt. Vernon Pl. NW
Renaissance Washington D.C.
MOUNT VERNON SQUARE
PS 7's
CHINATOWN
Full Kee
Matchbox
Red Roof Inn
Graffiato
Gallery Place/ Chinatown
6th Street
Zola
Hotel Monaco
Poste
Jaleo
Rasika
Oyamel
Wolfgang Puck
The Souc
The Capital Grille
Indiana Avenue
7th St.
8th St.
Madison Drive NW
Jefferson Drive SW
7th Street SW
D Street SW
L'Enfant Plaza

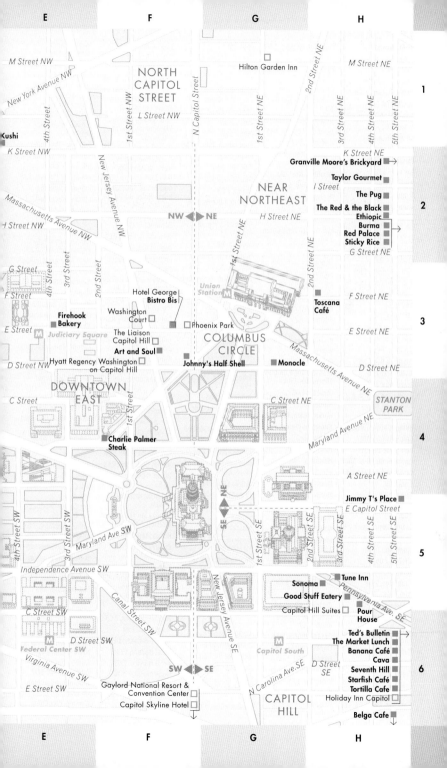

E   F   G   H

M Street NW

New York Avenue NW

NORTH CAPITOL STREET

Hilton Garden Inn ☐

M Street NE

1

L Street NW

1st Street NW

N Capitol Street

1st Street NE

2nd Street NE

3rd Street NE

4th Street NE

5th Street NE

Kushi ■

K Street NW

New Jersey Avenue NW

Granville Moore's Brickyard ■→

K Street NE

Massachusetts Avenue NW

H Street NW

Massachusetts Avenue NW

NEAR NORTHEAST

I Street

Taylor Gourmet ■

The Pug ■

The Red & the Black ■

Ethiopic ■

Burma ■

Red Palace ■

Sticky Rice ■

→

2

NW ◆ NE

H Street NE

1st Street NE

2nd Street NE

G Street NE

G Street

F Street

4th Street

3rd Street

2nd Street

E Street

Firehook Bakery ■

Union Station Ⓜ

Hotel George
Bistro Bis ■

Washington Court ☐

☐ **Phoenix Park**

COLUMBUS CIRCLE

Massachusetts Avenue NE

Toscana Café ■

F Street NE

E Street NE

3

Ⓜ *Judiciary Square*

The Liaison Capitol Hill ☐

Art and Soul ■

Johnny's Half Shell ■

Monocle ■

D Street NE

D Street NW

Hyatt Regency Washington on Capitol Hill ☐

DOWNTOWN EAST

C Street

1st Street

C Street NE

Massachusetts Avenue NE

STANTON PARK

4

Charlie Palmer Steak ■

Maryland Avenue NE

4

4th Street SW

3rd Street SW

Maryland Ave SW

A Street NE

Jimmy T's Place ■

E Capitol Street

5

NE

SE

1st Street SE

2nd Street SE

3rd Street SE

4th Street SE

5th Street SE

Independence Avenue SW

Canal Street SW

New Jersey Avenue SE

Tune Inn ■

Sonoma ■

Pennsylvania Ave. SE

Good Stuff Eatery ■

Capitol Hill Suites ☐

Pour House ■

C Street SW

D Street SW

Ⓜ *Federal Center SW*

Virginia Avenue SW

Ⓜ *Capitol South*

D Street SE

Ted's Bulletin ■→

The Market Lunch ■

Banana Café ■

Cava ■

Seventh Hill ■

Starfish Café ■

Tortilla Cafe ■

Holiday Inn Capitol ☐

6

E Street SW

SW ◆ SE

Gaylord National Resort & Convention Center ☐

Capitol Skyline Hotel ☐

N Carolina Ave. SE

CAPITOL HILL

Belga Cafe ■

↓

E   F   G   H

Where to Stay

WORD OF MOUTH

"We love the Tabard Inn near Dupont Circle for its quirky charm, great location, and good restaurant."

—macdogmom

Updated by
Beth Kanter

The Capital City's hotel scene can officially change its status from "up and coming" to just plain "up." Washington, D.C.'s vast array of lodging now offers something for everyone—and in many cases somethings for everyone—from historic properties to modern designer hotels to urban inns. You can pick your hotel based on the type of experience you set out to have when you arrive.

If you're seeking an experience steeped in pomp and circumstance consider one of the city's grand hotels, of which there are quite a few: the Jefferson, the Hay-Adams, the Fairfax at Embassy Row, the Willard, and the St. Regis, to name but a few. When you check in at any of these beautifully kept and storied properties, it is near impossible to forget the rich history that defines D.C.

If you prefer a more urban vibe you have a big choice: Hotel George, Hotel Monaco, and the Topaz Hotel are a few top favorites, and other contemporary inside-the-Beltway gems include the Donovan House, the W, and the Dupont Circle Hotel.

For a more traditional hotel experience consider checking into one of the many chain hotels located in strategic locations throughout and just outside the city.

Visitors in search of a more intimate lodging experience may do well to cross the threshold at one of the city's many charming bed-and-breakfasts. The Swann House, Akwaaba DC, or the off-the-beaten-path Intown Uptown Inn all offer exceptional personalized service, art-filled guest rooms, and the pleasure of waking up to a home-cooked morning meal. Over the years, the Embassy Circle Guest House and the Woodley Park Guest House have been luring guests back time and time again for very good reasons.

All the hotels listed here in this chapter reflect D.C.'s dazzling array of choices, and each one can help you upgrade your vacation status from good to great.

PLANNING

LODGING STRATEGY

With hundreds of D.C.-area hotels, it may seem like a daunting question. But fret not—our expert writers and editors have done most of the legwork. The 80-plus selections here represent the best this city has to offer—from the best budget motels to the sleekest designer hotels.

Scan "Best Bets" for top recommendations by price and experience. Or find a review quickly in the listings. Search by neighborhood, then alphabetically. Happy hunting!

RESERVATIONS

With more than 95,000 guest rooms available in the area, you can usually find a place to stay—though it's always prudent to reserve. Hotels often fill up with conventioneers, politicians in transit, families, and, in spring, school groups. Hotel rooms in D.C. can be particularly hard to come by during the Cherry Blossom Festival in late March or early April, and also in May, when many graduate from college. Late October's Marine Corps Marathon also increases demand for rooms. Rooms also book up fast and far in advance (and prices get raised) every four years when it comes time to celebrate the presidential inauguration.

FACILITIES

You can assume that all rooms have private baths, phones, TVs, and air-conditioning unless otherwise noted. Breakfast is noted when it is included in the rate, but that's not a typical perk at most Washington hotels. One feature you may well want to consider for a summertime visit is a pool (*see our Best Bets list for some of the most notable*).

WITH KIDS

From the free Smithsonian museums on the Mall to the cuddly pandas at the National Zoo, D.C. is a very family-friendly town. Major convention hotels (and those on the waterfront) don't always cater to families, so we recommend looking Downtown, in Foggy Bottom, or in Upper Northwest, where many hotels offer special panda packages for the zoo-bound. Also, the closer your hotel is to a Metro stop, the quicker you can get on the sightseeing trail. The Metro itself often ranks as a favorite attraction among the under-12 set. Consider a stay at an all-suites hotel. This will allow you to spread out and, if you prepare your meals in a kitchenette, to keep costs down. It gives the grown-ups the option of staying up past bedtime, too. A pool may well be essential for a stay with children, especially during D.C.'s notoriously humid summer months.

A number of well-known chains, including **Embassy Suites, Fairmont, Four Seasons, Ritz-Carlton,** and **St. Regis** also offer special programs or packages for kids and usually have babysitting services. **Holiday Inns** allow kids (typically under 12) to eat free in their restaurants and several of the Kimpton properties offer family-friendly rooms complete with bunk beds and child-sized bathrobes.

In the listings, look for the ☾, which indicates the property is particularly good for kids.

PARKING

Hotel parking fees range from free to $50 per night. This sometimes involves valet parking, with its additional gratuities. Street parking is free on Sunday and usually after 6:30 pm. But there are often far more cars searching than there are spaces available, particularly Downtown, in Georgetown, and in the upper Connecticut Avenue area.

During weekday rush hours, many streets are unavailable for parking; illegally parked cars are towed, and reclaiming a car is expensive and very inconvenient. Read signs carefully; some are confusing, and the ticket writers are quick.

PRICES

If you're interested in visiting Washington at a calmer, less-expensive time—and if you can stand semitropical weather—come in August, during the congressional recess. Rates also drop in late December and January, except around an inauguration. Weekend, off-season, and special rates (such as AAA discounts and Web-only promotions) can also make rooms more affordable. Hotels that cater to government workers and businesspeople, especially properties in the Virginia and Maryland suburbs, offer some especially sizeable discounts on weekends, even in busy tourist seasons. A little bit of research can pay off in big savings.

Prices in the reviews are the lowest cost of a standard double room in high season.

USING THE MAPS

Throughout the chapter, you'll see mapping symbols and coordinates (✛ 3:F2) after property names or reviews. To locate the property on a map, turn to the Washington, D.C. Dining and Lodging Atlas at the end of the Where to Eat chapter. The first number after the ✛ symbol indicates the map number. Following that is the property's coordinate on the map grid.

HOTEL REVIEWS

Listed alphabetically within neighborhoods. The following reviews have been condensed for this book. Please go to Fodors.com for full reviews of each property.

THE WHITE HOUSE AREA AND FOGGY BOTTOM

$ ⚏ **Aunt Bea's Little White House.** You won't find Aunt Bea when you step in to this cozy, accurately named little white house, but innkeeper Gerald will treat you like family. **Pros:** helpful innkeeper; affordable; home-cooked breakfast. **Cons:** can't walk to museums or attractions; not many amenities. **TripAdvisor:** "this is how it's done," "great breakfast and charm," "blown away by the service and comfort." ⑤ *Rooms from:* $50 ✉ 3619 12th St. NW, Brookland ☎ 202/629–2308 ⌁ 3 rooms ⑩| *Breakfast* Ⓜ *Columbia Heights* ✛ 2:C1.

$$ ⚏ **DoubleTree Suites by Hilton Hotel, Washington, D.C.** At this all-suites hotel close to the Kennedy Center and Georgetown, the roomy, one- and two-bedroom units have full kitchens and living-dining areas with

WHERE SHOULD I STAY?

	Neighborhood Vibe	Pros	Cons
The White House Area and Foggy Bottom	Charming residential and office area along Pennsylvania Avenue. Stately early-20th-century buildings.	Safe area; walking distance to Georgetown, State Department, and the Kennedy Center; good Metro access.	Paltry dining options and lots of traffic. Far from tourist attractions. Older hotels with few budget rates.
Capitol Hill and Northeast D.C.	Charming residential blocks of Victorian row houses populated by members of Congress and their staffers.	Convenient to Union Station and the Capitol. Stylish (if not cheap) hotels. Fine assortment of restaurants and shops.	Some streets iffy at night; parking takes some work; hotels are pricey. Chock-full of tourists and high-priced hotels.
Downtown	This once-abandoned part of town is undergoing a renaissance. It's packed during the day but a little lonely in places at night.	Right in the heart of the Metro system; easy access to the White House. Large hotel selection.	Can feel desolate at night; few browse-worthy shops; daytime street parking near impossible.
Georgetown	Wealthy neighborhood bordered by the Potomac and a world-class university. Filled with students and upscale shops and eateries.	Safe area. Historic charm on every tree-lined street. Wonderful walking paths along river.	Crowded; no nearby Metro access; lots of traffic. Challenging parking. Lodging options are limited and tend to be expensive.
Dupont Circle and Adams Morgan	Cosmopolitan neighborhood, filled with stylish bars, restaurants, and shops; center of late-night activity in Adams Morgan.	Modern design hotels and lots of them; plentiful nightlife; easy Metro access; wide selection of bars and restaurants.	Few budget options in Dupont; limited street parking; very crowded in summer months. Few worthy lodging options in Adams Morgan.
Upper Northwest	A pleasant residential neighborhood with a lively strip of good restaurants.	Safe and quiet; an easy walk to the zoo, Metro, and restaurants; street parking easier than Downtown.	A long ride to attractions other than the zoo; feels almost suburban. Few new hotels.

desks, dining tables, and sofa beds. **Pros:** near Metro; rooftop pool overlooks the Watergate; quiet neighborhood; good online deals available. **Cons:** far from the museums; too quiet for some. **TripAdvisor:** "nice room," "great staff," "fabulous location." ⑤ *Rooms from: $265* ✉ *801 New Hampshire Ave. NW, Foggy Bottom* ☎ *202/785–2000, 800/222–8733* ⊕ *www.doubletree.com* ⚲ *105 suites* ⏍ *No meals* Ⓜ *Foggy Bottom/GWU* ✛ *1:D6.*

$$ ⚑ **Embassy Suites Washington, D.C.** All accommodations at this pleasant and convenient hotel within walking distance of Georgetown and Dupont Circle have a livng room and bedroom and surround an atrium filled with classical columns, plaster lions, wrought-iron lanterns, waterfalls, and tall palms. **Pros:** family-friendly; in-house restaurant serves lunch and dinner; pool to keep the little ones—and sweaty tourists—happy. **Cons:** not a lot of character; museums not in walking distance. **TripAdvisor:** "perfect for us," "great front desk staff," "great breakfast." ⑤ *Rooms from: $278* ✉ *1250 22nd St. NW,*

BEST BETS FOR WASHINGTON, D.C. LODGING

Fodor's offers a selective listing of quality lodging, from the city's best budget motel to its most sophisticated luxury hotel. Here are our top recommendations by price and experience. The properties that provide a particularly remarkable experience in a price range are designated with a Fodor's Choice logo.

Fodor's Choice ★

Best by Price

Best by Experience

Mandarin Oriental, $$$$, p. 243

BEST POOL

Capitol Skyline Hotel, $$, p. 237

The Liaison Capitol Hill, $$$, p. 239

Omni Shoreham Hotel, $$, p. 255

Washington Marriott at Metro Center, $$$$, p. 246

HOT SCENE

Donovan House, $$, p. 240

The Dupont Hotel, $$$, p. 250

Hotel Madera, $$$, p. 251

Hotel Rouge, $$$, p. 252

The Liaison Capitol Hill, $$$, p. 239

Topaz Hotel, $$$, p. 254

W Washington, D.C., $$$$, p. 246

BEST FOR KIDS

Courtyard Chevy Chase, $$, p. 256

The Fairmont Washington, D.C., $$$, p. 236

Four Seasons Hotel, $$$$, p. 247

Marriott Wardman Park, $$$, p. 255

Omni Shoreham Hotel, $$, p. 255

MOST ROMANTIC

The Fairmont Washington, D.C., $$$, p. 236

Hotel Monaco, $$$, p. 242

Hotel Rouge, $$$, p. 252

Mandarin Oriental, $$$$, p. 243

Swann House, $, p. 254

BEST VIEW

Hay-Adams Hotel, $$$$, p. 241

JW Marriott Washington, D.C., $$$, p. 243

Key Bridge Marriott, $$, p. 257

Mandarin Oriental, D.C., $$$$, p. 243

Omni Shoreham Hotel, $$, p. 255

The Ritz-Carlton Georgetown, $$$$, p. 249

BEST HOTEL GYM

The Fairmont, Washington, D.C., $$$, p. 236

Grand Hyatt Washington, $$$, p. 241

The Liaison Capitol Hill, $$$, p. 239

Mandarin Oriental, $$$$, p. 243

Ritz-Carlton Washington, D.C., $$$$, p. 236

Willard InterContinental, $$$, p. 246

MOST ECO-FRIENDLY

Courtyard Chevy Chase, $$, p. 256

Hyatt Regency Washington on Capitol Hill, $$, p. 239

Willard InterContinental, $$$, p. 246

GRANDEST GRANDES DAMES

Hay-Adams Hotel, $$$$, p. 241

The Jefferson, $$$$, p. 243

The Mayflower Renaissance Washington, D.C. Hotel, $$$$, p. 243

The St. Regis, $$$$, p. 244

Willard InterContinental, $$$, p. 246

BEST LOBBY

Mandarin Oriental, $$$$, p. 243

The Mayflower Renaissance Washington, D.C. Hotel, $$$$, p. 243

Omni Shoreham Hotel, $$, p. 255

The Ritz-Carlton Georgetown, $$$$, p. 249

PET-FRIENDLY

Hay-Adams Hotel, $$$$, p. 241

Hotel Helix, $$$, p. 242

Hotel Rouge, $$$, p. 252

BEST FOR JOGGING BUFFS

Mandarin Oriental, $$$$, p. 243

Marriott Wardman Park, $$$, p. 255

Omni Shoreham Hotel, $$, p. 255

The Ritz-Carlton Georgetown, $$$$, p. 249

BEST HOTELS WITH WASHINGTON-INSIDER BARS

The Fairfax at Embassy Row, $$$$, p. 251

Hay-Adams Hotel, $$$$, p. 241

The Liaison Capitol Hill, $$$, p. 239

W Washington, D.C., $$$$, p. 246

BEST HOTELS FOR AFTERNOON TEA

Henley Park Hotel, $$, p. 241

The Jefferson, $$$$, p. 243

The Mayflower Renaissance Washington, D.C. Hotel, $$$$, p. 243

Park Hyatt, Washington, D.C., $$$$, p. 249

BEST-KEPT SECRETS

Akwaaba DC, $, p. 249

Embassy Circle Guest House, $$, p. 251

Inn at Dupont Circle South, $, p. 252

The Intown Uptown Inn, $, p. 255

BEST BOUTIQUE HOTELS

Donovan House, $$, p. 240

The Dupont Hotel, $$$, p. 250

Hotel George, $$$, p. 237

Hotel Monaco, $$$, p. 242

Topaz Hotel, $$$, p. 254

7

West End ☎ *202/857–3388, 800/362–2779* ⊕ *www.embassysuites. com* ⇆ *318 suites* ⦵ *Breakfast* Ⓜ *Foggy Bottom/GWU or Dupont Circle* ⌖ *1:D5.*

$$$ 🔲 **The Fairmont, Washington, D.C.** The large glassed-in lobby and about
☼ a third of the bright, spacious rooms overlook an elegant central courtyard and gardens; accommodation are comfortable and light, furnished with a stylish mix of traditional and contemporary pieces. **Pros:** fitness fanatics will love the health club and indoor pool; lots of kid-friendly features; easy walk to Georgetown. **Cons:** pricey; far from most major attractions. **TripAdvisor:** "excellent property," "exceptional customer service," "wonderful bed." ⑤ *Rooms from: $399* ⊠ *2401 M St. NW, Foggy Bottom* ☎ *202/429–2400, 866/540–4505* ⊕ *www.fairmont.com* ⇆ *406 rooms, 9 suites* ⦵ *No meals* Ⓜ *Foggy Bottom/GWU* ⌖ *1:D5.*

$ 🔲 **The George Washington University Inn.** Wrought-iron gates lead into a pleasant courtyard, setting the tone of this intimate, quiet getaway where the traditionally styled guest rooms are a few blocks from the Kennedy Center, the State Department, and the George Washington University. **Pros:** good price; close to Metro. **Cons:** basic accommodations; far from museums. **TripAdvisor:** "a wonderfully cozy luxury room," "a quiet corner of Washington," "so much to offer." ⑤ *Rooms from: $189* ⊠ *824 New Hampshire Ave. NW, Foggy Bottom* ☎ *800/426–4455* ⊕ *www.gwuinn.com* ⇆ *64 rooms, 31 suites* ⦵ *No meals* Ⓜ *Foggy Bottom/GWU* ⌖ *1:D6.*

$$$$ 🔲 **The Ritz-Carlton Washington, D.C.** Luxury oozes from every polished marble surface at one of Washington's most coveted hostelries: beds are dressed in 400-thread-count Egyptian cotton linens (and have earned the reputation as some of the most comfortable in town), large marble tubs are complemented by separate showers, and impeccable service makes you feel pampered. **Pros:** attentive service; convenient to several parts of town; attached to fabulous health club and pool. **Cons:** pricey room rates; expensive valet parking. **TripAdvisor:** "luxury in the District," "wonderful Ritz property," "it's worth it." ⑤ *Rooms from: $469* ⊠ *1150 22nd St. NW, Foggy Bottom* ☎ *202/835–0500, 800/241–3333* ⊕ *www.ritzcarlton.com/hotels/washington_dc* ⇆ *267 rooms, 32 suites* ⦵ *No meals* Ⓜ *Foggy Bottom/GWU* ⌖ *1:E5.*

$$ 🔲 **St. Gregory Luxury Hotel & Suites.** The handsome St. Gregory caters to business and leisure travelers with spacious accommodations that include fully stocked kitchens and such hotel services as turndown service, complimentary newspaper, and shoe shine. **Pros:** big rooms; good for long-term stays. **Cons:** far from museums; area is sleepy at night. **TripAdvisor:** "staff are super nice," "exceeds all expectations," "a lovely suite." ⑤ *Rooms from: $210* ⊠ *2033 M St. NW, West End* ☎ *202/530–3600, 800/829–5034* ⊕ *www.capitalhotelswdc.com* ⇆ *54 rooms, 100 suites* ⦵ *No meals* Ⓜ *Dupont Circle* ⌖ *1:E5.*

$ 🔲 **State Plaza Hotel.** No Washington hotel gets you quicker access to the State Department, which sits across the street; the surroundings are neither luxurious nor terribly atmospheric, but the spacious suites have kitchenettes and lighted dressing tables, and the hotel staff is friendly and attentive. **Pros:** all suites; free Internet access; walk to Metro. **Cons:**

far from museums; not a lot of character. **TripAdvisor:** "old-style rooms with great location," "extremely nice," "helpful staff." $ *Rooms from: $199* ⊠ *2117 E St. NW, Foggy Bottom* ☎ *202/861–8200, 800/424–2859* ⊕ *www.stateplaza.com* ⤵ *230 suites* ⦿*No meals* Ⓜ *Foggy Bottom/GWU* ✛ *1:E6.*

CAPITOL HILL AND NORTHEAST D.C.

$$ ⛉ **Capitol Hill Suites.** Contemporary suites here are done in blue and brown tones and have large work desks, flat-screen TVs, and spacious closets, and an eco-friendly sensibility extends from free-trade coffee in the lobby to water-saving showerheads in every bathroom. **Pros:** good for extended stays; free Internet access; close to Metro; breakfast included in rates. **Cons:** limited street parking; wings are not connected. **TripAdvisor:** "convenient and comfortable," "very helpful staff," "great location." $ *Rooms from: $233* ⊠ *200 C St. SE, Capitol Hill* ☎ *202/543–6000* ⊕ *www.capitolhillsuites.com* ⤵ *152 suites* ⦿*Breakfast* Ⓜ *Capitol South* ✛ *2:H5.*

$$ ⛉ **Capitol Skyline Hotel.** This boxy, glass and concrete hotel built in the
☼ 1960s is making a 21st-century comeback with its cool retro embodiment of its earlier heritage, with a gleaming lobby and inviting rooms done in red, white, and blue (some with views of the U.S. Capitol). **Pros:** big outdoor pool; spacious rooms; good value. **Cons:** area sketchy at night; out-of-the-way location; restaurant has uneven food and slow service. **TripAdvisor:** "friendly and convenient," "great location and staff," "nice spacious clean room." $ *Rooms from: $224* ⊠ *10 I St. SW, Southwest* ☎ *202/488–7500, 800/458–7500* ⊕ *www.capitolskyline.com* ⤵ *196 rooms, 7 suites* ⦿*No meals* Ⓜ *Navy Yard* ✛ *2:F6.*

$$$ ⛉ **Hilton Garden Inn/U.S. Capitol.** Bright and shiny, this new Hilton welcomes guests to the nation's capital with soothing, well-kept guest rooms and attentive service, and it's just a block away from the Metro stop and near Union Station. **Pros:** brand-new; near Metro; outdoor pool. **Cons:** some reports of noise at night; not in the center or town. **TripAdvisor:** "friendly staff," "quiet and friendly," "modern and clean." $ *Rooms from: $299* ⊠ *1225 First St. NE, Capitol Hill* ☎ *202/408–4870* ⊕ *www. hiltongardeninn.com* ⤵ *204 rooms* ✛ *2:G1.*

$$$ ⛉ **Holiday Inn Capitol.** One block from the National Air and Space
☼ Museum, this family-friendly hotel is in a great location for those bound for the Smithsonian museums and the comfortable guest rooms were recently remodeled with new drapes, bedding, and granite-top vanities in the bathrooms. **Pros:** family-friendly; rooftop pool; close to museums. **Cons:** limited dining options nearby; not much going on in the neighborhood at night. **TripAdvisor:** "great location," "great staff," "convenient." $ *Rooms from: $340* ⊠ *550 C St. SW, Southwest* ☎ *202/479–4000* ⊕ *www.hicapitoldc.com* ⤵ *532 rooms, 13 suites* ⦿*Breakfast* Ⓜ *L'Enfant Plaza* ✛ *2:H6.*

$$$ ⛉ **The Hotel George.** We cannot tell a lie—D.C.'s first contemporary boutique hotel is still one of its best; more than a decade after it first burst on to the scene, Hotel George still excels at providing a fun and funky alternative to the cookie-cutter chains. **Pros:** close to Union Station; popular in-house restaurant; updated fitness center. **Cons:** small

Park Hyatt, Washington, D.C.

Hay-Adams Hotel

Hotel Monaco

Mandarin Oriental Washington, D.C.

Sofitel Washington, D.C. Lafayette Square

closets; some reports of street noise; ultramodern feel not everyone's cup of tea. **TripAdvisor:** "comfortable and modern rooms," "lovely," "excellent service." ⑤ *Rooms from: $309* ⊠ *15 E St. NW, Capitol Hill* ☎ *202/347–4200, 800/576–8331* ⊕ *www.hotelgeorge.com* ⇨ *139 rooms, 1 suite* ⦿ *No meals* Ⓜ *Union Station* ⊕ *2:F3.*

$$ 🖬 **Hyatt Regency Washington on Capitol Hill.** A favorite for political events, fund-raising dinners, and networking meetings, this standard-issue business hotel is a solid choice if you're planning on spending a lot of time on the Hill. **Pros:** indoor pool; quick walk to Union Station; near the Capitol. **Cons:** busy; lots of groups; anonymous feel. **TripAdvisor:** "attentive staff," "great location," "comfortable." ⑤ *Rooms from: $279* ⊠ *400 New Jersey Ave. NW, Capitol Hill* ☎ *202/737–1234, 800/233–1234* ⊕ *www.hyattregencywashington.com* ⇨ *802 rooms, 32 suites* ⦿ *No meals* Ⓜ *Union Station* ⊕ *2:F3.*

$$$ 🖬 **L'Enfant Plaza Hotel.** At this attractive hotel two blocks from the Smith-
Ⓒ sonian museums and near several government agencies (USDA, USPS, and DOT), all of the guest rooms are large and well appointed and some have spectacular views of the river and the monuments. **Pros:** short walk to Smithsonian; good views from top floors; nice pool; pet-friendly. **Cons:** area is sleepy at night; not many nearby restaurants. **TripAdvisor:** "comfortable bed," "very accommodating," "perfect location." ⑤ *Rooms from: $359* ⊠ *480 L'Enfant Plaza SW, The Mall* ☎ *202/484–1000, 800/635–5065* ⊕ *www.lenfantplazahotel.com* ⇨ *370 rooms, 102 suites* ⦿ *No meals* Ⓜ *L'Enfant Plaza* ⊕ *2:C6.*

$$$ 🖬 **The Liaison Capitol Hill, An Affinia Hotel.** If the Liaison Capitol Hill wasn't steps away from the city's most stately buildings you could easily think you had checked into a sleek Manhattan hotel rather than one of D.C.'s more popular boutique properties, with a trendy buzz and guest rooms defined by modern chic. **Pros:** fantastic rooftop pool and deck; in-house Art and Soul restaurant is a choice dining destination; sidewalk patio for people-watching and summer cocktails; brand-new gym. **Cons:** some street noise at night; no great room views; expensive parking. **TripAdvisor:** "great location to see the city," "quaint facilities," "lovely rooms." ⑤ *Rooms from: $359* ⊠ *415 New Jersey Ave. NW, Capitol Hill* ☎ *202/638–1616, 866/233–4642* ⊕ *www.affinia.com* ⇨ *343 rooms* ⦿ *No meals* Ⓜ *Union Station* ⊕ *2:F3.*

$$ 🖬 **Phoenix Park Hotel.** If you prefer to be near the Hill but not in a convention hotel, this hotel named for a Dublin park may be for you: small but cozy guest rooms boast comfy beds with 300-thread-count Egyptian-cotton sheets and equally soft Irish-cotton bathrobes in the closets. **Pros:** perfect location; pleasant guest rooms. **Cons:** no swimming pool; small rooms. **TripAdvisor:** "perfect romantic hotel," "great location," "boutique gem in D.C." ⑤ *Rooms from: $274* ⊠ *520 N. Capitol St. NW, Capitol Hill* ☎ *202/638–6900, 800/824–5419* ⊕ *www.phoenixparkhotel.com* ⇨ *146 rooms, 3 suites* ⦿ *No meals* Ⓜ *Union Station* ⊕ *2:F3.*

$$$ 🖬 **Washington Court Hotel.** If you're searching for the city's newest "It" hotel, keep looking, but if you want a reliable, clean, comfortable place to stay—with soothing guest rooms done in soft grays and browns—then the Washington Court Hotel is for you. **Pros:** good location;

7

Capitol views from many rooms; executive king rooms have sofa beds. **Cons:** some reports of mixed service; expensive parking. **TripAdvisor:** "very classy," "high-end hotel with great service," "very good location." ⑤ *Rooms from: $369* ✉ *525 New Jersey Ave. NW, Capitol Hill* ☎ *202/628–2100* ⊕ *www.washingtoncourthotel.com* ⇥ *252 rooms, 12 suites* ⊺⊙⎮ *No meals* Ⓜ *Union Station* ⊹ *2:F3.*

DOWNTOWN

$$$ ⚏ **Capital Hilton.** Plush-top beds, flat-screen TVs, and black-and-white photographs of D.C. landmarks create comfortable and stylish surroundings—and with the hotel in walking distance of the White House, three Metro stations, and many restaurants and shops, the location is hard to beat. **Pros:** renovated guest rooms; desirable location; great gym. **Cons:** expensive parking; some reports of street noise; no views. **TripAdvisor:** "friendly and good location," "a benchmark for any Hilton," "amazing staff." ⑤ *Rooms from: $349* ✉ *1001 16th St. NW, Downtown* ☎ *202/393–1000* ⊕ *www.capital.hilton.com* ⇥ *544 room, 32 suites* ⊺⊙⎮ *No meals* Ⓜ *Farragut North* ⊹ *1:G6.*

$ ⚏ **Comfort Inn Downtown D.C.** These clean, roomy, and light-filled guest quarters overlook residential blocks and are near a fair number of restaurants and clubs. **Pros:** light-filled guest rooms; fresh cookies at check-in; pleasant staff. **Cons:** some reports of street noise at night; walk to Metro; no restaurants or stores in immediate area. **TripAdvisor:** "location and staff = A+," "excellent stay above expectations," "great hosts." ⑤ *Rooms from: $199* ✉ *1201 13th St. NW, Downtown* ☎ *202/682–5300* ⊕ *www.choicehotels.com* ⇥ *100 rooms* ⊺⊙⎮ *Breakfast* Ⓜ *McPherson Sq.* ⊹ *1:H5.*

$ ⚏ **The District Hotel.** Housed in a creaky 1920s apartment building, the District Hotel gives off something of a Europe-on-$25-a-day vibe—small, dark, run down in places, a fair share of students, and not much in the way of amenities—but it's a real bargain for the neighborhood. **Pros:** cheap; good location; free Wi-Fi. **Cons:** shabby not chic; stairs to get into the building and then again into the lobby; little natural light in rooms. **TripAdvisor:** "great for location," "just old," "you get what you pay for." ⑤ *Rooms from: $139* ✉ *1440 Rhode Island Ave. NW, Downtown* ☎ *202/232–7800, 800/350–5759* ⊕ *www.thedistricthotel. com* ⇥ *58 rooms* ⊺⊙⎮ *Breakfast* Ⓜ *McPherson Sq.* ⊹ *1:H4.*

$$ ⚏ **Donovan House.** You won't find anything remotely close to a colonial reproduction here; complete with its hanging egg chairs, iPod docking stations, and circular showers, the Donovan House seems more Manhattan than Washington. **Pros:** modern design; rooftop pool; near clubs. **Cons:** smallish rooms; 10-minute walk to Metro. **TripAdvisor:** "another great Kimpton property," "exceptional service," "different kind of hotel." ⑤ *Rooms from: $280* ✉ *1155 14th St. NW, Downtown* ☎ *202/737–1200* ⊕ *www.donovanhousehotel.com* ⇥ *193 rooms* ⊺⊙⎮ *No meals* Ⓜ *McPherson Sq.* ⊹ *2:B1.*

$$ ⚏ **DoubleTree by Hilton Hotel Washington, D.C.** Just off Scott Circle and ☽ only six blocks from the White House, the Doubletree offers spacious, recently renovated guest rooms that have comfortable beds, well-equipped workstations, clock radios with MP3 players, and coffeemakers. **Pros:** child-friendly; good location; newly renovated rooms. **Cons:** no pool; limited street parking. **TripAdvisor:** "boutique and modern," "nice service," "clean and nice rooms." $ *Rooms from: $269 ⊠ 1515 Rhode Island Ave. NW, Downtown ☎ 202/785–2000, 800/222–8733 ⊕ www.washington.doubletree.com ⤴ 220 rooms, 9 suites* ⊺◯⫻ *No meals* Ⓜ *Dupont Circle* ✛ *1:G4.*

$$$ Ⓣ **Fairfield Inn and Suites.** Bold contemporary decor provides a soothing retreat in a busy part of town, near many of the top attractions. **Pros:** complimentary breakfast and Wi-Fi; lots of restaurants, entertainment, and attractions nearby. **Cons:** some Fodorites complain about street noise; busy part of town not for everyone. **TripAdvisor:** "great service," "good breakfast," "clean rooms." $ *Rooms from: $299 ⊠ 500 H St. NW, Penn Quarter/Chinatown ☎ 202/289-5959, 866/599-6674 ⊕ www.marriott.com ⤴ 189 rooms; 9 suites* ⊺◯⫻ *No meals* Ⓜ *Gallery Pl./Chinatown* ✛ *2:D2.*

$$$ Ⓣ **Grand Hyatt Washington.** The staff here sometimes refers to this hotel with all the standard business comforts as a mini city, and with so many conveniences under one atrium-topped roof it's easy to see why; a Starbucks, deli, florist, ATM machine, gift shop, restaurants, sports bar, and even a lagoon are all clustered around the massive lobby area. **Pros:** great location for sightseeing and shopping; often has weekend deals; nice gym and indoor pool. **Cons:** often filled with conventioneers; chain-hotel feel. **TripAdvisor:** "great location," "nice bistro," "impressive." $ *Rooms from: $319 ⊠ 1000 H St. NW, Downtown ☎ 202/582–1234, 800/233–1234 ⊕ www.grandwashington.hyatt.com ⤴ 851 rooms, 37 suites* ⊺◯⫻ *No meals* Ⓜ *Metro Center* ✛ *2:C2.*

$$$$ Ⓣ **Hay-Adams Hotel.** With its elegant charm and refined decor, it's no
Fodor's Choice wonder that the Obamas chose this impressive Washington landmark,
★ with guess rooms decorated in a class above the rest, as their first Washington home as they got ready to move into 1600 Pennsylvania Avenue. **Pros:** plush guest rooms; impeccable service; almost in the shadow of the White House. **Cons:** expensive; no pool. **TripAdvisor:** "great property with really cool neighbors," "incomparable," "outstanding service." $ *Rooms from: $399 ⊠ 16th and H Sts. NW, Downtown ☎ 202/638–6600, 800/424–5054 ⊕ www.hayadams.com ⤴ 124 rooms, 21 suites* ⊺◯⫻ *No meals* Ⓜ *McPherson Sq. or Farragut North* ✛ *1:G6.*

$$ Ⓣ **Henley Park Hotel.** A Tudor-style building adorned with gargoyles, a National Historic Trust property, has the cozy feel of an English country house, and the atmosphere extends to the charming rooms, with nice touches like four-poster beds. **Pros:** historic building; privileges at nearby pool; frequent weekend specials. **Cons:** little parking; some street noise. **TripAdvisor:** "charming boutique hotel," "almost perfect," "great location." $ *Rooms from: $269 ⊠ 926 Massachusetts Ave. NW, Downtown ☎ 202/638–5200, 800/222–8474 ⊕ www. henleypark.com ⤴ 83 rooms, 13 suites* ⊺◯⫻ *No meals* Ⓜ *Metro Center* ✛ *2:C1.*

$$$ Ⓣ **Homewood Suites by Hilton, Washington.** The large family room–style
☺ lobby here often is abuzz with people in suits preparing presentations and tourists resting up from the day; the two-room suites have pull-out sofas, a work area that doubles as a table, and kitchens complete

with microwaves, dishwashers, and full-size refrigerators. **Pros:** roomy suites; reduced weekend rates; good for families and extended stays. **Cons:** no pool; difficult street parking; 10 minutes to Metro. **TripAdvisor:** "great amenities," "excellent customer service," "pleasant place to stay." $ *Rooms from: $339* ⊠ *1475 Massachusetts Ave. NW, Downtown* ☎ *202/265–8000* ⊕ *www.homewoodsuites.com* ↪ *175 suites* ⏹ *Breakfast* Ⓜ *McPherson Sq.* ✛ *1:H5.*

$ ⛭ **Hotel Harrington.** One of Washington's oldest continuously operating hotels doesn't offer any frills and the bathrooms and large guest rooms haven't seen a renovation in many a year—but the Harrington does have low prices and a location right in the center of everything. **Pros:** bargain prices; convenient location; free Wi-Fi. **Cons:** no real amenities; shabby but not chic; old rooms and bathrooms. **TripAdvisor:** "inexpensive and convenient," "basic clean hotel," "in the center of everything." $ *Rooms from: $149* ⊠ *436 11th St. NW, Downtown* ☎ *202/628–8140, 800/424–8532* ⊕ *www.hotel-harrington.com* ↪ *245 rooms* ⏹ *No meals* Ⓜ *Metro Center* ✛ *2:C3.*

$$$ ⛭ **Hotel Helix.** In the urban Logan Circle neighborhood, the Helix combines a hip vibe with colorful hospitality, offering contemporary-style guest quarters with flat-screens, colorful furnishings, and huge photos of surfing scenes and pop-culture icons ranging from Little Richard to Jackie O to Martin Luther King Jr. **Pros:** funky feel; good service; afternoon champagne "Bubbly Hour." **Cons:** a schlep to the Metro; no pool; small gym. **TripAdvisor:** "a fun place to stay," "in the heart of it all," "best family rooms on the planet." $ *Rooms from: $340* ⊠ *1430 Rhode Island Ave. NW, Downtown* ☎ *202/462–9001, 866/508–0658* ⊕ *www.hotelhelix.com* ↪ *160 rooms, 18 suites* ⏹ *No meals* Ⓜ *McPherson Sq.* ✛ *1:H4.*

$$ ⛭ **Hotel Lombardy.** From the European antiques to the Oriental wool rugs to the original oil paintings, Hotel Lombardy has lots of old-world charm. **Pros:** homey rooms; beautiful lounge; three blocks from the White House. **Cons:** old-fashioned; expensive breakfast; on busy street. **TripAdvisor:** "lovely stay," "welcoming staff," "great value." $ *Rooms from: $230* ⊠ *2019 Pennsylvania Ave. NW, Downtown* ☎ *202/828–2600* ⊕ *www.hotellombardy.com* ↪ *140 rooms 21 suites* ⏹ *No meals* Ⓜ *Foggy Bottom-GWU* ✛ *1:E6.*

$$$ ⛭ **Hotel Monaco.** Hotel Monaco is the perfect marriage of whimsy and
Fodor's Choice elegance—updated guest rooms are filled with eclectic prints and plush
★   furnishings, which harmoniously coexist with the 15-foot vaulted ceilings and other traditional architectural elements of this historic 1839 neoclassical landmark designed by Robert Mills of Washington Monument fame. **Pros:** fun Penn Quarter location next to the Spy Museum; near great restaurants and shops; convenient to the Metro. **Cons:** noisy part of town; no pool. **TripAdvisor:** "comfortable and relaxing room," "perfect location," "quirky but cool." $ *Rooms from: $359* ⊠ *700 F St. NW, Penn Quarter* ☎ *202/628–7177, 800/649–1202* ⊕ *www.monaco-dc.com* ↪ *167 rooms, 16 suites* ⏹ *No meals* Ⓜ *Gallery Pl./ Chinatown* ✛ *2:D3.*

$$$$ 🖫 **The Jefferson.** Once the top hat–clad doorman ushers you into the
Fodor'sChoice exquisite marble lobby and you settle into the stylish guest rooms
★ with plush Porthault linens, Italian marble walk-in showers, and televisions recessed into the bathroom mirrors, you may think you've
stepped into a different stately residence down the street—at 1600
Pennsylvania Avenue. **Pros:** exquisite historic hotel; impeccable service; prestigious location. **Cons:** expensive; some rooms have views
of other buildings; some street noise at night. **TripAdvisor:** "perfect
stay," "sobbed when I had to check out," "such an elegant hotel."
Ⓢ *Rooms from: $460 ⊠ 1200 16th St. NW, Downtown ☎ 202/448–
2300 ⊕ www.jeffersondc.com ⤶ 99 rooms, 20 suites* ⦿ *No meals*
Ⓜ *Farragut North � 1:G5.*

$$$ 🖫 **JW Marriott, Washington, D.C.** Despite the slick, upscale chain feel to
the place, from the location near the White House to the views from
the top floors, it's hard to forget you are in the nation's capital when
you stay here. **Pros:** in the heart of town; spiffy rooms with a luxuri-
ous, traditional feel; good views from top floors. **Cons:** very busy;
expensive for what you get. **TripAdvisor:** "great staff," "very nice
and well located," "gorgeous hotel." Ⓢ *Rooms from: $279 ⊠ 1331
Pennsylvania Ave. NW, Downtown ☎ 202/393–2000, 800/393–2503
⊕ www.jwmarriottdc.com ⤶ 737 rooms, 35 suites* ⦿ *No meals*
Ⓜ *Metro Center ɟ 2:B3.*

$$$ 🖫 **The Madison, Washington, D.C.** Luxury, meticulous service, and a great
deal of stylish comfort prevail at the stately Madison, which is why
the signatures of presidents, prime ministers, sultans, and kings fill the
guest register. **Pros:** exceptional service; central location, pretty guest
rooms with plush linens. **Cons:** pricey; no pool. **TripAdvisor:** "attractive and comfortable," "nice rooms," "spectacular hotel with an excellent location." Ⓢ *Rooms from: $339 ⊠ 1177 15th St. NW, Downtown
☎ 202/862–1600, 800/424–8577 ⊕ www.madisonhoteldc.com ⤶ 356
rooms, 9 suites* ⦿ *No meals* Ⓜ *McPherson Sq. ɟ 1:G5.*

$$$$ 🖫 **Mandarin Oriental, Washington, D.C.** Asian accents, an impressive
Fodor'sChoice art collection incorporated throughout the public areas and the guest
★ rooms, views of the waterfront or the Mall, beds so comfortable they
make you want to ignore your wake-up call, and a decadent spa all
set a new standard of sophisticated luxury and refined service. **Pros:**
excellent spa; beautiful views; best location for cherry-blossom viewing.
Cons: expensive; a bit out of the way; few nearby dining options. **TripAdvisor:** "good location," "sumptuous rooms," "outstanding spa and
service." Ⓢ *Rooms from: $495 ⊠ 1330 Maryland Ave. SW, Downtown
☎ 202/554–8588, 888/888–1778 ⊕ www.mandarinoriental.com ⤶ 347
rooms, 53 suites* ⦿ *No meals* Ⓜ *Smithsonian ɟ 2:B6.*

$$$$ 🖫 **The Mayflower Renaissance Washington, D.C. Hotel.** The magnificent
ↅ block-long lobby with its series of antique crystal chandeliers and gilded
columns is a destination in itself, and guest rooms at this grande dame
hotel, which opened its doors in 1925 for Calvin Coolidge's inauguration, are done in traditional style in soothing yellows, greens, tans, and
blues and have sheltered legions of distinguished guests. **Pros:** historic
building; near dozens of restaurants; a few steps from Metro. **Cons:**
rooms vary greatly in size; no pool; expensive parking. **TripAdvisor:**

7

"consistently high quality," "elegance in the city," "great service." ⑤ *Rooms from: $429* ✉ *1127 Connecticut Ave. NW, Downtown* ☎ *202/347–3000, 800/228–7697* ⊕ *www.marriott.com* ⇱ *583 rooms, 74 suites* ⦿| *No meals* Ⓜ *Farragut N.* ✛ *1:F5.*

$$ 🖼 **Morrison-Clark Inn.** In these two, attached 1864 Victorian town houses, antiques-filled public rooms have decorative marble fireplaces, bay windows, and medallioned ceilings, and rooms are furnished with neoclassical, French country, or Victorian pieces and have all the modern amenities. **Pros:** charming alternative to cookie-cutter hotels; historic feel throughout; fitness room and outdoor pool. **Cons:** some street noise; long walk to Metro; not ideal for young children. **TripAdvisor:** "quaint oasis in the Capital," "comfortable lovely place," "lots of character." ⑤ *Rooms from: $229* ✉ *1015 L St. NW, Downtown* ☎ *202/898–1200, 800/332–7898* ⊕ *www.morrisonclark.com* ⇱ *54 rooms, 12 suites* ⦿| *Breakfast* Ⓜ *Metro Center* ✛ *2:C1.*

$$ 🖼 **The Quincy.** Chic, contemporary style and a black, white, and orange color scheme carries throughout the studio-style rooms with various-size kitchenettes at this city-center inn that's popular with families and business types alike. **Pros:** central location; convenient to Metro; affordable weekend rates. **Cons:** much of the area shuts down at end of the workday; no pool. **TripAdvisor:** "excellent location," "comfy bed," "great rooms." ⑤ *Rooms from: $279* ✉ *1823 L St. NW, Downtown* ☎ *202/223–4320, 800/424–2970* ⊕ *www.thequincy.com* ⇱ *100 suites* ⦿| *No meals* Ⓜ *Farragut North or Farragut West* ✛ *1:F5.*

$$$ 🖼 **Renaissance Washington, D.C. Downtown Hotel.** Stylish contemporary decor, extensive business services, such touches as special mattresses and fine linens, and a 10,000-square-foot fitness center and a full-service spa elevate this chain hotel into the luxury realm. **Pros:** convenient to convention center; near Metro; popular part of town; extremely attractive surroundings. **Cons:** convention crowds; chain-hotel feel; expensive. **TripAdvisor:** "top quality," "great service," "staff goes above and beyond." ⑤ *Rooms from: $399* ✉ *999 9th St. NW, Downtown* ☎ *202/898–9000, 800/228–9898* ⊕ *www.marriott.com* ⇱ *794 rooms, 13 suites* ⦿| *No meals* Ⓜ *Gallery Pl./Chinatown* ✛ *2:D2.*

$$$ 🖼 **Sofitel Washington, D.C. Lafayette Square.** The French could not have
Fodor'sChoice   landed a better location for the Sofitel, a minute's walk from the White
★   House, and the luxury chain has maintained the 1920s style of the original Shoreham Building, with an understated, sophisticated lobby and chic, though slightly small, guest rooms and beautiful marble bathrooms. **Pros:** prestigious location; highly rated restaurant; lovely rooms. **Cons:** lobby on the small side; expensive parking. **TripAdvisor:** "fantastic service," "great food," "superb location." ⑤ *Rooms from: $330* ✉ *806 15th St. NW, Downtown* ☎ *202/730–8800* ⊕ *www. sofitel.com* ⇱ *237 rooms, 16 suites* ⦿| *No meals* Ⓜ *McPherson Sq.* ✛ *1:H6.*

$$$$ 🖼 **The St. Regis Washington, D.C.** The hand-painted ceiling in the lobby
Fodor'sChoice   of this 1926 Italian Renaissance–style landmark sets the stage for the
★   exquisite attention to detail that awaits in the handsome guest rooms—
☾   Pratesi linens line the beds, LCD TVs are recessed behind the bathroom mirrors, and personal butlers carry BlackBerrys, so while you're

St. Regis Washington, D.C.

Embassy Circle Guest House

Hotel Madera

W Washington, D.C.

CLOSE UP

The Mayflower Renaissance: Did You Know?

■ President Franklin D. Roosevelt wrote, "The only thing we have to fear is fear itself" in Room 776.

■ J. Edgar Hoover ate lunch at the Mayflower restaurant almost every weekday for 20 years. He almost always brought his own diet salad dressing.

■ Walt Disney once dined on the Mayflower's roof.

■ The state dinner celebrating the 1979 Arab-Israeli peace treaty was held here.

■ Winston Churchill sat for a portrait here.

■ Members of Congress interviewed Monica Lewinsky in the 10th-floor Presidential Suite while pursuing the impeachment of President Bill Clinton.

■ Former New York Governor Eliot Spitzer was allegedly visited by a high-priced call girl at his room here in 2008. The resulting scandal led to his resignation.

out you can email requests like "Please pack my bags." **Pros:** close to White House; historic property; exceptional service. **Cons:** no pool; most rooms don't have great views; very expensive. **TripAdvisor:** "the best of the best," "gracious service," "perfect in every way." ⑤ *Rooms from: $595* ⊠ *923 16th St. NW, Downtown* ☎ *202/638–2626* ⊕ *www.stregis.com/washington* ↪ *175 rooms, 25 suites* ⦿*No meals* Ⓜ *Farragut North* ✛ *1:G6.*

$$$$ 🍴 **W Washington, D.C.** From the DJ spinning tunes in the living room–
Fodor'sChoice style lobby to the oversize flat-screen TV near the doorway that
★ broadcasts an image of a flickering fireplace to the ultramodern room
furnishings, every detail here screams urban chic—and does so with style. **Pros:** new hip hotel; individualized and attentive service; fabulous location and restaurant. **Cons:** pricey; too modern for some; no pool. **TripAdvisor:** "posh style," "sexy property," "the best view of Washington." ⑤ *Rooms from: $455* ⊠ *515 15th St. NW, Downtown* ☎ *202/661–2400* ⊕ *www.starwoodhotels.com/whotels* ↪ *317 rooms, 32 suites* ⦿*No meals* Ⓜ *McPherson Sq.* ✛ *2:B3.*

$$$$ 🍴 **Washington Marriott at Metro Center.** Near the White House, the MCI Center, and the Smithsonian museums, the Marriott has many virtues, including attractive, comfortable guest rooms and an indoor pool and health club that are among the best in town. **Pros:** great location; popular restaurants; updated guest rooms. **Cons:** busy location; big-chain hotel. **TripAdvisor:** "great staff," "nice location and room," "outstanding customer service." ⑤ *Rooms from: $519* ⊠ *775 12th St. NW, Downtown* ☎ *202/737–2200, 800/393–2100* ⊕ *www.marriott.com/wasmc* ↪ *454 rooms, 5 suites* ⦿*Breakfast* Ⓜ *Metro Center* ✛ *2:C2.*

$$$ 🍴 **Willard InterContinental.** A favorite of American presidents and other newsmakers offers superb service, a wealth of amenities, and guest rooms filled with period detail and Federal-style furniture, and equipped with sleek marble bathrooms. **Pros:** luxurious historic hotel; great

location two blocks from the White House; decadent spa. **Cons:** expensive; no pool. **TripAdvisor:** "lobby is magnificent," "evoking the political spirit of Washington, D.C.," "wonderful luxurious hotel." ⑤ *Rooms from: $319* ⊠ *1401 Pennsylvania Ave. NW, Downtown* ☎ *202/628–9100, 800/827–1747* ⊕ *www.washington.intercontinental.com* ⤳ *335 rooms, 40 suites* ⦿ *No meals* Ⓜ *Metro Center* ✢ *2:B3.*

GEORGETOWN

$$$$ 🏨 **Four Seasons Hotel, Washington, D.C.** Impeccable service and a wealth
Fodor's Choice of amenities make Washington's leading hotel a favorite with celebri-
★ ties, hotel connoisseurs, and families—best of all are the luxurious,
☾ ultramodern rooms, offering heavenly beds and French limestone or
marble baths with separate showers and sunken tubs. **Pros:** edge of
Georgetown makes for a fabulous location; lap-of-luxury feel; impeccable service. **Cons:** astronomically expensive; challenging street parking; far from Metro. **TripAdvisor:** "premium experience," "exceptional service," "luxurious accommodations." ⑤ *Rooms from: $725* ⊠ *2800 Pennsylvania Ave. NW, Georgetown* ☎ *202/342–0444, 800/332–3442* ⊕ *www.fourseasons.com/washington* ⤳ *164 rooms, 58 suites* ⦿ *No meals* Ⓜ *Foggy Bottom* ✢ *1:C5.*

$$ 🏨 **Georgetown Inn.** A heart-of-Georgetown location, the feel of a quaint European hotel, and elegant guest rooms with plush bedding make this pleasant inn a favorite with return guests. **Pros:** shoppers love the location; good price for the neighborhood; some nice views. **Cons:** a hike to Metro; congested area. **TripAdvisor:** "perfect location," "all together average," "needs an upgrade." ⑤ *Rooms from: $259* ⊠ *1310 Wisconsin Ave. NW, Georgetown* ☎ *202/333–8900, 888/587–2388* ⊕ *www. georgetowncollection.com* ⤳ *86 rooms, 10 suites* ⦿ *No meals* Ⓜ *Foggy Bottom* ✢ *1:B5.*

$$ 🏨 **Georgetown Suites.** These suites of varying sizes, all with fully equipped
☾ kitchens and separate sitting rooms, are a welcome break from standard hotel rooms. **Pros:** spacious rooms; good choice for a family that wants to spread out; perfect location. **Cons:** parking can be challenging; not a lot of character. **TripAdvisor:** "great location with kitchen," "huge bedroom," "accommodating and gracious." ⑤ *Rooms from: $235* ⊠ *1111 30th St. NW, Georgetown* ☎ *202/298–7800, 800/348–7203* ⊕ *www.georgetownsuites.com* ⤳ *216 suites* ⦿ *Breakfast* Ⓜ *Foggy Bottom* ✢ *1:B5.*

$$ 🏨 **Holiday Inn Georgetown.** On the edge of Georgetown, this no-sur-
☾ prises chain hotel is a short walk from Dumbarton Oaks, National Cathedral, and Georgetown University, and some guest rooms offer a scenic view of the Washington skyline. **Pros:** quiet neighborhood; walk to restaurants; pretty outdoor pool. **Cons:** not near a Metro; far from Downtown; generic chain feel. **TripAdvisor:** "overall a good hotel," "enjoyed my stay," "average." ⑤ *Rooms from: $220* ⊠ *2101 Wisconsin Ave. NW, Georgetown* ☎ *202/338–4600, 877/863–4780* ⊕ *www. higeorgetown.com* ⤳ *281 rooms, 4 suites* ⦿ *No meals* Ⓜ *Foggy Bottom* ✢ *1:A2.*

7

Four Seasons Hotel, Washington, D.C.

The Latham Hotel

Ritz-Calton Georgetown

Omni Shoreham Hotel

$$ ⌂ **The Latham Hotel.** With many of the beautifully decorated rooms offering treetop views of the Potomac River and the C&O Canal and a refreshing rooftop pool, it's not surprising you'll find many diplomats overnighting here. **Pros:** fun location; lots of charm; great restaurant. **Cons:** some street noise; busy area at night and on weekends. **TripAdvisor:** "lovely room," "friendly staff," "pet-friendly elegance in Georgetown." ⑤ *Rooms from: $229* ✉ *3000 M St. NW, Georgetown* ☎ *202/726–5000, 866/481–9126* ⊕ *www.thelatham.com* ⌂ *124 rooms, 9 suites* � *No meals* Ⓜ *Foggy Bottom* ⊹ *1:B5.*

$ ⌂ **The Melrose Hotel.** Gracious, traditional rooms done in a soothing palette of creams and blues all have marble baths, and many have pull-out sofa beds, making this hotel a good choice for families. **Pros:** nice alternative to chain hotels; good location; walk to dining and shopping. **Cons:** street noise; no pool. **TripAdvisor:** "no frills," "comfortable room," "great D.C. hotel." ⑤ *Rooms from: $160* ✉ *2430 Pennsylvania Ave. NW, Georgetown* ☎ *202/955–6400, 800/635–7673* ⊕ *www.melrosehoteldc.com* ⌂ *249 rooms, 34 suites* ⎹ *No meals* ⊹ *1:D6.*

$$$$ ⌂ **Park Hyatt, Washington, D.C.** Understated elegance and refined service are much in evidence at this soothing city getaway, where the earth-tone guest rooms are a minimalist tribute to the American experience and feature chestnut floors, hard-covered books, and folk art accent pieces. **Pros:** spacious rooms; good for entertaining; lull-you-to-sleep beds; destination in-house restaurant. **Cons:** expensive valet parking; not convenient to Metro. **TripAdvisor:** "business mixed with pleasure," "great service," "like being at home." ⑤ *Rooms from: $595* ✉ *1201 24th St. NW, Georgetown* ☎ *202/789–1234* ⊕ *www.parkwashington. hyatt.com* ⌂ *216 rooms, 19 suites* ⎹ *No meals* ⊹ *1:D5.*

Fodor's Choice ★

$$$$ ⌂ **The Ritz-Carlton Georgetown.** Once an incinerator dating from the 1920s, this building still topped with a smokestack might seem the most unlikely of places for an upscale hotel, but settle into one of the large and chicly designed guest rooms (upper-level suites facing the river boast some of the city's best views) and you'll agree the concept works. **Pros:** hot design; steps away from restaurants and shopping; refined service. **Cons:** far from the Metro; very expensive. **TripAdvisor:** "always a pleasure," "low-key luxury," "off the beaten path." ⑤ *Rooms from: $559* ✉ *3100 South St. NW, Georgetown* ☎ *202/912–4200* ⊕ *www.ritzcarlton.com/hotels/georgetown* ⌂ *86 rooms, 29 suites* ⎹ *No meals* ⊹ *1:B6.*

Fodor's Choice ★

7

DUPONT CIRCLE

$ ⌂ **Akwaaba DC.** If your perfect vacation includes a having a good book, warm fire, and soft bed then the charming Akwaaba DC bed-and-breakfast is your dream come true. **Pros:** neighborhood location; nice breakfasts; well-kept historic home. **Cons:** smallish bathrooms; reports of some noise from street-facing rooms. **TripAdvisor:** "great accommodations," "wonderful surprise," "magical stay in a magical place." ⑤ *Rooms from: $175* ✉ *1708 16th St. NW, Dupont Circle* ☎ *877/893–3233* ⊕ *www.akwaaba.com* ⌂ *8 rooms, 1 apartment* ⎹ *Breakfast* Ⓜ *Dupont Circle* ⊹ *1:G3.*

HOT HOTEL BARS AND LOUNGES

Some of the most iconic examples of power bars, where inside-the-Beltway decision makers talk shop and rub elbows, are housed in many of this town's historic hotels. So grab a snifter of single malt and begin your people-watching at these classic D.C. hotel bars:

The **Jockey Club Lounge** at the **Fairfax at Embassy Row** made a comeback when it reopened after a long absence on the power bar scene. The original club started serving diplomats, politicians, lobbyists, and other notable individuals in the 1920s, and the reborn club continues that tradition today.

The **Off the Record** bar at the **Hay-Adams** advertises itself as the place to be seen and not heard, and being just steps from the White House, that couldn't be more true. Tucked away in the historic hotel's basement, you really never know who you might run into here.

Although they don't boast the same old-world dark wood and red-leather charm of the bars at the historic hotels, the lobby bar at the decidedly more modern **Liaison Capitol Hill** and **POV** on the roof of the **W Hotel** hold their own as stops on the seen-and-be-seen hotel bar scene.

$$ ⬚ **The Churchill Hotel.** At this historic Beaux-Arts hotel landmark near Dupont Circle, lounges and spacious guest rooms are comfortable and elegant and have small work and sitting areas; many have excellent views as well. **Pros:** friendly service; good-size rooms; frequent specials. **Cons:** far walk to Metro; uphill from Metro to hotel. **TripAdvisor:** "home from home," "nice rooms," "great staff and service." ⑤ *Rooms from: $238* ⊠ *1914 Connecticut Ave. NW, Dupont Circle* ☎ *202/797–2000, 800/424–2464* ⊕ *www.thechurchillhotel.com* ➴ *91 rooms, 82 suites* ⫶⚬⫶ *No meals* Ⓜ *Dupont Circle* ✦ *1:D3.*

$$ ⬚ **Courtyard Washington, D.C./Dupont Circle.** The standard Courtyard amenities come with a big plus here: some of the south-facing rooms on higher floors enjoy fantastic panoramic views of the city that take in the Washington Monument and other historic landmarks through the floor-to-ceiling windows. **Pros:** great views from some rooms; good location; outdoor pool. **Cons:** chain-hotel feel with few unique touches; older hotel design. **TripAdvisor:** "friendly and helpful staff," "comfy bed," "gracious management." ⑤ *Rooms from: $278* ⊠ *1900 Connecticut Ave. NW, Dupont Circle* ☎ *202/332–9300* ⊕ *www.marriott.com* ➴ *146 rooms, 1 suite* ⫶⚬⫶ *Breakfast* Ⓜ *Dupont Circle* ✦ *1:E2.*

$$$ ⬚ **The Dupont Hotel.** With its contemporary furniture, sleek color scheme, and clean lines, the Dupont pulls off *Mad Men*–chic without so much as a hint of kitsch—along with such amenities as heated bathroom floors, flat-screen TVs, and surprisingly effective noise-blocking windows. **Pros:** right on Dupont Circle; newly renovated; fabulous Level Nine concierge level. **Cons:** traffic and noise on Dupont Circle; guest rooms on the small side; limited closet space. **TripAdvisor:** "charming hotel," "comfortable and stylish," "calm perfection." ⑤ *Rooms from: $305* ⊠ *1500 New Hampshire Ave. NW, Dupont Circle* ☎ *202/483–6000,*

The Fairfax at Embassy Row: Did You Know?

The Fairfax at Embassy Row has a long connection to D.C. politics. Here are a few fun facts about the historic property.

■ Al Gore lived here as a child (it was not a hotel at the time).

■ Hillary Clinton held press conferences here when she was running for president.

■ The Steinway piano in the lounge was a gift from the Kennedy family.

■ Nancy Reagan was a Jockey Club regular (she liked the corner table), and back in the day had a chicken salad named for her.

■ The Jockey Club opened for business in 1961 on the day John F. Kennedy took the presidential oath of office.

800/423–6953 ⊕ *www.doylecollection.com/dupont* ⟿ *295 rooms, 32 suites* ❑ *No meals* Ⓜ *Dupont Circle* ✛ *1:F4.*

$$ ⊡ **Embassy Circle Guest House.** Owners Laura and Raymond Saba have
Fodor's Choice lovingly restored this former embassy, transforming it into a warm and
★ friendly home away from home—rooms are bright, with light wood
floors and Oriental rugs, and the house is filled with works by artists
who have been guests at one time or another. **Pros:** lovely hosts; personal service; good location. **Cons:** no bathtubs; too intimate for some.
TripAdvisor: "close to perfection," "cannot be beat," "the perfect base
for visiting D.C." Ⓢ *Rooms from: $240* ✉ *2224 R St. NW, Dupont Circle* ☎ *202/232–7744, 877/232–7744* ⊕ *www.dcinns.com* ⟿ *11 rooms*
❑ *Breakfast* Ⓜ *Dupont Circle* ✛ *1:D3.*

$$$$ ⊡ **The Fairfax at Embassy Row.** Light-filled hallways, invitingly bright
guest rooms, insanely soft bed linens, marble baths, decorator furnishings, and impeccable service make this hotel, which used to be
Al Gore's childhood home, a bastion of luxury. **Pros:** historic hotel;
larger rooms; great location. **Cons:** no pool; challenging street parking.
TripAdvisor: "spacious old-world charm," "very comfortable," "the
people are so friendly." Ⓢ *Rooms from: $407* ✉ *2100 Massachusetts
Ave. NW, Dupont Circle* ☎ *202/293–2100, 888/625–5144* ⊕ *www.
fairfaxhoteldc.com* ⟿ *259 rooms, 27 suites* ❑ *No meals* Ⓜ *Dupont
Circle* ✛ *1:E4.*

$$$ ⊡ **Hotel Madera.** Tranquil guest rooms at this unique inn in a quiet part
of town southwest of Dupont Circle sport grass-cloth wallpaper, Japanese-inspired patterned carpeting, and oversize wooden headboards
with indigo blue mohair padding. **Pros:** fun hotel; convenient location. **Cons:** no pool or gym; small bathrooms. **TripAdvisor:** "treated
like royalty," "oasis in the middle of D.C.," "comfortable room."
Ⓢ *Rooms from: $309* ✉ *1310 New Hampshire Ave. NW, Dupont Circle* ☎ *202/296–7600, 800/430–1202* ⊕ *www.hotelmadera.com* ⟿ *82
rooms* ❑ *No meals* Ⓜ *Dupont Circle* ✛ *1:E4.*

$$$ ⊡ **Hotel Palomar, Washington, D.C.** The Palomar is winning hearts and
minds not just with a hard-to-beat location but with space and style as

7

well—muted chocolate-beige rooms are some of the largest in town, and are decorated with cool animal prints (think tiger-striped robes, crocodile-patterned carpets, and faux-lynx throws) and plush purple and fuchsia furnishings. **Pros:** spacious rooms; outdoor pool; good for pet owners. **Cons:** smallish baths; busy public areas not cozy for sitting. **TripAdvisor:** "welcoming in every way," "wonderful customer service," "great for a romantic trip." $ *Rooms from: $339* ⌧ *2121 P St. NW, Dupont Circle* ☎ *202/448–1800* ⊕ *www.hotelpalomar-dc.com* ⚟ *315 rooms, 20 suites* � *No meals* Ⓜ *Dupont Circle* ✛ *1:E4.*

$$$ 🖵 **Hotel Rouge.** Hotel Rouge will have you seeing red and loving it; rooms are a sleek postmodern tribute to the color, from the red platform beds to the red velvet curtains, chicly offset with gray and white accent pieces. **Pros:** newly renovated rooms and lobby; gay-friendly vibe; good location. **Cons:** no pool; the scene is not for everybody. **TripAdvisor:** "beautiful hotel," "great location for going out," "classy." $ *Rooms from: $330* ⌧ *1315 16th St. NW, Dupont Circle* ☎ *202/232–8000, 800/738–1202* ⊕ *www.rougehotel.com* ⚟ *137 rooms* 101 *No meals* Ⓜ *Dupont Circle* ✛ *1:G4.*

$ 🖵 **Hotel Tabard Inn.** One of the city's oldest hotels is actually three connected town houses, featuring all kinds of hidden treasures and rooms along its dimly lighted hallways—you get the sense the place belongs to someone's fantastical albeit slightly eccentric great-aunt. **Pros:** affordable choice; lots of character; Sunday-night jazz in the hotel lounge; in-house destination restaurant. **Cons:** some shared bathrooms; limited privacy; steps to climb. **TripAdvisor:** "nice location and atmosphere," "funky and fun hotel experience," "exceptional customer service." $ *Rooms from: $165* ⌧ *1739 N St. NW, Dupont Circle* ☎ *202/785–1277* ⊕ *www.tabardinn.com* ⚟ *40 rooms, 25 with bath* 101 *Breakfast* Ⓜ *Dupont Circle* ✛ *1:F4.*

$ 🖵 **The Inn at Dupont Circle North.** A more modern version of its sister property, The Inn at Dupont Circle South, this small hotel offers such high-tech touches as flat-screen TVs, free Wi-Fi, and whirlpool tubs. **Pros:** good location; breakfast included. **Cons:** not as charming as other bed-and-breakfasts; some shared baths; steps to climb. **TripAdvisor:** "cute and great location," "perfect place to stay," "somewhat quirky." $ *Rooms from: $150* ⌧ *1620 T St. NW, Dupont Circle* ☎ *202/467–6777, 866/467–2100* ⊕ *www.thedupontcollection.com* ⚟ *7 rooms, 5 with bath* 101 *Breakfast* Ⓜ *Dupont Circle* ✛ *1:G3.*

$ 🖵 **The Inn at Dupont Circle South.** This is the inn where everybody knows your name: innkeeper Carolyn Torralba jokes that her guests are "her babies," and the personal attention shows in the featherbeds, doilies, bric-a-brac, and impressionist posters. **Pros:** personable innkeeper and many repeat guests; across from Metro; children welcome; airport shuttle. **Cons:** creaking floors; steps to climb; not all rooms have private baths. **TripAdvisor:** "home away from home," "quaint inn with charm and warmth," "wonderful breakfast." $ *Rooms from: $140* ⌧ *1312 19th St. NW, Dupont Circle* ☎ *202/467–6777, 866/467–2100* ⊕ *thedupontcollection.com* ⚟ *8 rooms, 3 with shared bath* 101 *Breakfast* Ⓜ *Dupont Circle* ✛ *1:F4.*

LODGING ALTERNATIVES

APARTMENT RENTALS

D.C. is a notoriously transient town, with people hopping on and off the campaign trail on a moment's notice often leaving their apartments in the sublets and long-term rental columns of local newspapers and websites. If you can't stomach the idea of another family vacation with you and the kids squeezed into a single hotel room with no kitchen, or if you are traveling with others, a furnished rental might be for you. Often these rentals wind up saving you money—especially on meals and snacks. Be warned, the allure of a full kitchen and room to spread out might get you hooked on apartment rentals for life. Here are some websites to help you find hotel alternatives, short-term apartment rentals, apartment exchanges, and other alternative ways to stay in town.

⊕ www.vrbo.com

⊕ www.washingtondc.craigslist.org

⊕ thehill.com/classifieds.html

⊕ www.militarybyowner.com

⊕ www.dcdigs.com

⊕ www.remington-dc.com

⊕ www.cyberrentals.com

International Agents
Hideaways International.
Hideaways International, membership $195. ⑤ *Rooms from: $195* ✉ 767 *Islington St., Portsmouth, New Hampshire* ☎ 603/430–4433, 800/843–4433 ⊕ www.hideaways.com.

Rental Listings
Washington Post
(⊕ www.washingtonpost.com).
Washington CityPaper
(⊕ www.washingtoncitypaper.com).

BED-AND-BREAKFASTS

Bed and Breakfast Accommodations, Ltd. To find reasonably priced accommodations in small guesthouses and private homes, try Bed and Breakfast Accommodations, Ltd. ⑤ *Rooms from: $195* ☎ 413/582–9888, 877/893–3233 ⊕ *www. bedandbreakfastdc.com.*

HOME EXCHANGES

If you would like to exchange your home for someone else's, join a home-exchange organization, which will send you its updated listings of available exchanges for a year and include your own listing in at least one of them. It's up to you to make specific arrangements.

Exchange Clubs
HomeLink International. HomeLink International; $119 for a listing published in a directory and on websites. ⑤ *Rooms from: $119* ☎ 954/566–2687, 800/638–3841 ⊕ *www.homelink.org.*

Intervac U.S. Intervac U.S.; $199.99 yearly for a listing, online access, and a catalog; $99.99 without catalog. ⑤ *Rooms from: $99* ☎ 800/756–4663 ⊕ *www.intervacus.com.*

HOSTELS

Hostelling International—USA.
No matter what your age, you can save on lodging costs by staying at hostels. ⑤ *Rooms from: $28* ✉ *8401 Colesville Rd., Suite 600, Silver Spring, Maryland* ☎ 301/495–1240 ⊕ *www.hiusa.org* ✛ *2:C1.*

$ ⊡ **The Normandy Hotel.** At this quiet bed-and-breakfast–style hotel nestled on a residential street near Embassy Row, rooms are stylish and cozy, breakfast is served in the pretty conservatory or on the terrace, and the staff bakes cookies each afternoon and hosts a weekly wine-and-cheese reception. **Pros:** quiet location; close to restaurants and shops; charming inn-like hotel. **Cons:** no pool on-site but use of one nearby; a bit of a walk to the Metro. **TripAdvisor:** "charming room," "most amazing beds," "lovely hotel and staff." $ *Rooms from: $159* ⊠ *2118 Wyoming Ave. NW, Dupont Circle* ☎ *202/483–1350* ⊕ *www.doylecollection.com/ normandy* ⇌ *75 rooms* ⦿*⃝ Breakfast* Ⓜ *Dupont Circle* ✛ *1:E2.*

$$$ ⊡ **Residence Inn Washington, D.C./Dupont Circle.** It's remarkable that a
☕   commercial chain can feel so cozy—a small fireplace sitting room is right off the lobby, kitchens come stocked with everything you need, and sleeper sofas are an added bonus for families looking for more room to spread out. **Pros:** free breakfast; good choice for families. **Cons:** chain-hotel rooms; few unique touches; no pool. **TripAdvisor:** "friendly service," "very comfortable," "pleasant staff." $ *Rooms from: $329* ⊠ *2120 P St. NW, Dupont Circle* ☎ *202/466–6800, 800/331–3131* ⊕ *www.marriott.com/wasri* ⇌ *107 suites* ⦿*⃝ Breakfast* Ⓜ *Dupont Circle* ✛ *1:E4.*

$ ⊡ **Swann House.** You'll be hard-pressed to find a more charming inn
Fodor's Choice   than Dupont Circle's Swann House and equally challenged to find more
★   delightful hosts than innkeeper Rick Verkler and his staff. **Pros:** perfect location; beautiful and lavish rooms; fireplaces in winter, a pool in summer. **Cons:** bed-and-breakfast style not for everyone; less expensive rooms are small. **TripAdvisor:** "perfect Washington accommodations," "a very special experience," "friendly staff." $ *Rooms from: $199* ⊠ *1808 New Hampshire Ave. NW, Dupont Circle* ☎ *202/265–4414* ⊕ *www.swannhouse.com* ⇌ *9 rooms, 4 suites* ⦿*⃝ Breakfast* Ⓜ *Dupont Circle* ✛ *1:F3.*

$$$ ⊡ **Topaz Hotel.** A marriage of cozy and whimsy lulls visitors with funky purple couches, green-and-white stripped walls, plush bedding, and contemporary accent pieces. **Pros:** newly remodeled rooms and lobby; good location; individual feel. **Cons:** funky style not for everyone; no pool. **TripAdvisor:** "excellent location," "nice boutique hotel," "great experience." $ *Rooms from: $330* ⊠ *1733 N St. NW, Dupont Circle* ☎ *202/393–3000, 800/775–1202* ⊕ *www.topazhotel.com* ⇌ *91 rooms, 8 suites* ⦿*⃝ No meals* Ⓜ *Dupont Circle* ✛ *1:F4.*

UPPER NORTHWEST

$ ⊡ **Adam's Inn.** At this cozy bed-and-breakfast spreading through three residential town houses near Adams Morgan, the zoo, and Dupont Circle, the Victorian-style rooms are small but comfortable; many share baths, but those that do also have a sink in the room. **Pros:** affordable rates; nearby Metro; lively neighborhood. **Cons:** some shared baths; steps to climb. **TripAdvisor:** "quiet island," "still a jewel," "perfect little getaway." $ *Rooms from: $129* ⊠ *1746 Lanier Pl. NW, Woodley Park* ☎ *202/745–3600, 800/578–6807* ⊕ *www.adamsinn.com* ⇌ *26 rooms, 16 with bath* ⦿*⃝ Breakfast* Ⓜ *Woodley Park/Zoo* ✛ *1:F1.*

$$ [icon] **Embassy Suites Washington D.C.–at Chevy Chase Pavilion.** If you are ☺ looking for an easy, family-friendly place to unpack your bags, these spacious two-room suites right at the D.C./Maryland border are for you—each is done in soothing earth tones and has two flat-screen TVs, a work space, and a sitting area. **Pros:** eco- and family-friendly; close to Metro; updated guest rooms. **Cons:** lots of families; chain hotel. **TripAdvisor:** "their staff is the best," "lots of perks," "excellent place to relax." ⑤ *Rooms from: $229* ✉ *4300 Military Rd., Upper Northwest* ☎ *202/362–9300, 800/760–6120* ⊕ *www.embassysuitesdcmetro.com* ↩ *198 suites* ⏏ *Breakfast* Ⓜ *Friendship Heights* ✛ *1:A1.*

$ [icon] **The Intown Uptown Inn.** If you consider hopping on a bus to get to the sights a small price to pay for the chance to stay at a charming B&B at a bargain price, then this beautifully renovated 1909 Victorian decorated with stylish antiques is the place for you. **Pros:** beautiful inn; laid-back and gracious host; great price. **Cons:** an approximate 25-minute bus ride to Downtown; almost no restaurants or shopping in walking distance; only accepts cash (can hold a reservation with credit card). **TripAdvisor:** "great innkeepers," "an oasis in D.C.," "historic charm." ⑤ *Rooms from: $140* ✉ *4907 14th St. NW, Upper Northwest* ☎ *202/541–9400* ⊕ *www.iuinn.com* ↩ *10 rooms, 2 with shared bath* ⊟ *No credit cards* ⏏ *Breakfast* ✛ *1:H1.*

$$ [icon] **Omni Shoreham Hotel.** This elegant hotel overlooking Rock Creek Park has been lovingly tended and is aging gracefully, still luring guests with light-filled guest rooms (many are larger than typical) done in a soothing garden palette and equipped with snazzy marble bathrooms. **Pros:** historic property; great pool and sundeck; good views from many rooms. **Cons:** not Downtown; extremely large. **TripAdvisor:** "feels like home," "historic hotel in nice neighborhood," "beautiful location." ⑤ *Rooms from: $275* ✉ *2500 Calvert St. NW, Woodley Park* ☎ *202/234–0700, 800/834–6664* ⊕ *www.omnihotels.com* ↩ *836 rooms, 16 suites* ⏏ *No meals* Ⓜ *Woodley Park/Zoo* ✛ *1:C1.*

Fodor's Choice
★
☺

$$$ [icon] **Washington Marriott Wardman Park.** You almost get the sense that ☺ you stepped into a mini city when you enter this huge, redbrick hotel behind the Woodley Park Metro, offering a modern wing, where contemporary-style rooms are done with splashes of bright color, or the lower-key 1918 Wardman Tower. **Pros:** on top of Metro; light-filled sundeck; pretty residential neighborhood with good restaurants. **Cons:** busy; loud; lines at restaurants when hotel is full; massive. **TripAdvisor:** "quiet," "spacious rooms," "lovely campus." ⑤ *Rooms from: $359* ✉ *2660 Woodley Rd. NW, Woodley Park* ☎ *202/328–2000, 800/228–9290* ⊕ *www.marriott.com* ↩ *1,189 rooms, 125 suites* ⏏ *No meals* Ⓜ *Woodley Park/Zoo* ✛ *1:D2.*

$$ [icon] **Woodley Park Guest House.** At this warm, peaceful bed-and-breakfast on a quiet residential street near the zoo, antiques-filled rooms are individually decorated, and most have private baths. **Pros:** close to Metro; near the zoo; breakfast included. **Cons:** a Metro ride away from Downtown; some shared baths; limited privacy. **TripAdvisor:** "excellent guest house," "very nice surprise," "a warm and welcoming place." ⑤ *Rooms from: $215* ✉ *2647 Woodley Rd. NW, Woodley Park*

7

☎ *202/667–0218, 866/667–0218* ⊕ *www.dcinns.com* ⌁ *13 rooms, 11 with bath* ¦○¦ *Breakfast* Ⓜ *Woodley Park/Zoo* ✦ *1:D2.*

SUBURBAN MARYLAND

$ ⊟ **Bethesda Court Hotel.** A vintage low-key, three-story motor inn, two blocks from the Bethesda Metro and near restaurants, shops, and an independent movie theater, has been carefully upgraded to offer comfortable, traditionally furnished rooms with good beds and marble bathrooms. **Pros:** free Wi-Fi; close to Metro; basic Continental breakfast included. **Cons:** far from Downtown and major attractions; parking is extra; no room service. **TripAdvisor:** "a classic and a gem," "ideally located," "trustworthy and friendly staff." ⑤ *Rooms from: $159* ⊠ *7740 Wisconsin Ave., Bethesda* ☎ *301/656–2100* ⊕ *www.bethesdacourtwashdc.com* ⌁ *74 rooms, 1 suite* ¦○¦ *Breakfast* Ⓜ *Bethesda* ✦ *1:A1.*

$$ ⊟ **Courtyard Chevy Chase.** Everything about this chain hotel is bright
Fodor's Choice and shiny, from the sleek lobby that features "media pods" for quiet
★ work sessions to good size, stylish rooms with all the high-tech ameni-
Ⓒ ties. **Pros:** new; green initiatives at work throughout the hotel; close to Metro, restaurants, and shops; outdoor pool; good for business travelers. **Cons:** a distance from Downtown. **TripAdvisor:** "well managed," "comfortable room," "exceeded our expectations." ⑤ *Rooms from: $229* ⊠ *5520 Wisconsin Ave., Chevy Chase* ☎ *301/656–1500* ⊕ *www.marriott.com* ⌁ *225 rooms, 1 suite* ¦○¦ *Breakfast* Ⓜ *Friendship Heights* ✦ *1:A1.*

$ ⊟ **Doubletree Hotel Bethesda.** The big plus at this business-oriented hotel are larger-than-typical guest rooms, equipped with firm, comfortable beds and ample working space. **Pros:** rooftop pool; hypoallergenic rooms; good value. **Cons:** outside the city; far from major attractions; a bit of a walk to Metro. **TripAdvisor:** "quite nice," "attractive rooms," "convenient." ⑤ *Rooms from: $170* ⊠ *8120 Wisconsin Ave., Bethesda* ☎ *301/652–2000* ⊕ *www.doubletreebethesda.com* ⌁ *269 rooms, 7 suites* ¦○¦ *No meals* Ⓜ *Bethesda* ✦ *1:A1.*

$$$ ⊟ **Hyatt Regency Bethesda.** Well-equipped guest rooms have sleigh beds and mahogany furnishings, along with plenty of welcome amenities, such as large desks, 32-inch TVs, and marble baths. **Pros:** at Metro station; easy walk to dozens of restaurants; indoor pool. **Cons:** often crowded; noise from lobby. **TripAdvisor:** "great staff," "great room," "perfect choice for D.C. visitors." ⑤ *Rooms from: $309* ⊠ *1 Bethesda Metro Center, 7400 block of Wisconsin Ave., Bethesda* ☎ *301/657–1234, 800/233–1234* ⊕ *www.bethesda.hyatt.com* ⌁ *391 rooms, 7 suites* ¦○¦ *No meals* Ⓜ *Bethesda* ✦ *1:A1.*

$ ⊟ **Residence Inn Bethesda Downtown.** If you're looking for an affordable home away from home, this is a sensible option: the recently renovated one- and two-bedroom suites come with fully equipped kitchens with a standard-size refrigerator and dishwasher, plates, and utensils. **Pros:** dozens of restaurants within walking distance; rooftop pool; walk to Metro. **Cons:** far from monuments; chain-hotel feel. **TripAdvisor:** "comfortable and homey," "great location and rooms," "friendly staff." ⑤ *Rooms from: $149* ⊠ *7335 Wisconsin Ave., Bethesda* ☎ *301/718–*

0200, 800/331–3131 ⊕ www.residenceinnbethesdahotel.com ⤴ 187 suites ⦁⦿⦁ Breakfast Ⓜ Bethesda ✛ 1:A1.

SUBURBAN VIRGINIA

$$ ▣ **Hilton Arlington Hotel.** At this popular outlying chain hotel, large guest rooms offer "serenity" beds, work desks, and comfy chairs, service is friendly, and a covered skywalk leads to the Ballston Common Mall and National Science Foundation. **Pros:** easy Metro access; big rooms; online check-in. **Cons:** far from attractions; chain-hotel feel; no pool. **TripAdvisor:** "nice room and great location," "very convenient," "friendly staff." Ⓢ *Rooms from: $242 ✉ 950 N. Stafford St., Arlington* ☎ *703/528–6000, 800/445–8667 ⊕ www.hiltonarlington.com ⤴ 205 rooms, 5 suites* ⦁⦿⦁ *No meals* Ⓜ *Ballston ✛ 1:A6.*

$$ ▣ **Holiday Inn Arlington at Ballston.** While rooms are typical chain-style, you can get into Washington quickly via the Metro, and Arlington National Cemetery and the Iwo Jima Memorial are nearby. **Pros:** free high-speed Internet access; near the Metro. **Cons:** outside the city; **TripAdvisor:** "welcoming staff," "good food and great people," "nice location." Ⓢ *Rooms from: $239 ✉ 4610 N. Fairfax Dr., Arlington* ☎ *703/243–9800 ⊕ www.hiarlington.com ⤴ 221 rooms, 2 suites* ⦁⦿⦁ *No meals* Ⓜ *Ballston ✛ 1:A6.*

$ ▣ **Hyatt Arlington.** This solid over-the-Potomac choice offers large, modern, well-equipped and stylish guest rooms; the hotel's restaurant, Cityhouse, serves classic American cuisine; and the lobby bar is a good place to relax with an early-evening martini or late-night drink. **Pros:** free Wi-Fi; across from Metro; newly updated rooms. **Cons:** outside the city; dull neighborhood; no pool. **TripAdvisor:** "very welcoming and helpful staff," "clean and modern," "great location." Ⓢ *Rooms from: $203 ✉ 1325 Wilson Blvd., Arlington* ☎ *703/525–1234, 800/908–4790 ⊕ www.hyattarlington.com ⤴ 312 rooms, 5 suites* ⦁⦿⦁ *No meals ✛ 1:A6.*

$$ ▣ **Key Bridge Marriott.** Guest rooms sparkle; the views from the Potomac ↻ side are camera worthy; and although the property carries a Virginia zip code, you can walk over the Key Bridge into Georgetown or hop on the Metro at the nearby Rosslyn station. **Pros:** good choice if traveling with kids; near the Metro; nice views from some rooms. **Cons:** outside the city; area dull at night. **TripAdvisor:** "great location," "comfortable accommodations," "courteous." Ⓢ *Rooms from: $229 ✉ 1401 Lee Hwy., Arlington* ☎ *703/524–6400, 800/228–9290 ⊕ www.marriott. com ⤴ 571 rooms, 11 suites* ⦁⦿⦁ *No meals* Ⓜ *Rosslyn ✛ 1:A6.*

$$$ ▣ **Residence Inn Arlington Pentagon City.** The view across the Potomac of ↻ the D.C. skyline and the monuments is magnificent from these suites in a high-rise adjacent to the Pentagon and two blocks from the Pentagon City Fashion Centre mall. **Pros:** a plus for families; easy walk to Metro; airport shuttle. **Cons:** outside D.C.; neighborhood dead at night. **TripAdvisor:** "spacious," "all the comforts of home," "what a wonderful staff." Ⓢ *Rooms from: $299 ✉ 550 Army Navy Dr., Arlington* ☎ *703/413–6630, 800/331–3131 ⊕ www.marriott.com ⤴ 299 suites* ⦁⦿⦁ *Breakfast* Ⓜ *Pentagon City ✛ 1:A6.*

7

$$$$ 🛏 **The Ritz-Carlton Pentagon City.** This Ritz has a more contemporary feel than one might traditionally associate with the luxury chain, with chic and large guest rooms that shine in gold, yellow, and blue. **Pros:** indoor walk to Metro; indoor pool; attentive service. **Cons:** outside D.C.; slightly less ritzy but more hip than other Ritz properties. **TripAdvisor:** "best service," "an oasis of comfort," "a lovely trip." ⑤ *Rooms from: $469* ✉ *1250 S. Hayes St., Arlington* ☎ *703/415–5000, 800/241–3333* ⊕ *www.ritzcarlton.com* ⇆ *409 rooms, 15 suites* ⦿ *No meals* Ⓜ *Pentagon City* ✛ *1:A6.*

Nightlife

WORD OF MOUTH

"Ethiopian restaurants, 930 Club, the Black Cat, jazz clubs whose names escape me—U Street is far more lively, and with distinctly local flavor, than Dupont these days."

—kayd

Updated
by Allison
Lombardo

From buttoned-down political appointees who've just arrived to laid-back folks who've lived here their whole lives, Washingtonians are always looking for a place to relax. And they have plenty of options when they head out for a night on the town. Most places are clustered in several key neighborhoods, making a night of barhopping relatively easy.

Georgetown's dozens of bars, nightclubs, and restaurants radiate from the intersection of Wisconsin and M streets, attracting crowds that include older adults and college students. Many restaurants here turn into bars after the dinner crowd leaves. Georgetown is one of the safest neighborhoods in D.C., with a large police presence on weekends.

Those seeking a younger and less inhibited nightlife may prefer the 18th Street strip in Adams Morgan, between Columbia Road and Florida Avenue, which offers a wide variety of places for dancing, drinking, eating, and everything else you can imagine. The best part of Adams Morgan is that there are so many bars and clubs around 18th Street that if you don't like one, there's another next door. At night the streets are so crowded you will have trouble weaving your way through the swarms of revelers. AdMo, as it's affectionately called, is best known as a drinking hot spot, but there are some underappreciated gems that make the strip worth the trip for anyone.

The U Street Corridor (U Street NW between 9th and 17th streets NW), historically D.C.'s hippest neighborhood and a regular stop for jazz greats, has undergone a revival and is now the hottest spot in town, with bars that appeal to all kinds of people. Wine bars, dive bars, hipster bars, gastropubs, and dance clubs make for a full night out.

For serious dance action, head to Northeast D.C. Huge crowds and loud music, ranging from hip-hop and Latin to techno and trance, await you at the ever-popular warehouse-turned-mega-clubs like Love and Ibiza. This is a rougher part of town, so be cautious.

Other hot spots include Capitol Hill and Downtown. The stretch of Pennsylvania Avenue between 2nd and 4th streets has a half-dozen

Capitol Hill bars. And thanks to massive recent development, Penn Quarter/Chinatown is burgeoning with squeaky-clean new bars.

The newest center of gravity for D.C. nightlife is the burgeoning H Street Corridor, home to a historic jazz club, a palace of wonders and oddities, and bars with the most personality in town. Difficult to get to, H Street remains undiscovered except to those in the know.

PLANNING

ADMISSION

Most nightlife venues in D.C. have cover charges for bands and DJs, especially those performing on Friday and Saturday. Expect to pay from $10 to $20 for most dance clubs. Jazz and comedy clubs often have higher cover charges along with drink minimums.

DRESS CODE

Despite how formally they might have to dress during the week, on the weekend District residents really let their hair down. Although many of the high-end clubs require you to "dress to impress," including dress shoes for men, most bars and pubs are slightly more casual. This is especially true during the summer, when shorts can be considered acceptable on an oppressively humid night.

HOURS

Last call in D.C. is 2 am, and most bars and clubs close by 3 am on the weekend and between midnight and 2 am during the week. The exceptions are after-hours dance clubs and bars with kitchens that stay open late.

8

NIGHTLIFE INFORMATION

To survey the local scene, consult Friday's "Weekend" section in the *Washington Post* and the free weekly *Washington CityPaper*. A terrific online site (with an accompanying cell phone app) for local happenings is the *Post*'s Going Out Guide (⊕ *www.washingtonpost.com/gog*). The free publications *Metro Weekly* and *Washington Blade* offer insights on gay and lesbian nightlife. Local blog DCist (⊕ *www.dcist.com*) posts daily on D.C. events. It's a good idea to call clubs ahead of time, as last week's punk-rock party might be this week's merengue marathon.

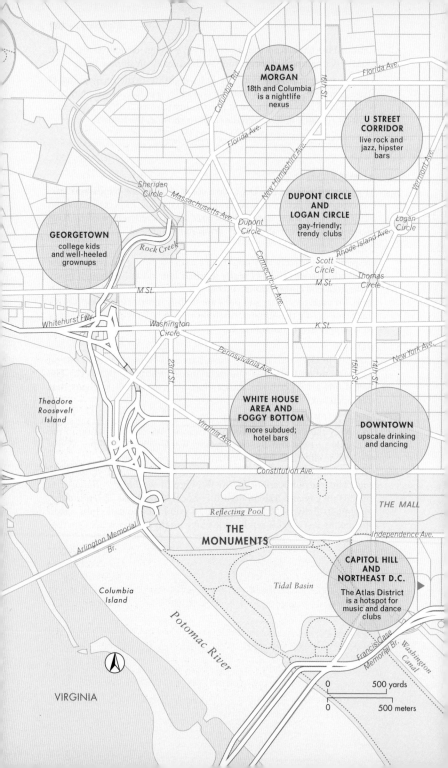

ADAMS MORGAN
18th and Columbia is a nightlife nexus

U STREET CORRIDOR
live rock and jazz, hipster bars

DUPONT CIRCLE AND LOGAN CIRCLE
gay-friendly; trendy clubs

GEORGETOWN
college kids and well-heeled grownups

WHITE HOUSE AREA AND FOGGY BOTTOM
more subdued; hotel bars

DOWNTOWN
upscale drinking and dancing

THE MONUMENTS

CAPITOL HILL AND NORTHEAST D.C.
The Atlas District is a hotspot for music and dance clubs

Theodore Roosevelt Island

Columbia Island

Potomac River

Reflecting Pool

THE MALL

Tidal Basin

VIRGINIA

Columbia Rd.

Florida Ave.

16th St.

Florida Ave.

New Hampshire Ave.

Vermont Ave.

Sheridan Circle

Massachusetts Ave.

Dupont Circle

Logan Circle

Rhode Island Ave.

Rock Creek

Connecticut Ave.

Scott Circle

M St.

Thomas Circle

M St.

Whitehurst Fwy.

Washington Circle

23rd St.

Pennsylvania Ave.

K St.

15th St.

14th St.

New York Ave.

Virginia Ave.

Constitution Ave.

Independence Ave.

Arlington Memorial Br.

Francis Case Memorial Br.

Washington Canal

0   500 yards

0   500 meters

FIVE GREAT NIGHTLIFE EXPERIENCES

9:30 Club: The best live music venue in D.C., the club showcases new and legendary performers from across the nation.

The Birchmere: Known for blue-grass, the club offers a variety of genres, with something for everybody—from Kelly Willis to Aaron Neville to Tom Rush and Jerry Jeff Walker.

Café Saint-Ex: There's an upstairs and downstairs for your wild and mild sides.

Blues Alley: D.C.'s classiest jazz club is the place to enjoy outstanding performers and Cajun food in an intimate setting.

Rock and Roll Hotel: Experience the H Street Corridor with locals-in-the-know, while enjoying indie acts and a great dance party.

WHITE HOUSE AREA AND FOGGY BOTTOM

The area near the White House and Foggy Bottom offers a less frantic nightlife environment because the center of the city empties out during the weekends, but in recent years, some interesting clubs and restaurants have opened, many near major hotels, making the area more attractive to the going-out crowd.

BARS AND LOUNGES

★ **P.O.V.** For decades, the perfect way to end a night out in Washington was a trip to the Sky Tavern on the Hotel Washington's 11th floor rooftop. When the W Washington, D.C. hotel replaced the Hotel Washington in 2009, the Sky Tavern was reincarnated as P.O.V. ("Point of View"). The trendy indoor lounge and outdoor terrace offer a tremendous view over D.C.'s low skyline; you can gaze at the monuments and the Capitol while enjoying a seasonal cocktail or a bite from Jean-Georges Vongerichten's menu. Unfortunately, the view here is no secret, so expect a long wait to get in. ■ TIP➔ Children are not always welcome at this posh lookout. P.O.V. stays open very late for D.C.: until 2:30 am on weekends. ⊠ 515 15 St. NW, White House Area ☎ 202/661–2400 ⊕ www. pointofviewdc.com Ⓜ McPherson Sq.

DANCE CLUBS

★ **Eden.** Located near the White House, this hot spot attracts Washington celebrities, foreign visitors, and the sophisticated elite. The two-story club hosts a variety of local and big-name DJs and is famous for its rooftop deck, attracting big crowds in the summer. Open on Sundays. ⊠ 1716 I St. NW, Foggy Bottom ☎ 202/785–0270 ⊕ www.edendc.com Ⓜ Farragut West.

Science Club. Quiet and relaxed early in the evening, this nerd chic–inspired, upscale dive gets loud and crowded after 10 pm. There are two floors with DJs spinning, and the music styles change depending on the night. ⊠ 1136 19th St. NW, White House Area ☎ 202/775-0747 ⊕ www.scienceclubdc.com Ⓜ Farragut West.

CAPITOL HILL AND NORTHEAST D.C.

Seemingly overnight, Capitol Hill has become a hot location. Great new restaurants and bars match time-tested steadies, allowing nighttime crowds to enjoy food from celebrity chefs and then dance away the night or relax in a casual dive bar. A four-block area in the H Street Corridor, known as the Atlas District, is home to some great music venues.

Northeast's industrial environment can be intimidating and caution is warranted for safety reasons. Make use of the premium parking—for about $20—that will put you close to the entrance. Even parking a few blocks away on neighborhood streets is risky at night. Taxis are another good option.

BARS AND LOUNGES

★ **Dubliner.** A Washington institution that offers cozy paneled rooms, rich pints of Guinness, and nightly live Irish entertainment make this place popular among Capitol Hill staffers and Georgetown law students. It is located near Union Station. ⊠ *Phoenix Park Hotel, 520 North Capitol St. NW, Capitol Hill* ☎ *202/737–3773* ⊕ *www.dublinerdc.com* Ⓜ *Union Station.*

H Street Country Club. The only D.C. bar to offer indoor miniature golf and skee ball, H Street Country Club's friendly, quieter vibe has made it a popular nightspot. Margaritas and fish tacos round out the fun mix. ⊠ *1335 H St. NE, Northeast* ☎ *202/399–4722* ⊕ *www.thehstreetcountryclub.com* Ⓜ *Union Station.*

Phase One. This long-standing lesbian club attracts an eclectic, laid-back clientele. The small dance floor and pool tables in the back make it an intimate and comfortable spot, although sometimes the place gets very crowded. ⊠ *525 8th St. SE, Capitol Hill* ☎ *202/544–6831* ⊕ *www.phaseonedc.com* Ⓜ *Eastern Market.*

Tune Inn. This hole-in-the-wall dive bar, attracts tourists but also Capitol Hill staffers and interns. It's burgers got 15 minutes of fame by being featured on a FoodNetwork show and are worth the hype. ⊠ *331 Pennsylvania Ave. SE, Capitol Hill* ☎ *202/543–2725* ⊕ *www.tuneinndc.com* Ⓜ *Capitol Hill South.*

DANCE CLUBS

Ibiza. Ibiza remains one of D.C.'s most popular dance clubs, with DJs and special guests announced a week in advance on the radio and online. This is a great space, but only if you like your music loud and your dance floor crowded, which it tends to be, even with its cavernous space and seven bars. When you need a breath of fresh air, Ibiza has a rooftop deck—a rarity in D.C. Saturday is 18-and-over night, which can attract a younger crowd. ⊠ *1222 1st St. NE, Northeast D.C.* ☎ *888/424–9232* ⊕ *www.ibizadc.com* Ⓜ *New York Ave./Florida Ave./Gallaudet U.*

★ **Love.** This four-story dance powerhouse looms over an industrial area far from Downtown. Elegant and minimalist, Love makes the most of its former warehouse home. The music changes from night to night, and from floor to floor, but you're sure to sample salsa, house, and trance. This wood-paneled club attracts a primarily upscale, but diverse clientele. Washington Wizards players and other celebrities are frequently spotted in the VIP areas. Love also has occasional concerts from performers such as Wyclef Jean and Alicia Keys. ■TIP➔ Plan ahead for taxis given the club's isolated locale. ✉ *1350 Okie St. NE, Northeast* ☎ *202/636–9030* ⊕ *www.lovetheclub.com.*

Remington's. Country-western dancing is all the rage at this cavernous club on Capitol Hill. The upstairs lounge features karaoke, pool, and foosball, attracting a laid-back crowd willing to try just about anything. Dance lessons are offered on Monday and Wednesday from 8:30 to 9:30 pm. ✉ *639 Pennsylvania Ave. SE, Capitol Hill* ☎ *202/543–3113* ⊕ *www.remingtonswdc.com* Ⓜ *Eastern Market.*

MUSIC CLUBS
JAZZ AND BLUES

★ **HR-57.** Named after a congressional resolution proclaiming jazz a "rare and valuable national treasure," HR-57 isn't just a club, it's a nonprofit cultural center. It spotlights musicians based in the D.C. area, many of whom have national followings. Fried chicken and collard greens are on the menu; beer and wine are available, or bring your own bottle (corkage is $3 per person). Open Wednesday through Saturday, weeknights feature jam sessions by local artists, and big names sometimes join in on the weekends. The warm and relaxed atmosphere makes this place worth a visit. ✉ *816 H St. NE, H Street Corridor* ☎ *202/667–3700* ⊕ *www.hr57.org* Ⓜ *Union Station.*

Mr. Henry's. This laid-back club is the last holdout of a once-thriving live-music scene on Capitol Hill. Roberta Flack got her start in the upstairs performance space, where a dozen or so tables are scattered around the wood-paneled room. There's never a cover. ✉ *601 Pennsylvania Ave. SE, Capitol Hill* ☎ *202/546–8412* ⊕ *www.mrhenrysrestaurant. com* Ⓜ *Eastern Market.*

ROCK AND POP

Red Palace. Divey, quirky, and sometimes downright weird, this eclectic theme club, offers a unique combination of indie rock music, vaudeville, burlesque, and more. While enjoying a drink, patrons can check out quirky artifacts in the Museum of Oddities. ✉ *1210 H St. NE, Northeast* ☎ *202/399–3201* ⊕ *www.redpalacedc.com* Ⓜ *Union Station.*

Rock and Roll Hotel. In the H Street Corridor, this venue offers some of the nation's best indie acts. Housed in a former funeral home, the multiple dance floors can get very crowded when well-known musicians perform. Live acts are in the main room and DJs spin on the second floor, called the Hotel Bar, hosting some of the most enthusiastic dance parties in town. Notable acts include the Walkmen, Andrew W.K., and Juliette and the Licks. It's a 15-block walk from the Metro and, in this still up-and-coming area, it's best to take a taxi. ✉ *1353 H St. NE, H Street Corridor* ☎ *202/265-6010* ⊕ *www.rockandrollhoteldc.com* Ⓜ *Potomac Ave.*

8

DOWNTOWN

You'll find plenty of bars and lounges in the Downtown area, which has been undergoing revitalization in recent years. Development around Chinatown and the Verizon Center has turned this into a lively neighborhood, especially when there's a sports or musical event at the arena. A few blocks south, Penn Quarter/Chinatown, formerly a quiet neighborhood, is seeing larger evening crowds, thanks to the opening of several terrific new restaurants, cafés, and bars. You can take the Metro, exiting at the Archives/Navy Memorial/Penn Quarter station (Green and Yellow lines).

BARS AND LOUNGES

Fadó Irish Pub. Built with authentic materials, dark and warm Fadó is really four pubs in one: the Library, the Victorian Pub, the Gaelic, and the Cottage. The pub's name comes from an old Irish expression meaning "long ago." Live Irish acoustic music is performed every Sunday afternoon, and there's live Celtic rock on Wednesday and Saturday nights. Monday night is quiz night, a local favorite, and sports are often screened, including English Premier League soccer. Fadó often pulls a crowd from the nearby Verizon Center. ⊠ *808 7th St. NW, Chinatown* ☎ *202/789–0066* ⊕ *www. fadoirishpub.com* Ⓜ *Gallery Pl./Chinatown.*

The Passenger. D.C.'s craft cocktail scene has exploded in recent years, and the Passenger is a magnet for cocktail connoisseurs and food critics alike. No longer the best-kept secret in Washington, this speakeasy has a frenetic vibe in its dark and crowded space. Inside, the intimate Columbia Room provides seating for about a dozen in a private area in the back of the bar for a unique mixology experience—you need a reservation for its two-hour seating, and with its high price tag it's a special occasion type of place. ⊠ *1021 7th St. NW, Downtown* ☎ *202/393–0220* ⊕ *www.passengerdc.com* Ⓜ *Mount Vernon/Convention Center.*

COMEDY CLUBS

Capitol Steps. Putting the "mock" in democracy, the musical political satire of this group of current and former Hill staffers is presented in the amphitheater of the Trade Center every Friday and Saturday at 7:30 pm and occasionally at other spots around town. This D.C. classic is fun for the whole family, no matter which side of the aisle you sit! Tickets are available through Ticketmaster. ⊠ *Ronald Reagan Bldg. and International Trade Center, 1300 Pennsylvania Ave. NW, Downtown* ☎ *703/683–8330* ⊕ *www.capsteps.com* Ⓜ *Federal Triangle.*

LIVE MUSIC INFO

D.C. Blues Society. The D.C. Blues Society is a clearinghouse for information on upcoming shows, festivals, and jam sessions in the metropolitan area. It also publishes a monthly newsletter. ⊕ *www.dcblues.org.*

Folklore Society of Greater Washington. At more than 200 events a year, the society presents folk and traditional musicians and dancers from all over the country. Venues around the D.C. area host events ranging from contra dancing to storytelling to open-mike singing. ☎ *202/546–2228* ⊕ *www.fsgw.org.*

DC Improv. The Improv, as everyone calls it, offers a steady menu of well-known and promising stand-up headliners—recent acts have included Jim Breuer, D. L. Hugley, and Gilbert Gottfried—as well as a bevy of funny amateurs. ✉ *1140 Connecticut Ave. NW, Downtown* ☎ *202/296–7008* ⊕ *www. dcimprov.com* Ⓜ *Farragut N.*

DANCE CLUBS

★ **Ultrabar.** Relatively intimate, this bar offers a fun and luxurious environment. The club comprises the metallic interior of Croma, a VIP room, warm wood paneling in the Bedroom, and spectacular lasers on the Main Floor, with multiple dance floors featuring hip-hop, Latin, and international music. A diverse crowd comes here; don't be deterred by the long lines of college students waiting to get into the lounge. ✉ *911 F St. NW, Downtown* ☎ *202/638–4663* ⊕ *www.ultrabardc.com* Ⓜ *Metro Center.*

> **EARLY TO BED**
>
> During a performance at Georgetown's Blues Alley, the headliner noted that the 8 pm shows at the club sell out, while the later 10 pm shows beg for patrons. She attributed this to the fact that "people in Washington have to get up at 5:30 am every morning and turn on the TV to see what is happening with the world." That remark is close to the truth, and explains a sometimes-lackluster nightlife during the workweek in D.C.

GEORGETOWN

Due to its proximity to the university, weekends are a happening affair in Georgetown. A number of bars serve as restaurants by day, until the college and intern crowds take over at night. Although most venues here tend to attract a younger set, the neighborhood still offers many options for patrons over thirty, such as the legendary Blues Alley. Most people come to Georgetown for the shopping, but there are plenty of good reasons to linger into the evening. There's little parking here, and no Metro access, so if you're not staying nearby your best bet is a taxi. In late spring and summer, head to the Georgetown waterfront for drinks and a riverside stroll.

BARS AND LOUNGES

Degrees. Hidden away inside the Ritz hotel, in what was once the Georgetown Incinerator, this modern bar is a breath of fresh air in the neighborhood's rather monotone scene. With an extensive wine and cocktail selection behind the black granite bar and a hip, well-dressed set of patrons in front of it, Degrees exudes elegance from all corners. If there's too much attitude in the bar, head out to the hotel's lovely lobby and sit by the fireplace. This is a perfect pre-movie, post-date, mid-shopping stop. ✉ *Ritz-Carlton, 3100 South St. NW, Georgetown* ☎ *202/912–4100* ⊕ *www.ritzcarlton.com.*

J Paul's. This is a great neighborhood saloon and a terrific place to go for a beer and a game. The menu is extensive, but stick to the great hamburgers and seafood dishes. J Paul's attracts a diverse crowd from students to lobbyists and politicians. ✉ *3218 M St. NW, Georgetown* ☎ *202/333–3450* ⊕ *j-pauls.com.*

8

Nick's Riverside Grille. Next to Tony and Joe's on the Georgetown waterfront, Nick's offers a great view of Washington Harbour and the Potomac while you enjoy fine food and drink. When the weather's nice, crowds flock to the restaurant-bar's outdoor tables. Location, location, location. ⊠ *3050 K St. NW, Georgetown* ☎ *202/342–3535* ⊕ *www. nicksriversidegrille.com.*

★ **The Tombs.** Visitors to Georgetown University looking for a pint or some upscale pub grub head down the stairs below 1789 restaurant to The Tombs. Adorned with rowing paraphernalia, the traditional collegiate watering hole has been serving Hoyas since 1962. It's the closest bar to campus so gets crowded with students at night. ⊠ *1226 36th St. NW, Georgetown* ☎ *202/337–6668* ⊕ *www.tombs.com.*

Tony and Joe's. Right on Georgetown's waterfront, this restaurant has a large outdoor patio where you can enjoy a drink alfresco on a spring or summer evening. The cocktails are a little pricey, but you can't beat the view of the Potomac River and Kennedy Center at night. ⊠ *3000 K St. NW, Georgetown* ☎ *202/944–4545* ⊕ *www.tonyandjoes.com.*

MUSIC CLUBS

JAZZ AND BLUES

Fodor's Choice ★ **Blues Alley.** Head here for a classy evening in an intimate setting, complete with great music and outstanding New Orleans–style grub. The cover charge is typically $25 for well-known performers such as Mose Allison, and more for top acts like Wynton Marsalis. There is also a $10 food or drink minimum. ■TIP➔ You can come for just the show, but those who enjoy a meal get better seats. ⊠ *1073 Wisconsin Ave. NW, near M St., Georgetown* ☎ *202/337–4141* ⊕ *www.bluesalley.com* Ⓜ *Foggy Bottom.*

DUPONT CIRCLE AND LOGAN CIRCLE

Dupont Circle is a longstanding weekend hot spot, with numerous bars and lounges for all ages and preferences. Home to some legendary classics, like Russia House and Kramerbooks & Afterwords, the expansion toward Logan Circle has introduced new favorites like Churchkey. P Street is Washington's answer to San Francisco's Castro Street, and remains the vibrant focal point of the city's gay and lesbian nightlife scene. Parking is difficult, but everything is walkable from Dupont Circle Metro stop.

BARS AND LOUNGES

Churchkey. There's an astounding selection of beers here—more than 500 varieties from more than 30 countries, including 50 beers on tap and exclusive draught and cask ales. It even has its own Beer Director. If you have trouble making a choice, bartenders will offer you 4-ounce tasters to help figure out what you like. The urban-vintage vibe balances unassuming and pretentious in pretty much equal measure, reflected in a menu that ranges from tater-tots through artisan cheeses to pork belly carbonara. The size of the weekend crowds attests to the popularity of this beer mecca. ⊠ *1337 14th St. NW, Logan Circle* ☎ *202/567–2576* ⊕ *www.churchkeydc.com* Ⓜ *McPherson Sq.*

Fodor's Choice
★

Eighteenth Street Lounge. Home to Washington's chic set, ESL's unmarked visage might be intimidating, but this multilevel club's array of lux sofa-filled hardwood coves makes it seem like the city's chilliest house party. On the top floor of this former mansion, jazz musicians often entertain. The back deck, complete with hanging chandeliers, provides summer visitors with two extra bars and a dance floor. Fans of techno music flock here because it's the home of the ESL record label and the renowned musical duo Thievery Corporation. ■TIP➔ The dress code here is strictly enforced by the doorman: no khakis, baseball caps, sneakers, or light-colored jeans. ✉ *1212 18th St. NW, Dupont Circle* ☎ *202/466–3922* ⊕ *www.eighteenthstreetlounge.com* Ⓜ *Dupont Circle.*

Gazuza. This bar, whose name means "lust" in Castilian Spanish, draws an attractive local crowd that attempts to chat over the throbbing house music. The tiny interior, done in an aggressively modern style, fills up early, spilling patrons onto the spacious balcony, a prime people-watching spot. Gazuza also offers the opportunity to smoke a hookah, with a choice of different flavors. ✉ *1629 Connecticut Ave. NW, Dupont Circle* ☎ *202/667–5500* ⊕ *gazuzalounge.com* Ⓜ *Dupont Circle.*

JR's Bar & Grill. On the 17th Street strip, JR's packs in a mostly male, mostly professional crowd. Patrons shoot pool, play video games, gaze at videos on the big screen, and chat with their neighbors. The weekend fill-up brings in a younger crowd, especially after kickball games played on a nearby field. ✉ *1519 17th St. NW, Dupont Circle* ☎ *202/328–0090* ⊕ *www.JRsbardc.com* Ⓜ *Dupont Circle.*

Number Nine. Number Nine is a simple, comfortable replacement for the former club-thumping Halo. In the heart of Logan Circle, it's a predominently male gay bar attracting guests of all ages, and its two floors each have a marble bar, a fireplace, and plush couches. The daily happy hour (5–9 pm) offers two-for-one drinks and at any time this is a great place for a cocktail and some good conversation. ✉ *1435 P St. NW, Logan Circle* ☎ *202/986–0999* ⊕ *www. NumberNineDC.com.*

Russia House Restaurant and Lounge. Transport yourself to Moscow by sampling shots from an entire menu devoted to vodka. Unlike any other bar in D.C.—or perhaps the U.S.A. for that matter—Russia House's brooding vibe, bizarre old-world charm, and authentic food might feel kitschy until you see real Eastern European revelers dancing it up late at night in one of the lounges (there are four floors, though they are not all open all the time). It gets crowded later on, but you can enjoy a more intimate meal in the restaurant of this singular spot earlier in the evening. ✉ *1800 Connecticut Ave. NW, Dupont Circle* ☎ *202/234–9433* ⊕ *www.russiahouselounge.com* Ⓜ *Dupont Circle.*

St. Arnold's Mussel Bar on Jefferson. This cozy space in the heart of Dupont is named after St. Arnold, held to be the patron saint of brewing, and it's certainly blessed with its choice of hard-to-find Belgian beers. The Belgian theme continues in the menu, including the required mussels, prepared in numerous ways, and it all makes for a casual evening out or a comfortable happy-hour spot. All this, together with its wood-lined basement location, is sure to transport you to the old world.

8

D.C.'S PARTY ANIMALS: STAFFERS

GENERAL DESCRIPTION

Prolific species endemic to the Washington area; similar species are present in state capitals throughout the country, but the Washington staffer is notably more rapacious. Republican and Democratic subspecies are distinct; Congressional, White House, and departmental varieties are less so, due in part to migration between offices every two to four years.

IDENTIFYING MARKS

BlackBerry; security badge, usually worn around neck. Dark suits, bland ties, hair neatly coiffed. Republican subspecies have been harder to find in the last few years and the males have extremely neat hair; Democratic subspecies is younger, with big idealistic eyes.

DIET

The bulk of the staffer's diet is coffee, but it also consumes takeout and martinis. Although staffers are technically omnivores, their actual intake depends on their environment and which other species are present. A staffer may eat lo mein with legislators or lobster with lobbyists, or both, in the same day.

HABITAT

Like other political species, staffers tend to stick close to the Capitol and White House during the day, although they can also be spotted at the **Union Pub** and the **Capital Grille** at lunchtime. After hours, the best places to watch Republican staffers are **Bullfeathers, Tune Inn,** and **Tortilla Coast,** all on the Hill. Democratic staffers now enjoying proximity to the White House can be found at **Potenza's bar, La Bar** at the Sofitel Hotel, and **BlackFinn. George** in Georgetown is also popular among both species, for those with the financial means. As populations of GOP and Democratic staffers shift, turf wars sometimes erupt; observe Democratic staffers moving in on Republican territory at the **Capital Lounge** on the Hill, and the reverse at **Stetson's,** in Adams Morgan.

BEHAVIOR

Remarkably intelligent and adaptable, though notoriously young, staffers are some of Washington's most interesting species to observe. It is not uncommon to observe a staffer simultaneously sending email on its BlackBerry, talking on a cell phone, and ordering in a restaurant or bar (the scientific name for this behavior is formulating policy). Staffers are gregarious among their own, but can become obsequious and competitive when in the presence of legislators.

A new location has also opened in Cleveland Park. ⊠ *1827 Jefferson Pl. NW, Dupont Circle* ☎ *202/833–1321* ⊕ *starnoldsmusselbar.com* Ⓜ *Dupont Circle.*

DANCE CLUBS

Cobalt. Popular among the gay and lesbian crowd, this lounge offers martinis in a swank setting. But don't pass up heading upstairs to the dance floor. The Tuesday night "Flashback" parties are always fun, although most of the songs are older than the clientele who pack the place. Weekend parties are known to be wild. ⊠ *1639 R St. NW, Dupont Circle* ☎ *202/232-4416* ⊕ *www.cobaltdc.com* Ⓜ *Dupont Circle.*

MUSIC CLUBS
JAZZ AND BLUES
New Vegas Lounge. Dr. Blues doesn't allow any soft-jazz-bluesy-fusion in his house. Even during the weekly open-jam session at this longtime favorite, it's strictly no-nonsense wailing guitar rhythms by seasoned local players. The resident Out of Town Blues Band attracts an eclectic crowd of longtime followers and young people just passing by in the trendy neighborhood. This could be the most unique dance party in town. ⊠ *1415 P St. NW, Dupont Circle* ☏ *202/483–3971* ⊕ *www. newvegasloungedc.com* Ⓜ *Dupont Circle.*

ADAMS MORGAN

Adams Morgan is Washington's (albeit much smaller) version of New Orleans' French Quarter. The streets are jammed on the weekends with people of all ages and descriptions. Bars and restaurants of all types line the streets, making it easy to find one that will suit your tastes. Be prepared for crowds on the weekends and a much tamer vibe on weeknights. Getting there is easy, with three nearby Metro stops: Woodley Park/Adams Morgan (Red Line), Dupont Circle (Red Line), and U Street/Cardozo (Green and Yellow lines). Taxis also are easy to find, except after last call when the crowds pour out of bars.

BARS AND LOUNGES
Bourbon. Bourbon diverges from the typical Adams Morgan scene by offering visitors a Southern-tinged drinking and dining experience. Though you can dance through midnight into the wee hours here, earlier in the evening you'll fine interesting whiskey, scotch, and bourbon options coupled with Southern goodies like barbecue chicken salads, grits, and mac-and-cheese. It's casual, sometimes crowded, and the open back porch in summer is a welcome respite from the 18th Street crowd. ⊠ *2321 18th St. NW, Adams Morgan* ☏ *202/332–0800* ⊕ *www. bourbondc.com* Ⓜ *Adams Morgan/Woodley Park.*

Chief Ike's Mambo Room. Chief Ike's is known for attracting a wild and eccentric crowd for the best dance-your-pants-off party in town, which doesn't start until midnight. The drinks may not be anything special, but the person sitting next to you may very well be. There's plenty of room to hang out, chat, and sip a cool cocktail, with dancing downstairs. Right off the 18th Street strip, you can't miss Chief Ike's gaudy entrance. ⊠ *1725 Columbia Rd. NW, Adams Morgan* ☏ *202/332–2211* ⊕ *www.chiefikesmamboroom.com* Ⓜ *Woodley Park/Zoo.*

Madam's Organ. Neon lights behind the bar, walls covered in kitsch, and works from local artists add to the gritty feel that infuses Madam's Organ. Its three levels play host to an eclectic clientele that shoots pool, listens to live music performed every night on the lower level, and soaks up rays on the roof deck. There are some who dislike Madam's Organ for its popularity, but, for most, it's a place that's hard not to like. ⊠ *2461 18th St. NW, Adams Morgan* ☏ *202/667–5370* ⊕ *www. madamsorgan.com* Ⓜ *Woodley Park/Zoo.*

8

D.C.'S PARTY ANIMALS: LOBBYISTS

GENERAL DESCRIPTION

Though currently plentiful, the lobbyist is a threatened species in Washington. Ironically, recent legislation and public awareness of the species have only deepened its endangerment.

IDENTIFYING MARKS

Lobbyists may look familiar to New Yorkers, due to their marked resemblance to investment bankers (the latter are extremely rare in Washington). Easy to identify by custom-made suits, stylish haircuts, and the occasional suspender or cigar (males only), they are distinguishable from lawyers by their habit of picking up the check and by the gaggle of out-of-towners that they often escort.

DIET

Studies of lobbyists' expense reports indicate a particularly voracious appetite, heavy on red meat, sushi, and fine wine. It is interesting to note, however, that lobbyists take virtually all their meals in restaurants, and thus have a limited ability to find food on their own; without an expense account, the lobbyist may starve.

HABITAT

The lobbyist's habitat is shrinking rapidly and is a source of some concern. Washington lobbyists are native only to K Street, but in recent years their normal range had extended to the Capitol, with a vast migratory range encompassing Scottish golf courses, Mississippi casinos, and the Mariana Islands. As pressure increases on the species, it is being driven back to K Street, but can still be reliably spotted at **Charlie Palmer, Sonoma, Bistro Bis, Central, Tosca,** and **Capital Grille.** Follow the sommelier.

BEHAVIOR

Lobbyists coexist symbiotically with legislators, each reliant on the other for protection and sustenance. Thus, the two species are often spotted together: the lobbyist feeding the legislator with food, trips, and campaign cash, the legislator reciprocating with spending bills. In such company, the lobbyist is at its most resplendent—charming and expansive. When alone or with members of their own species, however, lobbyists can be gruff and temperamental. Watch for them on cell phones in expensive restaurants.

Tryst. Bohemian and unpretentious, this coffeehouse-bar serves fancy sandwiches and exotic coffee creations. Comfy chairs and couches fill the big open space, where you can sit for hours sipping a cup of tea—or a martini, in the evening—while chatting or clacking away at your laptop. Some of D.C.'s many bloggers make this their home base during the day, and the management has no problem letting people relax for an hour or two . . . or eight. Tryst is best in the warm months, when the front windows swing open and the temperature matches the temperament. ⊠ *2459 18th St. NW, Adams Morgan* ☎ *202/232–5500* ⊕ *www.trystdc.com* Ⓜ *Woodley Park/Zoo.*

DANCE CLUBS

★ **Habana Village.** No matter what the temperature is outside, it's always balmy inside the unpretentious Habana Village. The tiny dance floors are packed nightly with couples moving to the latest live salsa and merengue music, and it's one of the only places in D.C. where you'll find older men twirling young women across the dance floor. When it's time to cool down, you can head to one of several lounges in this converted four-story town house and sip the house specialty: a mojito garnished with sugarcane. ✉ *1834 Columbia Rd. NW, Adams Morgan* ☎ *202/462–6310* ⊕ *www.habanavillage.com* Ⓜ *Woodley Park/Zoo.*

MUSIC CLUBS
JAZZ AND BLUES
Columbia Station. An oasis on the 18th Street strip, this unpretentious neighborhood bar attracts a diverse crowd, many of whom were pulled in off the street by the good vibes emanating from this place. Amber lights and morphed musical instruments adorn the walls, and high-quality live local jazz and blues fills the air. The large, open windows up front keep the place cool—much like the music—in summer months. ✉ *2325 18th St. NW, Adams Morgan* ☎ *202/462–6040* ⊕ *www. columbiastationdc.com* Ⓜ *Woodley Park/Zoo.*

U STREET CORRIDOR

Decades ago, the U Street Corridor was famous as D.C.'s Black Broadway. After many dormant years, today the neighborhood has come roaring back with a lively bar, club, and music scene that appeals to all ages. Almost as busy as Adams Morgan, U Street has become the new nightlife draw across the District. The U Street Corridor is easily accessible from the U Street/Cardozo Metro stop, on the Green and Yellow lines. Taxis also are easy to find.

BARS AND LOUNGES
Busboys and Poets. Part eatery, part bookstore, and part event space, Busboys and Poets is a popular local hangout that draws a diverse crowd. The three venues host a wide range of entertainment, from poetry open mikes to music to guest authors and activist speakers. The name is an homage to Langston Hughes, who worked as a busboy in D.C. before becoming a famous poet. This original location is open until 2 am on weekends—there's another Downtown (at 1025 5th St. NW) and one across the river in Arlington. ✉ *2021 14th St. NW, at U St. NW, U St. Corridor* ☎ *202/387–7638* ⊕ *www.busboysandpoets. com* Ⓜ *U St./Cardozo.*

Fodor's Choice ★ **Café Saint-Ex.** Themed after the life of Antoine de Saint-Exupéry, French pilot and author of *The Little Prince*, this bilevel bar has a split personality. The upstairs brasserie has pressed-tin ceilings and a propeller hanging over the polished wooden bar. Downstairs is the Gate 54 nightclub, designed to resemble an airplane hangar, with dropped corrugated-metal ceilings and backlit aerial photographs. The DJs draw a fairly young crowd nightly and an updated menu attracts an upscale evening clientele for dinner, too. ✉ *1847 14th St. NW, U Street Corridor* ☎ *202/265–7839* ⊕ *www.saint-ex.com* Ⓜ *U St./Cardozo.*

★ **Chi-Cha Lounge.** Insular groups of young professionals relax on sofas and armchairs in this hip hangout, while Latin jazz mingles with Peruvian and Bolivian folk music in the background and old movies run silently

8

The Lowdown on Late-Night Eats

Top off a night of barhopping with a stop at one of these delicious late-night haunts.

ADAMS MORGAN

Amsterdam Falafelshop. The menu at Amsterdam Falafelshop might consist of only three items—falafels in pita, Dutch-style french fries, and brownies—but the choices are far from limited. At this cash-only spot, choose from nearly 20 different garnishes and a variety of dipping sauces. This is late-night eating at its best. ⊠ *2425 18th St. NW, Adams Morgan* ☎ *202/234–1969* ⊕ *www. falafelshop.com* Ⓜ *Woodley Park/Zoo, Adams Morgan.*

El Tamarindo. As the bars clear out after last call, make your way off crowded and chaotic 18th Street and into the pleasantly low-key El Tamarindo for cheap heaping portions of Mexican and Salvadoran cuisine. You can enjoy a full sit-down meal at 3 am, including quesadillas, enchiladas, and Salvadoran-style *pupusas* (tortillas stuffed with cheese and other fillings). ⊠ *1785 Florida Ave. NW, Adams Morgan* ☎ *202/238–3660* ⊕ *www.eltamarindodc.com* Ⓜ *Dupont Circle.*

DUPONT CIRCLE

Annie's Paramount Steak House. Once a popular gay hangout, Annie's Paramount Steak House now attracts a more varied crowd. Anyone who craves steak and eggs in the middle of the night will appreciate this reliable and relatively cheap steak house, open all night on Friday and Saturday. ⊠ *1609 17th St. NW, Dupont Circle* ☎ *202/232–0395* Ⓜ *Dupont Circle.*

Kramerbooks & Afterwards. It's not only the literati who flock to the charming, independent Kramerbooks & Afterwards for a book and brew. This all-inclusive bookstore, bar, and café is a popular after-hours destination attracting hip, young Washingtonians. Open all night on Friday and Saturday, and late at night during the week, this is the perfect place to wind down after a long night. ⊠ *1517 Connecticut Ave. NW, Dupont Circle* ☎ *202/387–3825* ⊕ *www.kramers. com* Ⓜ *Dupont Circle.*

GEORGETOWN

Bistro Français. The name says it all at Georgetown's Bistro Français, where you can expect straightforward French fare. Open until 3 am Tuesday through Thursday and until 4 am Friday through Sunday, this neighborhood landmark is where many local chefs relax when they're finished cooking. ⊠ *3128 M St. NW, Georgetown* ☎ *202/338–3830* ⊕ *www. bistrofrancaisdc.com* Ⓜ *Foggy Bottom.*

Five Guys Burger and Fries. After a night of hobnobbing with politicos, stop in at Five Guys Burger and Fries—their award-winning ground-beef burgers with all the fixings and crispy, twice-fried fries hit the spot. If you're going to fill up on the free peanuts, make sure to select the "little" burger, which is one patty instead of the usual two. There are now ten locations in D.C., and the chain is rapidly expanding throughout the nation. ⊠ *1335 Wisconsin Ave. NW, Georgetown* ☎ *202/337–0400* ⊕ *www.fiveguys.com* Ⓜ *Foggy Bottom.*

—Carolyn Galgano

behind the bar. This lounge, modeled after an Ecuadorian hacienda, gets packed on weekends, so come early to get a coveted sofa along the back wall. Down the tasty tapas as you enjoy the namesake drink— think sangria with a bigger kick. For a price, you can smoke a hookah filled with imported honey-cured tobacco. ⊠ *1624 U St. NW, U Street Corridor* ☎ *202/234–8400* ⊕ *www.latinconcepts.com* Ⓜ *U St./Cardozo.*

Marvin. Trendy, trendy, trendy makes Marvin packed with young crowds on the weekend, but even if that's not your scene it's still worth a visit. The excellent gastropub menu—moules and frites, shrimp and grits— and a chill lower level offer a respite from the dance floors above, and the outdoor back porch (heated in chillier months) is another relaxing area. ⊠ *2007 14th St. NW, U Street Corridor* ☎ *202/797–7171* ⊕ *www. marvindc.com* Ⓜ *U St./Cardozo.*

Nellie's Sports Bar. An unlikely combination of a sports bar with a gay bar; everyone feels welcome in this establishment. Nellie's is very popular because of its support for the D.C. gay community, and draws crowds to its eccentric events, such as drag shows, drag bingo, and pop culture trivia. If that's not your cup of tea, you can always watch pro football and other sports on the bar's large-screen TVs. ⊠ *900 U St. NW, U Street Corridor* ☎ *202/332–6355* ⊕ *www.nelliesportsbar. com* Ⓜ *U St./Cardozo.*

The Saloon. A classic watering hole, the Saloon has no TVs, no light beer, and no martinis. What you can find are locals engaged in conversation— a stated goal of the owner—and some of the world's best beers, including the rare Urbock 23, an Austrian beer that is rated one of the tastiest and strongest in the world, with 9.6% alcohol content (limit one per customer). The Saloon is now offering a broader bar menu too. ⊠ *1207 U St. NW, U Street Corridor* ☎ *202/462–2640* Ⓜ *U St./Cardozo.*

U Street Music Hall. This basement dance hall hosts both DJs and live bands playing indie, dance, dub-step, and electro music. On nights with a band, cover charges start at $10, depending who's on. The drinks are reasonably priced here, and come with the option of a late-night hot dog. The diverse crowd really mirrors the night, with club kids on DJ nights and young hipsters for the bands, so check the website to make sure it's your kind of crowd. ⊠ *1115 U St. NW, U St. Corridor* ☎ *202/588–1880* ⊕ *www.ustreetmusichall.com/* Ⓜ *U St./Cardozo.*

U-topia. A colorful and offbeat dining establishment, U-topia offers culinary flair in a room filled with art. Customers enjoy an eclectic menu that includes such diverse choices as Cajun jambalaya, Moroccan seasoned lamb couscous, and cumin chicken. Meanwhile, the music tends toward acoustic jazz featuring piano trios. A neighborhood hot spot, the place has grown with the neighborhood, catering to those who prefer a place where one can converse while listening to softer jazz. ⊠ *1418 U St. NW, U Street Corridor* ☎ *202/483–7669* ⊕ *www.utopiadc.com* Ⓜ *U St./Cardozo.*

Vinoteca. The sophisticated set flock to Vinoteca for its solid list of around 100 wines, its menu of delicious small bites, and its weekend brunches. There's a daily happy hour (5–7 pm), and the flights of wine to sample are attractively priced. On Sunday nights there are live flamenco

D.C.'S PARTY ANIMALS: LEGISLATORS

GENERAL DESCRIPTION

The legislator's life cycle is one of migration, from its home state to Washington and back, during weekends, congressional recesses, and finally, election years. Natural selection has made it thus a particularly hardy and dynamic species; its struggles for dominance are among Washington's most dramatic and powerful.

IDENTIFYING MARKS

Prominent smile, entourage. Legislators are rarely alone, but outside the Capitol are seldom seen in the company of other legislators, preferring the company of staffers, lobbyists, and (sometimes) interns. They often travel in black SUVs and tend to be hard to catch, but can sometimes be lured by cameras and microphones. The Senate variety is almost exclusively white and largely male; the House variety is more diverse and vocal.

DIET

While in Washington, legislators eat a rich diet of porterhouse steak, Chinese takeout, and french fries. But in election years a legislator's epic journey of campaign migration results in significant culinary hardship, and during this time many subsist on donuts and pie.

HABITAT

Observe legislators in the Capitol itself, and around the Hill and White House at the Source, Capital Grille, and the Caucus Room, as well as in Georgetown at Café Milano and Citronelle. On Friday afternoons and Monday mornings, you may catch a glimpse of legislators migrating through Reagan National Airport. In election years their habitat changes dramatically, and although hard to find in Washington, they're easy to spot at county fairs and senior citizens' homes.

BEHAVIOR

This species is known for noisy and complex displays of principle, called speechifying. These displays are meant to simultaneously attract voters and intimidate competitors; occasionally, they also result in legislation.

performances. In good weather you can dine on the front patio, and out back there's a large bar and a bocce court. Vinoteca also offers wine classes for small groups in their private rooms upstairs. ⊠ *1940 11th St. NW, U Street Corridor* ☎ *202/332–9463* ⊕ *www.vinotecadc. com* Ⓜ *U St./Cardozo.*

DANCE CLUBS

Town. This gay club stands out by regularly hosting drag shows and cabaret performances. It even has its own dance troupe, X-faction, to get the crowd worked up. On the edge of the U Street Corridor—the club attracts a varied audience of gay men and lesbians in a friendly environment. There are two adjacent parking lots—a plus in Washington. ⊠ *2009 8th St. NW, U Street Corridor* ☎ *202/234–8696* ⊕ *www. towndc.com* Ⓜ *Shaw-Howard U.*

MUSIC CLUBS
JAZZ AND BLUES

Bohemian Caverns. The cramped stairway delivers you to a performance space designed to look like a cave, a complete and accurate renovation of the Crystal Caverns, once a mainstay of D.C.'s "Black Broadway" and the place to see Miles Davis and Charlie Parker. The club rightfully calls itself "the Sole Home for Soul Jazz." These days Friday and Saturday are given over to jazz; blues acts headline on Thursday; and open-mike night on Wednesday brings jazz-influenced poets to the stage. ⊠ *2001 11th St. NW, U Street Corridor* ☎ *202/299–0800* ⊕ *www.bohemiancaverns.com* Ⓜ *U St./Cardozo.*

Twins Jazz. For more than 23 years, twin sisters Kelly and Maze Tesfaye have been offering great jazz at their club on U Street. The club features some of D.C.'s strongest straight-ahead jazz players, as well as groups from as far away as New York. On the club's menu are tasty nachos, wings, and burgers. Connections with local universities also bring in new and experimental talent to match the more accomplished performers. ⊠ *1344 U St. NW, U Street Corridor* ☎ *202/234–0072* ⊕ *www. twinsjazz.com* Ⓜ *U St./Cardozo.*

ROCK AND POP

★ **9:30 Club.** When they come to town, the best indie performers, and a few of the bigger acts, play this large but cozy space wrapped by balconies on three sides. Recent acts have included current sensations as well as groups with a long history, such as the B-52s, George Clinton, OAR, Mos Def, and Joe Jackson. ■TIP➔ For the best seats, arrive at least an hour before the doors open, typically at 7:30. ⊠ *815 V St. NW, U Street Corridor* ☎ *202/265–0930* ⊕ *www.930.com* Ⓜ *U St./Cardozo.*

Fodor's Choice ★ **Black Cat.** Come here to see the latest local bands as well as indie stars such as Neko Case, Modest Mouse, Arcade Fire, and Regina Spektor. Dave Grohl, lead singer of the Foo Fighters, owns a stake in the club. The post-punk crowd whiles away the time in the Red Room, a side bar with pool tables, an eclectic jukebox, and no cover charge. The club also is home to Food for Thought, a legendary vegetarian café. ⊠ *1811 14th St. NW, U Street Corridor* ☎ *202/667–4490* ⊕ *www.blackcatdc. com* Ⓜ *U St./Cardozo.*

DC9. With live music seven days a week, this two-story rock club hosts up-and-coming indie rock bands and the occasional nationally known act. There's a narrow bar on the ground floor and a humongous concert space upstairs. Friday night is "Liberation Dance Party" night, playing the best of the last two decades to get the young crowd hopping. ⊠ *1940 9th St. NW, U Street Corridor* ☎ *202/483–5000* ⊕ *www.dcnine. com* Ⓜ *U St./Cardozo.*

Velvet Lounge. Squeeze up the narrow stairway and check out the eclectic local and national bands that play at this unassuming neighborhood joint. Performers ranging from indie mainstays to acclaimed up-and-comers rock the house with psychobilly, alt-country, and indie pop. ⊠ *915 U St. NW, U Street Corridor* ☎ *202/462–3213* ⊕ *www. velvetloungedc.com* Ⓜ *U St./Cardozo.*

8

SUBURBAN VIRGINIA

Just across the Potomac, Arlington and Alexandria boast some top-notch bars and lounges—with considerably more parking and less hectic traffic than D.C. Also accessible by the Metro, revitalized Ballston and Clarendon are interesting and enjoyable places to visit at night.

BARS AND LOUNGES

Carpool. "Andy Warhol meets General Motors" is how one magazine described this former-garage-turned-bar. Enjoy a brew and food from a kitchen run by Rocklands, which makes some of the best barbecue in the area. Carpool, which serves a local clientele, has 12 pool tables, seven dartboards, and a cigar room with a walk-in humidor. If you like sports, you'll love the multiple screens showing multiple games at the same time. ⊠ *4000 Fairfax Dr., Arlington, Virginia* ☎ *703/532–7665* ⊕ *www.carpoolweb.com* Ⓜ *Ballston*.

Fishmarket. There's something different in just about every section of this multilevel, multiroom space, from a piano-bar crooner to a ragtime piano shouter and a guitar strummer. The thirty- and fortysomething crowd is boisterous. If you really like beer, order the largest size; it comes in a glass big enough to put your face in. ⊠ *105 King St., Old Town, Alexandria, Virginia* ☎ *703/836–5676* ⊕ *www.fishmarketva. com* Ⓜ *King St*.

State Theatre. This is the place to go to see famous bands from the past like Leon Russell, the Smithereens, and Jefferson Starship. You have the choice of sitting or standing in this renovated movie theater, which is about 10 miles south of D.C. The popular 1980s Retro Dance Parties, featuring The Legwarmers tribute band, draw locals who like to dress the part. ⊠ *220 N. Washington St., Falls Church, Virginia* ☎ *703/237–0300* ⊕ *www.thestatetheatre.com* Ⓜ *East Falls Church*.

MUSIC CLUBS

ACOUSTIC, FOLK, AND COUNTRY MUSIC

Fodor's Choice
★ **The Birchmere.** A legend in the D.C. area, the Birchmere is one of the best places outside the Blue Ridge Mountains to hear acoustic folk, country, and bluegrass. Enthusiastic crowds have enjoyed performances by artists such as Mary Chapin Carpenter, Lyle Lovett, Bela Fleck, and Emmylou Harris. More recently, the club has expanded its offerings to include jazz performers such as Diane Schuur and Al Jareau, and blues artists like Robert Cray and Buddy Guy. ⊠ *3701 Mt. Vernon Ave., Alexandria, Virginia* ☎ *703/549–7500* ⊕ *www.birchmere.com*.

The Performing Arts

WORD OF MOUTH

"Don't miss the Kennedy Center, they have free shows the entire
family can enjoy."

—Epartida

Updated
by Allison
Lombardo

In the past 40 years D.C. has gone from being a cultural desert to a thriving arts center. The arts scene has exploded to meet the demands of young professionals who flock here for opportunities in government as well as the Washington establishment that demands a more highbrow experience. Visitors have the opportunity to view incredible theater, music, and dance in fresh, dynamic facilities, including a plethora of small, unique venues. When you include the classics—the Kennedy Center, the Washington National Opera, and the National Theatre—it's clear that Washington's art scene is a major draw of talent on the East Coast.

Most of the headline performers flock to the Kennedy Center or the Verizon Center, but Washington is also peppered with dozens of small- and medium-size venues. Performance halls tend to showcase musicians, but there's no shortage of dance and theater troupes, or stand-up comedians. Don't go looking for a theater district: the venues are spread across town and in the Maryland and Virginia suburbs.

With dozens of acoustically superior venues and majestic backdrops around town, D.C. sets a lofty stage for its musicians, who have the talent to match. Whether it's the four armed services bands marching in the footsteps of John Philip Sousa, chamber players performing beneath classic Renaissance art at the National Gallery, and choirs and organs matching the heights of the National Cathedral's buttresses, this city's musicians consistently lay down a fitting sound track for the landscape.

Perhaps as a counterbalance to all the political theater in town, D.C.'s playhouses, large and small, have grown into a force to be reckoned with over the past few years. Nearly every major theater in town has recently renovated its performance spaces or is in the process of doing so, and new small theaters are popping up all the time. Washington does offer some unique political performances that you won't find anywhere else—comedy shows with a partisan twist and socially focused dramas. However, the Washington arts scene has shaken the stodgy reputation of its formally dressed denizens and has recently introduced the Capital Fringe Festival and other events. The new Atlas Arts District in Northeast Washington and the explosion of venues, events, and bars in Chinatown has provided new centers to harness the city's bursting creative energy. As if all that weren't enough, D.C. often hosts some of the best touring companies from the East Coast and beyond.

Often performing in churches and other less-than-ideal settings (including some without air-conditioning), Washington's small companies present drama that can be every bit as enthralling as—and often more daring than—that offered by their blockbuster counterparts. No matter the size, all companies in town compete fiercely for the Helen Hayes Award, Washington's version of the Tony.

The solid performances of the Washington Ballet, generally considered one of the better troupes in the United States, and those of smaller companies around town are complemented by frequent visits from some of the world's best companies, including the Kirov Ballet and the Alvin Ailey American Dance Theater. Washington is also host to many festivals, and dance is often highlighted. The traditional Japanese dance featured during the Cherry Blossom Festival and the varied styles that come to town during the Smithsonian Folklife Festival are particular treats.

D.C.'s countless foundations, embassies, national museums, and institutions offer the visiting cinephile an unexpected side benefit—quirky, long-forgotten, seldom-seen, and arcane films on as many topics as there are special interests.

PLANNING

TICKETS

Tickets to most events are available by calling or visiting the venue's box office and website or through the following ticket agencies:

Ticketmaster. Ticketmaster sells tickets for events at most venues. You can buy by phone, on the Web, or in person at Macy's department stores and the D.C. Visitor Information Center. ☎ *202/397–7328, 703/573–7328, 410/547–7328* ⊕ *www.ticketmaster.com.*

TICKETplace. TICKETplace sells half-price, day-of-performance tickets for select shows. Hours are: Wednesday–Friday 11–6 and Saturday 10–5. A 12% service charge is included in the ticket price. ✉ *407 7th St. NW, Downtown* ☎ *202/842–5387* ⊕ *www.ticketplace.org* Ⓜ *Archives/Navy Memorial.*

Tickets.com. Tickets.com takes online reservations for a number of events around town. ☎ *800/955–5566* ⊕ *www.tickets.com.*

EVENTS INFORMATION

For information on events in D.C., the best listings are found at the *Washington Post Going Out Guide* (⊕ *www.washingtonpost. com/gog*) and the free weekly *Washington CityPaper* (⊕ *www. washingtoncitypaper.com*). Other events listings are found in the daily "Guide to the Lively Arts" and the Friday "Weekend" sections in the *Washington Post,* the Thursday *Washington Times* "Washington Weekend" section, and the "City Lights" section in the monthly *Washingtonian* magazine; *Washingtonian* also publishes an entertainment guide (⊕ *www.washingtonian.com/inwashington*). You can also check out the Greater Washington Cultural Alliance (⊕ *www.cultural-alliance. org*). DCist (⊕ *www.dcist.com*), a popular local blog, and Express Night Out (⊕ *www.expressnightout.com*) post daily on D.C. events.

WHITE HOUSE AREA AND FOGGY BOTTOM

South of Downtown D.C. and north of Georgetown, Foggy Bottom is home to the Kennedy Center and George Washington University's Lisner Auditorium—two great venues for the performing arts. Both facilities present drama, dance, and music, offering a platform for some of the greatest American and international performers, though visitors will have to travel to find a pretheater dinner or drink.

MAJOR VENUES

Fodor's Choice
★

John F. Kennedy Center for the Performing Arts. On the bank of the Potomac River, the gem of the D.C. arts scene is home to the National Symphony Orchestra, the Washington Ballet, and the Washington National Opera. The best out-of-town acts perform at one of three performance spaces— the Concert Hall, the Opera House, or the Eisenhower Theater. An eclectic range of performances is staged at the center's smaller venues, including the Terrace Theater, showcasing chamber groups and experimental works; the Theater Lab, home to cabaret-style performances; the KC Jazz Club; and a 320-seat family theater. But that's not all. On the Millennium Stage in the center's Grand Foyer, you can catch free performances almost any day at 6 pm. ■TIP→ On performance days, a free shuttle bus runs between the Center and the Foggy Bottom/GWU Metro stop. ⊠ *New Hampshire Ave. and Rock Creek Pkwy. NW, Foggy Bottom* ☎ *202/467–4600, 800/444–1324* ⊕ *www.kennedy-center.org* Ⓜ *Foggy Bottom/GWU.*

Choral Arts Society of Washington. From spring to fall the 200-voice Choral Arts Society of Washington choir performs classical pieces at the Kennedy Center. Three Christmas sing-alongs are scheduled each December, as is a popular tribute to Martin Luther King Jr. on his January birthday. ☎ *202/244–3669* ⊕ *www.choralarts.org.*

Washington National Opera. Founded in 1956, the Washington National Opera is one of the largest companies in the nation and presents eight works in fall and spring at the Kennedy Center Opera House. The operas, performed in their original languages with English supertitles, are often sold out to subscribers, but returned tickets are available an hour before curtain time. For standing-room tickets to each week's performances, inquire at the box office starting the preceding Saturday. Every fall the Opera presents Opera in the Outfield, a free live performance in Nationals Park (also broadcast). ✉ *New Hampshire Ave. and Rock Creek Pkwy. NW, Foggy Bottom* ☎ *202/295–2400, 800/876–7372* ⊕ *www.dc-opera.org.*

WORD OF MOUTH

"Each summer the Smithsonian sponsors a Folklife Festival, which features the food, music, dance, history, culture, etc. of several countries/states/groups."
                                    —longhorn55

Washington Ballet. Between September and May the Washington Ballet presents classical and contemporary dance, including works by choreographers such as George Balanchine, Choo-San Goh, and artistic director Septime Webre. The main shows are mounted at the Kennedy Center, but each December the company performs *The Nutcracker* at the Warner Theatre. ☎ *202/362–3606* ⊕ *www.washingtonballet.org.*

Lisner Auditorium. A 1,500-seat theater on the campus of George Washington University hosts pop, classical, and choral music shows, modern dance performances, and musical theater, attracting students and outsiders alike. ✉ *730 21st St. NW, Foggy Bottom* ☎ *202/994–6800* ⊕ *www.lisner.org* Ⓜ *Foggy Bottom/GWU.*

★ **National Gallery of Art.** The National Gallery offers a variety of music. On Friday from Memorial Day through Labor Day, local jazz groups perform to packed crowds in the sculpture garden from 5 to 9 pm. Loyal listeners dip their weary feet in the fountain, sip sangria, and let the week wash away. From October to June free concerts by the National Gallery Orchestra and performances by visiting recitalists and ensembles are held in the West Building's West Garden Court on Sunday nights. Entry is first-come, first-served, with doors opening at 6 pm and concerts starting at 6:30 pm. On Wednesdays, free midday performances of classical music begin around noon. ✉ *6th St. and Constitution Ave. NW, The Mall* ☎ *202/842-6941* ⊕ *www.nga.gov* Ⓜ *Archives/ Navy Memorial.*

Fodor'sChoice **Smithsonian Institution.** Throughout the year the Smithsonian Associ-
★ ates sponsor programs that offer everything from a cappella groups to Cajun zydeco bands; all events require tickets and locations vary; for a memorable music experience, try to catch one of the performances in the museum's third-floor Hall of Musical Instruments, where musicians occasionally play period instruments from the museum's collection. The Smithsonian's annual summer Folklife Festival, held on the Mall, highlights the cuisine, crafts, and day-to-day life of several different cultures. (Texas, Wales, Colombia and Bhutan are among the most recent ones to have been featured.) ✉ *1000 Jefferson Dr. SW, The Mall* ☎ *202/357–2700, 202/633–1000 recording, 202/357–3030 Smithsonian Associates* ⊕ *www.si.edu* Ⓜ *Smithsonian.*

9

MUSIC

ORCHESTRAS

National Symphony Orchestra. Under the direction of Christoph Eschenbach, the NSO performs from September to June at the Kennedy Center Concert Hall. In summer the orchestra performs at Wolf Trap and gives free concerts at Rock Creek Park's Carter Barron Amphitheatre. On Memorial and Labor Day weekends and July 4, the orchestra performs on the West Lawn of the Capitol. ✉ *New Hampshire Ave. and Rock Creek Pkwy. NW, Foggy Bottom* ☎ *202/462–4600* ⊕ *www.kennedy-center.org/nso.*

PERFORMANCE SERIES

Armed Forces Concert Series. In a Washington tradition, bands from the four branches of the armed services perform June to August on Monday, Tuesday, Wednesday, and Friday evenings on the East Terrace of the Capitol. Concerts usually include marches, patriotic numbers, and some classical music. The Air Force celebrity series features popular artists such as Earl Klugh and Keiko Matsui on Sunday in February and March at DAR Constitution Hall. ✉ *U.S. Capitol* ☎ *202/767–5658 Air Force, 703/696–3718 Army, 202/433–4011 Marines, 202/433–2525 Navy* ✑ *www.aoc.gov.*

Sylvan Theater. Other performances take place at 8 pm from June to August, on Tuesday, Thursday, Friday, and Sunday nights at the Sylvan Theater. ✉ *Washington Monument grounds, 14th St. and Constitution Ave., The Mall* ☎ *202/426–6841* Ⓜ *Smithsonian*

Washington Performing Arts Society. One of the city's oldest arts organizations stages high-quality classical music, jazz, gospel, modern dance, and performance art in halls around the city. Past artists include the Alvin Ailey American Dance Theater, Yo-Yo Ma, the Chieftains, Herbie Hancock, and Savion Glover. ✉ *Suite 510, 2000 L St. NW, Foggy Bottom* ☎ *202/785-9727* ⊕ *www.wpas.org.*

FILM

Hirshhorn Museum and Sculpture Garden. Avant-garde and experimental first-run documentaries, features, and short films are frequently screened here for free. ✉ *Independence Ave. and 7th St. SW, The Mall* ☎ *202/357–2700* ⊕ *www.hirshhorn.si.edu* Ⓜ *Smithsonian or L'Enfant Plaza.*

National Archives. Historical films, usually documentaries, are shown here daily. Screenings range from Robert Flaherty's 1942 coverage of the plight of migrant workers to archival footage of Charles Lindbergh's solo flight from New York to Paris. ■TIP➔ After catching a documentary, it's easy to stroll by the Constitution in this solemn and impressive venue. ✉ *Constitution Ave. between 7th and 9th Sts. NW, The Mall* ☎ *202/501–5000* ⊕ *www.archives.gov* Ⓜ *Archives/Navy Memorial.*

National Gallery of Art, East Building. Free classic and international films, often complementing the exhibits, are shown in this museum's large auditorium. Pick up a film calendar at the museum or online. ✉ *Constitution Ave. between 3rd and 4th Sts. NW, The Mall* ☎ *202/842–6799* ⊕ *www.nga.gov* Ⓜ *Archives/Navy Memorial.*

★ **Screen on the Green.** Every July and August this weekly series of classic films turns the Mall into an open-air cinema. People arrive as early as 5 pm to picnic, socialize, and reserve a spot. The show starts at dusk. ✉ *7th St., The Mall* ☎ *877/262–5866* Ⓜ *Smithsonian.*

Five Great Arts Experiences

CLOSE UP

■ **Arena Stage:** Housed in a state-of-the-art, audience-friendly facility, Arena Stage offers innovative new American plays as well as classic plays and musicals.

■ **Busboys and Poets:** This gathering place has become a mainstay for seeing cutting-edge poets, musicians, performing artists, authors, and political speakers. Something always seems to be happening at this combination restaurant, bookstore, fair trade market, and gathering place. ⇨ *For more information, see Busboys and Poets listing in Nightlife.*

■ **Kennedy Center:** The gem of the D.C. arts scene, this is the one performance venue you might take with you if you were stranded on a desert isle.

■ **Shakespeare Theatre:** Among the top Shakespeare companies in the world, this troupe excels at both classical and contemporary interpretations.

■ **Woolly Mammoth:** This remarkable theater company stages some of the most creative and entertaining new plays from the nation's best playwrights.

CAPITOL HILL AND NORTHEAST D.C.

The arts scene in Capitol Hill and Northeast D.C. has blossomed in recent years with the opening of several performance venues and the explosion of restaurants, bars, and stages along the emerging H Street Corridor. Leading the charge is the Atlas Center, at the cutting edge of dance, music, and drama. Lovers of classical drama will discover great performances and an authentic atmosphere at the Folger Shakespeare Library near the Capitol.

MAJOR VENUES

Atlas Performing Arts Center. Known as the "People's Kennedy Center," this performance venue located in a restored historic movie theater is community-based, encompassing four theaters and three dance studios. The Atlas is home to a diverse group of resident arts organizations, including theater troupes, dance companies, orchestras, and choral groups. The nearest Metro stop is Union Station, though at night it's best to take a taxi given the walk through dark streets. Parking is available on the street. ✉ *1333 H St. NE, Northeast D.C.* ☎ *202/399–7993* ⊕ *www.atlasarts.org* Ⓜ *Union Station.*

MUSIC

CHAMBER MUSIC

Coolidge Auditorium at the Library of Congress. Over the past 80 years, the Coolidge has hosted most of the 20th-century's greatest performers and composers, including Copland and Stravinsky. Today the Coolidge draws musicians from all genres, including classical, jazz, and gospel, and the hall continues to wow audiences with its near-perfect acoustics and sightlines. Concert tickets are free, but must be ordered in advance through Ticketmaster. ✉ *Library of Congress, Jefferson Bldg., 101 Independence Ave. SE, Capitol Hill* ☎ *800/551–7328* ⊕ *www.loc. gov* Ⓜ *Capitol South.*

9

Folger Shakespeare Library. The library's internationally acclaimed resident chamber music ensemble, the Folger Consort, regularly presents medieval, Renaissance, and baroque pieces performed on period instruments. The season runs from October to May. ⇨ *The library is best known for its theater productions.* ✉ *201 E. Capitol St. SE, Capitol Hill* ☎ *202/544–7077* ⊕ *www.folger.edu* Ⓜ *Union Station or Capitol South.*

Rorschach Theatre. Rorschach stages some of the most creative plays in Washington, featuring intimate and passionate performances on the stages of the innovative H Street Atlas Performing Arts Center. The company offers lesser-known works by such playwrights as Pulitzer Prize–winning Tony Kushner and Russia's Mikhail Bulgakov, as well as stage adaptations of literary classics such as *Lord of the Flies.* ✉ *1333 H St. NE, Northeast D.C.* ☎ *202/452–5538* ⊕ *www.rorschachtheatre.com* Ⓜ *Union Station.*

DANCE

Joy of Motion. Joy of Motion includes the resident Dana Tai Soon Burgess & Company (modern), Furia Flamenca, and Silk Road Dance Company (traditional Middle Eastern and Central Asian), among others. They perform in the studio's Jack Guidone Theatre, located in Atlas Performing Arts Center in Northeast D.C. ✉ *5207 Wisconsin Ave. NW, Friendship Heights* ☎ *202/276–2599* ⊕ *www.joyofmotion.org* Ⓜ *Friendship Heights.*

CHORAL MUSIC

Basilica of the National Shrine of the Immaculate Conception. Choral and church groups occasionally perform at the largest Catholic church in the Americas. Every summer the Basilica offers recitals featuring the Shrine's massive pipe organ. See the website for times and visiting performers. ✉ *400 Michigan Ave. NE, Northeast D.C.* ☎ *202/526–8300* ⊕ *www.nationalshrine.com* Ⓜ *Brookland/CUA.*

THEATER AND PERFORMANCE ART

Folger Shakespeare Library. The library's theater, a 250-seat re-creation of the inn-yard theaters in Shakespeare's time, hosts three to four productions a year of Shakespearean or Shakespeare-influenced works. Though the stage is a throwback, the sharp acting and staging certainly push the envelope. ⇨ *Folger Shakespeare Library music performances.* ✉ *201 E. Capitol St. SE, Capitol Hill* ☎ *202/544–7077* ⊕ *www.folger.edu* Ⓜ *Union Station or Capitol South.*

DOWNTOWN

Several of Washington's most prestigious performance centers can be found in Downtown D.C. The Verizon Center, Woolly Mammoth Theater, Sixth & I Synagogue, and other venues are surrounded by the bustling nightlife around Chinatown (itself mostly located in Dupont Circle).

FILM

Landmark's E Street Cinema. Specializing in independent, foreign, and documentary films, this theater has been warmly welcomed by D.C. movie lovers both for its selection and state-of-the-art facilities. It has an impressive concession stand, stocked to please the gourmand, the health-conscious, and those who just want a jumbo box of Milk Duds. The E Street is also one of the few theaters to serve alcohol. ⊠ *555 11th St. NW, Downtown* ☏ *202/452–7672* ⊕ *www.landmarktheatres. com* Ⓜ *Metro Center.*

MAJOR VENUES

DAR Constitution Hall. Acts ranging from Steve Harvey to Josh Gorban to B.B. King perform at this 3,700-seat venue, one of Washington's grand old halls. DAR is well worth a visit for both the excellent performers it attracts and its awesome architecture and acoustics. ⊠ *1776 D St. NW, Downtown* ☏ *202/628–4780* ⊕ *www.dar.org/ conthall* Ⓜ *Farragut West.*

Verizon Center. In addition to being the home of the Washington Capitals hockey and Washington Wizards basketball teams, this 19,000-seat arena also plays host to D.C.'s biggest concerts, ice-skating events, and the circus. If Lady Gaga comes to town, this will be the spot to see her! Parking can be a problem, but several Metro lines converge at an adjacent station. ⊠ *601 F St. NW, Chinatown* ☏ *202/661–5000* ⊕ *www. verizoncenter.com* Ⓜ *Gallery Pl./Chinatown.*

THEATER AND PERFORMANCE ART

Capital Fringe Festival. Brought to D.C. in 2005, Capital Fringe Festival sends every little theater in town into a frenzy every July. With tickets around $17, local performers display the strange, political, interesting, surreal, and avant-garde to eclectic crowds at all times of the day in venues throughout the city. ■TIP→ Just beware, not all of the theaters have air-conditioning, and Washington can be torrid in midsummer. ☏ *866/811–4111* ⊕ *www.capfringe.org.*

ⓒ **Ford's Theatre.** Looking much as it did when President Lincoln was shot at a performance of *Our American Cousin*, Ford's primarily hosts musicals, most with family appeal. Dickens's *A Christmas Carol* is staged every year. The historic theater, maintained by the National Park Service, is now more audience-friendly, thanks to a renovation that replaced hard wooden chairs with more-comfortable padded seats, added new restrooms, improved lighting and sound, and installed the building's first elevator. Tours of the theater and a renovated museum are available for free, but timed entry tickets are required. ⊠ *511 10th St. NW, Downtown* ☏ *202/426–6925* ⊕ *www. fordstheatre.org* Ⓜ *Metro Center.*

9

☾ **National Theatre.** Though rebuilt several times, the National Theatre has operated in the same location since 1835. It now hosts touring Broadway shows, such as *Jersey Boys* and *Movin' Out.* ■TIP➔ From September through April, look for free children's shows Saturday mornings and free Monday night shows that may include Asian dance, performance art, and a cappella cabarets. ⊠ *1321 Pennsylvania Ave. NW, Downtown* ☎ *800/447-7400* ⊕ *www.nationaltheatre.org* Ⓜ *Metro Center.*

Fodor's Choice ★ **Shakespeare Theatre.** This acclaimed troupe crafts fantastically staged and acted performances of works by Shakespeare and his contemporaries, offering traditional renditions but also some with a modern twist. Complementing the existing stage in the Lansburgh Theatre is the Sidney Harman Hall, which provides a 21st-century, state-of-the-art, midsize venue for an outstanding variety of performances, from Shakespeare's *Two Gentleman of Verona* to the hilarious *Abridged History of America*. For two weeks in late spring the group performs Shakespeare for free at Carter Barron Amphitheatre. ⊠ *450 7th St. NW, Downtown* ☎ *202/547–1122* ⊕ *www.shakespearedc.org* Ⓜ *Gallery Pl./Chinatown or Archives/Navy Memorial.*

Sixth & I Historic Synagogue. Known for its author readings, with guests ranging from comedian Tina Fey to Nancy Pelosi, the Sixth & I Historic Synagogue has been named one of the most vibrant congregations in the nation. The historic, intimate space, founded in 1852, hosts religious events as well. ⊠ *600 I St. NW, Chinatown* ☎ *202/408-3100* ⊕ *www.sixthandi.org* Ⓜ *Gallery Pl./Chinatown.*

Theater J. In recent years Theater J has emerged as one of the country's most distinctive and progressive Jewish performance venues, offering an ambitious range of programming that includes work by noted playwrights, directors, designers, and actors. Past performances have included one-person shows featuring Sarah Bernhard and Judy Gold as well as more edgy political pieces. Performances take place in the Aaron and Cecile Goldman Theater at the D.C. Jewish Community Center. ⊠ *1529 16th St. NW, Downtown* ☎ *202/518–9400* ⊕ *www.theaterj.org* Ⓜ *Dupont Circle.*

Warner Theatre. One of Washington's grand theaters, the Warner hosts Broadway road shows, dance recitals, high-profile pop music acts, and the occasional comedian in a majestic art deco performance space. ⊠ *513 13th St. NW, Downtown* ☎ *202/783–4000* ⊕ *www.warnertheatre.com* Ⓜ *Metro Center.*

Fodor's Choice ★ **Woolly Mammoth.** Unusual avant-garde shows with edgy staging and solid acting have earned Woolly Mammoth top reviews and 35 Helen Hayes Awards. The cast performs works with a social message and also welcomes Chicago's Second City annually for a political comedy show. The troupe's talent is accentuated by its modern 265-seat theater in the Penn Quarter near the Verizon Center. ⊠ *641 D St. NW, Downtown* ☎ *202/393–3939* ⊕ *www.woollymammoth.net* Ⓜ *Gallery Pl./Chinatown or Archives/Navy Memorial.*

GEORGETOWN

Georgetown is more than just bars on a Saturday night. Smaller drama groups stage productions in several of Georgetown's larger churches; check local publications for the latest offerings.

MUSIC

CHAMBER MUSIC

Dumbarton Concerts. Dumbarton United Methodist Church, a fixture in Georgetown since 1772 (in its current location since 1850), sponsors a concert series that has been host to such musicians as the American Chamber Players, the St. Petersburg String Quartet, and the Thibaud String Trio. ■ TIP➜ Before or after a performance, take a stroll through the nearby Dumbarton Oaks estate and park. ⊠ *Dumbarton United Methodist Church, 3133 Dumbarton Ave. NW, Georgetown* ☎ *202/965–2000* ⊕ *www.dumbartonconcerts.org* Ⓜ *Foggy Bottom.*

DUPONT CIRCLE

Dupont Circle's reputation has grown in recent years as a place for good drama, with the Studio Theatre offering outstanding productions from new writers and some of America's best-known playwrights. Talented troupes in unique venues, including the Keegan Theatre at Church Street and Washington Stage Guild, are sprinkled throughout the neighborhood. But a little-known secret are the free concerts offered at the Phillips Collection.

FILM

National Geographic Society. Documentary films with a scientific, geographic, or anthropological focus are shown regularly at National Geographic's Grosvenor Auditorium. An easy walk from Dupont Circle, "NatGeo" also hosts speakers, concerts, and photography exhibits year-round. ■ TIP➜ The annual All Roads Film Project showcases works by indigenous and underrepresented minority-culture filmmakers from around the world, usually in September. ⊠ *1145 17th St. NW, Dupont Circle* ☎ *202/857–7700* ⊕ *www.nationalgeographic.com/nglive/washington* Ⓜ *Farragut N.*

MUSIC

CHAMBER MUSIC

Phillips Collection. Duncan Phillips's mansion is more than an art museum. On Sunday afternoons from October through May, chamber groups from around the world perform in the long, dark-paneled Music Room. Phillips after 5, from 5 pm to 8:30 pm on the first Thursday of the month, offers a lively mix of jazz performances, food and drink, gallery talks, films, and more. ■ TIP➜ The free concerts begin at 4 pm; arrive early for decent seats. ⊠ *1600 21st St. NW, Dupont Circle* ☎ *202/387–2151* ⊕ *www.phillipscollection.org* Ⓜ *Dupont Circle.*

THEATER AND PERFORMANCE ART

The Keegan Theatre at Church Street. This tiny 115-seat black-box theater is tucked among the scenic rowhouses of Dupont Circle. The Keegan Theatre troupe stages both Irish and American plays, and visiting troupes also perform. ■TIP➡ Note that given the size and age of this unique venue, there is little access for those with limited mobility and long lines form for the bathrooms at intermission. ✉ *1742 Church St. NW, Dupont Circle* ☎ *703/892–0202* ⊕ *keegantheatre.com* Ⓜ *Dupont Circle.*

★ **Studio Theatre.** One of the busiest groups in the city, this independent company produces an eclectic season of classic and offbeat plays in four spaces: the original Mead and Milton theaters, the newer 200-seat Metheny Theatre, and the experimental Stage 4. The theater is part of the energetic 14th Street Corridor. ✉ *1501 14th St. NW, Dupont Circle* ☎ *202/332–3300* ⊕ *www.studiotheatre.org* Ⓜ *Dupont Circle.*

Washington Stage Guild. This company performs neglected classics and foreign plays in the Undercroft Theatre of Mount Vernon Place United Methodist Church, offering lesser-known works by Oscar Wilde and George Bernard Shaw, such as *Don Juan in Hell* and *Lord Arthur Savile's Crime*. The Guild also stages selections from the Lady Gregory plays, hilarious slices of Irish life that presage Yeats and Beckett. ✉ *900 Massachusetts Ave. NW, Logan Circle* ☎ *240/582–0050* ⊕ *www.stageguild.org* Ⓜ *Dupont Circle.*

ADAMS MORGAN

Adams Morgan has long been the hub of the city's best avant-garde performances, primarily offered by the D.C. Arts Center. You can enjoy an incredible meal at a nearby restaurant, see a performance, and then head to one of the neighborhood's colorful bars after the show.

THEATER AND PERFORMANCE ART

Gala Hispanic Theatre. This company attracts outstanding Hispanic actors from around the world, performing works by such leading dramatists as Federico García Lorca and Mario Vargas Llosa. Plays are presented in English or in Spanish with instant English translations supplied through earphones. The company performs in the newly renovated Tivoli Theatre in Columbia Heights, a hot spot for Latino culture and cuisine. ✉ *Tivoli Sq., 3333 14th St. NW, 14th and Park Rd., Columbia Heights* ☎ *202/234–7174* ⊕ *www.galatheatre.org* Ⓜ *Columbia Heights.*

U STREET CORRIDOR

The U Street Corridor is enjoying a renaissance and is starting to reclaim its former title of Washington's "Black Broadway." The Lincoln Theatre offers great productions from diverse sources. Try some of the smaller venues in this neighborhood for original and compelling dramas.

MUSIC

OPERA

In Series. Trademark cabaret, experimental chamber opera, and Spanish musical theater (also known as *zarzuela*) are among the hallmarks of this burgeoning nonprofit company, which performs at venues around the city. ✉ *1835 14th St. NW, U Street Corridor* ☎ *202/204-7763* ⊕ *www.inseries.org.*

THEATER AND PERFORMANCE ART

Lincoln Theatre. Once the host of such notable black performers as Cab Calloway, Lena Horne, and Duke Ellington, the 1,250-seat 1920s-inspired Lincoln is part of the lively U Street Corridor. It presents movies, comedy shows, and musical performers such as Harry Belafonte, the Count Basie Orchestra, and the Harlem Boys and Girls Choir. ✉ *1215 U St. NW, U Street Corridor* ☎ *202/328–6000* ⊕ *www. thelincolntheatre.org* Ⓜ *U St./Cardozo.*

UPPER NORTHWEST

Summer is when the performing arts come alive in Upper Northwest D.C. One of the city's gems is Carter Barron, an outdoor amphitheater that offers everything from classical music to jazz to rhythm and blues. Other venues include the refurbished Avalon Theatre, which features outstanding documentaries and hard-to-find independent films. Some of the biggest blockbuster films are presented at the historic Uptown Theatre, which has the largest film screen in town.

FILM

Avalon. The Avalon, built in 1923, is operated by a nonprofit group and offers some of the best and most unusual in independent and foreign film. ✉ *5612 Connecticut Ave. NW, Cleveland Park* ☎ *202/966–6000* Ⓜ *Cleveland Park.*

Filmfest DC. Twenty-five years running, this annual citywide festival of international cinema (officially known as the D.C. International Film Festival) takes place in late April or early May at venues throughout Washington. ✉ *Upper Northwest* ☎ *202/234–3456* ⊕ *www.filmfestdc. org* Ⓜ *Friendship Heights.*

Loews Cineplex Uptown 1. The Uptown is a true movie palace, with art deco flourishes; a wonderful balcony; and—in one happy concession to modernity—crystal clear Dolby sound. The theater boasts the town's largest movie screen, almost three times the size of a standard screen with triple the effect. ✉ *3426 Connecticut Ave. NW, Cleveland Park* ☎ *202/966–5400* Ⓜ *Cleveland Park.*

MUSIC

CHORAL MUSIC

Washington National Cathedral. Choral and church groups frequently perform in this breathtaking cathedral. Organ recitals on the massive pipe organ are offered every Sunday afternoon and the choir sings Evensong most weekdays around 5:30. Admission is usually free. ✉ *Massachusetts and Wisconsin Aves. NW, Cleveland Park* ☎ *202/537–6207* ⊕ *www.nationalcathedral.org* Ⓜ *Tenleytown/AU.*

PERFORMANCE SERIES

Carter Barron Amphitheatre. On Saturday and Sunday nights from June to September, this 3,750-seat outdoor theater hosts pop, jazz, gospel, and rhythm-and-blues artists such as Chick Corea and Nancy Wilson. The National Symphony Orchestra also performs here, and for two weeks the Shakespeare Theatre presents a free play. ✉ *Rock Creek*

9

Park, 4850 Colorado Ave. NW, Upper Northwest ☎ *202/426–0486* ⊕ *www.nps.gov/rocr/planyourvisit/cbarron.htm.*

SOUTHWEST D.C.

Arena Stage is reviving the performing arts scene in Southwest D.C. Housed in the dramatically renovated and reborn Mead Center for American Theatre, the Arena attracts connoisseurs of great American drama. Take in a play, walk around the waterfront, and then enjoy some great seafood at one of many neighborhood restaurants.

THEATER AND PERFORMANCE ART

★ **Arena Stage.** The first regional theater company to win a Tony Award performs innovative American theater, reviving such classic plays as *Oklahoma!* and also showcasing the country's best new writers. Arena's productions are held in the state-of-the art Mead Center for American Theatre, the second-largest performing arts complex in Washington, after the Kennedy Center. Located near the still-developing waterfront neighborhood in Southeast D.C., the Mead features three stages: a theater in the round, seating 650; a modified thrust stage theater seating 514; and the "Cradle," a new 200-seat black-box theater for experimental productions. ⊠ *1101 Sixth St., SW, Southwest D.C.* ☎ *202/554–9066* ⊕ *www.arenastage.org* Ⓜ *Waterfront/SEU.*

SUBURBAN MARYLAND

Several venues make it worth your while to venture outside the District for entertainment. Glen Echo Park, once an amusement park, is now an arts center, and the Strathmore, while farther out in Rockville, is easily accessed by Metro and well worth the trip.

FILM

Fodor's Choice
★ **American Film Institute Silver Theatre and Cultural Center.** This state-of-the-art center for film is a restoration of architect John Eberson's art deco Silver Theatre, built in 1938. The AFI hosts film retrospectives, festivals, and tributes celebrating artists from Jeanne Moreau to Russell Crowe. ■TIP→ The AFI Silver also hosts the annual Silver Docs festival, which features some of the world's best documentaries and appearances by some of the greatest filmmakers, such as Martin Scorsese. ⊠ *8633 Colesville Rd., Silver Spring* ☎ *301/495–6700* ⊕ *www.afi.com/silver* Ⓜ *Silver Spring.*

MAJOR VENUES

Montgomery College–Takoma Park/Silver Spring Cultural Arts Center. This brand-new facility boasts three stages that accommodate every type of perfomance: folk music, Asian festivals, children's plays, classical music, avant garde dramas, and more. ⊠ *7995 Georgia Ave., Silver Spring* ☎ *240/567–5775* ⊕ *www.cms.montgomerycollege.edu* Ⓜ *College Park.*

Fodor's Choice
★ **Music Center at Strathmore.** Located just outside the Capital Beltway in North Bethesda, this majestic concert hall receives praise for its acoustics and its audience-friendly design. Major national folk, blues, pop,

jazz, Broadway, and classical artists perform here. The center is home to the Baltimore Symphony Orchestra and the National Philharmonic. More-intimate performances are held in the 100-seat Dorothy M. and Maurice C. Shapiro Music Room. ■TIP➔ Consider taking the Metro to Strathmore; the center is less than a block from the Grosvenor Metro station. ⊠ *5301 Tuckerman La., North Bethesda* ☎ *301/581–5200* ⊕ *www. strathmore.org* Ⓜ *Grosvenor/Strathmore.*

MUSIC

ORCHESTRAS

Baltimore Symphony Orchestra. The world-renowned Baltimore Symphony Orchestra, under the leadership of Marin Alsop, plays both at the Music Center at Strathmore and also at the Joseph Meyerhoff Symphony Hall in Baltimore. ⊠ *5301 Tuckerman La., North Bethesda* ☎ *877/276–1444* ⊕ *www.bsomusic.org* Ⓜ *Grosvenor/Strathmore.*

PERFORMANCE SERIES

Institute of Musical Traditions. Emerging, near-famous, and celebrated folk performers such as Si Kahn, John McCutcheon, and the Kennedys perform at the Institute's concerts, most often held at the St. Mark Presbyterian Church in Rockville, a 30-minute drive from Washington. ⊠ *10701 Old Georgetown Rd., Rockville* ☎ *301/754–3611* ⊕ *www.imtfolk.org.*

THEATER AND PERFORMANCE ART

Ⓢ **Glen Echo Park.** The National Park Service has transformed this former amusement park into a thriving arts center. Every weekend the Adventure Theater puts on traditional plays and musicals aimed at children ages four and up. Families can spread out on carpeted steps. At the Puppet Company Playhouse, skilled puppeteers perform classic stories Wednesday through Sunday. ⊠ *7300 MacArthur Blvd., Glen Echo* ☎ *301/634–2222, 301/320–5331 Adventure Theater, 301/320–6668 Puppet Co.* ⊕ *www.glenechopark.org.*

Ⓢ **Imagination Stage.** Shows like the classic *Dr. Doolittle,* and such original fare as Karen Zacarias and Deborah Wicks LaPuma's *Cinderella Likes Rice and Beans,* are produced here for children ages four and up. The state-of-the-art center in Bethesda includes two theaters and a digital media studio. ⊠ *4908 Auburn Ave., Bethesda* ☎ *301/961–6060* ⊕ *www. imaginationstage.org.*

Round House Theatre. Each season on its Main Stage in Bethesda, Round House presents an eclectic body of work ranging from world premieres to great 20th-century works to contemporary adaptations of the classics. Round House's 150-seat black-box stage, home to more-experimental works, is in Silver Spring, adjacent to the American Film Institute Silver Theater. ⊠ *4545 East–West Hwy., Bethesda* ☎ *240/644–1099* ⊕ *www. roundhousetheatre.org* Ⓜ *Bethesda.*

SUBURBAN VIRGINIA

Suburban Virginia is home to a number of outstanding performing venues offering Shakespeare, opera, dance, popular music, and more. Some of the best musical productions are staged at the nationally lauded Signature Theatre in Arlington, only a short trip from downtown Washington. Some venues here are connected to the Metro, while you'll need a car to reach others.

MAJOR VENUES

Center for the Arts. This state-of-the-art performance complex on the suburban Virginia campus of George Mason University satisfies music, ballet, and drama patrons with regular performances in its 1,900-seat concert hall, the 500-seat proscenium Harris Theater, and the intimate 150-seat black-box Theater of the First Amendment. The 9,500-seat Patriot Center, site of pop acts and sporting events, is also on campus. ⊠ *Rte. 123 and Braddock Rd., Fairfax* ☎ *888/945–2468* ⊕ *www.cfa.gmu.edu.*

Wolf Trap National Park for the Performing Arts. Wolf Trap is the only national park dedicated to the performing arts. June through September, the massive, outdoor Filene Center hosts close to 100 performances, ranging from pop and jazz concerts to dance and musical theater productions. In summer, the National Symphony Orchestra is based here, and the Children's Theatre-in-the-Woods delivers 70 free performances. During the colder months the intimate, indoor Barns at Wolf Trap fill with the sounds of musicians playing folk, country, and chamber music, along with myriad other styles. The park is just off the Dulles Toll Road, about 20 mi from downtown Washington. ⊠ *1645 Trap Rd., Vienna* ☎ *703/255–1900, 703/938–2404 Barns at Wolf Trap* ⊕ *www. wolftrap.org* Ⓜ *Vienna.*

THEATER AND PERFORMANCE ART

American Century Theatre. Devoted to staging overlooked or forgotten 20th-century American plays, American Century has staged performances of Paddy Chafeysky's *The Tenth Man,* Orson Wells's *Moby Dick Rehearsed,* and even a rare Mel Brooks production, *Archy and Mehitabel.* ⊠ *2700 Lang St., Arlington* ☎ *703/998–4555* ⊕ *www. americancentury.org.*

Signature Theatre. Led by artistic director Eric Schaeffer, Signature has earned national acclaim for its presentation of contemporary plays and groundbreaking American musicals, especially those of Stephen Sondheim. The company performs in a dramatic facility in Arlington, Virginia, with two performance spaces, the 299-seat MAX and the 99-seat ARK. ⊠ *4200 Campbell Ave., Arlington* ☎ *703/820–9771* ⊕ *www. signature-theatre.org.*

Sports and the Outdoors

WORD OF MOUTH

"If you are into beautiful gardens, go to Georgetown and see Dumbarton Oaks. It is magnificent. And right down the street is another historic home and beautiful garden, Tudor Place. Neither one is the White House, but the gardens are sublime."

—con_brio

Updated by Allison Lombardo

Although Washington may be best known for what goes on inside its hallowed corridors, what's going on outside is often just as entertaining. Washingtonians are an active bunch and the city provides a fantastic recreational backyard, with dozens of beautiful open spaces in the District and the nearby Maryland and Virginia suburbs. The city's residents take full advantage of these opportunities, exploring by bike, running amid the monuments, and sailing up the Potomac. They're also passionate about their local teams—especially the Redskins and the Capitals, whose games are sold out year after year.

Visitors to Washington can enjoy a wealth of outdoor attractions. Rock Creek Park is one of the city's treasures, with miles of wooded trails and paths for bikers, runners, and walkers that extend to almost every part of the city. The National Mall connects the Lincoln Memorial and the Capitol and is one of the most scenic greenswards in the world. Around the Tidal Basin you can run, tour the monuments, and rent paddleboats. Theodore Roosevelt Island, a wildlife sanctuary that deserves to be better known, has several paths for hiking and enjoyable spots for a picnic. And these places are just a few among dozens.

PLANNING

Nationals Park. D.C.'s baseball team, the Nationals, plays in the spacious, state-of-the-art Nationals Park, on the Anacostia waterfront in Southwest Washington. The area is booming with entertainment venues, and the stadium offers the option of sitting or standing at a bar within sight of the field. ⊠ *1500 S. Capitol St. SE* Ⓜ *Navy Yard.*

Robert F. Kennedy Stadium. Uniquely, soccer is incredibly popular in the nation's capital, finding its fans in the international crowds who miss

FIVE GREAT OUTDOOR EXPERIENCES

Bird-watch on Theodore Roosevelt Island: Take in the spectacular scenery at this tucked-away wildlife sanctuary.

Get a new perspective on the cherry trees: Take a leisurely trip in a paddleboat around the Tidal Basin in spring.

Get moving with picture-postcard motivation: Run or bike on the Mall with Washington's monuments as a unique background.

See the National Zoo's giant pandas: Washington's love affair with the adorable pandas at the National Zoo has gotten a welcome extension; Mei Xiang and Tian Tian are extending their D.C. stay until December 2015.

Stroll through Washington's loveliest landscapes: Walk through Dumbarton Oaks' many acres of distinctive gardens modeled after classic French, English, and Italian designs.

the big matches at home. Robert F. Kennedy Stadium, the Redskins' former residence on Capitol Hill, is now home to Major League Soccer's D.C. United. ⊠ *2400 E. Capitol St. NE, at 22nd St.* Ⓜ *Stadium.*

WASHINGTON FOR EVERY SEASON

With every change of the seasons, D.C. offers new pleasures for sports and outdoor enthusiasts.

In winter you can have an old-fashioned afternoon of ice-skating and hot chocolate in the National Gallery's Sculpture Garden, or go to the Verizon Center to see the Wizards play basketball or the Capitals play hockey.

Come spring the city emerges from the cold with activities everywhere. Runners throng Rock Creek Park, softball and kickball games are a common sight on the Mall, and boats float down the Potomac.

In summer baseball fans head to new Nationals Park to see the Nationals play, and Washington Redskins fans check out their favorite football stars at training camp in Ashburn, Virginia.

When fall arrives the seasonal colors of the trees in Rock Creek Park are a spectacular sight for bikers, hikers, and runners. Tickets to see the Redskins at FedEx Field are some of the city's most prized commodities.

10

PARKS AND NATURE

Washington is more than marble and limestone buildings. The city is blessed with numerous parks and outdoor attractions that provide a break from the museums and government facilities. Rock Creek Park extends through much of the city; there may just be an entrance to the park nearby your hotel. Other outdoor attractions, such as the Tidal Basin, Potomac Park, and Constitution Gardens, offer a chance to see nature, combined with the beauty of nearby waterways and the majesty of the city's most beloved monuments, such as the Vietnam Memorial, World War II Memorial, and the FDR Memorial.

GARDENS

Constitution Gardens. Many ideas were proposed to develop this 50-acre site near the Reflecting Pool and the Vietnam Veterans Memorial. It once held "temporary" buildings erected by the Navy before World War I and not removed until after World War II. President Nixon is said to have favored something resembling Copenhagen's Tivoli Gardens. The final design was plainer, with paths winding through groves of trees and, on the lake, a tiny island paying tribute to the signers of the Declaration of Independence, their signatures carved into a low stone wall. In 1986 President Reagan proclaimed the gardens a living legacy to the Constitution; in that spirit, a naturalization ceremony for new citizens now takes place here each year. ⊠ *Constitution Ave. between 17th and 23rd Sts. NW, White House rea* ⊕ *www.nps.gov/coga* Ⓜ *Foggy Bottom.*

> **QUICK BITES**
>
> **At the circular snack bar just west of the Constitution Gardens lake, you can get hot dogs, potato chips, candy bars, soft drinks, and beer at prices lower than those charged by most street vendors.**

Fodor'sChoice ★ **Dumbarton Oaks.** One of the loveliest places for a stroll in Washington is Dumbarton Oaks, the acres of enchanting gardens adjoining Dumbarton House in Georgetown. Planned by noted landscape architect Beatrix Farrand, the gardens incorporate elements of traditional English, Italian, and French styles and include a formal rose garden, an English country garden, and an orangery (circa 1810). A full-time crew of a dozen gardeners toils to maintain the stunning collection of terraces, geometric gardens, tree-shaded brick walks, fountains, arbors, and pools. Plenty of well-positioned benches make this a good place for resting weary feet, too. You enter the gardens at 31st and R streets and there is a small fee. **Dumbarton House** houses world-renowned collections of Byzantine and pre-Columbian art. ⊠ *1703 32nd St. NW, Georgetown* ☎ *202/339–6401, 202/339–6400* ⊕ *www.doaks.org* ⌦ *Gardens: Apr.–Oct. $8, Nov.–Mar. free* ☉ *Gardens: Apr.–Oct., Tues.–Sun. 2–6; Nov.–Mar., Tues.–Sun. 2–5.*

★ **Hillwood Estate, Museum and Gardens.** Cereal heiress Marjorie Merriweather Post purchased the 25-acre Hillwood Estate in 1955. Post devoted as much attention to her gardens as she did to the 40-room Georgian mansion: you can wander through 13 acres of them, including a Japanese rock and waterfall garden, a manicured formal French garden, a rose garden, Mediterranean fountains, and a greenhouse full of orchids. The "Lunar Lawn," where she threw garden parties that were the most coveted invitation in Washington society, is planted with dogwood, magnolia, cherry, and plum trees, as well as azaleas, camellias, lilacs, tulips, and pansies. The estate is best reached by taxi or car (parking is available on the grounds). It's a 20- to 30-minute walk from the Metro. ⊠ *4155 Linnean Ave. NW, Upper Northwest* ☎ *202/686–5807, 202/686–8500* ⊕ *www.hillwoodmuseum.org* ⌦ *House and grounds $12* ☉ *Feb.–Dec., Tues.–Sat. 10–5* Ⓜ *Van Ness/UDC.*

Kahlil Gibran Memorial Garden. In a town known for it's political combat, this tiny urban park is a wonderful place to find some peace. The park combines Western and Arab symbols and is perfect for contemplation.

From the Massachusetts Avenue entrance, a stone walk bridges a grassy swale. Farther on are limestone benches, engraved with sayings from Gibran, that curve around a fountain and a bust of the Lebanese-born poet. The garden is near the grounds of the U.S. Naval Observatory. ⊠ *3100 block of Massachusetts Ave. NW, Upper Northwest* Ⓜ *Woodley Park or Dupont Circle.*

Kenilworth Park and Aquatic Gardens. Exotic water lilies, lotuses, hyacinths, and other water-loving plants thrive in this 14-acre sanctuary of quiet ponds and marshy flats. The gardens' wetland animals include turtles, frogs, beavers, spring azure butterflies, and some 40 species of birds. ■ **TIP➜** In July nearly everything blossoms; early morning is the best time to visit, when day bloomers are just opening and night bloomers have yet to close. The nearest Metro stop is a 15-minute walk away. ⊠ *1550 Anacostia Ave. at Douglas St. NE, Anacostia* ☎ *202/426–6905* ⊕ *www. nps.gov/keaq* 🎫 *Free* ☉ *Gardens and visitor center, daily 7–4; garden tours daily at 9, 10, and 11* Ⓜ *Deanwood.*

Tudor Place. A little more than a block from Dumbarton Oaks in Georgetown is this little-known gem, the former home of Martha Washington's granddaughter. The house has 5.5 acres of gardens that offer impressive replications of Federal-period gardens and include 19th-century specimen trees and boxwoods from Mount Vernon. Make time for a one-hour tour of the house itself, which features many rare possessions of George and Martha Washington. ⊠ *1644 31st Pl. NW, Georgetown* ☎ *202/965–0400* ⊕ *www.tudorplace.org* 🎫 *$8, garden $3* ☉ *House tours: Tues.–Sat. on the hr 10–3; Sun. on the hr noon–3. Garden: Mon.– Sat. 10–4, Sun. noon–4. Closed Jan.* Ⓜ *Woodley Park or Dupont Circle.*

United States Botanic Garden. Established by Congress in 1820, this is the oldest botanic garden in North America. The garden conservatory sits at the foot of Capitol Hill, in the shadow of the Capitol building and offers an escape from the stone and marble federal office buildings that surround it; inside are exotic rain-forest species, desert flora, and trees from all parts of the world. A special treat is the extensive collection of rare and unusual orchids. Walkways suspended 24 feet above the ground provide a fascinating view of the plants. A relatively new addition is the National Garden, opened in 2006, which emphasizes educational exhibits. The garden features the Rose Garden, Butterfly Garden, Lawn Terrace, First Ladies' Water Garden, and Regional Garden. ⊠ *1st St. at 100 Maryland Ave. SW, Capitol Hill* ☎ *202/225–8333* ⊕ *www. usbg.gov* 🎫 *Free* ☉ *Botanic Garden daily 10–5; National Garden daily 10–7* Ⓜ *Federal Center SW.*

10

Fodor's Choice ★ **United States National Arboretum.** During azalea season (mid-April through May) this 446-acre oasis is a blaze of color. In early summer, clematis, peonies, rhododendrons, and roses bloom. At any time of year the 22

original Corinthian columns from the U.S. Capitol, re-erected here in 1990, are striking. The arboretum has guided hikes throughout the year, including a Full Moon Hike at night. Check the website for schedules and to register. For a soothing, relaxing outing, visit the Cryptomeria Walk and Japanese Stroll Garden, which are part of the Bonsai and Penjing Museum. Admission to the grounds is free. On weekends a tram tours ($4) the arboretum's curving roadways at 10:30, 11:30, 1, 2, 3, and 4. It's a difficult walk from the Metro so driving or biking in is best. The **National Herb Garden** and the **National Bonsai Collection** are also here. ✉ *3501 New York Ave. NE, Northeast D.C.* ☎ *202/245–2726* ⊕ *www.usna.usda.gov* ⊡ *Free* ⊗ *Arboretum and herb garden daily 8–5, bonsai collection daily 10–4* Ⓜ *Weekends only, Union Station, then X6 bus (runs every 40 mins); weekdays, Stadium/Armory, then B2 bus to Bladensburg Rd. and R St.*

> **WORD OF MOUTH**
>
> "I guess the question is whether the point is just to see cherry trees or to see a larger context. The Arboretum is lovely (but not easy to get to if you don't know D.C.) but the Tidal Basin has the advantage, of well, being the Tidal Basin and on the Mall. The cherry trees are part of a larger experience visually. The Arboretum will be much less crowded."
>
> —MikeT

PARKS

C&O Canal. George Washington was one of the first to advance the idea of a canal linking the Potomac with the Ohio River across the Appalachians. Work started on the Chesapeake & Ohio Canal in 1828, and when it opened in 1850 its 74 locks linked Georgetown with Cumberland, Maryland, 184.5 miles to the northwest (still short of its intended destination). Lumber, coal, iron, wheat, and flour moved up and down the canal, but it was never as successful as its planners had hoped it would be. Many of the bridges spanning the canal in Georgetown were too low to allow anything other than fully loaded barges to pass underneath, and competition from the Baltimore & Ohio Railroad eventually spelled an end to profitability. Today the canal is part of the National Park System; walkers follow the towpath once used by mules, while canoeists paddle the canal's calm waters.

You can glide into history aboard a mule-drawn **canal boat ride**. The National Park service provides the hour-long rides from about mid-April through late October; tickets cost $5 and are available across the canal from the visitor center, next to the Foundry Building. The schedule varies by season, with limited rides in spring and fall. In summer the boats run at least twice a day from Wednesday through Sunday. Call the visitor center for the exact schedule on the day of your visit. Canal-boat rides also depart from the Great Falls Tavern visitor center in Maryland. ✉ *Georgetown Canal Visitor Center, 1057 Thomas Jefferson St. NW, Georgetown* ☎ *202/653–5190* ⊕ *www.nps.gov/choh* ⊗ *Visitor center: Apr.–Oct., Wed.–Sun. 9–4:30; Nov.–Mar., weekends 10–4, staffing permitting.*

10

Rock Creek Park. The 1,800 acres surrounding Rock Creek have provided a cool oasis for D.C. residents ever since Congress set them aside for recreational use in 1890. Bicycle routes, jogging and hiking paths, and equestrian trails wind through the groves of dogwoods, beeches, oaks, and cedars, and 30 picnic areas are scattered about. About twice the size of NYC's Central Park, the park stretches through much of the Northwest part of the city so it's very easy to enter and exit the park for a short or long exercise excursion.

Nature Center and Planetarium. Rangers at the Nature Center and Planetarium introduce visitors to the park and keep track of daily events; guided nature walks leave from the center weekends at 2. The center and planetarium are open Wednesday through Sunday from 9 to 5. The Planetarium hosts regular shows for children on Wednesday at 4 and weekends at 1 and 4. Adults can also look through the telescope one Saturday night a month. Information on other activities can be found at the Nature Center website. ⊠ *South of Military Rd., 5200 Glover Rd. NW, Upper Northwest* ☎ *202/426–6829* ⊕ *www.nps.gov/rocr/index.htm.,*

Klingle Mansion. The renovated 19th-century Klingle Mansion is used as the National Park Service's Rock Creek headquarters. Also in distant areas of the park are Fort Reno, Fort Bayard, Fort Stevens, and Fort DeRussy, remnants of the original ring of forts that guarded Washington during the Civil War, and the Rock Creek Park Golf Course, an 18-hole public course. ⊠ *3545 Willliamsburg La. NW, Upper Northwest* Ⓜ *Cleveland Park.*

Meridian Hill Park. Landscape architect Horace Peaslee created oft-overlooked Meridian Hill Park, a noncontiguous section of Rock Creek Park, after a 1917 study of the parks of Europe. As a result, the garden contains elements of gardens in France (a long, straight mall bordered with plants), Italy (terraces and wall fountains), and Switzerland (a lower-level reflecting pool based on one in Zurich). Meridian Hill is also unofficially known as Malcolm X Park in honor of the civil rights leader. On weekends you will find a mix of pick-up soccer games, joggers running the stairs, and the occasional drum circle. Drug activity once made it unwise to visit Meridian Hill alone; it's somewhat safer now, but avoid the park after dark. ⊠ *16th and Euclid Sts., Adams Morgan* Ⓜ *U St./Cardozo.*

Tidal Basin. This placid pond was part of the Potomac until 1882, when portions of the river were filled in to improve navigation and create additional parkland. The Tidal Basin is the setting for memorials to Thomas Jefferson, Franklin Delano Roosevelt, Martin Luther King, Jr., and George Mason, and can be enjoyed by strolling along the banks or paddling across the tame waters.

Two grotesque sculpted heads on the sides of the Inlet Bridge can be seen as you walk along the sidewalk that hugs the basin. The inside walls of the bridge also feature two other interesting sculptures: bronze, human-headed fish that spout water from their mouths. The bridge was refurbished in the 1980s at the same time the chief of the park, Jack Fish, was retiring. Sculptor Constantine Sephralis played a little joke: these fish heads are actually Fish's head.

Once you cross the bridge, continue along the Tidal Basin to the right. This route is especially scenic when the **cherry trees** are in bloom. The first batch of these trees arrived from Japan in 1909. The trees were infected with insects and fungus, however, and the Department of Agriculture ordered them destroyed. A diplomatic crisis was averted when the United States politely asked the Japanese for another batch, and in 1912 First

WORD OF MOUTH

"My suggestions would be to spend time in Rock Creek Park, the canal area in Georgetown, as well as possibly Dumbarton Oaks in Georgetown, and/or Hillwood Estate on the edge of Rock Creek Park, both of which have pretty grounds."

—Cicerone

Lady Helen Taft planted the first tree. The second was planted by the wife of the Japanese ambassador, Viscountess Chinda. About 200 of the original trees still grow near the Tidal Basin. (These cherry trees are the single-flowering Akebeno and Yoshino variety. Double-blossom Fugenzo and Kwanzan trees grow in East Potomac Park and flower about two weeks after their more famous cousins.)

The trees are now the centerpiece of Washington's two-week **Cherry Blossom Festival,** held each spring since 1935. The festivities are kicked off by the lighting of a ceremonial Japanese lantern that rests on the north shore of the Tidal Basin, not far from where the first tree was planted. The once-simple celebration has grown over the years to include concerts, martial-arts demonstrations, a running race, and a parade. Park Service experts try their best to predict exactly when the buds will pop. The trees are usually in bloom for about 10–12 days in late March or early April. When winter refuses to release its grip, the parade and festival are held anyway, without the presence of blossoms, no matter how inclement the weather. And when the weather complies and the blossoms are at their peak at the time of the festivities, Washington rejoices. ✉ *Bordered by Independence and Maine Aves., The Mall* Ⓜ *Smithsonian.*

West Potomac Park. Between the Potomac and the Tidal Basin, West Potomac Park is best known for its flowering cherry trees, which bloom for two weeks in late March or early April. During the rest of the year, West Potomac Park is just a nice place to relax, play ball, or admire the views of the water and the memorials that surround it.

10

ZOOS AND AQUARIUMS

National Aquarium. The aquarium has an incongruous location inside the lower level of the Commerce Department Building, near the massive Ronald Reagan Building. Established in 1873, this is the country's oldest public aquarium, with more than 1,200 fish and other creatures—such as eels, sharks, and alligators—representing 270 species of fresh- and saltwater life. Affiliated with Baltimore's National Aquarium, the Washington aquarium is operated by a nonprofit organization. However, it does not receive federal funding. As a result, the exhibits appear somewhat dated, but the easy-to-view tanks, accessible touching pool (with

DID YOU KNOW?

The mayor of Tokyo gave Washington, D.C., 3,000 cherry trees in 1912 honoring the friendship between the United States and Japan. The U.S. government reciprocated in 1915 with a gift of dog-wood trees.

crabs and sea urchins), low admission fee, and absence of crowds make this a good outing with small children. The Aquarium's cafeteria is also a great place to stop for a snack. ⊠ *14th St. and Constitution Ave. NW, White House Area* ☎ *202/482–2825* ⊕ *www.nationalaquarium.com* 🎫 *$9; children $4.50* ⊙ *Daily 9–5, last admission at 4:30; sharks fed Mon., Wed., and Sat. at 2; piranhas fed Tues., Thurs., and Sun. at 2; alligators fed Fri. at 2* Ⓜ *Federal Triangle.*

Fodor's Choice
★
Ⓒ
National Zoo. Since 2000, the giant pandas, Tian Tian and Mei Xiang, have been the zoo's most famous residents. Fans were concerned the adorable couple would be returning to China in 2011 when their contract ended, but a new agreement guarantees that Mei and Tian will stay in Washington until December 2015. This raises the possibility of another baby panda watch. In 2005 the pandas had their first cub, Tai Shan, who was moved to China in 2010.

The National Zoo has much to offer in addition to the pandas. Carved out of Rock Creek Park, it contains 2,000 animals, representing 400 species. The zoo is a series of rolling, wooded hills that complement the many innovative compounds showing animals in their native settings. Step inside the Great Flight Cage to observe the free flight of many species of birds; this walk-in aviary is open from May to October (the birds are moved indoors during the colder months). Between 11 a.m. and 2 p.m. each day you can catch the orangutan population traveling on the "O Line," a series of cables and towers near the Great Ape House that allows the primates to swing hand over hand about 35 feet over your head. One of the more unusual and impressive exhibits is Amazonia, an amazingly authentic reproduction of a South American rain-forest ecosystem. You feel as if you are deep inside a steamy jungle, with monkeys leaping overhead and noisy birds flying from branch to branch. Exciting new exhibits are always being added, such as the new Asia trail featuring sloth bears, fishing cats, red pandas, a Japanese giant salamander, clouded leopards, and other Asian species.

Part of the Smithsonian Institution, the National Zoo was created by an Act of Congress in 1889, and the 163-acre park was designed by landscape architect Frederick Law Olmsted, who also designed the U.S. Capitol grounds and New York's Central Park. Before the zoo opened in 1890, live animals used as taxidermists' models were kept on the Mall. ⊠ *3001 Connecticut Ave. NW, Upper Northwest* ☎ *202/673–4800, 202/673–4717* ⊕ *nationalzoo.si.edu* 🎫 *Free, parking $16* ⊙ *Apr.–Oct., daily 6 am–8 pm; Nov.–Mar., daily 6–6. Zoo buildings open at 10.* Ⓜ *Cleveland Park or Woodley Park/Zoo.*

SPORTS

Washington is well designed for outdoor sports, with numerous places to play, run, and ride. When the weather is good, it seems all of Washington is out riding a bike, playing softball and volleyball, jogging past monuments, or taking a relaxing stroll. Many of the favorite locations for participation sports are in the shadow of D.C.'s most famous spots, such as Capitol Hill and the White House.

Hop on two wheels to give your feet a break and explore the monuments by bike.

BASEBALL

Washington Nationals. Major League Baseball has returned to D.C., where the Washington Nationals of the National League play in their new spectacular home, Nationals Park. Tours ($15) of the state-of-the art stadium are available when the Nationals are on the road and in the morning when the team has night games. Individual game tickets may be purchased at the park or through the team's website. Seats range from $10 to $325 and inexpensive tickets are often available at the box office on game day. ■TIP→ The Metro is a hassle-free and inexpensive way to get to the ballpark. The closest and most convenient stop is the Navy Yard on the Green Line. Parking is scarce. ✉ *1500 S. Capitol St. SE* ☏ *202/675–6287* ⊕ *washington.nationals.mlb.com* Ⓜ *Navy Yard.*

BASKETBALL

Georgetown University Hoyas. Of the Division I men's college basketball teams in the area, the most prominent are the Georgetown University Hoyas, former NCAA national champions. The Hoyas became a national basketball powerhouse under their coach John Thompson III, and remain perennial contenders in the national tourney. The Hoyas often play at the Verizon Center. ⊕ *guhoyas.com.*

Washington Mystics. The WNBA's Washington Mystics play at the Verizon Center in Downtown Washington. The Mystics perennially lead the WNBA in attendance, despite a losing record. The games are loud, boisterous events. Ticket prices range from $17 to $70, with courtside tickets for $125. You can buy tickets at the Verizon Center box office or through Ticketmaster. The women's basketball season runs from late May to August. ⊠ *6th and F Sts., Downtown* ☎ *202/432–7328* ⊕ *www. wnba.com/mystics* Ⓜ *Gallery Pl./Chinatown.*

Washington Wizards. The NBA's Washington Wizards play from October to April at the Verizon Center and feature rising star John Wall. Tickets for individual games cost $40 to $850. The team also offers $16 seats in the upper level and courtside seats for a whopping $2,500. Buy tickets from the Verizon Center box office or from Ticketmaster. ⊠ *6th and F Sts., Downtown* ☎ *202/432–7328* ⊕ *www.nba.com/wizards* Ⓜ *Gallery Pl./Chinatown.*

BICYCLING

The numerous trails in the District and its surrounding areas are well maintained and clearly marked.

C&O Canal Towpath. For scenery, you can't beat the C&O Canal Towpath, which starts in Georgetown and runs along the C&O Canal into Maryland. You could pedal to the end of the canal, nearly 200 miles away in Cumberland, Maryland, but most cyclists stop at Great Falls, 13 miles from where the canal starts. The occasionally bumpy towpath, made of gravel and packed earth, passes through wooded areas of the C&O Canal National Historical Park. You can see 19th-century locks from the canal's working days, and you may catch a glimpse of mules pulling a canal barge. The barges now haul passengers, not cargo. ⊕ *www.nps.gov/choh.*

Capital Crescent Trail. Suited for bicyclists, walkers, rollerbladers, and strollers, the paved Capital Crescent Trail stretches along the old Georgetown Branch, a B&O Railroad line that was completed in 1910 and was in operation until 1985. The 7.5-mile route's first leg runs from Georgetown near Key Bridge to central Bethesda at Bethesda and Woodmont avenues. At Bethesda and Woodmont the trailheads through a well-lighted tunnel near the heart of Bethesda's lively business area and continues into Silver Spring. The 3.5-mile stretch from Bethesda to Silver Spring is gravel. The Georgetown Branch Trail, as this section is officially named, connects with the Rock Creek Trail, which goes to Rockville in the north and Memorial Bridge past the Washington Monument in the south. On weekends when the weather's nice, all sections of the trails are crowded. ☎ *202/234–4874 Capital Crescent Coalition.*

East Potomac Park. Cyclists might try the 3-mile loop around the golf course in East Potomac Park at Hains Point, the southern area of the park (entry is near the Jefferson Memorial). Though somewhat less scenic than a run around the Mall, it's a favorite training course for dedicated local racers and would-be triathletes. ☎ *202/485–9874 National Park Service.*

Mall. Each day bicyclists cruise the Mall amid the endless throngs of runners, walkers, and tourists. There's relatively little car traffic, and bikers can take in some of Washington's finest landmarks, such as the Washington Monument, the Reflecting Pool, WWII Memorial, and the Smithsonian's many museums, as they travel from the Lincoln Memorial all the way up to the Capitol and back (about a 4-mile loop). Those looking for a longer trek can extend their ride up and down Independence and Constitution avenues.

Mount Vernon Trail. Mount Vernon Trail, across the Potomac in Virginia, has two sections. The northern part, closest to D.C. proper, is 3.5 miles long and begins near the causeway across the river from the Kennedy Center that heads to Theodore Roosevelt Island *(⇨ see Hik-*

BIKING THE MALL

A pleasant loop route begins at the Lincoln Memorial, going north past the Washington Monument, and turning around at the Tidal Basin. Along the way are small fountains and parks for taking a break and getting a drink of water.

ing). It then passes Ronald Reagan National Airport and continues on to Old Town Alexandria. This section has slight slopes and almost no interruptions for traffic, making it a delightful biking route. Even relatively inexperienced bikers enjoy the trail, which provides wonderful views of the Potomac. To access the trail from the District, take the Theodore Roosevelt Bridge or the Rochambeau Memorial Bridge, also known as the 14th Street Bridge. South of the airport, the trail runs down to the Washington Marina. The final mile of the trail's northern section meanders through protected wetlands before ending in the heart of Old Town Alexandria. The trail's 9-mile southern section extends along the Potomac from Alexandria to Mount Vernon.

Rock Creek Park. Rock Creek Park covers an area from the edge of Georgetown to Montgomery County, Maryland. An asphalt bike path running through the park has a few challenging hills but is mostly flat, and it's possible to bike several miles without having to stop for cars (the roadway is closed entirely to cars on weekends). Bikers can begin a ride at the Lincoln Memorial or Kennedy Center, pass the Washington Zoo, and eventually come to the Washington, D.C., line, where the trail separates, with one part continuing to Bethesda and another to Silver Spring. Fifteen miles of dirt trails crisscross the park; these are best for hiking.

INFORMATION

Washington Area Bicyclist Association. WABA provides an organizational home for bike enthusiasts across the Washington metropolitan area. Members conduct local outreach to encourage biking, do advocacy for better bike lanes, and educate the public about bike safety. WABA also provides an institutional structure for those looking for organized longer rides. ⊠ *1803 Connecticut Ave., 3rd fl., Upper Northwest* ☎ *202/518–0524* ⊕ *www.waba.org.*

RENTALS AND TOURS

Big Wheel Bikes. Big Wheel Bikes, near the C&O Canal Towpath, rents multispeed and other types of bikes hourly or for the day. Rates range from $5–$10 per hour and $25–$100 per day. There is a three-hour minimum. Tandem bikes, kids' bikes, and bikes with baby carriers are also available. A second location is near the Capital Crescent Trail. There's also an Alexandria branch if you want to ride the Mount Vernon Trail. ⊠ *1034 33rd St. NW, Georgetown* ☎ *202/337–0254* ⊕ *www.bigwheelbikes.com* ⊠ *2 Prince St., Alexandria, Virginia* ☎ *703/739–2300.*

10

Bike and Roll. Bike and Roll is a tour company that offers three-hour, 4- to 8-mile guided tours of Downtown Washington. The company offers tours that range in cost from $35 to $50, and bike rental is included. Bike and Roll has locations at the Old Post Office Pavilion and at Union Station. Advance reservations are required. Tours start from the Mall. ⊠ *1100 Pennsylvania Ave. NW, Downtown* ☎ *202/842-2453* ⊕ *www.bikethesites.com.*

The Boathouse at Fletcher's Cove. The Boathouse at Fletcher's Cove, next to the C&O Towpath and Capital Crescent Trail, rents fixed-gear bikes for $7 per hour and $28 per day. ⊠ *4940 Canal Rd. NW, at Reservoir Rd., Georgetown* ☎ *202/244–0461* ⊕ *www.fletcherscove.com.*

Capital Bikeshare. One of the nation's largest bike-share programs lets you pick up a bike at one of 140 stations located around Washington and Arlington, Virginia, and then return it at a location near your destination. Using a credit card to pay the $7 24-hour membership fee at a bike station kiosk, you receive a code to unlock a bike. The membership entitles you to an unlimited number of rides during the 24 hours. The first 30 minutes are free, then different rates apply; a 90-minute trip is $4.50. Bikers provide their own helmets. ■TIP➔ Capital Bikeshare is designed for quick, short trips. A bike rental shop may be a better option for visitors needing a bike for a full day. ☎ *877/430–2453* ⊕ *www.capitalbikeshare.com.*

Thompson's Boat Center. In addition to its access to the river, Thompson's Boat Center allows easy access to the Rock Creek Trail and the C&O Towpath and is close to the monuments. Adult single-speed bikes are $7 per hour and $25 per day. Rentals are on a first-come, first-served basis. ⊠ *2900 Virginia Ave. NW, Foggy Bottom* ☎ *202/333–4861, 202/333–9543* ☾ *Nov.–Feb.* Ⓜ *Foggy Bottom/GWU.*

BOATING AND SAILING

The Chesapeake Bay is one of the great sailing basins of the world. For scenic and historical sightseeing, take a day trip to Annapolis, Maryland, the home of the U.S. Naval Academy. ■TIP➔ The popularity of boating and the many boating businesses in Annapolis make it one of the best civilian sailing centers on the East Coast.

Potomac River. Canoeing, sailing, and powerboating are popular in the Washington, D.C. area. Several places rent boats along the Potomac River north and south of the city. You can dip your paddle just about anywhere along the river—go canoeing in the C&O Canal, sailing in the widening river south of Alexandria, or even kayaking in the raging rapids at Great Falls, a 30-minute drive from the capital.

RENTALS

Belle Haven Marina. Belle Haven Marina, south of Reagan National Airport and Old Town Alexandria, rents two types of sailboats: Sunfish are $30 for two hours during the week and $35 for two hours on the weekend; Flying Scots are $46 for two hours during the week and $54 for two hours during the weekend. Canoes, jon boats, and kayaks are available for rent at $20 for two hours. Rentals are available from

April to October and prices for full-day rentals are available on the website. The marina takes reservations, which are useful during peak-season weekends. ✉ *George Washington Pkwy., Alexandria, Virginia* ☎ *703/768–0018* ⊕ *www.saildc.com.*

The Boathouse at Fletcher's Cove. The Boathouse at Fletcher's Cove, just north of Georgetown, rents 17-foot rowboats for $12 per hour and $22 per day. Canoes are available for rent at $12 per hour and $24 per day. Single kayaks are $10 per hour and $28 per day, while double kayaks are $17 per hour and $40 per day. ✉ *4940 Canal Rd., at Reservoir Rd., Georgetown* ☎ *202/244–0461* ⊕ *www.fletcherscove.com.*

Thompson's Boat Center. Thompson's Boat Center is near Georgetown and Theodore Roosevelt Island. The center rents canoes for $12 per hour and $24 per day. Single kayaks are $10 per hour and $28 per day, and double kayaks are $17 per hour and $40 per day. Rowing sculls are also available, but you must demonstrate prior experience and a suitably high skill level. Note: Thompson closes from Halloween through early March, based on the water's temperature. ✉ *2900 Virginia Ave. NW, Foggy Bottom* ☎ *202/333–4861, 202/333–9543* ⊕ *www.thompsonboatcenter.com* Ⓜ *Foggy Bottom/GWU.*

Tidal Basin Boathouse. The Tidal Basin Boathouse, in front of the Jefferson Memorial, rents paddleboats beginning in mid-March and usually ending in October. The entrance is on the east side of the Tidal Basin. You can rent two-passenger boats at $12 per hour and four-passenger boats at $19 per hour. ✉ *1501 Maine Ave. SW, The Mall* ☎ *202/479–2426* Ⓜ *Farragut W.*

FOOTBALL

Washington Redskins. The Washington Redskins has become one of the top three most valuable franchises in the NFL based on its 1983, '88, and '92 Super Bowl wins. As a result, despite the franchise's dry spell, diehard fans snap up season tickets year after year. Even though FedEx Field is the largest football stadium in the NFL with 91,000 seats, individual game-day tickets can be hard to come by if the team is enjoying a strong season. Your best bet is to check out StubHub (⊕ *www.stubhub*, the official ticket marketplace of the Redskins. Tickets can range anywhere from $75 to $1,200, depending on the match-up.)

10

■ **TIP→** Game tickets can be difficult to get, but fans can see the players up close and for free at training camp, held in August. The Redskins invite the public to attend their training camp in Ashburn, in nearby Loudoun County, Virginia. Camp begins in late July and continues through mid-August. The practices typically last from 90 minutes to two hours. Fans can bring their own chairs, and the players are usually available after practice to sign autographs. Call ahead to make sure the practices are open that day. A practice schedule is on the team's website. ☎ *301/276–6000 FedEx Field stadium* ⊕ *www.redskins.com.*

HIKING

Great hiking is available in and around Washington. Hikes and nature walks are listed in the Friday "Weekend" section of the *Washington Post*. Several area organizations sponsor outings, and most are guided.

Billy Goat Trail. The challenging Billy Goat Trail starts and ends at the C&O Canal Towpath below Great Falls and has some outstanding views of the wilder parts of the Potomac, along with some steep downhills and climbs. ⊠ *MacArthur Blvd., Potomac, Maryland* ☎ *301/413–0720* ⊕ *www.nps.gov/choh.*

Huntley Meadows Park. A 1,460-acre refuge in Alexandria, Huntley Meadows Park is made for birders. You can spot more than 200 species—from ospreys to owls, egrets, and ibis. Much of the park is wetlands, a favorite of aquatic species. A boardwalk circles through a marsh, enabling you to spot beaver lodges, and 4 miles of trails wend through the park, making it likely you'll see deer, muskrats, and river otters as well. The park is usually open daily dawn to dusk. ⊠ *3701 Lockheed Blvd., Alexandria, Virginia* ☎ *703/768–2525* ⊕ *www.fairfaxcounty.gov/ parks/huntley.*

Potomac-Appalachian Trail Club. The Potomac-Appalachian Trail Club sponsors hikes—usually free—on trails from Pennsylvania to Virginia, including the C&O Canal and the Appalachian Trail. ⊠ *118 Park St. SE, Vienna, Virginia* ☎ *703/242–0315* ⊕ *www.patc.net.*

Sierra Club. The Sierra Club has many regional outings; call for details. ☎ *202/547–2326* ⊕ *www.sierrapotomac.org.*

Fodor's Choice
★ **Theodore Roosevelt Island.** Theodore Roosevelt Island, designed as a memorial to the environmentally minded president, is a wildlife sanctuary off the George Washington Parkway near the Virginia side of the Potomac—close to Foggy Bottom, Georgetown, East Potomac Park, and the area near the Kennedy Center. Hikers and bicyclists can reach the island by crossing the Theodore Roosevelt Memorial Bridge or walking from the Rosslyn Metro. Many birds and other animals live in the island's marsh and forests. It's an easy but scenic stroll of good length, so surprisingly close to the city. ⊠ *Turkey Run Park, George Washington Memorial Pkwy.* ☎ *703/289–2500* ⊕ *www.nps.gov/this.*

Woodend. A self-guided nature trail winds through Woodend Nature Sanctuary, a verdant 40-acre estate that is the suburban Maryland headquarters of the local **Audubon Naturalist Society.** So bring those binoculars! On the grounds is a mansion, also called Woodend, designed in the 1920s by Jefferson Memorial architect John Russell Pope. You're never far from the trill of birdsong here, as the Audubon Society has turned the place into something of a private nature preserve, forbidding the use of toxic chemicals and leaving some areas in a wild, natural state. Programs include wildlife identification walks, environmental education programs, and a weekly Saturday bird walk September through June. A bookstore stocks titles on conservation, ecology, and birds. The grounds are open daily sunrise to sunset, and admission is free. ⊠ *8940 Jones Mill Rd., Chevy Chase, Maryland* ☎ *301/652–9188, 301/652–1088 for recent bird sightings* ⊕ *www.audubonnaturalist.org.*

HOCKEY

Fodor's Choice
★ **National Gallery of Art Ice Rink.** The National Gallery of Art Ice Rink, surrounded by the museum's Sculpture Garden, is one of the most popular outdoor winter venues in Washington. The art deco rink is perfect for a romantic date night, a fun daytime kid activity (when it's less crowded), or for just enjoying the wintry views of the National Archives and the sculptures as the sun sets. In spring the rink becomes a fountain. Admission is $8 for adults, skate rental is $3. ⊠ *Constitution Ave. NW, between 7th and 9th Sts., Downtown* ☎ *202/216–9397* ⊕ *www.nga. gov/ginfo/skating.htm* Ⓜ *Archives/Navy Memorial.*

★ **Washington Capitals.** One of pro hockey's top teams, the Washington Capitals play home games October through April at the Verizon Center and feature one of hockey's superstars, Alex Ovechkin. Seats on the main level range from $90 to $310, and those in the upper deck range from $35 to $60. Tickets can be purchased at the Verizon Center box office or from Ticketmaster. ⊠ *6th and F Sts., Downtown* ☎ *202/432–7328* ⊕ *www.washingtoncaps.com* Ⓜ *Gallery Pl./Chinatown.*

RUNNING

Running is one of the best ways to see the city, and several scenic uninterrupted trails wend through Downtown Washington and nearby northern Virginia. It can be dangerous to run at night on the trails or on the Mall, although the streets are fairly well-lighted. Even in daylight, it's best to run in pairs when venturing beyond public areas or heavily used sections of trails.

C&O Canal Towpath. The 89-mile-long C&O Canal Towpath in the C&O National Historical Park is a favorite of runners and, mostly gravel and dirt, is easy on knees and feet. Most popular is the stretch between the Key Bridge in Georgetown and the Boat House at Fletcher's Cove, about a 4-mile round-trip. ⊕ *www.nps.gov/choh.*

Fodor's Choice
★ **Mall.** The most popular running route in Washington is the 4.5-mile loop on the Mall around the Capitol and past the Smithsonian museums, the Washington Monument, the Reflecting Pool, and the Lincoln Memorial. At any time of day hundreds of runners and speed walkers make their way along the gravel pathways. For a longer run, veer south of the Mall on either side of the Tidal Basin and head for the Jefferson Memorial and East Potomac Park, the site of many races.

Mount Vernon Trail. Across the Potomac in Virginia is the Mount Vernon Trail. The 3.5-mile northern section begins near the pedestrian causeway leading to Theodore Roosevelt Island (directly across the river from the Kennedy Center) and goes past Ronald Reagan National Airport and on to Old Town Alexandria. You can get to the trail from the District by crossing either the Theodore Roosevelt Bridge at the Lincoln Memorial or the Rochambeau Memorial Bridge at the Jefferson Memorial. South of the airport, the trail runs down to the Washington Marina. The 9-mile southern section leads to Mount Vernon.

Rock Creek Park. The most popular run in Rock Creek Park is along a trail that follows the creek from Georgetown to the National Zoo,

10

about 4 miles round-trip. In summer there's considerable shade, and there are water fountains and an exercise station along the way. The roadway is closed to traffic on weekends.

INFORMATION AND ORGANIZATIONS

For low-key group runs, check the D.C. Road Runners' website (⊕ *www.dcroadrunners.org*). Pacers (⊕ *www.pacers.com*), a popular running-store chain, has weekly group runs at its six locations. Information on weekend races around Washington and comprehensive listings of running and walking events are posted online by a local publication, the *Washington Running Report* (⊕ *www.runwashington.com*).

Fleet Feet Sports Shop. Most Sunday mornings the Fleet Feet Sports Shop sponsors informal runs through Rock Creek Park and other areas. Runners gather at the store just before 9 am to embark on the 5-mile runs. ✉ *1841 Columbia Rd. NW, Adams Morgan* ☎ *202/387–3888* ⊕ *www.fleetfeetdc.com* Ⓜ Woodley Park/Zoo.

SOCCER

Fodor's Choice ★ **D.C. United.** D.C. United is one of the best Major League Soccer (U.S. pro soccer) teams. International matches, including some World Cup preliminaries, are often played on RFK Stadium's grass field, dedicated exclusively to soccer play. Games are April through September. You can buy tickets, which generally cost $23–$52 at the RFK Stadium ticket office or through the team's website, which offers special youth pricing. ✉ *Robert F. Kennedy Stadium, 2400 E. Capitol St. SE, Capitol Hill* ☎ *202/547–3134* ⊕ *www.dcunited.com* Ⓜ *Stadium.*

Shopping

WORD OF MOUTH

"Eastern Market is not that big and just reopened after a fire. But on the weekends, there is a huge flea market all around it. Fairly yuppified. Easy to get to by Metro in D.C."

—smetz

Updated by Kathryn McKay

Despite the fact that going to the "the Mall" in D.C. doesn't mean you're going shopping, Washington offers fabulous stores that sell serious or silly souvenirs, designer fashions, recycled and green goods, books about almost everything, and handicrafts. Even if you're headed to our nation's Mall, you'll discover that plenty of collections housed along the famous greensward, such as the Smithsonian museums and the National Gallery of Art, have plenty of interesting things to buy in their gift shops.

Beyond the Mall, many of the smaller one-of-a-kind shops survived the recession, including some designer boutiques, interesting specialty shops, and stores that have been part of the landscape for generations. Weekdays, Downtown street vendors offer a funky mix of jewelry; brightly patterned ties; buyer-beware watches; sunglasses; and African-inspired clothing, accessories, and art. Discriminating shoppers will find satisfaction at upscale malls on the city's outskirts. Of course, T-shirts and Capitol City souvenirs, with the city's iconic images on everything from candy bars to magnets, are in plentiful supply.

PLANNING

GALLERY HOPPING

Washington has three main gallery districts—Downtown, Dupont Circle, and Georgetown—though small galleries can be found all over in converted houses and storefronts. Whatever their location, many keep unusual hours and close entirely on Sunday and Monday. The *Washington Post* "Weekend" section (⊕ *www.washingtonpost.com*) and *Washington CityPaper* (⊕ *www.washingtoncitypaper.com*), published on Thursday, are excellent sources of information on current exhibits and hours.

HISTORIC WALKS

Shopping is the perfect way to acquaint yourself with some of D.C.'s distinguished neighborhoods. A quick diversion down a side street in Georgetown reveals the neighborhood's historic charm and current glamour. Peer around a corner in Dupont or Capitol Hill to see a true D.C. architecture classic—the row house. Wandering Downtown you are sure to bump into one of the nation's great neoclassical structures, whether it is the White House or the historic Hotel Monaco.

HOURS

Store hours vary greatly. In general, Georgetown stores are open late and on Sunday; stores Downtown that cater to office workers close as early as 5 pm and may not open at all on weekends. Some stores extend their hours on Thursday.

HOW TO SAVE MONEY

If you're willing to dig a bit, D.C. can be a savvy shopper's dream. Upscale consignment stores like Secondi in Dupont Circle and discount outlets like Nordstrom Rack in Friendship Heights provide an alternative to the surrounding luxury retail. Secondhand bookstores throughout the city provide hours of browsing and buying at welcoming prices.

WHITE HOUSE AREA AND FOGGY BOTTOM

In an area best known for the nation's most famous citizen, museums and the home of George Washington University are fun places to shop for official White House Christmas ornaments and Easter eggs, flags from all over the world, crafts made by living Native American artists and artisans, and even jewelry made from real government red tape. If you're looking for a tasty treat, two farmers' markets sell produce that's said to be as fresh as food grown in the White House garden. For an out-of-the-world treat, pick up a pack of astronaut ice cream at the National Air and Space Museum.

CRAFTS AND GIFTS

InfoShop. You won't find the *New York Times* bestsellers here, but you will find titles on world development issues, poverty, and other weighty issues along with fiction by writers from Africa, Central and South America, and Asia that are hard to find elsewhere. Lining the windows of this bookstore, stocked and run by the World Bank, are desk flags of countries from all over the world that sell for $5 each. Students, teachers, and government employees with IDs receive discounts. ⊠ *701 18th St. NW, White House Area* ☎ *202/458–4500* ⊕ *www.worldbank. org/infoshop* ⊗ *Weekdays 9:30–5:30* ⊗ *Closed weekends* Ⓜ *Farragut N, Farragut W.*

Museum Shop at Decatur House. Beyond the Web, there are only three places in D.C. to purchase official merchandise from the White House Historical Association: the temporary White House Visitor Center on the Ellipse, the Decatur House, and a small shop around the corner (740 Jackson Place NW). Decatur offers the greatest variety. From the popular Christmas ornaments to jewelry, ties, scarves, and accessories, the merchandise is well made. Ten dollars or less will get you cocktail

UPPER NORTHWEST
luxury & discount retailers in a suburban strip plus boutiques

ADAMS MORGAN
eclectic bohemian rummaging

U STREET CORRIDOR
small vintage, urban boutiques & chic home design stores

GEORGETOWN
retail chains, antiques & galleries, endless hours of cruising

DUPONT CIRCLE
books, coffee, galleries, perfect on the weekends

WHITE HOUSE AREA AND FOGGY BOTTOM
crafts, museum shops, and White House souvenirs

DOWNTOWN
modern home furnishings & specialty items

CAPITOL HILL AND NORTHEAST D.C.
Eastern Market plus neighborhood stores for unique gifts

Columbia Rd.

Florida Ave.

16th St.

Florida Ave.

New Hampshire Ave.

Vermont Ave.

Logan Circle

Massachusetts Ave.

Rock Creek

Rhode Island Ave.

Scott Circle

Thomas Circle

M St.

M St.

Whitehurst Fwy.

Washington Circle

K St.

New York Ave.

Pennsylvania Ave.

15th St.

14th St.

FOGGY BOTTOM

23rd St.

Virginia Ave.

Theodore Roosevelt Island

Constitution Ave.

THE MALL

Reflecting Pool

THE MONUMENTS

Independence Ave.

Arlington Memorial Br.

Columbia Island

Tidal Basin

Francis Case Memorial Br.

Washington Canal

Potomac River

VIRGINIA

0   500 yards

0   500 meters

napkins, bookmarks, or a wooden Easter egg. The more expensive merchandise includes silk scarves, hand-painted enamel boxes, and jewelry with cameos of the White House. But the charming staff offers fun facts about the White House for free. ✉ *1610 H St. NW, White House Area* ☎ *202/218–4338* ⊕ *www.whitehousehistory.org/decatur-house/* ⊙ *Weekdays 9–4* ⊙ *Closed weekends.*

National Air and Space Museum Store. Of course, one of the most visited museums in the world has a huge gift shop! The lower level of the three-floor, 12,000-square-foot store has a small clearance section, tons of toys and games, and glow-in-the-dark jewelry and nail polish. The upper level showcases higher quality goods that will appeal to more serious aviation fans, such as hardcover books and authentic flight jackets. Most merchandise is on the middle level. Space pens that work upside down and freeze-dried "astronaut" ice cream are best sellers. ■**TIP**➔ If the main store is too crowded, you can pick up the most popular inexpensive items at small retail outlets on the first and second floors of the museum. ✉ *Independence Ave. and 6th St. SW, The Mall* ☎ *202/633–4510.*

★ **National Archives Store.** In a town full of museum shops, the National Archives Store stands out, with bespoke merchandise that's only available here. Authentic-looking copies of the Constitution and other historical documents are printed in Pennsylvania and replicas of stationery used in the Civil War come from Maine. The popular "red tape" jewelry is crafted by an Archives employee who works in the building and uses real red tape that bound Government documents: hence the phrase "cut through the red tape." Other popular products feature Rosie the Riveter, Nixon meeting Elvis, and a vitamin doughnut. A 2012 expansion makes room for interactive games associated with special exhibits. When there's a line outside for admission to the Archives, store employees roll out a cart with cold water and cool merchandise. ✉ *Constitution Ave. between 7th and 9th Sts., The Mall* ☎ *202/357–5271* ⊕ *www. archives.gov* Ⓜ *Archives/Navy Memorial.*

MARKETS

FRESHFARM Market. Pick up a crab cake, an empanada, or a Mexican-style ice pop at this farmers' market on Wednesdays from 3 to 7, early April through November. Or pick up similar fare near Lafayette Park (810 Vermont Ave., NW) on Fridays from 11 to 2:30, May through October. Of course, both locations (and FRESHFARM markets in Dupont Circle on Sundays, H Street, NE, on Saturday mornings, and Penn Quarter on Thursday afternoons) sell local, organic fruits and vegetables. ✉ *Foggy Bottom, I St., between New Hampshire and 24th St. NW, White House Area* ☎ *202/362–8889* ⊕ *www. freshfarmmarkets.org.*

USDA Farmers' Market. Blueberry popcorn anyone? On Friday from early June until mid-November from 10 to 2, pick up fresh fruits, vegetables, breads, baked goods, and flavored popcorn across from the Smithsonian Metro station. Appropriately, the market is in the parking lot of the U.S. Department of Agriculture building. ✉ *12th St. and Independence Ave. SW, White House Area* ⊕ *www.ams.usda.gov* ⊙ *Early June–mid–Nov., Fri. 10–2.*

CAPITOL HILL AND NORTHEAST D.C.

Capitol Hill is a shopper's dream as Eastern Market and the unique shops and boutiques clustered around the historic redbrick building offer hours of browsing fun. Inside Eastern Market are produce and meat counters, plus the Market Five art gallery. ■ TIP → The flea market, held on weekends outdoors, presents nostalgia and local crafts by the crateful. There's also a farmers' market on Saturday. Along 7th Street you can find a number of small shops selling such specialties as art books, hand-woven rugs, and antiques. Cross Pennsylvania Avenue and head south on 8th Street for historic Barracks Row. Shops, bars, and restaurants inhabit the charming row houses leading toward the Anacostia River. The other shopping lure on the Hill is Union Station, D.C.'s gorgeous train station. Beautifully restored, it now houses both mall shops and Amtrak and commuter trains.

Keep in mind that Union Station and Eastern Market are on opposite sides of the Hill. The Eastern Market Metro stop is the midpoint between the Eastern Market strip and Barracks Row; Union Station is several blocks away. You can certainly walk to Union Station from the Eastern Market stop, but it might be taxing after the time already spent on your feet in the shops.

QUICK BITES

The Market Lunch. Locals line up for fried fish and crab-cake sandwiches at this greasy grill next to the fish counter in Eastern Market's food bazaar. Try their specialty, blueberry pancakes, on Saturdays from 8 to noon. ✉ *Eastern Market, 225 7th St. SE, North corner of market, Capitol Hill* ☎ *202/547–8444* ⊙ *Closed Mon.* Ⓜ *Eastern Market.*

SHOPPING MALL

Union Station. Resplendent with marble floors and vaulted ceilings, Union Station is a shopping mall as well as a train station. Upscale retailers include such familiar chains as L'Occitane, White House/Black Market, and Godiva, as well as a bookstore, restaurants, and a food court. The east hall is filled with vendors of expensive domestic and international wares who sell from open stalls. Making History sells a more eclectic selection of souvenirs than you'll find in most gift shops. The Christmas season brings lights, a train display, and seasonal gift shops to Union Station. ✉ *50 Massachusetts Ave. NE, Capitol Hill* ☎ *202/289–1908* ⊕ *www.unionstationdc.com* Ⓜ *Union Station.*

BOOKS

Capitol Hill Books. Pop into this three-story maze of used books to browse through a wonderful collection of out-of-print history books, political and fiction writings, and mysteries. ✉ *657 C St. SE, Capitol Hill* ☎ *202/544–1621* ⊕ *www.capitolhillbooks-dc.com* Ⓜ *Eastern Market.*

☺ **Fairy Godmother.** This specialty store, which opened in 1984, features books for children, from infants through teens, in English, Spanish, and French. It also sells puppets, toys, craft sets, and CDs. ✉ *319 7th St. SE, Capitol Hill* ☎ *202/547–5474* Ⓜ *Eastern Market.*

FIVE GREAT SHOPPING EXPERIENCES

11

Eastern Market, Capitol Hill Area: Artists, musicians, farmers, and more make this beautifully restored market a feast for the senses. Most vendors accept only cash, but ATMs are nearby.

Kramerbooks & Afterwords, Dupont Circle: Meeting up at Kramerbooks for a lazy Sunday afternoon of brunch and shopping is a quintessential D.C. experience.

Miss Pixie's Furnishings and Whatnot, U Street Corridor: The outside of the store may be bright pink, but everything inside is "green." Buyers flock to Miss Pixie's for vintage furniture, home goods, and clothes.

National Archives Store, The Mall: The building where you can see the Declaration of Independence is also home to a store full of all-American gifts, including jewelry made out of real "red tape."

Tiny Jewel Box, Downtown: Since 1930, one family has owned and run this gem of a shop. On the day that her husband was inaugurated, First Lady Michelle Obama presented former First Lady Laura Bush with a custom-made leather bound journal and silver pen from this shop.

CHILDREN'S CLOTHING

☺ **Dawn Price Baby.** The infant and toddler clothing at this friendly rowhouse boutique has been carefully selected with an eye for supercomfortable fabrics and distinct designs. The shop also stocks toys, gifts, strollers, and bibs for baby Democrats and Republicans. There's a second location in Georgetown. ⊠ *325 7th St. SE, Capitol Hill* ☎ *202/543–2920* ⊕ *www.dawnpricebaby.com* ☉ *Closed Mon.* Ⓜ *Eastern Market.*

CRAFTS AND GIFTS

Fodor'sChoice
★ **Homebody.** Original artwork, contemporary rugs, delicious-smelling candles, modern kitchen items, furniture, and an eclectic mix of jewelry, bags, and wallets crowd this sophisticated and irreverent boutique. ⊠ *715 8th St. SE, Capitol Hill* ☎ *202/544–8445* ⊕ *www.homebodydc. com* ☉ *Closed Mon.* Ⓜ *Eastern Market.*

Woven History/Silk Road. Landmarks in this bohemian neighborhood, these connected stores sell handmade treasures from small villages around the world. Silk Road sells home furnishings, gifts, clothing, rugs, and accessories made in Asian mountain communities. Woven History's rugs are made the old-fashioned way, with vegetable dyes and hand-spun wool. ⊠ *311–315 7th St. SE, Capitol Hill* ☎ *202/543–1705* ⊕ *www.wovenhistory.com* ☉ *Closed Mon.* Ⓜ *Eastern Market.*

MARKET

Fodor'sChoice
★ **Eastern Market.** Vibrantly colored produce and flowers; freshly caught fish; fragrant cheeses; and tempting sweets are sold by independent vendors at Eastern Market, which first opened its doors in 1873. On weekends a flea market and an arts-and-crafts market add to the fun. After the redbrick building was gutted by fire in 2007, a $22-million reconstruction project restored it to its original Victorian grandeur. Now it is a vibrant and lively gathering place, complete with

entertainment, art showings, and a pottery studio. ⊠ *7th St. and North Carolina Ave. SE, Capitol Hill* ⊕ *www.easternmarket-dc.com* ⊗ *Closed Mon.* Ⓜ *Eastern Market.*

WOMEN'S CLOTHING

Forecast. If you like classic, contemporary styles, Forecast should be in your future. It sells silk and wool-blend sweaters in solid, muted tones for women seeking elegant but practical clothing from brands like Yansi Fugel and Eileen Fisher. The housewares and gifts selection on the first floor is colorful and of high quality. ⊠ *218 7th St. SE, Capitol Hill* ☎ *202/547–7337* ⊗ *Closed Mon.* Ⓜ *Eastern Market.*

DOWNTOWN

Downtown D.C. is spread out and sprinkled with federal buildings and museums. Shopping options run the gamut from the Gallery Place shopping center to small art galleries and bookstores. Gallery Place houses familiar chain stores like Urban Outfitters, Bed, Bath & Beyond, Ann Taylor Loft, and Aveda; it also has a movie theater and a bowling alley. Other big names in the Downtown area include Macy's and chain stores like H&M and Banana Republic. With its many offices, Downtown tends to shut down at 5 pm sharp, with the exception of the department stores and larger chain stores. A jolly happy-hour crowd springs up after working hours and families and fans fill the streets during weekend sporting events. The revitalized Penn Quarter has some of the best restaurants in town peppered among its galleries and specialty stores.

The worthwhile shops are not concentrated in one area, however. The Gallery Place Metro stop provides the most central starting point—you can walk south to the galleries and design shops, or west toward Metro Center and Farragut North, though this trek is only for the ambitious. Although Gallery Place is a nightlife hot spot, Metro Center and the Farragut area are largely silent after working hours.

CRAFTS AND GIFTS

Après Peau. Local dermatologist Tina Alster sells her customized collection of moisturizers, perfume, and lotions in her bright and airy shop. ⊠ *1430 K St. NW, Downtown* ☎ *202/628–8855* ⊕ *www.skinlaser.com* ⊗ *Closed weekends* Ⓜ *Farragut N.*

Fodor's Choice
★

Fahrney's. What began in 1929 as a repair shop and a pen bar—a place to fill your fountain pen before setting out for work—is now a wonderland for anyone who loves a good writing instrument. You'll find pens in silver, gold, and lacquer by the world's leading manufacturers. ⊠ *1317 F St. NW, Downtown* ☎ *202/628–9525* ⊕ *www.fahrneyspens. com* ⊗ *Closed Sun.* Ⓜ *Metro Center.*

★ **Indian Craft Shop.** Jewelry, pottery, sand paintings, weavings, and baskets from more than 45 Native American tribes, including Navajo, Pueblo, Zuni, Cherokee, Lakota, and Seminole, are at your fingertips here—as long as you have a photo ID to enter the federal building. Items range from inexpensive jewelry (as little as $5) on up to collector-quality art pieces (more than $1,000). This shop has been open since 1938. ⊠ *U.S.*

11

D.C.'s Museum Shops

Would someone in your life love a replica of the Hope diamond? It's waiting for you at the gift shop in the National Museum of Natural History. With a wide range of merchandise and price points, from inexpensive postcards to pricey pottery, museum gift shops allow you the flexibility to bring home a small memento of your visit to the nation's capital or to invest in a piece of American art or history. Museum gift shops offer everything from period jewelry reproductions to science kits for kids, not to mention prints and postcards of the masterpiece paintings in the permanent collections. Prices are no higher than you'd find in comparable stores. Another bonus: You won't pay tax on anything purchased in a Smithsonian museum.

Department of the Interior, 1849 C St. NW, Room 1023, Downtown ☎ *202/208–4056* ⊕ *www.indiancraftshop.com* ☉ *Closed weekends, except 3rd Sat. of each month* Ⓜ *Farragut W or Farragut N.*

FOOD AND WINE

Fodor'sChoice
★
Cowgirl Creamery. A California original, this self-titled "cheese shop" has an educated staff that can help you find the perfect block (through many taste tests) as well as a matching wine or olive spread. Their artisan cheeses hail from the Bay area, from local cheese makers, and from points beyond. On Thursday, from 5 to 7 pm, a cheesemonger slices and pours at informal cheese and beer tastings; on Friday from 5 to 7 pm, the pairings continue, with wine rather than beer. ✉ *919 F St. NW, Downtown* ☎ *202/393–6880* ⊕ *www.cowgirlcreamery.com* ☉ *Closed Sun.* Ⓜ *Gallery Pl.*

JEWELRY

Fodor'sChoice
★
Tiny Jewel Box. Despite its name, this venerable D.C. favorite contains six floors of precious and semiprecious wares, including unique gifts, home accessories, vintage pieces, and works by well-known designers, including David Yurman, Penny Preville, and Alex Sepkus. The Federal Collection on the sixth floor features handmade boxes and paperweights with decoupages of vintage prints of Washington commissioned by the Tiny Jewel Box. In 2011, *InStore Magazine* named this family-run store "America's Coolest Jewelry Store." ✉ *1147 Connecticut Ave. NW, Downtown* ☎ *202/393–2747* ⊕ *www.tinyjewelbox. com* ☉ *Closed Sun.* Ⓜ *Farragut N.*

SPAS AND BEAUTY SALONS

Andre Chreky. Housed in an elegantly renovated Victorian town house, this salon offers complete services—hair, nails, facials, waxing, and makeup. And because it's a favorite of the Washington elite, you might just overhear a tidbit or two on who's going to what black-tie function with whom. Adjacent whirlpool pedicure chairs allow two friends to get pampered simultaneously. ✉ *1604 K St. NW, Downtown* ☎ *202/293–9393* ⊕ *www.andrechreky.com* Ⓜ *Farragut N.*

The Grooming Lounge. Most spas are geared to women, but guys are pampered here. You can find old-fashioned hot-lather shaves, haircuts, and business manicures and pedicures—everything a man needs to look terrific. The hair- and skin-care products—from Clarins, Billy Jealousy, and Malin and Goetz, to name just a few—are worth a visit even if you don't have time for a service. ⊠ *1745 L St. NW, Downtown* ☎ *202/466–8900* ⊕ *www.groominglounge.com* Ⓜ *Farragut N.*

WOMEN'S CLOTHING

Coup de Foudre. All the upscale lingerie in this inviting, elegant boutique hails from France. Coup de Foudre—which translates to "love at first sight"—specializes in friendly, personalized bra fittings. ⊠ *1008 E St. NW, Downtown* ☎ *202/393–0878* ⊕ *www.coupdefoudrelingerie.com* ⊗ *Closed Sun.* Ⓜ *Metro Center.*

Rizik Bros. This tony, patrician Washington institution offers designer women's clothing and expert advice. The sales staff will help find just the right style from the store's inventory, which is particularly strong in formal dresses. Take the elevator up from the northwest corner of Connecticut Avenue and L Street. ⊠ *1100 Connecticut Ave. NW, Downtown* ☎ *202/223–4050* ⊕ *www.riziks.com* Ⓜ *Farragut N.*

GEORGETOWN

Although Georgetown is not on a Metro line and street parking is non-existent, people still flock here to shop. This is also the capital's center for famous residents, as well as being a hot spot for restaurants, bars, and nightclubs.

National chains and designer shops now stand side by side with the specialty shops that first gave the district its allure, but the historic neighborhood is still charming and its street scene lively. Most stores lie east and west on M Street and to the north on Wisconsin Avenue. The intersection of M and Wisconsin is the nexus for chain stores and big-name designer shops. The farther you venture in any direction from this intersection, the more eclectic and interesting the shops become. Some of the big-name stores are worth a look for their architecture alone; several shops blend traditional Georgetown town-house exteriors with airy modern showroom interiors.

Shopping in Georgetown can be expensive, but you don't have to add expensive parking lot fees to your total bill. ■ TIP→ The D.C. Circulator is your best bet for getting into and out of Georgetown, especially if it's hot or if you are laden down with many purchases. This $1 bus runs along M Street and up Wisconsin, passing the major shopping strips. The nearest Metro, Foggy Bottom/GWU, is a 10- to 15-minute walk from the shops.

QUICK BITES

DolceZZa. The handmade gelato and sorbet at this all-white storefront are divine, especially during the heat of summer. The flavors, such as Valrhona chocolate amargo, are endlessly inventive. Strawberry-, peach-, apple-, and clementine-flavored sorbets are available seasonally. Espresso and churros will warm winter afternoons. ⊠ *1560 Wisconsin Ave. NW, Georgetown* ☎ *202/333–4646* ⊕ *www.dolcezzagelato.com.*

ANTIQUES AND COLLECTIBLES

Cherub Antiques Gallery & Michael Getz Antiques. Two dealers have shared this Victorian row house since 1983. Michael Getz Antiques carries fireplace equipment and silver. Cherub Antiques Gallery specializes in art nouveau and art deco. A glass case by the door holds a collection of more than 100 cocktail shakers, including Prohibition-era pieces disguised as penguins, roosters, and dumbbells. ✉ *2918 M St. NW, Georgetown* ☎ *202/337–2224 Cherub Gallery, 202/338–3811 Michael Getz Antiques* ⊕ *www.trocadero.com/cherubgallery* Ⓜ *Foggy Bottom/GWU.*

Fodor's Choice
★

Jean Pierre Antiques. Very Georgetown, but fairly close to Dupont Circle, this gorgeous shop sells antique furniture and gifts from France, Germany, Sweden, and Italy. In 2011, the charming owner added vintage American Lucite tables to his inventory. ✉ *2601 and 2603 P St. NW, Georgetown* ☎ *202/337–1731* ⊕ *www.jeanpierreantiques. com* Ⓜ *Dupont Circle.*

Marston Luce. House and garden accessories are in the mix here, but the emphasis is on 18th- and 19th-century French country furniture discovered by the owner on yearly buying trips in Europe. They also carry Scandinavian painted furniture. ✉ *1651 Wisconsin Ave. NW, Georgetown* ☎ *202/333–6800* ⊕ *www.marstonluce.com* ☉ *Closed Sun.* Ⓜ *Foggy Bottom/GWU.*

Opportunity Shop of the Christ Child Society. This Georgetown landmark, staffed by volunteers, sells fine jewelry, antiques, crystal, silver, and porcelain on consignment. Prices are moderate, and profits go to a good cause—the Christ Child Society, which provides for the needs of local children and young mothers. ✉ *1427 Wisconsin Ave. NW, Georgetown* ☎ *202/333–6635* ⊕ *www.christchilddc.org* Ⓜ *Foggy Bottom/GWU.*

ART GALLERIES

Many of Georgetown's galleries are on side streets. Their holdings are primarily work by established artists.

Addison Ripley. This well-respected gallery exhibits contemporary work by national and local artists, including painters Manon Cleary and Wolf Kahn and photographer Frank Hallam Day. ✉ *1670 Wisconsin Ave. NW, Georgetown* ☎ *202/338–5180* ⊕ *www.addisonripleyfineart.com* ☉ *Closed Sun. and Mon.* Ⓜ *Foggy Bottom/GWU.*

Appalachian Spring. The glossy wooden jewelry boxes displayed here are treasures in their own right. Traditional and contemporary American-made crafts—including art glass, pottery, jewelry, homewares, and toys—fill this lovely shop. There's also an outpost in Union Station's East Hall. ✉ *1415 Wisconsin Ave. NW, Georgetown* ☎ *202/337–5780* ⊕ *www.appalachianspring.com.*

Galleries 1054. Several distinct galleries live under one roof at this location. ✉ *1054 31st St. NW, Georgetown* ☉ *Closed Sun. and Mon.* Ⓜ *Foggy Bottom/GWU.*

Parish. Parish features contemporary work in all mediums by primarily African-American artists. ☎ *202/944–2310* ⊕ *www.parishgallery.com.*

Alla Rogers. Alla Rogers has contemporary Eastern European, Russian, and American art and photography. ☎202/333–8595.

Winter Palace Studio. This gallery features contemporary realism oil paintings by Russian painter Natasha Mokina and other artists, including her students. ✉*Georgetown* ☎*301/263–0000* ⊕*www. winterpalacestudio.com.*

BOOKS

Bridge Street Books. This charming independent store focuses on politics, history, philosophy, poetry, literature, film, and Judaica. ✉*2814 Pennsylvania Ave. NW, Georgetown* ☎*202/965–5200* ⊕*www. bridgestreetbooks.com* Ⓜ*Foggy Bottom/GWU.*

CHILDREN'S CLOTHING

Magic Wardrobe. This shop caters to kids (and parents) who prefer and can afford preppy clothes reminiscent of school uniforms—think collared shirts and jumpers for girls and cargo pants and button-down shirts for boys. Both American and European designers are on hand, plus clothes from the shop's own private label for kids from newborn to size 16. The shop also carries shoes. ✉*1661 Wisconsin Ave. NW, Georgetown* ☎*202/333–0353* ⊕*www.themagicwardrobe.com.*

Ⓒ **Tugoo Toys and Yiro.** One hundred percent organic, Yiro clothing (newborn to 10 years) is produced without chemicals and is colored only with natural dyes (and yes, the outfits are soft and attractive). A baby registry will help you pick the perfect eco-friendly outfit or toy for the environmentally conscious mom. ✉*1319 Wisconsin Ave. NW, Georgetown* ☎*202/333–0032* ⊕*www.yirostores.com.*

HOME FURNISHINGS

Fodor's Choice ★ **A Mano.** The store's name is Italian for "by hand," and it lives up to its name, stocking colorful hand-painted ceramics, hand-dyed tablecloths, blown-glass stemware, and other home and garden accessories by Italian and French artisans. There are even adorable kids' gifts. Items are now also available in their online catalog. ✉*1677 Wisconsin Ave. NW, Georgetown* ☎*202/298–7200* ⊕*www.amano.bz.*

Theodore's. A Washington institution, Theodore's is the place to visit for ultramod housewares, from stylish furniture to accessories, leather, rugs, and upholstery that make a statement. There's an excellent selection of wall-storage units for almost all tastes. ✉*2233 Wisconsin Ave. NW, Georgetown* ☎*202/333–2300* ⊕*www.theodores.com.*

MEN'S AND WOMEN'S CLOTHING

Hu's Wear. Ladies looking for just –off-the-runway looks to go with their Hu's Shoes will find designs by Sonia Rykiel, Alexander McQueen, and Proenza Schouler. ✉*2906 M St. NW, Georgetown* ☎*202/342–2020* ⊕*www.husonline.com.*

relish. In fashionable Cady's Alley, this dramatic space holds a women's collection handpicked seasonally by the owner. Modern, elegant, and practical selections include European classics and well-tailored modern designers, such as Jill Sander, Marni, and Dries Van Noten. ✉*3312 Cady's Alley NW, Georgetown* ☎*202/333–5343* ⊕*www.relishdc.com* ⊗*Closed Sun.* Ⓜ*Foggy Bottom/GWU.*

DID YOU KNOW?

Georgetown, one of D.C.'s oldest and storied neighborhoods, is a great spot for political celebrity sightings. Heavyweights like Senator John Kerry, political pundit George Stephanopoulos, and journalist Bob Woodward live here.

SHOES

Fodor's Choice
★

Hu's Shoes. This cutting-edge shoe store would shine in Paris, Tokyo, or New York. Luckily for us, it brings ballet flats, heels, and boots from designers like Chloé, Givenchy, Céline, Proenza Schouler, and Sonia Rykiel right here to Georgetown. ⊠ *3005 M St. NW, Georgetown* ☎ *202/342–0202* ⊕ *www.husonline.com* Ⓜ *Foggy Bottom/GWU.*

Sassanova. There are high-end shoes in this girly shop for every occasion—be it a walk on the beach or through a boardroom. Brands carried include the latest from Kate Spade and Sigerson Morrison. Jewelry, bags, and even a selection of upscale casual clothing round out the selection. ⊠ *1641 Wisconsin Ave. NW, Georgetown* ☎ *202/471–4400* ⊕ *www.sassanova.com.*

SPAS AND BEAUTY SALONS

Fodor's Choice
★

Blue Mercury. Hard-to-find skin-care lines—such as Laura Mercier and Trish McEvoy—are what set this homegrown, now national, chain apart. The retail space up front sells soaps, lotions, perfumes, cosmetics, and skin- and hair-care products. Behind the glass door is the "skin gym," where you can treat yourself to facials, waxing, and oxygen treatments. ⊠ *3059 M St. NW, Georgetown* ☎ *202/965–1300* ⊕ *www.bluemercury.com* Ⓜ *Foggy Bottom/GWU* ⊠ *1619 Connecticut Ave. NW, Dupont Circle* ☎ *202/462–1300* Ⓜ *Dupont Circle.*

WOMEN'S CLOTHING

The Phoenix. Owned and operated by the Hays family since 1955, here you can find contemporary clothing in natural fibers by designers such as Eileen Fisher and Flax, as well as jewelry from Germany, Turkey, and Italy, and fine- and folk-art pieces from Mexico—all under a roof with 30 solar panels. ⊠ *1514 Wisconsin Ave. NW, Georgetown* ☎ *202/338–4404* ⊕ *www.thephoenixdc.com.*

Urban Chic. It's hard to imagine a fashionista who wouldn't find something here—whether she could afford it might be another story. Gorgeous suits, jeans, cocktail dresses, and accessories from Shoshanna, Tibi, Ella Moss, Rebecca Taylor, and Susana Monaco are to be had. The handbags are a highlight. ⊠ *1626 Wisconsin Ave. NW, Georgetown* ☎ *202/338–5398* ⊕ *www.urbanchiconline.com.*

Wink. While the clientele and styles skew toward the young and trendy, women of all ages shop in this subterranean space for coveted jeans and colorful, sparkly tops, dresses, and jewelry. Theory, Diane von Furstenberg, and Rebecca Taylor are among the labels carried. ⊠ *3109 M St. NW, Georgetown* ☎ *202/338–9465* ⊕ *www.shopwinkdc.com* Ⓜ *Foggy Bottom/GWU.*

DUPONT CIRCLE

You might call Dupont Circle a younger, less staid version of Georgetown—almost as pricey but with more apartment buildings than houses. Its many restaurants, offbeat shops, and specialty book and record stores give it a cosmopolitan air. The street scene here is more urban than Georgetown's, with bike messengers and chess aficionados filling up the park. The Sunday farmers' market is a popular destination for organic food, fresh cheese, homemade soap, and hand-spun wool. To the south of Dupont Circle proper are several boutiques and familiar retail stores close to the Farragut and Farragut North Metro stops. Burberry and Thomas Pink both have stores in this area of Dupont.

QUICK BITES

Kramerbooks & Afterwords. Serving brunch in the morning, snacks in the afternoon, cocktails in the evening, and coffee all day long, Kramer's is the perfect spot for a break. Try to snag an outside table, drop your shopping bags, and watch the world go by. "Sharezies," appetizers served on tiered plates, are perfect for, well, sharing. ⊠ *1517 Connecticut Ave. NW, Dupont Circle* ☎ *202/387–1400* ⊕ *www.kramers.com* Ⓜ *Dupont Circle.*

ANTIQUES AND COLLECTIBLES

Burton Marinkovich Fine Art. You know you've reached this gallery when you spot the small front yard with two abstract sculptures by Lesley Dill and Leonard Cave. The gallery has works by modern and contemporary masters, including Ross Bleckner, Richard Diebenkorn, David Hockney, Kandinsky, Matisse, Miró, Picasso, and others. Rare modern illustrated books and British linocuts from the Grosvenor School are also specialties. ⊠ *1506 21st St. NW, Dupont Circle* ☎ *202/296–6563* ⊕ *www.burtonmarinkovich.com* ☉ *Closed Sun. and Mon.* Ⓜ *Dupont Circle.*

Geoffrey Diner Gallery. A must for hard-core antiques shoppers on the hunt for 19th-, 20th-, and 21st-century wares, this store sells contemporary fine art, Tiffany lamps, Arts and Crafts pieces from pivotal designers from Europe and the United States. It's open Saturday and by appointment only. ⊠ *1730 21st St. NW, Dupont Circle* ☎ *202/483–5005* ⊕ *www.dinergallery.com* ☉ *Closed Sun.–Fri.* Ⓜ *Dupont Circle.*

Fodor'sChoice ★ **Hemphill Fine Arts.** This spacious gem of a contemporary gallery shows mid-career and established artists in all media, such as William Christenberry, John Dreyfuss, Linling Lu, and Julie Wolfe. ⊠ *1515 14th St. NW, 3rd fl., Logan Circle* ☎ *202/234–5601* ⊕ *www.hemphillfinearts. com* ☉ *Closed Sun. and Mon.* Ⓜ *Dupont Circle.*

BOOKS

Fodor'sChoice ★ **Kramerbooks & Afterwords.** One of Washington's best-loved independents, this cozy shop has a choice selection of fiction and nonfiction. Open all night on Friday and Saturday, it's a convenient meeting place. Kramerbooks shares space with a café that has late-night dining and live music from Wednesday to Saturday. ■TIP➔ There's a computer with free Internet access available in the bar. ⊠ *1517 Connecticut Ave. NW, Dupont Circle* ☎ *202/387–1400* ⊕ *www.kramers.com* Ⓜ *Dupont Circle.*

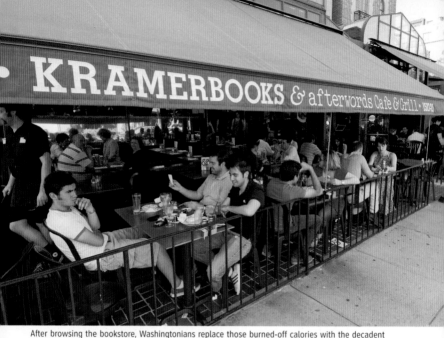

After browsing the bookstore, Washingtonians replace those burned-off calories with the decadent Dysfunctional Family Sundae at Kramerbooks & Afterwords.

★ **Second Story Books.** A used-books and -records emporium that stays open late, Second Story may lead bibliophiles to browse for hours. ✉ *2000 P St. NW, Dupont Circle* ☎ *202/659–8884* ⊕ *www.secondstorybooks. com* Ⓜ *Dupont Circle.*

CHILDREN'S CLOTHING

Kid's Closet. If filling a little one's closet is on your list, stop here for high-quality contemporary infant and children's clothing and toys. Open since 1982, the shop carries sizes 0–7 for boys and 0–16 for girls. ✉ *1226 Connecticut Ave. NW, Dupont Circle* ☎ *202/429–9247* ⊕ *www.kidsclosetdc.com* ⊗ *Closed Sun.* Ⓜ *Dupont Circle.*

CRAFTS AND GIFTS

Beadazzled. A rainbow of ready-to-string beads fills the cases at this appealing shop. They also stock jewelry as well as books on crafts history and techniques. Check their website for a class schedule. ✉ *1507 Connecticut Ave. NW, Dupont Circle* ☎ *202/265–2323* ⊕ *www. beadazzled.net* Ⓜ *Dupont Circle.*

The Chocolate Moose. This store is simple, sheer fun for adults and kids alike. Looking for clacking, windup teeth? You can find them here, along with unusual greeting cards, strange boxer shorts, and unique handcrafts. If playing with all those fun toys makes you hungry, you can pick up a select line of premium European chocolates. ✉ *1743 L St. NW, Dupont Circle* ☎ *202/463–0992* ⊕ *www.chocolatemoosedc. com* ⊗ *Closed Sun.* Ⓜ *Farragut N.*

HOME FURNISHINGS

Reincarnations. Reincarnations is a neighborhood favorite. It's hard to pinpoint one style that dominates—trendy, antique, funky—so everyone can find something to like. ✉ *1401 14th St. NW, Logan Circle* ☎ *202/319–1606* ⊕ *www.reincarnationsfurnishings.com* ☉ *Mon.* Ⓜ *Dupont Circle.*

Tabletop. Evoking a museum gift shop, this is a delightful place to find tiles by Canadian designer Xenia Taler, Marimekko accessories, and Daphne Olive jewelry, as well as modern accessories, pillows, and rugs. ✉ *1608 20th St. NW, Dupont Circle* ☎ *202/387–7117* ⊕ *www.tabletopdc.com* Ⓜ *Dupont Circle.*

JEWELRY

lou lou. A "blingful" boutique jam-packed with costume jewelry and bags at price points that please the purse draws lots of ladies looking for the latest trendy item. ✉ *1601 Connecticut Ave. NW, Dupont Circle* ☎ *202/588–0027* ⊕ *www.loulouboutiques.com* Ⓜ *Dupont Circle* ✉ *950 F St. NW, Downtown* ☎ *202/737–0545* Ⓜ *Gallery Place/Chinatown or Metro Center.*

MEN'S CLOTHING

J. Press. Like its flagship store, founded in Connecticut in 1902 as a custom shop for Yale University, this Washington outlet is resolutely traditional: Shetland and Irish wool sport coats are a specialty. ✉ *1801 L St. NW, Dupont Circle* ☎ *202/857–0120* ⊕ *www.jpressonline.com* ☉ *Closed Sun.* Ⓜ *Farragut N.*

WOMEN'S CLOTHING

Fodor'sChoice
★
Betsy Fisher. Catering to women of all ages and sizes in search of contemporary and trendy styles, this store stocks one-of-a-kind accessories, clothes, shoes, and jewelry by well-known designers like Diane Von Furstenberg. A small selection of up-and-coming designs is also available. ✉ *1224 Connecticut Ave. NW, Dupont Circle* ☎ *202/785–1975* ⊕ *www.betsyfisher.com* Ⓜ *Dupont Circle.*

Fodor'sChoice
★
Secondi. One of the city's finest consignment shops, Secondi carries a well-chosen selection of women's designer and casual clothing, accessories, and shoes. The brands carried include Marc Jacobs, Louis Vuitton, Donna Karan, Prada, and Anthropologie. ✉ *1702 Connecticut Ave. NW, 2nd fl., Dupont Circle* ☎ *202/667–1122* ⊕ *www.secondi.com* Ⓜ *Dupont Circle.*

ADAMS MORGAN

Scattered among the dozens of Latin, Ethiopian, and international restaurants in this most bohemian of Washington neighborhoods are a score of eccentric shops. If quality is what you seek, Adams Morgan and nearby Woodley Park can be a minefield; tread cautiously. Still, for the bargain hunter it's great fun. ■TIP➔ If bound for a specific shop, you may want to call ahead to verify hours. Adams Morganites are often not clock-watchers, although you can be sure an afternoon stroll on the weekend will yield a few hours of great browsing. The evening hours bring scores of revelers to the row, so plan to go before dark unless you want to couple your shopping with a party pit stop.

How to get there is another question. Though the Woodley Park/Zoo/Adams Morgan Metro stop is technically closer to the 18th Street strip (where the interesting shops are), getting off here means that you will have to walk over the bridge on Calvert Street. Five minutes longer, the walk from the Dupont Circle Metro stop is more scenic; you cruise north on 18th Street through tree-lined streets of row houses and embassies. You can also easily catch Metrobus 42 or a cab from Dupont to Adams Morgan.

QUICK BITES

Tryst Coffeehouse. Relax with a latte on one of the couches or cushiony chairs at this neighborhood hangout. They have a surprisingly large menu that includes sandwiches, bagels, pastries, and alcoholic drinks in addition to their coffee selections. Free Wi-Fi on weekdays is an added bonus. ☒ *2459 18th St. NW, Adams Morgan* ☏ *202/232–5500* ⊕ *www.trystdc.com* Ⓜ *Woodley Park/Zoo.*

BOOKS

Idle Time Books. Since 1981, this multilevel used-book store has been selling "rare to medium rare" books with plenty of meaty titles in all genres, especially out-of-print literature. ☒ *2467 18th St. NW, Adams Morgan* ☏ *202/232–4774* ⊕ *www.idletimebooks.com* Ⓜ *Woodley Park/Zoo.*

CHOCOLATE

Cocova. For chocoholics with a gourmet palate, this is one-stop shopping. The shop will feed your passions, with offerings both foreign (Valrhona from France) and domestic (Recchiuti from San Francisco and Vosges Haut Chocolat from Chicago). Selections from D.C.-area chocolatiers make for tasty souvenirs. ☒ *1904 18th St. NW, Adams Morgan* ☏ *202/903–0346* ⊕ *www.cocova.com* ☉ *mornings* Ⓜ *Dupont Circle.*

CRAFTS AND GIFTS

Toro Mata. Stunning black-and-white pottery from the Peruvian town of Chulucana is a specialty of this gallery; they directly represent six different artisans living and working there. The walls of the gallery are lined with elegant handcrafted wood mirrors, colorful original paintings, alpaca apparel, and other imported Andean crafts. ☒ *2410 18th St. NW, Adams Morgan* ☏ *202/232–3890* ⊕ *www.toromata.com* ☉ *Closed Mon.* Ⓜ *Woodley Park/Zoo.*

HOME FURNISHINGS

Skynear Designs Gallery. The owners of this extravagant shop travel the world to find the unusual, and their journeys have netted modern art, furniture, and home accessories. A staff of interior designers is on hand to help you identify and sort through the collection of treasures. ☒ *2122 18th St. NW, Adams Morgan* ☏ *202/797–7160* ⊕ *www.skynearonline.com* Ⓜ *Woodley Park/Zoo.*

MEN'S AND WOMEN'S CLOTHING

Meeps Fashionette. Catering to fans of retro glamour, this shop at the bottom of the Adams Morgan strip stocks a wide selection of vintage clothes and costumes for women and men from the '40s through the '90s. There's also an expanding selection of new, original designs by local talent. ☒ *2104 18th St. NW, Adams Morgan* ☏ *202/265–6546* ⊕ *www.meepsdc.com* Ⓜ *Dupont Circle.*

Mercedes Bien. Vintage 1940s through '80s clothes and retro-wear here includes everything from cocktail dresses to cowboy boots. You can also find a selection of jewelry and belts, all handpicked by the owner Mercedes. With no website, this small walk-up shop attracts buyers by offering exceptional, personal service. It's open weekends only. ⊠ *2423 18th St. NW, Adams Morgan* ☎ *202/360–8481* ⊙ *Mon.–Fri.* Ⓜ *Woodley Park/Zoo.*

Fodor'sChoice
★ **Nana.** A hip and friendly staff is one of the reasons why D.C. women love this store. Another is the stock of both new, repurposed, and vintage women's clothes at affordable prices, plus handmade jewelry and cool handbags. The owner Jackie Flanagan's own line of clothing, based on vintage patterns, is made in D.C. at the Bits of Thread studio. In 2012, Nana moved from the U Street Corridor to its current spot in Mount Pleasant. ⊠ *3068 Mt. Pleasant St. NW, Adams Morgan* ☎ *202/667–6955* ⊕ *www.nanadc.com* ⊙ *Closed Mon.* Ⓜ *Columbia Heights.*

Violet. Young women looking for fashion-forward styles will find plenty to love here at prices that fit their wallets. Short, seductive dresses, silky wraps and jackets, big funky earrings, and high-stepping shoes are sure to turn heads. Purchases are wrapped in—what else?—purple tissue paper. ⊠ *2439 18th St. NW, Adams Morgan* ☎ *202/621–9225* ⊕ *www.violetdc.com* ⊙ *Closed Mon.*

SHOES

Fleet Feet Sports Shop. The expert staff at this friendly shop will assess your feet and your training schedule before recommending the perfect pair of new running shoes. Shoes, apparel, and accessories for running, swimming, soccer, and cycling crowd the small space, where you might just bump into former Mayor Adrian Fenty (his brother and sister-in-law own the shop). ⊠ *1841 Columbia Rd. NW, Adams Morgan* ☎ *202/387–3888* ⊕ *www.fleetfeetdc.com* Ⓜ *Woodley Park/Zoo.*

U STREET CORRIDOR

In the 1930s and 1940s U Street was known for its classy theaters and jazz clubs. After decades of decline following the 1968 riots, the neighborhood has been revitalized. The area has gentrified at lightning speed, but has retained a diverse mix of multiethnic young professionals and older, working-class African-Americans. At night the neighborhood's club, bar, and restaurant scene comes alive. During the day the street scene is more laid-back, with more locals than tourists occupying the distinctive shops. ■TIP➔ On the third Thursday of each month, the area shops stay open late to offer light refreshments and special deals for the fun "Shopper Socials."

Greater U Street Neighborhood Visitor Center. Pick up brochures and maps of the neighborhood at this small visitor center next to Ben's Chili Bowl. Although the center is unstaffed, you can pose for a photo with a life-size picture of DC's Black Broadway most famous resident, Duke Ellington. ⊠ *1211 U St. NW, U St. Corridor* ☎ *202/661–7581* ⊙ *10–6* Ⓜ *U St./Cardozo.*

ANTIQUES AND COLLECTIBLES

GoodWood. Like a local Anthropologie, this friendly shop sells vintage and antique wood furniture, including wonderful 19th-century American pieces, along with mirrors, decorative items, dresses made by local designers—even a small but gorgeous collection of estate jewelry. ⊠ *1428 U St. NW, U Street Corridor* ☎ *202/986–3640* ⊕ *www. goodwooddc.com* ⊙ *mornings* Ⓜ *U St./Cardozo.*

Millennium. This eclectic shop sells what it calls "20th-century antiques," a unique blend of high-end vintage midcentury modern furniture and decorative art. ⊠ *1528 U St. NW, downstairs, U Street Corridor* ☎ *202/483–1218* ⊙ *Closed Mon.–Wed.* Ⓜ *U St./Cardozo.*

HOME FURNISHINGS

Home Rule. Here you can find some of the latest design elements from Europe for the bath, kitchen, and dining room. There are also playful tissue holders and other fun and affordable household items in cheerful colors. ⊠ *1807 14th St. NW, U Street Corridor* ☎ *202/797–5544* ⊕ *www.homerule.com* Ⓜ *U St./Cardozo.*

★ **Miss Pixie's Furnishings and Whatnot.** The well-chosen collectibles—handpicked by Miss Pixie herself—include gorgeous textiles, antique home furnishings, lamps and mirrors, glass- and silverware, and artwork. The reasonable prices will grab your attention, as will the location, an old car-dealer showroom. ⊠ *1626 14th St, NW, U Street Corridor* ☎ *202/232–8171* ⊕ *www.misspixies.com* Ⓜ *U St./Cordozo or Dupont Circle.*

Muléh. Exquisite contemporary Indonesian and Filipino home furnishings and trendy clothes from LA and New York fill this expansive showroom. The furniture pieces, which are the primary focus of the store, are made from fine organic materials. It's sort of like wandering through a luxury resort in Southeast Asia and finding a fabulous clothing boutique tucked in the back. ⊠ *1831 14th St. NW, U Street Corridor* ☎ *202/667–3440* ⊕ *www.muleh.com* Ⓜ *U St./Cardozo.*

Zawadi. The name means "gift" in Swahili, but you may want to buy the beautiful African art, textiles, home accessories, and jewelry for yourself. ⊠ *1524 U St. NW, U Street Corridor* ☎ *202/232–2214* ⊕ *www. zawadidc.com* ⊙ *Tues.–Wed.* Ⓜ *U St./Cardozo.*

WOMEN'S CLOTHING

Current Boutique. Don't be fooled by the new dresses in the front—this shop is a consignment shopper's dream. "Current" styles from brands such as Tory Burch, Citizens, True Religion, Banana Republic, Free People, and Diane Von Furstenberg just might fit better when you buy them at a third of their original price. ⊠ *1809 14th St. NW, U Street Corridor* ☎ *202/588–7311* ⊕ *www.currentboutique.com* ⊙ *Closed Mon.* Ⓜ *U St./Cardozo.*

Redeem. With street-smart clothes, boots, and accessories, women and men who are stuck in a fashion rut can find redemption here with brands like Funktional and Los Angeles–based thvm, plus Woolverine boots. A pop-up shop in the front with "Mad Men"–types of vintage accessories for men adds to the fun. ⊠ *1734 14th St. NW, U Street Corridor* ☎ *202/332–7447* ⊕ *www.redeemus.com* ⊙ *Closed Tues. and mornings Wed.–Mon.* Ⓜ *U St./Cardozo.*

UPPER NORTHWEST

The major thoroughfare Wisconsin Avenue runs northwest through the city from Georgetown toward Maryland. It crosses the border in the midst of the Friendship Heights shopping district, which is also near Chevy Chase. Other neighborhoods in the District yield more interesting finds and more enjoyable shopping and sightseeing, but it's hard to beat Friendship Heights for sheer convenience and selection. The upscale lineup includes Barneys CO-OP, Bloomingdales, Neiman Marcus, and two Saks Fifth Avenues—*the men's and women's collections are in separate buildings.* Stand-alone designer stores like Jimmy Choo, Louis Vuitton, Christian Dior, and Cartier up the luxury quotient. Although Filene's Basement closed, Nordstrom Rack joined the discounters Loehmann's and T.J. Maxx, who hawk the designer names at much lower prices. Lord & Taylor and chains like the Gap, Ann Taylor Loft, and Williams Sonoma occupy the middle ground.

Tightly packed into a few blocks, the big-name area is self-explanatory. However, there are also a few local gems in the surrounding neighborhood.

BOOKS

★ **Politics and Prose.** After being bought by two former *Washington Post* reporters in 2011, this legendary independent continues the original owners' tradition of jam-packed author events and signings, but they added another main attraction: Opus, the book-making machine that instantly prints out-of-issue books or self-published manuscripts. In their coffee shop downstairs, you can debate the issues of the day or read a book—of your own writing, perhaps. The nearest Metro is 15 minutes away. ⊠ *5015 Connecticut Ave. NW, Upper Northwest* ☏ *202/364–1919* ⊕ *www.politics-prose.com* Ⓜ *Friendship Heights.*

FOOD AND WINE

Calvert Woodley Liquors. This liquor store carries not only an excellent selection of wine and hard liquor, but also many kinds of cheese and other picnic and cocktail-party fare. Its international offerings have made it a favorite pantry for embassy parties. ⊠ *4339 Connecticut Ave. NW, Upper Northwest* ☏ *202/966–4400* ⊕ *www.calvertwoodley.com* ⊘ *Closed Sun.* Ⓜ *Van Ness/UDC.*

Rodman's Discount Foods and Drugstore. The rare store that carries wine, cheese, and space heaters, Rodman's is a fascinating hybrid of Kmart and Dean & Deluca. The appliances are downstairs, the imported peppers and chocolates upstairs. ⊠ *5100 Wisconsin Ave. NW, Upper Northwest* ☏ *202/363–3466* ⊕ *www.rodmans.com* Ⓜ *Friendship Heights.*

GIFTS

Periwinkle Inc. Warm and welcoming, Periwinkle Inc. offers a panoply of gift options: boutique chocolates, cases of nutty and gummy treats, handmade jewelry, Stonewall Kitchen snacks, hand-designed wrapping paper, scented bath products, printed note cards, and Voluspa candles. ⊠ *3815 Livingston St. NW, Upper Northwest* ☏ *202/364–3076* ⊕ *www.perwinklegiftsdc.com* Ⓜ *Friendship Heights.*

JEWELRY

★ **Ann Hand.** Catering to Washington's powerful and prestigious, this jewelry and gift shop specializing in patriotic pins may seem intimidating, but prices begin at $45. Hand's signature pin, The Liberty Eagle, is $195. Photos on the walls above brightly lit display cases showcase who's who in Washington wearing you-know-who's designs. ✉ *4885 MacArthur Blvd. NW, Upper Northwest* ☎ *202/333–2979* ⊕ *www.annhand.com* ☉ *Sat.–Sun.*

WOMEN'S CLOTHING

CatchCan. Bright and breezy clothes made of mostly natural fibers, plus comfortable but playful shoes and funky rain boots, make casual wear as fun as it is practical at this shop. The local owners' love of color continues with a sizeable collection of jewelry, greeting cards, housewares, and soaps. ✉ *5516 Connecticut Ave. NW, Upper Northwest* ☎ *202/686–5316* ⊕ *www.catchcan.com* Ⓜ *Friendship Heights.*

Julia Farr. Women who lobby on Capitol Hill and women who lunch at the country club look to Julia for a professional and polished look. Decorated in soothing sea shades, her boutique carries classic styles from emerging and established designers. Appointments are encouraged. ✉ *5232 44th St. NW, Upper Northwest* ☎ *202/253–3277* ⊕ *www.juliafarrdc.com* ☉ *Closed Sun. and Mon.* Ⓜ *Friendship Heights.*

Tabandeh. This avant-garde women's clothing boutique stocks an expertly selected cache of J Brand jeans, Rick Owens tops, and Ann Demeulemeester clothing, shoes, and jewelry. ✉ *5300 Wisconsin Ave. NW, Upper Northwest* ☎ *202/966–5080* ⊕ *www.tabandehjewelry.com* Ⓜ *Friendship Heights.*

Side Trips

WORD OF MOUTH

"Do go to Mt. Vernon and the Woodlawn Plantation up the road. Old Town Alexandria is on the way and worth several hours. You could even take a boat tour to Mt. Vernon from the Alexandria dock at the foot of King St. (go through the Torpedo Factory—it is studios of working artists, interesting and free)."

—con_brio

WELCOME TO SIDE TRIPS

TOP REASONS TO GO

★ **Walk in Washington's Shadow:** The minute you step onto the grounds of Mount Vernon, you'll be transported back in time to colonial America.

★ **Time Travel:** Delve into colonial history in Old Town Alexandria, then fast-forward to the 21st century with funky shops, artist's galleries, hot restaurants, boutiques, and bars. Don't miss Alexandria's farmers' market, held every Saturday, year-round, from 5:30 am to 11 am. Believe it or not, it has been around since George Washington's produce was sold here.

★ **Get Crabby:** Head east to Annapolis on the Chesapeake Bay and feast on a Maryland specialty: blue crabs by the bushel (the bib is optional).

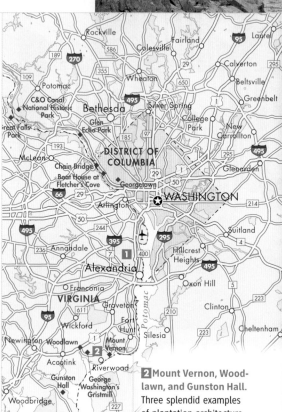

1 **Alexandria.** Alexandria is across the Potomac and 7 miles downstream from Washington. As a commercial port, it competed with Georgetown in the days before Washington was a city. It's now a big small town loaded with historic homes, shops, and restaurants.

2 Mount Vernon, Woodlawn, and Gunston Hall. Three splendid examples of plantation architecture remain on the Virginia side of the Potomac, 16 miles south of D.C. Mount Vernon, the most-visited historic house in America, was the home of George Washington; Woodlawn was the estate of Martha Washington's granddaughter; and Gunston Hall was the residence of George Mason, a patriot and author of the document on which the Bill of Rights was based.

12

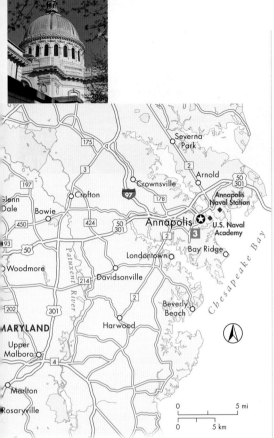

GETTING ORIENTED

There's no question that Washington, D.C., has enough sights, sounds, and experiences to keep you busy for a week or more without seeing everything on your itinerary. The three destinations highlighted here help enrich your experience whether you're a history buff, foodie, outdoor enthusiast, or boater. With just a bit of planning, any one of these trips can be done in a day or even an afternoon. Follow the locals' example and escape the heat of the capital with a trip to the countryside.

3 **Annapolis, Maryland.** Maryland's capital is a popular destination for seafood lovers and boating fans. Warm, sunny days bring many boats to the City Dock, where they're moored against a background of waterfront shops and restaurants. The city has one of the country's largest assemblages of 18th-century architecture. Its nautical reputation is enhanced by the presence of the U.S. Naval Academy.

Updated
by Kathryn
McKay

Within an hour of D.C. are getaway destinations connected to the nation's first president, naval history, and colonial events. Alexandria was once a bustling colonial port, and Old Town preserves this flavor with its cobblestone streets, taverns, and waterfront. Cycle 7 miles downriver along the banks of the Potomac to get here, or hop on the Metro for a quick 30-minute ride.

Mount Vernon, George Washington's plantation, is a mere 16 miles from D.C. on the Virginia side of the Potomac. Make a day of it, and visit the two other interesting plantation homes—Woodlawn and Gunston Hall—that are nearby.

Another option is to get out on the water in Annapolis, a major center for boating and home to the U.S. Naval Academy. Feast on the Chesapeake Bay's famous crabs, then watch the midshipmen parade on campus at the academy.

PLANNING

KID TIPS

No matter the ages of your children or the weather, Mount Vernon can keep everyone amused with activities that delight the senses. See where George and Martha Washington and their slaves lived, hear the Revolutionary rifles fired in animated movies, taste hoecakes, and smell the herbs in the garden. A dress-up room in the education center gives children the chance to look like colonial kids.

Find out what it takes to become a midshipman at the **U.S. Naval Academy's** new exhibit in the visitor center.

■ TIP➔ Even kids who don't "dig" history might like sifting through dirt for artifacts in Alexandria during Family Dig Days at the archaeology museum in the Torpedo Factory.

12

TO GET TO ...	BY CAR:	BY METRO OR BUS:
Alexandria	George Washington Memorial Pkwy. or Jefferson Davis Hwy. (Rte. 1) south from Arlington (10 mins)	The Blue or Yellow Line to the King Street Metro stop (25 mins from Metro Center stop)
Mount Vernon	Exit 1 off the Beltway; follow signs to George Washington Memorial Pkwy. southbound (30 mins)	The Yellow Line to the Huntington Metro stop. From there, take Fairfax County Connector Bus 101, 151, or 152 (45–50 mins)
Woodlawn	Rte. 1 southwest to the second Rte. 235 intersection; entrance is on the right at the traffic light (40 mins)	Bus 151, 152, or 171 from Huntington Metro station (45–50 mins)
Gunston Hall	Rte. 1 south to Rte. 242; turn left and go 3.5 miles to entrance (30 mins)	No Metro or bus
Annapolis	U.S. 50 east to the Rowe Blvd. Exit (35–45 mins, except during weekday rush hour when it may take twice as long)	Amtrak from Union Station to BWI; MTA Light Rail from BWI to Patapsco Light Rail Station; transfer to Bus #14 (2 hrs)

ALEXANDRIA, VIRGINIA

A short drive (or bike ride) from Washington, Alexandria provides a welcome break from the monuments and hustle and bustle of the District. Here you encounter America's colonial heritage. Founded in 1749 by Scottish merchants eager to capitalize on the booming tobacco trade, Alexandria became one of the most important colonial ports and has been associated with the most significant personages of the colonial, Revolutionary, and Civil War periods. In Old Town this colorful past is revived through restored 18th- and 19th-century homes, churches, and taverns; on the cobbled streets; and on the revitalized waterfront, where clipper ships docked and artisans displayed their wares. Alexandria also has a wide variety of small- to medium-size restaurants and pubs, plus a wealth of boutiques and antiques dealers vying for your time and money.

GETTING HERE AND AROUND

Take either the George Washington Memorial Parkway or Jefferson Davis Highway (Route 1) south from Arlington to reach Alexandria. ■TIP➔ Stop at the Alexandria Visitors Center at Ramsay House (221 King Street) for a 24-hour free parking permit good at any two-hour metered spot. You can get one even if you're visiting from elsewhere in Virginia.

The King Street/Old Town Metro stop (about 25 minutes from Metro Center) is right next to the Masonic Memorial and a 10-block walk on King Street from the center of Old Town. ■TIP➔ There's a free King Street Trolley between the King Street station and the Torpedo Factory Art Center daily from 11:30 am to 10 pm.

TOURS

Old Town Experience runs walking tours that leave from the Alexandria Visitors Center 10:30 am Monday through Saturday and 2 pm Sunday; tickets are $15. Another tour operator, Footsteps to the Past, also leads tours from the visitor center at 1:30 pm Monday through Saturday; tickets are $15. Alexandria Colonial Tours leads guided walks of historic Alexandria by reservation. Ghost-and-graveyard tours (reservations not required) are conducted Friday, Saturday, and Sunday nights, although in summer you can also take a tour on Wednesday and Thursday nights. Tours are nightly in October. Specialty tours include African-American history and faith and heritage.

ESSENTIALS

Visitor Information Alexandria Visitors Center ✉ *Ramsay House, 221 King St.* ☎ *703/746–3301, 800/388–9119* ⊕ *www.visitalexandriava.com.*

EXPLORING

TOP ATTRACTIONS

Appomattox Confederate Statue. In 1861, when Alexandria was occupied by Union forces, the 800 soldiers of the city's garrison marched out of town to join the Confederate Army. In the middle of Washington and Prince streets stands a statue marking the point where they assembled. In 1885 Confederate veterans proposed a memorial to honor their fallen comrades. This statue, based on John A. Elder's painting *Appomattox,* is of a lone soldier glumly surveying the battlefields after General Robert E. Lee's surrender. The names of 99 Alexandria Confederate dead are carved on the base. ⊠ *Washington and Prince Sts., Old Town.*

Boyhood Home of Robert E. Lee. This childhood home of the commander of the Confederate forces of Virginia is a fine example of a 19th-century Federal town house. The house is privately owned and not open to visitors. ⊠ *607 Oronoco St., Old Town.*

ALEXANDRIA'S FARMERS' MARKET

If it's Saturday and you're up early, join the locals at Alexandria's Farmers' Market, one of the oldest continually operating farmers' markets in the country—open for business since the 1700s. The market is held from 5:30 am to 11 am year-round at City Hall (⊠ *301 King St.*). In addition to incredible produce, you'll find artisans selling handmade jewelry, dolls, quilts, purses, sweaters, and more. You'll also find delicious baked goods and other snack items for a quick meal on the go or a picnic later in the day.

Carlyle House. Alexandria forefather and Scottish merchant John Carlyle built this grand house, completed in 1753 and modeled on a country manor in the old country. Students of the French and Indian War will want to know that the dwelling served as General Braddock's headquarters. The house retains its original 18th-century woodwork and is furnished with Chippendale furniture and Chinese porcelain. An architectural exhibit on the second floor explains how the house was built; outside there's an attractive garden of colonial-era plants. ⊠ *121 N. Fairfax St., Old Town* ☎ *703/549–2997* ⊕ *www.carlylehouse. org* ⊑ *$5* ☺ *Tues.–Sat. 10–4, Sun. noon–4, guided tour every 1/2 hr.*

Christ Church. George Washington and Robert E. Lee were pew holders in this Episcopal church, which remains in nearly original condition. (Washington paid quite a lot of money for pews 59 and 60.) Built in 1773, this fine example of an English Georgian country-style church has a Palladian window, an interior balcony, and an English wrought-brass-and-crystal chandelier. Docents give tours during visiting hours. ⊠ *118 N. Washington St., Old Town* ☎ *703/549–1450* ⊕ *www. historicchristchurch.org* ⊑ *$5 donation suggested* ☺ *Mon.–Sat. 10–4, Sun. 8:45–1.*

★ **Gadsby's Tavern Museum.** The two buildings that now make up this
☺ museum—a circa-1785 tavern and the 1792 City Hotel—were centers of political and social life. George Washington celebrated his birthdays in the ballroom. Other noted patrons included Thomas Jefferson, John Adams, and the Marquis de Lafayette. The taproom, dining room, assembly room, ballroom, and communal bedrooms have been restored to their original appearance. ⊠ *134 N. Royal St., Old Town* ☎ *703/746–4242* ⊕ *www.gadsbystavern.org* ⊑ *$5* ☺ *Nov.–Mar., Wed.–Thurs. and Sat. 11–4, Fri. 11–4 and 7–9:30, Sun. 1–4, last tour at 3:45; Apr.–Oct., daily 10–5, last tour at 4:45; tours 15 mins before and after the hour.*

★ **George Washington Masonic Memorial.** Because Alexandria, like Washington, D.C., has no really tall buildings, the spire of this memorial dominates the surroundings and is visible for miles. The building overlooks King and Duke streets, Alexandria's major east–west arteries. Reaching the memorial requires a respectable uphill climb from the King St. Metrorail and bus stations. From the ninth-floor observation deck (reached by elevator) you get a spectacular view of Alexandria and Washington, but access above the first and mezzanine floors is by guided tour only. The building contains furnishings from the first Masonic lodge in Alexandria. George Washington became a Mason in 1752 in Fredericksburg, and became charter master of the Alexandria lodge when it was chartered in 1788, remaining active in Masonic affairs during his tenure as president, 1789–97. ⊠ *101 Callahan Dr., Old Town* ☎ *703/683–2007* ⊕ *www.gwmemorial.org* ☜ *$5; $8 guided tour (includes observation deck)* ☉ *Daily 9–4; 1-hr guided tour of building and observation deck daily at 10, 11:30, 1:30, and 3.*

Lee-Fendall House. At historic Lee Corner at North Washington and Oronoco streets, the Lee-Fendall House was built in 1785; over the course of the next 118 years it was home to 37 members of the Lee family and served as a Union hospital. The house and its furnishings, of the 1850–70 period, present an intimate study of 19th-century family life. Highlights include a splendid collection of Lee heirlooms, period pieces produced by Alexandria manufacturers, and the beautifully restored, award-winning garden. ⊠ *614 Oronoco St., Old Town* ☎ *703/548–1789* ☜ *$5* ☉ *Wed.–Sat. 10–4; Sun. 1–4; sometimes closed for private events.*

Lyceum. Built in 1839 and one of Alexandria's best examples of Greek Revival design, the Lyceum is also the city's official history museum. Over the years the building has served as the Alexandria Library, a Civil War hospital, a residence, and offices. Restored in the 1970s for the Bicentennial, it has an impressive collection including examples of 18th- and 19th-century silver, tools, stoneware, and Civil War photographs taken by Mathew Brady. ⊠ *201 S. Washington St., Old Town* ☎ *703/838–4994* ⊕ *www.alexandriahistory.org* ☜ *$2 donation suggested* ☉ *Mon.–Sat. 10–5, Sun. 1–5.*

Ramsay House. The best place to start a tour of Alexandria's Old Town is at the **Alexandria Visitors Center at** Ramsay House, the home of the town's first postmaster and lord mayor, William Ramsay. The unusually helpful staff hands out brochures, maps for self-guided walking tours, and 24-hour permits for free parking at any two-hour metered spot. You can also use a free computer station to plan your travels. ⊠ *221 King St., Old Town* ☎ *703/746–3301, 800/388–9119* ⊕ *wwwvisitalexandriava.com* ☜ *Guided tours $10–$15* ☉ *Jan.–Mar. daily 10–5; Apr.–Dec. daily 10-8; tours Mon.–Sat. 10:30 and 1:30, Sun. 2.*

★ **Torpedo Factory Art Center.** Torpedoes were manufactured here by the U.S.
☾ Navy during World War II. Now the building houses the studios and workshops of about 160 artists and artisans. You can observe printmakers, jewelry makers, sculptors, painters, and potters as they create original work in their studios. The Torpedo Factory also houses the

12

Alexandria Archaeology Museum, which displays artifacts such as plates, cups, pipes, and coins from an early tavern, and Civil War soldiers' equipment. If digging interests you, call to sign up for the well-attended public digs (offered once a month from June to October). ⊠ *105 N. Union St., Old Town* ☎ *703/838–4565* ⊕ *www.torpedofactory.org* ⊠ *Free* ⊙ *daily 10–6, Thurs. 10–9.*

WORTH NOTING

Alexandria Black History Museum. This museum, devoted to the history of African-Americans in Alexandria and Virginia, is at the site of the Robert H. Robinson Library, a building constructed in the wake of a landmark 1939 sit-in protesting the segregation of Alexandria libraries. The federal census of 1790 recorded 52 free African-Americans living in the city, but the port town was one of the largest slave exporting points in the South, with at least two highly active slave markets. ⊠ *902 Wythe St., Old Town* ☎ *703/838–4356* ⊕ *www.alexblackhistory.org* ⊠ *$2* ⊙ *Tues.–Sat. 10–4.*

Athenaeum. One of the most noteworthy structures in Alexandria, this striking Greek Revival edifice at the corner of Prince and Lee streets stands out from its many redbrick Federal neighbors. Built in 1852 as a bank (Robert E. Lee had an account here) and later used as a Union commissary headquarters, then as a talcum powder factory for the Stabler-Leadbeater Apothecary, the Athenaeum now houses the gallery of the Northern Virginia Fine Arts Association. The Washington School of Ballet also offers dance classes here. This block of Prince Street between Fairfax and Lee streets is known as **Gentry Row,** after the 18th- and 19th-century inhabitants of its imposing three-story houses. ⊠ *201 Prince St., Old Town* ☎ *703/548–0035* ⊕ *www.nvfaa. org* ⊠ *Free* ⊙ *Thurs., Fri., Sun. noon–4, Sat. 1–4.*

Captain's Row. Many of Alexandria's sea captains once lived on this block, which gives visitors the truest sense of what the city looked like in the 1800s. The stone pavement is not original, but nicely replicates the stones laid down during the Revolution, taken from ships sailing to America and used to balance the vessels during the passage. ⊠ *Prince St. between Lee and Union Sts., Old Town.*

Friendship Fire House. Alexandria's showcase firehouse dates from 1855 and is filled with typical 19th-century implements, but the resident Friendship Fire Company was established in 1774 and bought its first engine in 1775. Among early fire engines on display is a hand pumper built in Philadelphia in 1851. Most everything can be seen through the windows even when the firehouse is closed. ⊠ *107 S. Alfred St., Old Town* ☎ *703/746–3891* ⊕ *oha.alexandriava.gov/friendship* ⊠ *Suggested donation $2* ⊙ *Sat. and Sun. 1–4.*

Lloyd House. A fine example of Georgian architecture, Lloyd House was built in 1797 and is owned by the City of Alexandria and used for offices for the Office of Historic Alexandria. The interior has nothing on display so it is best admired from outside. ⊠ *220 N. Washington St., Old Town.*

Old Presbyterian Meeting House. Except from 1899 through 1949, the Old Presbyterian Meeting House has been the site of an active Presbyterian congregation since 1775. Scottish pioneers founded the church, and Scottish patriots used it as a gathering place during the Revolution. Four memorial services were held for George Washington here. The tomb of an unknown soldier of the American Revolution lies in a corner of the small churchyard, where many prominent Alexandrians—including Dr. James Craik, physician and best friend to Washington, and merchant John Carlyle—are interred. The original sanctuary was rebuilt after a lightning strike and fire in 1835. The interior is appropriately plain; if you'd like to visit the sanctuary you can borrow a key in the church office, or just peek through the many wide windows along both sides. ⊠ *321 S. Fairfax St., Old Town* ☎ *703/549–6670* ⊕ *www.opmh.org* ✍ *Free* ⊙ *Weekdays 8:15–4:15.*

☾ **Stabler-Leadbeater Apothecary.** Once patronized by Martha Washington and the Lee family, the Stabler-Leadbeater Apothecary is among the oldest apothecaries in the country (the reputed oldest is in Bethlehem, Pennsylvania). Some believe that it was here, on October 17, 1859, that Lt. Col. Robert E. Lee received orders to lead Marines sent from the Washington Barracks to help suppress John Brown's insurrection at Harpers Ferry (then part of Virginia). The shop now houses a museum of apothecary memorabilia, including one of the finest collections of apothecary bottles in the country. In fact, they have so many that curators are still processing them all. ■**TIP**➔ Tours include discussions of Alexandria life and medicine, as well as the history of the family that owned and ran the shop for 141 years. Tours designed especially for children are available. ⊠ *105–107 S. Fairfax St., Old Town* ☎ *703/746–3852* ⊕ *www.apothecarymuseum.org* ✍ *$5* ⊙ *Apr.–Oct., Tues.–Sat. 10–5, Sun. and Mon. 1–5; Nov.–Mar., Wed.–Sat. 11–4, Sun. 1–4.*

WHERE TO EAT

More than 50 restaurants participate in Alexandria's biannual restaurant weeks in January and August, offering either a three-course meal for $35 or dinner for two at $35.

$ ✕ **Eamonn's A Dublin Chipper.** A nod to his native Ireland, this fish-and-
IRISH chips joint is Chef Cathal Armstrong's latest addition to his growing
☾ Old Town Alexandria empire—he also runs the acclaimed Restaurant Eve and Majestic Café. This 20-seat, counter-service chipper-with-attitude serves up crispy cod and fries with your choice of seven different sauces from classic tartar to curry. Down it with a pint of Guinness or an Irish soda and finish with a piping hot fried Mars bar, a weird-but-wonderful dessert that's the perfect end to a battered meal. ■**TIP**➔ When the pirate flag is flying and a blue light glows at an unmarked door, head upstairs to the PX, a 21st-century speakeasy operated by Armstrong and his wife. ⑤ *Average main: $10* ⊠ *728 King St., Arlington* ☎ *703/299–8384* ⊕ *www.eamonnsdublinchipper.com.*

King Street is the heart of historic Old Town Alexandria, Virginia, with lively restaurants and shops.

$$$ ✕ **Las Tapas.** A big, bright, authentic Spanish restaurant, Las Tapas spe-
SPANISH cializes in, what else? There are 59 tapas on the menu, such as tortilla
espanola, plus substantial entreés, including five kinds of paella. Indeed,
Paella Valenciana is the signature dish in this friendly restaurant. Order
a jug of the red, white, or specialty sangrias to accompany your meal.
Then sit back and watch the flamenco dancers, who perform Tuesday
through Thursday nights; Friday and Saturday nights bring Spanish
guitar music. $ *Average main: $30* ⊠ *710 King St.* ☎ *703/836–4000*
⊕ *www.lastapas.us.*

$$ ✕ **Le Refuge.** At this local favorite, run by Jean François and his wife
FRENCH Françoise for 25 years, enjoy lovingly prepared, authentic French
country fare with beaucoup flavor; popular selections include trout,
bouillabaisse, garlicky rack of lamb, frogs' legs, and beef Wellington.
Polish it all off with an order of profiteroles or crème brûlée. $ *Av-
erage main: $25* ⊠ *127 N. Washington St.* ☎ *703/548–4661* ⊕ *www.
lerefugealexandria.com* ☽ *Closed Sun.*

$$ ✕ **Majestic Café.** An art deco facade remains, but the stylish interior
AMERICAN brings a modern sensibility to a 1930s-era landmark. The cooking style
is rustic American, with an emphasis on simplicity, seasonal products,
and comfort food—home-style meat loaf and mashed potatoes, Amish
chicken two ways, and fried green tomatoes with burrata cheese and
basil puree. On Sunday, in addition to the regular menu, the café offers
a special family-style dinner for $22 per person, including dessert.
Themes for these dinners include "Summer Lovin'" and "The Har-
vest." The Majestic is about eight blocks from the Metrorail. $ *Aver-
age main: $25* ⊠ *911 King St.* ☎ *703/837–9117* ⊕ *www.majesticcafe.
com* Ⓜ *King St.*

$
BARBECUE
☺
✕ **Rocklands.** This homegrown barbecue stop is known for its flavorful pork ribs smoked over hickory and red oak. Sides like silky corn pudding, rich mac 'n' cheese, and crunchy slaw are as good as the meats, which cover everything from beef brisket and chopped pork barbecue to chicken and fish. The family crowd comes for dinner, but the place also does takeout. There is another branch in Arlington at 3471 Washington Boulevard. $ *Average main: $16* ⊠ *25 S. Quaker La.* ☎ *703/778–9663* ⊕ *www.rocklands.com.*

$$$
MODERN GREEK
✕ **Taverna Cretekou.** Whitewashed stucco walls and colorful macramé tapestries bring a bit of the Mediterranean to the center of Old Town. On the menu are *exohikon* (lamb baked in a pastry shell) and fish sautéed with artichokes, and the extensive wine list includes only Greek choices, such as the special Taverna Cretekou made near Kalamata. In warm weather you can dine in the canopied garden. ■ **TIP→** Thursday evenings bring live music, and if you are so moved, plates for breaking are free for the asking—opa! A buffet brunch is served on Sunday. $ *Average main: $27* ⊠ *818 King St.* ☎ *703/548–8688* ⊕ *www.tavernacretekou.com* ۞ *Closed Mon.*

$$$$
MODERN
AMERICAN
✕ **Vermilion.** Be sure to make reservations because foodies flock here for a taste of Chef Anthony Chittum's award-winning modern American menu. This upscale establishment puts an emphasis on the casual with its exposed brick walls, ceiling beams, and gas lamps. Chittum favors locally sourced, sustainable ingredients, though quality trumps local here so you may find an Alaskan halibut on this Mid-Atlantic menu alongside a braised short ribs and caramelized onion *crespelle.* Vermilion is also one of the area's favorite weekend brunch spots. Tuesday and Wednesday evenings bring live music to the first-floor lounge. $ *Average main: $37* ⊠ *1120 King St.* ☎ *703/684–9669* ⊕ *www. vermilionrestaurant.com* ۞ *No lunch on Tues.*

WHERE TO STAY

For expanded hotel reviews, visit Fodors.com.

$$
HOTEL
☺
🛏 **Embassy Suites Old Town Alexandria.** Adjacent to Alexandria's landmark George Washington Masonic Memorial, this all-suites hotel sits across the street from the Metro station and around the corner from the Amtrak station. **Pros:** large rooms; across from Metro station. **Cons:** outside city; small pool that is often crowded; popular with school groups. **TripAdvisor:** "always good," "worked for us," "great location." $ *Rooms from: $269* ⊠ *1900 Diagonal Rd., Old Town* ☎ *703/684–5900, 800/362–2779* ❘❍❘ *Breakfast.*

$$$
HOTEL
🛏 **Hotel Monaco Alexandria.** There's a fine line between history and modernity in Old Town Alexandria, and Hotel Monaco reflects that spirit in luxurious guestrooms where traditonal Americana takes on a sharp, contemporary look. **Pros:** central location to Old Town sights; guests enjoy a complimentary wine happy hour in the lobby between 5 and 6. **Cons:** thin walls mean you might hear conversations in adjoining rooms or barking dogs in the hallway. **TripAdvisor:** "service and comfort," "a beautiful hotel," "great location and fancy rooms." $ *Rooms from: $299* ⊠ *480 King St.* ☎ *703/549–6080* ⊕ *www.monaco-alexandria.com* ☞ *241 rooms, 10 suites* ❘❍❘ *No meals* Ⓜ *King St.*

$$$ ⊞ **Morrison House.** The architecture, parquet floors, crystal chandeliers,
HOTEL decorative fireplaces, and furnishings here are so faithful to the Federal
★ period (1790–1820) that the hotel is often mistaken for a renovation
rather than what it is: a structure built from scratch in 1985. **Pros:** in
the heart of Old Town, about a 15-minute walk from the train and
Metrorail stations; modern building with historic charm. **Cons:** can be
a little pricey; fireplaces are decorative only. **TripAdvisor:** "great ser-
vice," "perfection," "friendly staff and a clean room." ⑤ *Rooms from:*
$299 ⊠ *116 S. Alfred St.* ☎ *703/838–8000, 800/367–0800* ⊕ *www.*
morrisonhouse.com ⇴ *42 rooms, 3 suites* ⑩ *No meals* Ⓜ *King St.*

MOUNT VERNON, WOODLAWN, AND GUNSTON HALL

Long before Washington was planned, the shores of the Potomac
had been divided into plantations by wealthy traders and gentlemen
farmers. Most traces of the colonial era were obliterated as the capital
grew in the 19th century, but several splendid examples of plantation
architecture remain on the Virginia side of the Potomac, 15 miles or
so south of D.C. In one day you can easily visit three such mansions:
Mount Vernon, the home of George Washington and one of the most
popular sites in the area; Woodlawn, the estate of Martha Washing-
ton's granddaughter; and Gunston Hall, the home of George Mason,
author of the document on which the Bill of Rights was based. (Expect
the longest wait times at Mount Vernon, particularly in spring and
summer.) Set on hillsides overlooking the river, these estates offer mag-
nificent vistas and bring back to vivid life the more palatable aspects
of the 18th century.

MOUNT VERNON, VIRGINIA

16 miles southeast of Washington, D.C., 8 miles south of Alexandria, VA.

GETTING HERE AND AROUND

To reach Mount Vernon by car from the Capital Beltway (Route 495),
take Exit 1 and follow the signs to George Washington Memorial
Parkway southbound. Mount Vernon is about 8.5 miles south. From
downtown Washington, cross into Arlington on Key Bridge, Memo-
rial Bridge, or the 14th Street Bridge and drive south on the George
Washington Memorial Parkway past Ronald Reagan National Airport
through Alexandria straight to Mount Vernon. The trip from D.C.
takes about a half hour.

Getting to Mount Vernon by public transportation requires that you
take both the Metro and a bus. Begin by taking the Yellow Line train
to the Huntington Metro station. From here, take Fairfax County Con-
nector Bus 101, 151, or 152 ($1.70 cash or $1.50 with SmarTrip card).
Buses of each route leave about once an hour—more often during rush
hour—and operate weekdays from about 4:30 am to 9:15 pm, week-
ends from about 6:30 am to 7 pm.

TOURS

BOAT TOURS The *Spirit of Mount Vernon* makes a pleasant trip from Washington down the Potomac to Mount Vernon from mid-March through mid-October. Boarding begins at 8 for the narrated cruise down the Potomac River. Once you arrive at Mount Vernon, you'll have more than three hours to tour the estate before reboarding at 1:30. Tickets cost $48 and include admission to the estate.

BUS TOURS Martz Gray Line runs four-hour trips to Mount Vernon (with a stop in Alexandria), departing daily at 8 am from Union Station. A ticket is $55 and includes admission to the mansion and grounds. There's also a seasonal Mount Vernon–by-candlelight tour that departs at 5:30 on selected Friday and Saturday evenings in November and December for $55.

> ### THE VIEW OUT BACK
>
> Beneath a 90-foot portico is George Washington's contribution to architecture and the real treasure of Mount Vernon: the home's dramatic riverside porch. The porch overlooks an expanse of lawn that slopes down to the Potomac. In springtime the view of the river (a mile wide where it passes the plantation) is framed by redbud and dogwood blossoms. United States Navy and Coast Guard ships salute ("render honors") when passing the house during daylight hours. Foreign naval vessels often salute, too.

ESSENTIALS

Boat Information Spirit of Mount Vernon ⊠ *Pier 4, 6th and Water Sts. SW, Southeast, Washington, District of Columbia* ☎ *866/302–2469 boat reservations* ⊕ *www.spiritcruises.com.*

Bus Information Fairfax County Connector ☎ *703/339–7200* ⊕ *www.fairfaxcounty.gov/connector.*

Bus Tour Information Marz Gray Line ☎ *800/862–1400* ⊕ *www.graylinedc.com.*

EXPLORING

Fodor'sChoice
★
☾
Mount Vernon. This plantation and the surrounding lands had been in the Washington family for nearly 70 years by the time the future president inherited it all in 1743. Before taking over command of the Continental Army, Washington was an accomplished farmer, managing the 8,000-acre plantation and operating five farms on the land. He oversaw the transformation of the main house from an ordinary farm dwelling into what was, for the time, a grand mansion. The inheritance of his widowed bride, Martha, is partly what made that transformation possible.

The red-roof main house is elegant though understated, with a yellow pine exterior that's been painted and coated with layers of sand to resemble white-stone blocks. The first-floor rooms are quite ornate, especially the formal large dining room, with a molded ceiling decorated with agricultural motifs. The bright colors of the walls, which match the original paint, may surprise those who associate the period with pastels. Throughout the house are smaller symbols of the owner's eminence, such as a key to the main portal of the Bastille—presented to Washington by the Marquis de Lafayette—and Washington's presidential chair.

United States Navy and Coast Guard ships salute (render honors) when passing Mount Vernon during daylight hours.

As you tour the mansion, guides are stationed throughout the house to describe the furnishings and answer questions.

The real treasure of Mount Vernon is the view from around back: the home's dramatic riverside porch overlooks an expanse of lawn that slopes down to the Potomac. In springtime the view of the river (a mile wide where it passes the plantation) is framed by dogwood blossoms. In the 19th century, steamboats rendered honors when passing the house during daylight hours.

You can stroll around the estate's 500 acres and three gardens, visiting the workshops, kitchen, carriage house, greenhouse, slave quarters, and—down the hill toward the boat landing—the tomb of George and Martha Washington. There's also a pioneer farmer site: a 4-acre hands-on exhibit with a reconstruction of George Washington's 16-side treading barn as its centerpiece.

But some of the most memorable experiences at Mount Vernon, particularly for kids, are in the orientation and education centers. Interactive displays, movies with special effects straight out of Hollywood, life-size models, and Revolutionary artifacts illustrate Washington's life and contributions.

A National Treasure tour explores behind the scenes and includes a chance to see the basement of the house; the tour sells out quickly so reserve ahead of time.

Actors in period dress who portray General Washington and his wife welcome visitors at special occasions throughout the year, including President's Day, Memorial Day, and July 4. Evening candlelight tours are offered weekend evenings in late November and early December and during wine festivals held one weekend in May and in October.

George Washington's Gristmill and Distillery—both reproductions—operate on their original sites. Records kept by Washington helped archaeologists excavate the distillery in the late 1990s. During the guided tours, led by costumed interpreters, you meet an 18th-century miller and watch the water-powered wheel grind grain into cornmeal. The mill and distillery are 3 miles from Mount Vernon on Route 235 toward U.S. 1, almost to Woodlawn. Tickets can be purchased at the gristmill or at Mount Vernon. ⊠ *Southern end of George Washington Pkwy., Mount Vernon* ☎ *703/780–2000* ⊕ *www. mountvernon.org* ✉ *$15, gristmill $4, combination ticket $17* ☉ *Mar., Sept., and Oct., daily 9–5; Apr.– Aug., daily 8–5; Nov.–Feb., daily 9–4.*

MARTHA WASHINGTON: HOT OR NOT?

As hard as it may be to believe from the portraits of her in history books, Martha Washington was a hottie. Far from the frumpy, heavy-set woman we know as the *first* first lady, Martha wore sequined purple high heels on her wedding day, read romance novels, and had many admirers, not to mention a previous husband. A team of forensic anthropologists used a 1796 portrait of Mrs. Washington to digitally create an image of what she might have looked like in her twenties. The image inspired Michael Deas to create a portrait of the young first lady, which now hangs in the education building at Mount Vernon.

SPORTS AND THE OUTDOORS

An asphalt bicycle path leads from the Virginia side of Key Bridge (across from Georgetown), past Ronald Reagan National Airport, and through Alexandria all the way to Mount Vernon. Bikers in moderately good condition can make the 16-mile trip in less than two hours. You can rent bicycles at several locations in Washington.

A great place to rent a bike is the **Washington Sailing Marina** (☎ *703/548–9027* ⊕ *www.washingtonsailingmarina.com*), which is beside the Mount Vernon Bike Trail just past the airport. A 12-mile ride south will take you right up to the front doors of Mount Vernon. Cruiser bikes rent for $8 per hour or $28 per day. The marina is open 9–5 daily.

WOODLAWN, VIRGINIA

3 miles west of Mount Vernon, 15 miles south of Washington, D.C.

GETTING HERE AND AROUND

To drive to Woodlawn, travel southwest on Route 1 to the second Route 235 intersection (the first leads to Mount Vernon). The entrance to Woodlawn is on the right at the traffic light. From Mount Vernon, travel northwest on Route 235 to the Route 1 intersection; Woodlawn is straight ahead through the intersection.

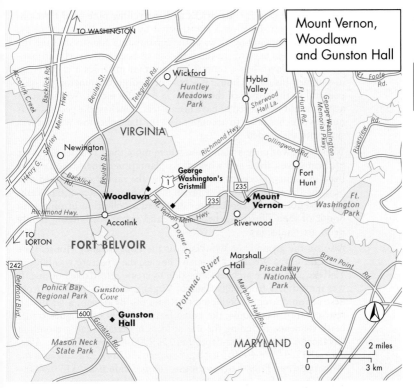

Mount Vernon, Woodlawn and Gunston Hall

To use public transportation, take Bus 151, 152, or 171 ($1.70 cash or $1.50 with SmarTrip card) from Huntington Metro station. Route 171 begins earlier and runs later than the other two buses and well beyond Woodlawn operating hours. Buses returning to the station have the same numbers but are marked Huntington.

ESSENTIALS

Bus Information Fairfax County Connector ☏ *703/339–7200* ⊕ *www.fairfaxcounty.gov/connector.*

EXPLORING

Woodlawn. This plantation home was once part of the Mount Vernon estate, and from here you can still see the five trees of the bowling green that fronted Washington's home. The house was built for Martha Washington's granddaughter, Nelly Custis, who married George Washington's favorite nephew, Lawrence Lewis. (Lewis had come to Mount Vernon from Fredericksburg to be his Uncle George's social secretary so that the statesman could have more time to manage his five farms.)

The Lewises' home, completed in 1805, was designed by William Thornton, a physician and amateur architect from the West Indies who drew up the original plans for the U.S. Capitol. Like Mount Vernon, the Woodlawn house is constructed wholly of native materials, including the clay for the bricks and the yellow pine used throughout the interior. Built on a site selected by George Washington, the house has commanding views of the surrounding countryside and the Potomac River beyond. In the tradition of Southern riverfront mansions, Woodlawn has a central hallway that provides a cool refuge in summer. Inside the house is a bust of George Washington set on a pedestal so the crown of the head is at 6 feet, 4 inches. Washington's actual height is believed to have been 6 feet, 2 inches; the pedestal was built two inches taller to accommodate for the inches lost when it was sunk into the garden.

Woodlawn was once a plantation where more than 100 people, most of them slaves, lived and worked. As plantation owners, the Lewises lived in luxury. Docents talk about how the family entertained and how the slaves prepared these lavish meals. As intimates of the Washingtons' household, the Lewises displayed a collection of objects in honor of their illustrious benefactor, and many Washington family items are on display.

Also on the grounds of Woodlawn is the **Pope-Leighey House.** One of Frank Lloyd Wright's "Usonian" homes, the structure was built in 1940 as part of the architect's mission to create affordable housing. It was moved here from Falls Church, Virginia, in 1964, to save it from destruction during the building of Route 66. By design, a small and sparsely furnished home, the home features many of Wright's trademark elements, including the use of local materials. Call a month in advance to arrange an in-depth tour. ✉ *9000 Richmond Hwy., Alexandria* ☎ *703/780–4000* ⊕ *www.woodlawn1805.org* 💲 *$8.50 each for Woodlawn and Pope-Leighey House, combination ticket $15* ⊗ *Mar.–Dec., Thurs.–Mon. 10–5; limited guided tours in Mar.; tours leave every half hr for each house; last tour at 4.*

GUNSTON HALL, VIRGINIA

12 miles south of Woodlawn, 25 miles south of Washington, D.C.

GETTING HERE AND AROUND

You'll have to use a car to get to Gunston Hall, because there is no bus stop within walking distance. Travel south on Route 1, 9 miles past Woodlawn to Route 242; turn left there and go 3.5 miles to the plantation entrance.

EXPLORING

Fodor'sChoice
★
🐾
Gunston Hall Plantation. Down the Potomac from Mount Vernon is the home of another important George. Gentleman farmer George Mason was a colonel of the Virginia militia and author of the Virginia Declaration of Rights, the model for the U.S. Bill of Rights, which called for freedom of the press, tolerance of religion, and other fundamental democratic principles. Mason was a framer of the Constitution but refused to sign the final document because it didn't stop the importation of slaves, adequately restrain the powers of the federal government, or include a bill of rights. Mason's objections spurred the movement for the inclusion of the Bill of Rights into the Constitution.

12

Mason's home was begun about 1755. The Georgian-style mansion has some of the finest hand-carved ornamented interiors in the country and is the handiwork of the 18th century's foremost architect, William Buckland, who also designed the Hammond-Harwood and Chase-Lloyd houses in Annapolis. The house is built of native brick, black walnut, and yellow pine, and follows the style of the time that demanded absolute symmetry, which explains the false door set into one side of the center hallway and the "robber" window on a second-floor storage room.

The interior, with carved woodwork in styles from Chinese to Greek, has been meticulously restored, with paints made from the original formulas and carefully carved replacements for the intricate mahogany medallions in the moldings. Restored outbuildings include a kitchen, dairy, laundry, and smokehouse, and a schoolhouse has also been reconstructed.

The formal gardens, recently under excavation by a team of archaeologists, are famous for their boxwoods—some were planted during George Mason's time, making them among the oldest in the country. The Potomac is visible past the expansive deer park, and Mason's landing road to the river was recently found. Special programs, such as archaeology tutelage and a plantation Christmas celebration, are available. A tour of Gunston Hall takes at least 45 minutes; tours begin on the front porch of the house. Buy tickets at the visitor center, which includes a museum and gift shop. ⊠ *10709 Gunston Rd., Mason Neck* ☎ *703/550–9220* ⊕ *www.gunstonhall.org* ✆ *$10* ☉ *Daily 9:30–5; last tour at 4:30, tours every hr on the hr.*

OFF THE
BEATEN
PATH

National Museum of the Marine Corps. Eighteen miles south on I–95, next to the Marine Corps Base Quantico, the glassy atrium of the National Museum of the Marine Corps soars into the sky. The design for this 118,000-square-foot homage to the military's finest was inspired by the iconic photograph of marines lifting the American flag on Iwo Jima. Inside the museum, visitors are able to see the flag itself, as well as experience the life of a marine. The museum is completely interactive, from the entrance where drill instructors yell at new "recruits" in surround-sound, to the Korean War exhibit, where visitors walk through a snowy mountain pass and shiver from the cold while listening to the 2nd Platoon fight on the other side of the mountain. The museum also has a staggering collection of tanks, aircraft, rocket launchers, and other weapons. There is even a rifle range simulator ($5) where guests of all ages can learn how to hold a rifle and practice hitting targets. Ooh-rah! ⊠ *18900 Jefferson Davis Hwy., Triangle* ☎ *877/635–1775* ⊕ *www.usmcmuseum.org* ✆ *Free* ☉ *Daily 9–5.*

ANNAPOLIS, MARYLAND

In 1649 a group of Puritan settlers moved from Virginia to a spot at the mouth of the Severn River, where they established a community called Providence. Lord Baltimore, who held the royal charter to settle Maryland, named the area around this town Anne Arundel County, after his wife; in 1684 Anne Arundel Town was established across from Providence on the Severn's south side. Ten years later, Anne Arundel Town became the capital of Maryland and was renamed Annapolis after Princess Anne, who later became queen. It received its city charter in 1708 and became a major port, particularly for the export of tobacco.

In 1774, patriots here matched their Boston counterparts (who had thrown their famous tea party the previous year) by burning the *Peggy Stewart*, a ship loaded with taxed tea. Annapolis later served as the nation's first peacetime capital (1783–84). The city's considerable colonial and early republican heritage is largely intact, and because it's all within walking distance, highly accessible.

Although it has long since been overtaken by Baltimore as the major Maryland port, Annapolis is still a popular pleasure-boating destination. On warm sunny days the waters off City Dock become center stage for an amateur show of powerboaters maneuvering through the heavy traffic. Annapolis's enduring nautical reputation derives largely from the presence of the U.S. Naval Academy, whose strikingly uniformed midshipmen throng the city streets in crisp white uniforms in summer and navy blue in winter.

GETTING HERE AND AROUND

The drive (east on U.S. 50 to the Rowe Boulevard exit) normally takes 35–45 minutes from Washington. During rush hour (weekdays 3:30–6:30 pm), however, it takes about twice as long. Also beware of Navy football Saturdays.

Parking spots on Annapolis's historic downtown streets are scarce, but there are some parking meters for $1 an hour (maximum two hours). You can park on residential streets free where allowable. You can pay $5 ($10 for recreational vehicles) to park at the Navy–Marine Corps Stadium (to the right of Rowe Boulevard as you enter town from Route 50), and ride a free Annapolis Transit shuttle bus downtown. Annapolis Transit also offers free shuttle transportation within the Historic Area. There are five parking garages in the downtown area with fees ranging from $12 to $16 per day maximum; Sunday mornings from 6 am to 1 pm parking is free.

TOURS

Walking tours are a great way to see Annapolis's historic district. The Historic Annapolis Museum rents four self-guided audio walking tours. Choose from the city's highlights, African-American Annapolis, or Annapolis during the Revolutionary War or Civil War. The cost for each is $5. Guides from Watermark wear colonial-style dress and take you to the State House, St. John's College, and the Naval Academy. The cost is $16.

Discover Annapolis Tours leads one-hour narrated trolley tours ($18) that introduce you to the history and architecture of Annapolis. Tours

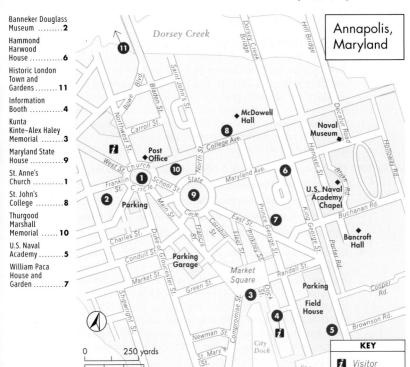

Annapolis, Maryland

12

KEY

i *Visitor information*

leave from the visitor center daily April through November and most weekends December through March.

Or see Maryland's state capital from the water. Annapolis Sailing Cruises' *Woodwind* and *Woodwind II* are twin 74-foot boats that make daily trips between April and October, with some overnight trips. Two-hour sails are $36 to $39. When the weather's good, Watermark runs boat tours that last from 40 minutes to 7½ hours and go as far as St. Michaels on the Eastern Shore, where there's a maritime museum, yachts, dining, and boutiques. Prices range from $14 to $72.

ESSENTIALS

Tour Contacts Discover Annapolis Tours. If you're using GPS, the address is 25 Northwest St. ⊠ *26 West St., Historic District* ☎ *410/626–6000* ⊕ *www. discover-annapolis.com.* **Historic Annapolis Foundation Walking Tours** ⊠ *99 Main St., Historic District* ☎ *410/267–6656* ⊕ *www.annapolis.org.* **Schooner Woodwind Cruises.** Schooner Woodwind Cruises. ⊠ *Annapolis Marriott Hotel dock* ☎ *410/263–7837* ⊕ *www.schoonerwoodwind.com.* **Watermark** ⊠ *1 Dock St., Historic District* ☎ *410/268–7601* ⊕ *www.watermarkcruises.com.*

Visitor Information Annapolis & Anne Arundel County Conference and Visitors Bureau ⊠ *26 West St., West Side* ☎ *410/280–0445, 888/302–2852* ⊕ *www.visit-annapolis.org* ☉ *Daily 9–5.* **Information Booth.** (open March through September) ⊠ *Dock St. parking lot* ☎ *410/280–0445.*

EXPLORING

TOP ATTRACTIONS

★ **Banneker-Douglass Museum.** Named for abolitionist Frederick Douglass
and scientist Benjamin Banneker, this former church and its next-door
neighbor make up a museum that tells the stories of African-Americans
in Maryland through performances, lectures, educational programs,
and changing exhibits and permanent shows. Audio and visual presentations and hands-on exhibits make the museum engaging for kids,
while also bringing home the hardships of slave life. ⊠ *84 Franklin St.*
☎ *410/216–6180* ⊕ *www.bdmuseum.com* ⊠ *Free* ⊙ *Tues.–Sat. 10–4.*

**NEED A
BREAK?**

The Annapolis Bookstore. A café and a garden provide the perfect place
for reading and storytelling. With its carefully selected collection of both
new and rare books, the store is an oasis from the ubiquitous chains. As
befits its Annapolis location, the shop specializes in maritime books. ⊠ *35
Maryland Ave.* ☎ *888/339–7370* ⊕ *www.annapolisbookstore.com.*

★ **Hammond-Harwood House.** Based on the Villa Pisani in Stra, Italy, by
Andrea Palladio, this 1774 home was designed by premier colonial
architect William Buckland and is considered America's greatest colonial high-style residence. Called the architectural "Jewel of Annapolis," the residence was greatly admired by Thomas Jefferson when he
sketched the house in 1783. The wood carvings surrounding the front
door and enriching the dining room are some of the best surviving of
their kind in America. The site today exhibits famous colonial art by
Charles Willson Peale, Rembrandt Peale, James Peale, John Trumbull,
John Hesselius, Jeremiah Theus, and John Beale Bordley, as well as an
extensive decorative arts collection covering everything from Chinese
export porcelain to Georgian period silver. Also on display is the world's
largest collection of colonial cabinetwork by Annapolis native John
Shaw. Noted landscape architect Alden Hopkins from Colonial Williamsburg created the property's Colonial Revival garden. Tours leave
on the hour; the last begins at 3 in the winter and 4 during the rest of
the year. Regular tours may be a bit dry for children under 12, but children's tours are available by special appointment. ■TIP➔ Call ahead to
see if special children's programs are planned for the day of your visit. ⊠ *19
Maryland Ave.* ☎ *410/263–4683* ⊕ *www.hammondharwoodhouse.org*
⊠ *$7* ⊙ *Jan. closed, Feb.–Mar. by appointment only, Apr.–Oct., Tues.–
Sun. noon–5; Nov–Dec. noon–4.*

★ **Historic London Town and Gardens.** The 17th-century tobacco port of London, on the South River a short car ride from Annapolis, was made up
of 40 dwellings, shops, and taverns. London all but disappeared in the
18th century, its buildings abandoned and left to decay, but the excavation of the town is underway, and buildings are continually being
restored. One of the few original colonial structures is a three-story
waterfront brick house, built by William Brown between 1758 and
1764, with dramatic river views. Docents conduct 30- to 45-minute site
tours; allow more time to wander the house grounds, woodland gardens,
and a visitor center with interactive displays. From April to December,
house tours are led approximately every hour. ⊠ *839 Londontown Rd.,*

Edgewater ☎ *410/222–1919* ⊕ *www.historiclondontown.com* ✉ *$10* ☉ *Apr.–Dec., Wed.–Sat. 10–4:30, Sun. noon–4:30.*

Fodor's Choice
★ **Maryland State House.** Originally constructed between 1772 and 1780, the State House is the oldest state capitol in continuous legislative use; it's also the only one in which the U.S. Congress has sat (1783–84). It was here where General George Washington resigned as commander in chief of the Continental Army in 1783 and where the Treaty of Paris was ratified in 1784, ending the Revolutionary War. Both events took place in the Old Senate Chamber, which is filled with intricate woodwork (attributed to colonial architect William Buckland), including the ubiquitous tobacco motif. The Maryland Senate and House hold their sessions in two other chambers in the building. Also on the grounds is the oldest public building in Maryland, the tiny redbrick treasury, built in 1735. Note that tours are self-guided and you must have a photo ID to enter the State House. ✉ *One Hundred State Circle* ☎ *410/260–6445* ✉ *Free* ☉ *Daily 9–5.*

St. John's College. The Annapolis campus of St. John's, the third-oldest college in the country (after Harvard and William and Mary), once held the last Liberty Tree, under which the Sons of Liberty convened to hear patriots plan the Revolution. Damaged in a 1999 hurricane, the 400-year-old tree was removed; its progeny stands to the left of McDowell Hall. St. John's adheres to a Great Books program, and all students follow the same four-year, liberal-arts curriculum, which includes philosophy, mathematics, music, science, Greek, and French. Students are immersed in the classics, through small classes conducted as discussions rather than lectures. Start a visit here by climbing the gradual slope of the long, brick-paved path to the cupola of McDowell Hall.

Down King George Street toward the water is the Carroll-Barrister House, now the college admissions office. Once home to Charles Carroll (not the signer of the Declaration but his cousin), the house was built in 1722 at Main and Conduit streets and moved onto campus in 1955. ✉ *60 College Ave., at St. John's St.* ☎ *410/263–2371* ⊕ *www.stjohnscollege.edu.*

Elizabeth Myers Mitchell Art Gallery. The Elizabeth Myers Mitchell Art Gallery, on the east side of Mellon Hall, presents world-class exhibits and special programs that relate to the fine arts. ☎ *410/626–2556.*

Fodor's Choice
★ **United States Naval Academy.** Probably the most interesting and important site in Annapolis, the Naval Academy occupies 329 waterfront acres along the Severn River and abuts downtown. Men and women enter the USNA, established in 1845 on the site of a U.S. Army fort, from every part of the United States and foreign countries to undergo rigorous study in subjects that include literature, navigation, and nuclear engineering. The centerpiece of the campus is the bright copper-clad dome of the interdenominational **U.S. Naval Academy Chapel.** Beneath it lies the crypt of the Revolutionary War naval officer John Paul Jones, who, in a historic naval battle with a British ship, uttered the inspirational words, "I have not yet begun to fight!"

On the grounds, midshipmen (the term used for women as well as men) go to classes, conduct military drills, and practice or compete in intercollegiate and intramural sports. Bancroft Hall is one of the largest dormitories in the world—it houses the entire 4,400-member Brigade

FIRST AFRICAN AMERICAN GRADUATE

In 1949 a man by the name of Wesley Brown made history as the U.S. Naval Academy's first African American graduate. Five others had tried before him but were forced out by intense racism and violence. Brown also suffered greatly in his years at the academy. A group of upperclassmen tried to force him out by piling him up with unwarranted demerits and ensuring that he was snubbed by his peers, but Brown never gave up. A veteran of World War II and the Korean and Vietnam wars, Brown served another 20 years in the Navy as a lieutenant commander in the Civil Engineering Corps before retiring in 1969. In 2008 the Naval Academy unveiled its $50 million Wesley Brown Field House, a state-of-the-art gymnasium that overlooks the Severn River—a fitting tribute to a man who is credited with not only helping to improve the Navy, but also the country. Today nearly one-fourth of the student body is comprised of minorities. To read more about Brown's fascinating story, check out *Breaking the Color Barrier*, by historian Robert J. Schneller Jr.

of Midshipmen. You can't see how shipshape the middies' quarters are, but you can go inside Bancroft to see the glorious Memorial Hall, a tribute to Academy grads who died in military operations. In front of Bancroft is the Statue of Tecumseh, a bronze replica of the USS *Delaware*'s wooden figurehead "Tamanend." It's decorated by midshipmen for athletics events; and for good luck during exams, students pitch pennies into his quiver of arrows. ■TIP➜ If you're here at noon on weekdays in fair weather, watch the midshipmen form up outside Bancroft Hall and parade to lunch accompanied by the Drum and Bugle Corps. ⊕ *www.navyonline.com* ✉ *Grounds tour $9.50* ☉ *USNA Armel-Leftwich Visitor Center: Mar.–Dec., daily 9–5; Jan. and Feb., daily 9–4. Guided walking tours generally leave Mon.–Sat. 10–3 on the hr and Sun. 12:00–3 on the ½ hr; call ahead to confirm and for Jan. and Feb. tour times.*

USNA Armel-Leftwich Visitor Center. Adjoining Halsey Field House is the USNA Armel-Leftwich Visitor Center. A new exhibit "The Quarter Deck," opening in early 2013, focuses on what it takes to become a midshipman. Walking tours of the Naval Academy leave from the center. Everyone 16 and older must have a government-issued photo ID to be admitted through the academy's gates. Park on the street or in Annapolis public parking and walk through Gate 1 or 3—on foot is the only way you can enter unless you're driving a car used for official Department of Defense business. ✉ *52 King George St.* ☎ *410/293–8687.*

U.S. Naval Academy Museum & Gallery of Ships. Near the chapel in Preble Hall is the U.S. Naval Academy Museum & Gallery of Ships, which tells the story of the U.S. Navy through displays of model ships and memorabilia from naval heroes and fighting vessels. The Rogers Ship Model Collection has 108 models of sailing ships built for the British Admiralty. Admission for the museum is free; hours are Monday through Saturday from 9 to 5 and Sunday from 11 to 5. ✉ *118 Maryland Ave.* ☎ *410/293–2108.*

William Paca House and Garden. A signer of the Declaration of Independence, Paca (pronounced "PAY-cuh") was a Maryland governor from 1782 to 1785. His house was built from 1763 through 1765, and its original garden was finished by 1772. The main floor (furnished with 18th-century antiques) retains its original Prussian blue and soft gray color scheme and the second

floor houses more 18th-century pieces. The adjacent 2-acre garden provides a longer perspective on the back of the house, plus worthwhile sights of its own: upper terraces, a Chinese Chippendale bridge, a pond, a wilderness area, and formal arrangements. An inn, Carvel Hall, once stood in the gardens, now planted with 18th-century perennials. You can take a self-guided tour of the garden, but to see the house you must go on the docent-led tour, which leaves every hour at half past the hour. The last tour leaves 1½ hours before closing. ⊠ *186 Prince George St.* ☎ *410/990–4543* ⊕ *www.annapolis.org* ✉ *House and garden $10, garden only $7* ☉ *House and garden mid-Mar.–Dec., Mon.–Sat. 10–5, Sun. noon–5; Feb.–mid-Mar., Fri. and Sat. 10–4, Sun. noon–4.*

WORTH NOTING

Historic Annapolis Museum. This light-filled, modern little museum is a good place to pick up tickets for tours by foot, carriage, or boat. A few paces away at 77 Main Street, the Museum Store sells maps, Maryland history books, ceramics, and nautical knickknacks in the site of a warehouse that held supplies for the Continental Army during the Revolutionary War. ⊠ *99 Main St.* ☎ *410/267–6656* ⊕ *www.annapolis. org* ✉ *Free* ☉ *Mon.–Thurs. 10–5, Fri. and Sat. 10–6, Sun. 11–5; shorter hrs in winter.*

Kunta Kinte–Alex Haley Memorial. A series of plaques along the waterfront recounting the story of African Americans in Maryland lead to a sculpture group depicting Haley, famed author of *Roots,* reading to a group of children. On the other side of the street, a three-sided obelisk and plaque commemorates the 1767 arrival of the African slave immortalized in Haley's novel. This is a lovely place that may inspire you to reflect on African American history and the importance of family, reading, and passing oral history from one generation to another. ⊠ *Market Sq.* ⊕ *www.kintehaley.org.*

St. Anne's Church. Residing in the center of one of the historic area's busy circles, this brick building is one of the city's most prominent places of worship. King William III donated the communion silver when the parish was founded in 1692, but the first St. Anne's Church wasn't completed until 1704. The second church burned in 1858, but parts of its walls survived and were incorporated into the present structure, built the following year. The churchyard contains the grave of the last colonial governor, Sir Robert Eden. ⊠ *Church Circle* ☎ *410/267–9333* ✉ *Free* ☉ *Mon.–Thurs. 8–4, Fri. 8–12; services on Sun.*

Thurgood Marshall Memorial. Born in Baltimore, Thurgood Marshall (1908–93) was the first African American Supreme Court Justice and one of the 20th century's foremost leaders in the struggle for equal rights under the law. Marshall won the decision in 1954's *Brown v. Board of Education*, in which the Supreme Court overturned the doctrine of "separate but equal." Marshall was appointed as U.S. Solicitor General in 1965 and to the Supreme Court in 1967 by President Lyndon B. Johnson. The 8-foot statue depicts Marshall as a young lawyer. ⊠ *State House Sq., bordered by Bladen St., School St., and College Ave.*

WHERE TO EAT

In the beginning, there was crab: crab cakes, crab soup, whole crabs to crack. This Chesapeake Bay specialty is still found in abundance, but Annapolis has broadened its horizons to include eateries—many in the Historic District—that offer many sorts of cuisines. Ask for a restaurant guide at the visitor center.

$ ✕ **49 West Coffeehouse and Gallery.** In what was once a hardware store,
ECLECTIC   this eclectic, casual eatery has one interior wall of exposed brick and another of exposed plaster; both are used to hang art for sale by local artists. Daily specials are chalked on a blackboard. Menu staples include a large cheese-and-pâté plate, deli sandwiches, and soups and salads. There's free Wi-Fi, and live music is performed every night but Sunday. Ⓢ *Average main: $12* ⊠ *49 West St.* ☎ *410/626–9796* ⊕ *49westcoffeehouse.com.*

$$ ✕ **Buddy's Crabs & Ribs.** Family owned and operated since 1988, with
SEAFOOD   a great location overlooking Annapolis Harbor, this fun and informal
♺   restaurant features all kinds of seafood and shellfish, including their famous "Big Buddy" crab cakes and all-you-can-eat buffets. Buddy's is the biggest restaurant in Annapolis. With each full-price entrée, one child 10 and under can eat free from the kids' menu. Ⓢ *Average main: $20* ⊠ *100 Main St.* ☎ *410/626–1100* ⊕ *www.buddysonline.com.*

$$$ ✕ **Café Normandie.** Wood beams, skylights, and a four-sided fireplace
FRENCH   make this French restaurant homey, and out of the open kitchen comes an astonishingly good French onion soup, made daily from scratch. Bouillabaisse, puffy omelets, crepes, and seafood dishes are other specialties. Breakfast is served on weekends. All offerings are sustainable and local. Ⓢ *Average main: $26* ⊠ *185 Main St.* ☎ *410/263–3382.*

$$ ✕ **Cantler's Riverside Inn.** Opened in 1974, this local institution was
SEAFOOD   founded by Jimmy Cantler, a native Marylander who worked as a waterman on the Chesapeake Bay. The no-nonsense interior has nautical items laminated beneath tabletops, and steamed mussels, clams, and shrimp as well as Maryland vegetable crab soup, seafood sandwiches, oysters, crab cakes, and numerous fin fish are served on disposable dinnerware; if you order steamed crabs, they'll come served atop a "tablecloth" of brown paper. Water-view outdoor dining is available seasonally. Boat owners can tie up at the dock; free parking spaces are rare during the busy summer season and carpooling is encouraged if you drive. Jimmy Buffett claims that it is one of his top 10 favorite places

to have a drink waterside. This place is easiest to find by boat, so if you're coming by car, use a GPS or check the website for directions. ■TIP→ Cantler's gets very crowded on summer weekends—prepare to wait. Reservations are accepted for parties of ten or more Monday through Thursday. $ *Average main: $20* ⊠ *458 Forest Beach Rd.* ☏ *410/757-1311* ⊕ *www.cantlers.com.*

$$$$
AMERICAN

✕ **Carrol's Creek.** You can walk, catch a water taxi from City Dock, or drive over the Spa Creek drawbridge to this local favorite in Eastport. Whether you dine indoors or out, the view of historic Annapolis and its harbor is spectacular. The all-you-can-eat Sunday brunch is worth checking out, as are the seafood specialties. Any of the entrées, including the herb-encrusted rockfish or grilled New York strip steak, can be turned into a reasoanbly priced four-course meal with the addition of soup, salad, and dessert. $ *Average main: $45* ⊠ *410 Severn Ave., Eastport* ☏ *410/263-8102* ⊕ *www.carrolscreek.com.*

$
AMERICAN

✕ **Chick and Ruth's Delly.** Deli sandwiches (named for local politicos), burgers, subs, crab cakes, and milk shakes are the fare at this very busy counter-and-booth institution. Built in 1899, the edifice was just a sandwich shop when Baltimoreans Ruth and Chick Levitt purchased it in 1965. Their son Ted and his wife Beth continue the business today. Don't plan on placing an order at 8:30 am on a weekday or 9:30 am on a weekend—that's when the place stops to say the Pledge of Allegiance. $ *Average main: $11* ⊠ *165 Main St., Historic District* ☏ *410/269-6737.*

$
MEXICAN

✕ **El Toro Bravo.** At this local favorite, an authentic Mexican restaurant, the wooden colonial exterior conceals Mexican tiles and the occassional bull's head on the walls. On weekends, there's often a line, but takeout is available. The guacamole is made on the premises. $ *Average main: $12* ⊠ *50 West St., 1 block from visitor center* ☏ *410/267-5949.*

$$$
SEAFOOD

✕ **Harry Browne's.** In the shadow of the State House, this understated establishment has long held a reputation for quality food and attentive service that ensures bustle year-round, especially during the busy days of the legislative session (early January into early April) and special weekend events at the Naval Academy. The menu clearly reflects the city's maritime culture, but also has seasonal specialties, and in a green approach to dining, everything used is recycled. Live Irish music is performed in the lounge once a month. The sidewalk café is open, weather permitting, April through October. There is a champagne brunch on Sunday. $ *Average main: $30* ⊠ *66 State Circle* ☏ *410/263-4332* ⊕ *www.harrybrownes.com.*

$
AMERICAN

✕ **McGarvey's Saloon and Oyster Bar.** An Annapolis institution since 1975, this dockside eatery and watering hole is full of good cheer, great drink, and grand food. A heritage of seasonal shell- and fin-fish dishes, the finest burgers and steaks, as well as unstinting appetizers, make McGarvey's menu one of the most popular in the area. The full menu is available daily until 11 pm. Choose to eat outside in good weather, at the bar, or in the light-filled atrium. $ *Average main: $17* ⊠ *8 Market Space* ☏ *410/263-5700* ⊕ *www.mcgarveys.net.*

$$ ✕**Middleton Tavern.** Horatio Middleton began operating this "inn for
AMERICAN seafaring men" in 1750; Washington, Jefferson, and Franklin were
among his guests. Today four fireplaces, wood floors, paneled walls,
and a colonial theme create a cozy atmosphere and seafood tops the
menu; the Maryland crab soup and pan-seared rockfish are standouts.
Try the tavern's own Middleton Oyster Ale, perhaps during happy hour
or during a weekend blues session in the upstairs piano bar. Brunch is
served on weekends, and you can dine outdoors in good weather. $ *Average main: $24* ⊠ *City Dock at Randall St.* ☎ *410/263–3323* ⊕ *www.
middletontavern.com.*

$$$ ✕**Osteria 177.** This might be the nicest restaurant in the capital that
MODERN ITALIAN doesn't serve crab cakes. It also might be the only local Italian restaurant that doesn't offer pizza or spaghetti. Instead, Osteria serves seafood
from all over the world, meat, and pasta made on the premises. Northern Italian owner and chef Arturo Ottaviano offers sea bass filleted at
tableside, lobster bisque served in generous oval-shaped bowls, and
his signature dish Linguine all' Osteria 177, surrounded by generous
servings of seafood. Local politicians and lobbyists like the $15 lunch.
$ *Average main: $26* ⊠ *177 Main St.* ☎ *410/267–7700.*

$ ✕**Rams Head Tavern.** This traditional English-style pub serves better-
BRITISH than-usual tavern fare, including spicy shrimp salad, crab cakes, beer-
★ battered shrimp, and daily specials, as well as more than 100 beers—15
on tap—including six Fordham beers and others from around the
world. Brunch is served on Sunday, and nationally known folk, rock,
jazz, country, and bluegrass artists perform some nights. Dinner-show
specials are available; the menu has light fare. $ *Average main: $14*
⊠ *33 West St.* ☎ *410/268–4545* ⊕ *www.ramsheadtavern.com.*

WHERE TO STAY

For expanded hotel reviews, visit Fodors.com.

There are many places to stay near the heart of the city, as well as area
bed-and-breakfasts and chain motels a few miles outside town. Prices
vary considerably. They rise astronomically for "Commissioning Week"
at the Naval Academy (late May), the week of July 4, and during the
sailboat and powerboat shows in October.

Annapolis Accommodations. Annapolis Accommodations specializes in
rentals as short as three days or as long as three years. Their office is
open 9–5:30 weekdays. $ *Rooms from: $14* ⊠ *41 Maryland Ave., Historic Area* ☎ *410/263–3262* ⊕ *www.stayannapolis.com.*

Annapolis Bed & Breakfast Association. Annapolis Bed & Breakfast Association books lodging in 12 bed-and-breakfasts in the old section of town,
which has many restaurants and shops, and in Eastport. $ *Rooms from:
$189* ⊕ *www.annapolisbandb.com.*

$$$ 🏨 **Annapolis Marriott Waterfront.** You can practically fish from your room
HOTEL at the city's only waterfront hotel, where rooms have either balconies
♻ over the water or large windows with views of the harbor or the historic district. **Pros:** a "pure room" is available for the allergy sensitive;
accessible for travelers with disabilities; a great place for children. **Cons:**
some rooms have no waterfront view, some have only partial views;

chain hotel lacks charm; parking is pricey. **TripAdvisor:** "room location a major factor," "wonderful visit," "great hotel with great views." $ *Rooms from: $349* ✉ *80 Compromise St.* ☎ *410/268–7555* ⊕ *www. annapolismarriott.com* ⇥ *150 rooms* ⟨○⟩ *No meals.*

$ 🏠 **Country Inn & Suites.** Rooms all have standard chain-hotel decor, but
HOTEL a large fireplace, wooden floors, and overstuffed sofas make the lobby an inviting place to linger. **Pros:** complimentary hot breakfast included; reliable and inexpensive option; near shopping. **Cons:** 4 miles from the dock; small gym. **TripAdvisor:** "great place for a family," "very nice lodging," "wonderful experience." $ *Rooms from: $129* ✉ *2600 Housely Rd.* ☎ *410/571–6700, 800/456–4000* ⊕ *www.countryinns. com* ⇥ *100 rooms* ⟨○⟩ *Breakfast.*

$ 🏠 **Gibson's Lodgings.** Three detached houses from three centuries—1780,
HOTEL 1890, and 1980—are operated together as a single inn, and all the guest rooms are furnished with pre-1900 antiques. **Pros:** conveniently located between the Naval Academy and downtown; half block from the water; free parking in the courtyards. **Cons:** only one of the houses can accommodate children; only one room is handicapped accessible. **TripAdvisor:** "great room," "fantastic location," "a true gem." $ *Rooms from: $149* ✉ *110–114 Prince George St.* ☎ *410/268–5555, 877/330–0057* ⊕ *www.gibsonslodgings.com* ⇥ *20 rooms, 18 with bath* ⟨○⟩ *Breakfast.*

$ 🏠 **Historic Inns of Annapolis.** Three 18th-century properties in the his-
B&B/INN toric district, the Governor Calvert House, Robert Johnson House,
★ and Maryland Inn, are now grouped as one inn, all offering guest rooms that are individually decorated with antiques and reproductions. **Pros:** historic properties; within walking distance of activities; lemonade or spiced cider served daily in the Calvert House. **Cons:** prices vary greatly; some rooms are small. **TripAdvisor:** "wonderful quaint accommodations," "lovely base in Annapolis," "charming." $ *Rooms from: $169* ✉ *58 State Circle* ☎ *410/263–2641, 800/847–8882* ⊕ *www. historicinnsofannapolis.com* ⇥ *124 rooms, 14 suites* ⟨○⟩ *No meals.*

$ 🏠 **Scotlaur Inn.** On the two floors above Chick and Ruth's Delly, rooms
B&B/INN in this family-owned B&B are papered in pastel colonial prints and furnished with high beds topped with fluffy comforters and lots of pillows. **Pros:** a chance to stay above one of Annapolis's landmarks right in the center of town. Half off in nearby parking garage. **Cons:** might not be your style if you prefer modern decor and don't like chintz; rooms are on the smaller side; no elevator. **TripAdvisor:** "amazing staff," "great people," "perfect location." $ *Rooms from: $95* ✉ *165 Main St.* ☎ *410/268–5665* ⊕ *www.scotlaurinn.com* ⇥ *10 rooms* ⟨○⟩ *Breakfast.*

$$ 🏠 **The Westin Annapolis Hotel.** The Westin Annapolis is part of a large
HOTEL redevelopment complex about a mile from the City Dock and offers luxurious accommodation, along with a business center and the largest ballroom in town. **Pros:** the complete Starwood hotel experience; modern hotel with many amenities. **Cons:** about a mile from the City Dock in a rapidly gentrifying neighborhood; Wi-Fi only free in public areas. **TripAdvisor:** "great service," "best place to stay in Annapolis," "convenient to everything." $ *Rooms from: $219* ✉ *100 Westgate Circle, Park Place* ☎ *410/972–4300* ⊕ *www.westin.com/annapolis* ⇥ *225 rooms* ⟨○⟩ *No meals.*

Travel Smart Washington, D.C.

WORD OF MOUTH

"We loved the Metro, and it worked seamlessly (except for the afternoon when all the Virginia Tech/Boise State football fans took over the trains on the way to the game)."

—MP07950

GETTING HERE AND AROUND

Although it may not appear so at first glance, there's a system to addresses in D.C., albeit one that's a bit confusing for newcomers. The city is divided into the four quadrants of a compass (NW, NE, SE, SW), with the U.S. Capitol at the center. Because the Capitol doesn't sit in the exact center of the city, Northwest is the largest quadrant. Northwest also has most of the important landmarks, although Northeast and Southwest have their fair share. The boundaries are North Capitol Street, East Capitol Street, South Capitol Street, and the National Mall.

If someone tells you to meet them at 6th and G, ask them to specify the quadrant, because there are actually four different 6th and G intersections (one per quadrant). Within each quadrant, numbered streets run north to south, and lettered streets run east to west (the letter *J* was omitted to avoid confusion with the letter *I*). The streets form a fairly simple grid—for instance, 900 G Street NW is the intersection of 9th and G streets in the NW quadrant of the city. Likewise, if you count the letters of the alphabet, skipping *J*, you can get a good approximation of an address for a numbered street. For instance, 1600 16th Street NW is close to Q Street, Q being the 16th letter of the alphabet if you skip *J*.

As if all this weren't confusing enough, Major Pierre L'Enfant, the Frenchman who originally designed the city, threw in diagonal avenues recalling those of Paris. Most of D.C.'s avenues are named after U.S. states. You can find addresses on avenues the same way you find those on numbered streets, so 1200 Connecticut Avenue NW is close to M Street, because *M* is the 12th letter of the alphabet when you skip *J*.

▌ AIR TRAVEL

A flight to D.C. from New York takes a little less than an hour. It's about 1½ hours from Chicago, 3 hours from Denver or Dallas, and 5 hours from San Francisco. Passengers flying from London should expect a trip of about 6 hours. From Sydney it's an 18-hour flight.

Airline Contacts AirTran ☎ 800/247–8726 ⊕ *www.airtran.com.* **American Airlines/ American Eagle** ☎ 800/433–7300 ⊕ *www.aa.com.* **Delta Airlines** ☎ 800/221– 1212 ⊕ *www.delta.com.* **jetBlue** ☎ 800/538– 2583 ⊕ *www.jetblue.com.* **Southwest Airlines** ☎ 800/435–9792 ⊕ *www.southwest.com.* **United Airlines** ☎ 800/864–8331 ⊕ *www.united.com.* **US Airways** ☎ 800/428– 4322 ⊕ *www.usairways.com.*

Airlines and Airports Airline and Airport Links.com ⊕ *www.airlineandairportlinks.com.*

Airline Security Issues Transportation Security Administration ☎ 866/289-9673 ⊕ *www.tsa.gov.*

Air Travel Resources in Washington, D.C. U.S. Department of Transportation Aviation Consumer Protection Division ☎ 202/366– 2220 ⊕ *airconsumer.ost.dot.gov.*

AIRPORTS

The major gateways to D.C. are **Ronald Reagan Washington National Airport (DCA)** in Virginia, 4 miles south of Downtown Washington; **Dulles International Airport (IAD)**, 26 miles west of Washington, D.C.; and **Baltimore/Washington International–Thurgood Marshall Airport (BWI)** in Maryland, about 30 miles to the northeast.

Reagan National Airport is closest to Downtown D.C., and has a Metro stop in the terminal. East Coast shuttles and shorter flights tend to fly in and out of this airport. Dulles is configured primarily for long-haul flights, although as a United hub, it's also well-connected regionally.

BWI offers blended service, with its many gates for Southwest Air, as well as international flights. Although the Metro doesn't serve Dulles or BWI, there is affordable and convenient public transportation to and from each airport. Be aware that the Mid-Atlantic region is prone to quirky weather that can snarl air traffic, especially on stormy summer afternoons.

Airport Information Baltimore/Washington International-Thurgood Marshall Airport (BWI). ☎ 800/435–9294 ⊕ www.bwiairport. com. Dulles International Airport (IAD). ☎ 703/572–2700 ⊕ www.metwashairports. com/dulles. Ronald Reagan Washington National Airport (DCA). ☎ 703/417–8000 ⊕ www.metwashairports.com/reagan.

GROUND TRANSPORTATION: REAGAN NATIONAL (DCA)

By Car: Take the George Washington Memorial Parkway north for approximately 1 mile. Exit on I–395 North; bear left onto US–1 North toward Downtown. For the city center, turn left on Madison Drive NW and turn right on 15th Street NW. The drive takes 20–30 minutes, depending on traffic and your destination.

By Metro: The Metro station is within easy walking distance of Terminals B and C, and a free airport bus shuttles between the station and Terminal A. The Metro ride to Downtown takes about 20 minutes and costs about $1.95, depending on the time of day and your final destination.

By Shuttle: SuperShuttle, a fleet of bright blue vans, will take you to any hotel or residence in the city. The length of the ride varies, depending on traffic and the number of stops. The approximately 20-minute ride from Reagan National to Downtown averages $14.

By Taxi: Expect to pay $20–$25 to get from National to Downtown.

Contacts SuperShuttle ☎ 800/258–3826, 202/296–6662 ⊕ www.supershuttle.com. Washington Metropolitan Area Transit Authority ☎ 202/637–7000, 202/638–3780 TTY ⊕ www.wmata.com.

TAXI TIP

If you plan to take a cab from Reagan National Airport, note that a $2.50 surcharge is added to the metered fare. Large items of luggage placed in the trunk cost an additional 50¢ per item. Taxi rip-offs have decreased since the District introduced meters, but if the fare seems astronomical, get the driver's name and cab number and contact the D.C. Taxi Commission.

Taxicab Commission. Taxicab Commission ☎ 311, 202/645–6018 ✉ dctc@dc.gov ⊕ dctaxi.dc.gov.

GROUND TRANSPORTATION: BALTIMORE/WASHINGTON INTERNATIONAL (BWI)

By Car: Exit BWI and follow I–95 West. Take Exit 2B to MD–295 South for 24 miles; exit on US–50 West toward Washington. Continue on New York Avenue for about 3 miles; continue on Mount Vernon Place NW for 2 miles. Continue on Massachusetts Avenue NW; turn left on Vermont Avenue NW at Thomas Circle. Turn right on K Street NW; take a left on 17th Street NW and you're now basically in the city center. The distance is about 34 miles and should take 50–60 minutes.

By Public Transit: Amtrak and Maryland Rail Commuter Service (MARC) trains run between BWI and Washington, D.C.'s Union Station from around 6 am to 10 pm. The cost of the 30-minute ride is $14–$54 on Amtrak and $6 on MARC's Penn Line, which runs only on weekdays. A free shuttle bus transports passengers between airline terminals and the train station (which is in a distant parking lot).

Washington Metropolitan Area Transit Authority (WMATA) operates express bus service (Bus B30) between BWI and the Greenbelt Metro station. Buses run between 6 am and 10 pm. The fare is $6.

By Shuttle: SuperShuttle will take you to any hotel or residence in the city. The ride from BWI, which takes approximately 60 minutes, averages $37.

By Taxi: The fare from BWI is about $90.

Contacts Amtrak ☎ 800/872-7245 ⊕ www.amtrak.com. Maryland Rail Commuter Service ☎ 410/539-5000, 410/539-3497 TTY, 866/743-3682 ⊕ www.mtamaryland.com. SuperShuttle ☎ 800/258-3826, 202/296-6662 ⊕ www.supershuttle.com. Washington Metropolitan Area Transit Authority ☎ 202/637-7000, 202/638-3780 TTY ⊕ www.wmata.com.

GROUND TRANSPORTATION: DULLES (IAD)

By Car: From Dulles Airport, exit onto Dulles Airport Access Road and follow this for 14 miles; merge onto VA–267 East. Merge onto I–66 East; follow this for approximately 6 miles and exit to the left on E Street Expressway. Take the ramp to E Street NW. Total distance from the airport to Downtown is about 27 miles and should take about 45 minutes.

By Public Transit: Washington Flyer links Dulles International Airport and the West Falls Church Metro station. The 30-minute ride is $10 one-way and $18 round-trip for adults, free for children under six. Buses run every half hour from 5:45 am to 10:15 pm. All coaches are accessible to those in wheelchairs. Fares may be paid with cash or credit card at the ticket counter near Door 4 at the Arrivals/Baggage Claim Level. Board the bus just outside the door.

The Washington Metropolitan Area Transit Authority (WMATA) operates express bus service between Dulles and several stops in Downtown D.C., including the L'Enfant Plaza Metro station and Rosslyn Metro station in Arlington, Virginia, just across the river from Georgetown. Bus 5A, which costs $6, runs every hour between 5:30 am and 11:30 pm from curb location 2E in the second lane on the (lower) arrivals level in front of the terminal. Make sure to have the exact fare or a rechargeable SmarTrip card, as drivers cannot make change.

By Shuttle: The roughly 45-minute ride from Dulles on the SuperShuttle runs $29 for one person, $10 for each additional person. Sign in with the attendants at the lower-level doors, down the ramp when you exit the terminal.

By Taxi: The fare to Washington D.C. from Dulles is about $50–$60.

Contacts SuperShuttle ☎ 800/258-3826, 202/296-6662 ⊕ www.supershuttle.com. Washington Flyer ☎ 888/927-4359 ⊕ www.washfly.com. Washington Metropolitan Area Transit Authority ☎ 202/637-7000, 202/638-3780 TTY ⊕ www.wmata.com.

❚ BUS TRAVEL

REGIONAL BUSES

Several bus lines run between New York City and the Washington, D.C. area, including BoltBus, DC2NY, Megabus, Tripper Bus, and Vamoose (these last two run to Metro stations in Bethesda, MD and Arlington, VA). All the buses are clean, the service satisfactory, and the price can't be beat. Believe it or not, with advance planning, you might be able to get a round-trip ticket for just $2. Several of the bus lines offer power outlets, Wi-Fi, and a frequent-rider loyalty program. Bus Junction is a fast and easy way to compare prices and times online.

Information BoltBus ☎ 877/265-8287 ⊕ www.boltbus.com. Bus Junction ⊕ www.busjunction.com. DC2NY ☎ 202/332-2691 ⊕ www.dc2ny.com. Megabus ☎ 877/462-6342 ⊕ www.megabus.com. Tripper Bus ☎ 877/826-3874 ⊕ www.tripperbus.com. Vamoose ☎ 877/393-2828 ⊕ www.vamoosebus.com.

CITY BUSES

Most of the sightseeing neighborhoods (the Mall, Capitol Hill, Downtown, Dupont Circle) are near Metro rail stations, but a few (Georgetown, Adams Morgan) are more easily reached by the blue-and-white buses operated by the Washington Metropolitan Area Transit Authority. The No. 42 bus travels from the Dupont Circle Metro stop to and through Adams Morgan. Georgetown is a hike from the closest Metro rail station, but you can take a Georgetown Metro Connection shuttle to any Metrobus stop from the Foggy Bottom or Dupont Circle Metro stations in D.C. or the Rosslyn Metro station in Arlington, Virginia. The D.C. Circulator is another option for getting around the city; it has five routes and charges $1. The Potomac Avenue–Skyland via Barracks Row, Union Station–Navy Yard via Capitol Hill, and Woodley Park–Adams Morgan–McPherson Square Metro routes cut a path from north to south; the Georgetown–Union Station and Rosslyn–Georgetown–Dupont routes go east to west.

Complete bus and Metro maps for the metropolitan D.C. area, which note museums, monuments, theaters, and parks, can be picked up free of charge at the Metro Center sales office.

FARES AND TRANSFERS

All regular buses within the District are $1.70; express buses, which make fewer stops, are $3.85. For every adult ticket purchased, two children under the age of four travel free. Children five and older pay the regular fare. You'll save 20¢ and transfer bus-to-bus for free by using a SmarTrip card, a rechargeable Farecard you can use on buses and Metro. Just touch the card to the SmarTrip logo on the fare box.

To transfer Metro-to-bus, take a pass from the rail-to-bus-transfer machine in the Metro station after you go through the turnstile and before you board your train. When you board the bus, you'll pay a transfer charge (75¢ on regular Metrobus routes and $2.50 on express routes). There are no bus-to-Metro transfers.

D.C. Circulator passengers can pay cash when boarding (exact change only) or use Metro Farecards, SmarTrip cards, and all-day passes. Tickets also may be purchased at fare meters or multispace parking meters on the sidewalk near Circulator stops. Machines accept change or credit cards and make change. You only have to wait about 5–10 minutes at any of the stops for the next bus.

PAYMENT AND PASSES

Buses require exact change in bills, coins, or both. You can eliminate the exact-change hassle by purchasing a seven-day Metrobus pass for $15, or the $5 rechargeable SmarTrip card online before your trip or at the Metro Center sales office, open weekdays from 8 am to 6 pm. The SmarTrip card can also be used on the Metrorail system.

Information D.C. Circulator ☎ 202/962–1423 ⊕ www.dccirculator.com. **Metro Center sales office** ✉ 12th and F Sts. NW ☎ No phone. **Washington Metropolitan Area Transit Authority** ☎ 202/637–7000, 202/638–3780 TTY ⊕ www.wmata.com.

▌ CAR TRAVEL

A car is often a drawback in Washington, D.C. Traffic is awful, especially at rush hour, and driving is often confusing, with many lanes and some entire streets changing direction suddenly during rush hour. Even longtime residents carry maps in their cars to help navigate confusing traffic circles and randomly arranged one-way streets. Most traffic lights stand at the side of intersections (instead of hanging suspended over them), and the streets are dotted with giant potholes. The city's most popular sights are all within a short walk of a Metro station, so do yourself a favor and leave your car at the hotel. If you're visiting sights in Maryland or Virginia or need a car because of reduced mobility, time your trip to avoid D.C. rush hours, 7 am–10 am and 3 pm–7 pm.

With Zipcar, an urban car-rental membership service, you can rent a car for a couple of hours or a couple of days from convenient Downtown parking lots. An annual fee of $60, plus $8–$11.25 per hour or $74–$83 a day (plus membership fees) buys you gas, insurance, parking, and satellite radio. Reserve online or by phone, get in, and go.

Information zipcar ☎ 866/494–7227 ⊕ www.zipcar.com.

GASOLINE

Gas is more expensive in the District than it is in Maryland or Virginia, and gas stations can be hard to find, especially around Pennsylvania Avenue and the National Mall. Your best bets are the BP station at the corner of 18th and S streets NW, the Mobil station at the corner of 15th and U streets NW, the Exxon station at 2150 M Street NW, and the Mobil station at the corner of 22nd and P streets NW. The no-name station at Wisconsin and Q in Georgetown has the cheapest gas in Northwest D.C.—cash only.

LAY OF THE LAND

Interstate 95 skirts D.C. as part of the Beltway, the six- to eight-lane highway that encircles the city. The eastern half of the Beltway is labeled both I–95 and I–495; the western half is just I–495. If you're coming from the south, take I–95 to I–395 and cross the 14th Street Bridge to 14th Street in the District. From the north, stay on I–95 South. Take the exit to Washington, which will place you onto the Baltimore–Washington (B-W) Parkway heading south. The B-W Parkway will turn into New York Avenue, taking you into Downtown Washington, D.C.

Interstate 66 approaches the city from the southwest. You can get Downtown by taking I–66 across the Theodore Roosevelt Bridge to Constitution Avenue.

Interstate 270 approaches Washington, D.C., from the northwest before hitting I–495. To reach Downtown, take I–495 East to Connecticut Avenue South, toward Chevy Chase.

PARKING

Parking in D.C. is a question of supply and demand—little of the former, too much of the latter. The police are quick to ticket, tow away, or boot any vehicle parked illegally, so check complicated parking signs and feed the meter before you go. If you find you've been towed from a city street, call ☎ 311 or 202/737–4404 or log on to ⊕ www.dmv.dc.gov. Be sure you know the license-plate number, make, model, and color of the car before you call.

Most of the outlying, suburban Metro stations have parking lots, though these fill quickly with city-bound commuters. If you plan to park in one of these lots, arrive early.

Private parking lots Downtown often charge around $5–$10 an hour and $25–$40 a day. There's free, three-hour parking around the Mall on Jefferson and Madison drives, though these spots are almost always filled. There is no parking near the Lincoln or Roosevelt memorials. The closest free parking is in three lots in East Potomac Park, south of the 14th Street Bridge.

RENTAL CARS

If you're staying in D.C., skip it. Public transportation in the city is convenient and affordable, and driving here is no fun.

However, if you're staying in Virginia or Maryland and your hotel doesn't have a shuttle into D.C. and isn't within walking distance of Metro, then a car may be your best transportation option.

Daily rental rates in Washington, D.C., begin at about $40 during the week and about $22 on weekends for an economy car with air-conditioning, automatic transmission, and unlimited mileage. This does not include airport facility fees or the tax on car rentals.

In Washington, D.C., many agencies require you to be at least 25 to rent a car. However, younger employees of major corporations and military or government personnel on official business should check with rental companies and their employers for exceptions.

Major Rental Agencies
Alamo ☎ 877/222–9075 ⊕ www.alamo.com.
Avis ☎ 800/331–1212 ⊕ www.avis.com.
Budget ☎ 800/527–0700 ⊕ www.budget.com. **Hertz** ☎ 800/654–3131 ⊕ www.hertz.com. **National Car Rental** ☎ 877/222–9058 ⊕ www.nationalcar.com.

ROADSIDE EMERGENCIES

Dial 911 to report accidents on the road and to reach police, the highway patrol, or the fire department. For police non-emergencies, dial 311.

Emergency Services U.S. Park Police ☎ *202/610–7500.*

RULES OF THE ROAD

In D.C. you may turn right at a red light after stopping if there's no oncoming traffic. When in doubt, wait for the green. Be alert for one-way streets, "no left turn" intersections, and blocks closed to car traffic. The use of handheld mobile phones while operating a vehicle is illegal in Washington, D.C. Drivers can also be cited for "failure to pay full time and attention while operating a motor vehicle." The speed limit in D.C. is 25 mph except on the Whitehurst Freeway.

Radar detectors are illegal in Washington, D.C., and Virginia.

During rush hour (6–9 am and 4–7 pm), HOV (high-occupancy vehicle) lanes on I–395 and I–95 are reserved for cars with three or more people. All the lanes of I–66 inside the Beltway are reserved for cars carrying two or more during rush hour, as are some of the lanes on the Dulles Toll Road and on I–270.

Always strap children under a year old or under 20 pounds into approved rear-facing child-safety seats in the backseat. In Washington, D.C., children weighing 20–40 pounds must also ride in a car seat in the back, although it may face the front. Children cannot sit in the front seat of a car until they are at least four years old and weigh more than 80 pounds.

▌ METRO TRAVEL

The Metro, which opened in 1976, is clean and safe and provides a convenient way to get around the city—if you're staying near a Metro stop. You can find a list of area hotels indexed with the closest Metro station at ⊕ *stationmasters.com.* The Metro operates from 5 am weekdays and 7 am weekends, until 3 am Friday and Saturday and midnight the rest of the week. Don't get to the station at the last minute, as trains from the ends of the lines depart before the official closing time. During the weekday peak periods (5–9:30 am and 3–7 pm), trains come along every three to six minutes. At other times and on weekends and holidays, trains run about every 12–15 minutes. Lighted displays at the platforms show estimated arrival and departure times of trains, as well as the number of cars available. Eating, drinking, smoking, and littering in stations and on the trains are strictly prohibited.

FARES

The Metro's base fare is $2.10; the actual price you pay depends on the time of day and the distance traveled, which means you might end up paying $5.75 if you're traveling to a distant station at rush hour. Pay with a SmarTrip card, a rechargeable fare card that can be used throughout the Metro, bus and parking system, for a 25¢ discount. Up to two children under age four ride free when accompanied by a paying passenger.

PAYMENT AND PASSES

Buy your ticket at the Farecard machines; they accept coins and crisp $1, $5, $10, or $20 bills. If the machine spits your bill back out at you, try folding and unfolding it lengthwise before asking someone for help. Many machines will also accept credit cards. You can buy one-day passes for $14 and seven-day passes for $47. To enter the Metro platform, insert your Farecard into the slot on the turnstile and take it out again at the back—you'll need it to exit at your destination. Locals use the SmarTrip card; touch your card to the SmarTrip logo on the turnstile. Passes or SmarTrip cards can be purchased at the Metro Center sales office or online.

Metro Information Washington Metropolitan Area Transit Authority (WMATA). ⊠ *12th and F Sts. NW, sales center* ☎ *202/637–7000, 202/638–3780 TTY, 202/962–1195 lost and found* ⊕ *www.wmata.com.*

▌TAXI TRAVEL

Taxis are easy to hail in commercial districts, less so in residential ones. If you don't see one after a few minutes, walk to a busier street; if you call, make sure to have an address—not just an intersection—and be prepared to wait, especially at night. D.C. cabs are independent operators and the various companies' cars all have a different look, some better than others! If you're traveling to or from Maryland or Virginia, your best bet is to call a Maryland or Virginia cab, which generally are more reliable. But they're not allowed to take you from point to point in the District or pick you up there if you hail them, so don't be offended if one passes you by.

FARES

The base rate for the first one-eighth mile is $3. Each additional one-eighth mile and each minute stopped or traveling at less than 10 mph is 27¢. There is a 50¢ surcharge per large piece of luggage in the trunk. During D.C.-declared snow emergencies, there is an additional $15 fee. Maryland taxis charge $4 for the first ¼ mile and $.50 for each successive ¼ mile, plus $1 surcharge for each additional passenger. Virginia cabs charge $2.75 for the first one-sixth mile, 30¢ for each one-sixth mile thereafter, plus $1 surcharge for each additional passenger.

Taxi Companies **Barwood.** (Maryland) ☎ 301/984–1900. **Diamond** ☎ 202/387–6200. **Mayflower** ☎ 202/783–1111. **Red Top.** (Virginia) ☎ 703/522–3333. **Yellow** ☎ 202/544–1212.

▌TRAIN TRAVEL

More than 80 trains a day arrive at Washington, D.C.'s, Union Station. Amtrak's regular service runs from D.C. to New York in 3¼–3¾ hours and from D.C. to Boston in 7¾–8 hours. Acela, Amtrak's high-speed service, travels from D.C. to New York in 2¾–3 hours and from D.C. to Boston in 6½ hours.

Two commuter lines—Maryland Rail Commuter Service (MARC) and Virginia Railway Express (VRE)—run to the nearby suburbs. They're cheaper than Amtrak, but they don't run on weekends.

Amtrak tickets and reservations are available at Amtrak stations, by telephone, through travel agents, or online. Amtrak schedule and fare information can be found at Union Station as well as online.

Amtrak has both reserved and unreserved trains available. If you plan to travel during peak times, such as a Friday night or near a holiday, you'll need to get a reservation and a ticket in advance. Some trains at nonpeak times are unreserved, with seats assigned on a first-come, first-served basis.

Information **Amtrak** ☎ 800/872–7245 ⊕ www.amtrak.com. **Maryland Rail Commuter Service** (MARC). ☎ 800/325–7245 ⊕ www.mta.maryland.gov. **Union Station** ✉ 50 Massachusetts Ave. NE ☎ 202/371–9441 ⊕ www.unionstationdc.com. **Virginia Railway Express** (VRE). ☎ 703/684–1001 ⊕ www.vre.org.

ESSENTIALS

▌BUSINESS SERVICES AND FACILITIES

Imagine two Washington monuments laid end to end, and you will have an idea about the size of the Washington Convention Center, the District's largest building. Recognized nationally for its architectural design, the center also has a $4-million art collection featuring 120 sculptures, oil paintings, and photographs from artists around the world.

FedEx Office, across the street from the Convention Center and at many other locations citywide, provides everything from photocopying and digital printing to shipping and receiving packages. In addition, several companies offer translation and interpretation services, including Capital Communications Group, Comprehensive Language Center, and MFM Conference Interpretation. Capital Communications Group also offers multilingual city tours.

Business Services FedEx Office Print & Ship Center ⊠ *800 K St. NW* ☎ *202/682-0349* ⊕ *www.fedex.com.*

Convention Center Walter E. Washington Convention Center ⊠ *801 Mt. Vernon Pl. NW* ☎ *202/249-3000* ⊕ *www.dcconvention.com.*

▌COMMUNICATIONS

INTERNET

Most major hotels offer high-speed access in rooms and/or lobbies and business centers. In addition, dozens of D.C. area restaurants and coffee shops provide free wireless broadband Internet service, including branches of Starbucks and Così all over town. The Martin Luther King Jr. Memorial Public Library and 21 other branches of the D.C. Library System offer Wi-Fi access free of charge to all library visitors. At Kramerbooks & Afterwords café you can check your email for free on the computer located at the full-service bar (and it's open all night on Friday and Saturday).

Contacts Così ⊕ *www.getcosi.com.* **Cyber-cafes** ⊕ *www.cybercafes.com.* **Kramerbooks & Afterwords** ⊠ *1517 Connecticut Ave. NW* ☎ *202/387-3825* ⊕ *www.kramers.com.* **Martin Luther King Jr. Memorial Library** ⊠ *901 G St. NW* ☎ *202/727-0321* ⊕ *www.dclibrary.org.*

▌HOURS OF OPERATION

If you're getting around on the Metro, remember that from Sunday through Thursday it closes at midnight, and on Friday and Saturday nights it stops running at 3 am. Give yourself enough time to get to the station, because at many stations the last trains leave earlier than the closing times. If it's a holiday, be sure to check the schedule before you leave the station, as trains may be running on a different timetable. Bars and nightclubs close at 2 am on weekdays and 3 am on weekends.

▌MONEY

Washington is an expensive city, comparable to New York. On the other hand, many attractions, including most of the museums, are free.

ITEM	AVERAGE COST
Cup of Coffee	$1 at a diner, $4 at an upscale café
Glass of Wine	$7–$10 and up
Pint of Beer	$5–$7
Sandwich	$5–$7
One-Mile Taxi Ride in Capital City	$5–$10
Museum Admission	Usually free

Prices in this guide are given for adults. Substantially reduced fees are almost always available for children, students, and senior citizens.

PACKING

A pair of comfortable shoes is your must-pack item. This is a walking town, and if you fail to pack for it, your feet will pay. D.C. isn't the most fashionable city in the country but people do look neat and presentable; business attire tends to be fairly conservative, and around college campuses and in hip neighborhoods like U Street Corridor or Adams Morgan, style is more eclectic.

The most important element to consider, however, is the weather: D.C.'s temperatures can be extreme, and the right clothes are your best defense.

Winters are cold but sunny, with nighttime temperatures in the 20s and daytime highs in the 40s and 50s. Although the city doesn't normally get much snow, when it does, many streets won't be plowed for days, so if you're planning a visit for winter, bring a warm coat and hat and shoes that won't be ruined by snow and salt. Summers are muggy and very hot, with temperatures in the 80s and 90s and high humidity. Plan on cool, breathable fabrics, a hat for the sun, a sweater for overzealous air-conditioning, and an umbrella for daily thunderstorms. Fall and spring are less challenging, with temperatures in the 60s and occasional showers. Pants, lightweight sweaters, and light coats are appropriate.

RESTROOMS

Restrooms are found in all of the city's museums and galleries. Most are accessible to people in wheelchairs, and many are equipped with changing tables for babies. Locating a restroom is often difficult when you're strolling along the Mall. There are facilities at the Washington Monument, the Lincoln Memorial, the Jefferson Memorial, and Constitution Gardens, near the Vietnam Veterans Memorial, but these are not always as clean as they should be. A better option is to step into the closest Smithsonian museum, all of which are free and have excellent public restrooms.

Restrooms are also available in restaurants, hotels, and department stores. Unlike in many other cities, these businesses are usually happy to help out those in need. There's one state-of-the-art public restroom in the Huntington Station on the Metro. All other stations have restrooms available in cases of emergency; ask one of the uniformed attendants in the kiosks.

SAFETY

Washington, D.C., is a fairly safe city, but as with any major metropolitan area it's best to stay alert. Keep an eye on purses and backpacks, and be aware of your surroundings before you use an ATM, especially one that is outdoors. Move on to a different machine if you notice people loitering nearby. Assaults are rare but they do happen, especially late at night in Adams Morgan, Capitol Hill, Northeast D.C., and U Street Corridor. If someone threatens you with violence, it's best to hand over your money and seek help from police later.

Public transportation is quite safe, but late at night, choose bus stops on busy streets over those on quiet ones. The DC Downtown Business Improvement District's free guardian angel SAM service will walk you to a taxi, Metro, or your car until 9:30 pm May to October (7:30 pm November to April); just call their dispatch service. They operate in the White House area, part of Capitol Hill, Downtown, Penn Quarter, and Chinatown.

Contact SAM ☎ *202/624–1550.*

TAXES

Washington has the region's highest hotel tax, a whopping 14.5%. Maryland and Virginia have no state hotel tax, but charge county hotel taxes of 5%–10%.

Sales tax is 5.75% in D.C., 6% in Maryland, and 4% state plus 1% local sales tax in Virginia.

▌ TIME

Washington, D.C., is in the Eastern time zone. It's 3 hours ahead of Los Angeles, 1 hour ahead of Chicago, 5 hours behind London, and 15 hours behind Sydney.

▌ TIPPING

TIPPING GUIDES FOR WASHINGTON, D.C.	
Bartender	$1–$5 per round of drinks, depending on the number of drinks
Bellhop	$1–$5 per bag, depending on the level of the hotel
Hotel Concierge	$5 or more, depending on the service
Hotel Doorman	$1–$5 for help with bags or hailing a cab
Hotel Maid	$2–$5 a day (either daily or at the end of your stay, in cash)
Hotel Room Service Waiter	$1–$2 per delivery, even if a service charge has been added
Porter at Airport or Train Station	$1 per bag
Skycap at Airport	$1–$3 per bag checked
Taxi Driver	15%, but round up the fare to the next dollar amount
Tour Guide	10% of the cost of the tour
Valet Parking Attendant	$2–$5, each time your car is brought to you
Waiter	15%–20%, with 20% being the norm at high-end restaurants; nothing additional if a service charge is added to the bill
Spa Personnel	15%–20% of the cost of your service
Restroom Attendants	$1 or small change
Coat Check	$1–$2 per coat

▌ TOURS

GUIDED TOURS

Collette Vacations has a seven-day "Exploring America's Capital" vacation, which includes guided tours of the National Cathedral, Ford's Theatre, National Museum of American History or Air and Space Museum, the World War II, Korean War, and Vietnam memorials, Mount Vernon and Arlington National Cemetery. The trip also includes visits to Annapolis and Baltimore. Monograms Travel offers itineraries of D.C., some including Boston and/or New York, as well as "The Historic East," a driving tour of D.C., Virginia, and Philadelphia. All trips include a full-day guided trolley tour and free time. Mayflower Tours offers a seven-day "Washington, D.C. and Williamsburg" tour that includes four nights in D.C. with visits to the U.S. Capitol, Smithsonian Institution, Arlington Cemetery, and an evening monuments tour, as well as stops at Shenandoah National Park, Mount Vernon, and Jamestown; springtime trips take in the Cherry Blossom Festival, too. In commemoration of the 150th anniversary of the Battle of Gettysburg, Mayflower is offering a seven-night tour in July 2013 that includes three nights in D.C. with tours of the U.S. Capitol; the FDR, Vietnam, Lincoln, and World War II memorials; and Ford's Theatre; as well as three nights at Gettysburg National Military Park, where travelers will experience an enactment of this decisive battle. The tour also includes a one-night visit to Harper's Ferry, WV, and a tour of Antietam National Battlefield. Tauck Travel, in conjunction with filmmaker Ken Burns, also has a "Civil War Event Tour" that includes visits to the National Building Museum, Library of Congress, Frederick Douglas House, Ford's Theatre, President Lincoln's Cottage, Arlington National Cemetery, and Manassas National Battlefield. Trip highlights also include an after-hours tour of the National Archives with a keynote address by Ken Burns and a farewell gala at the National Portrait Gallery. World-Strides, which specializes in educational student travel, has "Discover D.C." programs that are designed to enrich the study of U.S. history and government. There's even a tour during the 2013 presidential inauguration in January.

Recommended Companies Collette Vacations ☎ 800/340–5158 ⊕ www.collettevacations.com. **Mayflower Tours** ☎ 800/323–7604 ⊕ www.mayflowertours.com. **Monograms Travel** ☎ 866/270–9841 ⊕ www.monograms.com. **Tauck** ☎ 800/788–7885 ⊕ www.tauck.com. **WorldStrides** ☎ 800/468–5899 ⊕ www.worldstrides.org.

SPECIAL-INTEREST TOURS

Road Scholar, formerly Elderhostel, offers several guided tours for older adults that provide fascinating in-depth looks into the history and beauty of D.C. The nonprofit educational travel organization has been leading all-inclusive learning adventures around the world for more than 30 years. In addition to the programs listed here, Road Scholar also has several other world studies and history programs in D.C. All Road Scholar programs include accommodations, meals, and in-town transportation.

Presented in conjunction with the Close Up Foundation, the nation's largest nonprofit citizenship education organization, "Monumental D.C." is a four-night program that includes seminars on many of the figures memorialized on and near the National Mall. Prices start at about $999 per person.

"Spies, Lies and Intelligence: The Shadowy World of International Espionage" is a fascinating exploration of the country's intelligence operation. Retired CIA agents share secrets of high-profile spying cases on this three-night trip that costs about $799 per person. Highlights include visits to the International Spy Museum and the NSA Cryptologic Museum.

"Signature City Washington, D.C.: Historical & Cultural Gems" lets visitors explore some of the city's lesser-known marvels such as the Scottish Rite of Free Masonry, Georgetown's Tudor Place and Embassy Row, and H Street, one of D.C.'s most historic neighborhoods. This five-night program starts at about $1,225 per person.

Contact Road Scholar ☎ 800/454–5768 ⊕ www.roadscholar.org.

DAY TOURS AND GUIDES

We recommend any of the tours offered by A Tour de Force, DC by Foot, Smithsonian Associates Program, Spies of Washington, and Washington Walks.

For convenience, you can't beat the Old Town Trolley Tours, which take you to all the major historical and cultural landmarks in the city. What's great about these tours is that you can get on and off as you please and stay as long as you like at any spot; you can reboard for free all day long. From April through October, Washington Walks has two-hour guided tours that are interesting and, at $15 per person, affordable. From March to November, join a free tour of the monuments and memorials with DC by Foot. And on hot summer days, hop onboard Capitol River Cruises for a cool look at the city from the water.

For families we recommend the bike tours (or Segway tours if all kids are over 16), the DC Duck tour (younger kids will get a kick out of the quackers that are given to all riders), a mule-drawn barge ride on the C&O Canal, and any of Natalie Zanin's historic strolls, especially the Ghost Story Tour of Washington.

BICYCLE TOURS

Bike the Sites Tours has knowledgeable guides leading daily excursions past dozens of Washington, D.C., landmarks. All tours start at the Old Post Office Pavilion. Bicycles, helmets, snacks, and water bottles are included in the rates, which start at $40. Their Capital Sites and Monuments night tours cost $45 and there's even a Blossoms by Bike tour for $35 during the annual Cherry Blossom Festival. Capital City Bike Tours also offers day and night monuments tours priced $35–$40 for adults. The Adventure Cycling Association, a national organization promoting bicycle travel, recommends tours around the region. Capital Bikeshare rents bikes by the hour and is a great way to visit the memorials and monuments at your own pace. And, you can return your bike at any of the 140 stations throughout the city and in Arlington.

Contacts **Adventure Cycling Association** ☎ *800/755–2453* ⊕ *www.adventurecycling. org.* **Bike the Sites Tours** ☎ *202/842-2453* ⊕ *www.bikethesites.com.* **Capital Bikeshare** ☎ *877/430-2453* ⊕ *www.capitalbikeshare.com.* **Capital City Bike Tours** ✉ *624 9th St. NW* ☎ *877/734-8687* ⊕ *capitalcitybiketours.com.*

BOAT TOURS

During one-hour rides on mule-drawn barges on the C&O Canal, costumed guides and volunteers explain the waterway's history. The barge rides, which cost $8 and are run by the National Park Service, depart from its visitor center Wednesday through Sunday from April through October.

Capitol River Cruises offers 45-minute sightseeing tours aboard the *Nightingale* and *Nightingale II*, Great Lakes boats from the 1950s. Beverages and light snacks are available. Hourly cruises depart from Washington Harbour noon to 9 pm April to October. Prices are $14 for adults and $7 for children three to 12; purchase tickets online and save $2 off the adult fare.

Several swanky cruises depart from the waterfront in Southwest D.C. The *Odyssey III*, specially built to fit under the Potomac's bridges, departs from the Gangplank Marina at 6th and Water streets SW. Tickets are approximately $50 for the weekday lunch cruise, $64 for the weekend brunch cruise, and $96–$120 for the daily dinner cruise. As the prices suggest, this is an elegant affair; jackets are requested for men at dinner. The sleek *Spirit of Washington* offers lunch and dinner cruises that range from $43 to $90. Odyssey and Spirit, as well as a handful

of other companies, offer sightseeing boat tours from the new National Harbour on the banks of the Potomac River in Maryland. Just minutes from D.C., National Harbour is opening in stages with a convention center, hotels, shops, restaurants, and condominiums.

Departing from Alexandria, the glass-enclosed *Nina's Dandy* cruises up the Potomac year-round to Georgetown, taking you past many of D.C.'s monuments. Lunch cruises cost $47 Monday through Friday and $52 on Saturday. A Sunday Champagne brunch cruise costs $57. Boarding for these cruises starts at 11 am. Depending on the day, dinner cruises start boarding at 6 or 6:30 pm and cost $88 Sunday through Friday and $98 on Saturday. The *Nina's Dandy* and sister ship *Dandy* also offer special holiday cruises.

From mid-March through October, DC Ducks offers 90-minute tours in converted World War II amphibious vehicles. After an hour-long road tour of landlocked sights, the tour moves to the water, where for 30 minutes you get a boat's-eye view of the city. Tours depart from Union Station and cost $35.10 for adults and $26.10 for children ages 11 and under; seating is on a first come, first-served basis.

Contacts **C&O Canal Barges** ✉ *Canal Visitor Center, 1057 Thomas Jefferson St. NW, Georgetown* ☎ *202/653-5190* ⊕ *www.nps.gov/choh.* **Capitol River Cruises** ✉ *Washington Harbor, 31st and K Sts. NW, Georgetown* ☎ *301/460-7447, 800/405-5511* ⊕ *www.capitolrivercruises.com.* **Dandy Cruises** ✉ *Prince St., between Duke and King Sts.,*

Alexandria, Virginia ☎ *703/683–6076* ⊕ *www. dandydinnerboat.com.* **DC Ducks** ✉ *50 Massachusetts Ave. NE, Union Station* ☎ *855/323-8257* ⊕ *www.dcducks.com.* **Odyssey III and Spirit of Washington** ✉ *600 Water St. SW, D.C. Waterfront* ☎ *202/488–6010, 866/404-8439* ⊕ *www.entertainmentcruises.com.*

BUS TOURS

All About Town has half-day, all-day, two-day, and twilight bus tours to get acquainted with the city. Tours leave from various Downtown locations. An all-day tour costs $50–$62, half-day and twilight tours cost $36–$46.

Gray Line's nine-hour "D.C. in a Day" tour stops at the White House Visitor Center, U.S. Capitol, World War II Memorial, Martin Luther King Jr. National Memorial and Smithsonian museums. The cost is $45 for adults and $10 for children ages 3–11. There's also a family rate of $95 for two adults and two children. Another all-day tour, "Mt. Vernon/Arlington Cemetery" includes visits to George Washington's home, Old Town Alexandria, Tomb of the Unknowns, and the Iwo Jima, Pentagon, Air Force, and Jefferson memorials. It is priced at $65 for adults and $20 for children. There's also a 2½-hour tour on Saturday morning, presented in conjunction with the International Spy Museum, that showcases more than 25 sites used by infamous spies, with tickets priced at $59 for adults and $25 for children.

Gross National Product's Scandal Tours, led by members of the GNP comedy troupe, last 1½ hours and cover scandals from George Washington to Barack Obama. These extremely lively tours, held on Saturday from April through August at 1 pm, cost $30 per person; reservations are required.

On Board D.C. Tours offers a daily six-hour "D.C. It All" tour that lets you hop on and off with the guide at 12 locations. The cost is $85 for adults and $70 for children under 12. Their three-hour "D.C. The Lights!" nightlife tour costs $55 for adults and $45 for children.

Contacts All About Town ☎ *301/856-5556* ⊕ *www.allabouttown.net.* **Gray Line** ☎ *301/386–8300, 800/862-1400* ⊕ *www.graylinedc.com.* **Gross National Product** ☎ *202/783-7212* ⊕ *www.gnpcomedy. com.* **On Board D.C. Tours** ☎ *301/839-5261* ⊕ *www.onboarddctours.com.*

ORIENTATION TOURS

Old Town Trolley Tours, orange-and-green motorized trolleys, take in the main Downtown sights and also head into Georgetown and the Upper Northwest in a speedy two hours if you ride straight through. However, you can hop on and off as many times as you like, taking your time at the stops you choose. Tickets are $35 for adults, $25 for kids 4–12; purchase tickets online and save $2.50–$3.50 per ticket. Two-day tickets also are available. ANC Tours is the only bus company authorized by the National Park Service to offer riding tours through Arlington National Cemetery. Tours depart daily from the Cemetery Visitors Center, 8:30–6:30, April through September, and 8:30–4:30 October through March. Stops include the Kennedy gravesites, the Women in Military Service for America and Robert E. Lee memorials, and the Tomb of the Unknowns, where it is timed to coincide with the Changing of the Guard ceremony; tickets cost $8.75 for adults and $4.50 for children ages 3–11.

Contacts Old Town Trolley Tours ☎ *202/832–9800* ⊕ *www.trolleytours.com.* **ANC Tours** ☎ *202/488-1012* ⊕ *www.anctours.com.*

PRIVATE GUIDES

A Tour de Force has limo tours of historic homes, diplomatic buildings, and "the best little museums in Washington." Tours are led by local historian and author Jeanne Fogle. Anecdotal History Tours, led by author Anthony Pitch, offers walking tours in Georgetown, Adams Morgan, and Capitol Hill, as well as tours of the theater where Lincoln was shot and the homes of former presidents.

In business since 1964, the Guide Service of Washington puts together half-day and full-day tours of D.C. sights, including some off the beaten path. Nationally known photographer Sonny Odom offers custom tours for shutterbugs at $50/hour, with a four-hour minimum.

Contacts A Tour de Force 703/525–2948 ⊕ www.atourdeforce.com. **Guide Service of Washington** ⊠ 734 15th St. NW, Suite 70120005 ☎ 202/628–2842 ⊕ www.dctourguides.com. **Sonny Odom** ⊠ 2420F S. Walter Reed Dr., Arlington, Virginia22206 ☎ 703/379–1633 ⊕ www.sonnyodom.com. **Anecdotal History Tours** ☎ 301/294–9514 ⊕ www.dcsightseeing.com.

SEGWAY AND SCOOTER TOURS

Rest your feet and glide by the monuments, museums, and major attractions aboard a Segway. Guided tours usually last about two hours. D.C. city ordinance requires that riders be at least 16 years old; some tour companies have weight restrictions of 250 pounds. Tours cost around $65–$80 per person and are limited to 6 to 10 people.

City Scooter Tours rents scooters and wheelchairs for self-guided tours. Three-day rental prices start at $175 for scooters and $150 for wheelchairs.

Contacts Capital Segway ☎ 202/682–1980 ⊕ www.capitalsegway.com. **City Segway Tours** ☎ 877/734–8687 ⊕ www.citysegwaytours.com. **City Scooter Tours** ☎ 888/441–7575 ⊕ www.cityscootertours.com. **Segs in the City** ☎ 800/734–7393 ⊕ www.segsinthecity.com.

GOVERNMENT BUILDING TOURS

Special tours of government buildings with heavy security, including the White House and the Capitol, can be arranged through your U.S. representative or senator's office. Limited numbers of these so-called VIP tickets are available, so plan up to six months in advance of your trip. Foreign visitors should contact their embassy in Washington, D.C., as far in advance as possible. Governmental buildings close to visitors when the Department of Homeland Security issues a high alert, so call ahead.

WORD OF MOUTH

"Take advantage of the free docent-led tours of the museums and other places, such as the Library of Congress. The docents are very knowledgeable and make your visit so much more enjoyable than a quick run through the building."

—Devonmci

Don't miss the stunning Capitol Visitor Center. Before your tour of the Capitol, you can watch orientation films, view historical documents from the Library of Congress and the National Archives, learn about the history of democracy through interactive touch-screen displays, walk alongside statues of notable historical figures, and see models of the Capitol and the Dome. The center, which also features a gift shop and cafeteria, is open daily from 8:30 to 4:30. Tours fill up quickly; it's best to order Capitol tour tickets online in advance of your visit (if you haven't reserved through your U.S. House or Senate member). There will be a few same-day passes available at the information desks in the Center's Emancipation Hall. The Bureau of Engraving and Printing, where U.S. money is made, has tours that begin every 15 minutes from 9 to 10:45 and 12:30 to 2 on weekdays (as well as 2 to 3:45 and 5 to 7 in summer). The free tours are popular. During the peak season from March through August, tickets are given out on a first-come, first-served basis at the ticket booth on Raoul Wallenberg Place (formerly 15th Street). The booth opens at 8 am and closes as soon as all tickets have been handed out; lines form very early and tickets go quickly, usually by 9 am. From September through February, tickets are not required; you line up at the Visitor's Entrance on 14th Street.

Foreign dignitaries are received at the Department of State's lavish Diplomatic Reception Rooms, but everyone else can get a peek on weekdays on 45-minute tours that begin at 9:30, 10:30, and 2:45.

Grand halls showcase exceptional and rare 18th- and 19th-century furniture, a must for decorative arts fans, but not so much for kids. Reserve three months in advance to be sure of a spot.

Contacts Bureau of Engraving and Printing ✉ *14th and C Sts. SW* ☎ *202/874–2330, 866/874–2330* ⊕ *www.moneyfactory.gov.* **Department of State** ☎ *2201 C St. NW* ☎ *202/647–3241, 202/736–4474 TDD* ⊕ *diplomaticrooms.state.gov.* **United States Capitol Visitor Center** ☎ *202/226–8000* ⊕ *www.visitthecapitol.gov.* **White House Visitor Center** ✉ *15th and E Sts. NW* ☎ *202/456–7041* ⊕ *www.whitehouse.gov/about/tours-and-events.*

MEDIA TOURS

The Voice of America is the U.S. government's foreign broadcaster, beaming news and current affairs programming around the world in 44 languages. Get a look behind the scenes with tours weekdays at noon and 3 pm. Reservations are recommended and can be made either online or by phone.

National Public Radio leads tours of its broadcast facilities on Tuesday and Thursday at 11 am. Show up 10 minutes beforehand for a security screening. If you have more than five in your group, it's best to call at least four weeks in advance of your visit.

Contacts National Public Radio ✉ *635 Massachusetts Ave. NW* ☎ *202/513–3232* ⊕ *www.npr.org/about/aboutnpr/visit.html.* **Voice of America** ✉ *330 Independence Ave. SW* ☎ *202/203–4990* ⊕ *www.voatour.com.*

WALKING TOURS

The Smithsonian Associates program offers a range of fascinating guided walks around Washington, D.C., and nearby communities; advance tickets are required. DC by Foot offers free tours (the guides work for tips, which makes them lively and entertaining) to the major memorials and monuments. The 1½-hour tours are available year-round; days and times vary by season. Look out for the guides in blue T-shirts (jackets in winter) at the start of the tour on the north corner of 15th Street and Constitution Avenue NW; the tours end at the Lincoln Memorial.

Washington Walks has a wide range of tours for $15 per person, including the self-explanatory "Memorials by Moonlight"; "Get Local," which goes in-depth into one Washington neighborhood; "The Most Haunted Houses," a look at the city's most ghost-filled residences; and "Before Harlem There Was U Street," a walk along Washington's "Black Broadway."

The nonprofit group Cultural Tourism DC leads guided walking tours that cover the history and architecture of neighborhoods from the southwest waterfront to points much farther north: Or, if you'd prefer to explore neighborhoods on your own, their website features seven self-guided walking tours, all of which are highlighted with historic markers. You also can check out other cultural events, many free, happening around the city on the Cultural Tourism DC website. DC Metro Food Tours explores the culinary heritage of seven neighborhoods, with 3½-hour tours offered year-round on weekends. Spies of Washington Walking Tours, led by a retired Air Force officer and former president of the National Military Intelligence Association, visits sites in Washington associated with espionage over the past 200 years. The approximately two-hour tours cost $12 per person.

Step back in time on one of Natalie Zanin's interactive theatrical tours to visit Washington, D.C., during the Civil War, World War II, or the 1960s. Or you can sign up for a Ghost Story Tour, on which Zanin dresses as Dolley Madison's ghost and shares stories of hauntings around the city, including Lafayette Square Park, where Edgar Allan Poe's spirit is said to wander. Tours cost $12 for adults and $6 for children. One of the more popular tours in the city is the U.S. National Arboretum's Full Moon Hike, offered about three times a month, excluding July and

August. It's a brisk 4-mile walk through the grounds and hills by the Anacostia River, which afford beautiful views of the city at night. It costs $22/person and registration is required. The Arboretum also has a number of other delightful walking tours through the enchanting gardens.

Contacts Cultural Tourism DC ☎ 202/661–7581 ⊕ www.culturaltourismdc.org. DC by Foot ☎ 202/370–1830 ⊕ www.freetoursbyfoot.com/dc. DC Metro Food Tours ☎ 202/683–8847, 800/979–3370 ⊕ www.dcmetrofoodtours.com. Natalie Zanin's Historic Strolls ☎ 301/588–9255 ⊕ www.historicstrolls.com. The Smithsonian Associates ☎ 202/633–3030 ⊕ www.smithsonianassociates.org. Spies of Washington Tour ☎ 703/569–1875 ⊕ www.spiesofwashingtontour.com. U.S. National Arboretum ☎ 202/245–4521 ⊕ www.usna.usda.gov. Washington Walks ☎ 202/484–1565 ⊕ www.washingtonwalks.com.

▌VISITOR INFORMATION

Destination D.C.'s free, 85-page publication, the *Official Visitors' Guide,* is full of sightseeing tips, maps, and contacts. You can order a copy online or by phone, or pick one up in their office (enter on I St.).

The most popular sights in D.C. are run by either the National Park Service (NPS) or the Smithsonian, both of which have recorded information about locations and hours of operation.

Events and Attractions National Park Service ☎ 202/619–7275 "Dial-a-Park" ⊕ www.nps.gov. Smithsonian ☎ 202/633–1000, 202/633–5285 TTY ⊕ www.si.edu. White House Visitor Center ✉ 1450 Pennsylvania Ave. NW, White House Area ☎ 202/208–1631 ⊕ www.nps.gov/whho.

State Information State of Maryland ☎ 866/639–3526 ⊕ www.visitmaryland.org. Virginia Tourism Corporation ☎ 800/847–4882 ⊕ www.virginia.org.

Tourist Information Destination DC ✉ 901 7th St. NW, 4th fl., Downtown ☎ 202/789–7000, 800/422–8644 ⊕ www.washington.org.

ALL ABOUT WASHINGTON, D.C.

The **Smithsonian website** (⊕ *www.si.edu*) is a good place to start planning a trip to the Mall and its museums. You can check out the exhibitions and events that will be held during your visit.

Cultural Tourism D.C. (⊕ *www.culturaltourismdc.org*) is a nonprofit coalition whose mission is to highlight the city's arts and heritage. Their website is loaded with great information about sights, special events, and neighborhoods, including self-guided walking tours.

Billing itself as D.C.'s online community for the web, **dcregistry.com** (⊕ *www.dcregistry.com*) lists more than 4,000 home pages with everything from arts and entertainment to real estate. There are discussion forums and a chat room, too.

Downtown D.C. Business Improvement District (⊕ *www.downtowndc.org*) is a nonprofit that oversees the 140-block area from the White House to the U.S. Capitol. The website has special events, shopping, and dining listings and information about the wonderful red, white, and blue uniformed D.C. SAMs, roving hospitality specialists linked to a central dispatcher by radio. In spring and summer, SAMs (which stands for safety, administration, and maintenance) are available to help visitors with directions, information, and emergencies. You'll spot their hospitality kiosks near Metro stops and major attractions.

Gay and Lesbian Washington, D.C., is a very inclusive town, with an active gay community and plenty of gay-friendly hotels, nightlife, and events. In addition to news and features, both *Washington Blade* (⊕ *www.washingtonblade.com*) and *Metro Weekly* (⊕ *www.metroweekly.com*) have guides to gay bars and clubs, including a calendar of events.

Kids and Families washingtonfamily. com (⊕ *www.washingtonfamily.com*) features a "Best for Families" as voted on by area families. Families may also want to check out **washingtonparent.com** (⊕ *www. washingtonparent.com*) and **kidfriendlydc. com** (⊕ *www.kidfriendlydc.com*), a blog with loads of kid-friendly events, deals and activities

News and Happenings The website of the *Washington Post* (⊕ *www.washingtonpost. com*) has a fairly comprehensive listing of what's going on around town. Also check out the site of *Washington CityPaper* (⊕ *www.*

washingtoncitypaper.com), a free weekly newspaper. The *Washingtonian* (⊕ *www. washingtonian.com*) is a monthly magazine. For personalized emails of things to do, member reviews, and listings of half-price show and event tickets in D.C. and other major cities nationwide, register for free at ⊕ *www.goldstar. com*, an online entertainment company. The Cultural Alliance of Greater Washington (⊕ *www.ticketplace.org*) also has an online listing of half-price tickets to theater, dance, music, and opera performances.

INDEX

PHOTO CREDITS

1, Fristle/Flickr. 3,JTB Photo/Japan Travel Bureau/photo-library.com. Chapter 1: Experience Washington: 6-7, Hemis/Alamy. 8, Destination DC. 9 (left), Smiley Man with a Hat/Flickr. 9 (right), DymphieH/ Flickr. 12, AgnosticPreachersKid/wikipedia.org. 13 (left), Molas/Flickr. 13 (right), Architect of the Capitol/wikipedia.org. 14 (left), graham s. klotz/Shutterstock. 14 (top center), S.Borisov/Shutterstock. 14 (top right), Kevin D. Oliver/Shutterstock. 14 (bottom right), Wadester16/wikipedia.org. 15 (left), alykat/wikipedia.org. 15 (top center), taylorandayumi/Flickr. 15 (top right), Jeremy R. Smith Sr./Shutterstock. 15 (bottom right), Kropotov Andrey/Shutterstock. 16, George Allen Penton/Shutterstock. 17 (left), LWPhotography/Shutterstock. 17 (right), Nickomargolies/wikipedia.org. 18 and 19, Destination DC. 20, DC St. Patrick's Day Parade Photographers. 21, Zhong Chen/Shutterstock. 22. Andrew Lightman. 25 (left), John Keith/Shutterstock. 25 (right), Ben Schumin/wikipedia.org. Chapter 2: Neighborhoods: 29, ctankcycles/Flickr. 30, John Keith/Shutterstock. 31, PHOTOTAKE Inc./Alamy. 32, National Capital Planning Commission. 33 (top), POPPERFOTO/Alamy. 33 (center), Tramonto/age fotostock. 33 (bottom), Yoke Mc/Joacim Osterstam/wikipedia.org. 34 (#3), Dennis MacDonald/age fotostock. 34 (#1), Douglas Litchfield/Shutterstock. 34 (#11), Chuck Pefley/Alamy. 35 (#5), Smithsonian Institution. 35 (#9), P_R_/Flickr. 35 (#2), Sandra Baker/Alamy. 35 (#12), Stock Connection Distribution/Alamy. 35 (#7), Franko Khoury National Museum of African Art/ Smithsonian Institution. 35 (#8), Gordon Logue/Shutterstock. 35 (#4), David R. Frazier Photolibrary, Inc./Alamy. 35 (#13), United States Holocaust Memorial Museum. 36, Smithsonian Institution. 38 (top), DC St. Patrick's Day Parade Photographers. 38 (2nd from top), National Cherry Blossom Festival. 38 (3rd from top), William S. Kuta/Alamy. 38 (4th from top), San Rostro/age fotostock. 38 (bottom), Visions of America, LLC/Alamy. 39, Lee Foster/Alamy. 40, PHC C.M. Fitzpatrick/United States Department of Defense/wikipedia.org. 41, Wiskerke/Alamy. 43, Corcoran Gallery of Art. 45, Jake McGuire/Destination DC. 47, Brent Bergherm / age fotostock. 48, Jake McGuire/Destination DC. 51, Andreas Praefcke/wikipedia.org. 52, vittorio sciosia/age fotostock. 53, Jim West/Alamy. 55, Ilene MacDonald/Alamy. 57, Timothy Hursley/National Portrait Gallery and Smithsonian American Art Museum, Smithsonian Institution. 58, Kord.com/age fotostock. 61, vittorio sciosia/age fotostock. 63, Bill Helsel/Alamy. 65, Rudy Sulgan/age fotostock. 67, LOOK Die Bildagentur der Fotografen GmbH/Alamy. 68, Art Kowalsky/Alamy. 71, Destination DC. 72, PCL/Alamy. 74, Carrie Garcia/Alamy. 75, Susan Isakson/Alamy. 77, Poldavo (Alex)/Flickr. 79, NCinDC/Flickr. 81, G. Byron Peck/City Arts Inc. 82, Destination DC. 84, SUNNYphotography.com/ Alamy. 85, thomwatson/Flickr. 87, Asiir/wikipedia.org. Chapter 3: Museums: 89, William S. Kuta/ Alamy. 90, Alfred Wekelo/Shutterstock. 92, Corcoran Gallery of Art. 93, Richard T. Nowitz/age fotostock. 94, Gryffindor/wikipedia.org. 95, Prakash Patel. 96and 97, Eric Long/NASM, National Air and Space Museum, Smithsonian Institution. 98 (top left), NASA/wikipedia.org. 98 (top right), Son of Groucho/Flickr. 98 (bottom), Henristosch/wikipedia.org. 99 (top left), cliff1066/Flickr. 99 (top left center), dbking/Flickr. 99 (top right center), Eric Long/NASM, National Air and Space Museum, Smithsonian Institution. 99 (top right and bottom), Mr. T in DC/Flickr. 100-101, JTB Photo/Japan Travel Bureau/photolibrary.com. 102 (top left), Eric Long/NASM, National Air and Space Museum, Smithsonian Institution. 102 (top right), cliff1066/Flickr. 102 (bottom), by Mr. T in DC/Flickr. 103 (top), Pete Markham/Flickr. 103 (bottom), Jeffrey Johnson/Flickr. 104, Lisa Nipp for DELL. 105, F.T. Eyre/ National Building Museum. 106, Dennis MacDonald/age fotostock. 107, vittorio sciosia/age fotostock. 108, Dennis MacDonald/age foto-stock. 109, Lee Foster/Alamy. 110, Alvaro Leiva/age fotostock. 111, Chris Greenberg/Getty Images/Newscom. 112, Andre Jenny/Alamy. 113, Robert C Lautman. 114, Robin Weiner/U.S. Newswire. 115, United States Holocaust Memorial Museum. Chapter 4: Monuments & Memorials: 129, Graham De'ath/Shutterstock. 130, Hisham Ibrahim/age fotostock. 133, SuperStock/age fotostock. 134, Condor 36/Shutterstock. 135 (top left), Scott S. Warren/Aurora Photos. 135 (bottom left), Dennis Brack/Aurora Photos. 135 (right), vario images GmbH & Co.KG/Alamy. 136, Jeremy R. Smith Sr/Shutterstock. 138 (top left), Ken Hackett/Alamy. 138 (top right), Rough Guides/Alamy. 138 (bottom), National Archives and Records Administration. 139 (top left), William S. Kuta/Alamy. 139 (top right), Chris A Crumley/Alamy. 139 (bottom), Jeremy R. Smith/Shutterstock. 140, Robert J. Bennett/age fotostock. 141, vittorio sciosia/age fotostock. 142, Bruno Perousse/age fotostock. 143, Martin Luther King, Jr. National Memorial Project Foundation, Inc. 144, Kanwarjit Singh Boparai/Shutterstock. 145, idesygn/Shutterstock. 146, John Keith/Shutterstock. 147, S.Borisov/ Shutterstock. 148, Visions of America, LLC/Alamy. Chapter 5: Official Washington: 151, Gary Blakeley/Shutterstock. age fotostock. 152, Architect of the Capitol/wikipedia.org. 155 (left), Bartomeu Amengual/age fotostock. 155 (top right), kimberlyfaye/Flickr. 155 (bottom right), SuperStock. 156 (top left and bottom left), Library of Congress Prints & Photographs Division. 156 (top right), Classic Vision/age fotostock. 156 (bottom right), Prints and Photographs Division Library of Congress. 157 (left), Architect of the Capitol. 157 (top right), José Fuste Raga/age fotostock. 157 (bottom), Architect of the Capitol/wikipedia.org. 158, U.S. Capitol Visitor Center. 159 (left), Wadester/wikipedia.org. 159 (right), wikipedia.org. 160 (left), MShades/Flickr. 160 (right), Architect of the Capitol/wikipedia.org. 162 (left), U.S. Senate, 110th Congress, Senate Photo Studio/wikipedia.org. 162 (top right), DCstockphoto.com/Alamy. 162 (center right), SCPhotos/Alamy. 162 (bottom right), United States Congress/wikipedia.org. 163, Dennis MacDonald/age fotostock. 164, Alvaro Leiva/age fotostock. 169, Ng Wei Keong/Shutterstock. 171, Robert Byrd/Shutterstock.173, Gage Skidmore [Creative Commons Attribution-Share Alike 2.0 Generic license], via Wikimedia Commons. 174 (top left and bottom left), Library of Congress Prints and Photographs Division. 174 (right) and 175 (top left), Bettmann/CORBIS. 175 (bottom left), wikipedia.org. 175 (right), Hunter Kahn/wikipedia.org. 176 (left), (c) 1924, The Washington Post. Reprinted with Permission. 176 (right), Matthew Brady/wikipedia.org. Chapter 6: Where to Eat: 177, Clay McLachlan/Aurora Photos. 178 and 183 (left), Rasika. 183 (right), Michael J. Colella. 184, Belga Café. 185 (top), Nayashkova Olga/Shutterstock. 185 (bottom), Anosmia/Flickr. 186, Ceiba. 187 (top), Monkey Business Images/Shutterstock. 187 (bottom), Lourdes Delgado. 188, 1789 Restaurant. 189 (top), Brasserie Beck. 189 (bottom), Leonidas. 190, Michael Matsil. 191 (top), James Ostrand/iStock-photo. 191 (bottom), Abdullah Pope. 192, Capital Region USA (capitalregionusa.org). 193 (top), Monkey Business Images/Shutterstock. 193 (bottom), Vegetate. 194, Allison Dinner. 195 (top), Graca Victoria/Shutterstock. 195 (bottom), Joe Gough/Shutterstock. Chapter 7: Where to Stay: 229, Bruce Buck. 230, George Apostolidis/Mandarin Oriental. 238 (top), David Phelps Photography/Kimpton Hotels & Restaurants. 238 (center left), The Hay-Adams. 238 (center right), David Phelps Photography/Kimpton Hotels & Restaurants. 238 (bottom left), George Apostolidis/Mandarin Oriental. 238 (bottom right), Sofitel Lafayette Square Washington DC. 245 (top), Bruce Buck. 245 (center left), Jumping Rocks Inc. 245 (center right), Jumping Rocks Photography. 245 (bottom), Starwood Hotels & Resorts. 248 (top), Four Seasons Hotels and Resorts. 248 (center left), The Latham Hotel, Washington DC. 248 (center right), The Ritz-Carlton Company, L.L.C.. 248 (bottom), Omni Shoreham Hotel. Chapter 8: Nightlife: 259, Rough Guides/Alamy. 260, dk/Alamy. Chapter 9: The Performing Arts: 279, Bob Llewellyn/FOLIO Inc. 280, Karin Cooper. Chapter 10: Sports & the Outdoors: 295, Krista Rossow/age fotostock. 296, Visions of America, LLC/Alamy. 300, Anosmia/Flickr. 304-305, sneakerdog/Flickr. 307, William S. Kuta/Alamy. Chapter 11: Shopping: 315, Destination DC. 316, Michael J. Hipple/age fotostock. 327, Alex Segre/Alamy. 330, Lee Foster/Alamy. Chapter 12: Side Trips: 337, Olga Bogatyrenko/iStockphoto. 338, rpongsaj/Flickr. 339, 2265524729/Shutterstock. 340, Anton Albert/Shutterstock. 347, Krista Rossow/age fotostock. 351, Jeff Greenberg/age fotostock. 363, vittorio sciosia/age fotostock.

ABOUT OUR WRITERS

Beth Kanter is a travel writer who specializes in all things D.C. She is the author of *Day Trips from Washington, D.C: Getaway Ideas for the Local Traveler* and the forthcoming *Food Lovers' Guide to Washington, D.C.* Her articles and essays have also appeared in a wide variety of publications including *Parents, Wondertime, Shape, Kiwi,* and the *Chicago Tribune.* You can visit her online at ⊕ *www.bethkanter.com.* She updated the Where to Stay chapter.

Allison Lombardo—bureaucrat by weekday, city explorer by weekend—makes sure her weekends and evenings are packed with action in the city she loves. A Dupont Circle denizen for many years, Allison's adventures take her all over the city to old gems and also unexpected discoveries. She updated the Nightlife, Sports and Outdoors, and the Performing Arts chapters.

A fourth-generation Washingtonian, freelance writer Kathryn McKay is the author of *Fodor's Around Washington, D.C. with Kids* and the updater of the Monuments and Memorials, Shopping, and Side Trips chapters. She has written for many local publications, including *Bethesda* magazine, *Northern Virginia* magazine, the *Washington Times,* and the *Washington Post.*

Born and raised in Virginia, Mike Lillis now lives in Washington, D.C., where he covers politics for *The Hill* newspaper. Many weekends find him in a canoe, paddling the rocky streams of the region. He updated the Experience Washington, D.C. chapter.

Cathy Sharpe, a freelance writer with more than 20 years of experience in travel, has lived in the Maryland suburbs of Washington since 1998. She loves seeing the metro area's wonders through the eyes of her four children. She updated the Official Washington chapter.

Where to Eat updater Elana Schor was bit by the Washington bug at age eight, when she first applied to become a Capitol tour guide. She still delights in showing D.C. newbies the ropes as a staff reporter for *Greenwire* and restaurant reviewer for *The Hill* newspaper. A six-year resident of the capital, she has also covered politics for Talking Points Memo and the *Guardian* newspaper.

Renee Sklarew lives in Bethesda—think Brooklyn to Manhattan—and loves Washington, D.C., for many reasons, most particularly because she is a museum junkie: her kids often complain that they should be allowed to go to an amusement park instead of constantly being dragged to museums on the weekends ("But I know they will thank me someday, and, in fact, the older one already does"). She has covered museums and neighborhoods in some of her other work, including her travel articles for *Northern Virginia Magazine* (another DC suburb), the *DC Examiner,* and, for a national audience, *Adventure Biking, Park & Recreation Magazine,* and *Running Times.* She even won an essay contest in *The Washington Post* once called "Why I Love My Hometown"—about Washington naturally. For this edition, she updated our Museums chapter and our Neighborhoods chapter.